MW00447686

LOVE IS ALL THAT MATTERS

For M.J. and John —

LOVE IS ALL THAT MATTERS

By Ila Kelley Bench

*I'm glad you are one of
Rebecca's friends —
My love —
Ila Bench*

Copyright © 2019 by Ila Kelley Bench

Cover artwork by Audra Mote

(artwork reprinted with permission)

ISBN-13: 978-179 6584707

Imprint by CreateSpace

Printed in the United States of America

All rights reserved. No part of this book may be reproduced in any form or by any electronic or mechanical means, including information storage and retrieval systems, without permission in writing from the author.

This is a work of nonfiction. Everything written here is true and the events and experiences have been provided as the author remembered them. The stories were recalled for writing assignments during years of writing classes. Many of the people named are no longer living. Those people named who are still living will, the author is confident, be pleased to have been included as important to her life story. The author and publisher will not be liable for any loss of profit or other commercial damages, including but not limited to direct, indirect, incidental, personal, punitive and consequential damages. While every attempt has been made to verify the information in this book, neither the author nor her affiliates/partners assume any responsibility for opinions, errors, inaccuracies, or omissions.

All registered trademarks, brands, and product names are the property of their respective owners and are only used for reference. There is no implied or paid endorsement for mentioning any of these names.

This book may be purchased at
www.amazon.com

ACKNOWLEDGMENTS

There could have been no story without my family, and the many friends who made my life exciting and worthwhile! I thank them for their love and encouragement for these many years!

David and Michelle Bench also helped with collecting supplies and gave unending assistance with computer operation!

To Sharon Kelly I owe help for many hours of advising, printing photos into text, proof reading, fact-checking, enthusiasm, and requirements of locating and dealing with a printer.

To my friend Audra Mote for her vision and artistic skill in creating the design for the cover – giving a beautiful feeling of "soul" for these stories.

LOVE IS ALL THAT MATTERS

TABLE OF CONTENTS

Chapter 6 – Holidays

Chapter 7 – Other Family

Chapter 1: Childhood

A VOICE FROM THE PAST

I grew up in a family that not only saved all kinds of things "because we might need it sometime," but also, many things of purely sentimental value like locks of hair, baby teeth, first baby shoes, baby dresses, etc. My mother's largest mixing bowl—which she used every-other day for making her routine batch of five loaves of bread—was the large china wash bowl in which she was bathed when she was a baby. Under my wedding dress, I wore the skirt part of a petticoat Mom had made for herself with tucks, hemstitching, and wide crocheted lace around the bottom. (One of my sisters has the tucked and crocheted bodice part of it.) I sometimes serve candy or preserves from a cut-glass dish which belonged to my mother's grandmother. So it isn't surprising that I have one of the letters I received from my Dad when I was about three years old!

I was born in 1925, before the *worst* part of the Great Depression, but in that part of the country people seemed to be satisfied to have short-time work, so Dad worked around our little ten-acre farm some, to improve the land that was originally just woods—planting fruit trees, and such. Then he would go work on the railroad for awhile, or a road-building project, or whatever might be available without going too far from home. But in 1927 or '28, a pipe-line company came through our area, and pay was so much better than most work, that Dad stayed with them even as they moved along their route. That meant that he'd be away from home for several days at a time, living in boarding houses.

Communication with his family was by letter because we had no phone. He and Mom corresponded about once a week, and letters were an important part of our lives. When Mom sat down to write a letter, three-year-old Ila wanted to write a letter too. I think I had learned the alphabet and some numbers by then, so my letters were more than likely pictures I drew, with maybe my name printed on it somewhere, and maybe *"Dear Daddy"* printed with Mom's help. His letters to Mom always had messages of such things as *"Hello"* and *"Love"* to me and one-year-old Ross, or even a letter written just to me.

1

In my box of special memory things is one of those letters that still survives. It's written on the 5x8-inch tablet paper that he and Mom always used (and I still do!). He often used paper with lines on it—and this one might have had faint ones that have faded during the more than eighty years of its existence. Also, they often used paper that was called "linen weave"—a better quality, "nicer" paper than some ordinary tablets. I think this one might be "linen" weave. I have an idea it was so special to me that I might have kept it then to "play" with. It's coming apart at one of the folds, so I apparently handled it a *lot*.

The letter indicates that spelling wasn't one of Dad's "long suits," and his penmanship wouldn't have won a prize, but there's a one-half-page size drawing of our family, playing musical instruments and singing together that shows his love, even beyond the loving words that he wrote:

"Miss ILA MAY KELLEY

My Darling little daughter—I will take the pleasure in answering that letter you wrote and did not get to send.

Are you and Rossy having lots of fun? Dady would like awful well to be with you and Rossy and mama all the time but I have to work so that God will give us something to eat and pretty dresses and clothes to wear.

I want you to sing lots dear so that when I dady comes home you and mama can sing and play the Getuar and ukelale while dady plays the fiddle. Won't that be fun for us – we will have a good time then won't we. Learn to sing the right tune to 'Bring back my Bonney to me.' Mama will help you –then we can sing it all together and Rossy can listen.

Write soon please.   Your dady"

Then comes the picture—a pencil drawing—rather detailed—of Mom sitting, playing a guitar, I standing with a banjo-shaped uke, Ross sitting on the floor banging on an up-side-down pan with something that looks like an egg beater, and Dad sitting on a chair, playing a fiddle. Both he and Mom have one foot raised, as if patting it to keep time with the music. Over the heads of all of us are musical notes floating in the air, words of the song, and "bang, bang, Bang, BANG" enclosed in the balloon-like drawings with pointers like cartoon-characters' words. Underneath is written: *"Who are all these fellows."*

What a precious expression of my Dad's love! I'm glad we don't throw away things that "we might need sometime"!

Kelley Family First Home

Mother Bertha, Baby Ross & Ila in 1927

Ila, age 3, with her dolls

One of the songs that my parents helped me learn and that I was called upon frequently to sing publicly when I was about three, four and five years old is "Will the Angels Let Me Play?"

"WILL THE ANGELS LET ME PLAY!"
In our yard where children
Were playing games one day,
A little tot, so lonely,
Was watching wistfully.
It seemed so hard she could not play
As other children do—
They said that she would spoil their games,
And was a baby, too!
Her poor little heart was breaking,
For they wouldn't let her play;
And as she goes to Mama,
. She murmurs plaintively:
Chorus
"Mama, when I go to Heaven
Will the angels let me play?
Just because I am so little,
Will they say I'm in their way?
Here, the children all don't like me—
'I'm a bother,' they all say!
When I go to Heaven, Mama,
Will the angels let me play?"
"I'm so tired, dear Mama,"
The little darling said.
"Rock me just a little,
And then put me to bed.
I wish my Papa would come home
Before I go to sleep—
Just tell him how I waited
For his kiss upon my cheek."
That night while all was silent
The angels came that way,
And took the little darling

4

Whose sweet lips seemed to say:
Chorus

HOME IS WHERE THE HEART IS

I've lived in a number of houses and apartments: twenty-three—in six states and two foreign countries since I was married. Each one had its own character: country, small town, large city, military base; upstairs, downstairs, furnished, unfurnished; in northern cold, midwestern and southern humidity, Mediterranean sunshine, tropical breezes, and northwestern rain. Most were rented; six were owned. All of them furnished a wide variety of "learning experiences," and almost all needed some time and "elbow grease" applied to cleaning dirty stoves and dusty shelves. In all of those far-flung houses, Gene and I lovingly made happy, attractive homes for ourselves, our family, and our friends. Those adventures give me wonderful memories! But none of them did more to form my personality and philosophy than the place of my birth and childhood near Dixon, in mid-Missouri.

In another story I've told about the beginning of that one—ten acres my dad owned before he and my mom were married—and about their plans for building their house and making it into a "home." When I now think about that house, I wonder how seven people lived in such a small space! For their first three years, there was only one downstairs room to serve as kitchen, dining room, sitting room, bedroom, and nursery. The upstairs room was reached by a ladder attached to one of the walls, so it wasn't useful for very much more than storage. A galvanized metal roof made the sound of rain quite prominent, and as I grew old enough to be very aware of it, I could tell by Dad's expression of enjoyment of the "pitter patter," that it was something that should be appreciated! I expect that a good part of his appreciation was that he and Mom (along with some help from friends and neighbors) had built with their own hands a cozy place for their family!

I was born in June, soon after the completion of that first one-room house. In two more years came my brother Ross. In another year, baby Barbara was on the way, and more space was added—a two-story addition on the west wide, with a stair-way, which made two easily accessible bedrooms upstairs. The new downstairs room became kitchen-dining area, with one door (called the back door) leading west to the wood-pile. A side door to the south was useful to go to the cellar, barn, chicken yard, or outhouse. (In case you don't know what an "outhouse" is, perhaps I should describe that one. It was a very small house that was located in the barnyard. It had one door, and it was used like one uses a toilet in a bathroom. Instead of a roll of toilet tissue, an old Sears-Roebuck catalog was available most of the time to use for "paper." "Crunching" a page of it in your hands a few times made it more comfortable to use. There was room for no more than two people to be inside it at one time. Dad had built a seat with two oval-shaped holes across the back—one large, and one a lower, smaller child-size one. Two small windows high on the sides provided ventilation. Some outhouses had crescent-shaped windows.)

Dad dug a deep cistern near the house on the west side; and to Mom, who had grown up carrying water for some distance from a spring, getting water by a few turns of a crank, just four or five steps from the kitchen door, was a real luxury. (It now occurs to me to wonder about their source of water before the cistern was dug! Maybe the cistern was dug before the addition was built, and the addition was built out close to it??? If not, they must have carried water from the neighbors' house across the road, or from Grandpa Kelley's spring, the equivalent of about three or four blocks away.)

After another four or five years, and another two babies, (Joy and Sterling, Jr.) Mom's dream of a "summer kitchen" became a reality! It, too, was added on the west side, with several windows in each of its three outside walls—for maximum summer breezes and great light. Linoleum covered the concrete floor, and guess what! The cistern's pump was now in the kitchen! Even more luxury! And with all of the windows open in the summer, the jobs of canning and ironing using a wood stove, were not quite as hot as they had been before.

The original upstairs room, being the larger one, became the bedroom for Joy, Barbara, and me. From the north window we could see the garden and the road as it came over the hill. The south window overlooked the space we called the "cow lot," a field called "the bottom," the orchard, the vineyard, and the meadow. There was a honeysuckle vine that grew all the way up to our south window by the time I was a teenager, and provided a most wonderful fragrance, carried into our room by the soft, night breezes. Sounds from outside were whippoorwill songs and owl calls from the woods, katydids and what Mom called "jar-flies" came from nearer the house; frogs croaked from the creek and slough in "the bottom" field; and at times, we heard some neighbor's hound dog chasing a coon, a possum, or some other nocturnal creature in the distance. All of that made a very good setting for this young girl's imagination to envision a handsome prince on a white horse, carrying her away to some story-book kind of magical place!

Little did I realize in those happy years that my "magical place" was right there! And that my philosophy and appreciation of life was taking root and growing right along with the flowers and garden I had to help tend. Every season had special experiences: the earth coming to life in the spring with wild flowers, birds that were nesting and singing; a baby calf, and chickens and pigs were in the barnyard. In the warm, sunny summers we walked barefoot in the cool grass or soft soil while helping with tending the garden or picking wild blackberries and strawberries. School and bright colored leaves came in the fall, along with helping with harvesting, stacking wood for winter, and school homework done with the family gathered around the round dining table with an Aladdin lamp in the center for light. Winter brought cold weather, snow, long underwear, evenings indoors with time for board games, apples and popcorn.

We were poor, but so were our friends and neighbors. Dad worked at whatever he could find—sometimes away from home—and we had grown most of the food we needed. Still, there often wasn't enough money for all our needs, and credit accounts began to grow. That worried my parents, so when Dad got a job on WPA with a fairly regular paycheck, they worked out what they called their "Five-Year Plan" to get out of debt and "on their feet" in five years. This was done prayerfully and methodically, using labeled envelopes along with whatever other bookkeeping they used. I just especially remember the envelopes and the prayers. With each paycheck a certain amount of cash was put into each envelope. Into the first one went 10% "for the Lord." From this envelope we took money for Sunday school and church collections, or for helping some needy person. Next was 10% for savings. Others were for paying off credit, food for animals, clothing, food, home maintenance, etc. Mom usually sold a small can of cream each week, and in summer we sold "U-Pick" grapes from our vineyard. All incoming money was divided into the envelopes. What a great lesson in budgeting that was for kids!

We were almost always busy—if not doing chores, we read or created games to play; we learned to sing together and play stringed instruments; we usually walked to church and school, had no phone, and no radio until much later. And in all the "busy-ness" we were being lovingly taught manners, cooperation, and appreciation of nature, of country, of friends, of family, and of God—by parents with positive attitudes.

So, I'm thinking that the relationships of the people who lived in that little house was the thing that helped to make it a "home." I wonder how much different I might have felt about life if I had been rich, or abused, or maybe homeless. I'm inclined to believe what someone else has said: "It doesn't matter <u>where</u> you live, as long as you <u>live</u> where you are"!

The front yard flower garden

Kelley home painted by Sterling, Jr. in 1980

Dad under the rose arbor he built (1930s)

The new barn built by Dad about 1930

Mom & Dad Kelley at Dixon home in the 1970s. The front gate hung between the two large trees. The pine tree behind them stood in the middle of the circular driveway.

BONDING OVER BREAKFAST – OR LUNCH – OR DINNER

An article in the "Oregonian's" Food section this week was titled, "More Americans Bonding over Breakfast." As I read it, I not only thought I could "smell the coffee," I thought I might also "smell" a story—about what breakfast was like at my Ross grandparents' home, in about 1933 or '34 when I was eight or nine years old.

Grandpa's name was Joseph Everett; Grandma was Oda May, and her maiden name was DeLancy. They had twelve living children: Jesse, Nellie May, Herbert (called "Hub") Edna, Bertha (my mom, nicknamed "Bert"), Susie Lillard, Cora, Everett Arthur (known as "Pete"), Ernest Theodore ("Dutch," for some reason), Sylvia Ann (called "Sib"), Inez Mabel (would you believe "Bun"), and last was Percy Edwin (known as "Pert"). The first four of them, who were older than my mother, were married, and some had grown children of their own by this time. Aunt Nellie Shelden lived on a farm not far away from Grandma and Grandpa, and two or three of her older sons were often visiting and working for my grandparents who still had five of their own children at home. This gives you an idea of the number of people involved at a mealtime there—and when our family visited, there were seven more—including children aged one to nine years old. Uncle Pert was twenty; the Shelden boys were nineteen, twenty, and twenty-one.

When we visited, we stayed for two or three days, because we lived twenty-five or so miles away; and sometimes traveled there in a horse-drawn wagon. Most of a day was allowed for a wagon trip. Another story includes more details about that.

After spending a night at the Ross home, I knew it was morning when I awakened to the fragrance of coffee brewing, ham frying, and biscuits baking! I can see now, in my mind's eye, Grandma holding the coffee grinder on her apron-covered lap, grinding coffee beans to put into her coffee pot. It wasn't a "Mr. Coffee" with a drip filter—for her family of up to eight coffee drinkers, it was boiled in a large, blue and white-speckled enamel coffee pot—cooked long enough for the aroma to reach every part of the house. (Sometimes when coffee was made later in the day, I could have the privilege of turning the crank on the top of the wooden box that housed the grinder and pull out the drawer full of ground-up beans.)

The ham was cured in their smoke house, with meat from hogs they had raised and butchered themselves. Each generous slice was edged with a half-inch or more of fat, so after it was cooked in the big black iron skillet, there was a nice bowlful of "red-eye" gravy, made by pouring a little water into the pan to boil for a minute. That was very yummy spooned over a split-open biscuit or sopped out of your plate where it had mixed with "runny" egg yolk.

Biscuits were made fresh from "scratch" for every meal (except quite often there was corn-bread for noon dinner). Grandma had a wooden mixing bowl into which she placed several cupfuls of flour and made a nest in the middle of it. Into that nest went some milk (usually buttermilk), some cream, some salt, and some Clabber Girl baking powder or Arm & Hammer soda. With her right-hand fingers, she worked it into a soft dough—but not using all the flour. Meanwhile, a couple of large baking pans were in the oven of the generous, wood-fired cook stove—melting some dollops of lard. They were brought out to receive the biscuits which Grandma formed by squeezing off a chunk of dough, patting it flat with a little flour so it didn't stick to her fingers. She had put a table knife, or some such thing, under one end of the pan, so that the melted lard ran to one end. Each biscuit top was dipped into the melted lard, then laid dipped-side-up at the other end of the pan. She placed them with their edges touching, so that when they were done, their sides were soft, except for the ones around the edges of the pans. (I thought the ones that cooked along the edges of the pan, forming a brown crust, were especially good with her home-made butter and some kind of jam, molasses, or apple butter).

When the biscuits were nearly done, the eggs were fried—enough for each person to have two or three. Most were cooked "over-easy," but some were done "sunny-side-up," and some were fully cooked—all served on platters.

The table looked awfully long to my young eyes—I'm guessing it would seat at least six people on each side, with one or two at each end. It sat on the window-side of the long dining room—a room that was used for a lot more things than just dining—and between the table and the wall was a long bench for seating on that side. The covering was of oil cloth—whatever design happened to be available when Grandma bought a replacement, or more often just white. Food was put on the table for passing—at least two serving dishes of each thing: the biscuits, ham, gravy (red-eye, plus white gravy made with milk), eggs, butter, jam, and some kind of canned fruit. There was plenty of milk for kids, teen-agers, and anyone else who wanted some. (Grandma's favorite milk was buttermilk, but for breakfast she drank coffee.) Grandpa wanted his coffee "saucered." After he added the sugar and cream, he poured some out into a sauce-dish that was put by his plate. He said it needed to be cooled off some before he could drink it—out of the saucer!

Mealtime there was a joyful occasion—always a lot of good food, a <u>bunch</u> of people, and plenty of talking. Some of it was about work plans for the day—who would work where, etc.—or about something someone had seen while out around the farm. Often the older boys got teased about their love-life that Grandpa called "girlin." When our family was visiting there were twelve people; fourteen or fifteen if some of the Shelden cousins happened to be there, too. To make room for everyone to eat at the same time, some of the children stood, squeezed between some adults, or in the spaces at the corners. Very small children sat on someone's lap. (There were two aunties who liked to hold small ones!)

Yes, there was "bonding"! A Grandpa and Grandma with great senses of humor, aunties who adored the children, uncles and cousins who played music on guitars and French harps when meals were finished, chores we could help with, animals to meet, and acres to roam! Sometimes families besides ours were all there at the same time. On those occasions, there were at least two "sittings" at mealtimes: men always first, and maybe some women; children always second, along with women who had been servers at the first sitting. Some of the older children loaded up plates and took them outside, if weather permitted.

By the time I had children of my own, my grandparents were gone, as well as some uncles and aunts; cousins were scattered, and visiting became more difficult. Consequently, my children missed the joy of getting to know most of those people—and I have missed knowing the extended younger generations. I'm so very thankful for those "Good Old Days" that were called "Hard Times," but for the people who were gathered together there then, they were "The Best of Times"!

SANTA CLAUS

I grew up in a Christian home, so I always knew that the reason we celebrated Christmas was to remember when Jesus was born. The details of the occasion were often talked about in the family and at Sunday School. Mom or Dad frequently read us the story that Luke wrote in the Bible about Mary and Joseph finding shelter in a stable because there were no vacant rooms at Bethlehem's inn—about the angels singing and startling the shepherds who were tending their sheep in the hills nearby—about them following the angel's direction to find the stable where "they found Mary and Joseph and the babe, lying in a manger."

But there was another character in the Christmas season that didn't seem to have anything to do with Jesus—and that was Santa Claus. I could understand the part about Jesus and celebrating His birthday, because we celebrated <u>my</u> birthday, too—and Mom's and Dad's and my little brother's, and Grandpa Kelley's. But it was quite mysterious how a man with a white beard and a red suit could go all over the world in a sleigh pulled by reindeer, flying through the sky, go down a chimney while everyone was asleep, and put gifts in the stockings the children hung up before they went to bed. <u>We</u> didn't even <u>have</u> a fireplace chimney—just a small metal stove pipe, and for <u>sure</u> he couldn't get into the house through it! But Mom explained to my satisfaction that though she had never seen him herself, for people who didn't have chimneys she supposed he just came through the door.

Well, the Christmas Eve when I was four years old, we got to see him in person—at least Mom, Ross who was two, and four-month-old baby Barbara did. Dad always went out to the barn before bedtime to make sure everything was okay, and to spend his daily lengthy time in the outhouse. It was while he was out that there was a knock at the front door. Mom, with Barbara on her lap, was reading a bedtime story to us, and I resented having that interrupted. Then through the door window we saw a funny looking man with a wooly-looking beard. I was frightened! I'd never seen anyone who looked like that before! Mom later said my "eyes got as big as saucers." She didn't seem to be upset, though, and asked me to open the door because she was holding the baby. I had to be <u>urged</u> to do it, because I didn't really want that man to be in the house, but I had learned to do what I was told to do.

Once he was in, he sat down and put his lumpy looking sack down beside him. It was a big burlap bag we called a "tow-sack." Then he started asking Ross and me if we had been good. He said he was Santa, but he didn't have on a red suit like in picture books. He <u>did</u> have a beard that looked like a sheep's wool, a red stocking cap, a full-length brown wool coat with a black fur collar, black rubber boots, and pants that were navy blue with small blue-green stripes. They were tucked into the tops of his boots. I asked, "Why aren't you wearing a red suit like in the pictures?" He said, "I have a lot of different kinds of clothes, and this time I wanted to wear these because they're so comfortable." (I suppose he was glad I didn't insist on seeing the reindeer!)

After we talked more about the being good thing—yes, I helped my mother with work when she asked me, and did my "chores;" yes, I played with my brother and baby sister; yes, I helped my dad sometimes like bringing him a hammer or nails. He said he had brought some toys for us, and then he would have to be going to see other children. I couldn't see what all he had in his bag, but for me he pulled out a darling baby doll with a little pink coat and cap. For Ross there was a little truck that would dump its load when you pushed a lever, and for Barbara a little rubber cat's head that "mewed" when it was squeezed. He gave Ross and me an orange, some colorful hard candy, some candy corn, a couple of chocolate candies known in those days as "nigger toes," and a few nuts.

Not long after he left, Dad came in the back door and found Ross and me literally beside ourselves with excitement. We were both talking at once to tell him about Santa's visit and showing him our "goodies." Dad said, "Well, what did Santa look like?" Evidently the thing that really stuck in my mind was the pants. After describing the rest of his appearance, I excitedly said, "And Daddy! He had pants just like yours!" I can still "see" those pants in my mind's eye, but I didn't make the connection until some years later that Santa and Dad were both wearing those pants that same evening, and the coat with the black fur collar was Mom's.

I kept on believing that Santa filled our stockings until I was maybe eight years old, although soon after "the visit" I was told that peoples' exchange of gifts was to symbolize the gifts brought to Jesus by "the Wise Men from the East." While rummaging through some boxes of things Mom had stored in an upstairs closet, I found some cards of bobby pins—for holding hair in place. I probably was looking for some of Mom's old clothes for playing "dress-up" which was one of our fun things to do when we played "house" with our dolls. I just left the hairpins there without reasoning why they were there, but then, come Christmas, those very hairpins showed up in my stocking! That bothered me, and I kept thinking about it. When I had a chance to go upstairs without being noticed, I dug into that box of old clothes where I had seen the bobby pins before. They were gone! So I told Mom privately about my frustration. I so wanted to believe Santa had put them in my stocking, I almost didn't want to know the truth I was afraid those hairpins might reveal. She gently told me that Santa was a lovely myth that people in many different countries had told their children for generations. "But Mom!" I said. "We've seen him! He came right here to our house!" She laughed her little quiet kind of laugh and told me it was actually Dad just pretending to be Santa to have some fun with Ross and me. "A-ha!" said I. "That's why Santa had pants just like Dad's!" She suggested we keep my discovery as our little secret from the younger kids so they could enjoy the excitement of Santa a few years longer.

14

Well, that was quite a shocking experience, but with finding out it was all a myth relieved me of a lot of wondering about the flying reindeer and gave me a feeling of a sort of "rite of passage." I could now be a member of the grown-up group having fun with Santa surprises for the younger ones. It was quite amazing how that added to my feeling about myself as a real person!

WHERE'S THE BEEF?

I've heard of a radio program called "The Splendid Table." Those words stir my imagination, expecting to hear about gourmet recipes, exotic spices, and aromatic herbs. Food is one of our necessities for life, and it stands to reason that as long as we have to eat, why not add to the enjoyment of it with variety and enhanced flavor? I doubt if anyone would call my childhood table "splendid," but it was always well-attended by five growing children with big appetites, enjoying whatever was on the menu! (You might have to use your imagination, because there may be things described here that you haven't experienced! Life is different now!)

Living in the country, having a family garden, and sometimes harvesting various wild delicacies, certainly provided a variety of foods—and Mom did a great job of that! She also would often say while we might be helping with the cooking, "Let's put some of this in, to make it good." If it was extra butter she was adding, she'd say, "This will make it real good!"

Even until the day she went to the hospital the final time at age ninety-three, if she knew you were coming (or often, even if she didn't), you'd find a cobbler or a pie or two on the kitchen counter. The most frequent one was probably peach cobbler. The really best ones were in the summer, made with fresh peaches, but she had a winter's supply of home-canned fruit on the basement shelves. Grandpa Kelley had one peach tree that had early fruit—always ripe by my birthday—June 21st. His gift to me was a peach for each year of my age, but he also brought extra ones, enough for Mom to make a cobbler, and he'd always accept her invitation to stay for dinner. Peach cobbler seemed to be his favorite delicacy. Mom also made one for his birthday in November.

Blackberry cobbler was one of the uses for the products of our labors in the hot, summer sun. July was probably their ripening time. We'd get up extra early in the morning to try to get our buckets filled before the sun got high. Everyone had to have a hat, (or a bonnet), long sleeves, shoes, kerosene rubbed around ankles to keep off some of the chiggers, and a belt or strap to hold the bucket, in order to free both hands for picking. In the berry patch, we had to be aware of possible snakes, especially copperheads. There were many garter snakes, but they were okay—not poisonous, and they ate many unwanted bugs. Berries that were not used right away on cereal, in a bowl with sugar and thick cream, or for cobbler, were canned or made into jelly and jam.

Our meats came mostly from our barnyard or from the woods. Chicken was plentiful, but time had to be allowed for catching, killing, plucking feathers, removing inedible parts, and cutting it into useable pieces—or roasting it whole. I was never called upon to do the catching or killing, but I was often there; and often helped with the rest of the preparation. To make catching the chicken easier, Dad took a long piece of heavy wire, bent one end of it into a hook shaped like a shepherd's crook, and made the other end into a handle-shape. With that, a chicken's leg could be snagged without it having to be chased. The killing procedure would sound quite gruesome to many people, so I'll have to think more about how to describe it—or even if I will. Maybe it might best be left to my reader's imagination. The "tools" used were a wood chopping block and a sharp hand-axe. I suppose those things became commonplace and taken-for-granted by farm kids, for whom it's all just part of food preparation. Of course, all those procedures had to happen to other kinds of meat, too: pork, rabbit, and squirrel were our most common resources, as well as an occasional raccoon or quail. Our neighbors—the Hile's—sometimes gave us some back-bones (with delicious meat on them) or some steaks when they butchered beef. We didn't eat much beef because we had no refrigeration to keep it from spoiling. It would have needed to be canned, which would have been more work and time than Mom wanted to use. Fish (except for canned salmon) wasn't often on our menu. Sometimes in summer we went a few miles to the Gasconade River to camp for a couple of days, and if we were lucky, we might catch a few catfish or sunperch to fry over our open fire. A "preacher friend" (Brother O'Dell) who liked to fish, occasionally brought some small bass—very tasty when breaded and fried! Those visits were part of his socializing when he came to our community to preach at our church. He was a really jolly, white-haired man who loved to laugh and joke. He was probably no more than fifty or sixty years old, but we children thought of him as "old"!

Chicken came to the table in a number of different ways: fried was the most usual, because it was quicker. To make it really good, Mom used an iron skillet with a generous amount of lard, heated to a sizzling temperature; then in went the chicken pieces, dredged in a mixture of flour, salt, pepper, and maybe a little crumbled sage. That was browned on both sides, covered to "cook through", then uncovered for a few minutes to become crisp. As the chickens aged, a fat hen was often chosen to make the supreme sacrifice for a pot of chicken soup and dumplings—or maybe as a special treat—with home-made noodles that were dried for awhile in the sun. I don't remember any special effort being made to remove fat that rose to the top of the pot, either! Sliding into the hot soup, passing through that layer of fat on top, was probably what made the dumplings and noodles so tasty!

Rabbits and squirrels were cooked in those same ways—depending upon age: young ones fried, older ones made into stew or soup with dumplings. Rabbits were usually caught in traps made from pieces of a small hollow log or wooden boxes. An apple core made a good bait to throw into the trap—making sure it went all the way to the back. There was a "trigger" made of a slim stick, placed with one end going into the trap about half-way to the back of the trap—so it would move when touched by the rabbit's back. That released the raised door on the front of the trap to make it fall down, keeping the rabbit inside to enjoy his apple until my brothers "ran the trap line" before they went to school. If we needed some meat, one of those rabbits might be fried for the table; otherwise it was prepared for selling for a few cents. As I remember, ten cents was considered a quite good price.

Squirrel was more special because acquiring one required hunting and having great skill in using a rifle. Grandpa Kelley supplied some of those little animals, and my brother Ross enjoyed hunting with him—eventually becoming a good hunter himself.

Well, it's time to at least name some other menu items: beans (the dried variety) and cornbread—baked beans, was a use for the left-over beans. (Green onions with that were tasty!) Potato soup and dumplings was a frequent favorite. Actually, potatoes were an important "staple" for us. Bushels of them could be stored in the cellar for use all winter—baked, fried, mashed, creamed, stewed, or made into a very tasty salad. For breakfast we could expect biscuits and cream gravy; fried ham with "red-eye" gravy; sausage; fried eggs; pancakes with cream "syrup"; cream of wheat; oatmeal (often with raisins); and as a real treat, French toast—which Mom called "egg bread." Vegetables from the garden came to the table in summer, or from the cellar in winter. An early spring treat was green peas in cream sauce. Later came green beans, carrots, okra (usually fried), and tomatoes—sliced in summer, cooked and poured over chunks of bread in winter; corn on the cob in summer—canned in winter and cooked with cream sauce. In the summer we had watermelons and cantaloupe, cucumbers—sliced in summer, pickled in winter; and strawberries for cereal in a bowl with sugar and cream; and for delicious shortcake. Extra ones made jars of jelly and jam.

Every few days Mom made five loaves of yeast bread. She usually timed the baking so it was coming out of the oven about the time we came home from school. Imagine a thick slice of that warm bread, slathered with homemade butter or thick cream! A little sugar sprinkled on it—or some grape or blackberry jelly spread on top—made it really good. In summer when we were at home all day, we frequently had "fried bread" for lunch on baking day. Flattened, uncooked bread dough was used to cook that delicious treat!

In winter, we looked forward to scooping up a large bowlful of freshly-fallen snow, to which Mom added sugar, vanilla, and thick cream, to make "Snow Cream"! In summer, part of the Fourth of July celebration was taking a block of ice home with us, after we went to the public picnic at the park in Dixon and making ice cream in the evening! There was nearly always some delicious cake (maybe even decorated for the holiday) on hand to eat with it!

Maybe you're thinking: "But where's the beef?" Did we have a "Splendid Table"? Most definitely! And love made it extra splendid! Even without the beef!

INSIGHTS and LESSONS

I have written other stories about Santee School—the one-room country school where my dad was also a student when he was a child in mid-Missouri. It's interesting to think that the title of this story would take my thoughts back to those earliest experiences with "education," in order to compare some of them with modern-day school practices. My own children have long ago finished elementary and high school, so most of what I know about school these days is "what I read in the papers."

When decisions are made by teachers or school boards, or legislators, that there isn't time or funds for all the programs we've sometimes enjoyed, it seems that art and/or music programs are often the ones that are suggested for cutting. Then I wonder if people realize how much can be done in those areas with very little time and very little money. It may not even be necessary to have special teachers with degrees in art or music. At Santee, our one teacher taught all subjects in all eight grades in that one-room school! And that is where my appreciation of art and music began!

In my opinion, the first five or six grades are some of the most fruitful years for much of our very basic learning. The foundations are laid from which interests develop and curiosity is sparked. It doesn't mean that all of those kids are going to become artists or concert musicians, although many of them may. The important thing is that they have an introduction from which appreciation can develop. If there can be a development of the subjects with more personal participation, the students will benefit even more. (For instance, research now seems to show that knowledge of music and its rhythm actually improves the understanding of math.)

In Missouri at the time I was in grade school—1931 to 1937—the State Department of Education developed courses of study for all subjects that were to be taught. Kits of instructional helps were sent to the teachers periodically. Once a month our school received an art packet that included a large poster-print of some famous painting. The teacher tacked the poster to the middle of the bulletin board and left it there to be observed until the next one arrived the following month. Just having it there to see meant that it was more than likely being subconsciously imprinted into our young minds. In addition, each student received a leaflet with a small copy of the picture, a brief history of the artist, and an interpretation of the painting—what the artist might have been trying to portray; something of the techniques used in the painting; attention called to the lighting or perspective, etc. These leaflets were "graded"—appropriate level of language for the youngest students—but when it was time for the art class, the whole school participated at the same time so that ideas and feelings of all the different ages of children were heard and discussed.

Similar procedures were followed with music, when the once-a-month packet came to the teacher. In the packet were a picture of the composer, a description of his life, and a few seventy-eight RPM (revolutions per minute) records of samples of different compositions. Even on our hand-cranked Victrola (record player), with the imperfect transmission of sound, young souls were stirred by the majesty of Beethoven's *Fifth Symphony*; the beauty of Handel's *Hallelujah Chorus*; the mental vision of Chopin's flying fingers playing his *Minute Waltz*; the lovely mood felt with Schumann's *Traumerei*; or the quiet reverence one felt with hearing about Franz Gruber's writing of *Silent Night,* etc.

I had another interesting experience with classical music in high school—in typing class where we practiced typing in rhythm to the tune of a march from the opera *Aida*.

I remember that one of my feelings about Beethoven was wondering how he could write such wonderful music when he was deaf! Thankfully, I think he had learned how to put the notes on paper before he became deaf! The <u>world</u> wouldn't be the same without Beethoven's inspiring music!

I am not an artist in any sense of the word, nor am I a musician. But I am very thankful for my childhood exposures to art and music—however meager—that enabled me to develop an appreciation for them. I'm thankful for having my attention called to the mysterious smile of Leonardo da Vinci's *Mona Lisa,* to the special light in Rembrandt's *Night Watch,* to the lovely colors and expressions in *Blue Boy,* and in Degas' ballet dancers, to the feeling of participating in the *Creation* as God's finger almost touches the finger of Adam on Michelangelo's Sistine Chapel ceiling painting, of being able to understand Van Gogh's pain when I see his *Sunflowers* and his countryside landscapes!

Let us not let money or time deprive young children of exposure to classical art or music. It's an investment that pays great dividends on even a modest down-payment!

SANTEE SCHOOL
1931—1937

From the time I was three or four years old I was eager to learn to read and write, so I was really happy to become six—and old enough to begin going to school at Santee! My teacher, Miss Lorena Rollins, had to drive past our house to get to school, so she was agreeable to pick me up on her way each morning, and give me a ride home after school each day. It was another one and a half miles to school, so I was really happy to not have to walk alone along the busy highway!

It was a typical one-room school house that was well built with three large windows on each side, three steps up to the covered front porch, and a well-house nearby. Inside, at the back end, was a long blackboard with the teacher's desk on a platform that was one-step high across the width of the room. At one end of that space was a long bench that was called the "recitation" bench; at the other end were book cases. A round heating stove was in the middle of the room; and student desks were lined up along the sides of the room, facing the front. Each desk was wide enough to seat two students and had space under the slanted top to hold books and other supplies. Seats folded up when not in use. Hooks for hanging coats were on the back wall. There was a small table for the bucket of drinking water in one corner at the back of the room, and spaces for many other items to be kept handy for use.

All eight grades were taught—the seventh and eighth grades in alternate years. As soon as the students were seated, we heard the teacher say, "All rise, and pledge allegiance" to the flag that was hanging at the front of the room. Then each class had its turn to go sit at the front of the room to "recite" by answering questions asked by the teacher. Everyone else studied to prepare for their turn to go to the "recitation bench." I often used some of that time to listen to upper classes recite!

Half-way between beginning of classes and noon, we were given a few minutes to go outside to play, or "whatever." Sometimes simple games were organized; sometimes it was just free time, or rest-room visits. (Those were located a small distance from the back of the main building—one for girls and one for boys.)

Every Friday afternoon was used for some "fun" things—educational games using math, geography, spelling, art, music, etc.

Lorena Rollins resigned after two years, and our new teacher for the next few years was Irene Humphreys. Both of those ladies were excellent instructors!

From the time I was four years old I was eager to learn, and was soon able to read, write, and do simple math; so I was quite bored with <u>first</u> grade! The teacher let me recite with the second grade, and I began my second year of school in the third grade—being promoted soon to the fourth grade. By 1937, I was ready to graduate from the eighth grade! With "honors"!

SANTEE SCHOOL   Fall of 1939

TOP ROW *(left to right): Orpha Jones, Opal Withers, Aleen Vaughn, Ross Kelley, Bobby Withers, Christine Perkins (teacher)*

MIDDLE ROW: *Dola Kelley, Louise Jones, Barbara Kelley, Mary Ellen Evans, Oneda Boucher, Charles Hood Evans, Bill Switzer*

BOTTOM ROW: *Dean Withers, Norma Alexander, Marjorie Boucher, Maurice Alexander, Harold Switzer, Patsy Rollins, Joy Kelley, Billie Jones*

IN FRONT *(holding hands): Dale Kelley, Sterling Junior Kelley*

(Ages of the Kelley Children: Ross, 11; Barbara, 9; Joy, 7; Sterling Junior, 5; Ila was student in 1931-1937 and therefore is not in this picture)

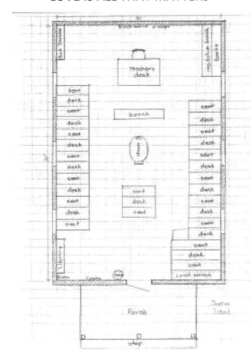

AUTUMN IN MY CHILDHOOD

Leaves that are now changing the colors of some of the trees into glorious shades of red, of yellow, of orange, of brown, and some of almost purple, remind me of autumn in my Missouri country home. (I have to include here the memory of a very dear Army chaplain friend, because there is a "leaf" connection. We lived at Fort Leonard Wood, Missouri, for a while during WWII. A Sunday church service was held in the community building of the housing area that was called Lenwood Place, and the Post Chaplain, Lt. Col. Leon M. Hall officiated. One autumn Sunday morning he used a description of the colorful leaves we were currently seeing for some point he wanted to make in his sermon. He was a very happy, jovial man with about three "chins," and a chubby face to go with his chubby body. In my mind's eyes and ears I can even now see and hear those words, slowly and expressively rolling out of his mouth in his wonderful, southern drawl, "red, orange, yellow, and purple." Purple was kind of emphasized by pursing his lips. Later at home we children laughed about his description, because he seemed sort of "carried away" with his list of colors—and we thought we had never seen "purple" leaves! Since then, I've seen MANY purple leaves!)

Conifer trees here in Oregon serve as dark backgrounds for deciduous ones, which seems to make the fall colors look even brighter. In my part of central Missouri, the only evergreens were occasional pines, and some red cedar, so more different colors surrounded us. There were sugar maple, silver maple, hickory, black walnut, elm, sumac, dogwood, red bud, gum, willow, wild plum, persimmon, sassafras, to name a few; and many kinds of oak—white oak, black oak, and post oak were the most common near our place. I often heard Dad speak of using post oak wood for making his fence posts because it was strong, had a straight grain that made it easy to split, and was durable enough to withstand weather for many years.

Behind our house, and along the cleared space that was used for pasture, fields, orchard, and garden, was what seemed to us children to be "deep" scary woods. It was easy to imagine there might even be bears back there among those trees—especially if one had to go to the outhouse in the dark! Mom and Dad assured us no bears lived in Missouri, but did they really know that for sure? There were other animals, though—squirrels, rabbits, possums, coons, and lots of birds, including noisy crows, hooting owls, large buzzards, and hawks that often lazily circled of the field looking for a snack of a field mouse or a chipmunk. A small creek ran through the woods and continued across our field, expanding the possibilities for adventures. Mom didn't like for us to wander <u>too</u> far into the woods, in case we'd get lost, but we made good use of the near part of it in all seasons. We even imagined that fairies lived in some of the mossy places and built play-houses under trees—outlining the "walls" of the rooms with rows of rocks or sticks.

Maybe the times I'm being reminded of now were times when we'd walk in the woods with Dad in autumn after the leaves had fallen. He frequently went looking for dead trees he could cut to use for firewood, and autumn and winter were good times to do that. Of course, the ground would be covered with fallen leaves, in some places, ankle-deep. Dad looked for—and found—enjoyment in just about everything he did. So while we were walking to look for the dead trees, he had fun along with us, shuffling our feet through the leaves—giving each step a "shushing" sound that was even louder later in the year when the leaves had dried.

Raking leaves from the lawn gave us games to play even while we worked! Colorful leaves from three large maple trees and from a couple of oaks were there. After the piles were gathered, we took turns burying each other for awhile before we had to finally pile them on the wheelbarrow and move them to be dumped in the woods. That took many trips with little brother or sister riding on them to help hold them down—and of course, especially entertaining for the ones who got to ride.

Writing here about raking leaves reminds me of a situation I once read about in a little book called *Love* by Leo Buscaglia, who at one time was a professor of education at the University of Southern California. He loved the beauty of the trees in his yard. And when the leaves had fallen he just left them on the ground and the sidewalk in front of his house. He enjoyed walking through them to and from his door—no doubt the same kind of "shuffling" I so enjoyed with my Dad. One day he was at home with some of his students who were there for a discussion session, when there was a knock on the front door. A group of neighbors had come to complain about what they saw as a neighborhood "eyesore." They asked him to clean up his leaves, and even offered to do it for him. He complied with the request, surprising his students who thought he had a right to enjoy his leaves. He told them that if they'd help him rake the leaves and put them into some baskets, they could reach a solution. When the leaves were finally collected, he gathered the baskets and poured the leaves over his living room floor—satisfying his neighbors with a cleared lawn, and still enjoying his leaves! (He must have lived alone—or else had a wife who shared his love of leaves!) For me, that story is really enjoyable, because I understand his "leaf thing"!

Well, life has given me quite a number of years in which to enjoy autumn leaves in many different places, and for that, I am truly grateful. From my adult viewpoint, however, I know they can be problems that have to be dealt with—they have to be cleaned out of the gutters, removed from the lawn and from the gravel driveway to keep them from killing grass and filling the gravel with debris that turns into mud. But that's okay. I still have plenty of time to "feast my eyes" on their beauty, and to "feed my spirit" with happy memories!

And now, I have two young grandsons, Thomas and Evan, who agree with me that playing in colorful leaves is a lot of fun! We pile them up, wade through them, iron them between pieces of waxed paper, and <u>they</u> roll around in them! Fortunately, my neighbors aren't ones to complain about the appearance of my lawn, so we won't be dumping leaves on my living room floor! We'll just enjoy them out there under the trees!

I WAS TAKEN *ABACK*!

The idea for this story came this week when I heard someone on the radio use the term "taken aback." From the time I began learning to read at about age three, reading has been one of my most enjoyable activities. Even when I played with my dolls before I was old enough to go to school, I had fun dressing and undressing them, pretending we were entertaining company or going visiting. But the best fun with them was sitting them down and reading to them. I'd even turn the book around so they could "see" the pictures!

As I became old enough (as the eldest child in the family), to have some rather major "chores" to do, I almost resented having to get my work done before I was free to read. I've often thought my mom was really smart to impose that discipline, because I was encouraged to work faster—and she got work done without having to do it herself. And why <u>shouldn't</u> I help with the work? I had "pay-back"—a loving family, a comfortable shelter, and good food to eat! But nothing dampened my joy of reading or quenched my thirst for knowledge.

When I was about middle-school age, I became fascinated with word meanings, and enjoyed using the dictionary. Looking up a word didn't stop at just finding what I wanted to know about <u>that</u> word. I'd notice some of the words before and after it or read about a picture that might be on that page of the dictionary. I decided that, for a New Year's resolution, I would read all the way through the dictionary! The one we had wasn't a complete unabridged, but it was maybe about the size of a *Webster's Collegiate.*

Well! I was "taken aback"! Look at those words that I'd never even heard of! A-a, a bed of solid lava in Hawaii! Aardvark, an animal I'd never heard of! And there was even a picture of it! Aback, I hadn't "heard" it before, but now I was "feeling" it! And I also felt a bit abashed!

After reading a few pages of "A" words, my interest abated, and I considered abandoning my project. It would be bondage to complete that task! Instead, I would dedicate my energy to being more flexible—giving attention to a habit of improving my jargon and knowledge by locating meanings when they were needed. It was obvious presently, that my quest was not rational. I would squander time that would be urgently valuable for more wholesome activity. Even Xerxes would consider that project a waste of youth! So my zeal amounted almost to zilch! After all, I hadn't yet heard of Zen or zucchini, either!

That year's resolution did accomplish something, though. It impressed upon my memory the meanings of some of those words I discovered during the short period of that reading project. And even after all those years, it reminds me of an exciting time of youthful enthusiasm! Please don't take my Dictionary away!

JOY'S DISAPPEARANCE

We aren't sure if anyone was assigned the job of supervising Joy, or not. It was more than likely just supposed that with all of the family around the house, two adults and five children, all could be accounted for at any given time.

It was a typical late summer day—too warm to be very active—but Mom and Dad didn't believe in being completely idle, so most of us were doing something, except for three-year-old Sterling, who was taking his afternoon nap, and five-year-old Joy who was "just resting." She was lying on the couch with a doll or two, singing to them and telling them some of her imaginary stories. Mom was busy in the kitchen, while Ross, Barbara, and I were in-and-out, doing who-knows-what. Dad's job that day was cleaning gutters and doing some minor things around the house and yard.

But you need to know a bit about the neighborhood. We lived in the country, two miles north of Dixon, Missouri, on a small ten-acre farm. I suppose most of the farms around us were quite small, too, because houses were something like a quarter, half, or as much as a mile apart. Except that <u>our</u> closest neighbors, Earl and Mary Hile, were just across the road. They were lovely, elderly people who had moved there from Trenton, Missouri, after retirement from his career with the railroad. In those days railroad men were considered to be quite "well-fixed." Not only did they earn a better-than-most pay check, but they retired with a nice monthly pension check. So Granddad and Grandma Hile (as we called them) seemed to us to be quite rich. They had beautiful wool rugs, a fancy lamp that pulled down over their dining table like a chandelier, a Model-T touring car, a team of horses, a cow, some chickens, a little dog, and numerous barn cats. We had a cow and chickens and cats, too, but they had <u>more</u>. And our floors were covered with linoleum. Of course, we <u>all</u> used kerosene for lights, wood for heating and cooking, and outhouse "bathroom" facilities. But <u>they</u> had factory-made covers on their toilet seats, and rolls of "tissue" instead of Sears Roebuck catalog paper! When our chickens slowed down their egg production, we bought eggs from Hiles for, I think, twenty cents a dozen. They also sold eggs and cream in town— got dressed up every Saturday and drove to Dixon for their shopping—then again on Sunday to go to church at the Baptist church. They encouraged us children to visit them, but Mom didn't let us go too often because she was afraid we'd "make a nuisance" of ourselves. It was our job, however, to go get eggs, and we traded milk when our cows were dry before calving. They always got up early, getting their work done before noon, and then relaxed all afternoon—in the summer, sitting on the shady side of their house in comfortable lawn chairs among all kinds of flowers. They also always saved the Sunday comics from their newspaper for us children to read.

Well, back to the Kelley's house. Instead of a well for storing water, Dad had dug a cistern when he built our house. It was rather small and round at the top (wide enough for a man to enter and go down into it with a ladder) and went straight down for several feet. Then it became wider, and went down to a rounded bottom, about twenty feet deep. The water was filtered through gravel and charcoal during the cold winter rains, being collected by the gutters off the metal roof. In the summer it was directed instead to barrels and used for laundry, watering plants, etc. We were known to have the coldest, sweetest drinking water in the community—and it was right outside the kitchen door, very handy!

LOVE IS ALL THAT MATTERS

On this summer day when the water was almost to its lowest point, Dad decided to go down into the cistern and check the concrete plaster, so he moved the pump from over the hole and went around to the other side of the house to get the ladder from where he'd been working earlier. At about that time I suppose Mom realized the living room was quiet and went in to see if Joy had fallen asleep. But Joy wasn't there! Mom called her, but no answer. Then she yelled to all of us, "Have any of you seen Joy?" We all began searching—out to the barn, the outhouse, upstairs, in the closets, in the cellar, by the woodpile. All of us were becoming frantic, even trying to remember if any cars had gone by that might have kidnapped her. Then Dad remembered the open cistern. He had only been away from it for a couple of minutes going to get the ladder…was it possible she could have fallen in? He looked and listened but could see no water movement nor hear any sounds.

Then, just when he was ready to put the ladder down into the cistern for a better look, Ross saw Joy coming down Hiles' long driveway towards home, walking carefully over the gravel with her bare feet. He and Barbara and I ran to meet her and asked, "Why did you go to Hiles' without telling someone?" She happily said, "Oh, I just went over to see if they had any new kittens!"

We were all so happy to find her, I don't think she even got scolded, but I'm sure she later heard some serious words from Mom and Dad, and we all learned some good lessons from the experience!

I WISH I HAD A . . .

When I was a child our family, and many others in our neighborhood, were quite poor. That is to say, there wasn't a lot of money, and it had to be wisely budgeted and used first for necessities. But we were rich if we considered the love and attention given to our "upbringing." Probably the lack of money added to our appreciation of values, as well as to the worth of things that cost a lot.

Mom and Dad both were musical—Mom had been an organist in the country church where she grew up. Her family had an organ in their home, similar to the one at their church—foot pedals pumped bellows that moved air over the reeds, which were opened by pressing various keys on the keyboard. The foot action had to be continuous to keep the air flowing while the fingers were busy at the keyboard. Dad played guitar, harmonica, banjo, and fiddle, read music, and loved to sing all kinds of songs from funny folk songs to the spiritually "touching" songs at church.

One day he brought home a mahogany cabinet-style Victrola (record player)—the kind that had to be wound up with a crank on the side in order for the record turntable to turn. To operate it, one lifted the top lid, let the metal lock-brace click into place to hold it up, placed a record called a "platter" on the turntable so the hole in the middle of the record went down over a small metal peg; turned the crank on the side as long as it would turn, then moved a small lever-type switch to "on." After the record began rotating "up-to-speed," an arm containing a sharp needle was set upon the record at the beginning, being careful to get it into the outer groove that led into the grooves that produced the sound. The lid could then be closed to shut out the "needle noise"—a small scratchy sound that sometimes had a "click" sound with each revolution if the record happened to have some damaged spots. Under the turntable mechanism was a compartment covered in front with fancy cloth behind a decorative wooden grill. That area contained a horn-shaped metal lining that came from the needle arm and amplified the sound. Below that were two doors that opened to reveal shallow shelves for storing the platters—each one encased in a paper cover to protect the fragile grooves from damaging scratches.

The previous owners were lovers of classical music, and their collection of records was included! What a treasure for country kids to begin to learn Music Appreciation! Dad and neighbor friends played violins, but they played them as "fiddles" for country music tunes. Imagine my fascination when I heard *Humoresque* played on the record player by a "violinist"! I wish I could remember the name of that artist. There were Sousa marches, piano concerts, operatic arias, and orchestra music we'd never heard before, except for the "Music Appreciation packages" at school that were part of the state's required curriculum.

About that time, at age twelve or so, I began to yearn for a piano I could learn to play. If only I could have a piano, I wouldn't ever want another thing! What a wish in a family with barely enough income for the food, clothes, and other necessities for five growing children! And a budget from which the first 1/10th of income was set aside for church contribution, and the second 1/10th went into savings. It seemed like a miracle when Dad came home from work one evening a couple of years later with news that "Mrs. Somebody" would sell her old piano for $10.00! And he had bought it!

The next Saturday Dad arranged with our cousin Lee Kelley, who was also a neighbor with a pickup truck, to haul it the few miles from town. Twelve-year-old brother Ross and Dad went along to lift and to help to steady it in the back of the truck. It was called "Upright Grand," was made of oak, and was <u>very</u> heavy. What excitement there was when we saw the truck coming slowly down the road with its precious cargo! But WAIT! For some mysterious reason the piano was falling out of the truck! Parts of it came loose and went flying every-which-way as it tumbled down into the ditch! No one seemed to know how it happened, but there was a bunch of sad people wondering if it would be possible to repair it. However, it was really solid, and fortunately the strings hadn't been damaged, so Dad was able to put it back together, get it tuned, and made it almost like new.

To learn to play was next. Piano lessons cost money, and we lived in the country with only one car that Dad had to drive to work. But, as Mom always said, "Where there's a will, there's a way," and she found a <u>great</u> one. We had a new neighbor lady, Mrs. Buss, who lived about a mile from us. She and Mom and Dad had become good friends through their mutual gardening interests, although many people in the community thought her quite strange. (What the neighbors thought "strange" was simply "class" that a lot of country folks didn't recognize!) She had come from St. Louis to learn to farm in order to get away from stress that had already caused what she called a "nervous breakdown." Being an energetic, enthusiastic, perfectionist kind of person, she read extension bulletins and asked all kinds of questions pertaining to farming from everyone, because she felt a need to do everything "right." She had a cow, a couple of pigs, some chickens, and a big garden. She hired neighbors to plow and plant and harvest some crops like corn and hay, and the rest, she did herself from early morning to late evening. She was a piano teacher, besides having worked in an office in St. Louis. Her grown daughter had recently married and was studying to be an organist.

To pay for my piano lessons, I was to spend the summer between my junior and senior years of high school staying with her from Sunday evening to Friday evening, helping with the farm and house work. Everything was done by a certain routine, and I <u>loved</u> it. Some chores, like milking (at 6:00 a.m.) and feeding cow, chickens, and pigs, were done before breakfast. Then came gardening—pulling weeds, hoeing, and harvesting, as things became ready for eating or canning. Lunch was the day's main meal—meat, potatoes, and often vegetables I'd never heard of before—Kohlrabi, for instance. I washed the lunch dishes and then we both took a lying-down rest for thirty minutes or so, after which we spent another half hour or more at the piano with her instruction and help with my practicing. Then more chores and a simple supper of cereal and fruit, followed with a little time for reading before early bedtime.

Needless to say, in that summer I learned much more than piano lessons! Just listening to stories of Mrs. Buss' experiences of living in the city, hearing her philosophy, enjoying her sense of humor, and being encouraged to value education and the arts was an education in itself! She even held a little "recital" for me at the end of the summer, inviting my family, some of my young friends and their families, and serving them fancy little sandwiches and sweets with tea and lemonade. I felt like a "star"! I continued with weekly lessons after school began until I graduated and we moved away.

But other good things came from that experience of mine—she also gave lessons to my two brothers and two sisters for a year or so, although Ross soon decided piano playing wasn't his "cup of tea." The only one of us who became a "pianist" was our youngest brother Sterling. We all soon learned that he was playing "by ear" rather than learning to read the music! At the end of each lesson Mrs. Buss would play our next assignment for us so we could hear how it should sound. That was all Sterling needed! That sound was stored in his head and was transferred to his small fingers. He soon stopped lessons and entertained himself (and everyone else in hearing distance) with any music he ever heard and some he "made up" himself. <u>Lots</u> of jazz! Later, one of his first furnishings in his home he designed himself, was a shiny, black, baby grand piano with which he has relieved stress and filled his home with music for many years. Now, as a "senior citizen," he is also learning to read music and to play classical guitar!

I'm really glad I wished for a piano! But it wasn't long after the piano, that I began thinking that <u>if I could just have a typewriter, I wouldn't ever want another thing!</u>

That will have to be another story! (Bless his dear heart, Dad provided one of those, too!)

CAMPING TRIP—ABOUT 1937 OR 1938

For a man with a family of five children during the Depression years, there weren't many vacations like what we might call a vacation now. Dad needed to work as many hours as possible to earn a livelihood, and he was indeed thankful to have any work at all for some of those years. When there was occasionally some time off, we needed to spend some of it visiting my mother's family on their farm twenty-five miles away. That seemed quite a long distance in those days, because we didn't always have a car, and the trip would be made with a wagon pulled by our team of mules. Those visits were fun, but Dad considered them to be more of an obligation than real recreation. His idea of a <u>real</u> vacation was a camping trip to a river!

One camping trip that I remember best was when I was twelve or thirteen years old. Dad had recently bought a dark green '29 Oldsmobile sedan (used, of course, but in good condition), so we had good transportation. There would be fishing with "trotlines"* as well as with poles, so some preliminary preparation was needed with the fishing gear, as well as with the food supplies. (I'm thinking the name "trotline" might possibly be derived from "trawl" fishing??)

A "trotline" was made of strong, tightly twisted cotton cord about 1/4th inch in diameter—long enough to reach across the river. From that line, short ones of about 1/8th inch cord, one or two feet long were tied, with a hook on the end of each one. Various things were used for bait—like pieces of liver, worms, grasshoppers, or dough balls. Mom helped with making the dough balls that were flavored sometimes with anise. I don't remember the ingredients, but they were boiled for awhile to give them some "body."

Grandpa Kelley, Dad's father, who lived a quarter of a mile from us, was going with us on this trip, as he often did. We were his only grandchildren and received a lot of wonderful attention from him. He was frequently available for playing games with us, making wooden whistles, and such. Dad liked having him along to help with the fishing, as well as for enjoying his company. Maybe you can imagine getting this outing off to a start with three adults, five children, and the camping gear, all stuffed into and tied onto that car that was no bigger than a modern-day "medium" size automobile—although it seemed like a limousine to us then!

In order to have the use of a boat, we got permission to camp on the property of a farmer that Dad must have known. Many people who lived near a river kept a boat tied up along the bank somewhere, and anyone was welcome to use it and put it back. This place was probably ten or twenty miles away, east of Dixon, where the river was fairly deep and wide. My brother, Ross, remembers the destination as Bowl Ford on the Gasconade River. To get there, he thinks we went down the Clifty Dale road.

Being midsummer, the river was lower than normal, so we were able to drive onto a lovely spot for setting up camp, near a channel that would be good for the fishing. There were some small trees that served as supports for our tarp that made a lean-to type of shelter, and places to hang gear that needed to hang—towels, tackle, and such. We found some large rocks to make a fire pit for cooking. These were arranged with some of them close enough together that the pans could sit on two of them with the fire between them.

As soon as we arrived, Dad and Grandpa set the trotline by tying one end to a tree on our side of the river, then carrying the line by boat across to the other side where it was anchored to another tree. As they rowed across, they baited each hook; and eventually all of the line was down to the proper depth for attracting the fish. (We hoped to catch some nice catfish, which were delicious to eat, and had fewer bones than most fish.) We spent the rest of the afternoon and evening exploring, playing, cooking and eating supper; and, of course, fishing from the bank with poles Dad cut from bushes along the bank and attached strings and hooks—no reels!

Clouds were beginning to show up by the time we curled up in our bedding rolls, but they didn't seem ominous. However, it was midsummer in mid-Missouri, and thunderstorms could sometimes appear seemingly "out of the blue." And this time, one did develop! We had to break camp, because Dad had discovered that we were on a spot that would be an island if the river should rise—and we wouldn't be able to drive off! There was no time to properly pack up—and it was raining, and dark, except for flashlights—so we moved some things to higher ground, put our bedding and us into the car, and drove to the farmer's barn to look for a place to sleep. There we found a newly harvested supply of hay in the hay-mow overhead, where we again spread our bedding rolls and enjoyed wonderful sleep on the sweet-smelling hay, with the sound of rain pattering on the roof!

By morning the rain was gone, and everything looked and smelled summertime-fresh. We children were all excited to see that there hadn't been enough rain to cause the river to rise after all!

The first thing to do back at the campground was to build a fire. Then, while Dad and Grandpa "ran the trotline," Mom cooked bacon and eggs, and made some coffee for Grandpa. Anything that's cooked on a camp fire seems to taste better than it does at home sitting at a table! I don't remember how many fish we caught, but sometimes just the "going fishing" is more important than the fish that might be caught! Sometimes the best "catch" will be the memories that enrich lives and bind families together for a lifetime!

*Here is some explanatory information I found in a Webster dictionary and on the Internet: In 1741 British naturalist William Bartram first recorded "trotlines" set by Florida Seminole Indians. The term "trot" was coined in Europe. The origin of the word is debated, but in all original forms it is associated with the bed of a stream or river with moving water. The name might have come from association with a "trawl" line which is moved through the water. The "trot" line with its bait is lowered to near bottom and left in place for the fish to find!

A SPECIAL "COMFORT FOOD" (*Bread and Butter*)

Almost everyone has a special "comfort food." I love to eat, so I think I have several—Mom's potato soup and dumplings; chicken noodle soup; anything chocolate; ice cream, when as a kid and we made it in a cranked freezer with a handle on the side; "snow cream" when there was a fresh snow; or "milk toast" for someone who happened to be sick. (It was worth being sick to get some of that!)

Mom made soups in a black, iron kettle that had a rounded bottom with three little legs. To use it, she removed one of the lids from the top of the wood stove and set the kettle in the hole where it would be closer to the fire. We grew bushels of potatoes every summer and stored them in a bin in the cellar. So potatoes, in one form or another, were on the table almost every day—maybe more than once. But the favorite supper food for us children was potato soup and dumplings. With the diced potatoes, she sometimes cooked some chopped green onions from the garden and added milk and butter to make it "soupy." Last came the rich dumplings (made with cream), dropped in by spoonfuls, and cooked with the lid tightly in place until they were done. Eating that was pure happiness! (Little did we know at the time that there might have not been too many other food choices in the pantry!)

On some winter days when there was new snow on the ground, we would promise to be good all day if Mom would make some "snow cream" for us. Part of the fun was bundling up and going out to get the snow! (Maybe bringing it into the house after a game or two of "Fox and Geese.") To a large bowl of freshly scooped snow, she added a rich mixture of sugar, beaten eggs, thick cream, and a few dashes of nutmeg. That had to be mixed and dished up quickly before it melted, but what a treat it was! (Thank goodness no one had yet heard of the possibility that raw eggs might carry salmonella! Or, that raw milk might not be healthy!)

Better than medicine was the extra attention a sick child would get by having some special servings of "milk toast"! To a couple of slices of toasted home-made bread, broken into chunks in a small bowl, Mom added warm, creamy milk, flavored with a little sugar and nutmeg. (Didn't I already say that "milk toast" made it worth being sick?)

Maybe more exciting than comforting, was Mom's peach cobbler—especially on my June birthday when Grandpa Kelley brought freshly ripened peaches from his orchard! That is still one of my favorite "memory" foods, because as long as Mom lived, there was almost always a fruit cobbler on her kitchen counter—more often than not, one made with peaches!

But for just a really good comfort food that was available often, without too much "fuss," it would be very hard to top warm, homemade bread and butter! With seven people in the family, most of them taking lunch buckets to school and work, it took a lot of bread to keep us all fed! Biscuits for breakfast, and sometimes cornbread for dinner, gave some variety, but without "light bread" for slicing, our home just wouldn't have been "home"! So every-other-day, Mom baked five loaves of white, yeast bread in her wood cook-stove oven. Of course, her yeast supply had to be started with a cake of "store-bought" yeast, but after that first yeast mixture was made, a small amount of it was set aside in a small bowl, topped with a saucer, and set on top of the kitchen cabinet to use for the next batch of bread. (We had no refrigeration, but evidently that yeast mixture didn't need it. Probably sitting on top of that cabinet—where warmer air collected near the ceiling—helped the yeast to live and "work" until time for its next use. Plus, it was out of the way of young, curious hands.)

The thing that made the bread special was the timing of the cooking. Early in the day she had mixed up the big bowl of dough—kneading flour into it until it was thick, and the surface had a "satiny" appearance. A large dishtowel—made from a cloth flour sack—was spread over it, and the bowl was set in a warm place for the dough to rise. When nearly double in size, she punched it down with her fingers, replaced the towel, and left it to rise again. After the second rising, there was more kneading, forming the loaves, rubbing the tops with lard, and putting them into the pans, where they waited for another rising—this time, doubling in size, ready for baking. The pans were not individual "loaf" pans. One was a large, oblong rectangle into which she crowded three loaves—rubbed with enough lard to keep them from sticking together. Into a smaller pan, she squeezed the other two. (I learned later in a college food preparation class that the kneading was necessary to "develop the gluten," which strengthened the texture of the bread while it cooked, helping it to hold the increased volume as a result of the gas bubbles formed by the yeast; thereby giving it the name of "light bread.")

There is still a very important part of Mom's "timing"! She had planned it all so that the bread would be ready to take out of the oven about the time we were coming home from school! What a fragrance greeted us as we came into the house, bubbling over with our stories of all that had happened in school, or things we had noticed along the mile and a half that we walked on the way home. Five young voices rang out at once: "I get the heel!" I don't remember how that was settled, but there could be at least two rewards of heels—one from each end of the loaf. (It would take most of one whole loaf for the five snacks!) On the oil-cloth covered table was the large dish of home-made butter, a covered dish of apple butter or blackberry jam, and the spreaders we'd need to cover that thick, warm, fragrant slice of bread! Sometimes, even tastier than the apple butter or jam, was a sprinkle of sugar on top of the warm, melting butter!

Where could one find any better expression of love—from a Mom whose life was totally given to the hard work of providing good, healthy food for her family—and to teaching them (by example, more than by "preaching,") to be thankful for the many blessings we all enjoyed! That was "comfort food"— for the body and the mind, but especially for the soul!

PRE-WORLD WAR II YEARS

For many people, including our family, life in the 1930's wasn't easy, if measured by present standards. In our Santee School community near the small town of Dixon in mid-Missouri, there was no electricity, no running water, no factories, and many families didn't even have a car. Farms were relatively small—mostly a hundred or so acres, or less. Ours was ten acres— enough to support a cow for milk, a couple of pigs, a few chickens, and for a few years, a couple of mules. Two mules could be used for heavy plowing and pulling the wagon—one mule was enough for light plowing and tilling. They were strong and didn't need as much food as horses; but patience sometimes reached a near breaking point for Dad, because these mules were very stubborn! And for reasons unknown to Dad, it was sometimes really difficult to get them going! (Dad's heart wasn't into farming in the first place, and the farm was too small to "make a living" anyway, so the mules were eventually sold, and a neighbor was hired to do plowing.)

Dad, and most of our neighbors, tried to find work of some kind as a supplement for the family support—even though our farms provided major food supplies. The small amount of work that <u>was</u> available would be of various kinds of manual labor which paid very little.

The WPA (Works Progress Administration) and CCC (Civilian Conservation Corps) programs provided some real economic benefits in our area, as they did in all of the country. Of course, there were many criticisms, and as happens in any government-financed activity, it was easy for many to take advantage of the available "easy money." I remember seeing political cartoons showing workmen leaning on their shovels or taking long breaks from work, even helping themselves to government-owned equipment or supplies. But the economy was stimulated, and a lot of beneficial work was done. Grandpa Kelley lived alone and for a while he worked in a CCC camp. I think the unit he was with did forestry work in southern Missouri; and room and board for the men was provided in the camp setting, in addition to a small wage.

Some people, including my dad, felt that a man who depended upon the government for a "living" was admitting lack of means, and might be looked upon as lazy or as being a "beggar." So Dad's pride kept him from joining the WPA work force for a while. Eventually, he felt it would be a good thing for him to do, since he would be <u>working</u> for the money he would receive. He was healthy and strong and didn't mind hard work. He had followed the Kansas wheat harvest, worked on the railroad, helped lay oil pipe lines, and done various jobs in road construction. To improve his skills, he took correspondence courses, studied algebra (including logarithms and other higher math), surveying, mechanical drawing, and drafting (to name a few) so that he came close to qualifying as an engineer. When he applied for road work, he was often given a Foreman or Supervisor title—earning a higher wage and giving his self-esteem a <u>big</u> boost. I think the projects that WPA financed were given to "civilian" contractors in the area where the work was to be done. In Dad's autobiography, when he describes his own work experiences, he gives the name of the contractor and the title of his job. If it was a supervisory one, for instance, one of his descriptions was, "The Government furnished me a lot of help, men who were on relief, and we improved a lot of the roads in our community."

One of his assignments was the building of the airport at St. Joseph, Missouri, in 1936. Of that work he said he was sent "to take charge of a crew of sixty-some men on an airport construction job. There were nine crews, and I was soon General Foreman over all of them—clearing, digging, grading, and building levees in the Missouri River bottom—until time to build the hangars."

Before the airport work, he had been elected Road Commissioner of our Maries County and appointed President of the Board. The road work he supervised there was WPA financed. In 1939, the WPA installed a sewer system for the town of Dixon, and in 1940, built a school gymnasium in Vienna, the county seat of Maries County.

Another interesting WPA project in our community was construction of mattresses. Our one-room Santee School became the "factory." Materials and equipment were brought in, and members of families were taught (with assistance) how to make mattresses for themselves. The materials were blue-and-white striped cotton twill for the covers, and many layers of cotton padding for the filling. Sewing machines were available for some of the special stitching, and to hold all those layers together, long needles were provided to pull heavy cord through from the top to the bottom. The cords were secured on the ends with buttons. Edges were reinforced with extra padding, rolled, and stitched into place. Mom was the one who did most of the work on one of them for our family.

With all our community working together, we survived the hard times—with the children not even realizing that it was all that hard! We had all we really needed, plus the joy of friendship and improving our circumstances!

(Many years later, when I lived in Oregon, I learned that the beautiful, famous Timberline Lodge on Mt. Hood was built by WPA between 1936 and 1938, by local people using local stone and large timbers. Native Americans hand-crafted many of the things used in the construction—such as weaving and decorative carving.)

LIVING IN ST. JOSEPH, MISSOURI — 1936-1937

In 1936, my family was beginning to recover from the worst of the Great Depression. Dad had been able to do road work and carpentry work to eke out an existence for our family—five children: young Sterling (nicknamed Junior), age 3; Joy, age 5; Barbara, age 7, Ross, age 9, and me, age 11.

I remember one of the projects that Mom and Dad put into use to help with finances. They called it their "Five-Year-Plan." They had credit accounts at a few stores where the merchants had generously allowed them to purchase necessities like groceries, clothing and shoes, food for our cow and chickens, and seeds for garden and crops. So getting out of debt was one of the major parts of "the Plan." Dad went to each creditor, telling each one that he appreciated their patience, and wanted to pay his bill, but would need some time, to which all agreed. With each paycheck, Mom and Dad sat at the dining table to apportion the money for the budget—to which the whole family was dedicated. Envelopes were arranged in a locked box that was kept on a shelf in one of the kitchen cabinets. Into designated envelopes went any money that was received: the first 10% was "for the Lord." The second 10% was for savings; the third 10% was divided among creditors; and the rest went into envelopes labeled Food, Clothing, Animal Feed, and Miscellaneous.

Dad had managed to buy a dark green '29 Oldsmobile to use for travel to work, and he invested in a correspondence course for studying surveying. I liked to watch him do his Drafting homework—using triangles, French curves, very accurately calibrated rulers, T-square, hard-lead sharp-pointed pencils, art gum erasers, and special adjustable pens that held India ink. Learning to use a transit and other surveying skills made it possible for him to get better paying jobs.

One of those jobs was with the contractor who was building the airport at St. Joseph, Missouri. He was offered a position as General Foreman for the work of grading and levee-building. According to his autobiography, when that part of the airport work was finished, he was appointed Superintendent of the roads in Buchanan County, where St. Joe is located. There he supervised thirty-six crews totaling 576 men, thirty-six foremen, and two assistant superintendents. The work included maintenance and construction—preparing the soil for proper levels and curves. The earth-moving machinery in those days was much less sophisticated than it is now, but in my memory, they were really miraculously giant machines—caterpillars, graders, steam shovels, and huge dump trucks! He sometimes took us children to watch some of the work from a safe distance, and he was "in seventh heaven" when he had opportunities to operate some of those machines himself! We young ones felt quite proud to think that our Dad was causing such important work to be done!

In the summer of 1936, he and Mom decided to make a temporary move from our little farm near Dixon, to a furnished apartment in St. Joe. We often went in the summer to stay short times with Dad, wherever he was working, but this time they planned to stay longer—into the beginning of school. It was our first experience of city living, so you can imagine our excitement! So many people! So many stores! So many cars!

Our apartment was located at 507 Independence Avenue, in a quite nice residential area. Our entrance was the back door of Mrs. Espey's home, where we had use of the large kitchen, the dining room, and two bedrooms. But the house had only one bathroom, and Mrs. Espey had to go through one of our bedrooms in order to use it herself. That bedroom had nicer furniture than the other part of the house that we were using, so she wanted it to be occupied by "the girls," ages eleven, seven, and five. We actually just used it for sleeping and dressing, as I remember, so we wouldn't be in Mrs. Espey's way. The two boys, ages nine and three, slept on the opened-out couch in our so-called living room. As we had always done before, the kitchen table was the gathering place for children's homework and Dad's study time. Mom's evening spare time was spent piecing quilts and reading to the pre-school children, Sterling and Joy.

Most city homes have much smaller lawns than the one we had "at our Dixon home," and this one seemed even smaller than some. Besides that, Mrs. Espey's sister, Mrs. Fosberg, lived next door, so her lawn came very close to the narrow concrete walk that went along the side of our house to our entrance door. We had been instructed by Mrs. Espey to not play on the lawn, which left only that walk to our door and the public sidewalk in front of the house for play surfaces. Sometimes we children thought that Mrs. Fosberg must have spent a lot of time all day watching us play, because it seemed that if we even as much as set a foot on her grass, she was yelling at us! Fortunately, there was a vacant lot across the street where we could get away from those critical eyes! Some trees and bare ground, some of it gravelly, made a fine place to play with toy cars, build roads for them, and such.

Nine-year-old Ross had a good time during the summer earning some money by selling ice cream bars door-to-door in the neighborhood. Mom made sure he had on a clean, white shirt and pants; and he had a special box with a strap over his shoulder to carry the ice cream—called "Cheerios"—with a piece of dry ice to keep it frozen. Without air-conditioned houses, many people sat on their front porches in lawn chairs in the late afternoon, and many of them welcomed hearing his happy "Cheerio-o-o-o-s—five cents!" (If he had any left over after he finished his route, we were the beneficiaries!

When fall came, we had a change of pace—going to school. Barbara was in the second grade and Ross was in fourth grade at Lindberg School; I was in eighth grade at Lafayette Jr. High, in the opposite direction. Barbara usually followed Mom's instruction to wait after school to walk home with Ross, but one day her teacher sent her class home early. She explained the way to our house to Barbara—telling her to go a certain number of blocks along a certain street, and then turn to go on our street. But Barbara got mixed up and turned one block too soon. While Mom was working in the kitchen, she happened to look out the window in time to see Barbara's red dress a block away on the next street. Mom ran to her rescue and calmed a very frightened little girl who had discovered she was lost!

After going to school all my life so far in a one-room school, I found the large city school to be quite overwhelming, but soon was able to find my way around and to make a few friends—all of them two years older than I because I had been promoted a couple of grades earlier at the beginning of my school experience. Even at eleven, I had "eyes" for a certain boy in my class named Henry Koch. He was <u>very</u> good-looking and popular, but as I remember, he didn't choose to give me any significant attention. Even now, I can remember his flashing smile, dark hair and eyes, and the little mole on the side of his chin just below his lower lip! I wasn't allowed to wear lipstick, but one of my girlfriends did, and let me borrow her tube of Tangee to put some on at school. Of course, I wiped it all off before going home! Once in a while I get a lipstick with a taste so similar to it, I have a memory flashback!

For several months my health had seemed to be less than good because of enlarged (or maybe diseased) tonsils and adenoids. I was getting a sore throat so often; the doctor decided those things should be removed. That frightening day came in early December. The surgery was to be done before noon in a surgical area of the doctor's office. Dad took the day off from work to take Mom and me there, and he entertained Joy and Sterling while Mom stayed with me. I had to stay there, lying down, for the rest of the day to be sure I would recover normally. I remember being quite nauseated after having ether used for the anesthetic. The extra attention after I got home was great—including ice cream and cool Jell-O that was carried to me in bed!

What fun we had at Christmas time! Never in our lives had we seen city Christmas lights; and the fabulous dolls and toys that filled so many store windows made it all seem like a dream world!

Dad was happy to have us all together; and he spent much of his time off taking us out to play in a park, to a library, and on various sight-seeing excursions—once to a Quaker rolled oats factory. Lots of noise there, with machinery running the belts and all the things that took the whole-grain oats and turned them out rolled—and in familiar boxes we'd seen for years in our own kitchen. Another favorite place was Krug Park where we had many picnic lunches and suppers, and played on wonderfully long slides, high-flying swings, and foot-powered merry-go-rounds!

In January, it was time for Mom and us children to go back to Dixon—I don't remember why—or maybe I never knew why. It was snowing the morning we left, but Dad said it was a dry snow that was blowing off the road, so he felt it was safe to drive. All was well until we reached Kansas City, a few miles to the south. Then, the snow was falling with freezing rain, which turned the road into a glaze of ice. Driving the rest of the way home was quite scary— and it was a little over a hundred miles! I remember hearing Dad say he felt confident of his own driving on ice, but going uphill was worrisome because he didn't know whether or not he could trust the drivers coming down hill meeting us. (He explained to us that when driving on ice, putting brakes on could cause the driver to lose control of making the car go where he wanted it to go—or to make it stop!)

What a relief it was when we arrived safely back to our country home again—feeling maybe just a little superior to our country neighbor playmates because we had seen such an exciting part of the world, and actually lived in a city!

SCHOOL BUS EXPERIENCES

My world changed dramatically in September 1937, when, at age twelve, I started high school—feeling quite grown-up, but very shy. Elementary school had been at Santee, a one-room school in our community, a little over a mile from our house. And to get there, we walked. But high school would be in town! No "little kids"—only teenagers, and all of them older and most of them taller than I! Dixon High was a consolidated school; so big, yellow buses brought loads of kids from outlying farms and villages from all directions. (Actually, the buses weren't really "that big" in comparison to ones used these days—but they just looked really big to me!)

The bus I rode came from Brinktown—a small village about thirteen miles north of Dixon, on graveled highway, two lanes wide, called a farm-to-market road that was built partly by WPA. By the time it reached my stop, it had already traveled nine of those miles, but I think miles have shrunk a lot in the last seventy years—they seemed a lot longer in those days! I walked north a quarter of a mile to Aunt Ada Kelley's house, where our little road intersected the highway, and the bus stopped there for me. I was welcome to wait on her front porch, or even to go inside in bad weather; which was a real luxury. If for some reason I didn't arrive there by the scheduled time, I could walk south on our little country road for the two miles to town, and <u>still</u> get to school on time, because the bus went "the long way." A short distance after my stop it turned to the right, off the highway for a few miles to a settlement called "The Pump Station." It was on the Ajax Oil pipeline, and the oil company had built some quite nice, modern homes for families of the people who "manned" the maintenance of the station. During the four years I rode the bus, we picked up several kids there, some of whom attended the grade school in Dixon. (I have fond memories of some of those young passengers—two of them were the Randall brothers—very nice, "city type," good-mannered, and really good-looking guys. The older one was named Homer, but Joe, the younger one, was <u>my</u> "heart-throb." He didn't know it, though, and of course never gave me any attention. Two of the Pump Station girls were Orpha and Louise Jones. They were cousins of Chadna Scott who lived in Dixon—and some years later, she became the wife of my brother Ross.

The driver of our bus was Garrett Veasman who lived in Brinktown. I can "see" him in my mind's eye—tall and thin, jovial and friendly, with a kind of long, thin nose. His son Marion (nicknamed Bud) was one of the passengers, and still in grade school, though he was about my age. He was another one of my "heart-throbs"—really cute and fun—and I think he even <u>liked</u> me! Sometimes he made room for me to sit beside him on the bus!

Seats on the bus were thinly padded, bench-type ones, along the sides of the bus, with a long board-seat through the middle. No seat belts. If the bus became crowded, Mr. Veasman encouraged boys to sit on the middle seat, because they could sit straddling it, thus making more room. Girls all wore dresses, so if they sat on that seat, they faced toward one side or the other. (I didn't like to sit there, because boys sitting behind me sometimes tugged on my hair braids.)

Our first stop when we reached town was at the Dixon grade school. I remember that Mrs. Petty was the principal there at that time—a short, chubby, middle-aged lady who was very well-liked and was active in community activities. I had met the Jones girls' cousin Chadna, so while stopped there, I liked to look out to the playground where kids were gathering, to see if I might see her—and I often did. She was a really cute little girl with dark brown hair. (Now, she's <u>still</u> cute—a great-grandmother with salt-and-pepper colored hair!)

In front of the high school, the buses lined up as they arrived to unload—then lined up again at four o'clock in the afternoon to take us home. Three girls who eventually became my best friends—Bernice Phillips, Lucille Cross, and Sue Hancock—rode Dewey Allen's bus that came from the little towns of Crocker and Hancock, west of Dixon. (Bernice has lived in Littleton, Colorado, for many years, has a son, a daughter, and several grandchildren. We've visited and kept in touch by letters and phone calls. She had a serious hearing loss, and hearing aids were not available to her when she was growing up. She was shy because of that, and not very popular, so we were "wallflowers" together—sometimes being called Mutt and Jeff because she was so much taller than I.

Gene Krone was one of the kids that I remember on my bus. He was quite tall and walked with a strange gait. In fact, he might have been a bit older than most of us. He was a very polite person, but not at all popular among our peers. Another one was Clarence Rohr who was older than most other students—maybe by three or four years, which seemed really old to me. I never knew the reason for his delayed education, but he was very smart, was friendly, and seemed very "wise."

When I now see school kids carrying books and many other belongings in backpacks, I'm reminded of what I carried with just my arms: always several books, a three-ring binder with sections divided for each class, maybe another spiral notebook or two, a lunch bag, an umbrella on rainy days, and frequently my musical instrument—a violin when a sophomore; a cello when a junior and senior.

During World War II our family lived for a while on the base at Fort Leonard Wood, Missouri. A special housing area was provided for civilian employees and military families, but there was no school on the base for children. I had finished school by that time and was working, but my two brothers and two sisters rode a bus that took children to the small town of Waynesville, near the Fort. Those buses were military troop-transport buses. Some were even trailer-trucks with benches for seats, and few windows. Drivers were Army personnel, and some older students were appointed to be "monitors," but that didn't prevent a lot of paper-wad throwing! Some buses that had forward-facing seats also had hand-holds for use when there was standing room only. One of my sisters remembers that with four Kelley kids getting on at the same time, other kids sometimes chanted, "Kelley, Kelley, Kelley, whoops! Kelley!—my brother Ross being the last one to board.

One can learn a lot about "life" by riding a school bus. Most of the kids are strangers at first. In a short time, people form small groups—some of them quite exclusive and "uppity." Some are friendly and like to talk; some are very popular and "cool"; some like to tease. You have to figure out ways to approach those you think would be good friends—and how to avoid the ones who don't share your interests. Sometimes it was possible to trade some snacks from lunch bags on the way home. Many of the exuberant types seemed to learn how far to test the patience of the driver who had to keep one eye on the kids, and both eyes on the road. On our bus, if people became too active or noisy, Mr. Veasman pulled to the side of the road and stopped. He didn't have to <u>say</u> much. Just his steely-eyed expression seemed to be enough to bring order.

More modern school buses came into my life when my own children became riders. In Hawaii the buses were gray-colored ones operated by Navy drivers when Becky and David attended school on the Pearl Harbor Navy Base. In Corvallis, their bus stopped near our house—one bus for high school; another for elementary and middle school. They were yellow, with forward-facing seats, and much larger than the one I rode. A special time of day for me was their arrival home from school—hearing about their day while they enjoyed some snacks. Even now, my heart leaps a bit when I hear and see the school bus going by—arousing memories of those happy times!

I'd like to see Garrett Veasman again, and thank him for those four years of driving that bus that was such an important part of my education, and my growing up!

THE KELLEY KIDS
PROFESSIONALLY KNOWN AS "THE KELLEY QUINTET"

This photograph of the children in our family was taken before we left for a singing engagement, sometime in the early summer of 1940, I think, between my junior and senior years of high school. I can remember that I was so happy to be posing in an open shade where we didn't have to worry about squinting in the sun, as photos in those days so often needed that extra light. We had already posed for several pictures in other locations around the yard—one photograph had the front yard arbor in the background. This one is at the southeast corner of our front porch with a spirea bush and tall maple trees in the background. Some flowers are visible in the lower right corner—in front of the porch foundation.

By this time, we had already been singing together for about four years—each playing a stringed instrument—and were enthusiastically received wherever we performed, in churches and gatherings called "singings." We mostly sang Gospel songs, many of which were written or arranged by Ozark country musicians, and had simple, lively rhythms with up-beat messages.

The youngest of us is Sterling (called "Junior" at that time because his first name is the same as Dad's). In this picture he was almost seven. His instrument is a ukulele, and he sang tenor. He definitely was the "star" of our group! From the very beginning he sang with great enthusiasm, confidence, and showmanship, strumming that uke for all it was worth!

The next older one is Joy who in 1940 was nine years old. She sang what we called "high alto" and played a little banjo ukulele that had been in Dad's family for a number of years. She had a very sweet voice and really enjoyed hitting those high notes—always smiling, and a little dignified. She later played a violin with us.

47

Eleven-year-old Barbara was next with a regular banjo, singing soprano, which was usually the "lead" part in most of our songs. She was (and still is) the "family clown," keeping us from ever getting bogged down with being too serious. Her voice was strong for her age, making it a good one for the rest of us to follow with our various harmonies. She later played a mandolin.

Ross was thirteen at this time and beginning to get a deepening voice, which made him <u>very</u> happy. He had always sung the bass harmony—which, of course, didn't sound at all "bass" until after his voice changed (into a really nice, <u>low</u> bass, I might add!). He took great interest in playing his guitar, gave me a lot of instruction and assistance with the various chords, and played much better than I played mine! In his spare time, he often played and sang cowboy songs, just for his own enjoyment.

I was fifteen and sang alto. If I <u>look</u> older than fifteen, it's because I <u>felt</u> like I was totally "grown-up," and had sort of "put away" any childish behavior I might have had, which wasn't much, because at that time I was often quite a serious person. My sisters had short hair—usually about shoulder length—but Mom wanted me to have long hair, and for most of my life had combed and "styled" it every morning before I went to school. Pigtails with ribbons or long curls were usual in grade school; by high school the long braids were often wrapped around my head. In this picture, when I was "dressed up," my hair was tucked into a hairpiece called a "rat" that circled my head. I later had a white guitar which I played as a Hawaiian guitar.

We frequently wore special clothes—the boys in white shirts and ties, or dark pants with their white shirts; the girls in matching dresses, which Mom made herself. A couple of years earlier than this, before I wanted to act so grown-up, one of our costumes for the very warm Missouri summer weather was white, fluffy dresses made of cotton dimity (not quite as sheer as organdy). They had ruffles over the shoulders like pinafore design; full gathered skirts, belted with a wide sash tied into a big bow in the back. And to think that Mom had the work of washing, starching, and ironing all those gathers and ruffles! She dressed the boys in starched, white trousers and shirts with open collars in the summer, and never, <u>ever</u> complained about all the extra work! After I started to high school and learned to sew, I could at least help with making our dresses. One set I especially remember was bright red pin-wale corduroy ones made with plain fitted bodice and circular skirt. They were fun to wear, even when we weren't singing together.

Dad was our coach and "agent." We had quite concentrated periods of rehearsals, which we called "practice," with his guidance. He knew how to read music, so he could teach each one of us the tune for our own "part"; and he also taught each of us how to play our instrument. Rewards of pieces of candy (often candy corn) followed a well-done practice, and <u>always</u> we received his generous praise! Here are a few of our song titles: *The Sunny Side of Life; The Paradise Valley; Don't Forget to Pray; I'll Fly Away; Just a Little Talk with Jesus;* and *Salvation Has Been Brought Down.* And here are the names of some of the communities in that mid-Missouri area where we sang: Vichy, Fairview, Hayden, Hancock, Swedeborg, Bland, Hazelgreen, Gospel Ridge, Flat Campground, Mt. Pisgah, and Big Piney (now on the Fort Leonard Wood grounds).

How thankful I am for this experience of performing as a family! That love of simple music led to further appreciation of all kinds of music for me, and the discipline of working together formed a bond that we still feel! Ross and his children now have fun singing and playing guitars together. Joy later played a violin, sang in high school chorus, and in adult years sang in church choirs. Sterling discovered more talent—playing a piano "by ear" and composing tunes himself. Barbara became a <u>real</u> clown, calling herself "Peaches," dressed as a "happy-go-lucky" man, often bringing joy to kids and others at parties, hospitals, and community gatherings. There really <u>IS</u> a <u>sunny side of life</u>! "Let us sing a song as we go along on the road that we must go, that the world may know as we onward go, there's a sunny side of life!"

A HIDDEN BLESSING (Beginning High School)

From the vantage point of my seventy-plus years of experience, I can now see that many of the disappointments along the way have actually been blessings in disguise. Learning to look for hidden blessings has contributed considerably to "serenity." But one disappointment at age thirteen was a BIG one, and at the time, seemed to threaten my whole plan for my life!

Being the first child born to doting parents and being a person eager for approval and eager to learn, I'm told that I was reading at age four and learning arithmetic at age five. Our country school began at grade one for children age six, and all eight grades were taught in one room. Naturally, I was bored in the class with the first graders who were just then beginning reading and numbers, so my teacher called me to recite with the second grade. She soon discovered I even fit into the third grade—an easy way to advance, because one had only to keep ears open while the older kids were reciting to learn whatever was being taught. So, by the second year in school, I was beginning the fourth grade. Consequently, I was two years younger than the average student was when it was time to begin high school.

I had done better than average academically in grade school, and with encouragement from parents reinforcing my own ambition, I had great plans for the future! I was twelve years old, felt very wise and practically all grown up! High school would be the wonderful place for me to begin learning what I needed to know to launch me into a career of big business. Of course, I would expect to be the manager in time, but I figured it would be wise to be a secretary first in order to learn "from the ground up." So my plan was to take all the courses I could get in math, typing, shorthand, bookkeeping, and such. Even my parents agreed that things like Home Ec and Art and English Literature would be less valuable. After all, Mom was a master homemaker and could teach me all I needed to know about cooking and sewing and keeping house, and other things I could just learn from my own reading when I had the time.

What a lump came into my throat when it came my turn in the line for registering that first day at good old Dixon High School! Various teachers were the registering officials, and I stood facing a smiling Miss Beckman—the music and freshman English teacher. She told me that my classes as a freshman would be Citizenship, Algebra, English I, Home Ec I, Related Science, and P.E. Disappointment and something akin to anger must have made me seem ridiculous to her, but I stood my ground, telling her my feelings about needing to learn all those business courses instead of the Home Ec, and now I've even discovered there was PE! I thought that was <u>definitely</u> a useless course! Miss Beckman said, "I'm sorry, but all those freshman courses are requirements, and the only thing I can do is suggest that you talk to the Superintendent, Mr. Kilburn." (He was also the high school principal.)

With tears in my eyes and choking on the lump in my throat, I found my way upstairs to his office. There I found one of the tallest, square-shouldered persons I had ever seen. But he had a very kind-looking face, with twinkling eyes, and he very patiently waited for me to tell him my problem. He said he fully realized how I felt, but since the state had established certain courses required for graduation, there was no way he could make any changes. He assured me that I could still have time later for the business classes, and just <u>maybe</u> there <u>might</u> be something in Home Ec that I would find to be of some benefit to me. He was so kind—even rose from his chair behind his desk to walk with me to his office door. I was afraid he was going to pat me on the head, which would have <u>not</u> helped my image of my grown-up self! It might have even started a <u>river</u> of tears, which were very close to coming anyway! He very kindly took me back to the registering table himself and helped me "save face."

Well, I <u>did</u> find Home Ec to be interesting. Miss Evelyn White was my kind of perfectionist and was soon my role model. I especially liked sewing and anything to do with textiles; but found the personality development, home nursing, child care, science as related to the home, meal planning and food preparation, and all the other parts of it to be very helpful and fulfilling. By the second year I was able to use Home Ec II as an elective and still find time for business courses. Then as a senior, I chose Home Ec III and Related Art! Great courses!

As valedictorian of my class I was able to choose a scholarship; and still standing my ground to be a businesswoman, I chose Draughon's Business College—their <u>complete</u> course. Very challenging experience, and exciting to master those wonderful bookkeeping machines and calculators! (All of them are now obsolete.) After graduation, I soon had a job as a secretary with nice paychecks!

In a couple of years, I began to realize that I still wasn't in my "<u>niche</u>." I felt there <u>had</u> to be more to life than sitting in an office, and I realized there had to be more school. But what? By then I knew I'd want to someday be a wife and mother, and from out of the blue came the idea of a career as a <u>Home Ec teacher</u>—easily combined with homemaking! My secretarial skills even made it possible for me to work part time for a wonderful Dietetics professor at the University of Missouri to pay for my college expenses!

I wrote Mr. Kilburn a letter a few years ago to tell him of my appreciation, my family, and what I consider to be my success. I've so often felt thankful to him for his wisdom and counsel that turned that terrible disappointment into such a great blessing! And besides…what's wrong with <u>Homemaking</u> as a career?

MORE ABOUT HIGH SCHOOL

I've already written about my frustrations with getting started in high school—my resentment about being required to take Home Ec—and the fact that I was only twelve years old. Of course, I *felt* quite grown-up and wise—

and in some ways I might have had a little bit of "wisdom beyond my years," but socially, I felt I was quite a misfit. Besides that, I lived in the country without the opportunity to bond with the town kids who could get together for movies, cokes, and just "hanging out."

Two boys who were "immature for their age," liked to tease me, so I had to try to stay out of their way. One time they put some drops of red ink in my chair, which I didn't notice before I sat down. They evidently had recently learned about a girl's monthly physical needs and made a point after class of chiding me about the red spots on the back of my skirt. I don't know when I was ever so embarrassed—for the rest of the day!

Being a sort of "loner" myself, it wasn't long until my friends became other country girls. Lucille Cross was one of them, and Bernice Phillips was another one who became my "bosom buddy," and we kept in touch by letter or by phone for as long as she lived. She also was shy, because she was taller than average, and had quite a severe hearing loss. I was so short; we looked like the cartoon characters, Mutt and Jeff, together!

Physical Education (P.E.) was one of the requirements I didn't like. I didn't mind the callisthenic exercises, but I wasn't at all athletic and dreaded the times when we had to play softball or volleyball. Thank goodness, we didn't have to play basketball—in those days basketball was thought to be physically bad for girls. My legs were too short to be able to run fast in softball, and I couldn't catch worth a darn. I seemed to be more of a hindrance than a help in volleyball; being so short, it was difficult for me to hit the ball over the net.

Glee Club and Orchestra were better activities for me. I really liked to sing, and I could call Dad's "fiddle" a "violin," and learn to play it. (Now, as an adult, sometimes listening to young children play, I can only imagine how patient our teacher must have been with me and other beginning musicians!) After the first year with the violin—and not really enjoying it very much—there was an opening for someone to play the cello that the school owned, so I tried that for the rest of my years there. I liked it better than violin, but I must have looked a little strange—the smallest person in the orchestra, playing one of the larger instruments. The music students went to county contests a couple of times a year, and sometimes played for local groups. For those occasions we had "uniforms"—for band, and for orchestra, a red cape with a large white "D" appliquéd on the left front. Underneath the cape, the girls wore white dresses; the boys wore white shirts and trousers. For Glee Club there were plain blue

52

cotton dresses with A-line skirts and blue- and white-striped tops. Hemlines had to all be the same distance from the floor.

I had made up my mind when I started high school that I would try to finish with a scholarship, which would be my best hope for going to college. Therefore, I put a lot of effort into studying. Mom and Dad gave me a little bit of an "edge" by allowing me time with my books when I might have otherwise been helping with chores.

I had some very good teachers: Evelyn White for Home Ec, Related Science, and Related Art; Rowena Beckman for English I, Glee Club and Orchestra; Curtis Barton for Algebra, Citizenship, and Geometry: Wilda Flint for English II and III, World History, and American History; George Bell for Shorthand, Typing, and Bookkeeping; Henry Kilburn (the Principal) for Business Arithmetic, and P.E. Mr. Barton taught with a lot of humor—very "informally." I remember that one time he told us that he saved a lot of money by cleaning his own teeth with *Bon Ami!* Miss Beckman was friendly, but rather reserved, and she was a wonderful musician. Miss White was a perfectionist, very considerate, and helpful with our Home Ec projects; Mr. Bell was energetic and added interest to typing class by playing classical band music. By keeping time to the martial music with our typing strokes, we developed rhythm and speed as we typed! Miss Flint was one of my favorites, with her very outgoing personality. She seemed to know everything about history and how to make it interesting, made Shakespeare "come alive," and dressed like she had just walked out of Vogue Magazine. I so wished I could be like her! Another teacher was James Bailey who took care of agriculture and shop classes for boys. He and Miss White were later married.

I especially liked Bookkeeping. After we learned some basics about assets, liabilities, accounts payable, accounts receivable, ledgers, and balance sheets, we were given a large packet called a "Practice Set." It contained the various stationery forms to use for the business of this imaginary company for one month. Each small envelope inside it contained the documents representing all that day's transactions, from which we made appropriate entries concerning the various accounts. I think one of the things that made it so interesting to me was the "order" it required. (I now sometimes wonder what has happened to that "orderly side" of me!)

There were two boys in my "Class of '41" named Charles Sease and Roy McGregor that I soon discovered would be my "scholarship opponents." They were leader-type young men—into athletics, class officers, and such—and both were very bright. Their grades were always high, seemingly with no effort. It so happened that I was the only girl in geometry class with six boys, including those two! With such a small class Mr. Barton often had us all doing work at the blackboard at the same time. One of those times that is still as vivid in my memory as if it were yesterday, was a pop quiz at the board. We were to list the seven ways of proving angles to be equal. I had memorized those ways, went confidently up to the board, quickly wrote down six of them, and suddenly had a mental block!

I happened to be standing next to Charles Sease, wondering if <u>he</u> would think of all of them. In all honesty, with no thought of cheating by copying, I just "glanced" over to see if he had written all seven of them. My eye just <u>happened</u> to fall on the one that I was missing! <u>Vertical angles</u>! I didn't feel like it was "right" to add it to my list—but <u>I did</u>! There are <u>six</u> ways to prove angles equal that I <u>don't</u> remember— the only one that I <u>do</u> remember is <u>vertical angles</u>!

Ila age 16 (1941)

A TEACHER'S INFLUENCE—MISS EVELYN WHITE

In another one of my stories I've written about the frustration I experienced when I entered high school. I wanted a career in business, and I had assumed that in high school I could concentrate on subjects that would be directly useful for things like typing, bookkeeping, shorthand, merchandising, filing, office management, and the like—several of which I knew were available at Dixon High. It had never occurred to me that there were state requirements for a certain number of common everyday things like English, Science, and History! And who would ever <u>dream</u> that Home Economics (which I interpreted as learning to cook and sew) could possibly be required? Even <u>Physical Education</u> was required, would you believe! Neither my mom nor my dad had gone to high school themselves, and I guess it just never occurred to them, or to me, to look into what to expect—consequently, my surprise and more than considerable disappointment! I actually had to swallow hard to keep from crying!

Right away, that freshman year, I had to take Home Ec I and Related Art, both taught by Miss Evelyn White. The classes were scheduled so that one of those followed the other, making it possible for some projects needing extra time could be finished during the next period. Other classes that year were English I, Algebra, Citizenship, and P.E.

Dixon High was an average sized school in that part of Missouri at that time. Dixon's population was around seven hundred, but students came by buses from other nearby small towns and farms. Class sizes—freshman, sophomore, junior, and senior—were from around twenty to forty students each. Thirty-five were enrolled in my class, which graduated in the spring of 1941. There were five teachers in addition to Miss White, all of whom were very good ones, I think; and students were for the most part respectful. I'm sure that all of the teachers added valuable influence to my school experience, but Miss White became one of my favorites. She had a quiet, matter-of-fact way of teaching, and sometimes used some humorous stories to explain or emphasize a point. One time in a Personality Development unit we discussed dating—its value, proper manners, and such. She said that she had always thought that one shouldn't go into serious, steady dating with someone you wouldn't want to marry. Well, that would take some critical evaluation early in a friendship, but it made some sense. She said she once stopped dating a boy because she "couldn't imagine him in the role of being a father to her children."

Our first sewing project in class included a dish towel, (called a "tea-towel"), an apron, and a potholder which we'd use when we began cooking classes. Techniques learned with these items were running a treadle sewing machine, straight machine stitching, measuring even hems, basting, using a thimble, stitching a bias facing on a curve, blind-stitching, embroidery (for sewing our name on the tea-towel, apron, and pot-holder); and for some girls, the first thing to learn was how to thread and hold a needle! Miss White showed us how to make a temporary cardboard gauge for measuring seam and hem widths—a simple tool that I've used for the rest of my life.

I think I grew up seeking adult approval, so I might have been an "easy target" for a teacher who soon recognized my desire to learn. She and I were both perfectionists, and that probably got me some special attention, too. The Home Ec program was called "vocational," which meant that part of the course was doing home projects of our choosing. Planning the project, time it would need, the cost, parental approval, and final evaluation went with each one. The teacher made home visits to acquaint her with each girl's family and environment, so she was able to help make the projects really worthwhile, living-learning experiences. Miss White always seemed to enjoy those home visits, as did my family. She also seemed to understand our low-income lifestyle and helped me do a lot with whatever I was able to afford.

One big opportunity for me was with several pieces of yard goods that my dad's sister had sent us. Some of it was very fine quality, light-weight cotton prints. One piece was a lovely, silky black and gray-blue stripe that I used for a dress that I both designed and sewed. Miss White came to my rescue with a way to repair a mistake that had me almost in tears. I had finished the dress— long full-gathered sleeves, perfectly fitted midriff waistline, a flared skirt with bias seams in front and back—requiring matched stripes on all four of them, and a zipper in the side. When I did the final pressing at home, I failed to test the temperature of the iron (the type that had to be heated on the stove because we had no electricity) before I put it down on the skirt to press the hem. The cloth was made of acetate, which meant that it immediately melted and stuck to the iron, leaving a hole the shape of the iron on the bottom of my new dress! When I showed it to Miss White, she shared my pain, but immediately began helping me with a solution. She suggested that if I had a left-over piece of fabric a little wider than the hole, I could cut along the edge of a stripe and sew a new piece to the bottom of the skirt, matching the stripes! What a wise lady! She restored my confidence in myself in such a positive way, at the same time teaching a lesson in problem solving!

One of my home projects was making matching dresses for my two younger sisters and myself, using one of the gift cotton prints—medium blue, orange, and pink flowers and green leaves. The dresses had square necklines, short puffed sleeves, and flared skirts with probably ten gores giving them their flare.

Another project was a home improvement one—building two flag-stone walks—a long one went from the front porch to the front gate; a short one from a door of the house to a side gate. The family all helped collect the flat rocks from several creek bottoms—many different colors, shapes and types of stone. To build those walks I had to stretch string to guide the outside edge, fit the rocks together according to their shapes, dig soil to proper depth from under each one, and settle it into a bed of sand; then fill in between them with soil. Miss White made several visits to check my progress—visits that all the family enjoyed.

One experience when I was a senior made me feel that I really had her approval. Our class was to go to a Home Ec gathering of some kind that involved several other schools. While we were in the Home Ec room preparing to leave, Miss White discovered a small rip in one sleeve of her dress under one of her arms. A Home Ec teacher, of all people, couldn't be seen with a rip in a seam! She found a needle and some thread and asked me to do the mending while she pulled the front of her dress open so I could reach the rip. My ego went up several degrees—being trusted to help her with that little problem that was a <u>big</u> one to her! (A <u>big</u> one for me, too, because it was so "personal"!) Maybe it was also one of my first realizations that teachers are just people, too! I should add that another thing that proved her "just people" status was her romance and marriage to the Ag teacher—James Bailey! (I've never had an opportunity to see if any of her children looked like their father!)

Her influence through three Home Ec courses, as well as the Related Science and Related Art along with them, eventually guided me to study to be a Home Ec teacher myself—after I had given the idea of a business career a trial for a couple of years!

WORLD WAR II

An often-asked question is "Do you remember where you were and what you were doing when you heard (or read) the news that the Japanese had bombed Pearl Harbor?" I was sixteen years old and, listening with my family to some Sunday evening radio programs—more than likely "Amos and Andy." (We hadn't had a radio very long, so it was quite a novelty, and listening times were controlled to keep it from dominating our time. Homework and chores had to be done first.) It was a great shock to have our program interrupted with the urgent news report. I knew that there was war in Europe, and that Japan was being aggressive in Asia and the Pacific, but I was too busy and too interested in my studies to be very aware of world news. In another story I've told about getting a scholarship to Draughon's Business College in Springfield, Missouri, and about our family moving there in late summer.

I really enjoyed my college courses because I was finally getting education that would qualify me to work in an office, which had been my high school ambition. Springfield was what one might call a small city—or maybe a very <u>large</u> town—not as busy and "frantic" as the few larger cities I'd experienced, so it was an enjoyable place to live. There were beautiful parks, a friendly church, movies, buses, and shopping for about anything we would need. The draft was calling for men to enter military service, but Dad was too old, and my brothers were too young, so life for us continued without much change for several months—even though the country began preparing for what was called "the war effort." Many people flocked to war products factories in various parts of the country where high-paying jobs were easy to find. A number of people in our part of the country had been out of work for a long time, so those good jobs were very much appreciated.

By summer, my dad had decided to work as a carpenter in Paducah, Kentucky, where a TNT ammunition plant was being built. We discovered that there was a Draughon's College there and that I could transfer my credits and scholarship, so we moved—in a large, open truck. Mom and the two younger children rode in the seat with the driver; Ross, Barbara, and I were in the back, surrounded with furniture and boxes. My main memory about that trip was the hot sun, and the constant wind, even though we were sitting in a small space leaning back against the cab of the truck. We managed to create a little shade at times, and stopped occasionally for bathroom, gas, food, and stretching legs; but it was a <u>long</u> day, and it wasn't what you'd call a "vacation"!

In Paducah, the house we moved into was in a low area of the city; and about three feet up on some of the walls were marks that we thought might have been left sometime in the past when the Ohio River flooded, but it was adequate for us. The school that I would attend was located in the downtown area. Dad could drop me there on his way to work, but that was rather inconvenient; so for my birthday I was given a bicycle that I could ride to school. Dad drove me along the streets he thought safest for me to travel before I was allowed to "go it alone." (By the way, the bicycle was pink, and had a generous, woven, white basket in front of the handlebars for my books.)

It wasn't long before rationing began, so that essential items and products could be used for military buildup. Each month a family was issued books of coupons to limit their purchases of the rationed foods, clothing, and gasoline, according to the size of their family. Restricted things that I remember were meat, coffee, sugar, leather shoes, tires and tubes, and gasoline. Farmers could get extra gasoline coupons for their tractors, because they had to produce as much food as possible. Soon we were able to buy shoes made of cloth uppers and some kind of composition soles. Being a clothes-conscious teenager, I welcomed those! Silk stockings were not available at all—the silk was needed to make military parachutes. Nylon hadn't yet been invented, so women wore stockings made of rayon—difficult to keep in place, baggy at the ankles, and got runs in them easily. Eventually nylon was created for parachutes, so after the war, stockings improved—even being made then of nylon!

By January 1942 I was ready to graduate, and Dad had heard that Fort Leonard Wood in Missouri was being activated, and that carpenters, as well as many other kinds of workers were needed. There had been a lot of rain in

Paducah, and the Ohio River was rising, so another move back to our Dixon home—about twenty-five miles from Fort Wood—seemed to Mom and Dad to be prudent. This time we didn't have to ride in the back of the truck! Dad was there to drive us in the car!

How exciting it was for me to go with Dad to Fort Wood to look for my first job! Right away we were both hired by the Post Exchange—Dad as a carpenter in their large maintenance department, and I as an office clerk right there in the personnel office! I felt like I was "somebody"! My pay was $70.00 per month! At first I did quite menial tasks like keeping records of who worked where in the various PX operations such as variety stores, beer gardens, barber shops, beauty shops, restaurants, gas stations, auto repair shops, shoe repair shops, bowling alley, a grocery store (called a commissary), and, of course, the maintenance shop. I also did typing, answering the phone, and endless filing. The Personnel Manager was a man from Nebraska named Paul Murphy. His wife, Arlene, worked in another department of the office. Mr. Murphy's secretary, Rita was married to a soldier who was soon transferred, so when she resigned, I was chosen to take her place—and I got a whopping salary increase to $90.00 per month! I loved the opportunity to use more of my new skills—taking shorthand dictation, typing letters, reviewing applications, keeping track of needed help in the various operations, etc. Personnel turnover was enormous, so our waiting room was often full of people seeking work or presenting papers for leaving.

Dad agreed to be "on call" for night maintenance needs, which meant that he would be authorized to live on the base. It was great to live near work and not have that 25-mile drive every morning and evening. Many military families also lived in the Housing Area. Our townhouse-style apartment in the officer quarters' section was at 11-B Rolla Street. Mom worked at the laundry, doing seamstress work for awhile, and later had plenty of work sitting with children of officer neighbors and sewing for several officers' wives. Sister Barbara was also a baby-sitter. Brother Ross did part time work at the gas station and was a pin-setter at the bowling alley. Both of my brothers and two sisters rode a bus to school at the nearby town of Waynesville.

At the Housing Area Chapel there was an active group of people where the Base Chaplain often conducted church services. Sunday school classes were available for all ages, and a number of high-school kids and young soldiers enjoyed a Sunday Evening Youth group. We all made many good friends there—and I was especially attracted to some of the young soldiers who came to our group! Our leaders were "very Swedish" Capt. Russell Johnson and his wife Margaret. They were from Minnesota, devoted Christians, and made sure we had fun things to do like early-morning picnic pancake breakfasts, to go along with our Bible studies and devotions. With my new-found salaried wealth, I bought some silverware for Mom and Dad's 25th Anniversary, and some new chairs to make our home a nice place to entertain the youth group and other friends.

You can tell that I, personally, didn't "suffer" much during the War, although it was often sad when there was news of some friend being killed in combat. People seemed to be very patriotic and united in keeping America strong. Even the rationing seemed to be taken into stride—just part of our duty. However, it was really good news when it was all over! A while before the War ended, I decided to begin attending the University of Missouri. I was there when the GIs began starting to college on the GI Bill, which paid for their tuition, living allowance, and books. And guess who was one of those GIs? Fresh-out-of-the-Marine Corps—Gene Bench! Meeting him was like beginning to <u>really</u> <u>live</u>!

THE SUMMER OF 1941

Some would probably call our family's summer of 1941 a really "far-out" experience, full of all kinds of inconveniences and risks, and totally unnecessary. Some might wonder, "<u>What</u> in the world were your parents thinking about?" Dad was earning more money than he had for many years (maybe <u>ever</u>) and could have easily afforded a nice place in town—but instead they chose a dilapidated old house in the middle of a big field of tall weeds, near O'Fallon, Missouri, with no other houses even in sight. The owner, Hodgen Bates, lived in town. It had long ago lost all its paint, and there were several holes where mice and/or rats could come and go at will. There were a few pieces of furnishings that Goodwill wouldn't even accept these days: a kerosene stove for cooking, some tables, and some chairs—and since we would only be there for the summer, we didn't need to move much from home—just some beds, minimum kitchen things, and a few clothes.

But what a very happy time it was! I was sixteen, had just finished high school as valedictorian of my class with an all-expenses-paid scholarship to Draughon's Business College, was old enough to learn to drive, and felt like my life was really getting ready to begin! We even had a new (well, "new" to us) car. It was a dark green '39 Oldsmobile four-door sedan with a gear shift on the right side of the steering column, just under the steering wheel, that would make learning to drive a <u>lot</u> easier. And it was <u>BIG</u>! Until then all seven of us had crowded into a '29 Olds two-door sedan—but five of us had been smaller then, and we appreciated even <u>having</u> a car. Many of our friends couldn't afford one, or at least not a very good one.

When a defense buildup began just prior to World War II, Dad left his highway construction work to become a carpenter, which paid more, and there was plenty of work building defense plants of various kinds, as well as new and/or expanded military bases. Fort Leonard Wood near our home was one of the first places he worked. Now he was helping build an ammunition plant near Weldon Springs. We always welcomed a chance to live temporarily where he was working—otherwise he'd be gone from home for one or two weeks at a time. So what did we care about the quality of the house? Life for us five children became an adventure—and we could all be together!

Housekeeping was a snap—no animals to tend—so Mom and her "brood" ranging from me at sixteen down to brother Sterling (called Junior then) at age eight, had many hours of spare time. No shopping malls, no public playgrounds, no parks, no television, no radio, and, since Mom couldn't drive, no transportation to anything anyway. But we hadn't learned to depend upon being entertained—our entertainment was "homespun." There was plenty of space to run and play our own ball-game inventions, explore the field and watch the hawks and rabbits, to hear the music of bird songs—quail, jays, red-wing blackbirds, robins, cardinals, larks, etc. We could try to keep cooler in the mid-day heat with games like checkers, dominoes, or marbles in the shade of the house, drawing pictures, cutting paper dolls, etc. But the activity we all seemed to enjoy most was reading time. Mom was usually the main reader, with me taking turns with her. I don't remember all of the titles, but we had several different subjects and levels that all of us could enjoy. *Gone with the Wind* was one I especially remember. It had recently been made into a movie, which we hadn't yet seen, and the book Mom had brought with us happened to be the movie edition with quite a number of color pictures of scenes from the movie. I could "see" myself as Scarlett, surrounded by all those admiring young men and then falling in love with the very adventurous Rhett Butler!

Mom had been a quilter all her life and had taken a sizeable box of scraps along—pieces left over from clothes she had sewed for us—so making quilts became another activity. It was a first experience for me and my sisters, Barbara and Joy. The design I chose to make was "nine-patch"; Barbara and Joy thought "four-patch" would be easier for them. That was very enjoyable—

61

probably because we had Mom's loving attention and guidance about combining colors, making tiny stitches, and keeping the pieces even. (And one person could read aloud while the others were stitching!) But don't ask me what Ross and Sterling were doing while we girls worked on our quilts! In all of that big field, and with their creative imaginations and talents for making their own entertainment, it could have been anything. At least they never came around complaining about having nothing to do!

We lived about a mile from a country store, and since we had no refrigeration, we needed some fresh food every day. Mom made a list, and some—or all—of us except Mom, walked to the store, allowing ourselves time to get there about the time Dad was coming home from work. Then came a very special part of the day for me—as soon as Dad turned the car onto the country road, he stopped and let me have some driving practice the rest of the way home! (It just occurred to me now while I'm writing this, why Mom stayed at home! I know my fourteen-year-old brother Ross was green with envy, and sisters were probably worried all the way!) There sure seemed to be a lot to think about all at once: being sure to put the clutch in before shifting, letting the clutch out at just the right speed and moment to accelerate smoothly, then shifting again a couple of times before you were really rolling. Of course, all this time the wheel had to be held steady to keep the car in the road! One time I somehow ran off the road, into a shallow ditch. It wasn't a dangerous situation, so Dad insisted that with his advice about the movements, I get it back on the road myself. I, of course, was devastated because I'd made the mistake, and worried that I might not be able to do it, but Dad was very patient and thought it was a worthwhile learning experience! The kids in the back seat were probably wondering if that was the place where they were "going to die"!

Some other learning experiences happened in downtown St. Louis where we'd gone shopping for school clothes near the end of summer. I would be leaving the family soon to go to Springfield to begin my college classes; Mom and the other kids would follow after packing up from our regular home at Dixon. I'd never been "on my own" before, so there in St. Louis I first experienced using a telephone. We found a couple of next-door stores that had public phones, so in one of them Dad showed me how to put in the coins into it and how to hold the receiver. It happened to be a quite modern one with the ear part and mouth part all on the same piece. Then we put the receiver back on its hook at the side of the phone, and Dad told me that when it rings to take the receiver off the hook, put it to my ear, and say "Hello." He wrote down the number of "my" phone and went next door to call me. After a very brief conversation he told me to write down the number of the phone that he was using, to hang up my receiver, and then to call him back. Wow! Modern technology! Other lessons that day were about safety in the city: keep my purse closed, put the strap over arm or shoulder, and hold it securely against my body; walk in the middle of the sidewalk (thieves could be lurking in doorways); walk wide around the corner of a building (someone could grab you before you could see them); and more advice about other city life circumstances.

For my transportation to Springfield to begin college, Dad made arrangements with the kind salesman who had come to our home to enroll me in school at Draughon's College. He and his wife would be driving across the state just before the beginning of school, and I could ride with them. They also helped me get checked into the YWCA that was near Draughon's, and where I would have room and board to stay until the family found a house for us. That was another very important learning experience for my new "adult" life! I suppose it was the first time I'd ever felt "loneliness"! I loved school and enjoyed working with capable professors and new friends. I felt like, "I can DO this!" And I felt new confidence about going shopping in nearby stores, cashing checks, riding a bus, etc. But—oh! Going home in the evening to that one small, sparsely furnished room was totally new, and totally lonely! I think I might have eaten lunch at school, but other meals were in the cafeteria (alone) at the "Y." In my room I studied at the small desk and slept in the single-size bed that wasn't all that comfortable. My books were my only company! For two weeks! When Mom arrived, I was so happy! I just clung to her and cried!

How thankful I am for that wonderful summer of togetherness in that old house! There was time for sightseeing in evenings and on weekends, sharing lazy days of leisure, and feeling the need to be responsible for my own self— another "rite of passage" into becoming an adult! And, as a bonus, I have a lovely quilt made of colorful scraps of dresses from my childhood, put together with soft yellow fabric, and now decorating one of our guest room beds to remind me often of those sunny summer days!

FAMILY TRADITIONS

Where do "traditions" come from? Why do they seem important? According to Mr. Webster's wisdom, a tradition is "a long-established custom or practice that has the effect of an unwritten law—a statement, opinion, or belief handed down orally from one generation to another." That definition seems to me to be describing the natural process of learning—from family members or from others who have "been there and done that." But soon we learn that there are <u>other</u> ways of living—that other families seem just as happy being different! Still, it's comforting to want to celebrate certain occasions in the way we learned from parents—who also learned from <u>their</u> parents, maybe for several generations. Why does that seem important? Could it mean that growing up means respecting the past? But doesn't growing up also include thinking about the future? When, and how, do we <u>make traditions our own</u>?

Traditions can be simple customs, or they can be extravagant productions. I believe the most significant thing about the celebration of an occasion is the effect it has upon the comfort, happiness, and the relationships of the people involved. I think I can use some of my memories for some examples.

Easter: Going to church was, and is, foremost. When I was younger, it seemed very important to have new clothes to wear. I no longer need that. As a child, the special Easter food was eggs—for breakfast, as many as we wanted, cooked to please! By the time my own children came, coloring eggs and hiding them was popular; and surprise baskets of candies left by the Easter Rabbit was morning excitement. (Church was still central.)

Fourth of July: When I was a child the family attended the "picnic" in the small Dixon city park. The weather was usually quite hot, and there were several kinds of entertainment: a Ferris wheel (first one constructed by engineer George W. G. Ferris for World's Fair in Chicago in 1893), and a couple of other simple rides; hot-dogs, hamburgers, ice cream, soda pop, cotton candy, and our own basket lunch, shared with relatives or friends. On the way home, we went by the ice plant, bought a large chunk of ice, wrapped it in a gunny sack, and carried it on the car bumper. At home, Mom quickly mixed together cream, sugar, flavoring, beaten eggs, a rennet powder, and maybe some crushed fruit, and filled the ice-cream freezer can. With the side of a hammer, Dad crushed chunks of the ice and layered it with salt into the outer freezer container (that was made of tapered slabs of wood held together by metal bands). From a hole near the top, water drained out as the ice melted. Then came what seemed the endless crank-turning! Mostly done by Dad. We children liked to put a piece of ice in our mouth, and then see how many times we could run around the house before it melted. That meant we were "out of gas," and we had to be towed by someone to the "station" for a refill of ice!

Usually it was sundown by the time we filled our bowls to enjoy that most wonderful treat! Often, we felt chilly enough for sweaters! But what fun!

Birthdays: A special dinner, of the birthday person's choice, was followed with a wonderful, beautifully decorated cake! Sometimes friends were invited to share it. Gene and I added to the dinner and cake tradition by placing gold-colored utensils on the table by the birthday person's plate.

Thanksgiving dinner is probably the one meal of the year that we try most earnestly to get right. It holds the hope of being a good meal whose ingredients, efforts, setting, and consumption are expressions of the best in us. Rather than the Thanksgiving table being a sanctuary from the world, could it be a representation of our best hope for it? For us, it has always been mostly a day for gathering the family—expressing our gratitude and enjoying some favorite foods. Usually the meat is turkey, with dressing, gravy, Brussels sprouts, corn, sweet potatoes, fruit salad, cranberry sauce (cooked by daughter Becky, with added sliced oranges and orange-flavored liqueur), and pie—pumpkin and apple. In 2009, we had a deviation from "tradition". The Butlers (Brian, Becky, Thomas, and Evan) stayed in Seattle, where they helped their church cook and serve dinner to over 150 homeless people, plus the volunteers who helped with the dinner. I was very pleased to have them celebrate in that way—making an opportunity for their children to serve and develop respect for people less fortunate than they! (Could we call that "hope for the world"?) David and Michelle served a turkey-with-all the-trimmings dinner to her mother and brother in their home at mid-day, then came to my house for an evening dinner. That year we experimented with cooking a goose! We thought it was quite tasty, with stir-fried Brussels sprouts, wild rice, mixed fruit salad, and pumpkin pie brought by David and Michelle. Could it be time for "new traditions"?

I've been part of other tradition changes, too. When I married into the Bench family, in 1948, I discovered their tradition of all the family often going to the ocean to dig clams—Mom and Dad, plus the families of daughters Lavada and Fern, and son Elby, all of whom lived in the area around Tacoma, Washington. (Youngest son, Gene, was in college in Missouri, and had just taken me for his bride, whom they were meeting for the first time!) Those gatherings continued into the next generation—sometimes camping overnight in the area just south of Copalis Beach. Finally, the clam seasons became fewer, and "development" came to the area. They could now stay in adjoining motel suites, with kitchens, at the Royal Pacific Resort in the new town of Ocean Shores! Right where they had previously camped! The motel is now named "The Sands," and there is seldom an open clam season, but on the weekend before Labor Day, the Bench family still gathers—and the people who were children then, now have grandchildren of their own!

Gene and I developed a New Year's Eve tradition that we hosted at our home after he retired from the Marine Corps. We had for several years enjoyed celebrating the evening with our square dance group, but because of Gene's back problems, we had to stop dancing. We didn't care for parties with loud music, ball room dancing, and alcohol; but we did really like playing bridge! We began inviting a few friends—five couples to make three tables of bridge, or three couples to make two tables. Each couple brought some finger-food for snacking throughout the evening, with which we served coffee, punch, or soft drinks. Around 11:45 p.m., we gathered in the living room to watch the Times Square's celebration on TV until the count-down, and "the ball" dropped. Then we toasted the New Year with sparkling apple or grape juice, hugs, and good wishes! But the New Year has to be started off <u>right</u>! What better way to start it than by playing one round (four deals) of bridge—for *Auld Lang Syne!*

Don't forget about the tradition of making popcorn! We really liked that one, beginning in childhood! One can now pop a sealed bag of it in the microwave, but that can't compare to the magic of putting hard kernels of corn into a hand-held pan, covering with the lid, and gently shaking it back and forth over a heat source while excitedly waiting for the "popping" to begin! When the popping stops, it is dumped into a large bowl and drizzled with melted butter. When I was a child it was often an after-dinner treat, made on the living room heating stove, because the wood fire in the kitchen stove was allowed to "go out" for the night. Popcorn must have been popular for many people, because it became almost a "necessity" for movie-goers!

Christmas: I've written some other stories about "Santa Claus" and Christmas Trees" that describe in some detail a few of my experiences with Christmas traditions. I have always considered Christmas to be one of my most treasured traditions—being the time to remember the birth of Jesus, and His life that was spent teaching the basics and importance of genuine love. Of course, many of the Christmas traditions include symbols of His life and teachings, <u>if</u> we <u>use</u> them properly. Even our American red-coated Santa Claus shows benevolence and kindness in bringing happiness to children, and in some other countries he is given the name of St. Nicholas or Father Christmas. Several years ago, after our children became adults, we agreed that instead of giving gifts to each other, we would use that money to make donations to charities in honor of each family member.

By now you get the idea how I feel about "tradition"! Maybe you can imagine how much I enjoy hearing Tevye sing the song called *Tradition* in the musical *Fiddler on the Roof!*

HAIR—AND—MY FIRST PERM

Hair styles seem to have been important to both men and women for goodness-only-knows how long. Ancient Egyptian art pictures show elaborate styles, rising high above the scalp, as well as elegant side arrangements that look quite sculptured. In medieval times, long hair seemed to be popular—maybe in poorly heated buildings, extra hair was good for holding in body heat. White wigs with long curls were "standard" for a time in France and England—and even in the American colonies. (I wonder about cave dwellers' hair styles? Was it long and straight—like the cartoons showing a man "taking a wife" by dragging her by her hair into his cave?)

Hair is mentioned in the Bible over fifty times. When Delilah cut Samson's hair, he lost his unusual strength (*Judges 16*). According to Jesus, "even the hairs of your head are all numbered" (*Matthew 10:30*). The apostle Paul taught the Corinthians: "Does not nature itself teach you that for a man to wear long hair is degrading to him, but if a woman has long hair it is her pride? For her hair is given to her for a covering." (*I Cor 11:14-15*). Jesus' friend Mary, the sister of Martha and Lazarus, must have had long hair. According to *John 11:2*, "It was Mary who anointed the Lord with ointment and wiped his feet with her hair."

For some time, hair styles have seemed to follow those of famous people: finger-waves of movie stars in the 1920's, Shirley Temple curls, Mamie Eisenhower bangs, Princess Diana's "bob," tiny "corn-row" braids, "rats" to add volume, halo braids. French braids, "up-do's," page-boy, and for a time it seemed that a lot of attention was given to making it look like it hasn't even been combed! U.S. Marines require a look of almost <u>no</u> hair, needing frequent attention to keep it short enough!

I've usually been right in there with all the rest, for whom hair seems to be quite a worry. My best years were probably from about age one to about age five, when it was cut with bangs straight across my forehead, then straight down the sides to just below my ears—and straight around the bottom. It was easy to wash and comb, didn't blow into my face in the wind, and wasn't affected if it got wet in the rain! (Maybe I should try that style again!)

I don't know if long hair became my wish, or if my mother thought it should be growing along with me. Eventually, by the time I was ten or eleven years old, it grew long enough I could sit on it. It became very difficult to shampoo, because we didn't have running water, so Mom usually helped with it. I suppose we didn't even know about special "shampoo" for washing hair. Mom just added vinegar to the rinse water to neutralize any remaining soap. In the summer it was fun to play outside in the sun while it dried. But, oh! The tangles that always had to be brushed and combed out! I don't know why I never lobbied for short hair. My two sisters, both younger than I, had short hair, as did most of my friends. My Mom must have wanted it so. She usually combed it in the morning for the day—braids with pigtails, braids wrapped around my head; or for Sunday—long vertical curls after sleeping all night with it rolled around rag strips. I envied the older neighbor girls and my aunts who curled their hair with curling irons—heated in the kerosene lamp chimneys.

By the time I graduated from high school and would be away from Mom when I began going to business college, we had to seriously consider my hair. We cut it to a long, shoulder length with some shorter hair on top for bangs. With a headband to keep it out of my face, it looked reasonably good, even though it was straight; and I could manage it myself.

Dad was working away from home then. He and Mom decided that the family might as well live in Springfield, Missouri where I would be in school for a couple of years; rather than Mom and the other kids on the Dixon farm, and Dad in some other place. I began college classes in September and lived in the YWCA boarding house for about a month while the family prepared for their move.

Our new home was a comfortable rented house on South Street, in walking distance from our different schools, and downtown. How nice it was to live in town, and to have electricity and running water! (But this story started out to be about "HAIR"!)

By then, people with straight hair who wanted curls could get a "permanent" wave, and not have to bother with curling irons heated in lamp chimneys! (Those with naturally curly hair, who wanted it straight, could have it straightened by pulling it through a device made with two flat surfaces, heated by electricity, and clamped onto a small section of hair at a time. I must admit that I often wondered why anyone who was blessed with natural curls couldn't be perfectly happy with it!) Well, I was tired of straight hair, so Mom and I decided I should get a "permanent."

That first one turned out to be kind of "scary," but I figured that I could survive if so many others did. In the first place, the machine that supplied the heat looked like it could be an execution device! Thirty or more metal clamps dangled from a round, dome-shaped thing on a stand that could be adjusted for height. In the air was a mixture of odors coming from the chemical in the perm solution (lots of ammonia); there were fragrances from various kinds of shampoo and other hair-fixing stuff being used around the salon—and, would you believe, the smell of bacon cooking!

After bundling me in towels and a cape, the hairdresser cleansed my hair and began the perm procedure. A small section of hair was gathered together and pulled through a slot in the center of a felt-looking pad about ¾" wide, a little more than an inch long, and about ¼" to ½" thick. The pad was pushed down firmly on the scalp, and the strand of hair was saturated with the perm solution and rolled around a roller to sit on the pad. (I don't remember what held it there.) When all the hair was rolled in this way, I could hardly hold up my head, it felt so heavy! Then it was time for the heat. I sat under the "execution machine" and each of the clamps was clipped over a roller. (Those dangling wires carried "hot" electricity to those rollers <u>on my head</u>!) I was warned to let the hairdresser know if I felt any hot spots—she meant any <u>really</u> hot spots! She also told me I'd smell something like bacon cooking, but not to worry—it would probably be a stray hair or two getting too hot, but no damage was being done. "After all," she said, "both hair and bacon are made of protein that makes an odor when it's heated." At frequent intervals a different roller was tested to see if the curl was "taking," then re-rolled and re-clamped. After several minutes, success was proclaimed, and I was led to a shampoo bowl where each roll was saturated with a neutralizing fluid (acid) and left to wait for the chemicals to react. (Neutralizing is the step that "sets" the curl.)

Then came the magical part! The rollers were all removed and the solutions rinsed out with what must have been <u>gallons</u> of running water! Fragrant conditioners followed, with the hairdresser combing everything into what they called "style." I felt like a princess with all of those wonderful curls that would stay curled for several months!

I suppose there have been well over <u>two</u> <u>hundred</u> perms in my hair since that first one. But no others under the "execution machine"! The "cold wave" was invented not long after that—simple enough that some packaged ones could be done at home. They contained chemicals that could react without applied heat—and some are made to automatically stop the action. For many years, I've chosen the local beauty college for my hair care. It's really inspiring to enjoy the enthusiasm of the students—and by the time the students are juniors or seniors, their skills are reaching professional levels. It's fun, too, to see the imagination they often use in experimenting with various hair styles and colors on themselves! (Green!? Orange!? Pink!? Short!? Shorter!?) This school sometimes displays their treasured antique perm machine with the dangling curling devices! It was my inspiration to record some memories of my own experience some seventy years ago with one of those monsters!

ECONOMIC DEPRESSION AND DOWNTURN

Early in college, I had a course called "Economics 101"—not because I wanted to learn about economics, but because it was a requirement for all students! The text was written by Professor Harry Gunnison Brown, the Chairman of the Economics Department at the University of Missouri. The year was 1945, and I would guess that more than half of the people in the class were young veterans returning from WWII. I remember that my instructor, Mr. Pinkney Walker—was himself a returning veteran. He was a tall, good-looking guy whose manner gave one the idea that he thought he was God's gift to women (and to everyone else); I was very naïve, shy, and "sheltered" from the "seamy" side of life, so you can imagine what the class was like for me, when Mr. Walker seemed to be telling more "off-color" jokes than he was helping us learn anything about Economics. (I didn't understand the jokes, but I knew they were off-color by the way all the guys guff-hawed!) Maybe there was one "economics" item that came from his teaching—something about the part of Professor Brown's income that came from managing to get his own book designated to be the text for that "required" class! I guess another economics principle I heard about was the law of "supply and demand." Well, at least I can balance my checkbook with my bank statements, and when I see my monthly investment statements, I can tell that lately I've been losing money!

My only qualification for writing about Depression and economic downturn is having lived in the time of what is now called "the Great Depression." I was born in 1925, and so my parents had a short time of enjoying the fruits of their labors before the stock market crash of 1929. They had worked in the Kansas wheat fields and in the Oklahoma oil fields for most of their first year of marriage and had saved enough money to build a small house on Dad's ten acres of land two miles north of Dixon, Missouri, before my birth. They put special thought into the location of the house—near the road, at the north end of the property from which they would have a view of all the rest of the acreage! Dixon was Dad's hometown where his father and many other relatives also lived. The Frisco railroad track maintenance work provided a small income for him. They had a Model T Ford that they had driven back to Missouri from Oklahoma. Now, they bought a team of mules, a Jersey cow, some Black Giant chickens, and some second-hand furniture. They planted a garden, an orchard, a small vineyard, and what they called a "truck patch" of crops like tomatoes, corn, beans, and potatoes for canning and storing for winter food.

I remember hearing their stories about many people who had lost homes and fortunes when the "crash" came. Millions of people were out of work; in cities there were soup lines, and drifters—no "unemployment insurance" then. If a man could even find work, the pay was often no more than a dollar a day. People who lived on farms were the lucky ones—at least they could grow some of their food. Mom sewed clothes for us, let down hems, turned collars on Dad's shirts, used the better parts of worn clothes for making quilts, made rugs of the rags that were left, and items of clothing from cloth feed sacks. We children created our own games and some toys, helped with chores, and read books. In Dixon, some of the merchants were kind enough to allow people to buy essentials on credit, and eventually even Dad had to go into debt. But through all the hardship, my parents kept a positive attitude—so that we children didn't realize that we were "poor." As far as we were concerned, the way we lived was just "life"! All our friends, neighbors, and relatives economized, too!

So—now, as I am writing, here we are in an "economic downturn," with the threat of another Depression. Of course, much has changed—especially lifestyles and standards of living! There are more people; our taxes pay for unemployment insurance; electronics has made it possible to communicate instantaneously world-wide; we can travel across the country or the ocean in just a few hours; products are imported and exported globally. We have become dependent upon electric power, upon indoor plumbing, upon ready-prepared foods; upon more than one car per family, Union wages, luxury homes, college educations—you name it!

But, by the end of this year—and no doubt by the end of another three or four—what I'm now feeling as "theory," will be revealing results of some major experiments and changes in economics and, no doubt in our standard of living. The American people seem to do their best work in hard times—overcoming hardships and difficulties to achieve prosperity and comfort. I can't help believing that the hard times in that other Depression formed the work ethic and patriotism that led to what Tom Brokaw described in his book, *The Greatest Generation.* Doesn't it make some sense that by learning now to live more economically, this present generation can also become a "great" generation?

While Americans were struggling with eking out a living for their families, some of the rest of the world was in other kinds of turmoil—Hitler was destroying Jews; Japan was in a genocidal war against the Chinese; in Russia, Stalin was sending people who disagreed with him to Siberia. In this country, Franklin D. Roosevelt was elected President, and began federal programs, called the New Deal, to get the American economy back on track. The creation of Social Security was one of them. Besides regulations for banks and industry, he promoted the Works Progress Administration, and the Civilian Conservation Corps. In both of those programs, people were paid for doing work—building schools, building and improving roads, clearing and creating parks, conserving forests, even building museums. One project here in our Oregon "backyard" is the beautiful, sturdy Timberline Lodge at Mount Hood. Native Americans were employed to furnish some of the art work in the form of crafts, such as weaving. From qualified architects to master stone masons, to landscape specialists, to road builders, and all the carpenters and other workmen, came that beautiful national treasure! Their help from the Government was the paycheck they received for their expertise and labor.

Of course, we know that World War II soon erupted; freedom was threatened, and Americans felt a need to not only defend our own people, but to help other oppressed nations. But wait! We weren't prepared for war! We would need ships and planes and tanks and guns! We'd need food and clothing and ammunition to support the thousands of young men and women who would sacrifice their own life plans to do the work required of their military commitment. The American Spirit rose to the occasion! In the name of defense, we lived with rationing—meat, sugar, butter, leather, gasoline, tires, etc. We planted "victory gardens" and collected things like used cooking grease, and various metals to donate to defense needs. We helped each other. We pulled black shades at night—especially in coastal cities where even the street lights were dimmed and shaded. The automotive industry made military vehicles instead of cars for civilians. Airplane factories sprung up—hiring thousands of people, even women! It was as if all of us suddenly changed our sense of purpose from our own needs to the needs of the nation as a whole.

No one wants to believe that fighting a war is necessary for prosperity and progress, but at least there were some good things that resulted from that awful experience. The nation as a people learned to work together; the veterans who had experienced "forced maturity" came home to a college education paid for by the Veterans' Bill of Rights; people seemed to have renewed ambition to live in peace and freedom—using creative energy to invent the many wonderful conveniences we've come to enjoy; to create programs to benefit the elderly, the disadvantaged, and the needy.

Now, as we rather suddenly face the hardships of unemployment, loss of wealth, and the need to "tighten our belts," I think this generation, too, will find strength of purpose and courage as they use their ingenuity to give new stability to a standard of living that will be based on sensible economics and cooperation—themselves becoming an even greater generation! Surely, by then, they will have learned one principle of economics—that to enjoy the convenience of a credit card, one needs to pay the balance in full each month!

LOVE IS ALL THAT MATTERS

Chapter 2: College Years

LOIS HANSEN DAHLBERG—MY COLLEGE ROOMMATE

Early in 1945, I decided I didn't want to be a secretary all my life, so more college would have to be the solution. After high school I'd chosen Draughon's Business College in Springfield, Missouri, as the place where I'd use my valedictorian scholarship; and that school qualified me for the office job I had at the Fort Leonard Wood Post Exchange in the personnel department. It was a fairly large office, and I felt quite honored when I was soon chosen to replace the Personnel Manager's secretary, Rita, when she resigned because her soldier husband was being transferred. Until then, I had been doing clerical work in the same department, with Mrs. Morton (a delightful lady who had a grown daughter working in the accounting department) and a couple of other girls. The new assignment would be a promotion, and would be much more challenging, giving me an opportunity to use dictation, letter-writing skills, review applications, help with placement of new employees, etc. It was even good pay for those days, and since I still lived with my parents, I'd been able to save enough for at least a start for college tuition.

The only thing that I found a bit "scary" about the college plan was the living arrangements. The University of Missouri was a much larger school than I had ever even imagined: all kinds of buildings spaced over acres of campus—housing for administration, classrooms for the many departments of study, several dormitories, boarding houses, apartments, even a small hospital-clinic. I imagined that dormitory life would be stressful to my small-town-farm-girl personality—more than likely, those girls would be looking to have a fun time rather than serious study time that I would want. I spent a day with Mom and Dad exploring the campus in Columbia, gathering applications, and looking at some boarding houses that were on the approved housing list. World War II was still going on, but veterans were already returning to attend college on the GI Bill, so many people who lived near the campus had qualified to provide rooms for students—even for freshmen.

After seeing several of them, we liked a two-story old-fashioned house on the corner of South Fifth Street and Conley, about three blocks from the west end of the campus. A widow named Mrs. Dunn was the owner and house mother, and she served breakfast and dinner. Breakfast was "to order;" dinner was served family style. Looking back, I have no idea how old she was—maybe as much as seventy, but at that time she seemed to me to be ancient. She'd been a housemother for a number of years, was very kind, and allowed male visitors in the living room and dining room during daytime and evening until 10:00 p.m. (midnight on Fridays and Saturdays) when girls were all required to be "in." There were three upstairs bedrooms to share one bath, and one downstairs room to share the bath with Mrs. Dunn. I chose the downstairs room. There was a front porch across the front of the house, with a swing at one end. It turned out to be a great place for "hanging out," or for lingering "good-nights," sheltered from rain or snow.

But that didn't solve the scariest problem for me: What would my roommate be like? I wasn't opposed to having fun—as long as it wasn't boisterous—but I did want to be able to devote plenty of time to study. I had never lived away from home—had not even gone to a summer camp of any kind—so I felt a little shy about suddenly living in one room with a strange girl! What if she were a sloppy "housekeeper"? What if she smoked? (Smoking was not banned in those days, and many young people seemed to think it was a way to appear "adult.") What if she liked "jazzy" music? Or what if she used "worldly" language that might insult my sheltered ears?

Well! I worried for nothing! We had to be on campus for a few days of orientation before classes began, and what a pleasure it was to meet and begin getting acquainted with Lois Hansen from Colorado! She was a junior and had come to Columbia for Journalism School—at that time, and more than likely still, considered the best in the country. You can guess that I had many questions for her to answer about what to expect of college life! How thankful I was to have her experience as a guide! I soon realized that she was the kind of person who would be one of the best friends I'd ever had—one from whom I'd learn new things, with whom I could share feelings or problems, and with whom I agreed about living conditions in our small, shared room.

One of our common experiences was being country girls, even though our farms were quite different—mine a ten-acre fruit and vegetable farm with a cow, a couple of pigs, and a few chickens—hers, a hundreds-of-acres mile-high ranch with cattle, horses, and grain fields. Another thing we shared was sewing skills—both of us made most of our own clothes, and I had a portable sewing machine we could use. But she was more fashion-conscious than I—a new attribute I could learn. I remember the outfit she sewed for Easter the first spring we lived together. It was a navy-blue crepe suit with a silky white blouse, but the design she created was new to me—three-quarter length jacket sleeves with puffy white blouse sleeves that came to her wrists. Until then, I'd only seen wrist-length jacket sleeves worn with wrist-length blouse sleeves. But she was tall and slender, so her design was very good for her. She topped it all with a _very_ wide-brimmed hat!

There was never any problem with having a messy-looking room—unless I left something out of place. I was quite an "organized" person in those days; she was even more so. We agreed on movies—musicals, historical, romantic, some comedies—and we both wanted plenty of study time. Even being a farm girl, she was quite sophisticated, having lived and attended college in Denver for a couple of years. I would also call her "cultured." She played the piano very well and liked classical music. One of her pieces that impressed me was a Grieg Concerto. Every Saturday afternoon her radio was tuned to "Saturday Afternoon at the Met," which even then was sponsored by Texaco! Appreciation of opera was one of the many things I learned from her. Until then my experience with music had been church hymns, gospel, country music, folk songs, and some popular "Hit Parade" tunes. The high pitched and foreign language opera music had heretofore been unpleasant. Soon I learned to like it, and to learn some of the stories it told. It was just like a play, except the words were sung instead of spoken!

The second year at Mrs. Dunn's, Lois and I decided to move into two single rooms upstairs that had a connecting door between. That gave us more space and the feeling of a suite. By then my sister Barbara and her friend Pat Innes were students at the University, too, and they had chosen to share one of Mrs. Dunn's other upstairs rooms.

After two years, Lois graduated in the spring and went back to Colorado to put to use her new expertise in journalism. We imagined what a great writer she would be. With her many interests she would soon be in the middle of all kinds of news reporting and feature writing! That year's Christmas letter told of her new job that she considered a temporary employment while she waited to find something in journalism. She was now the teacher in a one-room country school near Castle Rock—several miles from her family ranch. But there was more. A nearby bachelor rancher had been making sure she had a social life—square dancing, horseback riding, sleigh riding, skiing, pie suppers, etc. In another year she became Mrs. Russell Dahlberg, rancher's wife, gardener, homemaker, harvest hand, cow-girl, and eventually, mother of an energetic boy and a lovely girl! I've often wondered about the career dreams she had while in school—but after many years of correspondence with her, plus several visits to their ranch, I discovered that her happiness didn't need bright lights or glitz or fame. "Culture" doesn't need it either! Culture is of the soul! She treasured her piano, listened to "Saturday Afternoon at the Met," took family fishing vacations in the beautiful Rocky Mountains in the shadow of Pikes' Peak, went to grandchildren's games and school plays, and stood beside her "Rancher"!

Thank you, Lois, for enriching my life with your culture and love!

MRS. DUNN—1946-47

Today, as I'm writing this, is March 3, 2010. My diary entry for March 3, 1946, reads: "Lois and I lunched at the Virginia today. Mrs. Dunn was gone, so we had the boys up for supper." Where did this happen? Who is Lois? Who is Mrs. Dunn? Who are "the boys"?

At this time, I was in my first year of college at the University of Missouri in Columbia. WWII was over, and the campus was crowded with young male students who were veterans, returning to college with tuition and living expenses paid for by the Government's G.I. Bill of Rights. Many Columbia residents—especially in homes near the campus—were renting rooms to students, and Mrs. Dunn was one of those. She lived in a large, two-story frame house that was painted gray, and had a front porch with a swing at one end. Two or three wicker chairs took up some of the other space. Her spacious, old-fashioned carpeted living room was a place for students to entertain guests; and in the large adjoining dining room, she served breakfast and dinner for "her girls." The address was 507 South Fifth Street—just a block from the west edge of the campus, so it was a really convenient location for a boarding house.

Lois Dahlberg was my surprise roommate—a really delightful girl from Louviers, Colorado; a junior, and majoring in Journalism. (At that time the Journalism Department at the University of Missouri was the best one in the nation.) She really helped me learn how to "navigate" a campus and learn some of the ways of college students. We shared the one downstairs room.

Upstairs were two large bedrooms, each of which housed two girls. Two smaller single rooms, with a connecting closeable door, were at the east end of the hall. Eight young women put their feet under the dining table each morning and evening. Mrs. Dunn was a "grandmother" type, who seemed really old to me, but was probably no older than sixty or so; however, cooking and serving that many people was quite a chore. She asked Lois and me to give her some help with the serving, for which we received our meals without charge.

Anyone with some extra space for students was making money renting to the young veterans, and for the men, there were less rigid requirements for the quality of the rooms. Mrs. Dunn had some spare space in her basement, which she turned into a room for a couple of guys to share. (I don't remember if there was already a bathroom down there, or if she had one put in for them to use.) Soon we were introduced to Terry Hendrix (nickname T.D.) and Jerry, whose last name I don't remember. Terry had dark hair, a Clark Gable-style mustache, drove a Chevy sedan, and was shorter than sandy-haired Jerry. Both boys were Missourians, enthusiastic about school, and liked out-door adventures. With the two added students, Mrs. Dunn rearranged the dining room for two smaller tables, and it seemed that they often chose to sit at the same table with Lois and me. Those two were "the boys we had up for supper" that March evening when Mrs. Dunn was gone.

It wasn't long until the four of us became "two couples," double-dating for movies or bowling, or late evening snacks and coffee. Lois, who had grown up on a ranch, and I, also a country girl, liked getting out of town with Terry and Jerry, in Terry's car on weekends. Not far from campus was a beautiful little stream called Hinkson Creek. It was a favorite gathering place for beer parties for some. But the four of us just liked walking along its banks and wading in its usually clear water that bubbled and murmured over the rocks and gravel. We liked taking picnic lunches along, and had fun getting acquainted— hearing, of course, many tales from the boys of their wartime experiences. Lois had lived in Denver during her first two years of college, so had become somewhat sophisticated; so for her, Jerry was a guy with whom to spend casual time, but not serious or romantic time. It was different for Terry and me. We soon liked each other a lot! He had grown up on a chicken-farm near Odessa, Missouri, which was about half-way between Columbia and Kansas City. He was majoring in Engineering, and we soon discovered many shared interests. After a movie we often drove out of town to a "parking place" on a hill overlooking Columbia and the farms below. It was a really good place to watch the moon come up and make its way across the sky—until time for us to get back to Mrs. Dunn's before she locked the door! Mrs. Dunn liked Terry a lot, and thought we made a "cute couple"! One of our outings was taking Mrs. Dunn to visit her son who had a mushroom farm near the small town of Avauxsse. Part of the deal was for her son to give us a tour of his mushroom gardens. It was a new experience for Terry and me—walking through the rows and rows of trays of white button-mushrooms, growing in black rich soil, in a very darkened cave-like building. (We suspected that Mrs. Dunn's interest was more for a ride to visit her son, than for giving Terry and me a treat—but we didn't mind. He and I were together, and that was all that mattered!) My diary tells of many fun dates. One little recorded episode is on August 7th: "Washed this afternoon. (Terry 'punished' me with a kiss for flipping water on him!") Another entry on August 10th reads: "This was one of the happiest days (nights) of my life, as well as a sad one. T.D. and I went to a carnival and rodeo at Moberly. Got home at 5:00 a.m. There was a perfect full moon, and everything was wonderful!" It so happened that my Mom and Dad were coming to pick me up that morning, to go home for the rest of the summer. But I didn't expect them to be there when Terry and I got back to Mrs. Dunn's!

Terry decided to leave school temporarily to help his family on the farm at the end of summer school in August, so the next semester was a little lonely for me, although we had agreed that we were free to date others. He came for an occasional weekend, but it wasn't like having him there all the time—even living in the same house! For Christmas that year his gift to me was a lovely, matching necklace and bracelet, set with pale blue-green stones.

On January 26, 1947, I exercised my freedom to date others, and went on a blind double-date with my sister Barbara and her boyfriend, Joe Belshe. My date was Gene Bench, an ex-Marine who had just started school at the beginning of the winter semester. That date was the beginning of a longer story of adventures that lasted through the next _very_ happy, almost fifty-four years!

I LEARNED MORE THAN CHEMISTRY!

After working for a couple of years as a secretary to the Personnel Manager of the Post Exchanges at Fort Leonard Wood in Missouri, I began feeling that there must be something more challenging and interesting that I could learn to do for a career. Maybe something concerning chemistry?? I didn't know "beans" about what chemistry was, except that I thought it concerned the elements that, mixed together in different ways, made up everything in the world. Well, that was an idea that could be "put on the back burner" to think about. Later, I thought it would be "noble" to become a missionary to the "Indians" in the southwest—teaching them some ways to have better health, and a better standard of living. To do that, it seemed that studying Home Economics might be a basic background. And, of course, I wanted to eventually get married and have a family, so Home Economics would also be helpful for that. I'd also work some Bible study into it somehow.

Military friends I'd met while living at Fort Wood and being involved with the community church and youth group, talked about Wheaton Bible College near Chicago being a good place to go for that type of "dual" education. A BIG disappointment came when I wasn't accepted! (I think the reason was that they didn't have room for any more students for that fall term.) But I wasn't a "quitter," so I decided to enroll at the University of Missouri in Columbia until I could go to Wheaton. I could at least work on some "basic" courses.

From taking Home Ec in high school for three years, I knew I enjoyed learning about home-making, child training, some science, some art, foods, sewing, budgeting, and such—so learning to teach it should be quite interesting! The "catch" to that was that the teacher should know more about the subject than the students did! That meant getting substantial "background" information in all the different areas that are part of the course called "Home Economics." Some of those would be art—its principles, history, famous artists and their work; for child care—things like psychology, hygiene, biology, and bacteriology. Background for sewing had to include the nature of various fabrics, wardrobe planning, following directions on patterns and designing original patterns, the use of a sewing machine, and hours and hours of practice. For interior decorating—some architecture, use of spaces, artistic use of color and proper fabrics, needs of all the members of the family, and such. To teach foods, one needed to have courses in botany, zoology, biology, and both organic and inorganic chemistry! Much more to it than just learning to cook! And knowing chemistry would also help in general housekeeping—like using cleaning compounds, etc.

All this, to lead up to what a CHEMISTRY class had to do with my life! It turned out that, even though I had at one time thought chemistry would be a good thing to study, I discovered that it was a very difficult subject for me! Having not even had it as a course in high school, it was totally foreign—the nomenclature of elements and compounds, their atomic weights, their relationships to each other in combinations, atomic structures, etc. AND both organic and inorganic chemistry were required! Especially since the organic compounds were essential to the study of foods, fabrics, and the human body! Because it was so difficult, it wasn't one of my favorite courses, though I did appreciate what I was learning about and its relationship to all of life!

About the time I began college, World War II ended, and with the GI Bill available to veterans, the campus was inundated with young military veterans. In all the "general" types of courses, like the required Economics 101 and Inorganic Chemistry 101, there were many more men than women. Lectures for a class of a hundred or more students would be in a huge auditorium-style room, with everyone madly trying to take notes of the formulas and diagrams the professor rapidly drew on the far-away blackboard behind his podium on a stage. (Remember that there were no laptop computers in those days!) In a couple of small lab classes each week there was a better chance of getting some personal help to hopefully learn what we needed to know.

I can tell you that for this small-town country girl, that lab was a really scary place! Here I was, learning about all these various elements I'd never heard of—and the things that mixing them could do! Many of the mixtures turned out to be just every-day things—like two parts of hydrogen and one part of oxygen produced water! How great was that! One mixture that was popular was combining some things (I don't remember what) that made an awful odor like rotten eggs! (That experiment was discouraged!) And, of course, some mixtures would be explosive!

Another interesting thing about the lab class was that I was the only girl— the other twenty-five or thirty people were those just-home-from-the-war men. That was actually not so bad! They were mostly "gentlemanly"—glad to be there, many very knowledgeable about chemistry because they'd had it in high school, some were married with families, almost all of them my age or older— giving the lab a comfortable atmosphere of camaraderie. The guys were very friendly and respectful of me, and with a lot of "burning midnight oil," I made better than average grades.

But there was one guy who soon became a problem for me—the lab instructor! He was a thin, short, "nerdy" sort of man who had dark, unkempt hair, and some kind of physical problem that made him sort of shaky—maybe palsy, or at least some kind of involuntary tremors. That didn't bother me—I just felt sorry for his condition, but it evidently didn't affect his professional expertise because he was very patient and helpful with any chemistry problems. What did bother me, though, was the way he often let one arm sort of rest on my shoulder while he helped with whatever was giving me a problem with an experiment. I didn't <u>like</u> it, but at the same time, it didn't seem to be anything more than just a friendly gesture. Before long, however, some of the other students joked with me about his friendliness sometimes when we were leaving class. And then one day he put his arm around my <u>waist</u> instead of over my shoulder! By then, I decided I needed to make some kind of reaction, so I stepped away, looked him in the eye, and said, "I don't like that! Please don't touch me again"! He looked surprised but went ahead with giving me help with my experiment. On the way out of class that day, the guys congratulated me on facing up to him, and we all had some laughs about it—but my grades on my lab work went down after that! I probably should have reported his behavior to his superior, or to someone in the University administration; but I was <u>so naïve</u>! I don't even know if there were any laws then about harassment, or if it would have been of any benefit to anyone else to know about it! I just chalked it up to "learning a new lesson"—and it was <u>more</u> than Chemistry! Or maybe it was a lesson in a different <u>kind</u> of Chemistry!

OUR WEDDING DAY

Today is August 1, 2001, the fifty-third anniversary of our marriage in 1948, and the first wedding anniversary since Gene went to be with the Lord on June 22nd this year. Naturally, I'm doing a lot of remembering today, so it seems appropriate that I write down some of those memories.

We lived in Columbia, Missouri, then—I with my Kelley family at 1421 Hickory Street, and Gene with three college friends in a tiny little house on Paquin Street. (I remember that one of his housemates was named George Baker.)

We agreed the night before that we would observe the tradition of the groom not seeing the bride on their wedding day until she walked down the aisle at the ceremony, so he was relaxing and visiting with Doc Halmbacher's family who had come for Doc to be Gene's best-man. They had been best buddies in the Marine Corps during World War II and had agreed to be best-man for each other if they ever got married—although at that time, marriage was the farthest thing from their intentions. At nineteen and twenty years of age, there were places to go, things to do, and too many available girls to imagine a lifetime with just one! Doc was the first one to "weaken," and Gene had gone to Michigan a few weeks before to support him for his marriage to Mary. Now Doc, Mary, and Doc's parents were here to be with Gene—naturally staying at the Daniel Boone Hotel on Broadway where Gene worked as night auditor.

The day dawned beautifully clear, and I was up early because I had a lot to do—and was too excited to sleep anyway, once I awoke. We had chosen Sunday afternoon at four o'clock for the wedding, which would make attendance easier for many of my relatives who lived several miles away. I knew I had to do some personal things before the out-of-town people began to arrive, and one thing was to make a hat to wear with my going-away-outfit! My dress was medium blue crepe printed with white bunches of grapes; and of course, in those days, to be properly "dressed," one had to wear a hat, white gloves, heels, and hose. I always had a problem with finding clothes and accessories to buy because I'd get an idea in my head about something special that no one else had yet imagined, so I'd have to make it myself. I took an old hat, cut out the crown, shaped a narrow brim, and covered it with blue taffeta the color of my dress, then made a band with a small bow in the back from a piece of pale gray taffeta.

The next thing was doing my nails so they'd be dry before time to go downstairs. Our overnight bag had been packed the night before, Gene's going-away clothes were waiting in a downstairs bedroom, and my wedding dress that Mom and I had made was hanging up waiting for slipping into later. It was white crepe with a circular skirt that was extended in the back to make a train. The top of it was strapless with boning on the sides to keep it in place. Then there was an over-blouse made of embroidered white lace. It had long sleeves with points over my hands, large scallops just below the waist, and small scallops around the wide neckline where it attached to a white tulle yoke that extended on up to the neck. The scallops were outlined with seed pearls, and the same size of pearls edged the neckline. It was designed with the idea that I could later leave off the lace over-blouse, cut off the train, and have a nice strapless formal gown. (And sure enough, it was often used with various cover-ups, jewelry, and scarves.) My shoes were high-heeled silver sandals, and the veil was finger-tip length tulle held in place with a poufy white lace double ruffle attached to a headband.

LOVE IS ALL THAT MATTERS

I often noticed and admired the various colors of the sky at sunset. Frequently, if there weren't many clouds, there were soft shades of rosy pink and golden yellow against the pale blue sky. Once when I was sky-watching and those colors were "putting on a show," I decided I'd like those colors for bridesmaids' dresses. They were as beautiful as I'd imagined they'd be! Barbara, my oldest sister, was my maid-of-honor and wore the slightly greenish pale blue; my sister Joy wore the light dusty-rose; and a good friend, Mary Bourn, wore the pale yellow. For the flower girl, Aunt Cora's little daughter Corina, we chose the same blue because her pretty eyes were so blue! Her dress was also long and designed like those of the older girls.

Mary Lou and Don Myer were two of our best friends—themselves, married just a short time before, so they were special "helpers." Mary Lou was in charge of the reception, which would be at our house after the wedding, and they would drive the "get-away-car" when we were ready to leave. The three-tiered wedding cake was decorated with white roses and topped with three "sugar" wedding bells. Mrs. Frank Wyatt (Ella Mildred) and Mrs. Enoch Baldwin (Mabel) assisted with serving it and the fruit punch. The napkins were white cocktail size on which we had designed and stenciled three pink wedding bells—yellow on the inside and tied with blue ribbons (the colors of the three bridesmaids' dresses).

It was a very busy day with many relatives gathering to visit with our family, so there was noon-time cooking to do and get cleared away in time for the reception preparations. It's a good thing it was a nice day, because our house wasn't very large and many people chose to be outside.

When it was time to go to the church, my cousin Clarence Miller, who was like an older brother to me, came in his new black Kaiser sedan to pick up Mom, Dad, and me. I felt like a princess, I was getting so much special attention!

Friends had decorated the church with lovely multi-colored garden flowers, and on the altar was a large fan-shaped arrangement of pastel colored Glads, flanked by a pair of tall candelabras and large potted ferns. We didn't have many "florist" flowers because we were trying to be as economical as was reasonable and still have a nice, creative setting for our very special occasion. I wanted a white orchid to carry on top of the white Bible I was borrowing from sister-in-law Chadna. She had carried it for her wedding to my brother Ross two years before. To go with the orchid, the florist prepared various lengths of narrow white ribbon streamers into which she tied sprigs of fragrant white tube roses and light blue delphinium blossoms. For the attendants to carry, we made for each girl a fan covered with "her" taffeta, trimmed with white lace. Each dress had a satin ribbon sash into which were tied pastel flowers to match the nosegay flowers at their necklines. Barbara's were pink rosebuds; Joy's and Mary's were pastel sweet peas. Corina's little basket was hand-made, too, and was filled with rose petals from Kelleys' garden. Mom wore a gardenia corsage with her new pink dress. The men all had carnations for their lapels—Dad had a white one for his gray pin-stripe double-breasted suit; Gene had a red one for his white formal coat, and there were white ones for Doc and the ushers—Bob Bourn and Bill Wyatt. (Bob was Mary Bourn's brother, and Bill was engaged to my sister Barbara.)

Gene had invited his Political Science professor, Dr. Robert Karsch, to provide organ music which included *Tea for Two*, *Always*, and *I Love You Truly*. A friend, Mrs. Leroy Cox (Mary Frances), sang *Ah! Sweet Mystery of Life*, *Because*, and *The Lord's Prayer*. Our beloved pastor at the First Baptist Church, Dr. Lee C. Sheppard, performed the ceremony, into which he incorporated Kahlil Gibran's writing on "Marriage" from *The Prophet*. And, of course, my dad lovingly walked down the aisle with me. After the words, "Who giveth this woman to be married?" he said, "Her mother and I do," before he took his seat in the pew beside Mom. (I think he had a big lump in his throat! I know I did!)

So far, I haven't mentioned my teen-aged brother Sterling (called "Junior" at that time) or my married brother Ross. Ross had set up a sound-recording system for the ceremony, and then was standing by with a movie camera to take pictures. Sterling worked as a delivery boy for Western Union and was waiting at the door with a couple of telegrams for us as we walked out after the ceremony. The telegrams were from Gene's family in Washington State who had not been able to be with us for the wedding! What a wonderful surprise it was, and it brought tears to my eyes to know that they were thinking of us and being with us "in spirit"! The one from Mom and Dad Bench said, "Heartiest congratulations! May all your days be as happy as this one! Love, Mom and Dad Bench." The other one read, "Congratulations and every good wish for your happiness. Love, the rest of the Gang."

We stayed at the church for a while, getting pictures made after greeting guests at the sanctuary door as they left, so our time with people at the reception was cut quite short. Of course, there were more pictures there—cutting the cake, and then later as we made our departure for our wedding trip which was to drive to Tacoma, Washington for me to meet Gene's family.

It was sort of standard procedure then for a train of cars to follow the bride and groom for a few miles, but we thought we had figured out a way to outsmart them. Gene and Don Myer had taken our car, luggage stowed in the trunk, to Booneville—the next town to the west—and hid it. Then Don and Mary Lou were to take us there to pick it up. While we were changing clothes, Don did a good job of listening to the various plans being made at the reception while people were wondering how we would be planning to leave. Don pretended to be helping them and suggested that he pull his car up to the front of the house to block the street. Then Gene and I and Mary Lou hurriedly jumped into it and were gone before anyone realized what was happening. Unfortunately, I soon remembered that we didn't have our over-night bag! We had to go back—but how?

We decided to drop Mary Lou off at a taxi stand, she would go back for the bag, hope the cab driver could lose anyone who might follow, and meet us at the Post Office. She said she almost had to fight to get it, then wondered if she'd have a heart attack while the cab driver drove down the railroad track and through a bunch of back streets and alleys, but we soon noticed that some cars had picked up our trail. Don drove as fast as he dared to try to lose them, or to get them to give up, but on they came and some tried to crowd us off the road, taking some very dangerous chances. I was really worried, so I pretended to feel faint and asked them to stop. People crowded around the car—Bill Wyatt's face was pale and ashen after having just missed a collision! They let some of their adrenaline settle down while there was joking, tying some cans to Don's car, and writing "Just Married" all over it. (Don told us later that some of the soap they used for writing had some kind of abrasive in it that left it permanently scratched.) After a while we were finally able to proceed west to Booneville where we picked up our car and treated Don and Mary Lou to fried chicken dinner with us at Pete's Café.

Because Gene was working at the hotel in Columbia, his manager made a gift to us of a room at the Hotel Muehlebach in Kansas City for our wedding night. There we found a lovely room decorated with flowers and bowls of fruit. It was very late by then, and we were tired, but so very happy to finally be able to relax alone! As Gene would say, we felt like "we had the world by the tail, with a down-hill pull"!

That was the beginning of our almost fifty-four years of a wonderful life of adventures, which I will try to describe in other stories!

LOVE IS ALL THAT MATTERS

SECRETARY – STUDENT- WIFE

I've heard my mother say so often: "It never rains, but it pours"; and "If it isn't one thing, it's another." But she didn't complain about or even <u>think</u> about all the different roles she was always playing. I imagine life would be rather boring if we didn't have a variety of interests, and a variety of things that need our own attention. I'm thinking now about the beginning of <u>my</u> life as a wife. I had already been a college student for three years at the University of Missouri, with one more to go—and to be able to do that, I worked part-time as a secretary to Dr. Bertha Bisbey, who was the School of Home Economics Professor of Dietetics. <u>Wife</u> was added to my jobs on August 1, 1948, when I became Mrs. Gene Bench.

Our first home together was an upstairs apartment at romantic-sounding 1410 Rosemary Lane, near the campus. It was an upstairs, furnished space in a large old brick home—really inconveniently arranged, with a tiny kitchen space, and a shared bathroom; but love was there, and we were together! Then, after about a month, the pastor of our church—Dr. Lee Sheppard—offered us a rent-free house at his farm about ten miles south of Columbia, near a little wide-place-in-the-road called Deer Park. Our part of the deal was to feed and care for a couple of horses, some chickens, and several head of beef cattle. Dr. Sheppard paid for the animal food, and we would keep money we received from selling eggs that were left over after supplying the Sheppard family, and keeping some for our own use. We decided it would be worth whatever we were paying for rent in town and interesting to live in the country again—even considering the extra work involved and the quite long distance from campus.

It would require us to get up earlier, fit our class times together during the day, since we'd have only one car, and to get a few essential items of furniture—but a table and chairs, two beds, a dresser, a round heating stove, kitchen stove, and refrigerator were already there. So, in October, we moved in! Our car was a 1937 Ford '60 (which meant it had six cylinders)—not much good for hauling animal feed, so Gene traded it for a red International pick-up truck. I don't remember the model of the truck, but it was <u>quite</u> "used"!

We borrowed a rattan couch that my parents used on their front porch in the summer and made use of a number of free orange crates. Draped ones made end tables, and stacked ones made shelves for several different uses. Cow feed came in printed cloth sacks that I laundered and used for making window curtains, coverings for the orange crates, and pretty dish towels! Cooking was on a kerosene stove in the large, sunny country kitchen; heating would be with fire in the wood stove in the living room. There was electric power for lights, refrigerator, and water pump in the house and in the barn for light and water for the animals. It was very refreshing to be able to live in a "real" house!

The people who had lived at the farm before us had planted a very large garden that still had a few things growing, although they had harvested most of it. There were still some tomatoes, carrots, and a few green beans and potatoes. Cabbage heads had been cut out of each plant, but by now some very small little "heads" were growing from the stalks at the stem of each leaf. They were delicious—we just called them "Brussels Sprouts."

Gene suggested that as long as we had to feed chickens anyway, why not get a few dozen baby chicks of our own which would soon grow into "fryers" that could be sold? It sounded reasonable to me, until we realized it would be too cold for them in the unheated chicken house at night while they were so tiny; but we made a little pen for them in the living room near the heating stove, after covering the wood floor under the pen with many layers of newspaper. They added a fair amount of work—feeding, watering, and replacing newspapers. Their water had to have potassium (I think) added to it, which involved dissolving a little purple pill in the watering device—a jar turned upside down which allowed a small amount of water to come into the bowl around it as the chicks drank. The pen kept them from running all over the house, but we missed their chirping when it came time to move them to live in the chicken house!

As Christmas approached, we decided to extend our hospitality to my family for one day during the holiday season. Guests were my mom and dad; my brother Ross, his wife Chadna, and their 2-year old daughter Karen; my sister Barbara and her boyfriend Bill Wyatt; my sister Joy, and my brother Sterling. It was a pot-luck menu which turned into an old-fashioned country dinner—with rabbit from our own woods for the meat, cranberry sauce, and mixed vegetables from our garden. Others brought apple-walnut salad, home-made rolls and butter, and gingerbread. Mom brought a large peach cobbler, which was one of her delicious specialties. People really enjoyed the rabbit meat because we'd eaten rabbit often when we were growing up near Dixon!

Our Christmas tree was a small table-size one that Gene cut in our woods. Our budget wouldn't handle "store-bought" ornaments for it, so we strung garlands of cranberries and popcorn, and made many ornaments from milk bottle caps. One of the dairies in town used foil caps of different colors to cover their different kinds of milk: gold, bright blue, bright green, and orange.

All of them were silver colored on the underside, and Mom saved theirs for us, too. An amazing variety of designs and shapes could be made using a few snips with scissors, turning, flattening, rolling, or twisting them. Gene made a large star-shaped tree-topper by covering a cardboard shape with gold foil. With a tree as special as that one, it didn't need lights!

Cold weather brought a few surprises—unusually low temperatures that froze the ground deeply, and freezing rain that broke limbs from trees. Ice was so heavy on phone and light wires some poles which supported them toppled, and, of course, the roads were solid sheets of ice. Naturally we were without power for a while and used kerosene lamps for light. We missed some school before roads were sanded enough for driving; and we had to use chains on the truck for getting from the farm to the highway.

Then, spring brought an even more inconvenient situation! When the frozen ground thawed, we had mud! One morning when Gene backed the truck out of the garage for us to go to school, the back wheels sank into mud almost to the hubcaps. He walked about a quarter of a mile to a neighbor's house to get some help. The two of them had traded help sometimes—and he seemed happy to bring his tractor to pull us out of our long driveway. After that, we parked on the road, put on boots, and walked to and from the truck until the ground began drying out.

Sometime during that winter I was enrolled in a class called "Home Management." Along with class work, another requirement was to live in the Home Management House near the campus for a month. The "family" there consisted of seven female students (also enrolled in that course) and the class instructor, Miss Fern Staggs. The idea was that we would put to practical use the things we were learning about managing a home—taking turns with being responsible for cooking, cleaning, record-keeping, shopping, and such. (One new thing we learned was to flatten tin cans before putting them in the trash! Of course, to do that, both ends of the can had to be removed with a can opener!) I tried to talk my way out of actually living there, using for my reason the fact that I was married and already doing all those things in my own home! But I was up against that monster "it's a requirement" thing that I'd battled when I first started high school and tried to talk my way out of even taking Home Ec in the first place! So...for a month I became a "weekend wife." Gene wasn't happy about the arrangement either, but we managed. He was actually quite a good cook and didn't use too much of his time with dishwashing and cleaning, so we both survived and felt relieved to be back together when that part of my class was finished.

It wasn't what one might call an "easy" winter, but we <u>might</u> have saved a little money by working out our rent. That phase of our early adventures ended when I became ill with pneumonia and had to spend a few days in the little University hospital. We decided then that tending a farm didn't give us enough time for school, which, after all, was our most important goal. Dr. Sheppard agreed, and we planned to move back to town. But where? Apartments just weren't available at mid-term, and the town's housing needs were bursting at the seams with veterans and their families returning from World War II for education financed by the G.I. Bill. Ross and Chadna lived in a small upstairs apartment in Boonville—farther to the west from Columbia than we'd been to the south on the farm—but they generously offered to let us move in with them!

Living in Booneville is another story, and the months at the farm were chalked up to "experiences." But, my, oh my! We sure had lots of good fried chicken!

LOVE IS ALL THAT MATTERS

Chapter 3: Early Marriage

I REALLY WAS A TEACHER!

It was spring in 1949, and we would be graduating from the University of Missouri early in June, with Bachelor's degrees in Education. Gene would remain another year and a half in graduate school to study for a Master's degree in Education, focusing on Guidance and Counseling; but it was time for me to try my wings as a Vocational Home Economics teacher. Wow! What a challenge!

The first challenge was finding a <u>place</u> to teach! We'd <u>hoped</u> I might be able to work within commuting distance of Columbia (Missouri), since Gene would still be in school, but there weren't many locations that would meet that requirement—and, of course, there would have to be a <u>vacancy</u>. During my last year of college, I worked closely with my advisor—Mrs. Polly Garrett—who supervised my student teaching, as well as kept in touch with many of the area high schools; so she would be the one to assist with my applications.

There was Hickman High School in Columbia, of course, but Mrs. Powell was teaching there indefinitely. In fact, she had coached my practice teaching course there the year before. The other closest locations were at Pilot Grove, and New Franklin—both about thirty miles away in different directions—so they were my targets. Pilot Grove was little more than "a wide place in the road," being a <u>very</u> rural type community. The town of New Franklin was quite small, but it was at least a <u>town</u>, and the school had a larger enrollment. It also offered a little more pay. It so happened that my first invitation to an interview was at Pilot Grove, and I knew I couldn't afford to be very "picky," so I accepted the interview opportunity. It was a well-kept school and a friendly Superintendent—definitely a possibility, but I asked for some time to think about it.

Soon came the interview at New Franklin—happy day! This was a quiet little town that had been built on higher ground than the original town of Franklin—which was on the Missouri River, and had suffered from a severe flood not long after having been the

93

starting point for several western-bound wagon trains. But the town had a lot of "spirit"—including a winning basketball team—and great interest in their schools. The Superintendent was Mr. Pointer—a very pleasant, active man who was soon to become a father for the first time after ten years of marriage. I thought to my recently-married self, "What a long time to be married! I wonder what it's like to be married that long and just now having a baby!" He introduced me to some of the other teachers and showed me all around the campus with so much interest and enthusiasm; I decided to accept the offer, which would have to have School Board approval. The only thing that wasn't in my favor was Gene being a student at the University. Their last two Home Ec teachers had also been wives of students, and each stayed only one year—so I knew they'd <u>prefer</u> someone who might give them more time. You can imagine my joy when I received news of my selection!

The next need was a place to live—in walking distance of high school for me, because Gene would need our only car, a blue-green '38 Dodge sedan that replaced the red pick-up truck. It made sense to us for him to be the commuter for a number of reasons: his hours would be more flexible than mine, and I'd need to stay after school sometimes for conferences, etc. The apartment we chose was the upstairs level of a quite large bungalow that was surrounded by trees. School was within walking distance to the west—downtown was about the same distance to the east. And the homeowners were delightful people.

One of New Franklin's faults was its water—a source of quite a few jokes. For instance, two of the teachers' wives became pregnant soon after the Pointers' baby was born—and someone said, "It must be the water!" We, and many other teachers, took our white laundry to the nearby town of Booneville to the Laundromat—otherwise, the things would soon become ivory colored. There seemed no problem with the water being healthful, although it had a "flavor" that took some "taste" adjustment. These days they would probably do more filtering, or whatever would be necessary to clarify it and change the taste. But ... we survived.

My job description called for teaching Home Ec I, II, and III, a Related Science course, a Related Arts course, and Home Room. Part of each student's work was called Home Projects, which required me to visit each one in her home at least once during the year to learn of the best way to give any needed extra help, and to confer with parents. (Home visits was the part that gave the program the name "Vocational," and added an extra month of employment for me—including an extra month of pay—a really big $3,600.00 for ten months!)

LOVE IS ALL THAT MATTERS

Another activity I would be required to supervise was running an evening lunch-room for a week during an invitational basketball tournament that was a tradition of several years. The Home Ec department cooked and served hot dogs (with all the trimmings), chili, and coffee. Desserts—pies, cakes, and cookies were donated, and someone else took charge of cold drinks and ice cream bars. During that week my students became chili chefs by day and servers during the evening games. You can imagine the odors all over school throughout the day—ground meat, onions, and beans, cooking the chili that was made from scratch! Quite a "bonus" learning opportunity for me! It was predicted that by the end of the week I'd vow never to eat chili again. Gene was amused that the last thing I did when I was free on final night was to sit down and eat a bowl of chili!

What a delight it was to get to know all those young people, to visit in their homes, and use that information to help them with any learning needs. Some had never held a needle; many had never used a sewing machine; many had never cooked anything more than fudge or popcorn for their own pleasure. Before the year was over, all of them had sewed several things, including dresses for themselves; learned about colors and designs of clothing becoming to themselves; how to take care of various fabrics; and good grooming. They had planned and cooked breakfast, lunch, and dinner that would meet a day's nutritional needs; what makes bread, cake, and biscuits rise; a bit about home furnishings; a bit about child care; some things about budgeting money and planning time; and, of course, much more.

One thing that was a bit of a "pain" for me was that during this first year of teaching I was required to be supervised by my college counselor. Actually, it was a great provision in case I needed help with any problems! Her visit required showing her my lesson plans, some reporting of accomplishments, and allowing her to sit in on classes whenever she visited. My problem with it was that I didn't believe in following a set plan for the sake of following the plan! If some need arose one day that needed extra discussion, I felt that <u>that</u> was a good <u>opportunity</u> to discuss the information needed at that time. "The Plan" could wait! But, of course I soon discovered that I could "do it my way," and still satisfy the rules.

Gene and I had a very enjoyable social life with the other teachers and townspeople—potluck suppers, etc…even learned to play Canasta which was the rage at that time. A local auto dealer had the privilege of selling us our first new car—a Starlight Coupe Studebaker, with the sort of "bullet-shaped nose" in the middle of the grill. Not only was it an enjoyable sort of "status symbol," it made Gene's daily long drive to Columbia much safer.

A couple of classroom things stand out in my memory: one of the third-year students asked me, "Mrs. Bench, why do different Home Ec teachers teach different ways of doing things, like cutting cloth with pinking shears—or not?" (She had had a different teacher for each of her three years of Home Ec.) I said, "Because we  are different people and we've learned different things that we think work best. While I'm your teacher, I will expect you to learn <u>my</u> way, and then you can later choose for yourself what the best way is for you."

Another thing that was amusing, as well as a bit embarrassing, was with a magazine salesman the office had sent to my room to ask if I would like to order any magazines for my classroom. When I answered his knock at the door, he said, "May I see your teacher, please?" In my smartly tailored gabardine suit, silk blouse, and sporty shoes, I felt very happy to reply, "Yes! <u>I</u> am the teacher—please come in!"

As we expected, I resigned at the end of that very eventful year because we would need to be free to live wherever Gene would be working after he finished graduate school at the University of Missouri. How thankful I am to have had my first (and only) experience with teaching at New Franklin, Missouri!

WESTERN STATES TRIP II (With Kelley's)

On August l, 1948, Gene and I began our honeymoon, which was my first trip west. On August 4, 1950, we began my second trip—this time including my mom and dad (Sterling and Bertha Kelley), my sister Joy, and my brother Sterling who were both teenagers. The number one highlight of the trip would be for the Kelley's to meet the Bench family in the Tacoma, Washington area; but we wanted all of us to enjoy sights and experiences of special interest to us along the way. In 1948, Gene and I had traveled due west through Denver and Salt Lake City; angled northwest through part of Idaho to Portland, Oregon;

then went north from there to Tacoma. For <u>this</u> trip, we all agreed that we should go northwest from Kansas City—with Mt. Rushmore, Yellowstone Park, and the Grand Coulee Dam to be our special sights as we traveled in the states of Nebraska, South Dakota, Wyoming, Montana, Idaho and then Washington. Of course, in almost <u>every</u> mile there were special sights, because none of us had ever been that way before!

Looking back now, I'm amazed to think about it! There were six full-grown people—each of whom had to have clothing enough for two weeks, some of which would be in weather cooler than in Missouri, and some of it warmer; we wanted to be able to camp when convenient, in order to save money, so that meant carrying bedding rolls (we didn't have compact sleeping bags!), some simple cooking utensils, a small camp stove, and a tarp. I think we might have also included a couple of handy-dandy folding camp stools of Gene's—useful not only for sitting, but for small tables. For cooking, Mom's black iron skillet would be a necessity, and other utensils fit nicely together as a camp cook-set: an aluminum bucket with a lid that could be used as a skillet, another cooking pot with lid, a coffee pot, four plates, four cups, and two kinds of handles to use with the pots and lids all, tucked inside the bucket. We'd be riding in the new car Gene and I had recently bought—a 1950 Starlight Coupe—Studebaker's newest two-door model, designed with wrap-around rear window. The back-seat area wasn't very spacious, but the trunk was fairly large, and managed to hold our strange collection of "stuff"!

The car was all packed and ready to roll as soon as we got home from Gene's graduation ceremony where he received his Master of Education degree at the University of Missouri in Columbia. With so many miles to cover, and so many stops we'd want to make, we had to make the most of our time, which meant driving long days. When camping wasn't practical, we stayed in low-cost motels that had cooking facilities—fairly popular those days in western small towns.

It didn't take long for us to realize that each person noticed things that were of special interest to them: For Dad, it was <u>everything</u>! And almost everything seemed worthy of a photo! We decided he should have the front seat by the door—easy for his photo-shooting! When we first came in sight of mountains, he was really excited—wanted photos from distance, and from all angles once we were closer to them! Mom seemed especially interested in flowers—wild and cultivated. She noticed the many different varieties as our landscapes and elevations changed. Her sitting place was behind Dad, an easier place for her to get in and out. I, being the wife of the driver, and having the shortest legs for fitting over the hump that ran through the middle of the car, used the front middle seat. My interests were somewhat like Dad's—everything—but I was also the designated navigator and map-reader. And having a good view from the front, I could alert the back-seat people when to watch for special sights—using clock hands positions to describe the direction to look. Joy and "Junior" took turns with getting the left window seat. Joy liked scenery, flowers, and historical aspects of the towns and architecture. The teen-age Junior didn't seem highly impressed with most sights along the road but did especially notice cars.

One early stop was to visit the sculptured Mt. Rushmore Monument in the Black Hills.

It was awesome to think about the vision of the artists, and about the many hours they spent so skillfully sculpting the excellent likenesses of those four presidents! Seeing it up close meant a lot to all of us. Dad really liked Gene, and the two of them often "battled wits" with each other. I'll just quote from Dad's autobiography, *Coonrod*, to give you an idea about his enthusiasm and thoughts about a couple of happenings on this trip: "I remember we saw a wild porcupine while driving along a mountain road [in Black Hills]. Gene jumped out, grabbed up a soft pine board, tapped the porcupine lightly, and gave me a long quill from the porcupine. I have never been able to understand how Gene can so often be at the right place at the right time with the right equipment with the right know-how! Whether it's a steelhead, a bear, cougar, elk, deer, a canasta hand, a parking place or a rest room—or a porcupine by the road in the night with a soft pine board lying handy, miles from lumber mills or civilization—he seems to have a magic wand up his shirt sleeve! Then on to Yellowstone Park where there was again a scene at the right time and place: a mamma bear with a couple of babies. Gene got out of the car and drove the bears around while I was taking their picture with my movie camera. The mamma stood up straight as an Indian! I got wonderful pictures of it all!"

In Yellowstone Park we were all impressed with the animals—bear, elk, deer, and birds—the boiling mud-pots, rock formations, and, of course, the show that Old Faithful geyser puts on so regularly for anyone who is willing to wait for a few minutes!

Grand Coulee Dam on the Columbia River in eastern Washington was an unbelievably huge, "grand" sight to see! "Coulee" means a ravine or a deep gully, so the ravine the dam fills must have been really deep! It is said to be made with enough concrete to build a four-foot wide, four-inch deep sidewalk that would reach twice around the equator! Built during the nineteen-thirties depression, the water it backs up is named Franklin Delano Roosevelt Lake for F.D.R. who was president at the time.

We spent three wonderful days with the Bench family in Tacoma, Washington! Mom and Dad Bench had a big yard full of flowers—to the delight of my mom and dad—Gene's two sisters and brother all had children—a total of six, ranging from age two to six—and we were welcomed as if we were long-lost cousins! On one of the days the men took my Dad and Junior out fishing in Puget Sound. That was especially exciting for Junior—catching fish bigger than he had ever seen, in the

Mom and Dad Bench around their 49th wedding anniversary

first ocean water he had ever experienced, every time he put his hook in the water! They cleaned their "catch" and brought them to the picnic area at Point Defiance Park where the women were visiting and playing with the children. In just a few minutes Mom Bench fried a bunch of the fish to add to the waiting baskets of picnic food!

Another day we all drove to an ocean beach where the Bench family frequently dug razor clams. It was located near what is now the town of Ocean Shores where the Bench family has gathered for a four-day family reunion for probably the last forty years. Digging clams was one of the special things to do there—digging with the special long, slim, pointed shovels called "clam guns." A dimple in the sand indicated that a clam had gone down at that spot, after feeding during higher tide. Digging was great fun for all of us—especially for the Kelley family! We all slept on the beach that night to be able to dig clams again early the next morning as the tide went out. A bear came into our camp during the night—rummaged around the garbage can and left as quietly as he had come. Sleeping under stars to the rhythm of nearby waves gave the Kelley family some wonderful memories!

At the ocean we were several miles south of Tacoma, so the plan was for us to continue our trip from there while most of the Bench family returned home. But Mom and Dad drove with us for several miles to share lunch with us before we parted. They took us to a park for another picnic, where we cooked some of the crabs and clams we'd caught—making it a very special seafood feast! My Dad remembered that as we were getting ready to leave, Dad

Bench said to Mom Bench, "Zula, did you kiss the Kelley's goodbye?" She said, "Yes, and I think I'll kiss them all again!" Gene and I were really pleased for our two families to also be good friends, as we had expected them to be! No one could resist the Bench family hospitality!

On our way south, we stopped to see Crater Lake in Oregon, and then drove on into the Redwood country in California. That was another experience that was as awesome for the Kelley's as it had been for me when I had been there for the first time a couple of years before! Dad, being a carpenter and a lover of wood, was especially impressed—realizing that those very trees had been growing at the time Christ was living on earth! A novelty Dad and the kids liked was driving through the "tunnel" that had been cut through the base of one of the living trees!

San Francisco and the Golden Gate Bridge were on our route, as we drove to Merced for a short visit with Dad's Uncle Frank Warren and wife Serena. Someplace in that northern part of California, we had quite a surprise. While we were stopped for gas, Mom said, "That man sure looks like Bruce Richey!" (Bruce was an old family friend from Dad's childhood in Dixon, Missouri.) Sure enough—it was Bruce! He told us his brother Wayne also lived fairly nearby, so we stopped to visit a few minutes with him.

Yosemite Park was another stop; then Hoover Dam where we first saw the famous Colorado River. The dam was originally called Boulder but was later named Hoover for the President who helped with managing the funding for it during the Depression. It backs up the Colorado River to form Lake Mead and rises over seven hundred feet above the river.

The Grand Canyon was another sight that was unbelievable to country folks from Missouri! Really awesome! Even to Junior! From there we caught the legendary Highway 66 at Kingman, Arizona for the rest of the way east as far as Springfield, Missouri, where we headed northeast back to Columbia, and home. On 66 we were in desert for many interesting miles that included the Painted Desert and the Petrified Forest. Camping one night someplace in the desert was memorable for all of us. The sky seemed so high—and seemingly more stars than we'd ever seen before! The morning sunrise was glorious and thrilling! Dad and Gene heated water in the camping bucket for shaving, after we had cooked some breakfast and enjoyed the fresh breezes. Someplace in the Texas panhandle, we stopped for a picnic of watermelon—a favorite thing for the Kelley family. Crossing Oklahoma reminded Mom and Dad of visiting friends and working there for a while when they were on their honeymoon in 1924. Gene was reminded of living near Adam, when he was young.

Of course, we were all tired of riding by the time we were back in Columbia, but that trip was an experience of a lifetime for us! Remembering it is special for me, and for Joy and "Junior," too! By the way—when Junior grew up, and served in the Army, he began using his "real" name by which he is called to this day—Sterling!

A GREAT SALMON FISHING TRIP

Gene and I had been married for ten years in August of 1958, and lived in Bloomington, a southern suburb of Minneapolis, Minnesota. This year's vacation, in September, would be a trip to visit Gene's family in Tacoma, Washington, with time enough to do some sightseeing along the way. We decided to go through North Dakota, Montana, the northern tip of Idaho, then through eastern Washington, after a side trip to Yellowstone Park. In Missoula, Montana, we stopped to spend a night with long-time Marine Corps friends— retired Lt. Col. Bob Brown and his wife Cid. We had been neighbors several years before when Gene and Bob had duty together at Quantico, Virginia. You can imagine the expanse of blue sky and the miles of wide, open spaces we enjoyed as we drove across the northern prairie grasslands! Then we came to the steaming hills, bubbling mud-pots, and Old Faithful geyser in Yellowstone Park! Next were the majestic Rocky Mountains, on the western side of which was the very lovely Lake Coeur d'Alene!

The Benches are "out-door" people, and every time we visited, they kept busy showing us (especially for my benefit) the things they enjoyed there in the Pacific Northwest—a part of the country which was, to me, a fantastic wonderland! One time we drove up to the snow-line on Mt. Rainier; another time, from a row-boat with a small motor on the back, we fished for "bottom fish" in Puget Sound (near where the Narrows Bridge now crosses); we went digging for razor clams on the beach near Moclips; and there were frequent picnics and a camp-out at the beach. Their plans for us this year included a salmon fishing trip in the ocean from a charter boat. That would be quite exciting stuff for this Missouri gal whose fishing experience was mostly in rivers and lakes!

We had to go to Westport, near Aberdeen, to board the boat, so that meant very early rising, and dressing for any kind of weather. I wondered if I'd be sea-sick but was encouraged to keep some crackers handy to nibble now and then—and to stay in the fresh air where I could see the horizon as much as possible. In our bag of supplies were various kinds of snack things, and delicious sandwiches that Mom Bench had prepared for us.

Our boat was named the *Susan*—with a crew that included the pilot, and a couple of deck hands who helped with baiting hooks and taking care of the fish that were caught. Besides

Gene and me, our "party" included Gene's brother Elby, and brother-in-law Harry Evans both of whom lived near Tacoma.

Some sixteen or eighteen other people were also hoping to stand along the rail on the deck which encircled the boat and catch their limit of two salmon per person. In the center of the boat was an enclosed cabin with large windows, some seats and tables, and spaces for the passengers' gear. The boat crew provided the bait (small, silvery fish about the size of sardines), and the very large rods and hooks we would use to snare the salmon.

The pilot took us out into the ocean for about ten miles, and kept the boat slowly moving while the fisher-people readied their hooks and lines with bait and took their places along the rails of the deck. There were instructions given for the procedures to follow when someone felt a fish pulling on their line: first, yell out, "Fish on!" Then everyone else was supposed to reel in their lines to keep from getting them crossed and tangled, because the hooked fish would keep swimming all around—sometimes going away really fast; sometimes going in large circles; sometimes diving deeper; sometimes coming toward the boat—always trying to throw the hook out of its mouth—and often succeeding, if the fisherman allowed his line to go slack! My "station" was on the right side of the boat, a short distance from the bow, and Gene was next to me on my left. We hadn't had our lines out very long until I felt my line begin to spin out! I quickly jerked my rod up to "set" the hook and to keep the line taut. Right away Gene was beside me saying, "Here, let me help you!" I'm sure he knew it would take some "muscle" and some time to reel the fish up to the boat close enough for it to be netted, and just wanted to be sure I didn't lose the fish; but

I said, "Oh! No! This is my fish!" and kept turning my reel! But he stayed right there beside me! The deck hands came running with their very long-handled nets, while others cheered and watched as I struggled to hold the rod braced against my body with my left hand, turning the reel with my right hand, sometimes allowing the fish to swim away, then reeling it back again until it finally became tired enough to allow me to pull it up within reach of the net! What a thrill! My first salmon—largest fish I'd ever caught!

The next challenge would be getting our four fish back home to Minnesota! We knew of a grocery store near our place that rented freezer storage place where we could keep them once we were there. If we had been flying, it would have been simple to just have them packaged to carry as checked baggage on the plane; but we were driving and would be on the road for at least three days! It also would have been simple to trade them at a cannery for an equal weight of canned salmon; but I wanted to share whole ones with friends back home! Maybe a special dinner party! Harry was a builder, so he and Gene put their heads together and built an insulated wooden box that we could carry on top of our '54 Buick. (The fish had been frozen in relatives' big home freezers, and dry ice—enough, we thought, to get home—was put into the box with it.)

The first night on the way home we camped at Flat Head Lake near Glacier National Park in Montana. We made a point of NOT cooking bacon, which might be an odor that would attract a bear and got on our way early the next morning. The second night, we needed to stay in a motel, and noticed that a pink fluid was running out of the box down over the rear of the car! The dry ice was already almost gone, so we began watching for any place where we might buy more. Gene thought that in that part of the country where many people hunted big game and needed ice for preservation, we could easily find some—but we didn't. In one town in Wyoming we found a refinery that emptied CO_2 from some fire extinguishers into the box, and that lasted for a while. In North Dakota, a grocery store had some wet ice frozen in gallon sizes that they gave us. In another place, we found wet ice at a Dairy Queen. The fish were thawing but were still frosty enough that they could be re-frozen!

Finally, as soon as we reached Bloomington, we went to the grocery store with the freezer space for rent before we even went home—only to discover that they no longer provided that service! Now what! Gene called his Marine Corps assistant, Capt. Bill Rice, and told him of our sad predicament. Fortunately, Bill said that he and his wife had room for them in their chest-type freezer! What luck! Now we could plan our dinner party—but there was no way I could get one of those fish into my oven to bake it! The solution to that was to call the local Officers' Club where we could reserve a room for our party—and they would cook the fish—two of them! We gave Bill Rice one of the fish as a "thank you" for the use of his freezer, and cut the other one into smaller pieces for the two of us! Quite an exciting memory for me!

Chapter 4: Marine Corps Years

TRANSITION — FROM CIVILIAN TO MILITARY

I've heard it said that the only thing we can be sure of is change. Some changes are small, insignificant ones—some are large enough to require adjustment to a whole new "life style," needing a period of time to accomplish. I would call this kind of change a "transition." Some transitions are planned; some are surprises; some are just a combination of experiences that gradually turn into a transition. That's pretty much the way it happened that Gene became a "Career Marine," and I, of course, became a "Marine wife."

Life was going along according to our plan—very busy but leading to our first goal of finishing college at the University of Missouri. Gene had enrolled in the School of Engineering on the G.I. Bill at the end of World War II, and I was in the School of Home Economics to become a teacher. Gene's studies included all kinds of math and physics that engineers need to know—and that he loved; but about the time we married in 1948, he had begun to be aware of many students who were feeling a need for help to get their lives "on track." After conferring with our pastor and some professors in the field of psychology, he decided to change his major to Education with emphasis on Guidance and Counseling. We both graduated in the spring of 1949 with Bachelor's degrees in Education. I accepted the offer to teach Home Ec in a nearby high school at New Franklin, and he continued at the University for another year, plus a summer term, for the Master's degree he needed for counseling.

A small, upstairs apartment just a few blocks from school, and about the same distance from downtown, was available for us to rent; so I could walk to most places I'd need to go, and Gene could have the car to commute the thirty-or-so miles to the University at Columbia. (The car was a 1938 Dodge sedan we'd bought from Mr. Brummell in nearby Booneville. My brother Ross, a professional with autos from motors to bodies, had made sure it was in very good condition, and then gave it a new blue-green color which he called, "the best paint job I ever did!"). Gene still had G.I. pay coming for school, plus a Fellowship in the Educational Psychology department to cover the graduate tuition. I was earning $3,600 per year, for ten months of work in the Vocational

Home Ec program. That was a good year for us—but that will be another story.

Sometime in April 1950, Gene sent out applications to several high schools and received packets of information describing each one. An especially interesting one was from Esther High School, located near Flat River, in southeastern Missouri. The economy in the area was good, and the community gave a lot of interest to their schools. At Gene's interview with the Superintendent, Mr. Jeff Sarff, he was impressed with Mr. Sarff's vision of creating a Guidance and Counseling Department which would occupy half of his time—the other half would be teaching math. The beginning pay was good and included a retirement funding plan. The two men liked each other, so a contract was signed, and we began looking forward to our new opportunities while finishing our work in Columbia and New Franklin.

When the New Franklin school year was finished, we moved back to Columbia to live temporarily for Gene's final term, which was the beginning of summer school at the University. A friend told us of a vacancy in one of Mrs. Goodson's houses where she rented rooms to male students. For us, she had a two-room furnished apartment—living room and bedroom—which we paid for by emptying wastebaskets from all the rooms and serving meals in the dining room to students who lived in that house, as well to those who came there for meals from two of Mrs. Goodson's other nearby houses. We also set and cleared the tables; other people did the cooking and dishwashing. Mrs. Goodson was a very kind and jovial person and was bothered frequently with pain she called angina. She wasn't very active but enjoyed "her boys" and quite professionally and creatively dealt with all the meal-planning and food orders.

Late in August, after Gene's graduation, we moved again—to our new home in southeast Missouri where Gene would begin work at Esther High School. The house we found to rent was in the nearby little town of Desloge, and it was exciting to finally be "settling in" at a real house where we would have our own furniture—everything new! No more draped orange crates and apple-box shelves! We had bought a new Starlight model Studebaker coupe when we lived in New Franklin and had my income; now, with Gene's pay, we could buy furniture! (There had to be credit, of course, but that seemed easy to handle.) For the living room we selected simply designed oak tables—two end tables and a coffee table—finished in black with white rubbed into the grain (very sophisticated looking!); also, a couch and an easy chair with our choice of upholstery, which would be delivered later. We also bought a new bed, a dresser, a chest of drawers, a kitchen table and four chairs. I would make draperies and curtains for the windows, and the house would really feel like "home"!

At school, Gene found some changes. Jeff Sarff had been seriously injured and disabled in a car wreck in May when he and some friends were on their way to the Indy-500 auto races. The high school principal, George Pallo, was now in charge of administration, and would be Gene's boss. He was helpful, and we enjoyed making friends with the faculty members and their families. One couple became special, long-lasting friends—Margie and Diddle Powell. Margie was a P.E. teacher and coach for the school's champion girls' volley ball team. Diddle and Gene became Masonic "brothers." Gene had joined the lodge in New Franklin and was still working on learning the necessary ritual to become a third-degree Mason, so Diddle became his coach. One of the faculty social activities was gathering with spouses at the Pallo home every Friday evening for a pot-luck supper. The Pallos were Catholic and couldn't eat meat on Friday, so Mrs. Pallo always baked a ham for us to enjoy for a snack <u>after midnight</u>. Of course, strategic window blinds were closed, because it wouldn't be appropriate for the community people to see that there was also beer being served!

Along about this time the Korean War started, and the Marine Corps began recalling Reserves. Gene had come out of World War II as a Staff Sergeant and had applied for a commission on the basis of his college degree. So he wasn't surprised in October to get his letter of "Greetings," recalling him to Marine Corps active duty. George Pallo insisted that he ask for a deferment, so he did—thinking in his heart, and hoping, that it wouldn't be granted—but it was! New problem! It is said that "once a Marine, always a Marine," and Gene was no exception. He was confident he was fully qualified and had really looked forward to the new challenge of high school counseling; and also felt an obligation to his contract. But, at the same time, his patriotism and Marine Corps experience gave him a strong feeling of duty there. After serious consideration, he decided to turn down the deferment. Mr. Pallo was <u>furious</u>! And well he should have been, I think. He was being left without the new counseling program, and maybe even more importantly, a math teacher. They didn't part on friendly terms—Gene being told that he shouldn't expect to ever come back to teach at Esther High School!

This decision brought on another situation (Gene defined problems as "situations"). He was totally uncertain as to where, or what assignment he would be given when he reported for military duty—or what kind of housing to expect. In the meantime, what should we do with as-yet-unpaid-for new furniture? Fortunately, the furniture store agreed to take back all except the bed mattress and springs which, once used, they couldn't re-sell. We had not yet received the upholstered pieces, so that order was cancelled. My mom and dad agreed to buy the bed, and to let us store our other few things at their house until we found out where we'd be and what we'd need.

During the few days in Columbia with my folks, Gene decided we should have a better car. The new Studebaker had already given us a few problems, so we traded it in on a new '50 Pontiac Catalina—metallic blue with a cream-colored top. Its large trunk would serve us well for moving.

After Gene's orders were adjusted, we found that he was to report for duty at Camp Lejeune, North Carolina, on November 9, 1950. What better day to be back in the Marine Corps! The next day was the Marine Corps birthday! The Marine Corps was "born" in 1776, and its birthday is a very important day for Marines. A message from the Commandant is read to every unit, after which an appropriately sized, decorated cake is ceremoniously cut and shared. The serving of the cake is truly a ceremony in itself! It's an annual renewal of each Marine's commitment to the Corps, and the Corps' commitment to the nation's quest for peace and freedom worldwide. Of course, the procedure has to be adjusted to fit the location, so this description is what I have observed when space permits—all participants wearing dress-blue uniforms: A formal detail (group) performs a "colors" (flags) posting ceremony. Then the cake enters on a rolling cart covered with a scarlet cloth edged in gold fringe, preceded by an adjutant, with a Marine at each corner of the cart, and followed by a Marine shouldering a sword. The guest of honor, the oldest Marine present, and the youngest Marine present come to stand by the table; a brief history of the establishment of the Corps, followed by the message from the Commandant are read. The Marine with the sword cuts three pieces of cake; the first piece is presented to the guest of honor; the second piece is presented to the oldest Marine, symbolizing the honor and respect accorded to experience and seniority. The eldest then passes it to the youngest Marine, signifying the passing of knowledge from the old to the young. The third piece of cake, also received by the eldest, further emphasizes the fact of care for young Marines before looking to one's own needs. A formal retiring of the cake entourage ends the cake-cutting ceremony.

On the birthday evening we joined the festivities, starting with dinner at the NCO (Non-Commissioned Officers) club, followed by a cake-cutting, and dancing. I don't remember if any of the ladies wore formal dresses; I certainly didn't, having just arrived on the base, but the usual evening celebration is often called the Birthday Ball—banquet, cake ceremony, and dancing—formal dress. (I always thought the 10th was a fortunate day and evening for the celebration because November 11th was at that time Armistice Day, a holiday which later became Veterans' Day—and some people who had attended the Birthday Ball had to deal with hangovers! A day off from duty was appreciated!

There was one more problem: a place to live. No housing was available within fifty miles of the base. Gene could always live in the barracks, but we wanted to be together. Our first night was in a motel in the little off-base town of Jacksonville. (It was at my first breakfast in a little restaurant there that I first met up with "grits." My order was for bacon, eggs, toast, and juice; but what was that glob of white stuff on the side! When I asked the waitress what it was, she said—with a southern accent you could "cut" with a knife—"Honey, it's grits! You always get grits with bacon and eggs." I said, "How is it eaten?" She said, "Well, some people like it with some butter, and salt and pepper; and some like it with a little bit of sugar." I said I'd try the butter, and salt and pepper. I decided grits is a good thing for any meal! And can be cooked many different ways!)

The next day the guest house on the base had a vacancy for a couple of nights. After that I "hung out" there every day, waiting to see if there would be a cancellation. I did a lot of reading, writing letters, and visiting with the guest house receptionist, Helen Waldrep. After a couple of days, she felt well enough acquainted with us to ask if we'd like to have board and room with her parents, Mr. and Mrs. Gillette, who lived on a tobacco plantation a few miles from the base near the little town of Swansboro. It seemed like a boarding house, with breakfast and dinner included—a "working" farm setting with typical farm animals, barns, etc. Even a dear Negro hired man who was descended from slave parents. All the Gillette children had grown up and left, so they rented out their three extra bedrooms and served breakfast and dinner.

What an opportunity! Just getting to know the Gillettes turned out to be like being with our own parents! They wanted to be called "Papa" John and "Miss" Grace. No finer people ever lived! And no finer meals were ever served! Miss Grace was rightfully proud of her "southern cooking." There were biscuits for every breakfast—unless there were pancakes; and biscuits with every dinner—unless it was seafood-Friday with hush-puppies! And her biscuits weren't like any others—they were made with cream and "patted" just right, until they were melt-in-your-mouth delicious! Papa John's Christmas holiday treat was syllabub—home-made wine (made with blackberries, I think), whipped with thick cream. We made friends with some of their family, too: Helen's husband was Earl; son Milton's family lived across the road, with a young daughter named Kay, and son whose name I don't recall; daughter Lucille's family lived in a nearby town.

How is it possible that such a close friendship could develop in only the couple of months until Gene was transferred again! Getting to know the Gillette family was like living in a dream of "southern hospitality" with real, down-to-earth, truly loving people! While writing this story I began to wonder if Kathleen and Milton might still live there, so I called—and they do! Milton said that their children are both married and live on farms adjoining theirs— and they have children and grandchildren! Helen is no longer living, but Lucille is. Mrs. Grace was in a nursing home for her last three years of life.

Gene's assignment at this time was 1st Sgt of "C" Company, 8th Marines. But early January brought still another change: he was commissioned a 2nd Lieutenant on December 4th, 1950! Just when I was beginning to learn how to be an NCO wife, I'd have to learn to be an officer's wife! Really scary! Protocol seemed to be more important in those days than it is now. We had to have "calling cards" and make social calls on commanding officers; women wore hats and gloves for important occasions like parades and receptions; there were frequent "teas" and cocktail parties; and even in seating at dinner, rank was recognized. But this country girl soon realized that they were all just people, too—most of them were friendly and interesting, and all of us were sharing similar problems.

A new assignment soon came with the commission! It was to attend Basic School at Quantico, Virginia, effective January 6, 1951. When that was over in, I think, three months, Gene was retained at Quantico for another several months to be a Basic School Instructor. (He thought that assignment came as a result of his record that showed the education degree.)

Early in 1952, he was ordered to Naples, Italy, and assigned to be a guard officer for the Allied Forces Southern Europe (AFSE) Headquarters, which had moved there from London. That lasted for two-and-a-half wonderful years (described in another story), then it was back to Quantico, Virginia, for him to command a company with the Schools' Troops. In all this time, when we expected he'd be going to the war in Korea, he was doing other things where I could be with him—enjoying a lot of travel, meeting new people, and living quite an exciting life! So when he was offered a permanent commission, and sought my approval before he would accept it, I didn't have to think about it very long to be in agreement with him that he should say, "Yes." The background of having been enlisted gave him an understanding of the needs of the troops, and the counseling degree gave him skills in dealing with the problems of the young men he would command.

In the Marine Corps Gene seemed to have found his "true calling"—and the "Gypsy" in me was very happy to look forward to new friends, new places, and new challenges!   And, you know what? I've been happy for many years that we didn't keep that very unusual black furniture!

USMC BASIC SCHOOL, QUANTICO, VIRGINIA

We had time for a few days of leave before Gene had to report for his Basic School assignment at Quantico, Virginia; so he had a chance to show off his new Second Lieutenant bars to the Kelley family in Missouri at Christmas time. I remember on this trip we drove through Chattanooga, Tennessee, and noticed a large, lighted Christmas decoration on a nearby mountain. Another memory is about the newly popular song, "The Tennessee Waltz." I don't remember who sang it—I think that it probably was sung by several different artists. When we stopped for meals along the road, there seemed to always be someone playing it on the nickelodeon, and it was often on the radio in the car. I began to feel sorry for the guy who "lost his lil' darlin' the night they were playing the beautiful Tennessee Waltz!" because Gene and I were so happy being together and looking forward to an exciting future!

The Quantico base was used especially for educational training for Marines. There was one school for officer candidates, and another one called Basic School for newly commissioned second lieutenants. As a person's rank increased, there were schools for more advanced training for command and staff work. At the time Gene received these orders, the Korean War was in progress, and the Basic course was shortened, so that the new officers could be prepared faster for combat duty. His assignment was to the 3rd Special Basic Course that began January 6, 1951 and would last three months.

Again, finding local housing was a problem, so we took a second-floor furnished apartment in Alexandria, on the south side of Washington, D.C.— about thirty miles from Quantico. I've written another story about living there where the street in front of our building was U.S. Highway One, the main north-south route that is now Interstate 95.

111

This place brought me my first experience of living without Gene! Until then we had never spent even one night apart since our marriage three years before. I can still feel the shock I felt when I brushed my teeth—and my toothbrush was all alone in the toothbrush holder! Talk about <u>lonely</u>! The sudden "frogs" in my throat even brought a couple of tears! (Sometime later Gene just kept an extra toothbrush in his travel kit that was stocked and ready for taking away from home!)

Within a couple of months, we were able to get another furnished apartment in the town of Quantico, within walking distance of the Headquarters buildings. The apartments were in two brick buildings owned by a Mr. Ferlazzo and were called Ferlazzo Apartments. In each building were four apartments downstairs, and four upstairs—built less than a block from a quite often-traveled railroad. We lived downstairs, on the side away from the railroad, which wasn't any shelter from the noise of the trains that, legally, had to whistle not far from our location. There were many jokes about the train situation—including the timing of the conception of children!

The occupants there gave us a sort of ready-made neighborhood. I remember one couple who had a little boy about four years old. He was a quite outgoing child, and I liked to play with him. One day he was happily telling me what he considered a joke, saying, "Take off those striped pajamas!" Then he would go into almost a fit of laughter, and I, of course laughed with him. I later told his mother about it, and that I wasn't able to figure out what he found so funny. She laughed, and said it was a line in a story he had heard his dad tell, after which everyone laughed. It was about a zebra that escaped from a zoo and came to live on a farm. It went around the barnyard asking all the animals what they did on the farm—chickens produced eggs; cows produced milk, etc. When he came to the horse, the horse said, "Take off those striped pajamas, and I'll <u>show</u> you what I do!"

To keep from being bored, and to earn some money for what we called a "vacation fund," I answered an ad for a secretarial job at the Civil Service office on the base. Of course, I had to take a Civil Service test and get a "rating," after which I became secretary to Mr. Schoettler, the superintendent in that office. He liked to talk and had many stories about working in Alaska—in Ketchikan, Sitka, and Juneau—stories that further whetted my longing to travel!

Gene's classes were held at an outlying camp where there was space for them to do field command training. The "enemy" in their tactical training was provided by experienced Marines called Schools Demonstration Troops, also housed on the Quantico base. (A few years later, Gene became part of that organization for a while.) There was a quite large man-made lake that provided water for amphibious vehicle training, and an air station nearby that helped with the training that was often coordinated to learn about air support given to troops in combat. Until then, my only exposure to Marine Corps activity had been watching news reels and movies about them landing on beaches facing enemy fire, so I naturally sometimes wondered how soon I might become a widow! An invitation to watch a demonstration of how those landings are coordinated with air and navy support, to do what they call "soften up" a beach before the Marines arrive in their open landing craft, gave me some reassurance of their longevity. Members of Congress, high-level business people, and family members were guests at some of those demonstrations.

At the end of Gene's three months of training as a student, he received orders to continue working there and to be a Basic School instructor. He supposed that assignment to be based upon his record of the Master's degree in Education received the year before; and he assisted with the next three Basic classes. Then, in December of 1951, he received orders to a guard unit that would be stationed in Naples, Italy. That meant that we could have leave and spend Christmas with my family in Missouri before he had to report for duty the 11th of January 1952.

My sister Barbara's husband Bill Wyatt had, in the meantime, been recalled to active duty in the Navy; and they were also on the east coast. Bill was an officer assigned to a Destroyer Escort that operated out of Norfolk, Virginia, and he was also taking Christmas leave to spend in Columbia with his family and ours. As Gene and I were driving to Columbia, we wondered if they might also be someplace along the road west. We stopped at one of our favorite restaurants—the Southern Air—near St. Louis for dinner, thankful to be resting for awhile from riding, and talked again about Barbara and Bill. Gene was sitting facing the entrance, and just matter-of-factly said something like, "Who knows, they might just coincidentally stop here to eat, too!" About that time the two of them walked up behind me and spoke!

It was a great family reunion at the Kelley home! We were looking forward to telling about Gene's orders; Barbara and Bill had special news, too! We suggested they tell theirs first: they were excitedly expecting their first, longed-for baby in July! Then it was our turn. Gene said, "Dad, if you could take Mom for a long vacation to any place in the world, where would you go?" Dad thought a minute and said, "Well, there's a little island in the

Mediterranean Sea—I think it's called Capri. That's where I would like to take her!" What a set-up for Gene! He replied, "Well, that's where Ila and I will be living for awhile—just on the Italian shore in sight of it!" Living there, in Naples, will be another story!

TWO KELLEY SISTERS IN NEW YORK CITY

A weekend in New York City was an adventure of a life-time for my sister Barbara and me with our handsome husbands! Gene and I lived in Quantico, Virginia, where he had reported for duty on January 6, 1951, at the Marine Corps Base as a student in the Special Basic Course, having recently been commissioned 2nd Lt. When he completed the three-month course, he was assigned to stay on as a Marine Corps Schools instructor. In the meantime, Barbara's husband, Bill Wyatt, had been recalled for active duty, an officer in the Navy, and was stationed at the Navy Yard in Philadelphia. It was only natural for us two fun-loving couples to want to spend some time together while we were all living not far apart, there on the east coast. We chose to meet for a weekend in New York City, which was only a hundred miles north of Philadelphia.

Our husbands had been to New York before, so they made the plans. We would all travel there by train on Saturday, April 21, to arrive at Grand Central Station, and stay at the Dixie Hotel which was in the Times Square district. (It is now Carter Hotel.) Our train would arrive later than theirs, so the guys agreed that we would meet them on Times Square, under the large Camel cigarette sign that periodically blew smoke rings. Sure enough, there they were! It seemed to me a miracle to find those two familiar faces among all those thousands of others, in that <u>canyon</u> of surrounding sky-scrapers! What a <u>thrill</u>!

It was kind of surprising, too, to discover that several of the locations important to us were relatively close together—the railroad station, Central Park, Times Square, Broadway, Rockefeller Plaza, and our hotel—not many blocks apart. Other sights were easy to reach by subway—an adventure in itself! Can't you just imagine what it was like for us two country girls to be in that forest of such tall buildings? Our parents had taught us that it was bad manners to "gawk" at things that seemed unusual, and we didn't want to call attention to ourselves acting like hillbillies; but we just <u>had</u> to absorb the experience of feeling so tiny in the midst of that unbelievable steel and concrete jungle!

LOVE IS ALL THAT MATTERS

How can four people even <u>begin</u> to experience New York City in just two days! We had to choose a few places and things that were really important to us, plan travel to make the best use of our time, and keep going, going, going! I don't remember the order of the sights, but I do remember how important it was to find a way to rest now and then, and fortunately, the weather was good.

The Statue of Liberty was one of our choices to see. On Sunday morning, we took the subway to the south end of Manhattan Island, and then rode a ferry out to Liberty Island. What an impressive sight that was—to view from the distance, and gradually come closer to the monumental "lady" that means so much, to so many millions of people! In those days it was possible to go inside the statue and go by elevator to the top—to the "crown" to walk around and look out over the city and the bay! It was breath-taking! To descend, we decided to walk down the stairs! Oh, me, oh my! My legs were so weak and trembling by the time we were on the ground, I could hardly walk! And very sore the next day!

Fortunately, we could sit down for the ferry and subway trip to the next stop—the Empire State Building. When Barbara was a child, she had a metal "piggy bank" shaped like the Empire State Building. Dad had given it to her because of its importance as the tallest building in the world. I don't remember how it ranked in height in 1951, but we thought it important. No stair climbing there! Just a ride in the elevator to the top, and walk around the banistered viewing place, to again be shocked to be looking <u>down</u> on all the steel and concrete jungle!

(I remember walking on Wall Street among those skyscrapers some time—but that might have been on a later adventure.)

To enjoy some of the atmosphere of Central Park, we rode in a horse-drawn carriage for a while, watching people walking dogs, children playing, athletic groups, lovers strolling, birds of many kinds, and most of all, the wide-open space in the sunshine and fresh air! Fifth Avenue runs along one side of it, so after the carriage ride that ended at that corner of the park, of course we wanted to stroll along some of it to see some of the famous Fifth Avenue stores—windows filled with lovely stylish clothing!

Seeing a Broadway show was another thing of interest. Our hotel was very near many of the theatres, and we chose to see *Kiss Me Kate*, by Cole Porter on Saturday evening. The extent of theatrical drama for Barbara and me had been high school plays, and later, movies. (I had even been one of the characters in a high school play myself! The play involved a family, and I was chosen to play the part of one of the children, because I was the smallest person in school. I had only one short line to say—and I had trouble making my voice be loud enough. Mom helped with my costume, an above-the-knee fluffy dress with a big sash, and my long hair combed into spiral curls!) It was very exciting to see this "real-life" musical show—right there on Broadway! Some of the songs were *Another Opening of Another Show*, *Wunderbar*, *Too Darn Hot*, and *From This Moment On*.

At Rockefeller Center we saw the Rockettes and other dancers on the Radio City Music Hall stage, had tours of the NBC studios and the RCA Building, and walked around the Plaza to enjoy the statuary, waterfall, and many activities, which I don't remember.

We found interesting places to eat at the Rockefeller Center, our hotel, and the Crossroads Tavern in Times Square. One of the places—I don't remember where (and Barbara doesn't either)—at lunch time was a cafeteria where the food was located in compartments with glass doors. We don't remember how we gained access to each food selection, unless it was by using some kind of coin shaped thing???

Four tired people went back to Grand Central Station late Sunday, to board the train that would take us back to our homes and work! What a wonderful adventure we'd had together. Other visits followed later while we were all on the east coast. Those will be other stories!

NAPLES, ITALY
1952 — Part 1

Gene and I were both really happy when he received orders to Naples, Italy, to be part of a Marine guard detachment. While he helped with preparing some Marines for the assignment, I went for a short visit with my family in Missouri. Returning to the east coast by air gave me my first travel by plane! That was truly an exciting experience! For many years I had tried to imagine what it would be like to be flying so high I would be able to "see the "tops" of the clouds! What a thrill to be up there among them, and to look down at the scenes below! By 1:30 p.m. we were in "the Windy City" of Chicago which was not only windy but was also cold that day! I was happy to be able to stay at the airport out of the bitter wind.

After a two-hour wait, I boarded a four-engine DC-6 for the nonstop flight to Washington, D.C. We were above the clouds for a while before sunset, and the beauty of it was breathtaking! Nothing visible but blue sky and golden, fleecy clouds! It was pretty, too, when the clouds cleared, and the lights began to sparkle here and there seven thousand feet below, creating patterns in all colors in the towns and cities. On the way, a stewardess served a most delicious dinner—hot bouillon, breaded pork chops, green peas, parsley-potatoes, lettuce and tomato salad, rolls, ice cream, and coffee. Oh, yes! And a mint!

The best sight of all was the view of Washington, with the lights on the Capitol and the Washington Monument; because I knew that we were nearing that very handsome, smiling Marine who would be waiting to "sweep me off my feet" again, the minute I was back on *terra firma*!

On February 14, 1952, we left D.C. with Gene's detachment of Marines in tow. There were twenty-eight of them. They would be sailing with us to Naples, where they would work with Gene. After a ham dinner on the train, and a pleasant, uneventful trip, we arrived in Jersey City, boarded a bus, ferried over to Manhattan, unloaded the men at Brooklyn Navy Yard, and then went to our hotel—the St. George, in Brooklyn. We had a few days of waiting there, giving Gene time to see to the needs of his men.

Highlights of the stay in New York were: *South Pacific* on the stage, Rockefeller Center, Radio City, and the New York premiere of *Retreat, Hell!* In between activities we took turns "doctoring" each other's colds and trying to "stay up." We were surely lucky to get "front and center" seats for *South Pacific*. It was every bit as exciting as we had heard, imagined, and hoped; and the songs that have become so popular took on real meaning and seemed to come to life. Particularly impressive was Lt. Cable's *You've Got to be Taught to Hate* which he sang after his decision not to marry the lovely native girl, Liat, whom he had grown to love. Her little pantomime and dance, accompanying Bloody Mary's *Happy Talk* was an interesting exhibition of meaningful, delicate gestures. Those songs fit very well into our positive philosophy of life. Truly, the things we are taught as children are more than likely the things that shape our beliefs and ways of dealing with all kinds of situations. And who doesn't like to engage in "happy" talk! Like the song says, "You gotta have a dream—if you don't have a dream—how you gonna have a dream come true?"

At Rockefeller Center we were taken on a guided tour, ending atop the seventy-story RCA Building, from which we saw a good portion of New York. (The Queen Mary had docked just a while before.) There was an especially interesting mural on the ceiling of the RCA Building lobby; and three large pillars, at the tops of which were figures of men who represented time: to the left was "The Past"; to the right was "The Future"; the other one was "The Present" who was looking directly at us. He was balancing some heavy timbers on his shoulders, representing present work, influenced by the past and by the future.

At Radio City, a guided tour took us behind the scenes of NBC. The newsroom, television studios, sound effects demonstrations, and control boards were some of the highlights. The original NBC control board was on display just outside the present one. Quite a contrast!

February 23rd was the big day for going aboard the *USNS Johnson*! Our driver took us from our hotel to Pier 26, where we joined other Navy personnel scheduled for sailing; then by bus to a pier in Brooklyn where the *Johnson* was docked. Our stateroom was B-5, located on the starboard side at almost midship. The ship was delayed because of engine repairs, so we spent Saturday and Sunday becoming acquainted with our new environment. The Marines came aboard Sunday morning, Army troops and dependents Sunday afternoon, Navy troops on Monday morning.

The name of the ship, in a way described its size, as one of the smaller ships that were designated for transport of personnel. Pvt. Johnson, for whom the ship was named, was a recipient of a Medal of Honor; some of the larger personnel transport ships were named for Generals. The *Johnson* was <u>much</u> smaller than an ocean liner and less "smooth-riding".

We "shoved off" about 2:00 o'clock in the afternoon on February 25th. A couple of tugs maneuvered us out into the stream, and very shortly we were steaming out to sea under our own power—followed by thousands of sea gulls. Leaving the skyline of New York behind was quite emotional for me, having never before been out of my country. We had been to the Statue of Liberty as tourists and learned something about how immigrants had been processed there through the years; but now we were able to see her from "the water", as she would have appeared to those so eager to have the life of freedom that "she" promised. It gave us a new appreciation of what that statue means! By evening we were out of sight of American shores and beginning a new adventure that made it all ever so interesting!

On February 27th, the third day at sea, I wrote, "The dining room is telling a sad story today, with its many vacant chairs at mealtimes! Many a head is seen with its nose and mouth covered with a paper bag! Although the water doesn't <u>look</u> rough, the ship seems pretty much at the mercy of the sea today, pitching and rolling almost constantly. I haven't fallen a victim of seasickness yet (as I 'knock on wood'), but prevention of it has been no small effort. Gene had told me that being in the fresh air as much as possible, and being able to see the horizon, would probably help to avoid it. The food is very good, we have a private bath and porthole, very comfortable beds, and a well-equipped lounge, so it isn't difficult to keep oneself busy, and by tomorrow, I will probably be a regular sailor!"

Because this is a military ship, Gene was assigned the Provost duty that involved the passenger troops. Some of them will be going to Trieste as replacement personnel. Some will be going to Casablanca. (At this time there are still remnants of U.S. military involved in Europe after World War II.) Here is a quote from a letter Gene wrote home about some of the work he did as Provost:

"I have used my men (Marines) to stand the guard duty for the whole ship and have received nothing but compliments on them. The other troops are catching KP and clean-up details. There are no laundry or dry cleaning facilities for the troops, but through a little skullduggery I arranged for my men to use the crew's washing machine at 4:00 o'clock in the morning, and checked out a DC iron for ship's current. The Chief Steward loaned me an ironing board and the First Mate, who is the first man below the Master of the ship, arranged for us to use a small compartment for a pressing room. I keep one man busy doing nothing but pressing clothes. The result is a sharp-looking group!" (The troops had a dining hall—they call it a 'mess' hall—separate from the passengers traveling with families.)

"It's February 29, the fifth day, and we are approximately half way to our first stop—Casablanca. Yesterday was a rough one! The sea was rough—about twenty-foot waves, and the strong wind blew water onto the deck so badly that we had to stay inside. The lack of fresh air and walking on the deck took its toll of victims of seasickness; however, today the sun is shining and more people are enjoying it. For an idea of the speed we traveled, according to the little newspaper published daily on the ship, on a 24-hour day we went a little more than 400 miles, but we lost an hour every other day. The average speed was about seventeen knots, which is equivalent to about 24 $\frac{1}{4}$ miles per hour. We played bridge with Major Wiley and Major Flick last evening. Major Flick is from Lincoln, Nebraska, and knows Colonel Delaney (whom I knew when I lived with my family at Fort Leonard Wood, Missouri during World War II).

"This is March 2nd, the seventh day. Just after noon we came in sight of some of the islands of the Azores. Flores, the larger of the two in that group, appeared on the starboard side; and Corvo was off the port side. We were closer to Flores, and could see communities of houses, terraced farms, and several waterfalls. The island's northwest side came down to the sea in sheer cliffs, over which the rivers from higher up the mountain tumbled down to the water. It was a beautiful, green 'hunk' of land—so peaceful and 'rural' looking and provided us with lovely views that were ever-changing for about three hours."

At about 2:00 p.m., Tuesday, March 4th, we pulled into Casablanca in French Morocco. (Our reason for stopping there was because the ship carried personnel and supplies for the U.S. military facilities, still there since World War II.) The port's pilot came aboard, and then shortly two tugs came out to pull us up to the pier. It was one of the happiest, and most exciting, days so far. Happy for those who were joining their husbands, with all the rest of us happy for them; exciting for us who were going to have an opportunity to go ashore for a look around! We joined one of the sightseeing tours, which took all the rest of the day, and included lunch.

The bus took us through the main part of the city's shopping area. On the right side of the street we saw small shops which opened to the street, displaying their hundreds of different articles—from rugs to jewelry to ethnic clothing to picture post cards. Our guide warned us to stay away from those shops, if we didn't want to be "fleeced," because the natives were clever and tricky with their bargaining. On the left side of the street there were modern looking stores and more specialty shops.

The first stop was at the Sultan's palace. There we saw expansive gardens, lawns, and buildings of "story-book" beauty. Many kinds of flowers were in bloom—fuschia, geraniums, and marigolds—and the walks were lined with palm and tangerine trees, including ripe tangerines. It was quite refreshing after having left a cold and snowy New York only eight days ago! Our guide said the Sultan had twenty-some wives in his harem; the Prince had his separate house and harem on the same grounds.

From the palace we went to the Arab section. More open-front stores—even the meat markets and bakeries had their wares displayed in the open! Succulent pieces of meats roasting over open rotisseries gave off delicious fragrances! Our guide told us the Arabs keep their feet clean, but they only wash their faces when it rains—a story one could not doubt after seeing them. In this section, the people were almost all dressed in the national clothing—robes and turbans with shoes that look like scuffs. The women added a veil, which covered all of the face except for a narrow strip for the eyes.

We went on through the various sections of the city—French, Spanish, wealthy. The better homes were built up on the hill; beautiful villas and gardens overlooking the beaches, around the bend from the harbor. On top of the hill was the city's best hotel, at which Roosevelt and Churchill had their conference during World War II.

From there, along the beach to a café, from which we could see all of Casablanca while we ate some lunch and sipped refreshments—the choice of which was French champagne. It was the first time I had ever tasted champagne, but even though I didn't really care for the taste, I sipped for a while just to be sociable. I don't know if it was the champagne, or if I was experiencing "reverse seasickness" brought on by being stopped after my equilibrium system had adjusted to movement, but before long, the champagne came right back up! That gave me <u>another</u> new experience—the local restroom! Co-ed. A man came out, and I hurried in. After the champagne was gone, I stayed a bit longer to further use the facility. There was no "seat," just foot pads upon which to stand while bending the knees. A little "scary," but necessary. <u>And</u>, it was a long time before I was able to tolerate another glass of champagne!

Another interesting stop was the Court House. The walls surrounding the courtyards and the passageways were made of plaster, with cedar wood above—all intricately hand-carved. The "recession room" was a long, lavishly decorated room, furnished with brocade furniture and inlaid tables.

Before the tour ended, our guide took us to the "factory" where we could shop without having the prices doubled. Our choices of souvenirs were a bag, a belt, and a green and tan round hassock (without the stuffing) made of camel skin and embroidered with gold thread. (The hassock was used until 2012.)

Casablanca—population about 900,000—was a quite modern city, so far as buildings were concerned. Most of the homes and apartments had a very "20th century" look. There were all makes of cars are to be seen, and many bicycles and horse-drawn carriages. We saw Mobilgas, Texaco and Shell gas stations, and, of course, many familiar red and white Coca-Cola signs.

On Wednesday, March 5th, about one o'clock, we came to Gibraltar. For several hours we had been in sight of the Spanish mainland, and had been among schools of porpoise, blackfish, and a few whales. We were impressed with the apparent strength of the huge rock. In a way, it seemed almost to have "personality"—after centuries of time, still guarding with a watchful eye the narrow strait, which is the gateway to the Mediterranean area. Not only did it look <u>naturally</u> formidable, but military strength was also apparent in the many radar screens, radio towers, gun emplacements, etc. On the eastern slope a huge, smooth slab aroused our curiosity. We learned that it was the watershed for the port. Rain water was thus collected and stored for later use.

At 8:00 a.m., Saturday, March 8th, we tied up at the pier in Naples! The decks were a-flurry with eager "tourists" (those who were to return to the ship after a tour), customs officials to clear our passports, and hasty good-byes. The weather was quite disagreeable, with a cold wind and misty rain—even a snow flurry now and then—but we were assured it was very unusual. It was a great relief to find our Marine Corps friend, C.P. Clark, there to meet us!

NAPLES, ITALY
1952 — Part 2

As soon as Gene had his Marines settled in their quarters, our friend C.P. Clark and his driver took us to our hotel—Pensione Panorama—where we were given room #6 on the seventh floor, overlooking the Bay of Naples. We had a little balcony with vines trailing along the banister and furnished with a table and two beach chairs. Built-in closets seemed to be unheard-of.

Electricity was quite expensive, so it was conserved as much as possible. The halls were only dimly lighted at night, and not at all in the daytime. Heat was turned on only after noon. Jean Clark came before lunch time, so she and I had a long visit before Gene and C.P. were back from Gene's business of reporting in.

In the afternoon we met the Spicers—Ray and Carla—and the Porters—Chuck and Barbara. Ray was a Marine Captain who would be Gene's Commanding Officer of the guard unit. C.P and Gene would be his two lieutenants. We had known Barbara on the ship, and Clarks knew Chuck (USN) from their trip over. In the evening, we, with the Clarks and Porters, had dinner at "Le Arcate"—appetizers including octopus, soup, salad, steaks, dreamy desserts, and delicious red wine. The meal took two hours, but the atmosphere with terraces of flowers, orchestra, and happy people made the time pass altogether too quickly.

On Sunday, March 9th, we were lazy and slept late, but took advantage of the sun in the afternoon. We walked in the park on the waterfront, watched children playing strange ball games, admired the numerous pieces of sculpture and fountains, and watched the laughing, chattering people who were also having Sunday afternoon walks. Dinner that night was with Clarks at the Allied Officers' Club.

Saturday, March 15th, was a very eventful day. We moved into our new home—Apartment #11, at 12 Parco Lamaro. Signor Lamberti (our landlord) had flowers sent up and introduced us to our porters (building keepers), Papino and Fiorita, Papino's wife. ("Fiorita" means "Little Flower.") Our rooms are on the fifth floor, affording beautiful views. From our bedroom window we can see the Island of Ischia; from the three living room bay windows, we see Capri, Mount Vesuvius, and the beautiful blue bay, with the Sorrento peninsula in the distance. From the terrace on our roof, almost all of Naples is visible. Clarks are "next-door" neighbors in Building #13. (Mr. Lamberti is from South America, and has traveled extensively in the U.S. Here, he is in the export-import business, and assured us over and over again that he wants to help us "be happy in a strange land.")

Our apartment has a combination living-dining room, a bedroom, kitchen, maid's room, bathroom, and large entrance hallway. The floors are of marble-like tile, called terrazzo, which seem now to be awfully cold and hard! However, they're easy to keep clean, and will be cool for the summer months just around the corner. The beds are more like cots, with woven springs and thin, "fluff" mattresses—no head-board. If we fasten them together, we can use our double-bed size linens. Also, in the bedroom we have the usual large wardrobe-closet, plus a desk and a small chest of drawers.

The kitchens are obviously built for use by maids and show no concern for "labor-saving conveniences" such as built-in-cabinets or even hot water faucets! Next to the small sink is a deep concrete tub with a washboard molded into the side. It has a board cover to make it into counter space when not in use. The gas stove has three burners and a midget oven—about large enough for a cookie sheet and maybe eighteen inches high. A work table is furnished with a marble top and a drawer. There is a cabinet with a top compartment containing a small shelf halfway across. The middle compartment lid opens out to form table space, and it's equipped with a full-size dough board with a rolling pin beside it, and a small meat board. The lower compartment has shelves for storing pans and food. There is a small icebox, but we will eventually have a refrigerator. (Gene says he can build some shelves to fit under the table and sink.)

The bathroom has tile floor and walls, a built-in tub, but no shower. There is an "extra fixture" that flushes and is about the size of the stool. I've heard that American tourists use it for a "foot bath." Europeans use it for bathing the "seat" part of the anatomy. The hot water is heated as it runs through the coiled copper tubing in the gas heater and is thermostatically controlled.

After a day of moving in, we went with the Porters to our first opera— *Rigoletto*—at the Teatro di San Carlo in downtown Naples. The opera house was lavishly furnished and decorated with red velvets, gilded carvings, crystal chandeliers, and such. The stage scenery was especially interesting. The outdoor backgrounds were so realistic one could almost imagine feeling soft breezes blowing! It had such depth—river, sky, stars, bridge, distant lights, even moving clouds, and for one scene, thunder and lightning. We especially enjoyed the Duke's singing of *La Donna e Mobile* in Act III. (Translation: "Woman is fickle!")

Our landlord began working right away on giving us more conveniences. He had a new electric hot water heater (called *scaldabagno*) put in and added a hot water pipe to the kitchen. He had a special transformer made for my sewing machine (his wife had one just like it—a small-size Singer portable), and he paid half of the cost of transformers for it and the refrigerator we had shipped from the States.

Every time I looked out one of our windows, my heart sang! The view was seldom the same, but always there was the utterly beautiful blue Mediterranean water! One day just before sundown when I looked out over the bay, a cloud was hanging low over our hill, and I couldn't see the sun. However, the sun was shining through a hole in the cloud and sending golden rays over to the foot of Mt. Vesuvius, picking up the white and yellow and orange colors of the buildings, and greens of the trees. Two white sailboats near the shore fit right into the scene! I wished to be an artist! I did take a picture with the camera, but that didn't really do it justice.

It was good to have the Clarks living just next door. Jean and I sometimes had lunch together, went shopping, or just spent time relaxing together. Before our refrigerator arrived, it was necessary to shop for fresh food almost every day. The street that Parco Lamaro intersected, led up the hill to an area called Vomero where there were several shops of all kinds—fruit and vegetable markets, butcher shops, bakeries, cafes, pizzerias, shoe shops, etc. We could go on a bus, but after getting back to the stop nearest our place, we still had to climb many steps up hill, so we had to limit purchases to what we could carry. Usually, it was just food supplies of meat, vegetables, and fruit for one or two days, carried in a sizeable straw shopping basket. We "stood out like sore thumbs" among the local Italian shoppers—most of them women, many of whom were maids. It was interesting to watch and listen to their selecting and bargaining for the things they wanted to buy. We learned to do it, too.

Soon after we arrived, the commissary that was provided by the American military services began to expand, so that we were able to get many familiar products there, including nylon stockings, which were not available in Italian stores. It was housed in a warehouse type of building in what was called the Industrial Area, several miles from where we lived. There was also a gasoline station there where we could get subsidized gas for a few cents per gallon that would have cost Italians about three dollars. The commissary was a good place to stock up on staples, but shopping there was better done when a husband and a car were available to help.

We had very good Italian neighbors—Aldo and Maria Minozzi—whose apartment was on the same floor as ours. They were citizens of Rome but had come to Naples to live where Aldo worked as a pharmacist. They had a four-year-old son named Massimo who was very smart and enthusiastic. I enjoyed playing with him, and we could understand each other most of the time because he was learning to speak English. Visiting with them was special for all of us, because they wanted an opportunity to practice the English they were learning, and we really valued being able to learn and practice speaking Italian. Needless to say, our handy-dandy little English-Italian dictionary got a lot of use.

Soon after we met, the Minozzies suggested that we meet them in Rome for Easter in April. It is one of the major holidays in Italy, and the numerous candy stores were very colorful with their foil-wrapped eggs filled with little candies and trinkets. Gene had to stand duty Saturday morning, but we took the express train and were in Rome in two hours.

Aldo and Maria met us at the station, took us to check in at a cozy little Pensione that they knew about, then for the rest of the afternoon, they took us in their car all over the city. At the Villa Borghese gardens were acres and acres of beautiful green lawn, flowers, and lakes. We drove by the Sport Center which Mussolini had built, St. Peter's Cathedral, other cathedrals, Castel Sant' Angelo, Tomb of the Unknown Soldier, Mussolini's "balcony" (from which he made his famous speeches), the Forum, the Coliseum, the Trevi Fountain, triumphal arches, temple ruins, and everything between, and then out to the Appian Way. Most of the time we only looked at things from the car as we passed by, and were able to take a few pictures, but on the Appian Way we stopped for a while and felt the thrill of walking on some of the original pavement stones! A chapel was built at the spot on the old road where God spoke to Peter as Peter was leaving Rome during one of the Christian persecutions, and asked, "Quo vadis?" (which I think means, "Whither goest thou?"); whereupon, Peter returned to Rome to be crucified. You probably know that the Cathedral is supposed to be the resting-place of his remains.

The Minozzies treated us like a king and queen. We wanted to host them for dinner Saturday evening, but Aldo—in his broken English, accompanied by many meaningful gestures—insisted that, "When I visit you in Missouri, you pay—now you are in Roma!" (He pronounced *Roma* with a lovely, rolling "R!") He loves Rome, and after a weekend there, we understood why—beautiful, clean, wide streets; nice shops; lovely parks; and an indescribable atmosphere, blending B.C. history with the 20th century! I don't remember where or what we ate that evening, but I had to keep "pinching" myself to make sure that this wonderful adventure was really happening!

By then we were about to drop, we were so tired—had been on our feet for four solid hours—so we decided to go to the station, take the next train to Naples, and have dinner on the train. We learned, however, that that particular train had no diner, so we went around the corner to a nice little restaurant and spent the next two hours enjoying a late lunch that just happened to be on Gene's birthday. We had tasty appetizers, with Italian bread that is <u>so</u> good, spaghetti, steak with mushrooms, delicious red wine, and rum cake that seems to be an Italian specialty for dessert! It <u>takes</u> two hours to eat <u>that much</u>!

It was a really wonderful weekend, with possibilities of adventures only just touched! Soon we would have our car and be able to explore more things more thoroughly—and in the meantime we could do some research to learn more history of this exciting part of the world we would be experiencing for the next couple of years!

The next Sunday, April 20th, was our first visit to Capri—which many people consider to be "the Isle of Paradise." We had made plans to go with Jean and C.P. Clark, but when we wakened that morning it was very cloudy, so we decided against the trip and went back to bed for an hour. However, when we were ready to sit down to eat breakfast, the Clarks came over, all ready to go, so we swallowed our eggs and were ready to go in thirty minutes. The only boat before afternoon left at 9:00 a.m. and was just pulling out when we puffed onto the dock! Our first thought? "We missed the boat"—literally! But we were not to be left behind! Some dock hands began hailing the boat, named "Capri," while two more loaded us into a rowboat. Sure enough, the "Capri" had stopped to wait for us and was lowering the side gangway! We pulled alongside, paid the rowboat men a young fortune for their trouble, and in a flash we were aboard and the "Capri's" engines began churning again.

After landing, our first plans were to take the funicular (cog-train) up from the Marina Grande to the town of Capri, but for the same price, an enterprising driver offered us a ride in his limousine (which he said had been one of Mussolini's fleet). So, we took him up on his offer. We wanted to do some shopping and leisurely "looking," but our driver (named Salvatore) was a salesman first class and persuaded us to permit him to give us a tour of the island, including some shopping time and dinner in the "nicest restaurant in Capri."

By the time Jean and I had found some Capri sandals we liked—hers, white; mine, gold—all of us were ready to hunt some food. And Salvatore was the one who knew where to find it. He took us to his sister's restaurant, called "La Pigna," where we went to the kitchen to select our food. The sight of the immaculately clean kitchen with the half-prepared raviolis, zucchini, mashed potato balls filled with Mozzarella cheese, all kinds of fresh fish, and steaks, made our appetites grow to ravenous states. In no time at all we were enjoying all of it in the quaint little dining room lined with brother-in-law Luigi's paintings of scenes around the island. In the kitchen we were especially impressed by the wall covered with shining copper pots and pans, and with the built-in wood range across one end with a couple of open charcoal pits. The restaurant was named for the one wind-blown pine tree in the middle of their stone-paved terrace. The terrace was also furnished with tables and chairs. We were told that brother Luigi lived in New York, owned a restaurant of his own there, and painted when he came to Capri to visit.

After a stroll through their garden of all kinds of flowers, including honeysuckle, we were off for the drive around the island. We saw Gracie Field's beach, the rocks called the Faraglioni which are just off the southern coast, Tiberius' castle remains on top of the highest part of the island's eastern end, Mussolini's daughter's villa, and terrace after terrace of lovely flowers. Then we were driven up to the western side of the island called Anacapri, seeing the three-thousand-year-old steps that were built by the Phoenicians, some Roman ruins, the Hotel Eden Paradiso, and the Villa San Michele. There was a fantastic view from that high hill that is called Monte Solaro. I'm sure Salvatore received a sizeable tip when we got back to the little central village. Many more visits to that island followed during the next two years! And many more lunches and dinners at La Pigna. The best visits were the ones for more than one day, because after the one-day tourists leave on the last boat of the evening, the place really "comes alive"! As night falls, the tables of the sidewalk cafes fill up, accordions and mandolinos accompany strolling serenaders, "vino" flows, and there's dancing in the streets!

On May 4th, a few days after our car arrived, we spent a Sunday at Pompeii. We left Naples on the "Autostrada"—a toll highway about the width of an American two-lane road but serves as three lanes for the small Italian cars. Our first stop in Pompeii was at the museum, which houses some of the articles unearthed during the many excavations. The city was covered by volcanic ashes in the year A.D. 79 when Vesuvius erupted violently. Plaster casts have been made of many people and animals by pouring liquid plaster into the cavities discovered during excavation. The positions of some of these seem to indicate that life was extinguished by gas, before the rain of ashes covered the city. In the museum we saw gold dental instruments (similar to the type used in America in the 1700's), charred loaves of bread, cakes, beans, peas, chicken bones, pieces of cloth, glass, coins, pans, etc.

A walk around part of the city took us to the Public Forum, baths, temples to various gods, shops, residences, and amphitheaters. The baths were plumbed with lead pipes (as were the residences)—warm baths for women; additional steam and frigid ones for men. We were told the athletic-type men thought that plunging into cold water made muscles stronger. The steam rooms were built with arched ceilings, grooved so that the condensed steam would run off, rather than drip! The walls were insulated and were double-thickness.

One of the best-preserved houses was the "House of Vettii," two bachelor brothers. It had many rooms—sitting rooms, dining rooms, bedrooms, kitchen, and a beautiful enclosed garden. The walls showed lavish decorations, painted with many masterpieces of art. Most residential buildings had enclosed gardens with decorative personalized tiled "floors." The figure of a dog, ready to attack, was inlaid at the "House of the Tragic Poet." Lettering on the tile warned, "Beware of the Dog." It was a strange feeling to stand amid the ruins of the once-thriving commercial city where life was so suddenly snuffed out! With only a little imagination, one could almost "hear" the street vendors, chariots bumping along the rock-paved streets, guiding their wheels between the raised "stepping stones" at pedestrian crossings, or see a sacrifice being offered in one of the many temples! One wonders how much civilization was lost with those people!

A couple of weeks later, we spent a day exploring the ruins of Herculaneum, a seaport city near Pompeii. It was a summer resort for wealthy Romans when it suffered burial under hot mud and lava during the A.D. 79 eruption of Vesuvius. Formerly occupied by the Greeks, much of the architecture was of Greek style. Many outside walls were of diamond-shaped rock. An earthquake in A.D. 63 had damaged the city considerably, and the repairs showed Roman building techniques.

NAPLES — POZZUOLI, PHLEGRAEAN FIELDS, SOLFOTARA, BAIA

Our first visit to the Phlegraean Fields and Pozzuoli, seven or so miles northwest of Naples, was with Ray and Carla Spicer in May 1952. The Phlegraean Fields is a highly active volcanic area which includes the crater of a half extinct volcano called Solfatara, which has not been in full activity since A.D. 1198. The ground around was quite hot—even through shoes—and sounded hollow when stamped on; steam jets, charged with sulphurous gases emerged continuously from numerous fissures in the ground. A guide was required because some places were dangerous to walk across. Inside the crater were many fissures with hot air and steam blowing out, and in one place, a pool of black lava was boiling—not just simmering but boiling—making big "pops" like the thick apple-butter we used to stir for Mom at canning time!

Our guide showed us a hole that had caved off about two weeks ago—a man had been standing there and fell about two feet into the lava. That area was roped off, and we were assured that where we were walking, the safe ground was ten feet thick. Several times the guide threw a rock about the size of a man's fist down on the ground, and it sounded like pounding the side of a huge tank—hollow. For once, I got my feet warmed up, because the ground all over was very warm. A German scientist once tried to harness the steam for power and dug a hole in which to place his machinery, but after a little time, he discovered that the minerals had ruined the metal, so he gave up the idea.

We went into some nearby caves where the Romans had built mineral steam baths for health purposes—supposed to cure arthritis or skin diseases. And, we were told that in the past, when that Solfatara area became inactive, there would be action going on in Vesuvius. When Vesuvius became quiet, Solfatara again came to life. It was all very interesting, but we were a bit more relaxed when we got back to where we could "cool our heels," stomp on the ground, and have it sound <u>solid</u>!

That same guide took us over to the little coastal town of Pozzuoli, which was the first settlement in that area, and became the main southern seaport for ancient Rome. It was founded in the 6th century B.C. by Greeks. St. Paul spent seven days there on one of his journeys to Rome in A.D. 62 (*Acts 28:13-14 -- And from there we made a circuit and arrived at Rhegium; and after one day a south wind sprang up, and on the second day we came to Puteoli. There we found brethren and were invited to stay with them for seven days. And so we came to Rome.)* (Puteoli is now known as the modern city of "Pozzuoli.")

Part of the city ruins show evidence of having been under water for some time, but arose in 1538 when an earthquake caused a 455-foot "mountain" (Monte Nuovo—"New Mountain") to appear overnight. In 1838 an amphitheatre was unearthed, which was built to seat about 35,000 people. There were a number of passageways underground where wild animals were kept for the fighting—and a damp, dark prison where some of the early Christians awaited fights with the beasts. At times, great gates were closed and the arena was flooded for naval fights. There were separate entrances for the Emperor and the common people. Many beautiful statues were found when it was unearthed, and the entire thing is very well preserved. (For several years I had a sprig of a plant from one growing there. I dried it and kept it in my Bible.)

It was beginning to seem that every "rock we turned over" had a thousand or so years of history under it, and by December of 1952, we'd met a person who had helped to discover a lot of it in the past few years. Her name was Mrs. Raiola. (I can't believe I didn't record her first name!) She was working with the Virgilian Society in Naples and had been closely associated with many archaeologists. She was probably sixty or seventy years old, but she could outlast me, scampering around through ruins and restorations! Some of our American groups often engaged her for a guide because she had lived in that area for so long, had studied the ancient history of it, and even helped with some of the excavations, that we felt the wonderful stories she told were authentic.

We were part of a small group with her to this area after the visit I've just described. Our first stop with her was to the top of a hill from which we could see the towns of Miseno, Pozzuoli, and Baia; and the Islands of Procida and Ischia to the south in the Bay of Naples. She pointed out the mountain which rose up in four days during volcanic action in the area, some castles, and described how the Romans used to use those places. The weather here was so pleasant that the people of royalty and wealth liked to spend about nine months out of the year down here on the Mediterranean Sea shore. It was also an important seaport for commerce, and a naval station.

Straight across the bay from where we stood was a castle built by Augustus, and the hillside nearby was literally covered with apartments for royal guests. This castle wasn't large enough to give him the privacy he wanted, so he built another one on another point nearby and put a golden-paved bridge between the two. The city became known as the "golden shore of Baia." It must have been <u>something</u> to see! The rich people who came were to leave gifts of money to "the gods" to be used in building and improving the city. When we arrived to see it "close-up," we saw architectural structure characteristic of the time of 500 years B.C. One wall showed some original Greek decoration of <u>very fine</u> design that had been plastered over by the Romans later on. Each "apartment" had a private bath, with the water pumped up from below so hot it didn't need to be heated!

Nearby was the water reservoir that supplied the cities and the fleet with drinking water. It was carved out of solid rock and vaulted for support—fed by aqueduct from a mountain lake. The volume was 200-some cubic meters. Each year when the fleet went out for maneuvers, the "cistern" was drained and re-plastered with disinfectant plaster made from terra cotta, sulphur, and arsenic.

It was an experience of a lifetime to live in Naples, in the midst of ancient history, among people who seemed to love life—taking "siestas" every afternoon, treasuring their "bambinos," their good food, and plentiful "vino"!

CLIMBING MT. VESUVIUS

Long ago in grade school I first learned about Mt. Vesuvius in Italy, and I remember that I was unbelievably impressed with learning about the eruption on August 24, A.D. 79 that buried the city of Pompeii in its explosive rain of ash. I wondered what it might have been like for the people who must have been awfully frightened with the earthquakes and rumblings, then the sudden presence of ash and deadly gases from which there was no escape! There had been many other eruptions, but the people then living there weren't likely to have known about those—and certainly didn't have the scientific knowledge of geology that has been developed for us. Living in Naples from early 1952

131

to late 1953 gave me the rewarding opportunity to see the mountain up close, and to visit the excavations of Pompeii and Herculaneum to get an idea of how the people there lived, and to imagine their experience on that terrifying day!

Our apartment was high on the Vomero hill and from our windows we had a great view of the mountain, as well as the entire beautiful, unbelievably blue Bay of Naples that included the islands of Capri and Ischia. The 3600-foot mountain had erupted many times through the centuries, most recently in 1944. There was a railroad station at the base of it, and at one time a cog train ran from there to the summit; but it was destroyed in the 1944 eruption, which significantly enlarged the crater and lowered the summit about one thousand feet. A large museum nearby was a great tourist attraction.

The lower hills were a lovely patchwork of vineyards and fruit trees on cultivated ground. The very fertile soil was perfect for the growth of citrus fruits, and of the grapes from which a delightful white wine called La Crema di Christi ("Tears of Christ") was made. Higher vegetation included wild shrubs and prickly pears in black lava fields.

Gene's duties there with the Marine Corps were to help supervise the Marines who were assigned to guard the high-level offices of multiple military people connected with NATO after WWII. The Marine Corps required the enlisted men to meet certain levels of physical training and use of weapons, so finding places and ways to meet those needs required some imagination. Gene was just recently out of officer basic training himself and was very happy to be chosen to be the training officer. Climbing to the summit of Mt. Vesuvius, carrying back-packs, was one of the activities that gave them a challenging hike to keep themselves physically fit. The men enjoyed being out in the "boon-docks," and had a lot of respect for Gene's leadership.

I, of course, wished I could do it too! A guide had told Gene that very few women have the endurance to make it to the top, but Gene thought I wouldn't have a problem if we took our time—and I was determined to do it! So, on May 18th, 1952 Gene and I decided to make the climb ourselves, with a required guide. We were able to drive about a third of the distance up the side of the mountain to a place where we could park our American Jeep. The day was sunny and warm, but quite breezy as the altitude increased; and I was so busy enjoying the view, I soon realized that I should pay more attention to my steps! A walking stick helped with walking along the cinder path, but it was strewn with various sizes and kinds of stones that made it possible to turn an ankle or lose one's balance by a shoe rolling on one of those loose ones. The incline was gradual enough that an occasional brief stop to survey the view made the walk comfortable—but I'm sure, it took considerably more time for us than it did for the Marines!

Never in all my life had I seen such a view! And it constantly changed as our trail curved around the mountain's cone-shaped top. There was all of the great city of Napoli spreading beneath us—hills and valleys; roads and villages; cathedrals, parks, mansions, and slums; the port, outlined with docks, merchant ships, military ships, fishing boats, ocean liners, sail boats, and yachts. Farther out in the bay were the islands of Ischia and Capri and Procida—playgrounds for the rich and famous, supported by pleasant people providing for them the hotels, restaurants, quaint shops and beautiful villas all among hundreds of varieties of beautiful flowers! Our view included the colorful coastal towns of Sorrento, Positano, and Amalfi; the unearthed ruins of Pompeii and temples that had been covered with ash; and inland lay miles of green tree-covered mountains and beautiful blue lakes.

At the summit we walked part way around the south rim of the huge, three-hundred feet deep crater, taking time to examine the view into its rocky depths with steam issuing from some of the crevices. There was a fresh breeze coming from the sea, and we lingered for a bit while our guide served a cool bottle of La Crema di Christi wine! Gene told us that the Marines took an hour and a half to climb up the trail, and only seven minutes to come down— running straight down the slope through cinders over ankle deep. Well, Gene and I decided to come down, to where our car was parked, the same way! For us, it wasn't so much <u>running</u> as it was digging in our heels and sliding to a stop; then digging in and sliding again! For me, it was the first, and <u>I hoped</u>, the last time of moving in that manner!

The vegetation on lower slopes included many honey-locust trees, which were in full bloom! Wonderful aroma! On the way driving down, we rewarded ourselves with a stop at a small road side restaurant for what was quite a late lunch. We sat at a table on the terrace, shaded with arbors of vines and trees— again, a great view of scenes below. Just thinking about it, I can almost "feel" the refreshing breeze, smell the honey-locust, and taste the delicious wine— another bottle of La Crema di Christi! It is a fragrant white wine, said to be made from grapes grown on the slopes of Mt. Vesuvius; and so named for its uniquely delicious flavor. It was another one of the many times I've pinched myself, trying to believe all this was happening to ME!

LOVE IS ALL THAT MATTERS

EASTER IN ROME — 1952

This Easter season, in 2005, has been a little different from most for me, and has stirred memories of some other ones that were also different. This year I spent Palm Sunday weekend with Becky and her family in Seattle, visiting at both grandsons' schools, and going to church with them on Sunday. David, Michelle, and I celebrated Easter with a mid-day dinner at my house on Saturday, the day before Easter. On Good Friday evening I spent an hour experiencing a beautiful, contemplative prayer walk at my church—Calvin Presbyterian. I had never before done that sort of spiritual exercise, and I found it to be a very meaningful way of concentrating thoughts on the scriptures describing the last few days in the life of Christ on Earth—His last supper with His apostles, His trial, crucifixion, burial, and resurrection.

The several chilly days of almost continuous rain around Easter this year reminded me of an Easter when I was fourteen or fifteen years old, and had a beautiful new, ready-made spring coat from the Sears catalog that I had hoped to wear for Easter. It was a three-quarter length, rose-color novelty-weave, with a stitched stand-up collar that extended down the no-button front.

I don't remember the dress I wore with it, but the shoes were white sandals. At that age, new Easter clothes were very important to me—and on the family income at that time, there might have been some budget sacrifice made for me. As it so often happened in Missouri in April, Easter Sunday was quite cold and windy, but I so wanted to wear that new coat! Mom advised me that it wouldn't keep me warm, but she wisely allowed me to make my own decision—and I wore the coat anyway. By the time I had walked the one-and-a-half miles to church, I realized the importance of being comfortable—never mind the fashion! This Easter I wore a raincoat over a jacket and carried an umbrella—and drove my car to the convenient parking lot at church! Of course, I remembered my dear, very wise mother!

But Easter in 1952 was very different from any other I've ever experienced! Gene and I had lived in Naples, Italy, for a couple of months, and were ready for adventure. We had neighbors in our apartment building who were Romans—Aldo, Maria, and young son Massimo Minozzi. Aldo was a pharmacist in Naples, but they often spent time with their families in Rome and invited us to spend some of Easter weekend with them. Our car hadn't yet arrived, so we took a train to Rome on Friday, checked into a convenient pensione (hotel) that they had recommended, and met them for dinner.

LOVE IS ALL THAT MATTERS

On Saturday afternoon they took us in their car all over the city—clean, wide streets, that in comparison to Naples, had <u>cars</u> on them rather than people <u>walking</u> in them! There were lovely parks, and an indescribable atmosphere, blending B.C. history with the 20th century! Some of the things we saw were the Villa Borghese gardens, the sport center that Mussolini had built, St. Peter's Cathedral, Castel San't Angelo, Tomb of the Unknown Soldier, Mussolini's "balcony" (from which he made speeches), and the Appian Way. Mostly, we just observed from the car, but we took a few photos, and walked on some of the <u>original</u> pavement of the Appian Way! There is a chapel built at the spot on the Appian Way where Peter had a spiritual experience as he was leaving Rome during one of the Christian persecutions. According to a legend, Peter had a vision of Jesus meeting him, and he said to Jesus, "Quo vadis?" ("Whither goest thou?") Jesus replied, "I am coming to Rome to be again crucified." To which Peter replied, Lord, I will return and will follow Thee." Whereupon, Jesus ascended, and Peter returned to Rome to be crucified.*

(On later trips when Gene and I drove on the highway along which are the remains of the Appian Way, I always experienced special "feelings" when I saw those remains that were once that very famous route for travelers so many centuries ago! The Apostle Paul, and others about whom we read in the Bible, no doubt once traveled there—probably walking—on their trips from the Mediterranean shores to Rome and other locations in that area!)

The Minozzies suggested that we join an early-morning tour of the catacombs of St. Peter's Cathedral on Sunday morning, in which case we would be <u>inside</u> while the thousands of other people were gathering in the piazza to view Pope Pius XII's appearance on his balcony to give his Easter blessing. We didn't take time for all of the cathedral tour that day but went back other times to see more of it—a truly magnificent work of architectural art! The first stone was laid on April 18, 1506, and the completed basilica was consecrated on November 18, 1626—120 years in the building under the supervision and workmanship of the artists Bramante, Maderno, Michelangelo, and Raphael, among others. It was sort of an eerie feeling to see, and walk among, the many entombments of people – some of whom had been wealthy, most of whom had been middle class or poor. Some bodies had been placed in decorative sarcophagi; others were in various wrappings or containers. There were passageways between the burial areas, and those areas looked like spaces that had been carved out of earthen walls at different levels. We were told that during the times of persecutions of the early Church, Christians frequently met in the catacombs areas for their secret worship services.

Pope Pius XII came out on the balcony at noon and spoke to the 300,000 or so pilgrims and tourists gathered almost as far as the eye could see. For an hour before the Pope appeared, a choir sang, and officials read services—none of which we understood, of course, but nevertheless enjoyed. After the Pope spoke, an Associated Press reporter interviewed us and said he would send us a translation of the message—but I don't remember ever seeing it.

One of the most phenomenal experiences that day was coming out of the cathedral, finding ourselves inside of a special area that was roped off and guarded from the general public. It was interesting to visit with tourists and others standing near us, when suddenly, Gene noticed a familiar face—a man standing a few feet away from us—it was the man who was Captain of the ship Gene was on in the South Pacific during World War II!** What a coincidence! Needless to say, that was a most remarkable, surprising, reunion! A never-to-be-forgotten experience!

*George Edmundson in *The Church in Rome in the First Century* (London, 1913)

**The ship was a carrier—USS *Block Island.*

NAPLES — HERCULANEUM

Another city that suffered the fury of the 79 A.D. eruption of Mt. Vesuvius was Herculaneum, on the Gulf of Naples, northwest of Pompeii, and even nearer to the slopes of the mountain. (Its Italian name is Ercolano.) Our first visit there was on May 31, 1952. According to mythology, the town was founded by Hercules, but its first historical inhabitants were the primitive Oscans in the 6th century B.C. Later, the more civilized Greeks moved in, and after a few more "occupations" came the Romans, who used the seashore town as a summer resort.

Unlike Pompeii, which was buried under a rain of ashes, Herculaneum was covered by a stream of mud, mingled with pumice stones and ashes that penetrated into all cavities, and in time, solidified to a kind of stone, forming one single mass with the existing constructions. This mass preserved the priceless treasures until the relatively recent unearthing. Some private excavations were made in the 1700's by rummaging in the ruins using pick-axes and shovels, removing many valuable objects, then covering it all back again for the safety of the overlying village. We saw some of these treasures in the National Museum in Naples: sculptures of *Mercury Resting, Drunken Faun,*

136

Augustus, Claudius, and a *Bust of Plato.* In a house supposed to have been owned by Julius Caesar's father-in-law, Calpurnius Piso, a great number of rolls of papyrus were found. These too are in the Naples museum. Unrolling them is almost impossible, they are so fragile. In 1927, excavations were begun, using modern techniques, under the direction of Professor A. Maiuri. (We met a lady named Mrs. Raiola who knew Professor Maiuri and had helped with excavations and study of the history of the area. It was a joy to be a member of many of her guided tours!)

In some places the mud stream was as much as eighty feet deep. Only four skeletons were found after one third of the city had been unearthed, indicating that it wasn't destroyed until several hours, or perhaps days, after Pompeii, giving the people enough warning to escape. Much of the architecture was of the Greek type and had outside walls of diamond-shaped rock; but an earthquake in 63 A.D. had damaged the city considerably, and the repairs showed Roman building techniques.

Herculaneum was evidently wealthier than Pompeii—the houses were more lavishly decorated, with colorful walls having a lot of a rich red color in the frescoes, mosaic tiles in floors, and family altars that were built into walls. There were also very advanced things like under-ground sewers, running water, indoor toilets with water, wooden bed frames, and other furniture made of wood. There was quite a lot of the original charred wood—especially furniture and stairways. In one of the bath houses, some of the original glass was preserved—as clear as the original glass we saw in Williamsburg, Virginia. In one house was an iron door similar to our contracting and expanding lattice-type elevator doors—the only one of that period ever found. Only the bolts holding together the sliding bars had been replaced because they were missing—which indicated they might have been made of wood for quiet operation.

In one building—upstairs—we were shown a room supposed to have been occupied by a Christian slave. A cross was carved on the wall, under which was a little wooden altar with a place for kneeling.

One thing that aroused our curiosity was the fact that they used "Meridian sundials"—concave, half-globe looking ones—and that in a gymnasium in Pompeii there were military emblems using a globe and eagle! That seemed to be a very long time before people believed the earth to be round! Could it be that more civilization than we know was lost with those people?

Not long after this trip to Herculaneum, Gene had an interesting experience one day when he was out in town in Naples—maybe going to work.

He saw an American flag being used for an awning over one of the sidewalk shops—in a pouring rain, at that! You can imagine what a sight like that does to the "insides" of a Marine, to say nothing of being an American citizen. His first thought was to get it away from them, but to walk up and take it could cause big trouble. So he went to his office to get his Captain's permission to try "diplomacy" first; and if that didn't work, to see the American Consul. He then went to the ship (an American military vessel berthed in the harbor to provide support for American military personnel in the area) to see if he could get a piece of canvas to trade for the flag; and when the ship's supply officer heard the story, he, too, was very enthusiastic. While looking over possible substitutes in the ship's supply room, they decided the shop-keeper should be very happy to trade it for some waterproof mattress covers, so Gene took the covers, along with one of his Marines who spoke fluent Italian and went back to the street shop. A crowd immediately gathered when the Navy car and an American officer stopped. It took only an offer to make the exchange—the shopkeeper evidently was a little frightened—and both parties were benefited! The flag was awfully dirty and smelly, but the Marines thought it would be a nice souvenir for the Detachment after it was cleaned up!

NAPLES–TRIESTE

One of the requirements for a Marine is an annual weapon qualification, which for most of them is their rifle. That means a test of their accuracy in hitting a target from certain distances, and from certain positions—like standing, kneeling, and prone. But, in Naples, where Gene was working with a detachment that provided guard duty for the high-level military offices in the Mediterranean area, there were no rifle ranges suitable for this kind of testing. The closest range was at an army post near Trieste, all the way at the northeast "corner" of Italy. Gene was the detachment training officer, so he and the C.O. worked out a plan with the people at the rifle range for Gene to go to Trieste and stay for a month. Each week, one-fourth of the detachment would travel to Trieste for the four days required for the men to do the practice and testing required for the qualification. The wonderful part of that for us was that I could go, too! Gene was given extra pay (called *per diem*) to cover his travel, lodging and food—so I just "shared"! He had three-day weekends free, and we could do a little local sightseeing, too.

138

LOVE IS ALL THAT MATTERS

Trieste is a beautiful city on the Adriatic Sea, not far from Venice, and near the border of what was then Yugoslavia. The climate was comfortably warm and sunny, and with many buildings made of local white stone, along the shores of that very blue water, it had been for many years an ideal place for good living. It became an important seaport for the Austrian and Hungarian empires; developing industries of shipbuilding, steel mills, and oil refineries. Emperor Maximilian built a beautiful white castle as a vacation spot for himself in the mid- 1800's that eventually became a museum. For centuries the population had become a mixture of Italian, Slovenes, Croats, Austrian, German and Jews, as nations fought over ownership. After World War I, it became part of Italy; then, the Germans occupied it in 1943. Two years later, Tito claimed it for Yugoslavia. The World War II treaty made it a free territory, divided into two zones with U.S. and British troops maintaining one zone; and Yugoslavia maintaining the other. We were there during that time, and the U.S. Army troops were exceptionally "sharp" and well- liked, said to be the "sharpest" in the Army. Gene gave his men quite a pep-talk before coming here: to the effect that there would be NO "unfriendly arguments" with the soldiers, and that the Marines would be at all times looking and acting their very best!

With Gene's authorized travel time, plus a weekend, we were able to make some sightseeing stops on the way there, driving our dark green Jeep station wagon we'd bought especially for the Naples assignment. We left Naples after work on Friday afternoon (February 20th), and spent the first night in Rome. Lunch the next day was in Siena, where we drove off the main road into one of the town's piazzas. At the little restaurant, we had a table by a huge window where we could watch the people strolling around. It was interesting to see that almost all of them stopped to have a look at our car and license plates. We couldn't hear their comments, so we made a game of imagining comments they might be making!

The next stop was Florence, about four o'clock in the afternoon. We checked in at the hotel, put the car in the garage, and took off on foot to do some shopping and "looking." Darkness fell soon, so we had a chance to see some of the "Saturday night" crowd, doing last minute shopping, because shops would be closed on Sunday.

It was too foggy the next morning for photos we'd planned to make, so another stop there was planned for the trip home. Lunch that day was in Farrara, a little town just northeast of Bologna, after a delightful drive through the Appenine Mountains. There was a lot of snow, though the roads were clear, and the sights were really beautiful. Now and then a little town nestled on a sunny slope, many people were on bicycles, or just taking Sunday strolls, snow-covered peaks glistened in the sun every direction we looked! We saw several signs of skiers along the way. One was especially interesting—for some distance, two parallel ski tracks just abruptly stopped, and then were followed by <u>foot</u> tracks! We wondered what had happened there!

We were very disappointed when we reached Venice, where we would spend the night. Fog was so thick, we couldn't see much farther than across the road, and sometimes not that far. Everyone has to leave his car at the garage and take a gondola or a "bus-boat" over to the city. It was so miserable out that we stayed in that evening. The next morning the fog was no better, but after a good breakfast, we bundled up and went for a walk down to St. Mark's Cathedral, through some places where people were making Venetian glass and hand-made Venetian lace; along some of the canals; over bridges; through some market squares; and just <u>looking</u>. It was so foggy we couldn't see the top of the Cathedral! When the bells rang (on the hours), they sounded like they were coming from nowhere, because the towers were all shrouded in fog. One time, for about ten or fifteen minutes, there were many bells ringing all at once—all different sizes and tones. It really made pretty "music." Tired of walking, we had lunch at the hotel and decided to drive on—planning to come back to Venice for a weekend while in Trieste. We could more conveniently make that trip by train.

I don't remember much about the place we stayed in Trieste, but it must have been a hotel or guest house that was maintained for military people. There were many such places at, or near, the American military bases at that time. I do remember that no double room was available for us when we arrived, so they put us in two adjoining single rooms with a connecting door. The next day a double just down the hall was vacated, so a porter and I moved our things. Gene had to bring a lot of heavy clothes for his work outside, so we had three suitcases and a foot-locker full of "stuff."

C.O. Captain Ray Spicer and wife Carla, soon arrived with the first week's group of Marines, so while the men worked, Carla and I could spend time exploring. She was Italian, which made communication much easier! She had been there before, sometime before the war, and said the city and its atmosphere had changed a lot.

I must describe one of our favorite places to eat—called "The Hole in the Wall." They served <u>won</u>derful steak in a <u>won</u>derful atmosphere, complete with music! First, we had antipasti: pickled baby octopus, devilled eggs, mushrooms marinated in oil and vinegar, little anchovies, and various other items, impossible to describe on paper. Then a waiter rolled a little table over by our table and cooked the filet mignon steaks over a portable burner. Into the pan went butter, sage, pine needles, Worcestershire sauce, salt, pepper, steaks, mustard, lemon juice, and a dash of brandy. When the steaks were cooked, the waiter removed them to hot plates, and poured a spoonful of flaming brandy on top, so that they were aflame when served! There's just <u>no</u> way to describe that flavor! (We ate there often, so when the waiter said he couldn't make the recipe available, I secretly made notes of the amounts of the ingredients, and that became one of the special things Gene liked to cook.)

One day I went along for the ride when Gene had a meeting with a General whose office and home was in the Castle Miramare. We had been told that sight-seeing inside isn't possible, so I was amusing myself with a book while Gene was busy. When he came out, there was a Major with him who had been on the ship with us and asked me if I'd like a look inside! He took us through the rooms that aren't occupied, explained the portraits, original uses of the rooms, etc. It was a real treat, and a very wonderful surprise! We drove up the plateau for Gene to show me where they do their shooting, and then went over to the Yugoslavia border. We couldn't cross with a "visa," but we got information for going later.

A Liaison Officer (Captain Masterson) in Trieste introduced Gene to the "head" man at the Yugoslavia embassy (Mr. Nickovitch), and after a pleasant visit in his office he gave Gene a letter to the customs officials at the border, saying that if anyone questioned him, just say that Mr. Nickovitch had given authorization. (Masterson told Gene that "Nick" was very enthusiastic to have Americans visit Yugoslavia, and we assumed the reason was to negate some of the adverse propaganda that gets around about the Communist government.

On March 20th we drove to Postumia—about forty miles from Trieste—where there is (according to the guide) the fourth largest cave in the world—Mammoth in Kentucky, Carlsbad in New Mexico, and a cave in Austria being larger. The guide spoke eight different languages, but English wasn't one of them. He did speak Italian, so with our little bit of Italian, we were able to understand some of his explanations, which he gave to us while we walked to the next stop. We rode into the cave for quite a distance on a little rail train, then walked through several rooms and passages, and back to the train to go out. It's hard to describe a cave—they are all different, yet essentially the same. One huge room was called the "ballroom" and was lighted with several crystal chandeliers, which oddly enough, didn't look out of place at all! The delicate formations of rock and limestone seemed to just all blend right in!

We had lunch at a restaurant near the cave—looking for "local" flavor. They said they had a French cook, so it wouldn't be real Serbian flavor. Whatever it was, one meal of it was enough: dry brown bread, soup with lots of dark grease on top, meat patties, unseasoned mashed potatoes, white bean and onion salad with olive oil and vinegar and NO lettuce, and for dessert thin soggy pancakes spread with plum jam and folded over into fourths. Anyway, it was an interesting experience, and that was our goal, after all!

We must have seen the worst part of the country—rocky, barren, mountainous terrain that was just good for nothing. There were some small farms, but nothing that looked prosperous at all. We got some money changed at the first little town, then looked and searched for souvenirs to spend it, because it can't be taken out of the country! We were just flabbergasted to fine no souvenir shops! Not even at the cave! We walked up and down the main street of Postumia looking for something nice to remember it by, but there were very few window displays of any kind, and those weren't anything at all artistic. Things seemed to be of quite poor quality. We finally found a wooden bowl and a wooden vase—hand carved—that looked reasonably fair. The first time I ever remembered having money to spend and nothing to spend it for! On the way out, the money changer gave us a receipt for what we had left and said we could cash it in Naples for lire, but he couldn't return any of our "green"!

To sum it all up—it was an interesting day, but our impression was: "Go to Yugoslavia if you want to, but we'll go someplace else!"

NAPLES — RETURN FROM TRIESTE

By March 20, 1953 it was time to return to "normal" life in Naples, but we thought we just had to play some golf before we left Trieste, because it was such an unusual golf course. It wasn't the manicured grass that we'd seen back home—just really "natural" terrain. For instance, the "greens" were leveled, bare ground that was packed and sort of sandy. So, while Gene was waiting for the sergeants to get things ready for him to turn in, we went around for nine holes. It was a beautiful day—warm enough for only a sweater, and we thoroughly enjoyed it. The course was sprinkled all over with various tiny little spring flowers—little miniatures among the grass, and I had trouble sometimes deciding whether to look at my ball or the flowers! Gene shot 46 on the 35-par course. (My score was 77, but my reward was having fun and getting some exercise doing it!)

We got away from Trieste just after lunch Wednesday and stayed all night at Ferrara. After we checked in at the hotel we put the car in a garage and walked around town, partly looking for a nice place to eat, and partly just looking. The hotel restaurant seemed good, but we noticed a very spiffy looking restaurant about a half block away on the other side of the street. After we were inside, we discovered it was the same place where we'd eaten lunch one day going to Trieste! Coming in from a different direction, and at night, it looked different from the outside, and we hadn't noticed the nearby hotel on the first visit.

Thursday morning we crossed the mountains. Quite different scenery from a month ago! Where there had been snow covered hills, patterned with ski trails, there were now green hills splashed with early spring colors and blossoming fruit trees. And such wonderful air!

It was lunch time when we reached Florence, so we had some "Bistecca alla Fiorentina" (Florence steak, charcoal grilled, ultra-good) before we went looking and picture taking. That night we ate at a place called "Zi Rosa," which had a Neapolitan atmosphere, especially the music. We chatted with a very nice couple at the next table—Mr. and Mrs. Taylor, from Connecticut. He must have been in his late sixties, and really enjoying his life! Said he had studied singing in Vienna, Austria, forty years ago. Mrs. T. was a younger woman—a concert pianist. I was so amused soon after they first sat down: he bestowed a happy, loving look upon his wife, and said, "This is livin', isn't it!" The reason for my amusement—I couldn't count the times I'd heard Gene say those exact words to me, with almost the same tone of voice and expression! They and we asked the pianist (an old man with long, bushy white hair—I called him Beethoven) for some classical music. He seemed in the heights of heaven with that, so we kept extending our meal and enjoying it.

The next morning we joined an American Express tour group for visits to the Medici family chapels, the Cathedral, Giotto's Tower, Pitti Palace, and Michelangelo Piazza, from which we got a really breathtaking view of the city below and some beautiful estates above. Florence is probably the world's most famous "City of Art," but we didn't have time to go to the other art galleries. In college art classes I had been introduced to pictures of many famous paintings and outstanding architecture, so you can imagine the thrill I felt with being able to be in the presence of some of them! The Cathedral's bronze doors, by Ghiberti in the mid-1400's were especially inspiring—depicting ten scenes from the Old Testament. They were declared by Michelangelo "worthy to be the gates of Paradise," and their creation occupied twenty-seven years of Ghiberti's life. Another special piece of art to me was Michelangelo's "David," an enlarged copy of which stands in Florence's Piazza della Signoria. It was Michelangelo's first great sculpture, completed in 1503 out of a gigantic, solid block of local Carrara marble, which had been abandoned as spoiled. It is said that when it was set upon its pedestal, a chief member of the Signoria came to see it. After expressing his great admiration of the marvelous work, he remarked that the nose seemed to him too large, whereupon Michelangelo climbed a ladder, chisel in hand, and after pretending to work for a few moments, during which he let fall some of the marble dust which he had taken up in his pocket, turned with a questioning face to the critic, who responded, " Bravo! Well done! You have given it life." (I could have stayed in Florence forever—if Gene were with me!)

After lunch we headed down the Arno River to Pisa. There we shot pictures like mad before the sun got too low, then climbed to the top of the Leaning Tower. It leans even more than I had imagined from seeing photos! It was quite an unusual sensation climbing the circular stairway which goes up on the inside between the inner and outer walls! It isn't always the same degree of incline because of the slant, so sometimes it seems very hard to climb, then in a few steps, it becomes really easy! There are seven bells on top, toned up the musical scale. They are only rung on New Years'—no doubt a wonderful sound! I think it was said to be about fourteen feet out of vertical and has since been reinforced.

We drove to Leghorn, on the coast to spend the night—on the top floor of a very nice resort hotel—with a beautiful view of the sea, and the sound of the waves splashing all night long. The drive south down the coast with its many beaches was beautiful, and we were very thankful to be back to our own "foam rubber mattress," even though we enjoy "gadding about" so much!

Naples has its faults and some discomforts, but there's something about it that seems to "grow" on you—someplace around the region of your heart!

NAPLES — Joy's Visit #1

One of our most exciting experiences while living in Naples, was my sister Joy Kelley's visit! During her first year of teaching high school Home Ec in

Plattsburg, Missouri (which was also her first teaching position out of college), she made plans to travel to Naples during her summer vacation of 1953—sailing on the *SS Andrea Doria*, traveling in Europe with Gene and me, then flying home from England.

In April, we learned that Clare Booth Luce was sailing on that same ship, on the way to her office as the U.S. Ambassador to Italy! We went down to the dock the day she arrived—didn't get to see Madam Luce, but the ship was really beautiful. She was named for Signore Andrea Doria, who lived in Genoa, Italy, during the time of Columbus, was very active in maritime warfare, and became Admiral of the Genoese Fleet. The ship made her maiden voyage January 14, 1953, to New York from her homeport of Genoa. It was considered to be one of the most beautiful ocean liners ever built, with a million dollars spent on art work. There were three outdoor swimming pools (one for each class—first, cabin, and tourist), ten decks, and a crew of five-hundred-sixty-some people. When Joy arrived in mid-June, she was bubbling over with stories of her shipboard experiences—happy that her first voyage had been on such a beautiful, new ship! (Sadly, three years later, after more than one hundred crossings, the *Doria* capsized and sank on July 25, 1956, after colliding with the *MS Stockholm*. All passengers and crew—1,660 people—were rescued and survived, while forty-six died as a result of the collision.)

Our time with Joy was like a dream come true! It was so much fun showing her the things that we were finding interesting; and there were so many, and she was so appreciative, we were constantly on the go. We invited Mrs. Raiola to go with us some days. She's the elderly American lady of Swiss descent that I've mentioned before—a living, walking expert in classical literature and history. She had even done some excavating in the area when she was younger. She was about seventy years old, and so crippled, you felt like you should help her in and out of chairs, but when Joy and I were tired out from a day of sightseeing, she was still going strong. With her, we explored Pozzuoli where the Apostle Paul landed on his way to Rome, the remains of two temples to Apollo, and the remains of the first Christian church that Paul established in Italy. It was built on the foundation of the latest of the two temples to Apollo. At the Cave of the Cumaean Sibyl near Cuma, Mrs. Raiola enjoyed explaining to us the rituals practiced by the Sibyl, who was a great prophetess in the B.C. days when people were worshipping their various gods and goddesses. In the cave we saw the place where the Sibyl lived and received the priests and priestesses who were among the few allowed to see her. Then we went down into a further underground passage to a huge room where she officiated. It was very dark in the big room, except for (I think) seven holes that went up to the temple above the ground. The light coming through cast very mysterious, bluish circles of light directly under them—the "tunnels" above being long enough to direct the light rays just straight down, instead of spreading out enough of them to light the "room." When the Sibyl delivered her "oracles," she supposedly inhaled gases and smoke that came up out of the ground directly under the "hole" (the place being still partially an active volcano). This put her into a trance so that she began mumbling her "prophecies," which the priest, standing in the temple by the other end of the hole, delivered to the people waiting for her message. The message was worded in a negative way. Thus, the people lived by a conscience of fear, and kept pouring their money into the upkeep of the Sibyl and her cohorts, in return for her prophesies.

All of our friends wanted to meet Joy, so there had to be some "gatherings" of various kinds in other homes, or ours—some daytimes, and some evenings. On a day when we needed to just rest, we went with Gene to the beach for a Mediterranean swim; and then to the Officers' Club for a buffet dinner for Joy to see and hear the "Strolling Troubadours." They were two "ugly" twin brothers who played really fine music on their violin and Spanish guitar most evenings at the Club. On my birthday, Sunday, June 21st, we explored the Royal Palace at nearby Caserta, with good friends Chuck and Barbara Porter. (We had met Barbara on the ship when we went to Naples. Chuck was a Navy officer, and we frequently played bridge with them.) After strolling through the English garden, and looking at the falls and pools, we enjoyed a picnic lunch under the trees. Back at our house, we had angel food birthday cake that Barbara had made for me!

In a few days that followed, we kept busy doing day trips to Pompeii, Paestum, and Salerno, with Gene taking a couple of days off for the three of us to go to Capri. On a weekend in Rome, we showed her such sights as St. Peter's Cathedral, the Sistine Chapel in the Vatican, the Coliseum, the Forum, the Arch of Constantine, and the Appian Way with a few stretches of ancient paving (reminding us of the movie *"Quo Vadis"*). Of course, we had to put some coins in the Trevi Fountain—to assure our return to Rome someday! We dined once at Alfredo's for the fettuccine—which someone said was so delicious, it deserves to be eaten with a gold spoon." (One lady at each table gets the privilege of using a golden spoon. At our table we gave the honor to

Joy.) Of course, one needs many days to experience that beautiful, historical city, but we were thankful for the little that we had!

While in Rome, Joy and I made plans with a travel agency for a month-long tour of Europe with American Express. Gene would join us in Paris, to continue on to England, Scotland, and Ireland.

Seeing the size of Joy's small bag—no larger than many "carry-ons" now used on planes—and her method of packing, helped me with my own packing as we prepared for the bus tour we would share! For toilet articles, she had transferred the products to small plastic containers that took up minimal space and could be tucked into corners. Pantsuits for women were not yet fashionable, so we planned for only a few dresses, some made of nylon that could be hand-washed, dried overnight, and wouldn't need to be ironed. (I remember that one of Joy's "dressiest" dresses was one she made herself of dotted Swiss—navy blue, with woven-in dots of red. The bodice was fitted and sleeveless, with a low-cut neck, and gathered skirt. With movement, the raised red dots caused the fabric to have changeable, almost iridescent colors. I thought it one of the most beautiful dresses I'd ever seen—and so simple and practical!) In case of rain, we each carried a plastic poncho that folded into a small package, and a sweater for occasional cool weather; also, each brought one pair of extra shoes—dressy, but comfortable, sandals. For "everyday," we wore low-heeled walking shoes. Our cameras were small, but photos could be developed into slides. We were able to carry all of our "belongings" ourselves, so souvenirs would need to be light, and small!

The journey on the very large tour bus began on July l, in Rome. Luggage was stored in the "under-belly" area of the bus, and passengers were seated in roomy seats, with great views from the very large windows which curved into the overhead space. We soon learned our daily routine: stop at some towns for short sightseeing tours, lunch, or shopping—maybe several in one day. We had some time for ourselves when we stopped for overnight, most of the time just for one night, but sometimes for two. We were always given directions in the evening for the time and place to meet for the next day's tour, with a reminder that our luggage should be outside our hotel room door by a certain time. Before we went to breakfast!

It was wonderfully relaxing to have details taken care of, so we could just sit back and see the changing scenery—farm land, villages, bicycles, ox carts, mountains, lakes, people going about the business of their lives. Many farms in hill country and mountain foothills had crops growing on terraces—making use of every bit of tillable soil. Villages that had originally been built centuries ago were often on high ground for easier defense, leaving the low land with better soil for farming. Enemies could be seen as they approached. Orvieto was one of those interesting stops. The old town was on quite a high tufa stone hill, with cobble-stone streets, quaint buildings, battlements, and an impressive cathedral. In the middle of town was a huge, deep pit called the Well of San Patrizio. Actually a cistern, it is over 200 feet deep, with two spiral tracks so ingeniously entwined within each other that one file of donkeys can descend towards the water, while another is ascending with its load. It was considered an important "strong-hold" because of its protected water supply and mild climate.

Another stop was at the small town of Viterbo to see their Gothic fountains and medieval-style Papal Palace where Cardinals were shut in until the vote for a pope was completed. Signals of black smoke were sent up if not yet elected, white smoke when elected.

We especially enjoyed spending the first night in Assisi and imagining what life there must have been like when St. Francis lived there. The Cathedral of St. Mary of the Angels houses St. Francis' original chapel, grotto, rose garden of "thornless" roses. His tomb is in a 14th century monastery on the hill.

The second night in Perugia at the Palace Hotel was fun. After seeing sights and hearing history most of the day, we had roast pigeon for dinner. The City Hall had a relic of a lock and chain captured from Siena in the 12th century, and there was a painting by Perugino who lived in the time of Michelangelo and helped with some of the painting in the Vatican Sistine Chapel. Our special memory of Perugia, however is of its famous chocolate! We decided it was the best we had ever tasted, and even yet, we use the memory of that taste to judge our chocolate! We bought several samples of it to enjoy along the way and had a "chocolate party" for ourselves in our hotel room that night!

At Siena's cathedral we saw "graffito" floors—solid marble, carved and filled with black stucco. At that time, it was said to be the only work of its kind in the world. The Piazza del Campo was interesting and original for its shape, resembling a sea-shell. Also, that day we stopped in San Gimingnano. A small town, but some of the best-preserved medieval atmosphere, walls, and buildings. I remember being impressed by the many towers, and it is said to be one of the best-preserved art cities of Tuscany.

LOVE IS ALL THAT MATTERS

NAPLES — Joy's Visit #2

In Florence, July 3rd, 4th, and 5th, we had a wonderful rest from the road—and time to get a "feel" for this beautiful old city that is considered "Italy's Art Museum"! There was so much to see, we needed much more than three days! It's location in the region of Tuscany made even the environs interesting to see—peaceful vineyards and gardens, olive groves, tall cypress trees, and what I like to call "personality pines"—spreading into various shapes that have been guided by sun and wind. It was fun to try to imagine what life there must have been like for the many artists and powerful families who've lived there through several centuries: names like Medici, daVinci, Michelangelo, Botticelli, Dante, Pisano, and so many others.

In the numerous cathedrals, palaces, and art galleries we were able to see with our own eyes the many displays of the magnificent architecture, paintings, and sculptures we'd admired only in pictures before! We felt transported back in time to the lives of the artists who created these masterpieces and felt thankful for appreciative people who have managed to preserve so many of them.

In the Uffizi Gallery we liked Botticelli's painting called *Spring*, with the Three Graces dancing in filmy, flowing veils. Also there we liked *The Wrestlers*, *Venus di Medici*, and Rembrandt's self-portraits. Ever since Joy was a child, she has especially loved yellow finches, so she took a long look at DaVinci's *Madonna of the Goldfinch*!

At the Santa Croce cathedral we saw the tombs of Michelangelo and Dante, and a memorial to Galileo and Vespucci. There was much to see at the cathedral Santa Maria dei Fiori. First was Michelangelo's last work, *Deposition from the Cross* with Nicodemus, Mary, and Mary Magdalene; then the guide showed us the doors through which Lorenzo DiMedici escaped a plot to kill Michelangelo while he was in church. The dome, when built, was the world's largest, built with double walls, and without inside support. At that cathedral's Baptistery we saw Ghiberti's famous bronze doors—called by Michelangelo the "Gates of Paradise"—depicting stories from the Bible. Inside its dome we saw Byzantine mosaic, also using Bible story designs. The architect for the bell tower was Grotto, with the commission to prepare plans "to be built so as to exceed in magnificence, height and excellence of workmanship everything of the kind that had been achieved of old by the Greeks and Romans when at the zenith of their greatness." It is 276 feet high, using a variety of colors of marble in statues and other ornaments. In the Pitti Palace gallery, our favorite painting was Raphael's *Madonna of the Chair*. The model is thought to have been his girlfriend.

A walk across one of the bridges called "Ponte Vecchio," across the Arno River, could take as long as one wanted to be there (*vecchio* means "old"). It's an enclosed bridge, with small shops displaying every imaginable product along both sides of the interior. It is located in the old section of the city, close to major piazzas, and the Palazzo Vecchio—where the famous statue of *David* by Michelangelo, originally stood. At the gallery of the Academy of Arts, we saw the original *David*, which was moved there for conservation in 1873.

A very interesting stop on the tour of the city was at the Florentine Mosaic Factory. To see the details of this procedure of making designs of inlaid pieces of such things as colored stone, glass, or tile, gave a person a greater appreciation of the grand designs we'd been seeing in artistic architecture. Of course, I wanted some of the beautiful samples, but in order to keep my luggage manageable, I settled for a colorful, oval shaped brooch, designed with flowers and shells.

On July 4th our tour took us on a day-trip to Pisa. One of the main attractions there, of course, is the Leaning Tower, part of the Cathedral Santa Maria Maggiori begun by Pisano in 1173. It is 178 feet high and leans fourteen feet at the top. It contains seven bells tuned to scale. The heaviest bell weighs six tons, and one that was cracked by a bullet is dead. Joy and I found it quite difficult to walk up the steps to the top because of the variation of gravity due to the leaning of the tower. (Since it was the Fourth of July, we talked about what fun it would be to do fireworks from it!) In this cathedral, Galileo discovered the principle of the pendulum. The baptistery at one time was open to catch rain water for baptism. It has unusual acoustics (72 vibrations in 14 seconds), and the echo sounds like an organ. Its cemetery contains many shiploads of earth from Mt. Calvary which is near Jerusalem. (The name Calvary is simplified from the Latin "Calvaria." In the Bible, the place where Jesus was crucified is called "Golgotha".)

We were back on the bus on July 6th, enjoying scenery of pine forests and rolling hills through the northeastern part of Italy, on the way to Venice. One stop was in Ravenna, where, as in so many of the European small towns, the cathedral is like an art museum. Sometimes we were awed by the architecture and fine decorations of these sturdy structures for which the people were willing to sacrifice their labor and wealth because they felt that it was built to the glory of God! In most of them, women showed respect for the building by entering with head and/or upper arms covered. We had anticipated the need for head covering, but it was very warm, midsummer weather and most of our dresses had no sleeves. At one such place that required covered arms, we were fortunate to find some vendors of scarves near the entrance! (How convenient! Clever business people!) I bought a pale-yellow silk one, which became a favorite one to wear to keep my neck cozy for many years after it first served as my "admission" to a few "houses of God"!

In Ravenna we visited the church of Sant' Apollinare Nuovo, built in the 6th century, with walls decorated in Byzantine mosaic, using a lot of gold leaf. The poet Dante's tomb, preserving his remains, is also in Ravenna, where he died in 1321. We drove along a lovely pine grove near a canal—its beauty said to be a place of inspiration for some of Dante's poetry. Through a tiny door we entered the humble mausoleum of Galla Placidia and saw there a surprising array of very colorful mosaics, called the oldest mosaics in the world. The colors were vibrant blues, green, gold, eggplant, red, silver, and orange—arranged on walls and domed ceilings—showing figures of Christ, apostles, sheep, doves, deer, and stars. Galla Placida was a sister of one of Rome's emperors, and thought to be one of history's most powerful women. She died in A.D. 450.

Next came two exciting days in the magical city of Venice! It was founded in the fifth century as a place of refuge during the invasions of Italy by the Huns, and by the seventh century became a great maritime republic. As one glides along the Grand Canal, it's hard to imagine the labor involved in building the many grand palaces—many made of marble—the bridges, cathedrals, hotels, and shops supported by piles driven into the earth of the city's many small islands—all those centuries ago! It would take a book to describe the beauty of the architecture and the acres of art work, so if you're interested in that, you'll have to research it for yourself! I'll mainly tell a bit about our impressions, and of the "atmosphere" we felt.

Except for the occasional motors of the boats I'll call "water buses," the sounds were surprising—people talking, occasional music, pigeons doing their cooing, and flying with "whispering wings" here and there. The graceful gondolas and other rowboats gave a feeling of quiet leisure—no hurry to get to "the other side of town"! There were, of course, many pedestrians—shoppers carrying various kinds of cloth shopping bags; people in the piazzas slowly strolling, resting on a bench, or throwing food to the busy pigeons; children laughing, playing, and enjoying the sunshine. We wouldn't think of being in

Venice without taking time for a gondola ride along several of the canals, enjoying the opportunity to see some of the palaces up close, to see occasional laundry hung from windows, and to be down near the surface of the water while we listened to the gondolier tell about the sights—or sing some Italian songs. We were told there are about four hundred bridges spanning canals for pedestrians to be able to cross without the help of a boat. The Rialto Bridge across the Grand Canal in the area that is called the "old town," is one of the oldest ones.

We had a guided tour to see some of the more famous places. The Piazza San Marco, surrounded by the Byzantine-style cathedral of St. Mark, belfry, and the clock tower was a special place. Four bronze horses at the entrance were brought from Constantinople in 1204. (Constantine had had them brought to his capitol from the Acropolis in Greece.) Inside, the altar piece is studded with precious- and semi-precious stones, and many Byzantine mosaics decorate the walls and arched ceilings. The clock tower, erected in 1496-99, has a dial of blue and gold adorned with the signs of the zodiac. On a platform on the top are two giant bronze figures of men holding large hammers which strike the hours on the bell. It's called "Bell of the Moors," and the figures are Moorish slaves. The Doges' Palace was the ancient seat of justice and the home of the current Duke. On one of its walls we saw Titian's painting of *The Last Judgment*, said to be the world's largest canvas. Many prison cells are located in its basement. The palace is connected to the criminal courts building by the Bridge of Sighs, arching over the canal below at about the third-floor level. Its interior is built with a double passage. Criminals, when taken out of the prisons to suffer death, were led across this bridge to hear their sentences, and then to their execution. Byron slept in one of the prison cells for poetical inspiration. Our tour took us to see some of the prison cells—dark, damp, and cold.

Another day we went with a tour group to see the masterful glass blowing on the island of Murano; and to Burano to see their famous lace being made by hand.

Automobiles, buses, and trains have their parking places outside of the city, of course, so on July 9th, we packed ourselves onto one of the "water bus" boats to get back to our bus. The first stop that day was in Vicenza, after scenic driving through some hills and mountains. More churches, towers, and paintings. One significant sight there was an Olympic theatre—said to be the first roofed theatre in the world. It was built in 1580 of wood and plaster, with a stage that represents a town. The perspective of that work of art was very realistic.

Lunch that day was in Verona—in Juliet's "summer home," in sight of Romeo's villa. Juliet's tomb is in the monastery where she and Romeo were secretly married, and, of course, our tour guide took us to see Juliet's balcony, where we could imagine her delight when Romeo came to speak his words of love to her from the ground below!

NAPLES — Joy's Visit #3

July 10 was our final day in Italy. Being on the tour bus for ten days, in a foreign country, with fifty or so people we'd never met before, was a totally new experience for both Joy and me! It was good that we shared many likes and dislikes, were open-minded, and felt deeply rewarded for the opportunity to see with our own eyes some places we'd only studied in history. Sense of humor was helpful, too! As we became acquainted with other people on the tour—from different countries, of various economic levels and interests, it was as if that group of people was almost like family. But I have to admit, we had our own secret, humorous ways of sort of "analyzing" some of them! There were two sort of "feisty" sisters from Texas—older than we, and obviously from an upper-class kind of life—who we found quite interesting. Nothing "casual" about them! Every day they were "dressed to the nines," bedecked with apparently expensive jewelry; and frequently were describing to persons sitting near them on the bus, the "ritzy" hotels where they had stayed and personalities of important people they had met. They described how they shipped their furs and other clothing ahead of their arrival in other cities and countries; making it sound like being on our tour bus was an adventure in a life-style quite beneath their level of usual life. Well—duh! Of course, anyone traveling for extended lengths of time, or going from one climate to another, might find it convenient to ship clothing ahead. But, to Joy and me, the amusing thing about all that, was why they felt a need to "broadcast" such personal information to all the rest of us! The two of us were just happy we didn't have all those furs and jewelry to worry about!

Milan was our last stop in Italy. It is considered to be the principal financial center of Italy, and one of the richest manufacturing and commercial cities in the country. As we drove through the countryside in that area, we saw distant snow-capped mountains, sparkling lakes, and agriculture supported by fertile soil. There were small towns and modern industries alongside ancient buildings, medieval piazzas, colorful homes, and specialized crafts. For instance, the town of Cremona was noted for crafting fine violins as long ago as the 17th century, and many of them are preserved in a museum.

In the center of Milan, we visited the famous cathedral—beautiful Gothic style that took several centuries to build, with labor and contributions of patrons giving generously as a tribute to God. Begun in 1386, it was completed in 1897 and is said to be one of the largest and most magnificent churches in the world. To me, with its unusual vertical design and many soaring spires, it gives one an "uplifting" feeling! And the hundreds of delicate carvings into the light-colored marble give an apparent "lightness" to the massive structure. Milan suffered much damage in World War II, but the cathedral miraculously survived intact. Its interior is awesome! Towering carved columns that hold up the marble roof are connected with stately, gothic arches; and beautiful, dim light streams through the many colorful stained-glass windows. Extravagant carvings on the slim exterior wall sections seem to continue on above the edge of the roof, to form the many delicate looking spires—the central tallest one topped with a statue of the Virgin Mary. It's just impossible to describe its awesome beauty with mere words!

We also explored the La Scala Opera House, one of Europe's most famous and the largest opera house in Italy. It was externally unimpressive but is known for its magnificent interior arrangements for operatic art, and capability of seating 3600 spectators. We liked to imagine being there to enjoy an opera or a ballet, watching famous singers and dancers, dressed in colorful flowing robes, or in dramatic costumes, floating lightly and rhythmically, seeming to barely touch the floor upon delicate tip-toes.

In the 1400's Milan was the home of Leonardo da Vinci, who painted the beautiful *Last Supper* mural between 1495 and 1498 in the Church of Santa Maria della Grazie. It represents the dramatic moment when Jesus announced his approaching betrayal with the words, "One of you shall betray me." (*Matthew 26:21*) The painting's composition—groupings of the thirteen figures, colors of their clothing, and the expressions of their bodies and their faces— tells of their passionate feelings and surprise. One can almost "hear" their questions—"Who can it be!" "Lord, is it I?" It was painted directly upon the wall in tempera with egg-white base, and much pigment has crumbled away with attempts to restore it. The church was mostly destroyed in war, except for the wall with the painting which so well defines the artistic depth and creativity of da Vinci.

LOVE IS ALL THAT MATTERS

The next day we entered Switzerland by way of the St. Bernard Pass. We were told that the elevation there is 8,000 feet, but it is closed from October to June. (Remember, I'm writing this in 2008, over fifty years later.) It was used in Roman times, around 57 B.C., and a road was built in A.D. 69. Since around the 12th century there has been a hospice there, founded by St. Bernard of Menthon, and maintained by a monastery to aid lost travelers, using St. Bernard dogs. Photos of them show them with a small container of brandy being carried on the underside of their collar. In 218 B.C, on his way from Spain to conquer Rome, Hannibal crossed here, leading his army of 40,000, with cavalry and a number of elephants carrying baggage later used in battle.

On July 12th we began our sightseeing around Lake Geneva. First stop was at the Castle of Chillon, built in the 9th century upon a huge rock at the edge of the lake. Lord Byron's and the poet Shelly's autographs are on a wall in the prison hall. It was there that Byron began the poem *Prisoner of Chillon*, about a prisoner who was chained to a post for six years. Inside were many colorful vaulted ceilings, Savoy decorations, 15th century furniture, pewter, arms of many kinds and periods, a gun decorated with inlaid ivory and pearl, and a reliquary found in the chapel, dating to the time of Charlemagne.

The next day was spent in Geneva. There were very many historical buildings and churches to see, as well as beautiful shops filled with lovely, costly jewelry. Many famous clock and watch shops. John Knox and John Calvin preached there; and the Red Cross was officially begun in 1864. After World War I Geneva, with its tradition of independence and Swiss neutrality, was chosen as the seat of the League of Nations. Even though the organization wasn't able to prevent future wars, at least it was a start. We were impressed by the building itself—especially the paintings in the Council Room to represent Work, Health, and Cooperation. The skylight in the Assembly Hall provides always uniform light, which changes gradually from day to night. One of the views from our hotel in Geneva included Mt. Dents du Midi, named for its shape that someone thought looked like "middle teeth."

There is absolutely <u>nothing</u> that can compare to one's first sight of the <u>grandeur</u> of the Swiss Alps! Majestic, snow-covered peaks as far as one's eyes can see—streamlets to white-water rivers flowing down mountain sides covered with green meadows and colorful wild flowers! Farther down, shepherds were tending sheep, goats, or cows brought to high meadows to graze. Some of them had rustic cabins in the area for shelter and making cheese; and with long, alpine horns they could "say good-night or good-morning" to families below.

On July 14th, on the way to Lucerne, we changed trains in Interlaken—a small "touristy" town of about 5,000 situated between two lakes; hence, its name. With some time to spare between trains, we picked up some "goodies" (bread, cheeses, and fruits) at a deli, and walked to a nearby park to eat a picnic lunch while we enjoyed a great view of the snow-covered 13,000-ft Jungfrau, and watched men cutting hay in a small field close by. (No resource wasted!)

Then, on to Lucerne, where we stayed at the Hotel Montana. On guided tours for the next couple of days we felt like we were in a mountain wonderland—the freshest air imaginable; vast scenes of rugged peaks and deep, green valleys; and happy, energetic people seeming to really appreciate the joy of freedom! Lucerne had its beginnings around A.D. 750 with a monastery on the bank of the Reuss River where it flows out from Lake Lucerne. The river is still crossed by two old wooden bridges, built in the 14th and 15th centuries. They're adorned by many paintings illustrating the history of Switzerland and the town, one of the famous ones being called *The Dance of Death*. An important building is the twin-towered Hofkirche, which contains a 17th century organ, and originally formed part of a Benedictine monastery. The 16th century town hall now houses a regional museum, and we saw The Lion monument—the form of a dying lion, hewn out of the living sandstone, and designed by Thorwaldsen. It was dedicated in 1821 to the officers and men of the Swiss Guard who were slain while defending the Tuileries in Paris in 1792.

Switzerland long ago declared neutrality and maintains a strictly defensive army of one million men. Planes are jet planes, but no bombers. Our guide joked that the 'Swiss Navy" consists of the pleasure boats and commercial boats used on their lakes. Men keep their own weapons at home and can be mobilized in forty-eight hours. The top General is elected by the government. Universal military training for all men begins at age twenty, with four months the first year, three weeks per year until age forty-eight, and then they attend inspections until age sixty. Population is a mixture of Swiss, German, French, and Italian. The government is a seven-member executive body—one member is president for one year, with no power—and a two-house congress. Many communities vote for each law. Along roads, emergency phones are located at intervals—no numbers, no charge. Help comes from nearest point. We had two breath-taking trips up mountain sides! At Engleberg, we went up 6000 feet on Mt. Truebsee by cog train and cable car to a beautiful, blue lake. In Grindelwald Valley we traveled by chair lift to 8000 ft. for a glorious view of Jungfrau and glaciers. We thought about how much fun skiers must have when the pure, fresh snow covers slopes of many different heights and shapes! At Trammelbach Falls, we took an elevator 300 feet up through an underground gorge to see the top of the Falls.

In town, one of our dinners was at the Stadtkeller (which means "beer cellar"). There was wonderful "fondue" to dip, plus yodeling music, and dancers wearing native costumes. It was a real delight to see homes as our tour bus drove through the city and villages—cottages with colorful gardens and flower-filled window-boxes, small shops, many "cheese houses." The city was, of course, surrounded by many small, colorful villages where peasants retained many traditional customs. One of those villages, called Weggis, dates back to 1380. We were reminded of a lovely little folk song we'd learned some years ago:

From Lucerne to Weggis fair, Hol de ri de ah, Hol de ri ah;

Shoes and stockings we need not wear, Hol de ri de ah, Hol de ah!

Hol de ri de ah, Hol de ri de ah, Hol de ri ah! Hol de ri de ah, Hol de ri di ah, Hol de ah!

NAPLES — Joy's Visit #4

On July 17th we were back on the train on the way to Vienna, Austria—a thirteen-hour trip, with great scenery all the way—more mountains and clear, bubbling streams; small harvest fields with whole families cutting, stacking, and carrying hay—just like a story book! Some cities along the way were Zurich, Salzburg, and Linz—in the Russian zone much of the way, but we didn't see much difference.

After World War II, Vienna was divided into four zones—American, British, Russian, and French. It was quite an unusual sight to see all four flags flying on the same building. A police Jeep often had an M.P. from each army in it.

On Saturday we toured the city, seeing and hearing about architecture and history. Especially interesting was seeing the homes of Schubert, Beethoven, and Strauss; and monuments to Mozart, Hayden, and Beethoven. Did the people who lived there in those times appreciate how fortunate they were to have those great composers living among them and playing the music that we now consider to be immortal?

No one could be in Vienna without experiencing the Vienna Woods!—peaceful and natural, growing almost every tree imaginable. No wonder Johann Strauss was inspired to compose the beautiful *Tales from the Vienna Woods!* But

I wonder what <u>tales</u> he had in his mind! We also saw the Danube River, but it had turned quite green since Strauss described it in the *Blue Danube Waltz!* Still, it was a real inspiration just to <u>be</u> there!

The Imperial Palace, lavishly decorated, was quite impressive, and contained the crypt where many of the Imperial family members are buried. The city had been bombed quite heavily during World War II, and many buildings were still in ruins—many others had scars. We enjoyed the veal chops we had for lunch, as well as the Vienna sausage for dinner—much like our "wieners."

On Sunday, we were on the train again—on our way to Amsterdam. We had a three-hour layover in Munich, so we hired a taxi to drive us through the city and explain some of the things we were seeing. It must have been very beautiful at one time, but it was somewhat distressing to see large marble museums and domes, residence buildings, and government buildings so torn to pieces by bombs. There was much new construction, so it will no doubt "rise from its ashes." During the night we passed through Cologne—also with many wartime ruins. Amazingly, however, the cathedral was standing almost unharmed!

In Holland there were many wonderful, interesting things to see—like a story-book, again. Canals and dikes; fields of flowers, vegetables, and Holstein cattle; an airport—the only one in the world located twenty-five feet below sea level. Our guide explained how they reclaim land from the sea, and how the canals and dikes work. It is probably the only place in the world where birds fly below sea level, and fish swim above land level! (How fortunate we should feel for our spacious land!) It was also intriguing to see six thoroughfares running side by side: a side-walk for pedestrians; a narrow pavement for bicycles; a highway for cars; a canal for boats, a rail for street cars; and a railroad for trains.

We really enjoyed time at the Amsterdam flower market—the largest in the world! The market house covers 12,000 square meters, and it was practically filled with three-tiered tables, each heaped with cut flowers and potted plants. The cut flowers were carnations, roses, mums, dahlias, gladiola, and zinnias, to name a few. Potted plants had twenty or thirty huge blooms per plant. We watched the auction for a while—very interesting, with buyers from New York, England, Canada, South America, and almost every European country.

All of Amsterdam is built on piles. We saw several windmills, but they are not being built anymore. The last one was constructed about a hundred years ago, and they're used for water pumping, grinding flour, and sawing wood. The steady stream of unemployed people in Holland are put to work reclaiming the land, building parks and roads, and such—with pay of about sixteen dollars per week.

We had lunch in The Hague, in a seaside resort area, then visited the Hall of Knights (now the Parliament building) and the once Royal Palace. Most interesting, however, was the Peace Palace where the World Court presided—a beautiful building, built largely with Andrew Carnegie's $1,500,000, with furnishings given by members of the court. The U.S. gave light oak for the wood paneling in many of the major rooms; Brazil gave rose-wood for one room; Japan gave some beautiful tapestries; China, a large vase; the Netherlands gave the rugs and lamp fixtures; France, paintings and tapestries—one of which is incomplete because the artist was killed in the war; the marble floors are from Italy; iron gates from Germany, bronze statue of the *Christ of the Andes* from Argentina; stained glass from England; and a green jasper vase weighing five tons from Russia.

We returned to Amsterdam via the old town of Haarlem. Holland was a delightful place. We saw housing areas with freshly scrubbed walls and green, blooming gardens—one of the tidiest and cleanest places one can imagine. The people seemed happy, content to work for a living—efficient, but unhurried, and riding bicycles everywhere they went. There was one car for every eighteen families, and two bicycles per family, swarming the streets at busy hours. On bicycles were big, little, old, and young; dignified old ladies to very small children; mothers double-riding their children behind them; lovers holding hands as they rode—really quite a sight!

We went to the Tower of Tears where the wives used to watch their husbands sail away to sea—and from which Henry Hudson sailed on the expedition to find the Hudson River. At the National Art Gallery, we saw many lovely famous paintings; and a grand collection of Rembrandts, which we liked most of all. His *Night Watch* was especially interesting—with so many different types of people, and special use of light.

But during World War II there was much suffering. The old Jewish section was almost desolate—the Germans having taken all the Jews away during the war, imprisoning them for a while in a large theater building. There, they were not fed or given a place to sleep, so many of them died. Homes were torn down in order to get wood for fuel and building material for military needs.

Schools were closed for five years, with the buildings being used for German barracks, spy schools, etc. Dairy cattle worth $300 a head were slaughtered for food for the German army, and the dairy herds decreased from five million to about one-and-a-half million. And, of course, the peace-loving Dutch men were forced to fight and die in the German Army. However, by the time we were there, the two countries were getting along—the Dutch even furnishing some electricity for the Germans.

In Volendam we had a delicious, typical Dutch meal served by waitresses in lace caps, aprons, and long dresses—appetizers of tiny shrimp, tomato, cucumber, potato salad, boiled egg and lettuce—then vegetable soup, salad, pork chops, sautéed new potatoes, four vegetables, and grease-gravy with banana for dessert. Breads were delicious—black bread, gingerbread, Holland Rusk, different kinds of rolls, and sliced white bread. While in Holland, our breakfasts often were of a variety of breads, with cheeses, ham or salami, jam, butter, and chocolate.

Holland of course is famous for its Edam cheese, and we visited a small cheese factory to see how it is made—with whole milk and rennet, molded, and pressed—the process taking three weeks. And what of the cows? They are kept in the same building, in small stalls for five months during the winter without any exercise. The stalls were very clean and painted white. They even had a wire hook to hold their tails up when they lie down, so that they don't become soiled! A trough is provided for manure and kept constantly cleaned. Built into the wall, in the same room with the cows, were beds for the hired help. In the front of the building, the farmer's family lived. The hay loft was in the center of the building. From the outside, no one would suspect it was a barn, for it looked like a large dwelling.

On the Isle of Marken—near the mainland in the Zuider Zee—we felt like we were in the old Holland that we'd read about as children. It was practically a civilization of its own. The people were very conservative, wore long dresses, wooden shoes, long hair, and the "winged" caps. We were told that they mix very little with other communities, so that about thirty percent of the inhabitants there have the same name. The tour took us to a supposedly typical home—very small, and the main room had painted plates all over the walls, with a bed built into the wall. There was a small electric stove in the kitchen and a little gas burner to keep the tea pot hot. The sink was small but had running water. The clothes were folded and put into shelves and drawers. The lady of the house had a large stack of black aprons, worn because of her husband's death in the war. People hoped that by about 1985, a draining project would give them about 400,000 more acres of land.

For supper we found a small native café—really more of a sandwich shop and had ham and eggs on toast with a tomato and lettuce salad. Coffee was good, too. And before going to bed we had some real Dutch apple pie and ice cream!

On our last day there we did a lot of walking—to the Municipal Museum to see some Van Gogh paintings, to the house where Rembrandt spent his most successful years, and out to the harbor to watch the sea activity. One's imagination could wander indefinitely there—thinking about the lives of the fishing boat people; from where the merchant ships had come, and where they would go next; and watch the gulls and other sea-birds sailing and dipping for their dinners while the sun was dropping lower into the western sky.

On Friday, July 24th we went by train from Amsterdam to Brussels, in Belgium. It was just a nice, scenic trip through Rotterdam, Antwerp, and many small towns, except when a stray cow strolled in front of the train and was made into immediate hamburger. That was somewhat of a tragedy there, as the war and recent floods had depleted the stock, and a cow was worth between $300 and $400.

We had two days in Belgium. A guided tour Saturday morning took us to the main square in Brussels, the Grand Place—surrounded by guild houses, King's house, and the fabulous town hall. Brussels means "Home in the Marsh," which might account for the description we were given of the foundation of the town hall—built upon ox skins and sand. The skins were specially treated to be waterproof, filled with sand, and located eight meters deep under the foundation. The very large square provides a gathering place for ceremonies and festivals, and for open-air markets of every kind: birds, flowers, antiques, fresh produce, cheeses, hams, chickens, rabbits, seafoods, etc, etc. In that short tour we saw very little of the splendor of that great city of more than a million people that was founded as a fortress by a grandson of Charlemagne in the 10th Century. Now it is the home of NATO, of the EU (European Union), and of many other large international offices. The Palace of Justice is said to be the largest of its kind in the world, and the architecture of the parliament buildings, other palaces and the many churches and cathedrals was most impressive.

One piece of statuary that tour guides like to show has become a sort of famous symbol of the city. It's called *Manneken Pis*—a bronze fountain showing a small boy, urinating. It is said that in the 14th century when the city was under siege, attackers were planning to place explosives at the city wall. A little boy named Little Julian, from Brussels, happened to be spying on them as they were preparing. He urinated on the burning fuse, and thus saved the city!

We especially enjoyed a visit to one of the many lace factories. Girls and women of all ages were working diligently (and seemingly happily), holding pillows into which many straight pins were sticking straight up. With deft fingers they patiently moved tiny threads around them, forming the delicate designs of flowers, leaves, shells, scrolls, and such. The finished products were quite expensive, but we just had to splurge on a couple of small ones!

In the afternoon we drove through some beautiful parks and forests of tall, straight beech trees which were inspiring, and came to the famous battlefield of Waterloo. There we had tea and visited the panoramic painting of the battle while listening to a description of how Napoleon was defeated. In the middle of the two-and-a-half-mile field was an artificial hill built by the wives of the war dead in memory of the fallen husbands. A bronze lion was standing on top of it. Forty-three thousand lives were sacrificed in that one battle.

On Sunday, our tour went to Ghent and Bruges—more cathedrals, intricate medieval architecture, historical museums, beautiful small-farm scenery, and busy shopping plazas. One of the attractions in Ghent was the Gravensteen Castle—a formidable fortress, built around A.D. 1180. It later housed the Education Administration, some guild halls, and other offices. Guild halls were very prominent examples of architecture, especially in Belgium—and Ghent was for centuries one of northern Europe's largest and richest cities. In medieval times a guild was a union of men in the same craft or trade, to uphold standards and protect the members.

Bruges was once a busy seaport, but silt eventually filled in some of the area and ocean ships later were able to reach its harbor by way of a river and canal. Inside one of the cathedrals we visited the crypt where there were several wooden statues of Christ's crucifixion, and a place where one could buy small candles in the shape of various body parts. By burning the candle in a certain place and smelling the fumes, one was supposed to be healed in the part of his body which the candle represents. A woman in a wheel chair, without her legs, was coming from the crypt when we left.

At St. John's Hospital, erected in the 12th century and still in use, we visited an interesting chemistry room. They were still using some of the original equipment—wooden cabinets, and a bronze mortar and pestle. Many pottery jars and test tubes and old scales were not in use.

Other stops were at a convent on the bank of the beautiful Lake of Love; another lace factory; and a place where a family had a very unusual technique of painting with colored sand—quite effective and beautiful.

On Monday, July 28th we took a train from Brussels to Paris, where Gene would be meeting us—to celebrate Gene and Ila's fifth wedding anniversary, and to go on with us to the British Isles.

London was our first stop there. From our home in Naples, Gene had ordered a new 1953 MG which was going to be ready for us to pick up in London. (I called it "the sexiest car I had ever seen"— cream colored with a black canvas convertible top, and red leather interior and seats! The photo isn't  "our" car—only the same body! You have to imagine the red seats, black top, and white sidewall tires!) Picking it up was our first activity, followed by figuring out how to fit the three of us (and our luggage) into it—not luxuriously comfortable, but possible! From there, to Scotland, to Ireland (by boat), and back to more sightseeing in England. It was time for us to part company with Joy—she to board a plane to fly home to Missouri, and we to drive back to Naples. Truly, a "visit of a lifetime" for the three of us!

MARINE CORPS SCHOOLS, QUANTICO, VIRGINIA
October 1954 — December 1955

On September 3, 1954, we left Naples by plane, and I'm not sure where we landed in the U.S.—probably in New York or New Jersey. Our 1953 MG had been shipped ahead, so it was waiting for us in New York.

What an interesting drive it was—Labor Day weekend—as we traveled from New York to the Kelley home in Columbia, Missouri! Sometimes it was kind of scary—being on the Pennsylvania Turnpike in that tiny car among the large, speeding, American cars, and huge trucks! Having been out of the country since January of 1952, there were three years of new American models that we hadn't even seen before. We made a "game" out of trying to guess the make of approaching new cars that we didn't recognize! That experience of having so little luggage space, and feeling our vulnerability in case of an accident, convinced us that—as much as we loved our beautiful little "toy" car—it wasn't a practical one in the U.S.; and there was no way we could afford two cars at that time! So, we sadly traded it in on a new blue Buick sedan with a white top. It was one of the smaller models called "Special."—I remember that it had three holes along the side of hood. (The larger Buick had four holes.)

On October 8th Gene began his new assignment: Executive Officer (XO) of "A" Company, Schools Demonstration Troops (SDT), Marine Corps Schools (MCS), at Quantico, Virginia. This was Gene's second assignment at Quantico and he was now a Captain. We rented a two-bedroom house in a new development called Melrose Gardens at the north edge of the base; thankful to be near Gene's work, as well as to the many base activities.

One of Gene's lieutenants, Lou Delaine, was a neighbor who lived about four houses away with his Norwegian wife Wenke, and four-year-old son. They were great fun—all three of them. Son was allowed to play alone in his own back yard, and to come on over to our house, as long as he didn't go on the street. I liked to play with him and listen to his stories—and I had permission to offer him a cookie. He came to my house frequently and called me "Tanta" Ila—I don't know whether he really liked me, or if my cookies were the attraction! Wenke and I frequently enjoyed an afternoon "tea time," sometimes at my house, but more often at hers. She had met Lou when he was assigned to guard duty at the U.S. Embassy in Oslo, where she also worked. Her stories of her life in Norway always interested me.

Other good friends were the Swaynes and the Hoffs. Bob Swayne was another one of Gene's lieutenants. His family—wife Evelyn, sons Mike and Tim, and daughter Barbara, lived in quarters on the base. Bob became one of Gene's favorite officers—very energetic, bright, and deeply devoted to the Marine Corps. Each one of them had a great sense of humor and had a lot of fun exchanging witticisms! Evelyn was a dedicated wife, mother, and homemaker—quietly and gently "keeping the home fires" for her family, teaching and disciplining children while they felt loved and nurtured.

For some reason I seemed to be especially attracted to "foreign" Marine Corps wives. There was Carla Spicer, an Italian in Naples; Norwegian Wenke at Quantico; and another one at Quantico was Athena, Greek wife of Major Frank Hoff. I don't remember how we met the Hoff's—most likely through a duty connection between Gene and Frank. They lived on the base, but within walking distance of our place. Athena and I frequently met each other halfway, went to one house or the other, then walked together half-way when one of us went back home. They later adopted two children—Francis and Kathryn. Athena always went back to Athens once a year to visit her family; and after Frank retired they often spent time at some Greek island resort with grandchildren as their guests.

One of Gene's main duties while stationed at Quantico was Honor Guard Commander for visiting dignitaries. One of his "loves" was watching, or participating in, a parade with every Marine immaculately dressed in appropriate uniform—shoes shined to a mirror finish, creases as sharp as knife blades in pants and shirts, hair cuts exactly to regulation length, the Marines marching in perfect step, and rifles being handled in perfect unison! Visitors to the base were often high-ranking officers or civilians from the D.C. area, as well as from other countries. For instance, one of the honor guards that he commanded was for Vice President Nixon, and one was for Lt. Gen. Henry Wells, Chief of Staff of the Australian Army. I've heard Gene talk about learning the military protocol of foreign visitors in order to adjust his own technique of leading them through the "inspection of troops" that was a custom in the honors reviews. French officers included a sort of "cheek to cheek" movement (otherwise known as "air kiss") along with their salute, which he felt seemed rather awkward.

In February of 1955 he became the CO (Commanding Officer) of the company in an unusual turn of events. For some reason that I don't remember, the former CO was reprimanded, and Gene was given the command of the company. There was evidently some question then about an assignment for the demoted person, and Gene suggested that he become Gene's "Exec." A colonel friend advised Gene that he was asking for trouble, but Gene insisted that he would like to try. They had never been devoted friends, so their relationship was able to continue satisfactorily, on a strictly business basis.

Besides the honor guards, "A" Company also provided troops for assisting in the training of new officers that were attending the Basic Schools. The SDT troops acted as the "enemy" for the students that were learning battle techniques, while at the same time keeping their own readiness "honed" for combat duty, should it arise. Occasionally there was a demonstration of some military procedures given for the information of government officials and other interested persons, including dependents. I was invited to be a spectator once when Gene was in Basic School. From bleachers in a large field near the bank of a small lake, our group watched what was called a "typical landing" (1951-style) of a group of Marines—maybe a platoon or a company. First, we heard explosions simulating protective Navy gun-fire, "softening up" the beach, and saw fighter planes flying low over the beach. Marines with rifles began wading ashore from landing craft, some finding places to take cover, and others advancing on towards "enemy" engagement. The "show" was really educational for me—seeing and hearing the cooperation of air and sea maneuvers to provide some cover for the riflemen wading ashore—helped me realize the protection for riflemen in the cooperation of other services.

For a short time while we lived at Quantico, I worked as secretary to the Law Specialist (it was a Civil Service assignment). At that time the Marine Corps didn't offer specific training for law officers, so the Navy supplied these needs, as they also supplied doctors, corpsmen, and chaplains. My boss was a Lieutenant Commander, who managed the various kinds of courts and wrote up the descriptions of the courts' proceedings. There were many, many, <u>many</u> trials for AWOL's. It seemed strange to me that some of the young Marines never seemed to learn the problems they could face by being absent without leave! Marine officers sometimes acted as "defense lawyers" or the "prosecutors" in a court martial, so they often came into the office of the Law Specialist to discuss matters of law with him—at times both defense and prosecuting officers were discussing cases together with him. It was important for them to be sure that the Marines in court were getting a fair trial.

In December we left Quantico. Gene had orders to the 3rd Marine Division that was based in Japan—a Fleet Marine assignment where dependents weren't allowed to go. We stored our household belongings, and I moved—with my piano and steamer trunk—to live with my Mom and Dad in Columbia, Missouri, for the year Gene would be gone.

I — IN MISSOURI; GENE — IN JAPAN

In the spring of 1956, Gene received orders to go to Japan with the Fleet Marine Force for a year, and it seemed to be an opportunity for me to spend some time with my parents in Columbia, Missouri. Mom and Dad insisted that I move back into my old room instead of finding an apartment, and they even permitted me to bring my piano for continuing with lessons I'd started in high school and continued in Naples, where I had bought the piano.

Mom and Dad both worked, so my week days were free to do as I pleased. We planned a way to share housework—I cleaned high places so Mom wouldn't have to climb on the step stool, she cooked breakfast, I cooked dinner, and Dad packed up his own lunch. Dad was a very enthusiastic person—got up at 5:30 a.m. to give himself time to read and do some writing, so by breakfast time he was wide awake and well into his day. I'm not what you'd call "a morning person," so I didn't feel up to carrying on much of a conversation at the breakfast table. Poor Dad tried his best to "charge my battery," evidently thinking that some of his own exuberance would surely rub off on me, but to no avail. I finally decided I should just explain my feelings— hoping I wouldn't hurt his. I said, "Dad, I'm really sorry I'm such poor company at breakfast. I guess it just takes awhile to "wake up", but I'll try to do better." After that, we seemed to reach a "happy medium."

I had expected that I might soon be able to go to Japan on my own to spend some time with Gene. I knew that wives were discouraged from going, so I wouldn't expect to have housing furnished or my transportation paid. But after all, I was "free, white and 21"—I thought it would be simple for me to get a passport and stay in an apartment in town; maybe even get a job at a nearby Army base. Gene talked to his Commanding Officer about it and discovered that doing that would be highly unadvisable. I could understand the military point of view, but it <u>was</u> disappointing to feel that I couldn't exercise what was "my freedom." The reason for the rule, of course, was that the Marines were there to be ready to defend the Persian Gulf or Suez Canal, or whatever trouble might arise. They would need to be able to move upon very short notice and having dependents in the area who might need attention would slow the process. Also, if war should happen, American citizens might have problems in a foreign country. As I learned more about military life, I realized that I had my own kind of commitment to the Marine Corps, and part of my job was to be support for Gene. My life wasn't <u>entirely</u> my own.

I missed Gene, of course, but I had no trouble keeping busy. I worked half-time at the Baptist church office as financial secretary, and as assistant to the executive secretary. It was the church we'd attended as students, and where we were married, so I knew many of the people already. Once a week I had a piano lesson and a voice lesson, so I used some time practicing those things at home. I'd hoped that with some training I could enjoy, even more, singing in the church choir. My instructor was a professor at Stephens College who also worked with college students at our church—a <u>very</u> patient, talented, "fun" person. After a few months of lessons, he asked me one day, "Ila, have you ever shouted or yelled?" I thought a minute and said, "You know, I probably never have, now that I think about it! Why?" He gently told me that I probably shouldn't aspire to be a concert singer—that my vocal chords had never matured. I have a little girl's voice, but he didn't "kick me out." He still let me try and helped me learn to "lift my palate" and "tighten my diaphragm." I think one of the values to me was that those exercises also "lifted my spirits." Singing can do a lot to chase away "blues"!

One really valuable activity that was a lot of fun, was frequently "baby sitting" for my sister Barbara's family who lived in Columbia. Their daughter Debbie was four years old, and their son Randy was one. Playing with those lively kids and enjoying watching them grow helped to satisfy my longing for children of my own. And, of course, gave us a lasting "bond."

In those days, anyone who had traveled out of the country, and brought back photo slides, were candidates for group "programs." One of those invitations came from my church circle. We'd lived in Naples for two-and-a-half years, and had visited several countries on short trips, so I had quite a varied selection of slides. For that group I tried to associate some of the historical pictures with biblical history—such as a town near Naples—Pozzuoli—that is mentioned in the Bible as the port where the apostle Paul landed in Italy on his way to Rome. Other sites in Rome were the Vatican, the Coliseum where Christians were imprisoned and tortured. There were many examples of artistic, scenic, and historical interest in Florence, Venice, Switzerland, and other European countries. I liked doing that because it gave me an opportunity to "relive" the many happy, exciting hours of exploring those new places, "soaking up" some unfamiliar cultures, learning history, and understanding better how other people lived.

Another invitation to show slides came from my sister-in-law, Chadna, who thought it would make a good program for her Extension Club that would be meeting at her home in Salisbury—a few miles north of Columbia. I loved to play with their children, and this would be a good "outing" for me. My brother, Ross, worked in Columbia, so I could ride to Salisbury with him the evening before the ladies' club meeting and back to Columbia with him the next morning. For this group I chose slides to emphasize home and family life, farms, history—Pompeii, Rome, Florence, Venice, Naples, and interesting little medieval towns built on the tops of high hills with farms and fields below. Their idea had been to concentrate the people behind a wall around the town for better defense—they could see an enemy approaching and fight from a better vantage point.

I gathered together my toothbrush and needs for a couple of nights and put that bag and my slide case near the door so I wouldn't delay Ross when he came to pick me up. I'd made a new dress recently that I'd wear for the ladies' program and didn't want to wrinkle it by packing it in the bag—I'd just hang it in the car.

Ross and I had a good time visiting as we drove, and then, in Salisbury, we had a delicious dinner and fun playing all kinds of games—some rough and tumble ones—with the kids. As I prepared for bed, I decided to lay out clothes for the program tomorrow—shoes, stockings, underwear, jewelry ... but <u>where</u> was my <u>dress</u>! It was still hanging on the door back in Columbia! But the ladies wouldn't care what I was wearing, so why should I! We still had fun with the slides, and <u>delicious</u> cookies and coffee!

Even though that year without Gene seemed long—and lonely, I think it was well-spent in Columbia with my mom and dad. We had a somewhat "different" relationship than we had had before my marriage, but it was still rewarding and enjoyable for all of us. Gene wasn't in combat—just standing by in case of need—I had interesting things to do in my hometown with family and old friends, and my mom and dad seemed to worry less about Gene's safety because we could share our feelings. Staying busy with them helped the time go faster, and all of us were excited near the end of it to learn that his next assignment would be Officer Selection officer, stationed in Minneapolis, Minnesota! Those next three years would be especially memorable!

MINNEAPOLIS, MINNESOTA 1957—1960

April 1957 was a <u>very</u> happy month! Gene came home from a year in Japan with the Fleet Marine Force, Pacific—an assignment that didn't permit dependents to accompany him.

Some of Gene's month of leave was spent visiting Gene's family in Washington State, then, on April 27, we arrived in Minneapolis. It was an unusually warm day for that time of year, and we were delighted to see many families outside as we drove along residential streets lined with neat bungalows. Some people were doing yard work, many were gathered around picnic tables, or visiting over their fences, enjoying the sunshine. Our first home there was a comfortable little rented house in the suburb of St. Louis Park. It was on the west side of the city, near a major street for Gene to drive to his office, which was in the main post office downtown.

Minnesota is called "the Land of 10,000 Lakes," which I could believe, and our house was quite near a rather large one called Minnetonka. That was quite an elite neighborhood of lakeside homes with private docks and lovely landscaping; and included specialty shops, motels, and upscale restaurants. In winter, it froze over with very thick ice, and then became a colony of every imaginable kind of ice-fishing shelter—from temporary tents to small cabins built on runners and situated in some favorite place for the season. Some were furnished with radios and TV's; and most had heating and cooking stoves with comfortable seating around the fishing hole they had made in the floor, by cutting a hole through the ice. I think Northern Pike and Walleye Pike were the main fish caught there. The first time we drove out there in the winter, I couldn't believe my eyes! It was amazing to see all of those little houses, arranged along named streets, and cars and trucks driving around on the lake surface! Gene was an avid fisherman, but for some reason didn't like ice fishing as much as fishing for bass from a boat, in warmer water, in a warmer season.

When weather permitted, I frequently had a picnic supper packed up when Gene got home from work, and as soon as he could quickly change clothes, we headed for some small nearby bass lake to fish until sunset. There was a lot of tranquility out there on the water with loons swimming and "talking" to each other, frogs croaking and diving, birds singing evening songs, and gentle breezes making ripples on the water. Sometimes we trolled, but most usually anchored in some cove among cattails and lily pads—chatting when we felt like it, and otherwise just quietly enjoying each other's company away from city sounds. And, I should say, we used a lot of mosquito repellent! Everyone in Minnesota had their own descriptions of the sizes of Minnesota mosquitoes. And while some of the stories were comical and crazy, the "skeeters" there really were the largest ones I'd ever seen, and there were countless billions of them!

Gene's work consisted of traveling with a team of Marines to colleges in a five-state area, where they presented, and hoped that students would sign up for, what was called the Marine Corps Officer Selection Program. A student (male or female) who signed up became a member of the Marine Corps Reserve, and went to Quantico, Virginia, in the summer for active duty training to become a Second Lieutenant. Their commission came with college graduation, followed by active duty in the Marine Corps for a few years—I've forgotten how many. A candidate had to pass several examinations, including a physical, some of which the team could do on the spot. The simple physical was done by a Navy corpsman who traveled with them; then a more thorough one was later done by a doctor. Gene's assistant officer was a Marine aviator named Bill Rice, who was available to discuss flying with interested students.

A couple of sergeants who did administrative work also belonged to the team. Two of them that I remember were Dick Coerber and Cy Lepak—both of whom were very capable, young, single men. A corporal stayed behind to do the office work. A trip out of town, in a Marine Corps sedan, usually was from early Monday morning until late on Friday, to someplace in North Dakota, South Dakota, Michigan, Wisconsin, or Minnesota.

In the spring we decided to buy a house and found one—at 9306 10th Avenue South—that had been a model home in a new development south of Minneapolis that has become a town called Bloomington. We had great fun with planning and planting the landscaping, making a garden, and organizing interior decorating more than we'd been able to do previously. An important addition that we made was having a one-car garage built. In the frequently below-zero weather, our car needed to be kept from freezing, and to be warmed up before driving. One way to manage that was to use a warming device that could be plugged into an electrical outlet that warmed the engine block, but, of course, it was good to have it under cover from the snow and frost, as well. (We went back to see the house a few years ago and happened to be able to talk to the young man who is now the owner. He told us he really loved the house and had remodeled the basement into a comfortable family room, but he was sorry we didn't build a larger garage!)

We had very fine neighbors, once we became acquainted, but that didn't happen immediately. When we'd lived in Marine Corps communities, a new neighbor was immediately welcomed, and we wondered why that wasn't happening here. So, we began the "reaching out," discovering, from what one of the neighbors told us, that most of the men in the neighborhood had been in World War II as enlisted men, when it hadn't been appropriate to socialize with officers. So, when they saw Gene going and coming in an official car, often in dress uniform, they still felt a sort of "class distinction." We then began inviting friendship and maintained connections with several of them for many years.

With Gene traveling so much of the time, I soon ran out of interesting things to do. It was really exciting to have the new home—everything so new and clean! (Usually, when we moved into a different house or apartment, there'd be a greasy old stove to deal with!) So it didn't take very long to make draperies and get "settled in." There were occasional day-time activities with the church women—a Bible study group, a monthly luncheon, even sometimes rolling bandages for some missionary group—and coffee visits with neighbors were fun, but I still was bored. The best answer seemed to be for me to get a job—with the idea that my income would be used for special things other than usual living expenses. That job was at INA in Minneapolis!

I don't remember how I came to be employed by the very large insurance company called INA—Insurance of North America—maybe I answered an ad. I was assigned to be secretary to the manager of the Safety and Audit Department—Ed Lawrence. I took dictation, typed letters, answered the phone, and helped to coordinate the work of the safety inspectors. INA insured several large companies, many of which were upper mid-west grain farms who operated grain elevators and various kinds of machinery. That meant that there had to be periodic safety inspections of the work areas—and that was done by inspectors from our department. There were several men who traveled in several states to do that work, then brought back their reports that had to be typed up into "legible" form to pass on to the underwriters. The inspectors maintained desks in our office—and I remember only parts of the names of two of them: Norm, a tall, stocky man whose shirt tail usually seemed to be just barely tucked into his lower-than-waistline belt; Mr. Peterson was tall and slim, had thin nose and lips, and was always neatly dressed. All of the men were delightful, outgoing people; and everyone in the office had a lot of fun— hearing about some of their travels, as well as much joking while we worked.

There were maybe five or six typists—and I remember only two of them: Mai Treude, whose desk happened to be directly in front of mine, and Marie Norby. Marie was sweet and reserved, and we three often took coffee breaks at the same time—thus becoming very good friends. I still have a "sort of connection" with Marie.· When she left INA, it became my responsibility to buy a small going-away gift for her. I selected an ivory colored, good quality leather wallet that had space for a few cards (this was before the days of multiple credit cards), a nice sized coin purse, and it opened along the side for holding bills. One could even pull bills out by the end through a slot just inside the coin purse! A really handy, compact, easy-to-use little wallet! For some reason that I also don't remember, I didn't get to give it to her; I decided to keep it for myself. I'm writing this story in February of 2017; and for the last fifty-nine years, that wallet has been in whatever purse I happen to be carrying! One of my friends (whom I won't name), and some of my family, think I should replace it—and I'll admit that I have shopped for a new one for the last several years in stores from Florida to Oregon; but so far, I haven't found one that I thought I could "live" with! (Besides, I like the memories of Marie that it gives me!)

The other typist that I remember has never been out of my life since we met—Mai Treude! She had recently been married to husband Arvi and was still a "starry-eyed" bride. Working at a nearby desk with her was always delightful! She and Arvi were both refugees from

Estonia when they were children. Her parents had lived for a while in Germany before being sponsored to live in Minneapolis, and Arvi's family had come there by way of one of the Scandinavian countries. Several other Estonian families lived in the Minneapolis-St. Paul area, giving them enjoyable activities for ethnic socializing besides high school together. Arvi went to college while Mai worked, then she earned a Master's Degree in Library Science and became a special map librarian at a college in St. Paul for many years.

Mai and I soon discovered that our shared interests were many. She longed to travel, to see parts of the world she'd only read about—and so did I. It was even exciting to her that I had already had the good fortune of living for a couple of years in Italy with my adventurous husband. We had similar interests in art, in drama, and good food; so, before long the four of us became best friends. (One thing we didn't share was their devotion to sports cars! They had a sleek, brown and tan Corvette — "va-voom" sound, and all! On many weekends they joined other enthusiasts in sports car rallies!) In fact, "style" was a way of life for them—in cars, homes, and clothes! When they retired, they moved to a lovely home in Florida—where they grow many varieties of beautiful orchids—entertain "northern" friends in winter, and travel to visit cousins in Estonia, as well as to many other places to satisfy Mai's adventurous spirit. When they've visited us in Oregon there have been many walks in cool forests, ocean trips for salmon fishing and crabbing, and overnights at a few Oregon beaches. When we've gone to Florida, we've found deep-sea fishing, great beachcombing, shopping fun, museums, tropical gardens, and thought-provoking plays. Always—wonderful memories! And yes—a Jaguar in their driveway!

I don't remember how long I worked at INA—about a year, I think. I loved the work and the people, but because we had begun the counseling necessary to adopt a baby, it seemed advisable for me to show them that I was ready to be a "stay-at-home-mom" upon short notice. It was time for me to "move on," and many wonderful memories moved on with me!

JOY VISITS US IN MINNESOTA

Gene came home in the spring of 1957 from a year in Japan with the Fleet Marine Force. His next assignment would be Officer Selection Officer, stationed in Minneapolis, Minnesota. His work would involve travelling with the OSO team to colleges and universities in five states, offering students an opportunity to volunteer to work toward becoming an officer in the Marine Corps upon graduation from college. It was easy to "settle in," because we looked forward to an expected three years in the land of 10,000 lakes! You can imagine what that would be like for a "dyed-in-the-wool" fisherman! We bought a house—our first one—in the suburb of Bloomington on the south side of town, planted a garden, and became acquainted with the neighbors. We even began the long process involved with adopting our first baby—but that will be another story.

This story is about a vacation of exploring in the north of the state with my sister Joy when she came to visit during her time off from Instructor of Textiles and Clothing at Ball State University in Muncie, Indiana. It was in the summer of 1959, and the plan was to drive all the way to the Canadian border, fishing and enjoying points of interest along the way. We had a brand-new nylon umbrella tent that would be easy to set up; so, into our light blue "three-hole" Buick sedan we also packed up utensils and a few cooking supplies for camping, because we'd sure want to fry some of the fish we expected to catch!

The Gunflint Trail and nearby Sea Gull Lake was one of our first targets, where we'd stay in a cabin. That was in the far northeast "point" of the state, so our route would take us along the scenic western shore of Lake Superior (Indian name was "Gitche Gumee"). That meant we could have a chance to stop for awhile in Duluth—Minnesota's major port. There we saw huge freighters loaded with wheat, coal, iron ore, taconite, and who knows what else, that would travel to the Atlantic Ocean through the Great Lakes' waterway and down the St. Lawrence River. The drive northeastward along the lake shore was beautiful! Split Rock Lighthouse was one of our sights to see. That lighthouse is important to ships in that part of the lake because magnetic rock in that area distorts ships' compasses. Joy soon realized, as we drove farther north, that her legs needed something warmer than the skirts and shorts she'd brought with her, so we stopped at one of the local country stores where she found some black twill jeans that she has told me she enjoyed wearing for many years.

At Grand Marais we traveled north and northwest for several miles along the Gunflint Trail. It was like a wonderful, big nature trail—many birds and wildflowers were scattered through a forest of white birch trees. That was a quite different kind of woods from the oak and walnut ones in mid-Missouri where we all grew up. That trail was used by trappers and traders in an area that had been inhabited by the Ojibwe Indians for many thousands of years and was used for portage between lakes and rivers. Logging had also been an early industry. Formations of flint rock in that part of the state no doubt was a source of flint for guns, which in those days used flint to spark their powder.

We had reserved a cabin with a kitchen near the end of the trail on Sea Gull Lake, so we stopped at a nearby grocery to pick up some steaks for dinner and some items for tomorrow's breakfast. By now it was evening, and one of the first orders of business was to build a fire and start dinner. We soon noticed that a <u>cloud</u> of mosquitoes had come into the kitchen and were really swarming around Gene, who often seemed especially attractive to them. He began wildly swatting them, and soon we were all three in the mosquito fight. I don't remember how we got rid of the ones that were already inside—probably with repellent that we would have been carrying with us, but we discovered that they were <u>pouring</u> through a small hole in the wall—a hole that might have once served as an opening for a stove pipe. Stuffing paper into that hole fixed <u>that</u> problem.

We stayed there for a couple of days. Gene enjoyed fishing; Joy and I had time to explore the nearby woods, to pick some blueberries for breakfast pancakes, to relax and watch life along the lakeshore, and for Joy to sketch some landscape views that she liked. (She later painted some of them with water colors on pieces of birch bark Gene peeled from some trees for her and sent one to him when he was in Vietnam in 1966.) Of course, we couldn't be on a lake without doing some exploring by boat, and this one was especially interesting with many small islands and inlets. In the evening we were entertained by loons (Minnesota's state bird) that were diving for food, swimming, and "laughing" like loons do. One evening we loitered long enough to begin losing daylight while we were still some distance from our dock. One problem was that it was difficult to see if the water was free of obstructions beneath the surface. Joy and I perched in the bow of the boat to keep a sharp watch for stumps and rocks and such, but Gene had to reduce the speed, and darkness was rapidly approaching. It was a great relief to see the light at our cabin's dock!

The next part of the journey went through mining country as we traveled west across the state. There are underground iron ore mines near Ely in the Vermillion Range, and in the Mesabi Range near Hibbing we saw the world's largest open-pit mine. A lot of taconite is mined. It's a low grade of ore that requires extra refining to extract the iron. Farther west, around Bemidji, we were in Paul Bunyan country and, of course, snapped photos of each other standing by the giant statue of the legendary lumberjack and his blue ox, Babe.

One of our planned destinations was Lake Itasca, from which flows the Mississippi River. We had read that there, one could "step" across the river. We definitely wanted to add that to our list of experiences, and we did! There were actually several steps—maybe five or six stepping stones—leading the short distance to the other side, across the very shallow little stream of clear, cold water. More photographs of this significant accomplishment! (Gene picked some watercress to add to our supper salad.)

There were many campgrounds around the lake, so we found a secluded one we liked near the lake where the thick woods made great privacy in a beautiful setting among birch trees with "woodsy" fragrance. Gene found a slightly sloping place where we pitched our tent and unloaded our camping gear. Some large rocks at the edge of the campfire location was a good place to cook our breakfast bacon and eggs and fry some freshly caught Walleye Pike. The weather surprisingly changed during the night before we planned to leave, and we were awakened by rain! That new tent leaked! Every drop of rain that hit the top of it became a small spray of heavy mist on the inside! Gene had trenched around the tent, but soon there were puddles in the corners from the inside!

Back at home, with wet things spread to dry, we took time to read the directions that came with the new tent. Before being used, it was supposed to be set up and sprayed with water to "condition" it! Well ... it sure must have been well-conditioned by the time we got it dry!

And so it was for us, exploring
In the land of Hiawatha
By the shores of Gitche Gumee;
By the shining Big-Sea-Water.

LOVE IS ALL THAT MATTERS

We saw the Falls of Minnehaha,
Lovely wife of Hiawatha—
Heard the sound of "Laughing Water"
In the Land of Sky-Blue Water!

Thank you, Joy for your companionship—for sharing our fun, the sunsets, the Mississippi River crossing, the birch forest, even the mosquito swarms and the wet tent! You're a real "trooper"!

OUR FIRST CHILD

We had been married for nine years by the time we moved to Minnesota. For a long time, we had hoped for children, but it was still seeming to not be possible. So with the prospect of being in one place for three years, we decided to try for adoption with the Children's Home Society. We had to wait a few months for our turn to even be interviewed; then there was more waiting for our counselor to find a "match" for us. Interviews required really "baring our souls." They wanted to visit in our home, and to know family background, our philosophy of child rearing, health, financial stability, etc. We realized right away that we needed to be very open and natural, willing to disclose feelings that we might not have shared with just ordinary acquaintances. Some questions were: our choice of girl or boy; would we consider a child of a different race; would we consider a child older than a baby. We thought that with a natural birth there would be no choice of sex, so we would be happy with either. We thought that because of Gene's having no choice of future assignments, a child of a different color could possibly experience discrimination. As to an adoptive child's age—we would certainly prefer to have the experience of beginning with an infant.

This time of waiting was very useful for turning one of our bedrooms into a cute "nursery" with the new crib, chest of drawers, a bath/diaper changing table, window draperies, and (of course) a Mommy-sized rocking chair!

I've wondered if our descriptions of our growing up in what later was called "hard times" might have made a kind of background of our experiences that could have prepared us for dealing with problems and difficult situations that we'd be faced with as life progressed? It was interesting that after our interviews were over and we had been accepted for prospective parents, our counselor told us that from the time when she first began this work of child placement she had thought that she would never choose a military family for adoptive parents—but getting acquainted with us, changed her mind! How thankful we were! It was almost like there was a Higher Power in control of the whole experience!

After a few more weeks of waiting, you can imagine that we felt <u>greatly</u> rewarded in October of 1959, to receive the call that a <u>BABY GIRL</u>, born on August 24th, had been selected for us! She had the most beautiful blue eyes we had ever seen, reddish-blonde hair, and she even rewarded us with some of

her really sweet smiles! We named her Rebecca Anne—which, of course, soon became "Becky."

Important phone calls were in order! People in both of our families had been hoping for such a long time for us to become parents, some of them had almost given up! This would be quite a surprise for them! And, we knew they would be happy to hear the news! My mom and dad drove from Missouri to Minnesota the next day to visit! (Mom said Dad wanted them to pack their bags and leave right away—but she persuaded him to wait until morning!) Letters and phone calls came from others who were really happy for our new family! Expect to read a lot more about Rebecca Anne in stories that follow!

118 MAPLE LEAF LANE , WOODBRIDGE, VIRGINIA

In the summer of 1960, Gene received orders to the intermediate school for officers, which was then called "Junior School" located at Quantico, Virginia. He was a senior Captain, and this nine-month school would be training for a higher level of leadership. We sold our much-loved, first-owned home in Minneapolis, and found a new one to buy in Woodbridge, about halfway between D.C. and Quantico. Gene would have a fifteen-or-so-mile commute to the south, but the house was an interesting one, and in a community that was popular for military people. Many were also Junior School students, so it would be easy for them to carpool, giving me some freedom with our one car. Other advantages for us might be the  proximity to Washington, in case his next assignment would require him to work at Marine Corps Headquarters or the Pentagon; or to make it easy to sell.

Woodbridge was a fast-growing little town then, with houses of various styles and price ranges in several recently developed areas. A few of the homes that were still available in this particular development, Marumsco Village, were carved out of the side of a fairly high hill. The one we chose had a short, somewhat inclined driveway that provided off-road parking space for our new car. (It was a light brown Buick station wagon with a white top, that Gene had recently driven out of the factory, having special-ordered a "Wednesday" car. He had been told that a car assembled in mid-week was more likely to have no "bugs" than one assembled on a Monday when a worker might be tired from the weekend, or a "Friday" car when workers were in a hurry to begin their weekend off!) Several steps rose from the driveway to the front entrance, which opened into what we used as a family room; and also on that level were a bedroom, a bath, a laundry, and a furnace room with storage space. Upstairs were a living-dining area, a kitchen, two bedrooms, and a bath. The kitchen door opened at a higher ground level to a good-sized yard where we could have a picnic table and an "umbrella" clothes line. We had a dryer, but I liked to hang laundry outside when weather permitted. Those times were fun for both Becky and me—she was just learning to walk and enjoyed handing me clothespins for hanging things. At take-down time, I let the clothespins fall on the ground for her to pick up and put into the side pockets of the laundry carrier.

On the back of the deep lot—on top of a steep hill—were ten tall oak and maple trees that gave us nice afternoon shade in the level part of the back yard; and all of us had fun there when the leaves fell! Bushels of them! The real fun was hearing Becky's little screams of laughter as she played in the leaves— delighted to burrow into the pile, throw them up, or be covered with them! That was a good place for barbequing, and sitting in the shade, too! Mowing the lawn was quite a challenge for Gene, though. The hill was dangerously steep, so he attached a long rope between a tree and the lawnmower handle as a safety measure to prevent the mower from falling or sliding out of control as he mowed horizontally across the side of the hill.

Heating for the house and water was fueled by oil which was stored in a tank at the end of the house near the furnace room. The "furnace" was actually a small housing for a series of coiled copper pipes encircling a large jet burner that burned with a blue flame. A thermostat controlled its coming on and going off. As the water passed through the coils, it went on through specially designed "heater" pipes along the floor on the outside walls in the house. It seemed like a very good way to silently provide good, clean heat. Another feature we thought especially practical was that there was no holding tank for hot water to supply the faucets in the kitchen and bathrooms. When a hot water faucet was turned on, the oil burner began to flame under the coiled pipes, and hot water came very quickly, as needed! I've often wondered why this type of system isn't used in more homes. We also experienced a similar type of heating for water in Italy and Hong Kong. When we were first examining the house with our realtor, I remarked that it had no doorbell! His answer was: "Do the math! How much does a doorbell cost? Multiply that by the over one hundred houses in this development!" I decided that the builder was evidently trying to keep costs down! (After we moved in, Gene installed a pleasantly chiming doorbell himself!)

One of our next-door neighbors was a Sergeant's family that included a three-year-old daughter. She was a good playmate for Becky—and her Mom was a very helpful occasional babysitter! We soon realized, however, that the neighbor's TV was one of the reasons Becky liked playing at the neighbor's house so much! We'd lived in Italy when TV became popular in this country, so it was totally "new" to us. Until now we'd thought that, based on the available programming we'd experienced in homes of friends, the "boob-tube" was a very anti-social thing that might have some worthwhile news programs, but was otherwise a big waste of time. For instance: friends would invite us to come over for an evening visit. The host quickly hung up our coats and stuck drinks into our hands, in order not to miss too much of their TV program that was in progress. During commercials we'd "visit" a bit, or hosts would refresh the drinks. When a program ended, they chose the best of whatever show came next, whether anyone really wanted to watch it or not. When we'd decided to take our leave, we had to wait for the current program to end, or quickly depart during a commercial, feeling that we'd pretty much wasted an evening. But, with Becky preferring to play at her friend's house where the two of them could watch cartoons on TV! And, without a TV for her to watch at home, it became difficult to get a babysitter! Are you surprised that we soon became owners of a new TV?

We were happy to learn that some Marine Corps friends we had lived near before would be in the same school with Gene. One of those, who even lived in our neighborhood, was Luther "Lute" Troen with wife Marilyn, and sons David and Ricky. (Another son named Charley came later.) The Troens were bridge players, and we soon discovered others who played bridge and lived nearby. It didn't take long for a two-table group of us to get together once a month in each other's homes to play.

Several students in Gene's class were visiting officers from various foreign military services. One of them that he greatly admired was Rafael Eitan from one of the Israeli military services. Rafael had a great sense of humor, was very bright, and contributed greatly to the class. Gene had a lot of respect for him. Often there would need to be classified information presented to the class, so when that occurred, the foreign students had to be excused with the explanation, "The information for this period is above the classification for which some in the class are qualified." Sometimes a foreign student gave a presentation concerning his own country's service. Gene said there wasn't much of any importance, but lots of humor, when Mr. Eitan gave one of his own presentations. He would lead up to a critical point in a description, then say, "But further information is above the classification of this group," deliberately making fun of the situation he considered to be discriminatory. Not long after that, in June 1967, his name was given in our newspaper as being an important leader during the Six-Day War in which Israel captured the Golan Heights, Gaza Strip, and the West Bank. Reading the paper, Gene remarked, "I'm not surprised; with Eitan in charge, they couldn't lose."*

Well, living in Woodbridge was good. Frequently carrying a toddler, or wet laundry, up and down stairs made my back muscles stronger; we did sightseeing in Washington, and on weekends took side trips to historical places; we met new people, and formed lasting friendships with many of them; Gene had his very own bathroom downstairs; I improved my bridge game; and for many years we had the bright orange and orange-striped towels we used to brighten the downstairs bathroom that had no window! We had no problem selling the house the next summer—even made some money on it—took a month's leave to visit our families in the Midwest and the Pacific Northwest—and prepared to live next at Camp Lejeune, North Carolina.

*(From *Six Days of War,* by Michael B. Oren. In this book I found a couple of references to Rafael Eitan. Dates of that war were from June 5-10, 1967. Eitan was Commander of the 35th Airborne Brigade. On page 134, the author calls him "a commander in the paratroopers.")

CAMP LEJEUNE, NORTH CAROLINA 1961 — 1963

In July 1961, we were at Camp Lejeune, N.C. again! Ten years had passed since I had become a Marine Corps wife—there at that very base—in November 1950! Gene was a T/Sgt then, recently out of college as a veteran of World War II; and we had board and room in the home of John and Grace Gillette, tobacco farmers near the little coastal town of Swansboro. A month later Gene was commissioned as 2nd Lieutenant, and was transferred to Basic School at Quantico, Virginia. Now, he was a Major, assigned to the 2nd Battalion, 2nd Marine Division as a staff officer; with an almost-two-year-old daughter; and again, looking for a place to live! During this second time of living at Camp LeJeune, he was an S-4 (Logistics and Supply System) until June 1, 1962; an S-3 (Operations and Training) until May 3, 1963; and Battalion Executive Officer from May 6, to June 23, 1963.

Our two-year stay there was a quite eventful time—very enjoyable and rewarding, but not without some stress. Camp Lejeune is one of the largest of the Marine Corps bases, with some of the best military training areas, comfortable family quarters, and good support facilities for the Marines stationed there; but there was also a waiting line for quarters on the base, so our first home there was a well-worn furnished apartment off-base in the little town of Jacksonville, at 1806 South Street.

I don't remember much about the Jacksonville house (except that it was quite small), but I do remember that we celebrated Becky's second birthday there on August 24th. One of her gifts that proved to be a very useful one was a child-sized table with a couple of chairs. They had sturdy metal legs, table top made of Formica, and chairs upholstered in vinyl seats and backs—so they were easy to keep clean, and light enough to move easily. That grouping became a center for playdough sculpting, crayon art, and many, many tea parties for dolls—with Mommy and Daddy as frequent guests, as well! Another favorite gift that year was sunglasses in her size.

A week later, the end of August, we were able to move into quarters on the base in a newly completed area called Capehart Housing. The address was MOQ (short for Married Officers' Quarters) 2984. It was a 3-bedroom, 1½-bath unit with a fireplace in the living room, and a dining "ell" that connected to the kitchen. One of the bedrooms served as a combination office-sewing-TV-family room. We even had neighbors who were bridge-players! There was a spacious back yard—and the lawns were mowed and maintained by base maintenance crews. We installed a new gym set for Becky that had a couple of swings, a glider unit, and a slide. Right away we realized it would be well to double-check the liability clause in our insurance policy—the play set was a "magnet" for neighborhood children! One day we noticed that a boy a year or so older than Becky was on one of the swings, and Becky was running towards the house, where she picked up a sizeable stick of some kind, and then was headed back towards the boy. It was tempting to wait to see what she had planned to do, but Gene decided that he should intervene—just in case someone might get hurt. Sure enough, she meant to "defend her turf," so Gene's "intervention with mediation" turned into a learning experience for both kids!

One interesting experience (Gene frequently said, "There are no problems—only interesting experiences!") with the new house happened the first time we turned on the furnace. Dark smoke boiled out of all the heat vents! I called Maintenance and the Fire Department, not knowing what to expect. A search for the problem revealed a fireplace chimney clogged with trash that seemed to have been left behind from builders' lunch garbage! Heat was supplied by fuel oil to a furnace that was vented into the fireplace chimney! As a result of the smoke, the wall around the heat outlet in the master bedroom was quite discolored, so the room would be re-painted; and I could have my choice of color: its present color, which I would call a "battleship" gray; a rosy peach; or a "hospital green." I was glad <u>that</u> bedroom was the one that needed new paint, because I really hated that gloomy gray! I chose the green! Much more pleasant! That house was a really pleasant "home" for us, and it was very convenient to live on the base!

Among our new friends were Don and Sylvia Diamond who had three sons, a bit older than Becky—David, Mike, and Scott. Camp Lejeune had a beautiful ocean beach, some of which was used for military training to give Marines practice in making combat landings from ships. The part that was maintained for recreation was wonderful for family outings—and we made good use of it—for ourselves, as well as with friends.

Diamonds were bridge players, and their children and ours were almost always with us when we played together (which was often). If they were at our house, when it was time for Becky to go to bed, the boys went to sleep on a floor in their sleeping bags. The bridge game could continue. Sometimes we went to their house in Swansboro—again, snacks, bridge, kids to bed, and more bridge. Don had a boat which they often used for water skiing or fishing. One night, after playing bridge until midnight, Gene and Don decided it would be fun to go fishing for awhile. I don't remember what kind of fish they were hunting, but it was a two-person activity. One held a light in order to see the fish in the shallow water; the other used a spear to capture it. We had fish for dinner the next day.

Once while we lived there, a hurricane threatened the area. All Marines were ordered to stay on the base in their assigned units during the hours of the "watch," which turned out to be around thirty-six hours. We invited Sylvia and the boys to come to stay with Becky and me, thinking the base might be a safer place than their home in Swansboro. We gathered candles, flashlights, and canned food; and made sure the camp stove was in working order, in case we should lose power. Of course, we kept a radio on all the time—one that could also be powered by battery—to keep up with the weather news. Also, we knew the base would turn on sirens in case of danger. The boys were very excited and looked forward to a great "adventure"! They seemed quite "let down" when the hurricane turned into just a windy, rainy storm, but the grown-ups sure were thankful!

Gene was happily busy with Marine Corps work at Camp Lejeune. For a while his duties involved plans concerning logistics—the moving, supplying, and housing of troops at the battalion level that involved several hundred people. Then, for the next eleven months his classification was "S-3" with duties involving the battalion operations and training. That was his favorite work as a staff officer.

One of the activities of training was a practice landing on the island of Vieques, which is a short distance southeast of Puerto Rico. One end of the island was maintained at that time by the U. S. for the purpose of military training that would involve two battalions, transported on Navy ships. When one battalion landed—using procedures that they would use in an actual combat experience, they were met on the beach by a battalion already there, enacting the presence of enemy. When that sequence was completed, the "enemy" troops loaded onto the ship for their return to their home base at

Camp Lejeune. That operation was very significant for training—giving a good test of what the troops had learned about a combat experience.

For Gene's battalion, all went well getting there, and with whatever training they did in the two weeks or so that they were ashore. The Caribbean climate made living enjoyable and allowed for some exploring of the area. Once, a small group that Gene was with discovered an old abandoned bunker in which honey bees had built <u>enormous</u> numbers of combs filled with honey! They later went back to the site—with some containers borrowed from the mess hall, and with protective covering while dealing with the bees, and harvested some honey to add interest and flavor to their mess hall rations. Gene saved some of it in a jar to bring home with him. It was maybe the best honey I ever ate! Having been collected from various very fragrant tropical flowers, its flavor retained some of those fragrances—different from any of the flavors of honey gathered from our local blossoms of blackberries, fireweed, or fruit orchards.

The biggest surprise for the battalion came as they were loading onto the ship for their return to Camp Lejeune. On October 22, 1962, President Kennedy announced an air and naval blockade of Cuba, following discovery of Soviet missile bases on the island. He was in communication with Russian officials concerning the missiles in what had become known as a "Missile Crisis"! Instead of returning home, the ship—loaded with the "combat-ready" battalion of Marines—was ordered to "proceed with all speed" to Guantanamo Bay, Cuba! Dependents of the military people then stationed there had been evacuated, on such short notice that some had left laundry hanging on the clothes line! It would now become a base for waiting—in case military action would be needed for dealing with those missiles. My mom and dad were worried about the news they were hearing about the situation and urged me to bring Becky to be with them in Missouri, but I felt that my place was to stay put, to help with the morale (and family needs) of other wives. The young Marines were so ready to do whatever needed to be done, their officers were challenged to keep them occupied, without causing some <u>new</u> crisis! There was not much more than a fence between them and Cuban troops, and sometimes the two sides "entertained" each other by throwing rocks over the fence. The Marines played many military-related games, one of which was driving a tank through the area, repainting the number on it, and then driving the same one by the next day. (The Cubans might then think there were <u>many</u> tanks.) They even had a mustache-growing contest! Gene left his "handle-bar"-shaped one on for his return home to surprise Becky and me. It was such a surprise for

Becky that she didn't even <u>know</u> him! Needless to say, the mustache didn't last long!

The battalion came back to Camp Lejeune just a couple of days before Christmas. It was truly a happy time for the men and families who had been "standing by"! Gene's presence back at home was especially appreciated on Christmas Eve. After Becky went to bed we were up until after midnight putting together a pink colored metal toy kitchen set I'd ordered for Santa to leave for Becky! There was a stove, plus a unit that included a sink and some little cabinets—the height for a toddler to feel like she was in a real kitchen. I thought we would <u>never</u> get finished putting all those small Phillips-head screws into the holes that were provided to convert those slabs of pink metal into 3-dimensional objects! But Becky's delight on Christmas morning made it all worthwhile.

While Gene was enjoying his "day job" with Marines, I was enjoying Becky—watching her grow and learn <u>so</u> many new things in the world around us! Indeed, I was experiencing life from a whole new viewpoint— sharing with her the thrill of discovery and accomplishment of things adults just take for granted. When grownups walk along a path or a road, maybe planning tomorrow's activities, what things do they actually <u>see or hear</u>? A bird singing in a nearby tree, or flying across the path? Some tiny little colorful wild flowers? Or how about an ant hill? <u>That</u> is worth stopping and watching for a while! She was so cute, squatting down to watch the ants following each other in lines—some were carrying a piece of food or something larger than they themselves! She seemed totally absorbed in watching them to see where they were going! At age three, she liked doing things for herself, so I wasn't surprised to see her pull a step-stool up to a kitchen counter to make herself a peanut butter sandwich. Having experienced some moves to new homes, she liked a pretend game she invented by making the couch into a "moving van," piling it up with some dolls and toys, then sitting at the front end, and "driving" it! (Forever, a "can-do" girl!)

It was good, too, that we were able to socialize and get acquainted with other Marines, their wives, and children—most of them younger than we. We learned to square-dance; and that became an important activity for many years. We had an opportunity to belong to a bowling team. There was no shortage of bridge players, and I wouldn't even <u>attempt</u> to estimate how many games of bridge we played! Being able to visit again with Mr. and Mrs. Gillette, with whom we had stayed ten years ago, was like "coming home"! Such sweet, friendly people, with their lovely North Carolinian accent—still dishing up that southern-fried chicken, grits, and melt-in-your-mouth biscuits! Becky was fascinated with their dog, and cats, and chickens!

In the winter of 1962-63, we decided to make a "space-available" trip to the Panama Canal. Navy transport ships carried personnel and supplies to many ports around the world, and, if space was available, military people could travel along for a small fee to cover the cost of food and services. Traveling with orders on one such ship, the *Private Johnson*, we had gone to live in Naples, Italy. The ship we were on <u>this</u> time was the *General Callahan*—quite a lot larger than the private class ship.

We drove to New York City to begin the voyage—leaving our car parked in the Brooklyn Navy Yard parking area. Becky was very excited to be looking forward to riding on such a big ship. A Navy transport's facilities aren't as "plush" as a cruise liner, but the ships are very clean and comfortable. Our stateroom had a porthole, bunk beds, a couple of chairs, a couch that could be made into a bed, a desk, and a bathroom. Rooms were cleaned daily. An attendant came in each evening to turn down our bed covers, and to leave an apple on each pillow. He amused Becky by posing her teddy bear in various places around the room. Dinner was served at two different "sittings." People with children were given preference for the first one. Every day a small newsletter was left in our room, telling of activities available at certain times, any sights we might see, temperature and weather report, distance and speed traveled so far, and a few news reports that had come in on the office radio. A supervised play room was maintained at certain hours for children—and that was a fun place for Becky to spend some of her time.

Gene and I took advantage of the opportunity to play bridge (surprise?) when Becky was in the children's activity room. One of the bridge players was a lady whose husband was a Navy officer—not with her on this trip. Her father had been a ranking State Department person—so she had lived in many different exotic places, spoke seven languages, and we really enjoyed hearing her tell stories about some of their experiences. One time at a bridge table she showed us some of her very beautiful jewelry that she carried in a little brocade bag tucked into her purse. One quite unusual piece—a brooch—she said was a gift to her from a Persian Sultan (or maybe a Shah). It was an oval shape (about an inch long and a quarter-inch wide) with two ivory-looking tiger claws forming the rounded ends with a green colored polished gem-stone between them. <u>Most</u> unusual! She also had several items set with blue star sapphires that Gene especially liked. (In fact, he liked them so much that when he was in Thailand a few years later, he brought back a ring for me that was set with a large black star sapphire!)

Several of the "space-available tourists" on board were leaving the ship in San Juan, Puerto Rico, staying in a resort there for the few days until the ship came back on its return to New York; but <u>our</u> aim was to <u>see</u> the Panama Canal, even though the ship wouldn't go <u>through</u> it! It was mid-morning when the ship docked in San Juan, so we had all day to see some of the sights there, and to have a swim in the pool at the Officers' Club. A guided tour took us all over the city, and to visit some castles: El Morro, San Cristobal, and Casa Blanca. We also saw the cathedral that contains the tomb of Juan Ponce de Leon who founded San Juan in 1508. El Morro Castle, that interested Gene from a military standpoint, is high on a hill, surrounded by many fortified walls.

The ship docked at the Caribbean end of the canal fairly early in the morning and would be in port for several hours—overnight and would begin the trip back to New York the next evening. Gene had been in touch with Major Dillow, the CO of the Marine Barracks, located at the Pacific end of the canal. We had time to go there and still get back in time for the ship's return sailing. We took a bus across the Isthmus and were at Dillows' in time for lunch with them and their family in their home on the base. They had a daughter about Becky's age, and the two of them had great fun together. Mrs. Dillow phoned for reservations for us at a hotel in Panama City for the night; and then took Gene and me shopping, leaving Becky with their daughter and her "nanny." She said that embroidered linens were <u>the</u> best buy there, and she had an "in" with a special store. I chose a set of twelve place mats with napkins, and a tablecloth, with napkins, that was called an "Army-Navy" cloth—large enough for twelve place settings. It has "checkerboard" design with alternating nine-inch squares of lace and linen embroidered with a grape design. Two of its special occasions have been for covering the cake table at the wedding receptions for Becky and David.

LOVE IS ALL THAT MATTERS

It was interesting to see the house in which the Dillows lived—a typical design for the tropical climate. There was no air conditioning—just wonderful breezes coming through windows and screen-covered vents. They said that every home there had a "dry closet," with light bulbs to keep the air dry enough to prevent mold. In it they stored leather goods and other things subject to mold.

All three of us enjoyed the tropical atmosphere, sounds, and scenery that we "ogled" during the bus rides. The hotel was especially interesting and delightful—no glass for windows—just shutters that would keep out rain, and lock for security, while permitting ventilation. The songs of tropical birds all day and into the night were delightful—and they were beautifully colorful if we were able to spot them. Of course, the air that was filled with the fragrance of tropical flowers made everything feel like I was living a lovely dream!

In the spring of 1963, Gene received orders for his next duty station. The assignment called for him to be the Marine Officer Instructor in the NROTC Department at Oregon State University in Corvallis, Oregon! That assignment was especially appealing to us, because we loved the Pacific Northwest—not only for the climate, but also because we could be near Gene's family in Washington!

CALL ME A "BENCH BUG"

"My life began in a Volkswagen factory in Germany, but it became more interesting after I landed on the sales lot of a dealer named John Riddick in Columbia, Missouri, in 1963. Sterling W. Kelley was one of the salesmen there, and I might say he was a very good mechanic, too—keeping me "in tune" and cleaned up so my lovely blue-green coat would be sparkling, and I'd be "ready to roll" for my very first owner!

"About mid-July, an energetic-looking Marine Lt. Colonel named Gene Bench—whose wife, Ila, happened to be Sterling Kelley's sister—came in to look over Riddick's supply of automobiles. He said he had recently driven Ila and daughter Becky to Corvallis, Oregon, where he would be the Marine Officer Instructor at Oregon State University for three years. Their family car was a big, brown 1960 Buick station wagon he'd ordered when they lived in

Minnesota; and he had driven it out of the factory himself. The Buick was a very good car—they just needed another smaller one for a <u>second</u> car. I thought to myself, "How small are we talking about? Have you noticed <u>me</u>?" It wasn't long until Sterling was opening my doors and compartments to show this Bench person all about me. One thing that was <u>very</u> different from most cars was that my engine was in the rear; my cargo space was in the front, where you'd look for the engine in other cars. Sterling was really tall and towered over me, but Gene's legs were a little shorter, so sitting in me was fairly comfortable for him if he pushed my driver's seat all the way back. I was happy when he wrote a check and became my first owner!

"Before we could go home to Oregon, though, Gene had to go to Northwestern University, near Chicago, for about a month of special training for his new job. I was ideal transportation for him there—easy to fit into small parking spaces, and I didn't use much gas.

"At the end of that training, which Marines called "charm school," we were ready for the <u>long</u> trip—from Chicago, across the plains and mountains, to Oregon. We were a little slower than the bigger cars were, especially in the mountains, but Gene seemed to enjoy driving me—and really liked that I didn't need as much gas as that big Buick guzzled! I heard him joking to friends that I used so little gas, he had to stop once in a while and have some taken out! (I also noticed that we stopped to "rest" every couple of hours or so while he walked around a bit to "stretch his legs.")

"Ila and Becky stayed with Gene's mom and dad in Orting, Washington, while Gene and I were busy in Chicago and traveling back home. Becky was just four years old, so she had a good time getting acquainted with grandparents she hardly knew; and she and Ila had plenty of time to play together, as well as to visit Bench aunts and uncles and cousins who lived nearby.

"Our home in Corvallis was a brand new, ranch-style house at 1645 Arthur Circle. It was one of the first ones built in that development, and we frequently saw pheasants in the field in front of the house. Gene really appreciated me when he went to work on the OSU campus. His office was in the Navy Armory, which was a Quonset hut—no doubt considered a temporary arrangement at the time. Parking space was <u>very</u> limited, so I was a perfect car for him to drive to work.

"While we lived in Corvallis, I learned a lot about rivers and fishing. Very often Gene would change into his outdoor clothes before he even left his office, and we'd go straight to the Alsea River after work. (His fishing gear was always in my baggage compartment.) Sometimes we brought home a nice string of trout. In the winter, we brought home one or two big steelhead each time we went!

"In February, the family got a new baby boy—David Eugene! He was adopted and was already seven months old—actually born on the 4th of July! As soon as David was able to walk, Gene put a little child-harness on him and fastened the "leash" to his belt. That way, David could play and splash in the edge of the water while Gene cast his fishing lure over into the river's current— or to a deep hole where the fish would be lurking. (Ila always sent a change of clothes for David, because she knew he'd get soaking wet enjoying that adventure!)

"One Saturday I took Gene and David to their new farm on the Alsea River where Gene wanted to plant some apple trees on top of a hill in the woods where several acres of young fir trees were growing. He said the apples that would grow on those trees would attract deer and elk to the area. David was still wearing diapers, being fed baby food from a jar, and drinking from a bottle—so Gene had more to do that day than plant young apple trees! Actually, I think he must have been a very good "daddy"!

"In the summer of 1966, Gene had orders to go to Vietnam; but the family decided they should live in Columbia, Missouri, while he was gone so they could be near Ila's family. Becky and David could get to know their Kelley grandparents, and some aunts, uncles, and cousins. By then they had traded the brown Buick for a new green Oldsmobile station wagon. It would be needed to drive the family to Missouri, but Ila wanted me to go, too. I could be her "everyday" transportation. Gene knew of an Oregon State student who needed to travel east at about that time, so he was hired to drive me across country. Ila's other brother, Ross, was also living in Columbia then, so between him and Sterling, they kept me in good shape for Ila's chores of shopping, visiting around, bowling, and taking Becky to ballet lessons. Ross would sometimes take me out on a nearby highway where I could be driven faster than Ila could drive me around town. He said it was good for me to get the "carbon blown out of my carburetor" occasionally!

"A year later, Gene was back from Vietnam—this time with orders to Hawaii! I wondered what would happen to me! Would I get to go, too? The Marine Corps would pay transportation for one car, but not for two. And they'd definitely need a bigger car than I. Gene knew that sometimes Navy ships traveled from California to Hawaii without a full load of cargo, and that they would sometimes take a serviceman's car if space was available—and if he could get it to the dock. So, here I was, going west again, over those mountains, driven by a student from the University of Missouri this time, to the home of Ila's cousin in Long Beach, California. Gene signed the necessary papers for Cousin Clarence Miller to get me a ride on a ship. The Bench family stayed in Missouri several days to visit Kelley family people and to sell the nice brick house that had been our home during the year Gene was gone. They also acquired a used Chevrolet sedan to take to Hawaii. (That car was also bought from brother Sterling; and by now, he had his own dealership called "Kelley Pontiac.")

"I landed in Hawaii before the family arrived and was picked up by another Marine officer who was called their "sponsor." (A sponsor located temporary quarters—usually an apartment—stocked the refrigerator with food enough to last for a couple of days and served as a contact person for anything else an incoming family might need.) This sponsor happened to live across the street from Navy folks who had been good friends with my Bench family in Corvallis! Bruce Bryer was a Commander who had taught classes in the Navy department at Oregon State. Wife was Garnet; daughters were Judy and Susie—only a little bit older than Becky and David. One day in Hawaii, Garnet noticed a blue-green VW Bug parked in the yard across the street from the Bryer home. It looked very familiar to her, and when she saw the OSU sticker that was still attached to me, she said, "That car has to belong to Gene Bench!" "Yes," said the neighbor. "I'm his sponsor!" Bryers then found out when the Bench family would be arriving by plane, and all of them were waiting at the airport with colorful leis for each Bench person when they arrived! For some reason, the two families had not been in communication since they were together in Corvallis, so everybody was very excited and surprised! Needless to say, their next two years together in sunny Hawaii were wonderful ones—described in another story.

"But then, in 1968, Gene got orders to be a student at the National War College in Washington, D.C., and this time I wouldn't get to go with them. I wasn't too disappointed, though, because I really liked Hawaii—no snow or ice to bother with—and I soon discovered that my next owner was another young Marine officer who had recently come to Hawaii. I could still be happy, useful transportation to those warm, tropical beaches with people who would love me just as much as the Bench family did!"

LOVE IS ALL THAT MATTERS

CORVALLIS, OREGON — MY FIRST IMPRESSION

In the spring of 1963, Gene received change-of-duty orders to serve for three years as the Marine Officer Instructor at Oregon State University. The assignment called for him to go to Northwestern University for a month of some special preparation, prior to assuming duties at OSU at the beginning of the fall term; so before he went to Chicago, we wanted to find a house to buy.

We left Camp Lejeune, N.C. in our brown Buick station wagon, packed with essential accommodations for our almost-four-year-old Becky. We had a small tent, a portable stove, an ice box, and fit-together utensils for some camping along the way; plus clothing for the month of traveling which would include visiting Kelley relatives in Indiana and Missouri. With an energetic young passenger, we tried to limit our actual driving time—stopping for play time lunches and providing activity to work off energy in the morning and evening. Camping for a few of the nights made that very enjoyable, especially since we sometimes drove off the freeway to scenic places we all enjoyed. (If you ever do that, think about places with running water!)

I have since learned to appreciate deserts—noticing, when I look more closely, a lot of plant and animal life there, not immediately visible. In fact, I have come to realize that life there shows great courage and strength because survival requires more effort and even "cunning" than where nature endows the land with plentiful water.

So ... during the days that we drove for m-i-l-e-s and m-i-l-e-s through country that seemed so barren and desolate, I'd feel somewhat bored, and maybe wonder why the people in the few homes we saw would choose to live where life must be so difficult. You therefore can imagine the impact of almost suddenly coming upon the majestic Ponderosa pine forests on Highway 20! Yes! We got out the picnic lunch and spent some time walking (and running) on the pine needle-covered forest floor, among the ferns and tall trees—listening to the cool wind whispering through their towering branches! In a few more miles we came to the breathtaking view of the snowcapped Cascades—the Three Sisters, Mt. Washington, Mt. Jefferson, and Black Butte! Soon we saw small streams along the sides of the road—and sometimes stopped there to watch the clear, cold water from the melting mountain snow, tumbling over large and small rocks, sometimes murmuring—sometimes crashing and splashing! Spotting rainbow trout became especially exciting. Gene could hardly wait to be able to unpack his fishing gear!

Finally, we were on a long, straight stretch of road headed west out of Lebanon, Oregon. From there we could see the distant hills of the Coast Range—with Mary's Peak seeming to guide us like a beacon. What a valley! All the way across country I had tried to imagine what that trip must have been like for the pioneers in their covered wagons. (We had a "covered wagon", too! But what a difference! We had paved roads, bridges, motels, service stations, restaurants, and grocery stores—and no weary oxen to feed and tend!) Now, here we were in this verdant, green valley! No wonder the pioneers were willing to sacrifice so much! I could almost feel their joy, while feeling my own!

Driving into Corvallis, nestled with a view of tree-covered hills was like a "spiritual" experience! And it still is! "I will lift up my eyes unto the hills" (*Psalm 121*) always comes to mind.

We hoped we could find a house that would be convenient to the campus and Gene's work, so that's where we started looking. A lovely split-level home was for sale on Merrie Drive, but the price of it was above our budget. Mr. Harmon (Jim Harmon's father) was just beginning to develop Arthur Circle, and we discovered that with him we could have our choice of the lot, and our choice of several different house designs and finishes, in our price range. They would concentrate on the building of it while Gene was gone for the month to Northwestern! What an opportunity for me to be somewhat creative—choosing floor coverings, colors for inside and out, light fixtures, countertops, etc. We even asked for a couple of expansions and a cantilevered fireplace hearth—so our 12x18 carpet wouldn't have to be altered. We had heard about the wind that frequently blows from the west in the late afternoon, so we chose a lot upon which our backyard would be somewhat protected, as well as shaded. The yard was large enough for a great fenced-in play area for Becky and the son we hoped to soon adopt, and we could easily visualize a sandbox and a garden. Mr. Harmon built a curved concrete patio outside the sliding glass doors from the dining area to the family room, and Gene later designed a canvas awning to cover it.

Becky and I spent that month of August with Gene's mom and dad who lived in Orting, Washington, at that time. It's a very sleepy little town in the Puyallup Valley. His brother and two sisters also lived nearby, so it was a good time for me to enjoy in-laws, and for Becky to get acquainted with Bench relatives after being with Kelley families along the way. She was four, and in two months' time she was meeting all of her cousins, from east to west, and getting wonderful attention from doting grandparents, aunts, and uncles!

LOVE IS ALL THAT MATTERS

By the time Gene returned from Northwestern, our house was almost finished. A Navy NROTC staff member, Bruce Bryer, who was still on summer cruise—wife, Garnet, and daughters, Judy and Susan, with her parents in California—had left their house key with another staff member with instructions to rent it temporarily to incoming personnel who might need a place to stay! That became our home for a couple of weeks! Judy was Becky's age, so there were even toys to play with! I discovered some "interesting feelings" about living in another family's home—trying to analyze their interests by noticing the wall art, books, dishes, etc.! When we finally met them, we became really close friends—sharing many interests from playing bridge to being outdoors! (A few years later, we again "connected" when our two families lived in Hawaii at the same time!)

Soon we were in our new brown, L-shaped home with white roof and shutters at 1645 Arthur Circle! Before other homes were built around us during the following year, we often enjoyed watching pheasants fly up out of the tall grass nearby, and hearing songs of meadow larks when Gene went out to get into his car to go to work. Most evenings gave us glorious, golden-red sunsets; and always, those beautiful hills continued to give inspiration!

I often thought about the old song that goes:

"With someone like you—a pal, good and true, I'd like to leave it all behind … and let the rest of the world go by!"

OUR SECOND CHILD

Ever since Becky was about two years old, we had been hoping to adopt another child; and at Camp Lejeune, where Gene expected to have a two-year tour of duty, we made an appointment with a social worker in nearby Jacksonville who was connected with an organization who could help us. The disappointing part was that we found there was a waiting list for a baby, but older children were available sooner. We thought it wouldn't be fair to Becky to bring into the family a sibling older than she, and it seemed best to keep family additions as natural as possible. Mixed-race children also were readily available, but we decided against that, because we'd never know where we might need to live; and while we ourselves were not racially prejudiced, it wouldn't be fair to a child to risk living with discrimination in those days if it could be avoided. The waiting period for us could be as long as two years—but life was good, and I was in "Seventh Heaven" experiencing our beautiful, growing daughter! A lovely ocean beach was nearby, and I even conquered my fear of water and learned to swim because I didn't want her to know that I was afraid! Sure enough, Gene's transfer came before a baby became available.

So as soon as we were settled on Arthur Circle, we looked into the possibilities and procedures for adoption in Corvallis and decided to work through the Welfare Department. They had specialized social workers, as well as connections with other areas in the state. With our first baby, we'd decided to let ourselves be like anyone else having a baby—in those days no one knew the baby's sex until it's birth. Why should we be any different! But this time, with a choice possible, we thought it might be good to have a boy.

Our counselor—a Mrs. Nelson—was especially interested in discovering Becky's personality, and how she would react to a new baby in the family. So home visits included conversations with Becky while the two of them played together. Her first visit was a couple of weeks before Christmas, and one of her questions to Becky was, "What do you think Santa will bring when he comes?" Becky replied, "Well, in my stocking he usually puts some candy and nuts, and an apple, and a little toy. And he <u>might</u> bring me a new doll, or a real kitty cat!" Then she said to Mrs. Nelson, "Will Santa come to your house?" "Probably not," was the answer, "Because we don't have any children at our house." To which Becky loudly reasoned, "Then you should <u>adopt</u> some! <u>We're</u> going to adopt a new baby!"

That, of course was an excellent opening for Mrs. Counselor. "What do you think it would be like to have a little brother?" Becky's enthusiasm was building as she said, "I would <u>like</u> it! Let me show you where he would sleep, and he could use my old high chair because I'm getting bigger and I don't need it anymore. I can help take care of him, and we can play!" The meeting of adult eyes indicated that there would be no problem for Becky!

Gene and I thought it would be nice to spend Christmas with Mom and Dad Bench in Washington, because we hadn't been with them at Christmas time for so many years, but Becky was worried about it. She was afraid Santa wouldn't be able to find her! We had to leave a note to let Santa know where she'd be and told her she could take her stocking with her to hang up at Grandma's house, if she'd like. She was quite impressed on Christmas morning to find her stocking filled, and to find a new doll in a little bed waiting for her! It was great fun for her grandparents to share her joy, but after that, we decided to celebrate Christmas <u>day</u> in our own home where kids could enjoy new toys in their own surroundings; we could visit other family <u>after</u> Christmas!

Early in February we received a call to come to our counselor's office for a conference about a seven-month-old baby boy. We (just Gene and I) saw some pictures and heard some basic information about his parentage and health background. In his present foster home there were other children, so he was accustomed to family activity. Everything was seeming to be favorable—so the next thing for us was a visit with <u>him</u>!

Before we went to see him, Becky said she would like to take him a present, so we went shopping, agreeing that such a little baby would need something soft that wouldn't hurt him, and something that he could bite, because a baby likes to put things in its mouth. Finally, she spotted a small rubber fish squeeze-toy. "Oh, Mom! We <u>have</u> to get this! If he's going to be in <u>this</u> family, he has <u>got</u> to like fish!"

Adoption visits at that time were on "neutral" ground, without the presence of the foster mother, and this one was in a motel room in Portland. Our counselor was with us but excused herself so we could have time alone with the baby. We all fell in love with him right away—a chubby little guy with expressive brown eyes, lots of brown hair, and he seemed to like playing with Becky! We even thought he looked a bit like me. It was also customary to wait a few days before the final delivery—a time for adoptive parents to make last minute preparations, and to further adjust their mental feelings about a new member of the family. It was a time, as well, for the foster family to prepare for his departure, because they usually have made some significant bonding.

And so it was, that on February 13th, in 1964, we brought home our very precious and special "Valentine," who had been born on the 4th of July, 1963! On the way out of the motel where we met to receive him, I noticed that just near the door was a small rose bush with a coral-colored blossom! A rose! In February! Immediately, into my  mind came the tune of *Lo, How a Rose E're Blooming*! It seemed to be a spiritual promise to us that this new child was approved by a Higher Power to be <u>our</u> son—David Eugene Bench!

Becky was ecstatic, of course! And our home now felt "complete" with our beautiful new brown-eyed son to occupy that empty nursery room! His comfort had to be our number one priority—and that was to take him to our doctor for attention to his very bad cold. Even though he seemed to be a really good-natured baby, the whole thing must have been quite a confusing experience for him, and a "stuffy nose" sure didn't help!

As soon as his cold was better, his next surprise was a haircut by Gene's favorite barber! (Gene wanted to be sure that with all that beautiful hair, he wouldn't be mistaken for a girl!) While I held him, sitting erect on my lap, the barber entertained him for a little while—letting him hear, and even touch, the clippers—and then he slowly shaped the hair lock-by-lock. It wasn't a "Marine-style" haircut, but now, David definitely looked like a happy, beautiful little boy!

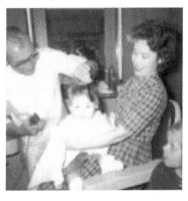

When he was able to walk, Gene began taking him fishing—using a child-harness with a leash that Gene fastened to his belt—giving David space to play in the edge of the water near his feet! Much great fun—splashing water and throwing rocks! A change of clothes, dry diapers, and snacks were waiting in the car for David's ride home. Are you surprised that fishing became one of David's favorite activities! (And I don't need to tell you that the Fourth of July became an even more special holiday for our family!)

In winter, we could find good places to play in the snow, just over the Cascade pass; and many weekends found us at the ocean, playing joyfully in tide pools, picking up shells, building sand castles, watching the sea lions, and eating clam chowder at Mo's. Other times we went to the mountains for some camping and fishing or exploring in the woods. At one spot, when I caught up with David, he had caught some salamanders and had their tails and heads and legs sticking out from between his chubby little fingers! We soon managed to get them untangled and set free to look for some bugs for their dinners! ("Boys will be boys"—whatever their age!) When we fished, Gene could keep David entertained if he tied a bait minnow to a string at the end of a long stick for David to do his "pretend" fishing. Day trips were more comfortable than camping for me—disposable diapers hadn't been invented yet!

BUT BABIES GROW UP!

Our family felt complete and compatible as David and Becky seemed to grow really fast, enjoyed school, and the frequent travelling necessary to follow

Gene's transfers every two or three years—including some time in England. We kept hearing about families whose children had to move so often frequently discovered problems adjusting to new locations—different schools, making new friends, etc. When Becky and David were in high school, I once asked them how they felt about frequent moves—leaving old friends, etc. Both of them said that they really liked living in new places and finding new friends— so we were pleased that evidently all the "adjusting" they had to do was just "adventures" for them! They were always excited about the "sight-seeing" that went with living in new places—and as they grew up we never worried about giving them new homes.

David was ten years old when Gene retired, and we moved to Overlook Drive, north of Corvallis, Oregon. He longed to be old enough to ride a motorcycle, but here in the country he could ride a small one—and had fun making trails through the tall grass in the vacant lot next door. Another interest was playing a bass guitar, which he taught himself to play. That eventually became "boring" without someone else to play melody with him.

After high school he enjoyed working in an assisted living place for awhile, then in service stations—becoming a manager of one in Corvallis—but needed something more rewarding. Some Computer Science in college made it possible for him to work for several years with Symantec, and do more college education.

His marriage with Michelle, their home, and other activities are in other stories.

CORVALLIS, OREGON — 1645 ARTHUR CIRCLE

It was great to have Gene back in Corvallis, ready to begin work at the University, and great, too, to be moved into our new home! The water main and street were still not complete, but we were able to get our cars to the front of the house; and our water supply came through a hose across the back yard from the Griswold's house on 17th street. Of course, when winter rains came, and building around us progressed, our view became a "sea of mud," but we were too busy to mind, and on sunny days the lovely sunsets were still there! At least, by that time our driveway was accessible.

It wasn't long until we had a great collection of friends. Membership in Folk Club (a University "connection") was practically "automatic." Those people welcomed new OSU staff members of all departments into special interest groups of many kinds. We chose to belong to bridge and bowling. I bowled on Monday mornings with wives—Gene on Wednesday evenings with men—at Highland Bowl, which then had only twelve lanes. Bridge groups were organized to meet once a month in various homes.

Another source of friends was the Newcomers'—also with interest-oriented groups of townspeople as well as Folk Club members new to Corvallis. (We played bridge with some of them many years later when we returned to live in Corvallis after Gene retired from the Marine Corps.)

We had already learned square dancing in North Carolina and were glad to discover very active square-dancing groups in Oregon. We became members of the Corvallis Squares who met in the very nice gym at the Benton Center on the second and fourth Saturday evenings. Square dancers seem to be the world's happiest people, and the people we met there (townspeople mostly) were really wonderful friends. Adding interest to square dancing are the wonderful outfits we wear—full, swingy skirts over petticoats, and special dancing shoes for ladies; a "western" type shirt that often matches his lady's dress, and western shoes and trousers for men. (When we returned to Corvallis for retirement, the Corvallis Squares were still dancing, and we became members again for several years.)

A fairly large number of retired military officers' families lived in Corvallis. Some had also had active-duty assignments in the University's reserve officer training programs, enjoyed living here, and stayed after retirement. Many of them, with their wives, met once a month for dinner and visiting—which, of course, included trading "sea-stories"! We never experienced a dull moment! We even became P.T.A. members. Becky began Kindergarten our second year. Her teacher was Miss Ruth—who was delightful, and very capable. The next year (our third and last one) she was in Mrs. Harmon's first grade class—at Garfield School for both years. Mrs. Harmon was a sweet, lovely, silver-haired "grandmotherly" lady, with great patience. Becky also began ballet classes that continued for several years when we lived in other places.

Gene's work at OSU was called Marine Officer Instructor, which was within the Naval Reserve Officer Training Corps (NROTC); and he was very excited about the assignment! He had had combat experience in World War II, and had a Master's degree in Education that prepared him for high school guidance and counseling, so he felt quite well qualified for training young people for military leadership. His classes were made up of Navy Midshipmen who had selected an option for duty in the Marine Corps, and Marine enlisted people—usually Tech Sergeants or Gunnery Sergeants—who had been selected to study for a college degree, while also earning a commission upon graduation.

The six courses were spread over three years; and included Evaluation of Warfare I, which I thought would be really interesting—learning things about Alexander the Great, the Roman Legions, the Crusades, and about weaponry that began with darts and spears and bows and arrows! Evaluation of Warfare II—modern tactics and related things like politics, U.S. foreign policies, Marine Corps history, and relationship of the Marine Corps with Naval services. Naval Science III included field exercises, and preparation for Officer Candidate School. A Leadership and Ethics class; Amphibious Warfare I; Amphibious Warfare II—necessary, of course, considering the dependence of cooperation between the Marine Corps and Navy that provided transportation to scenes of action. The Korean War and trouble spots around the Persian Gulf that were in the news at that time gave opportunities for discussions.

Besides teaching courses about military strategy and history, he was also in charge of the drill team, and of students' practice with personal weapons. A healthy competition developed between the regional drill teams who met at different colleges periodically to match skills of precision marching and rifle handling. The OSU team became one of the best!

But it wasn't "all work and no play." At least a couple of times each year we invited the Marine Option students to our house for an evening or a Saturday afternoon that included dinner. And each spring the combined ROTC departments had a formal dance at the Student Union ballroom that served two purposes—a good time socially, while giving the students experience with protocol connected with social occasions. The officers wore formal uniforms, and students wore their dress uniforms.

Navy Captain Ralph Locke was the head of the NROTC Department and held the University position of Professor of Naval Science. His Executive Officer (Assistant Professor of Naval Science) was Commander Americus Bacon—called "Merrick." For Gene's third year, the Exec was Marine Lt. Col. H. D. Fredericks—known as "Bud." (He retired after twenty years of service when he finished the OSU assignment, got a PhD in Education of the Handicapped, and remained in Corvallis doing international work in that field. The Fredericks family remained very good friends of ours. Other military people from those years were Cdr. Bert Sperling and wife Dorothy; Air Force Col. "Frosty" Fross and wife Ona; and Lt. Cdr. Bruce Bryer and wife Garnet, in whose house we lived for our first couple of weeks. (We were surprised to find ourselves stationed together again in Hawaii, from 1967 to 1969.)

Nearby Camp Adair was an Air Force base at the time we were in Corvallis, so we also had some social contacts with officers and wives from there—plus, there was access to a small commissary and military medical clinic. The Timm family had a child daycare in their home, which later became the Little Beavers Pre-School, on highway 99W at Lewisburg. I often drove out Highland Drive when I went to the commissary for groceries and dropped Becky off at Timms' on the way. Sometimes Mrs. Timm came to babysit for us in evenings.

When he wasn't at work, Gene liked to be holding a fishing rod—on the bank of a river, or from a boat on a river, a lake, or the ocean. In early spring the opening of the trout season was a very important date. Sometimes he went to the water with a friend, and often our family went to Diamond Lake, East Lake, or Paulina Lake, and stayed in the lodge for a couple of days; or tent-camping along some river. Fishing for steelhead was possibly his favorite rod-and-reel challenge. A steelhead is a rainbow trout that has gone to the ocean for a few years and grown into a fish the size of a salmon. They, too, come back to spawn in the stream where they were hatched, but unlike salmon, they go on living after spawning. They aren't easy to catch—so therein is the fisherman's challenge! We liked East Lake and Paulina Lake in eastern Oregon—fun places for family outings—especially with friends who liked to play bridge, as well as to fish!

A chapter of the Izaak Walton League was a group in which Gene found people with outdoor interests that included conservation, as well as hunting and fishing. They did a lot of volunteering for things like cleaning up the Alsea River after careless tourist-types had left behind all kinds of trash; building and placing bird houses and water-fowl nesting boxes; taking kids fishing; and giving nature talks at schools. Their January meeting was wild-game dinner—pot-luck style. It was always fun to see and taste the many creative ways of cooking venison, elk, antelope, duck, goose, bear, moose, fish, grouse, clams, crab—whatever! Some people made sausage using various kinds of meats; desserts included venison mince-meat pies, pies and cobblers made of wild blackberries, blueberries, etc. Homemade wines were also brought for sharing. In June a picnic provided the meeting they used for installing new officers.

CORVALLIS, OREGON — 1645 ARTHUR CIRCLE
(Continued)

In 1964 we bought an eighty-acre farm on the Alsea River. The very scenic Highway 34 runs through it, about fifteen miles inland from Waldport. The twenty acres south of the highway was bottom land along a large, horse-shoe bend of the river. There was a small house for residence; and many outbuildings for animals, equipment, and storage for hay and grain. One area was equipped for an apartment. Several acres of pasture land were fenced and planted with grass that could be harvested for hay, as well as for being good grazing for animals. Sixty acres on the north side of the road rose to a high hill of mixed timber that had recently been replanted with Douglas fir. Near the top of the hill was a fairly high-volume spring of wonderful, cold water. Some of it was piped into a holding tank, from which more pipes carried water under the highway to the house, to an apartment the former owner had created at the end of a row of outbuildings, and to a couple of watering troughs for animals. Hence, there was "indoor-outdoor plumbing" without a powered pump! And, there was electricity! My mother jokingly said to Gene, "A-ha! You bought yourself a fishing hole, eh?" The first steelhead he caught there happened to be a ten-pound wild one (meaning that it wasn't a hatchery fish). You may be sure it became beautifully mounted, and ever after had a place to hang over our fireplace!

One Saturday Gene took six small apple trees to plant on the hill at the farm, expecting that their fruit would eventually attract wild life. But he also took David—including diapers, baby food and extra clothes—in the VW, on the logging road to his chosen spot! He really liked "being a Dad"!

"The Farm" became a part of our lives for many years. Of course, Gene's Marine Corps assignments kept us from enjoying being there for several years, but a friend helped with maintenance and with keeping it rented until Gene's retirement in 1973. Besides fishing, we liked to pick wild blackberries that grew at the edge of the pasture along the river. They were extra-large, juicy ones that had plenty of warm, morning sun and cool shade in the afternoon! Our part of the river was also home for thousands of crawdads! Not only were they fun to catch by hand in summer when the water was low, they were also very tasty when cooked! And they were cute! They looked like baby lobsters! Catching them was a special activity for granddaughter Leah and Grandpa Gene to share!

Years later, after David graduated from high school he wanted to try living on his own—on the farm, with a friend. He had a new Datsun truck, and found some work to do in the area; so he fixed up the apartment, bought some chickens, and became a "farmer" for a couple of years while he tested his independence, and learned a lot about country living—that he liked it and chickens!

Our pets when the children were young were goldfish. Dogs or cats or birds just didn't seem to be practical when we moved often. Besides, Gene and I had grown up with families who considered cats and dogs to be outside animals, and Gene, for some reason just really didn't like cats! One time when Becky was nearing age six, and was cuddling with Gene in his lounge chair, she sweetly said, "Daddy, I really would like to have a pet." He replied, "Well, Princess, we have some goldfish that are pets." "But, Daddy, you can't play with a fish! I mean a pet like a kitty cat!" He didn't pursue the subject then, but we decided that a kitten might be a possible gift for her birthday which was coming soon.

After work the day before her birthday, he drove out to a nearby farm, answering an ad in the paper for kittens. The kittens were "barn" cats, so catching one was the first problem; then handling it, with it doing a lot of scratching, was another one! He had secretly put a litter box, food, and water in the garage, so we could surprise Becky with the kitten the next day. But when we looked for it in the morning, it was nowhere to be seen! Soon I heard a mewing sound above the ceiling over the family room which was behind the garage. Gene went up there, and somehow got it down; but we quickly decided it was <u>not</u> a good pet for a little girl! So, he boxed it up and took it back. Becky was sad but looked forward to the promise of a replacement. Another ad was answered, and this time Daddy came home with <u>two</u> kittens! One was a calico color, and the other was gray-striped. He said, "Well, there are two kids, might as well have two cats!" Becky named hers "Trendi," and David called his "Patches." It wasn't long until I noticed that often, after the children were in bed and Gene was watching TV, there were two kittens curled up in his lap!

In the early spring of 1966, Gene received orders to go to Vietnam in July. He was promoted to Lieutenant Colonel on April 1st, so would be assigned to command a battalion there. We decided that it would be well for the children and me to live in Missouri to be near my family for the year Gene would be gone, so we took advantage of my brother Sterling's offer to look for a house we could buy in Columbia—specifying that it should be a three-bedroom one that would be an easy sale when Gene returned—and that it should not have a steep driveway that might become icy in winter. Instead of selling the house in Corvallis on Arthur Circle, we learned that Camp Adair was looking for homes to lease and use for officers' quarters. The income from that was enough to cover the mortgage payment and taxes for the next three years until we needed to sell it.

A student of Gene's who was going home to the Midwest at the end of spring term, agreed to drive our Volkswagen "Bug" to my parents' home in Columbia. A Mayflower van, hired by the Marine Corps, came to do our packing, and on June 2nd we loaded ourselves into our green Oldsmobile station wagon for visiting Bench family in Washington, and doing sightseeing along the way to our new home in Missouri!

COLUMBIA, MISSOURI—VIETNAM 1966 —1967

I suppose the prospect of Gene preparing to go to Vietnam, and of me to be living in a new home I hadn't yet seen—with children aged three and seven—taxed emotions I had never before experienced! All subconsciously, of course, because I needed to accept—with apparent courage—whatever assignment Gene was given. My body reacted with what the doctor diagnosed as "depression," and gave me a prescription for Valium which kept me more or less "without feeling" for several days before we left Corvallis. But there were many positive aspects for the kids and me—we'd be living in the same town with my parents, and the families of my brother Sterling and my sister Barbara. Sterling had already found a house for us to buy—313 Proctor Drive—just about three blocks from a school for Becky. And when I'd been able to put the depression thing behind me, the cross-country trip together and "making a new nest" became a pleasant experience. Gene had to report for duty in California on July 7th to prepare for transportation to Vietnam. So we had the month of June together for traveling, visiting families, signing papers for buying the house, and for getting all the boxes and furniture under our new roof.

When traveling on orders, we usually planned to see some new part of the country; and this time we drove through the salt flats west of Salt Lake City, and then to I-70 for the rest of the way to Columbia, Missouri.

Sterling's choice of the house for us on Proctor was really great—a corner lot on a quiet, lightly-traveled street, with a large yard of at least a quarter of an acre. Landscaping was mature and well kept, and several lovely trees gave us cool shade in the summer, leaves to toss and pile up in the fall, nesting for many different birds, and families of squirrels to entertain us.

David's 4th birthday (L to R) Dad Kelley; Becky; Bill, Randy, Barbara, and Frank Wyatt; Mom Kelley; Mom's Aunt Minnie

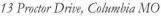

13 Proctor Drive, Columbia MO

(One tree in the back yard—a mulberry—was a bit of a problem, however. In the summer, I hung the laundry to dry on a clothesline not far from that tree where birds filled their tummies to over-flowing with berries just before they flew over the drying laundry! Quite often there were purple stains to remove!) People before us had built a cyclone fence enclosure for their dogs, but David found it useful for a temporary home for a terrapin he found. Grandpa Kelley drilled a small hole at the edge of its shell in which to tie a long string leash. Inside the fence it was protected from animals that might cause harm, and David kept it fed with bugs and vegetable pieces. In the fall we decided to set it free to spend the winter with its terrapin friends in some safe hibernating place.

The downstairs had a large family room that opened out to a level concrete area that could be used for parking, but Becky and David used it for a place to play with cars and dolls and neighborhood friends. Friends were mostly girls, but they were generous enough to let David play with them. I got some "boy" dolls for him to mix with their Barbies, and other girl-doll people—and David had cars and trucks and animals to fill out their imaginary activities.

Also downstairs were family room, furnace room, storage space, and a room that could be a good bedroom. At school, Becky's second-grade class had a project to learn about how to be safe in a tornado or other wind storm. She wanted us to make up a survival kit, so we did, and chose that downstairs room for our safe place. There were frequent announcements on the radio of tornado warnings in various areas over the state, which worried David, but he felt better  about it when I explained that many of those places were far away from us. I didn't let the children watch news on TV because there were real-life pictures of war and injuries in Vietnam—too graphic for their eyes, I thought. But I did have the radio on a lot, and one time when there was a report of the number of people killed that day in Vietnam, David's face became seriously sad, and he said, "My Daddy's in Vietnam! Is he going to get killed?" What to say?? I heard myself saying, "Vietnam is a big place. Daddy was probably in a different place from where those people were."

Becky had some school friends who were in "Bluebirds"—the beginning group of Campfire Girls, so we thought it would be a good activity for her. One of her friends was Julie, whose mother was the sister of Sterling's wife, Jeannette.

It was very good for us to be near my Kelley family; partly for me, but especially for Becky and David to get acquainted with cousins, grandparents, and aunts and uncles that they usually had visited only once a year. There were many birthday parties and "play dates"; and time with Grandpa in his shop, or on hikes to look for wild flowers and birds. My dad often made bluebird boxes that he placed in parks and along hiking trails and going with him to "check" on them was a real treat. David had two birthdays there—July 4th—when several family members gathered with us in our back yard for a picnic dinner and small fireworks. On his fourth birthday, Mom's Aunt Minnie Sutton gave him a large turtle-shaped "floor pillow" she had made for him while she had been staying for a while with my mom and dad.

Mom and Dad came on Christmas Eve to spend the night with us, to "help Santa," and to play with us on Christmas. On Gene's birthday, April

13ᵗʰ, the kids and I made a cake, covered it with cherries (which he loved) and put two candles on it. He was forty-two years old, and we thought all forty-two candles would be too many! A picture of it was one of many we sent to him in Vietnam.

Christmas dinner 1966. The bird was probably roasted duck.

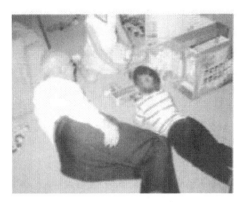

What fun to have Grandpa play with us!

David is holding his "Little Kiddle" fireman doll. First thing he wanted to do with it was play "barber." He was the barber, I was the mother. He asked me "how much to take off!"

Gene felt very fortunate to be assigned as Commanding Officer of a Battalion called 2/4: 2ⁿᵈ Battalion, 4ᵗʰ Marine Regiment. Some years before, it had been named "The Magnificent Bastards." Gene's Company Commanders called themselves "Bench's Bastards," and they called him "The Big Bastard." (The C.O. of "E" Company was Captain Walt Boomer, who later became a General, and was selected to be an Assistant Commandant of the Marine Corps.) Email for communication hadn't been invented yet, so we both wrote

209

postal letters almost daily. I saved the ones I received from him, and a few years ago we went through them and compiled a document he called "The Legacy Continues," describing the year he commanded the battalion.

They had a break after six months when they went to Okinawa for a few weeks to receive reinforcement. A normal time for a battalion commander to serve was six months, but Gene's request for continuing for another six months was honored, and he felt that his men were accomplishing what they were assigned to do, under very difficult circumstances. There were several Medals of Honor awarded; and to Gene's personal medals were added a Silver Star, two Bronze Stars, a Purple Heart, a Legion of Merit, and a couple of Vietnam medals. He called me by using a radio connection a few times. In one call he warned me that I would be receiving a dramatic communication from the Marine Corps that would tell me that he had been wounded in the line of duty—but that I shouldn't worry, because it was just a shrapnel wound in his arm that was taken care of by his Corpsman and wouldn't be a problem. Sure enough, one day while I was away from home, a Marine in "blues" uniform and an official car came to the house! The whole neighborhood was worried that the news might be bad, so all were relieved when I told them I'd heard already about it from Gene, and it wasn't serious. In fact, I feel like telling about a "spiritual" experience I had not long after he went to Vietnam: I was doing something at the sink in the kitchen—thinking about Gene, as usual, when I "heard" a voice coming from a little higher than my head on my left. It said, "You take care of the children—I'll take care of him!" That gave me freedom to present a positive attitude without worrying! I told my Mom that she was doing enough worrying for both of us!

Needless to say, we were all happy to hear in the spring that Gene's next assignment would take us to Hawaii for two—maybe three years! The kids and I made a "For Sale" sign for the front yard, and I listed the house with a realtor. It was an easy sale, and we were very happy. When Gene let me know when he would get back, we made arrangements for me to meet him alone in Kansas City—at the Muelbach Hotel where we'd spent our wedding night. I told the kids I was taking a little vacation, and that they would get to stay with Grandma and Grandpa Kelley for their vacation. I thought maybe it would be for two or three days, at least, but the very next day Gene was so anxious to see the kids, we went back to Columbia. Joy for the whole family!

I had sold our station wagon and had used the VW for myself while in Columbia, so one preparation for living in Hawaii was to buy a used Chevrolet sedan from my brother who was now in business for himself. A student from the University of Missouri ROTC drove the VW to California for my cousin to take to Long Beach for transport to Hawaii, and we soon had another cross-country, across-ocean trip to another home—and another story!

LIVING IN HAWAII 1967 — 1969

Gene was still in Vietnam when orders for his next assignment came in the spring of 1967, and all of us were exceedingly happy to find that he would be stationed in Hawaii! On July 17 he ceremoniously passed the battalion flag of the "Magnificent Bastards"—2nd Battalion, 4th Marines—to Lt. Col. Wes Hammond; leaving behind the two thousand-some Marines with whom he had spent the last thirteen very busy, combat months. He was leaving part of his heart with them; but was happy to be bringing the other part of it to be with his family again!

It was a great relief to have Gene safely at home with us, and he had about a month of leave time before getting all of us back to the west coast for the flight to Hawaii! We made good use of those days—visiting with all the Kelley families in Columbia, Missouri, and the Bench families in Tacoma, Washington on the way to San Francisco.

I had made arrangements with a student from the University of Missouri to drive our VW "bug" to California, and leave it with my cousin Clarence, who lived in a suburb of Long Beach. Gene stopped there on his way back from Vietnam and arranged for a "space-available" ride for that car on a Navy transport ship to Pearl Harbor. We'd need a second car in Hawaii, and were entitled to have one shipped on orders, so we bought a good used white Chevrolet Impala from my brother's automobile business in Columbia.

At that time, everyone arriving in Hawaii for duty was assigned a sponsor who helped the new family with getting settled—doing such things as reserving a hotel housekeeping suite and stocking its refrigerator with enough food for a couple of days, meeting the arriving family at the airport with leis, giving transportation to the temporary quarters, and giving other assistance as needed. So the sponsor was the one who had picked up our VW and kept it parked in his own driveway until we arrived. It so happened that one of <u>his</u> neighbors was the Bruce Bryer family, in whose house we had lived temporarily when we first came to Corvallis, and then became good friends!

We were to fly on a Pan American plane from San Francisco on August 21st, so we did some sight-seeing along the coast on our way there. One stop was for a short visit with friends in Corvallis. Another one was to see the Redwood trees near Crescent City in Northern California. That was very exciting for Becky and David—and it was a sentimental visit for us, because the Trees of Mystery Park there had been an inspiring place to us on our wedding trip in 1948. Then, in San Francisco we went to Chinatown, rode the trolleys, and explored some of the waterfront, while we waited for our scheduled time to board the plane.

You can imagine our surprise when we landed in Honolulu and found the <u>Bryer family</u> waiting there for us with leis in hand! We hadn't been in touch with them for several months and hadn't told them that Gene would be stationed there! But they soon told us the story of their sleuthing: Garnet had noticed our VW parked in their neighbor's driveway and saw the Oregon State parking permit still on the bumper. Her first thought was, "That just <u>has</u> to be Gene Bench's car!" When they asked about it, they discovered that the neighbor was sponsoring us, and in that way, had learned the details of our arrival! That was really like "Old Home Week"!

Becky's eighth birthday came three days after we arrived. We were living temporarily in an apartment near Waikiki Beach, so her birthday was celebrated with a party in the nearby park and consisted of a "bought" cake and cups of ice cream—with Susie and Judy Bryer as her guests ——and moving the party to the nearby beach for a romp in the sand and water!

When Gene checked in for duty, he found that Navy quarters would be available for us at McGrew Point, near Pearl Harbor, and not far from Hickham Air Force Base. It was a ranch- style house with a screened-in porch which Hawaiians call a "lanai." Windows were jalousie style that could be tipped to keep out rain or opened to level position for the breeze to come through. The address was 166 McGrew Loop—a corner lot with a large lawn, landscaped with

Entrance to Quarters – 166 McGrew Loop

212

banana trees, palm trees, several plumeria bushes, philodendron, bird of paradise, hibiscus, and several varieties of ferns. Part of our view was out to Pearl Harbor with the Arizona Memorial in the distance. The house wasn't large but was very comfortable with a kitchen open to the living room, three bedrooms, two bathrooms, and a storage room. The hall closet was equipped with shelves—no coat closet necessary! No furnace, either! (Some of the homes in higher elevations had fireplaces, because the temperature there could get down to the 50's, but it was seldom that cool at our sea-level location.) That house became "home" on August 29th.

Having a sponsor to help us with getting settled was a really wonderful experience, and it was all free! We insisted that we at <u>least</u> pay him and his wife for the food in the refrigerator, but the answer was that the only way we could repay would be for us to be a sponsor to someone else! There was an allowance from the Marine Corps to help with the expense of the hotel, and then the rent and upkeep for our permanent quarters were provided by the Navy.

We soon discovered that we were not alone in the house—David was really excited when we discovered that small, friendly, pinkish-white geckos were helping us keep the cockroach population under control! The geckos were harmless, didn't bother any food; and they mostly kept out of the way up in the exposed beams of the "vaulted" ceilings, or off in corners someplace. Once when we noticed some white eggs, about the size of peas, along one of the beams, Gene retrieved them for the kids to put into a box where they could watch for the hatching.

This might be a good time to tell about some other "indoor wildlife" I caused! With all the philodendron growing on the little wooden fence near the front door, I didn't need to have potted plants in the house. The vine had to be pruned frequently, so I just stuck some small branches of it into pots of water—and I had trouble-free greenery! One of these arrangements was in a nice little brass pot we'd fallen in love with and brought from Italy. It was perfect on the top of the piano that sat in one dimly lighted corner of the living room. After some time, we noticed that mosquitoes were bothering us at night, but we just figured that was one of the things people live with on a tropical island. One day, while I was dusting, I noticed quite a large number of the little creatures congregating around that pot of philodendron on the piano. A closer look revealed that there was a community of them—in various stages of growth: some were larvae wigglers, some were in the pupa stage, and others were trying their new wings! I said, "A-ha! That's what happens when water is just added to a pot, and not changed!" I saved it for an educational experience for the kids when they came home from school, and then made a practice of changing the water in the pot every week or so!

School started early in September, and a gray Navy bus came by on our street, picking up elementary students for Pearl Harbor Kai School that was on the Navy base. We were happy that Becky could be with military children, because we'd heard that the local Hawaiian school standards were somewhat lower. She was in the third grade that year. The school was large, in a long, two-story building. The hallways were outside on one side, with classroom doors opening off of them. It made a good place for the children's parade to show off their costumes as part of the Halloween celebration!

Traffic in the housing area was light, so it was an excellent place for David to ride his scooter and play with neighborhood kids. Becky took ukulele lessons at school, and also learned Chinese jump-rope, to "click" bamboo poles, and to use gourds and shells as percussion instruments. We had frequent beach picnics, and Girl Scouts. On Sundays, there was Sunday school (Gene was Superintendent for awhile), and church in a nearby chapel where a Navy Chaplain led the service. With a friendly neighborhood and looking forward to life in this beautiful island environment, we soon "settled in" to living—school, work, and fun!

OUR HAWAIIAN NEIGHBORHOOD

Living in Hawaii seemed like a long, wonderful vacation! So different from any other place we'd lived. It seemed strange to not have obvious seasons of winter, spring and fall, but there were some subtle differences. Birds sang more energetically in the spring; poinciana trees and poinsettia bushes bloomed in the winter; and some other flowers seemed to recognize their seasons. Breezes were usually pleasantly cool, but sometimes in summer, there were very warm, stronger ones that were called "Kona winds." Those didn't last more than a day or two, as I remember. We tried to make the most of our good fortune to be living in that lovely place, so on weekends and days off from school we could be found enjoying one of the many great beaches, or exploring museums, local craft shows, or relaxing with some of our many new friends.

Gene's work was what they called "Purple Suit," because the staff was made up of people from several different services. He was assigned to the Briefing Section of the staff of CINCPAC—Commander in Chief of the Pacific Command—who at that time was Admiral McCain (father of Senator John McCain). Other members of the staff were, of course, many Generals and Admirals of Navy, Air Force, Army, and Marines.

As Briefing Officer, he was to read and review daily messages that came in from all over the country, and to describe them to the early-morning gathering of that "star-studded" staff (affectionately called "The Milky Way" because it had so many stars). To do that, he had his own staff of communications people, experts of various warfare classifications, and people I'll call "map keepers," because I don't know what else to call them—although they no doubt had special titles.

He went to his office at midnight to prepare for the morning presentation—maybe 7:00 a.m., or so—I don't remember specifically, if I ever even knew. I do know that in order to describe the messages, he had map assistants and projection people to help with showing the senior officers the specific areas involved in the messages. Of course, there were always descriptions of the work of his beloved "Two-Four" Battalion that was still in Vietnam, and his heart ached when there were reports of difficult battles they were experiencing. One of those battles was in a place called Dai Do. The Battalion Commander, Lt. Col. Bill Weise, was wounded and had to be evacuated. The Sergeant Major, John Malnar (called "Big John"), was killed

215

performing duty that was worthy of receiving the Medal of Honor, which was awarded posthumously.

Of course, Gene's work schedule required him to sleep during the day, which had a few problems—like living in a house with thin walls and having young children around the neighborhood who were playing nearby. The solution for getting him comfortable for sleeping was to put some dark shades on our bedroom window, and to install a window air-conditioner that would not only cool the room but would "cover" the other sounds. He could usually get enough sleep to be able to get up in the late afternoon for dinner and evening family times with us. At one point we discovered <u>exceptional</u> sounds! Part of the movie *"Tora, Tora, Tora!"* was being filmed right there in Pearl Harbor. Our house happened to be directly under one of the pathways of the "Japanese" fighter planes, flying low to make "pretend" bombing runs! (We learned that one of the ways the filming crews made their <u>few</u> ships and planes appear in the movie to be <u>many</u>, was to repaint the numbers, and to make some other changes to the outward appearance of the equipment they were using. Some barrels of burning fuel oil simulated a bomb strike on a ship.)

Most of our neighbors were Navy people—all of them interesting. A Navy officer, Mike Dasovitch, lived next door with wife Gloria, son "Scooter," and daughter Gigi. Gloria was my "walking partner," a source for an emergency cup of flour or sugar, a morning cup of coffee, or just "talk." She was a somewhat dominant type and didn't like the kids to be too "rambunctious" in their play. Naturally, that made the boys in the neighborhood like to tease her, probably just to get her attention! In her yard was a tree that produced long seed pods that dropped to the ground when they dried, making great "missiles" for boys to play with—especially for throwing. (I was glad our four-year-old David was too young to be very much a part of that.) One interesting thing about Gloria was that she couldn't stand living with geckos, so they put window air-conditioners in their house so they could keep it closed up. Well, geckos are natural roach-control creatures, so without geckos, their house soon became infested with roaches. Their problem—not ours! <u>We</u> had geckos!

Another Navy family who became good friends, lived around the corner from us—Dick and Margie Jones, Valerie, and Steve. Their kids and ours liked each other, and Dick and Margie were good bridge-playing buddies. Our friendship continued, and they became neighbors again in Virginia. Margie and I have continued to keep in touch.

Some other friends who didn't live nearby, but were friends through Gene's work, were Gin and Don Watterson, and Rudy and Theresa Enderle. Our bowling partners were the VanDuesens. Del and Ann Delcuse became neighbors again in Virginia, where Ann was Becky's piano teacher.

A family who lived on a nearby side street had a pair of guinea pigs, and also were kids that our kids enjoyed playing with. When their dad received orders to move, we inherited the guinea pigs which they couldn't take with them. I sometimes wondered how many homes those guinea pigs had after we, too, had to pass them on.

One day there was considerable excitement in the neighborhood when a wild mongoose ran into the pipe under our driveway. Quite a large gathering of kids and parents came to watch, and to help Gene get it out of the pipe with some kind of long pole.

Some of our own family members and friends sometimes came to visit, and we became "tour guides" for them. Ira and Betty Stauss of Corvallis spent a day with us when they had a stopover during their trip with Rotary to someplace in the Far East. Gene's sister Fern and her husband Harry came for a few days, and their daughter Helen was there for a while another time. Helen's "goal" was to see a Don Ho show! He was making his song *Pretty Bubbles in the Wine* famous at that time. We were happy to have a long-time friend, Jean Brand, stop for a surprise visit on her way home from one of her frequent adventures! (She once said that she only worked in order to have money for traveling! Having "itchy feet" for travel myself, I understood!

Mom and Dad Kelley came for a couple of weeks with us, including Christmas, in December 1968. Dad, Gene, and our kids went on a tuna fishing boat one day, after which we enjoyed the delicacy of sashimi (raw fish) appetizers. Mom was a little squeamish about eating "raw" fish, but she was a good sport, and found it to be "good, but different"! The island's New Year's Eve celebration was quite spectacular—and loud! There were many fireworks displays lighting up whole communities, and enough firecracker explosions to make it sound like the middle of a battle! For our Christmas tree the first year, we bought a sizeable potted Norfolk Island pine and moved it outside after enjoying it for the Christmas season, where it grew about another foot in height. This year, we could move it back inside to enjoy again, with Mom and Dad— but decided it was time to plant it outside after Christmas. Gene and Dad planted it in our yard, between the house and the street corner. We called it "Dad's Hawaiian Tree" because one of his hobbies was planting a tree in every country and state that he visited. His countries included Israel, England, and

Ireland. Eventually, he had put one in almost all of the states, including Alaska. Gene visited this tree again sometime in the 1980's, and it had grown to be four or five times taller than the house!

Ila's dad planting our Norfolk Island Pine   *Here it is in the 1980s*

We were always happy to guide our visitors to an afternoon and evening at the Polynesian Cultural Center. It is part of the Church College of the Pacific, established by the Mormons, especially for education of students from Polynesian countries. Students maintain "villages" at the Center to show types of homes and crafts of hundreds of years ago in Samoa, Fiji, Tahiti, Hawaii, Tonga, and of Maori tribes in New Zealand. In the evening there is a two-hour musical show and an opportunity to dine on typical foods from all of those cultures.

Another favorite place to learn about the development of Hawaiian culture was the Ulu Mau Village, located near Waikiki Beach. There we enjoyed watching tapa printing, poi pounding, cooking, various games, quilting—a unique kind of appliqué—and, of course, hula dancing.

One of the most significant experiences for all of our family was the beginning of school for David. He had been really eager to ride in the big gray bus the Navy supplied for transportation to school! So, on September 11, 1968, he proudly joined Becky and his friends to climb aboard and ride to his Kindergarten class at Pearl Harbor Kai Elementary! He and Becky frequently attended a childcare group that provided hot lunches and good activities for the children when I had shopping or social events to do. Becky described one of their lunch experiences where they had a choice of stew or soup to go with their sandwiches. The lady who was serving said to David, "Do you want soup, or stew?" David said, "Yes." Again, she repeated, "Do you want soup, or stew?" Again, David said, "Yes!" By then Becky realized David's problem and came to his rescue and repeated the question to him more slowly. "David, do you want soup, or do you want stew?" David then realized that he thought the choice was "super-stew"! Our family all still chuckle about that memory!

Gene always felt that "the Mama" needed a break from the kitchen occasionally, so for many years we ate Sunday dinners "out." In Hawaii, one of our favorite places was at the Pearl Harbor Tavern which had a monkey-bar. The long wall behind the beverage bar was glass, behind which lived several small monkeys with all of their needs for feeding, sleeping, and playing visible. We all thought that to be very entertaining, and our food was good, too. On the Tavern roof was a Bonsai garden. Some of those artistically pruned little trees were very old and creative.

For Chinese food, we liked a small restaurant in Aiea—a kind of "family" place where some of the staff often were sitting at one of the dining room tables wrapping won- tons, or shaping egg rolls, or some other delicacy. On some Sundays we went to brunch at the officers' club at Fort Shafter, which was nearby when we finished activities of the worship service and Sunday school at the military chapel.

Grocery shopping was fun—especially choosing fresh foods that were not only locally grown, but were ones typically used in Polynesian, and other Far East cooking. Being locally grown, fruits and vegetables were tasty and "fresh" the year round. Each time I shopped I bought pineapples and papayas to keep out on the kitchen counter to reach their prime ripeness. Fish of many kinds from nearby ocean waters were wonderfully tasty and plentiful. And we used Kona coffee that had a really rich, full-bodied flavor!

A haircut for Becky became a quite important event in the spring of 1969. It had been growing for four or five years, and was about waist length—beautiful, silky, platinum blonde! She decided she'd like to have it shorter for easier shampooing and brushing, but at the same time, she was concerned about how she would look. These days she would have probably donated it to make wigs for cancer patients, but instead, we just tied it up with a ribbon and saved it—one of the things preserved in my steamer trunk, along with baby shoes and clothes, and other memory "stuff"!

Lotys and Toni, friends of Gene's sister, owned a condo apartment at Waikiki where they regularly came for a few weeks each winter, and occasionally invited Gene and me for dinner when they were there. One evening they asked us to come in time to watch the sunset from their deck, which was on the third (or maybe fourth) floor. Tony said the atmosphere seemed about right that evening for seeing "the green flash." Gene had heard sailors describe the phenomenon but had never seen one himself. It is a brief flash of green, just as the red sun sinks below the horizon. We were told to wait until Toni said it was near, so as not to get our eyes blinded by the sun beforehand. And sure enough! There it was! We later watched for it other times when we saw sunsets over the ocean, but we never saw it again.

Well, living in Hawaii truly must have been like living in Paradise! We even found square dancers! From the time we'd learned that activity early in our marriage, we had found it to be available in almost every place we'd lived!

HAWAII — VISITING THE "BIG ISLAND"

Our first trip to the "Big Island" (Hawaii) was a vacation that included David's fifth birthday—July 4, 1968. We stayed in one of the housekeeping cabins at Kilauea Military Camp, near the rim of Kilauea Crater. It was originally a campsite to be used by the National Guard of Hawaii, and as a resort for regular Army personnel of the Hawaiian Department. It was abandoned as a resort on December 7, 1941; and during World War II, it was used to house Japanese internees, and to quarter some Army tactical groups. In July 1943, the camp became a "Rest and Rejuvenation" (R&R) camp for combat personnel and was eventually developed into a peacetime recreation camp for members of all the Armed Forces and their dependents. Rates depended upon rank—from $3.50 per day for single enlisted personnel to stay in a dormitory facility; to cabins and apartments at $4.25 per day for lowest enlisted rank; up to $7.00 per day for senior officers. Gene's rank was Lieutenant Colonel, so we paid $6.50 for our cabin.

The higher altitude there at the camp on the mountain side made our otherwise comfortable cabin feel quite cool, and when we arrived Gene built a fire in the small, round heating stove. Becky and David had never seen that kind of stove, so we warned them that it would get very hot—and to be careful when they were near it. I continued with our unpacking while the children acquainted themselves with our "home-away-from-home." After a few minutes I noticed David looking at the end of his right forefinger, which was burned with a white blister! He was trying hard to not cry, though it must have been very painful. Instead, he held it up in the air and said, "Kentucky Fried Chicken"! His innocent bravery brought tears to my eyes, as I gave first aid to his cute finger! I suppose it was a natural experiment for a kid to discover for himself "how hot is hot?"

Many recreation facilities and conveniences were available: a golf course (with rental equipment), tennis courts, a theater, laundry, library, a nursery, beauty shop, cafeteria, dispensary, gift shop, car rental, and equipment for many games. The cafeteria would prepare take-along lunches or prepare special things like birthday cakes.

Bus tours were scheduled every day from Monday through Saturday; and we made use of some of those which included a guide to point out and describe places of interest. All along the way we often saw lava flows—some of various colors—and rain forests of giant ferns and colorful blossoms. There were frequent stops for giving extra time to explore; to "feel" the tropical air, to hear sounds of birds, and to enjoy the fragrance of the earth and flowers. Becky and David really enjoyed playing at the Black Sand beach. In one of the eruptions many years ago, a large lava flow continued on into the ocean; and as it was eroded, a long stretch of beach became just black sand. On another side of the island a similar lava flow turned the beach into green sand. At one stop we visited the Hale Manu Craft Shop. It was originally sponsored and subsidized by the Tuberculosis Association of Hawaii through sales of Christmas Seals. At the time we visited, it had changed ownership and now employed men who had completed treatment at the T.B. hospital.

Gardens were delightful stops. One was an authentic Japanese tea garden named Liliuokalani Gardens in honor of Hawaii's last queen. At Kong's Flora Leigh Gardens, there were over one hundred varieties of tropical plants artistically arranged along walks, with pools and varied vegetation, all identified and marked. It was started by a Mr. Kong as a hobby, and as it grew in size it was opened to the public.

Banyan Drive was started in 1933. One of the first celebrities to plant a tree along this scenic drive was George Herman "Babe" Ruth. In 1934, Franklin D, Roosevelt became one of the most prominent persons to plant a tree. Others were some members of his Cabinet—Secretary of War George Dern, Postmaster General James Farley, and Secretary of the Treasury Henry Morgenthau—as well as many other well-known people. Each tree is identified by a small sign at the base. It's an "eerie" kind of drive—the banyan trees so large and wide, with "roots" going down into the ground from the wide-spread branches, they look "other-worldly."

We went to parks that showed "tree molds" of hardened lava, formed around trees that were living—forming lava "tubes" to walk through; fern jungles, orchid gardens, and a bird park. Stopping at a macadamia nut orchard, we saw a movie of the production operations from planting to harvesting. This one, the Keaau Royal Macadamia Nut Factory, had about 72,000 trees. Of course, part of the tour included samples of their delicious products! At the Mauna Loa Orchid Farm, we observed the workings of another large industry of the Big Island. Each lady in our group received an orchid lei, and the men received boutonnieres!

One of the tours stopped for lunch at a park named Harry K. Brown "Waikoloa" Park. The name is derived from the pond in the park ("wai" meaning "water"), and the migratory birds that visit each year from the Arctic Circle ("okolea" meaning "golden plover"). A Mr. Hall supervised the construction of the park during WPA days. He brought to the park many stones important to the Hawaiian people, and which were in danger of being lost or destroyed. Some of those were stones that were used for tying prisoners in a sitting position; the feet being tied to smaller stones, and the back placed against the taller ones.

One stop that was very aptly named was "Devastation Trail," created when winds blew hot pumice and ash through a forest during the 1959 eruption. (There were several small eruptions during the years we lived in Hawaii, but they always broke out from someplace on a side of the mountain). After driving for a time along the Chain of Craters Road, and seeing sites of other eruptions, by far the most exciting sight was the Kilauea Crater, still bubbling and steaming, glowing red at night! Our tour guide knew that David was having his fifth birthday while we were there, and asked David what he thought about that display of fire and smoke to celebrate his birthday? He made it seem to David like it was all there just to honor his birthday! Very special memories for him! A guided walking tour that went into the crater was available, but we decided to let that tour wait for another time!

To celebrate David's birthday, we ordered a decorated cake from the bakers at the cafeteria, and invited some children at the camp, who had become playmates for Becky and David, to come to our cabin for a little party!

This whole experience (except David's birthday party) was duplicated in January of 1969, when my Mom and Dad came for a Christmas visit with us. We took them for a stay at Camp Kilauea, and for tours on our own time in our rented car—then to the airport for them to return home, carrying boxes of anthuriums and orchids with them! (Gifts for their friends!) The Big Island was a really great experience for them, and a very rewarding one for us to think about as we flew back to our home in Oahu!

HOW I BECAME A GIRL SCOUT
Or
"ON MY HONOR, I WILL TRY…"

As a child growing up in the country during the depression, Boy Scouts and Girl Scouts were totally unknown to me, or to my family. I first learned about Boy Scouts at age sixteen in 1941, when we moved to Springfield, Missouri for me to go to Business College. My brother Ross was a couple of years younger than I and joined a Boy Scout troop that met at his school. He was so proud to be wearing a uniform and worked hard to get badges to display on it. He was very particular about all the regulations—like getting his scarf tied just right—and learned many skills while working for those badges. I could see the benefits of a young person belonging to such a group.

Many years later, when our daughter Becky became old enough to start in a scouting program, we wanted her to experience the group friendship and to learn special skills while having fun doing it. We lived in Columbia, Missouri, by then, and some of her neighbor friends belonged to the Bluebirds, which was the beginner group for Campfire Girls. One of her Bluebird pals was Julie, daughter of Martha, the sister my brother Sterling's wife, Jeannette. Bluebirds was a great activity for her during all that school year when she was seven, and she liked wearing their cute red, white, and blue uniform!

In the summer, Gene came home from Vietnam with orders for duty in Hawaii. We were fortunate there to live in Navy base housing at McGrew Point, just outside the little town of Aiea. Becky rode a bus to school at the Hickam air base, but the Bluebirds met in Aiea; so that meant a once-a-week trip after school to take her to her meetings—a small inconvenience for me that was worth the time and effort for Becky's benefit. Of course, each trip also meant getting three-year-old David into the car, too.

I soon noticed that the Girl Scouts had a special meeting place near our house that was called "The Scout Hut." That started me thinking that if it would be okay with Becky to change groups, she could walk to meetings. Besides that, many of our military neighbors' daughters who had become Becky's friends were Girl Scouts. The idea of changing became even more desirable when we discovered at the beginning of the next year that the Bluebird leader was leaving, and no one would volunteer to take her place. I felt a little guilty that I wasn't volunteering, but I still didn't know very much about the Campfire Girls' program, and besides, I had to take care of David.

After talking to Becky about the situation, she was happy to go with Girl Scouts instead. I went with her to the first meeting, which was to enroll the girls and line up some volunteer help. Guess what? You're right! They didn't have a leader, either! What had I done? I still didn't want to volunteer to lead anything—especially knowing nothing about the Scout program! And, of course, I still had David, now age four, to consider. I finally hesitantly opened my mouth and explained my ignorance and my boy child's needs; but agreed to try to learn if we could have a co-leader, and if I could bring David to meetings, in case I couldn't find a sitter for him. He was quite well behaved, and I thought would play quietly in a corner with some books or toys. The co-leader who volunteered was a very capable lady with at least some experience, and most of the mothers agreed to help out "in any way they could." I thought to myself, "If you're all so willing to help, why wouldn't you help by being a leader!" But I didn't say it. At least, we were all friendly.

I found that periodically there was an all-day class for leaders not far away in Honolulu. It was an opportunity for me to learn "the Girl Scout way" for teaching the skills involved with working out the many badges that would help the girls become well-rounded people. I don't remember very many of them, but the categories included nutrition, cooking, sewing, community service, camping, family relationships, and even a category in religion. (In those days it was "politically correct" to admit that religion was okay.)

Gene's work was from midnight to mid-morning, so after a few hours of sleep he could be up to take care of David most of the time, and even helped me learn some needed skills—like tying knots! I really enjoyed learning about scouting and managed to keep a couple of steps ahead of the girls. I even felt a special responsibility when I, too, wore the uniform. It was a different design from the girls' but was made of the same green fabric.

Our troop was #145, and the girls were all eager, happy "troopers." I always got a "frog in my throat" when we said the Pledge of Allegiance at the beginning of each meeting, but the girls probably didn't notice. There were special names for almost everything—for instance, for hikes, each person carried snacks in a "nosebag." For cooking when camping, each one made a little "cooker" out of an empty #10 (tall) tin can. A can opener was used to make some triangular shaped holes around the open end, and more holes were cut around the side at the other end. The end that hadn't been removed became the cooking surface when it was turned upside down over the heat source. The heat source was also a project for each girl—corrugated cardboard strips, a little over an inch wide, tightly wound around to fit into an empty tuna fish can. Paraffin was then safely melted in a container sitting in a pan with boiling water, and then poured into the tuna can to almost cover the cardboard. This step in the project was done by one of the adults. It worked quite well for cooking bacon right on the top of the cooker, and for frying an egg in the grease left by the bacon. Each girl also had to learn how to build a fire before time to go camping, and how to put up and take down a tent, among many other things.

When it came time for the troop to camp, Gene planned to stay at home with David; but at the last minute, he found that he had to make a trip with the Admiral to Thailand, or Hong Kong, or someplace. The only thing I could do was to take David along with me on the overnight camping trip! We had two patrols (groups) of girls in the troop, with the co-leader and a volunteer mother to be in charge of them, so that I had some freedom to help with David—although he was a star attraction for all the girls, too. At that time, I hadn't realized that cocoa was somewhat of a stimulant, so I was happy to go along with the very popular activity of hot chocolate and making "S'mores" at the evening campfire. Two forms of chocolate just before bedtime! That, plus the excitement of the outing, made getting to sleep a little late! When it was time to award badges, I made a special camping badge to give David at the awards ceremony. He was quite a fine little "trooper," and sure added interest to the activity!

An awards ceremony was quite a formal occasion with special candles, formations, and procedures, followed with refreshments. I think I mentioned that a lump came into my throat when I said the Pledge of Allegiance. (It always has, and still does.) Well, when it came time to award the badges, with me feeling so proud of the work the girls had done, and describing some of the many skills they'd learned in the process, the lump in the throat turned into actual weeping! Embarrassing!

I wouldn't take anything for that year of experience in scouting! There's nothing that can compare with working and playing with eight-nine-ten-year old girls, full of enthusiasm, and eager to please and learn!

When summer came it was time for Gene to get orders again, and we were to travel back to the mainland on the "Lurline," one of the Matson ocean liners.

After we were in our stateroom, several friends came on board to bid farewell, but what a surprise it was when Troop #145, wearing their uniforms and accompanied by the troop co-leader, appeared with a special surprise gift for me! It was a lovely linen handkerchief upon which the girls had embroidered, in shades of Girl-Scout-green: "Aloha, Mrs. Bench—from Troop 145"! The little girl, who presented it said, "Mrs. Bench, this gift is for your tears!" Well, I <u>sure</u> needed it then—and I could even use it now, while I'm writing about it!

LEAVING HAWAII

Gene had expected a three-year tour of duty in Hawaii, but in the early spring of 1969, he received orders to attend the National War College in Washington, D. C. Selection for an assignment to that high-level school was a distinct honor, so he was very excited! Study there would include a Master's degree in International Affairs from George Washington University; and many of its graduates became Generals, Admirals, and Ambassadors. For <u>that</u>, we would certainly give up the joy of our year-round summer life in Hawaii! Duty there would begin August 2nd, which would give him about six weeks of combined leave and travel time that we could use for visiting families, and for finding a new home in the vicinity of Washington.

However, there was still time for more island fun—more luaus, hula lessons, visits to pineapple fields and the sugar cane mill, a glass-bottom boat ride over coral reefs, and frequent beach picnics to search for beach glass and unusual shells! Gene took some golfing and sailing lessons; and I enjoyed some classes in "Island and Asian" cooking. Looking back to some deep-sea tuna fishing trips, the tropical bird songs, and our many new and different experiences, made the remaining time seem even more special. (I probably should tell about a friend's myna bird that amused all of us. When the doorbell rang, it very plainly said, "Come in!" When the door opened, it was ready with, "Hello!" Then sometime soon, we heard it say an interesting sentence its mistress had taught it: "Birds don't talk!" It said those words with really nice voice inflections—and one couldn't help laughing! Becky and David liked visiting at their house and playing with their children.)

And, there was work to be done, too! Gene frequently accompanied Admiral McCain when he went to Washington for conferences, and he was able to use some of his spare time there to look for a house for us. We made a list of some features we would like, which gave a real estate agent an idea of possible selections: three bedrooms, two baths, garage (preferably attached), good school district, reasonable distance from D.C., and on the south side—expecting that the next year's assignment would more than likely be at Marine Corps Headquarters in Arlington, or maybe at Quantico. Prices of homes in that area were so high that we soon realized we'd have to shorten our list! One thing that "bit the dust" was a garage! Other things had to be considered, too: we still owned a house on Arthur Circle in Corvallis that we had contracted to Camp Adair for use as officers' quarters, with the rent making our mortgage payments on it. It would need to be sold in order for us to have more financial freedom when investing in another higher-priced one. It so happened that soon after Gene received his orders, a letter from Camp Adair told us that our house would no longer be needed, and they were ready to terminate their contract with us. So that was an easy hurdle, and a perfect time of year to sell a house in Corvallis!

Again, there was "car-shipping" to consider. We were authorized to ship a car on Gene's orders, so he made arrangements for it to go early, to be there for our transportation when we arrived in Los Angeles. We chose to ship the Chevrolet sedan, and sell the VW Bug in Hawaii. That was an easy sale, and we could keep it to use until our departure.

For this change of station travel, we were to sail on the Matson Line's USS Lurline, leaving Honolulu on Monday, June 16th. The packers came to pack our household effects on May 19th, so for the remaining month we were able to use beds, a table and some chairs furnished by base quarters; plus a few pots, pans and basic housekeeping items of our own that would go later in a separate shipment. One thing about living in military quarters was that before leaving, cleaning had to pass what we called a "white-glove" inspection. After doing that, I always felt that now that my house was this clean, I'd like to move back into it! In all the moving that we did, I deep-cleaned my share of kitchen stoves and shelves of houses we moved into! It was often unbelievable how much cooked-on grease the previous occupants left behind!

On sailing day, we went aboard the ship in the afternoon, and had two or three hours to receive guests in our stateroom. Several friends came to bid us "Bon Voyage" with flowers, leis, snacks, cards, and travel games for the kids. According to legend, tossing one's lei into the water when leaving Hawaii assures your future return, so of course we did that! And we joined others along the guard rail who were throwing streamers down to friends at Pier 10.

Becky and David were really impressed with being on that big ocean liner! The swimming pool was a favorite place, and there were planned activities for children every day and evening. They even enjoyed getting "dressed" for dinner! Our room steward came in every evening while we were at dinner to prepare our beds for sleeping, and always did some special thing for the kids' amusement. Gene had his little rubber good-luck toy with us that he called "The Man on My Shoulder," and the steward used that, or one of the kids' toys to make novel arrangements. They were very happy with the bunk beds—a new experience for them. Gene and I enjoyed a real vacation for those few days—many bridge games, evening entertainment in the lounge, visiting with other travelers, and just relaxing.

One night, somewhere in mid-ocean, we felt some unusual movements of the ship, and learned the next day that there was an engine problem that would slow our speed but was not a danger. I think we all felt that we were just getting some extended vacation time on our way to our Los Angeles destination!

My cousin, Clarence, who lived in a suburb of Los Angeles, had picked up the car we'd shipped, met us at the ship and drove us to his place where we stayed for a few days with him and his wife Evelyn. At his workplace he could get guest tickets for Disneyland, and for two days he was our guide for adventures there—endearing himself to Becky and David, of course—while we "caught up" on visiting.

Then we began another cross-country drive with stops to visit friends in Corvallis, Gene's family in the Tacoma area, new sights along the road, and Kelley families in Kansas, Missouri, and Indiana. In Columbia, Missouri, we did more car business with brother Sterling—traded the trusty Chevy for a new green Pontiac Catalina and bought a new Datsun for Gene to use for commuting to work. From there, the rest of the way to Springfield, VA, where our next home was waiting for us, I got my first experience with long-distance driving. David usually rode with Gene in the Datsun, with Becky and me following in the Pontiac. Sometimes we could manage to stay fairly close together, but for the sake of safety, we always planned for a meeting place along the road ahead.

At the end of that journey was our new home! It was a lovely, comfortable, two-story brick house with a patio and a deck; and a wooded, fenced back yard that extended to the bank of a shady little creek!

There was no garage! But there was a spacious, concrete, adjoining parking place!

LIFE IN SPRINGFIELD, VIRGINIA
MOVE TO CORVALLIS, OREGON—1969-1973

Again, I was moving into a house I had not seen, except for photos. While still living in Hawaii, Gene had had time to fly to Washington to do some house-hunting—enough to discover that real estate in the D.C. area was very "spendy"! He wanted to find a place in one of the suburbs on the south side of the city, because the assignment to the National War College would be for only one year; and in order to save expenses, the Marine Corps would more than likely send him to fill one of the many offices in the area—Marine Corps Headquarters, the Pentagon, or Quantico, Virginia, all located to the south. Our new address was 7308 Calamo Street, in Springfield, Virginia—very conveniently located about a mile west of I-95, and about a mile south of a large shopping center—easy access to the freeway for Gene's commute. Becky and David would be a short distance from Francis Scott Key Elementary school—Becky in fifth grade, David in first.

The house was a lovely two-story red-brick one on a half-acre wooded lot, with a back yard that extended quite a distance to an all-weather creek. The kids and I could hardly wait for Gene to get the door open for us to see the inside! The double-door opened to a split-level entrance, with steps going down on the left to a large family room, two bedrooms, a half-bath, utility, and storage room. Steps to the right led up to a living room, dining room and kitchen to the left; three bedrooms, and a bathroom to the right. Double sliding glass doors from the dining room opened upon a wide deck that extended the length of the house; and underneath was a concrete patio, and a tool shed. The first bedroom to the right of the entry became David's room; Becky's was the right front corner; and the master bedroom and connecting bath were in the right rear corner.

The fenced back yard was a wonderful place with several tall pine trees, some wild flowers, and small bushes. The trees were populated with scampering gray squirrels, chickadees, cardinals, mocking birds, blue jays, and song sparrows—to name a few. A back gate gave access to the bank of the creek and the wooded hill on the other side of it—a great place for a six-year-old boy to play with his new neighbor friends—and after about a year, with a Beagle and her puppies. (One of the years we lived there happened to be one that the seventeen-year Cicada locusts awakened, climbed the trees, shed their shells, and made their all-day squawking sound. Just one of them sounded like

"Pha-raoh!," but the sound of the millions of them altogether, was just a maddening roar! David and his friends made a game of collecting the shells they left behind on the trunks of the trees. The locust damage was in the form of cutting off ends of branches—by making splits in tender bark in which to deposit their eggs. When the damaged twig, holding the eggs, fell to the ground, the eggs hatched into grubs which went underground to live until time to emerge and finish the life-cycle.)

At the War College (later renamed National Defense University), located at Fort McNair in Washington, D.C, Gene discovered very interesting and challenging courses—many of them taught by high-level officials from State Department, military services, and businesses. A lot of emphasis was placed upon "community," with the idea of future "net-working" among peers. Students were assigned to small groups that were frequently revised, so that by socializing within one's group, by graduation each one would come to know all the others. The result—success might often depend more upon whom you know than upon what you know! It made life there very busy, interesting, and rewarding. Graduates went away with a Master of Science degree in International Affairs, equipped for becoming admirals, generals, or ambassadors. One off-campus trip, which included wives, was three days in New York City, attending meetings at the United Nations Building. There were other trips just for students, with a major one for Gene to several countries in Africa where their group was hosted by the local State Department people. Graduation in May, 1970, included a lovely formal dinner-dance.

His next assignment, in July, 1970, was to Marine Corps Headquarters in Arlington, Virginia, where he was an Assistant Team Chief in the Joint Planning Group. On October 6, the kids and I were invited to come to be with him there when he was promoted to Colonel, by his friend General Chaisson. Eight days later he was given a temporary assignment in London, with permission for the children and me to be with him (at our own expense). That experience will be described in another story called "London Assignment."

Other assignments while still stationed at Headquarters were: Plans Officer, Eastern Regional Team; G-3 Division, Assistant Head of Training and Education Branch A03; Head of Training and Education Branch AO3; and finally to Head of Inspection Team "B," Inspection Division, MCC 010, from which he retired June 30, 1973. Work on the inspection team required him to be away from home several times during the last year and a half of his time at Headquarters. The team traveled to all places in the world where Marines were stationed, in order to inspect their working conditions. Travel was provided by a Marine Corps plane that was designated for their use.

In about a week we were able to get unpacked, to begin getting acquainted with the neighborhood, and to discovering opportunities for exploring. We were happy to find it a very friendly neighborhood that included several children near the ages of our kids. Next door on our left lived the Hardin family: Ed, Bonnie, and children Karen and Wesley. Ed worked at the Department of Education in Washington, and used one of the then "new" computers that took up considerable space. He was a jovial person and liked to visit with Gene with all kinds of discussions and jokes. He called himself a "Dove," and called Gene a "Hawk." Their house was small but had a large "living" deck with an above-ground swimming pool. Bonnie was from West Virginia, had a lovely southern accent, and was a happy stay-at-home mom. Our kids liked playing together, but if Becky and David were invited to swim in the pool with Karen and Wesley, there was a rule that parents would be nearby. So Bonnie and I spent many hours sipping orange-flavored iced tea on their spacious deck while we talked about everything from cookies to "you-name-it." We four grownups played countless games of bridge, while we snacked and visited, and we still keep in touch.

Next door on the other side was the Ahmed family—Valerie was the American mother, and the father—whose name escapes me—was of some middle-eastern nationality. Jamal was a son about Becky's age, and there was a daughter a few years older.

The family across the street had a diabetic daughter named Jackie who was Becky's age, and in the same Girl Scout troop. I was quite impressed with her. She was very outgoing, and had learned to live actively with the diabetes—she responsibly chose her food, and expertly gave herself the needed insulin shots. Jackie's grandmother, named Mrs. Stocks, lived with them. She was a kind, gracious, and fairly active person; and became a frequent, favorite sitter for our children.

We always took advantage of learning about the history, activities, and cultural opportunities in every place we called "home," and this place was one that was really rich! Gene and I had done a lot of exploring when we had lived in that part of Virginia early in Gene's Marine Corps career, but now, with a couple of curious kids, we could do a lot of it all over again, from a different perspective—helping them to enjoy it while we appreciated it all the second time around!

Even in four years, we still weren't able to do much more than "scratch the surface." There were trips to homes of famous people: Thomas Jefferson's Monticello at Charlottesville, George Washington's plantation at Mt. Vernon, Robert E. Lee's mansion in Arlington, to name a few. On one long weekend we went for a tour of the restored colonial village of Williamsburg where the guides are dressed in colonial style, and seem to enjoy giving demonstrations of many of the colonial ways of doing work. Not far from there we went to Jamestown to see where an English settlement had been established in 1607. We had a good laugh with ourselves on that trip while we were traveling from one place to another. I was the map-reader, and we thought we were watching closely for the road to turn to where we wanted to go; but the radio was on for listening to music, and when "Drift Away," one of our favorite songs began playing, we all started singing along with it, and having great fun. We soon realized that while we were "drifting away," we had drifted right past the turn we thought we were looking for!

During spring break in 1973, we took a trip that we thought was really interestingly "unique." Disney World in Orlando, Florida, was in its early stages—nothing like all the adventures that are there now, but plenty to make it a worthwhile visit. And we wanted to give Becky and David a Florida experience before we moved away from the east coast. It so happened that the railroad was offering a special rate for a trip in which they provided special transport for the passengers' <u>cars</u> to also ride on the train—overnight from Washington, D.C. to Orlando! What a perfect convenience, as well as fun! We'd have our car to travel to the more southern parts of Florida, plus it simplified the luggage situation because we packed everything except our small carry-on bags in the car—a very real convenience with children who liked having games, toys, snacks, and "stuff" traveling with them! The departure station was at Lorton, a small town a few miles south of D.C.—actually quite near our place. The directions were for us to arrive at Lorton between 5:00 and 6:00 p.m., drive to the automobile loading dock, and then board the train ourselves where we had reserved seats. Soon a train attendant took us to a dining car where we were served a full, leisurely, "white-tablecloth" dinner, by stewards in sharp, white-coat uniforms. The train was equipped with some tall observation cars, as well as the usual lounge and snack-bar cars, so just being <u>on the train</u> was an adventure in itself! For two or three hours after dinner was finished, a lounge car was set up to show movies and put on entertainment for children.

We were seated in coach class, but the seats were large, and reclined into a very comfortable place to sleep. Each person was given a pillow and a blanket, so when it was "bedtime," Becky and I cuddled into two adjoining seats, with Gene and David sharing two others nearby. When morning came, there was still time for breakfast in the dining car, for exploring on the train, and for "watching the world go by" from our windows. The conductor reminded us that we would be arriving in Orlando about 11:30 a.m., and that as we left the train we would receive a sack lunch. And suddenly, it was summer! Florida weather!

Usually, before we went on a family trip, we did some research to discover some things about places or things we'd enjoy there. Seldom would we all be in total agreement, so in the planning, each person could list some choices— with the idea that we'd need to stay within our budget. Animals and science were often among David's favorites. Becky liked history and shopping. In Florida, of course, she especially wished for some time to lie on a beach and get a really good suntan! So we planned a route that would take us through orange groves and farm land, across the state to the Gulf of Mexico at Tampa; then we'd continue around the shoreline on our drive back home.

Of interest near Tampa, was Busch Gardens—called an "Africa Experience." There were many acres of activities, displays, boat rides, train rides, exotic birds, animals, bazaars, and food. (The admission price of $3.75 for adults and $2.50 for children included all rides, shows, attractions, and parking for a day!) One of our favorite things there was riding the Trans-Veldt Railway, patterned after African trains of the late 1800's. From it we saw close-up views of hundreds of African animals roaming free. Their African Veldt is also a survival center for many vanishing species of animals which are near extinction. One of the shows that gave the kids many laughs was the bird circus—watching the clever antics of trained cockatoos and macaws.

In Sarasota, we picnicked and played for a while on the Gulf beach and had a tour of the home of the Ringling Brothers' Circus. It was even better than going to one of their road shows! We liked being able to see them in their home setting, to find out some of their history, meet some trainers, get an idea of what it's like to maintain large animals in captivity.

The Everglades was one of David's choices for a place to visit. He wanted to see the alligators and crocodiles "up close"! To do that, we took a tour in a boat with a guide, through miles of swamp that was populated not only with alligators and crocodiles, but with exotic birds, jungle-like vegetation, turtles, frogs, and snakes. It was quite an unusual experience for us to be in a small boat, quietly moving slowly among the cypress and mangrove trees that grew in the shallow water—watching animals and fish living in the water that was warm and almost "steamy" with humidity. It was really exciting when the guide fed some crocodiles and alligators near our boat! (A souvenir entrance permit to the Everglades National Park, shows that we were there on March 8, 1973, and paid $2.00 for the day.)

Our next destination was the Keys. I don't remember how much time we spent there, but we did drive all the way to Key West, stopping along the way to picnic and play along some of the beautiful white sand beaches, look for shells, and watch the water skiers and fishing boats. With one tall fisherman and one short one in our family, we had to stop to see some fishing boats up close; and where there are fishing boats coming and going, one can see a few people proudly standing beside their catches of very large fish—Marlins or Tarpons! I could tell that Gene would have really enjoyed a day on one of those boats, but this wasn't the time. (That time did come, but a long time later.) When it was time to eat—none of us turned down Key Lime Pie, no matter what time of day it was! And there's nothing more beautiful than a Gulf-Coast sunset!

After spending time with the jungle animals in the Everglades, which was one of David's choices for sightseeing, it was Becky's turn for one of her wishes—to lie on a beach, and get a good suntan! We found time for that at the Homestead Air Force Base, a few miles south of Miami. (Being a military officer, Gene was entitled to lodging on a military base, for much less cost than "market" accommodations, if space was available. Some of the guest quarters were motel or hotel type rooms or suites, usually with coffeemakers and small refrigerators; some were apartments where families might be able to stay while waiting for more permanent housing; and often when we traveled, we took advantage of this privilege.) The beach was nearby—sand and ocean just as beautiful as the Miami beach, and much less crowded. I remember that we visited with some other military families relaxing there, and Becky was quite impressed with one of the teen-age girls who was very tan and beautiful; and being taller than most girls her age, Becky was able to enjoy getting her tan "in style," probably pretending that she, herself, was a teenager! That was much more rewarding than frolicking in the waves and building sand castles with her little brother!

While there we drove up to Miami, and took the Rickenbacker Causeway across an arm of Biscayne Bay, out to the Seaquarium on Virginia Key. None of us ever tired of spending time observing the beauty, and watching the antics, of creatures in the under-water world. This park, covering sixty acres was especially interesting, being in tropical waters.

Of course, we couldn't miss an opportunity to visit the Kennedy Space Center! Things there were so exciting, we could have spent much more time than we had to spare. We saw movies and saw exhibits and demonstrations of many kinds. Then on a guided bus tour we saw the launch sites, the vehicle assembly building, and the Air Force museum. Our young David had an imagination that perhaps he, too, could some day ride into space in front of one of those great rockets!

All the way north along the eastern coast, we made frequent stops "to play," and tried to turn lunch stops into short beach picnics.

Another sightseeing adventure was in St. Augustine. There we enjoyed a tour of the city which included the oldest Spanish house in the United States. St. Augustine was founded in 1565, as a Spanish military outpost. For almost two hundred years it was the scene of violence and political intrigue—raided and burned by Sir Francis Drake, sacked by English pirates, and burned by English troops. The oldest house shows continuous occupancy from early 1600's to the present. From the original crude structure of palm thatch and wood—which had burned—the present house "evolved" with many additions that tell the story of its long and colorful past. The first floor walls are made of coquina, a natural shell-stone found on Anastasia Island, across the bay. Some tapia floors, a mixture of lime, sand and shell, are typically Spanish, of a very early period. The Spanish covered their windows with projecting lattices of wood, and used wooden shutters to keep out enemies and weather. Secluded patios were located to the rear of their houses, and were well stocked with orange, lemon, pomegranate, fig, and other fruit trees suited to the climate.

But every vacation has to come to an end, and for us it was back to Calamo Street, for school and work—tanned and rested, our heads and hearts filled with rich memories of our southern adventures!

Living in Springfield for four years gave our family invaluable experiences—in a part of the country steeped in history and culture, all available within not too many miles. In Pennsylvania, there were Philadelphia, Gettysburg, Amish country in Lancaster County, and chocolate delights in Hershey. No history book could imprint the feeling gained in Philadelphia— standing in Independence Hall, in the very room where the Declaration of Independence was signed, the Constitution was written, and our nation was born! All of us were thrilled to be able to see the Liberty Bell up close, and to imagine the joy felt by our "founding fathers" who gave their energy, thought, and treasure to establish a nation that would be based upon freedom!

Being in Lancaster County, experiencing the life of the Amish people, was like going back in time—fertile farmlands, horse-drawn buggies, people simply dressed in mostly black clothing, doing their farm work and housework by hand. They carefully guard their privacy, but tourists are able to learn of their way of life at certain homes and shops that are operated for that purpose, including places to enjoy their simple, old fashioned, but delicious food.

But not far away, the food in Hershey was a different matter! What kind of chocolate would you like to sample? It was like being in "Willie Wonka" land! "Chocolate Town, U.S.A.," began with the return of Milton S. Hershey to his place of birth in central Pennsylvania. In 1903, he built his first plant and began manufacturing milk chocolate products on a large scale. From two small buildings, the plant had grown to more than two million square feet of floor space in 26 separate buildings. It was an educational adventure for all of us, to say nothing of breathing the delightful fragrance while watching the production of the hundreds of delicious chocolate delicacies. For a "chocoholic" like me, it was like I had "died and gone to Heaven"! This area was early settled by German and Scotch-Irish—hard-working people, creative in making useful items for living; such as fine cut-glassware, Stiegel stoves, canal boats, Conestoga wagons, various Pennsylvania Dutch crafts, pewter, spinning wheels, clocks, and sewing machines.

Farther west in Pennsylvania was Gettysburg. There we found another experience of history not possible to imagine without being there "on the ground." To begin, we had a simulated ride as if on the train upon which President Lincoln journeyed from Washington to Gettysburg on November 18, 1863, for the dedication of the National Cemetery. One actually "feels" the motion of the train, seeing and hearing events that took place on this historic trip—including the welcome for the President and his party upon arrival. But seeing a movie portraying one of the famous battles, hearing Lincoln's address, then actually walking on the very ground where so many brave men lost their lives, gives one "goose-bumps"! It was another time to say a prayer of appreciation for the freedom that we enjoy, and too often take for granted!

One of Becky's favorite books was *Misty*, a story about the Wild Pony Refuge on Chincoteague Island, across Chesapeake Bay from the mainland. I don't remember how we got to the island—by ferry boat, or by the seventeen-mile Chesapeake Bay Bridge-Tunnel, which is said to be among the seven engineering wonders of the world; but once there, we found more things than ponies of interest. The larger island of Assateague was discovered in 1608 by Captain John Smith, and we saw many well-preserved buildings of the colonial culture of the Eastern Shore that date to the 1700's.

The experience of living so near Washington, D.C. gave us all an opportunity to "feel" the best parts of government, as well as history of the development of the capital. We spent many hours in museums of all kinds, touring the capitol, the White House, monuments to presidents, and various historical buildings. It was like being in a different world to walk in a park in Cherry Blossom time! It's beyond words to "feel" springtime, surrounded by those beautiful pink flowers, away from the hustle and bustle of traffic and the work-a-day scene!

Some of the little things that David remembers about living in Springfield are about his friend, Wesley Marshall, and playing along the creek behind our house. Once he found a snapping turtle in the creek. He remembers Dad taking black snakes out of a woodpecker hole in one of the trees. He and Gene frequently went to a nearby Beagle farm where they did some fishing and hunting. Gene even helped him fire a shot-gun for the first time—he remembers the "kick" that wasn't very comfortable! When my dad visited, David took him fishing along the creek; and one day David caught, with his hands, a Carp that was ready to spawn! He carried it to the house—eggs spewing out—to keep in water in the laundry tub for his dad to see!

Becky had many friends and activities, and was on the threshold of becoming an adult. I'm afraid I might have been overly protective and hesitant to allow her as much freedom as she might have been able to handle. I had to "give in" to things like shaving legs and piercing ears that were really difficult for me. And I had a real eye-opener one day when her reply to me, about some discussion I don't remember, was, "Mom! How can you think that I don't "notice" boys!" (She was thirteen years old! It was time for Mom to wake up!)

Early in 1973, Gene had decided it was time for him to retire from the Marine Corps. Having lived in Corvallis before, we thought it would be a good place to "plant" our family while the children would soon be ready for high school and further education. The rest of the Bench family lived in the Tacoma, Washington, area, within easy visiting distance; and very important— there were wonderful streams for fishing! In May, he drove one of our cars to Corvallis, to look for a house, but he wanted me to be able to help make the final decision. I flew out to make the rounds with him and the realtor, and on Mother's Day we signed on the dotted line for the country home with a couple of acres at 910 NW Overlook Drive! There was even a backyard fence under tall fir trees for our beagle, Trimmie!

910 NW Overlook Drive, Corvallis

View from kitchen window
Tree David planted

But we had added another family member! When Gene picked me up at the airport, I discovered that a very young baby red squirrel was living in Gene's Datsun! On the way across country, in Tarkio, Missouri, he had discovered this tiny thing struggling in the middle of the street. It had evidently fallen out of its nest and wasn't even able to walk. He rescued it, gave it some banana left over from his lunch, and some water—all of which it ravenously devoured—and named it "Tarkio." Soon he discovered that Tarkio was infested with fleas, so on the way to his motel he picked up some flea powder, and shook the squirrel and some powder together in a paper bag. He said that the powder left in the bag looked like salt and pepper! We drove to Tacoma, to leave the car with Gene's mom and dad, and the two (actually three) of us flew back home from Sea-Tac. One of our "carry-ons" was a gallon plastic milk carton with a closeable door cut into the shoulder of it for putting Tarkio inside with some bedding and some food. More food could be dropped in through the air-hole left with the lid removed. He, and we, naturally attracted a lot of attention! When we got back home, we bought a tall, small-animal cage to be Tarkio's home on our patio. Gene made a wheel upon which he could run for exercise, and placed small pieces of tree limbs for him to climb. When we moved to Corvallis in July, Tarkio rode inside his cage in the back seat of our Pontiac, between Becky and David.

Four years in Springfield was the longest time Gene and I had lived in one place for the almost twenty-five years of our marriage! What in the <u>world</u> would it be like to live in the same house for maybe the rest of our lives! My heart couldn't help pondering that question. On the surface, it felt good—to be able "invest" in things like draperies and carpets, rather than economizing on something to "make do" for a couple of years; to be able to remodel if we wanted a change; for the children to be able to finally "put down some roots." But at a deeper level, there was a strange feeling of "finality." And what about Gene? Would he miss the military way of life, or become restless? I even voiced some of those feelings to Gene, hoping I was doing it in a positive way. He assured me that he was looking forward to a change—to more time to spend with the kids, to being able to do more fishing and hunting, to being free of career responsibility 24/7; and to being a common, everyday citizen. With those ideas in mind, we were able to present the whole deal to Becky and David with enthusiasm in a spirit of a great adventure!

Selling our house was no problem. We even did it ourselves, with the help of an office that specialized in helping with the proper papers. Officers coming to new assignments in that area were almost "standing in line" for a good deal on a good location. (However, we soon got some criticism from a neighbor who was a real estate agent—she said she could have got our asking price for us, plus a commission for herself! We thought that she might have been worried about who would be her new neighbors. I think that by law, we were not able to be "selective." She could have chosen the people to whom she showed it, with consideration given to the color of skin, which in those days, in that area, was important to many people.)

Some planning had to happen for our two animals. We wanted to take the kids into Canada—just so they could say they had been there, and we all had passports from the earlier travels in Europe—but Tarkio would have to have some shots, although he could ride in his cage in the car. When it came to Trimmie, the beagle, either she or I would have to fly, because my stomach didn't tolerate beagle dog odor very well. The group decided that it would be best for me to ride in the car, because Trimmie wouldn't be able to pour drinks and hand out snacks! She stayed with friends who put her on a plane after we were settled.

Finally, on July 2nd, our furniture was on its way with Mayflower, the house was the cleanest it had been since we moved into it, the 69 Pontiac Catalina was loaded up with Tarkio riding in the middle of the back seat—which gave a good definition of the "my side-your side" space between the kids. Becky was sitting behind me, Gene was under the steering wheel, and David was behind him. As we pulled out of the driveway for the last time, Becky was weeping buckets of tears because she was so sad to be leaving her friends! And I was crying because Becky was crying! David piped up with a cheerful, "Let's GO, DAD!" And go, we did for the rest of July!

The aim of this cross-country trip was for the children to experience being in as many states as reasonable, historical and scenic adventures, and visiting friends and family along the way. In each state we found more than enough to enjoy in the time available, but Becky and David were good travelers, and most of the time were even friendly with each other! Picnic lunches and time to get some exercise each day helped.

Special things to see in New York were the Statue of Liberty and the UN. Special adventure was riding on the subway. One of the significant things for me at the UN was a very large bronze statue that was a gift from the U.S.S.R.—"Man Beating Sword into Plowshare"! If only that could become a universal reality!

In Connecticut, we saw ships; drove across Rhode Island; in Massachusetts, Cape Cod, historic Boston and baked beans; a lobster dinner in Maine; and wonderful scenery in New Hampshire and Vermont.

A significant stop was in the Thousand Islands area of the St. Lawrence River at the eastern end of Lake Ontario; after we had entered Canada a few miles down-river, and driven along the Canadian shore. Tarkio was a novelty when we crossed the border, but his presence was no problem! A boat tour with a guide seemed to be the best way to learn about the island area, and that was great fun. Of course, there wasn't time to visit every one of the 1000, but some seemed significant. Many were privately owned, some had castles, some were migratory bird sanctuaries. We liked the smallest one, upon which grew a couple of shrubs of some kind, and one small, very wind-blown tree that looked like it was hanging on for dear life to that rocky place! Another unique island had only one house, with a few small trees, and no other space to spare. Between two of the islands was a foot-bridge, the tour guide called the world's shortest bridge.

A few hours at Niagara Falls were exciting ones. It's a sight that is hard to imagine without seeing—and hearing! Gene and I had been there before, so we weren't surprised to see the "wonder" that the kids experienced.

Ohio was the next state on the road west, then Indiana. There, in Muncie, we spent a couple of days with my sister Joy's family—including three cousins of similar ages of ours. In Illinois, were tours of Lincoln-land. In Missouri, we spent time with Kelley family—with grandparents, uncles and aunts and cousins our children usually saw only once a year.

LOVE IS ALL THAT MATTERS

Western state sights included the Badlands and Mt. Rushmore* in South Dakota; we stopped at Yellowstone in Wyoming and the lovely lake and town of Coeur d'Alene in Idaho. The night we spent there was in a large field where Winnebago had set up thousands of their campers to help with tourist lodging. We thought that would be fun to do—and it was! David liked to pretend he was driving it! Next came a few days with the Bench family in the Tacoma area, where we picked up the Datsun that Mom and Dad Bench had kept for us, and headed south to Oregon.

On August 1, our 25th wedding anniversary, we opened the door to move into our new home at 910 NW Overlook Drive, Corvallis, Oregon! For the first few days our sleeping bags were our beds, and the picnic cooler was our refrigerator, but the kids had a wonderful time exploring the woods and the field, where there was grass that was taller than their heads! Somehow, in the years that followed, it was a long time before it ever seemed important to live in any other place!

*(Becky must have been quite impressed with Mt. Rushmore. Later, in the 8th grade—when she had an assignment to write about what she would like to "be" when she grew up—she included a picture of it with a photo of herself added to the lineup of faces! When I saw that, I was quite impressed with her!)

LIVING IN LONDON—1970

This assignment began in October 1970, when we lived in Springfield, Virginia, near Washington, D.C. Gene had recently finished a senior-level course at the National War College at Fort McNair in Washington, had been promoted to Colonel, and was awaiting assignment to some duty appropriate for his new rank. It just so happened that an unexpected vacancy occurred on the Staff in London—a need for a Marine Colonel for three months until the man slated for that assignment finished a special school. We were overjoyed when Gene was selected to fill that vacancy! The Marine Corps couldn't authorize and pay for family to accompany him on such a short assignment, but we considered it a great opportunity, and were able to make arrangements to take the children and me at our own expense. Becky was in grade six, and David was in grade two. Their teachers agreed with our decision, and sent assignments they would need for them to keep up with their classes. Part of Becky's homework was a weekly letter to her class, telling of her "adventures"! I even learned a bit about "home-schooling"!

241

After Gene was settled at his new office, he made the arrangements for our family to go. Our transportation was planned to be by space-available on a military plane, leaving from Andrews Air Base on Sunday afternoon; but Gene was able to get back a day early to accompany us, so that gave us some other possibilities: 11:00 p.m. Saturday, and 4:30 a.m. Sunday. Waiting for space-available travel requires quite a lot of patience, time, and willingness to just _wait_. I was a little concerned about how it would be for seven-year-old David and eleven-year-old Becky, but I soon discovered we had a couple of young "gypsies" in the family! After we discovered we couldn't get on the 11:00 p.m. plane, the children reasoned that probably most people wouldn't want to get up at 2:00 a.m., so if _we_ did, we'd have a better chance! With that kind of "Bench positive thinking" prevailing, we went to bed for four hours, and sure enough, we were on the plane that left at 4:30! The plane was a military jet C-141 that lacked the plush and quiet of a commercial plane, but it was comfortable—and free (except for some minimal fees). We were served a hot meal and supplied with pillows and blankets, so we slept as much as possible, and were thankful to be moving!

We landed in Frankfurt, Germany, about 6:00 p.m., their time, and got on the list for space out of there for London. Gene had borrowed a friend's car for leaving England when he went to pick us up, so it was at the airport for us to use to get the rest of the way to London. The kids were interested that we had to drive on the left side of the road. That traffic pattern was important for us to "absorb" to even make pedestrian street crossing safe: instead of first looking left before crossing, one must first look to the right!

Our home-away-from-home became a small second-floor flat in the old Embassy Hotel, on Bayswater Street, not far from down-town London, but in a lovely neighborhood across from Hyde Park, and Kensington Gardens. It was only half a block to a subway entrance, and we were on a bus line, so it was easy to go just about anywhere—as long as we carried a map. David's favorite mode of travel was the "tube," (their subway) and he always made a point of figuring out the route to take! For the first few days we just looked around our neighborhood, played in the park, did laundry at the nearby Laundromat, and met neighbors.

Shopping in the nearby grocery store was an adventure—strange looking packages and cans until we learned to recognize the containers. The kids liked peanut butter mixed with molasses for a spread on their bread, but I didn't see molasses on any of the shelves. After asking a store clerk, I learned that it was called "Treacle" and came in a tin can. It was darker and thicker than our molasses, but tasted the same.

In our apartment the toilet was in a little room separate from the rest of the bathroom and had less heat. There was even a screen-covered open vent to the outside. The small kitchen, which wouldn't be used all day every day, could be closed off to conserve heat. There was one bedroom where Becky and David slept; and Gene and I slept in the living room on the sofa that opened into a bed.

The winter holiday season was exciting for all of us. Thanksgiving, of course, was a rather private one since it is not celebrated in England, but we had a traditional dinner with all the trimmings at the American Club (which was within walking distance from our apartment). Christmas was a holiday shared by both American and English people and was really special for Becky and David. There were wonderful decorations, special entertainments such as plays and concerts, and crowds of joyful shoppers! Some of our favorite places for shopping and just "looking," were toy stores—one of them was seven stories of every toy imaginable, and all of them fascinating! We found a small Christmas tree for our apartment, and discovered quite an assortment of tree decorations that were actually colorful, foil-covered chocolate candy! The children thought it was quite a novel experience after Christmas when we all sat around eating the decorations we took off the tree! St. Nicholas seemed to realize that we were away from home and had to keep our possessions to a minimum, so he didn't leave many toys—but he quite generously filled the stockings that they hung up!

When the Marine Corps Birthday was celebrated on November 10, we met the Commandant of the Royal Marines, Sir Peter Hellings, and his wife, both really charming people. A few days later, Gene and I were invited to their home for a luncheon. That was an exciting experience for this country girl! I'm thankful for the experience of spending even so short a time in that private home, which, of course, was far from an average English home; but it was good to experience the ambiance of elegant furnishings, and the gracious atmosphere of having servants available to give the hosts freedom with guests. I don't remember the menu, but the important part of the occasion was the experience of sitting at that table with its lovely linens and crystal and china, with the charming host and hostess, sharing conversation with Knights and Ladies! I felt like I was a <u>long</u> way from the Ozarks!

Early in November we took a "green bus" to Windsor Castle, up the Thames River west of London. It's a favorite vacation spot for the royal family because it affords total privacy in many acres of space where they can relax and enjoy their riding, hunting, or whatever. The most interesting display for Becky and David was Queen Mary's doll house, given to her in 1923 as a symbol of good will. Everything is made to the most minute detail—even a toy sewing machine that actually sews. The tiny books are actually printed, etc.

The children really enjoyed living in England. For a while, Becky visited a girls' school that was near our apartment, but she said that in class work they were behind her in most things. I think we might have found a way to spark David's enthusiasm to read! He reads quite well, but should do better, and never seems to really <u>want</u> to read. A few days ago we found a copy of *Dick Whittington and His Cat* at the library, and checked it out with the provision that David would read it <u>himself</u>. He sat down and read half of it when we got home (with help on some of the words), then finished it quite eagerly that evening. I think it was sort of a revelation to himself that he can read things other than his school reader! Then, out of a clear blue sky, he said with sparkling eyes, "I'm going to make a book report on this! Be sure to not take it back to the library until I do that"!

Getting ready for Christmas was fun while we waited nervously for Santa Claus. We planned our own special party for Christmas Eve. In our new "family organization" David was the President who conducted our occasional meetings where anyone who had grievances could air them for discussion, and suggestions could be made for better family relations. For the Christmas Eve party I was in charge of refreshments—English Christmas Pudding and hot chocolate. Becky did the decorations and Daddy was responsible for the entertainment. Becky wanted to read the Bible Christmas story, and we read stories from Christmas cards that we had received; then we sang some carols and played some games.

With the end of our time in London coming soon, we had to "crowd in" a few more things we wanted to do. During a walk on Bayswater Road to see the weekly art display, we found a large oil painting of some big, bold, red cactus flowers that we "need" for one of our walls—got it for the price we would have paid for a frame alone at home, and this one includes the frame! And we bought a couple of street lanterns that David liked.

After a bite of lunch, we spent the rest of the day at the British Museum. It's one of the world's best, and a person could spend many days there. (We've already spent a few.) Things are labeled well, so that just by looking, you can also "study." David was especially interested in the mummies—and there were several. One body, which was from someplace in south Arabia, was displayed in its burial box. It still had some of the hair, and you could see the pores in the skin. It hadn't been mummified or embalmed—just being buried in the hot, dry sand had produced "desiccation" which just dried it up. It was 5000 years old! There was a display of the jars the Egyptians used in their embalming process. In order to delay the body's decay, its insides were removed and stored in special shaped jars—liver in one with a lid shaped like a human's head; lungs in a jar with an ape-shaped head; stomach in one with a jackal head; and intestines in a jar with a lid like a falcon's head.

Also at the museum we saw the Rosetta stone, which was quite exciting! We bought a little book that describes how it was used as a key to the translations of the Egyptian Hieroglyphics. David was so impressed; he decided he'd make up an alphabet of his own!

One day we got up at 5:00 a.m. and went down to the wholesale fish market at "Billingsgate" on the Thames River. What an array! Every kind of fish and shell fish you can imagine. We even found out that those big, ugly Manta Rays are good to eat—it's what they often use for "fish & chips"! There were busy people with carts loaded with boxes, going through the aisles at a pretty fast clip, but no one seemed to be unhappy with we four "tourists" strolling around ogling the merchandise! In fact, there were many smiles and "good mornings" from stall keepers and shoppers as well, and people seemed happy to tell us about where their fish came from, or something about them.

From there we went across the river to a little community called Bermondsey where there is an antique market every Friday morning. It was still dark when we arrived, but already many people were there with flashlights, examining the wares—from the most delicate jewelry to many kinds of furniture and hardware. We used some Christmas money we'd received from family for some things we thought special: a pair of silver candelabra with removable "arms" is really special, really useful, and really beautiful! Another treasure was a blue-green Cloisonné vase—an old Chinese and Japanese art that is disappearing. David called our attention to some old railroad lamps— kerosene burners—with changeable red and green shades for signals. (They eventually found a "home" in David's house.) "History" was everywhere, and I think both David and Becky enjoyed it, and will remember a lot of it!

My mind was often occupied with thoughts about values of living in London for a short time. It was a great living experience for all of us, especially for Becky and David—history, geography, a different monetary practice, a variety of landscapes and architecture, travel without our own car, language with a different accent, new foods, and maybe most especially just the "feel" of the customs and cultures of part of the rest of the world, plus watching the children mature! David challenged himself with figuring out the subway routes, and each time we rode on what Londoners call "the Tube," we let David be our guide (with adult supervision and approval). Becky, at age eleven—and having always shown independent tendencies—sometimes seemed to not want to be identified as part of our "group." We did a lot of walking, of course, and she frequently walked a little ahead of us, or even on the other side of the street. And that was O.K. We could tell she was watching us "out of the corner of her eye." One time, to let her feel a bit more freedom, we arranged for her to ride the bus, by herself, to Gene's office to have lunch with him downtown. She boarded the bus at the street corner a few steps from our apartment, and had no changes before her stop at Marble Arch. I called Gene to let him know she was on the way, so he met her at the bus stop. She became his guest for lunch, then spent the rest of the day with him at his office.

Early in November we took a "green bus" to Windsor Castle. ("Green" buses were for traveling in the countryside; red double-decker buses ran locally in the city of London.) The Castle is up the Thames River thirty miles or so west of London. The site was chosen by William the Conqueror (William I), 980-some years ago when he needed good protection from the new "subjects" that had recently come under his control. Through the years various kings and queens have ordered building onto, or rebuilding of it. It's a favorite vacation spot for the royal family because it affords total privacy in acres and acres of space where they can relax and enjoy their riding, hunting, or whatever.

The Queen frequently entertains with a state dinner at Windsor Castle in the "Waterloo" chamber. The room was originally an open court where herbs were grown to "sweeten the air" of the king's private apartments. Later, antlers were hung on its walls, and it was called "Horn Court." The present chamber was constructed in 1830 to display Sir Thomas Lawrence's portraits of the sovereigns, statesmen, and generals who had contributed to the downfall of Napoleon. The carpet is a beautiful, soft-rose colored design (with some green and tan)—is seamless (80x40 feet), and was made for Queen Victoria in Agra, India. The table is made in sections which, when fitted together, will seat 150 people. All the rooms of the State Apartments are furnished with old things— many of them the original ones: lovely paintings, chandeliers, etc. The royal family occupies a different, more modern-type section when they live there.

The most interesting display for Becky and David was Queen Mary's doll house, given to her in 1923 as a symbol of good will. It's a model of Buckingham Palace, made to scale so that the people are five or six inches high. It was done under direction of Sir Edwin Lutyens who got everything made to the most minute detail by actual artisans and artists—miniature paintings, dishes, cars, furniture—even a sewing machine that actually sews. The tiny books are actually printed, etc.

The next weekend, on Saturday, was the Lord Mayor's Parade. A new Lord Mayor of London is appointed each year, and his installation is the occasion of an elaborate procession including his stop in the Hall of Justice, luncheon, and his eventual arrival at his official residence, the Mansion House. "Communications" was the theme of the parade this year, carried out by floats entered by various organizations—T.V., radio, newspapers, post office, sports groups, etc., accompanied by military groups and marching bands. We stood for an hour in the rain (along with thousands of others)!

Sunday was cold, but was sunny most of the day, so we boarded a bus for Greenwich—down the Thames a few miles. It, you know, is the place where east is divided from west—at the Greenwich meridian. We walked up quite a high hill to the observatory where we saw many old telescopes and instruments used in years past for calculating time, navigation, etc. Becky and David got a big charge out of standing across the meridian line with one foot in the Eastern Hemisphere and one in the Western! There's a little garden at one end of their marker that makes a nice background for pictures.

Down at the dock in Greenwich is the old sailing ship, the *Cutty Sark* which used to be on frequent merchant runs between London and China. We were told that she was the fastest merchant ship in her day, and was therefore very popular. We were able to go through the living quarters of the captain and crewmen, and onto the upper deck. The main deck is used now as a museum showing drawings from which the ship was built, log books, pictures, instruments, carvings, souvenirs, and history of the ship and its various captains.

Gene was invited to a memorial service on Sunday for the 41st Commando—the group of Royal Marines who fought side-by-side with American Marines in the Chosin Reservoir in Korea. They had been able to locate over 140 of the people who had participated—most of them retired now. And there were parents, relatives and friends of many who were killed in that battle. Soon after that, we went to Plymouth to visit Capt. John Ripley and wife Molin (pronounced Mo-leen'). He was a Company Commander for Gene in Vietnam and is now a CO of a Company in the British Marine 45th Commando at Plymouth—part of an "exchange" program between the Marines of the two countries.

John met us at the train station and took us out to the little village where they live. They are at the edge of it—actually in the country on a hill overlooking the village. It probably looks just like it did in the days of Sir Francis Drake and Sir Walter Raleigh! The roads are mostly "Devon Lanes" (County of Devon) which are wide enough for one car. Passing when meeting the infrequent traffic involves one car finding the widest spot and carefully squeezing by. One almost has to see them to believe them—but I'll try to describe with words. The rock-based roads are so strong, Army tanks won't faze them! The road bed in most places is lower by thirty or forty feet than the field level because of the years of wearing down. The high hedge rows at the sides of the road are used for fences to divide fields, too, making the land look like a big patchwork quilt. Grass and most shrubs are green the year around, although they do have some leaves that give autumn color.

The next day the Ripleys took us in their two cars to see the sights. In Plymouth we saw the very steps where the Pilgrims loaded into the Mayflower! The sister ship to the Mayflower is at another dock nearby. I would sure have to have a very important reason to give me courage to start across the Atlantic in one of those ships! Sir Francis Drake also sailed from Plymouth on his round-the-world cruise. There are many monuments and things there in his honor.

John's son, Steve went with John and us out to the Moor. It's a low, rolling mountain range, very unique in that its elevation is high, but the ground is like a sponge. It rains in showers in various areas very often, so it's always wet, and a wind like nothing you've ever felt, chills you all the way into your very marrow! And so hard, you have to lean into it. The Royal Marines go up there to train, hike, practice map reading, sleep, and the like. They have to keep corpsmen handy to treat exposure because death can follow quite shortly if a man does go into shock from the chill.

It's a wonderfully "small world" when one can visit friends in other parts of the world!

Gene went to Naples last Monday to attend a NATO conference until Wednesday. He had a wonderful time re-visiting some old "haunts"— especially the little restaurant called "Il Grottino." It's an ancient cave that has been used in times past for various things, including a church. It is "decorated" inside to look like the interior of Capri's Blue Grotto, the natural stalactites and even some cobwebs just add "atmosphere." It's operated by a couple of brothers who do the cooking, table service, and music for dining. The father was part of the establishment when we lived there, but he has since died. Gene said it was like a homecoming when he showed up for lunch. One of the brothers instantly recognized him and hugged him saying, "Hello, Mister Bench! Where is Mister Clark?" (Mister Clark was C.P. Clark—another Marine lieutenant in the office with Gene when we lived there in the fifties.) He and the brothers had a wonderful time, re-living those previous years.

That evening we took the kids to a concert at St. James Church (on Piccadilly Street), given by the Westminster Choral Society—a Christmas program. We had a chance to join with them for some carols—some familiar to us, and some new ones. There was one especially lovely one, for which I plan to try to find some music. The name of it was "Standing in the Rain."

Friday evening we went to a program, which compared to our P.T.A., at the school Becky has been visiting. Our children went to stay with the Lauff children, and we went on with Metta, the mother. Ben, the dad, wasn't feeling well and stayed home. Becky really enjoyed the experience of school there, with only girls—but in class work they were behind her in most things.

We spent the day Saturday at the Tower of London, Tower Bridge, and walking around down there. It was chilly, and the very large hot-dogs we got at a "street wagon" tasted really good—steaming hot, and dressed up with mustard and relish. We tried to explore the Billingsgate Fish Market, but it was closed. We did get to see the monument to the Great Fire which burned London practically to the ground in 1600 something.

Sunday started out being a sunny day, so we asked the Lauff girls to join us for a visit to the zoo in the afternoon. About the time we arrived, a fog started forming which got quite dense before we got home. It was very pretty and exciting, but dangerous for travelers. We were in a good position on the zoo grounds to just enjoy the feeling of envelopment, and the soft shadows of trees; people walking past us soon disappeared into it.

On Monday the kids and I went to the library to get some new books to read up about things to do and see soon: Wednesday we hope to go out to Stratford-on-Avon to see some Shakespeare country. Becky is also going to read a short biography on Charles Dickens as one of her reading requirements, and when she's through, we'll take a walking tour of part of the city in the neighborhood where he used to live.

On the way home we bought a small Christmas tree, so now I'm even more aware of several Christmas cards that still aren't on their way! That must be tomorrow's project. It's hard to write when the kids are up—they need so much attention.

My! What a <u>lovely</u> birthday party you had, Dad! How we wish we could have been there! Your description of it served a double purpose—one, of course, to tell us about it—the second was a very good opportunity to teach some much needed "music appreciation"! We had taken the children to see the play "The Great Waltz" (about Strauss), then to a children's birthday party for Beethoven at the American Embassy. David came to the conclusion that he thought "musicals" were very dull and that music or the people who create music are unimportant. Well, when you told about the Kelley's singing for you the song that <u>you</u>, Dad, wrote about the train wreck you witnessed from the railroad repair car that you were on, you should have seen David perk up! Creating music suddenly took on a new meaning! He wanted to know if I had ever heard you sing it, and if you'll sing it for him sometime! I'll bet he would be impressed, as well, with some of your poetry if it's handy some time when we're visiting you.

We've been pretty well ready for Christmas for a few days now, and it's sort of a matter of waiting nervously for Santa Claus. We were afraid this might be the year David would need a new explanation of the Spirit of Santa and Christmas, but he's still "playing the game" with us. This evening we're planning a family party. In our new "organization," David is the President who conducts our occasional meetings where anyone who has grievances can air them for discussion, and suggestions can be made for better family relations. For tonight's party, I'm in charge of refreshments—English Christmas Pudding and hot chocolate. Becky is to do the decorations, and Daddy is responsible for the entertainment. Becky wants to read the Bible Christmas story and we'll read the stories from your Christmas cards, sing some carols and play some games.

We went to an Anglican church Sunday, which is only two doors away from our flat. The morning service was very formal with lots of singing—for instance, the responsive readings were sung rather than read. We went to their coffee-and-juice time after the service and visited with some of the people, and with the Vicar. He is a large "portly" type, and a very jolly sort. He spent twenty-five years as a Chaplain in the British Army, and was asked to preach the Victory sermon at the American service in Paris at the end of WWII. That evening was their Christmas program—the story in drama. The actors posed in "tableau" scenes while the appropriate reading was being done. There was carol singing with the audience, and altogether, a lovely service. Unfortunately, we have to move, so we may not get to enjoy the fellowship there anymore. Maybe the new place will have another interesting group.

About the move—we had been told by the maids that our building was to be replaced by a new high-rise hotel this spring, but there are problems with the heating system now, and evidently it isn't worth repairing for the short period, so we're having to vacate. It won't be too inconvenient—in fact, we'll be able to escape the rent during the trip we're taking to the Continent for the week between Christmas and New Year's. The hotel is putting us into one of their other Embassy flats on the other side of Kensington Park from where we are now—an even nicer place, for the same money. They'll let us leave our extra gear in a storage room until we get ready for it. We're leaving the day after Christmas—by train to Dover, then ferry to Ostende, Belgium, where we have an Avis rental car waiting—then until January 3rd, we'll be visiting Belgium, Holland and Paris. Haven't decided yet what order. We're trying to get in touch with friends who live in Brussels before we plan an itinerary so we can fit our plans to theirs.

Christmas Morning: Guess what we saw when we opened the draperies this morning! SNOW! Probably about an inch—right on the roses that are still blooming here and there. I think that added almost more excitement for the kids than Santa's visit! David said, "That is Santa's gift to EVERYONE"! Becky and David were up at 3:00 a.m. to see if Santa had been here yet, and stumbled over their filled shoes during the process, but we persuaded them to go back to bed. (They didn't hang up stockings this time, because they thought that in Europe, Santa fills shoes instead.) Surprisingly, they were able to get back to sleep until 7:00 o'clock. Santa had to consider our problem of getting things back home to Virginia, so he wasn't as generous as he is sometimes. There were a few things that can become souvenirs, and some small playthings for now; for instance, some real Made-in-England puppets that will be appreciated for a long time. Both of them enjoy building with Legos, which are easy to pack and to carry, besides, they sometimes hold creative interest for hours.

We plan to go to the Columbia Club for dinner early this afternoon, and then spend the rest of the day packing for our trip and for moving while the kids play with their new "treasures." We especially look forward to spending New Year's Eve in "Gay Paree"! Gene and I spent an anniversary in Paris once—now it will be nice to celebrate a New Year there, too! Sharing our travel experiences now with the children is SO much more meaningful than before!

FAMILY TRAVELS IN EUROPE — 1970

With the end of our time in London coming soon, things are happening so fast these days, we all have to keep on our toes to keep up, but I think we're going to be able to accomplish most of the things we set out to do. On our last Sunday in London, we went for another walk on Bayswater Road, along the west side of Hyde Park to look at the weekly art display—blocks and blocks of paintings, and all sorts of artistic things like pottery, jewelry, stuffed toys, and much more. From there we took a subway to the East End, to a Sunday street market called Petticoat Lane. It is a place where vendors of all sorts of things set up shop right in the street. Most things were quite "junky," but seeing it was an experience.

Before we leave, we'll be entertaining about thirty people, most of them ones who have entertained us. We decided that rather than try to crowd that many into our apartment, it would be easier to ask the Columbia Club (the American guest house) to set up a room for us with a buffet table with all the trimmings. They can also include a chef to slice a nice hot beef roast. Becky and David haven't decided yet whether they want to go along or not. If they go, they'll most likely spend most of their time in the lounge watching color TV. (Color TV is a novelty to us—the TV at home is black-and-white.) We took them to two plays last week—Thursday afternoon was *Aladdin*, and Saturday morning was *Winnie-the-Pooh*. In *Pooh* most of the characters were the toy animals that Christopher Robin played with, so the actors were real people in animal costumes. It was just charming! And, it followed the stories in the book quite accurately.

One Saturday afternoon Gene took the kids to the Wax Museum while I did some shopping, then we all went to see the movie *Waterloo*. It took quite a lot of explaining for David, but maybe some history rubbed off for him—especially having recently been on the very spot where the big battle was fought. Next week we hope to have time to see *Cromwell*—the story of the English revolution when the king was overthrown, and parliamentary government got its start. After a few years they went back to having kings and queens but kept the parliament.

LOVE IS ALL THAT MATTERS

We still had three weeks of adventures ahead of us in France, Germany, Austria, Switzerland, Italy, and Spain. We are so very thankful for such rich opportunities!

We didn't get on the plane Saturday, January 29. When the authorities got more information about it, they found that it was carrying dangerous cargo of some sort and wouldn't allow passengers. So…we caught the next train back to London and bought tickets to fly from Heathrow to Frankfurt, Germany, and reserved an Avis rental car to be waiting for us at the airport there. Gene asked the Communications Office to call to reserve a room at the Frankfurt American Guest House, so after a rather busy day of chasing transportation, we were happy to have a lovely, comfortable room waiting for us.

Sunday morning, we walked over to the Officers' Club for a leisurely breakfast, packed up the little white Ford we'd rented, and headed for Munich. It was a lovely, sunny day, brisk, but not really very cold. We travel with a book by Arthur Frommer called *Europe on $5.00 a Day*, which is quite a money-saver. He gives the names, addresses, and phone numbers of inexpensive hotels and restaurants in several major European cities—and we've enjoyed all we've used of his selections—besides saving at least half or often more on lodging and food. The places he recommends are nice, clean, little out-of-the-way ones that you'd never find without a guide. In Munich we enjoyed a comfortable, convenient room, "liver dumplings" at a friendly little Bavarian restaurant; and then some Lederkase (liverwurst) sandwiches, and a museum he recommended. The museum is called the world's largest technical museum. We didn't have time to halfway do it justice but enjoyed seeing many things and how they "work." We had planned to stay there until about three p.m. before starting on for Berchtesgaden—an American military rest center near Salzburg—which Gene and I visited in 1953. But about one o'clock we looked out a window and noticed snow falling. We decided we'd better get going, since we had mountain driving ahead of us, and we wanted to arrive before dark.

After a few miles, the snow stopped, and the highway was dry, so we had a faster trip than we'd expected—arriving about 3:30 and were able to get a lovely room in the General Walker Hotel, high up on the Obersalzberg Mountain near where Hitler had his vacation home. It's lovely country, but people are sad because there still isn't enough snow for skiing. By the time we got our suitcases into the hotel, it started snowing, and tonight it's about maybe four inches deep. Becky and David were too excited to sleep!

Gene is trying to get some news of the Apollo 14, but there's no TV, and on our portable radio the news reports are mostly in German! He did hear that Apollo got off but wasn't able to understand what problem they encountered.

February 15, 1971.   Our stops at Berchtesgaden and Garmisch in Germany were quite special for Becky and David. They took a two-hour ski lesson and decided it's a pretty special sport! There hadn't been enough snow for skiing until the night we arrived; then came enough of the beautiful, powdery stuff to make the woods and mountains look like a fairyland, and even support some skiers. Some people at the lodge thanked us for bringing the snow with us!

Another highlight there was a trip into a very old salt mine near Berchtesgaden. We rode a cog train deep into the mine, and then traveled to lower levels inside sitting down on slides.   In some places they had built some walls of "slices" of various types of rock from the mine and put lights behind which glowed through the translucent rock.   Beautiful! There were varying shades of

7th from the left is Gene, David, Becky, and Ila

red, orange, yellow, purple, and brown—arranged in a sort of "modern art" scheme of blocks of different sizes and shapes.

Part of the fun of the trip was wearing uniforms over our clothes—old-style salt-miners' pants, coats and hats, and a leather apron worn backwards which protects miners from the dampness when they sit down. (The apron also was helpful on one's backside for going down the slides!) The mine is still active—furnishing salt for Germany and Italy in substantial quantities. To get it out they make a cavern, and then flood it with water and wait for it to soak up the salt to make brine. This is then pumped out and evaporated, leaving a very clean salt that doesn't require very much more refining.

At Garmisch we enjoyed the comforts of a lovely lodge in the scenic little town that looked like we had traveled back in time a century or two. I must describe our trip to what we'd hoped would be the summit of Zugspitze—the very rugged peak which towers over Garmisch. After skiing until mid-afternoon, we went to the cable car station for the trip up, but found it wasn't operating because it had been snowing up on the mountain all day—though it was clear then. There was one more cog-train run left for the day, and it only stayed at the top for ten minutes before returning, so we wouldn't have much time, but we decided to take it anyway. It didn't go all the way to the summit, but after going through a long tunnel towards the top, it came out on the eastern side of the mountain at a big hotel ski lodge. When I want to fill my mind with a beautiful thought, I can remember that view! If I were an artist, I'd try to paint it—if I were a poet, I'd compose a poem—if a musician, maybe I'd try to put it into a symphony! As it is, all I can do is keep it in my head, because it almost defies description! The snow was freshly fallen, and there were still some misty effects in the distance toward some other peaks. The sun was low, casting a "golden-pink" glow through the mist, and reflecting off the distant peaks and the soft foreground! We were so high; we were looking down on the other mountains.

The snow was cleared from the roads very soon, so by the time we were ready to go over the Alps to Italy the next day, it was good driving. It was even a perfectly clear, sunny day to give us what must have been a very unusual view of the mountains for the winter season! It was like being in a wonderland world of snow-covered peaks of varying heights, on a road with many curves, so that just around the next bend of the road was a totally different, magnificent view!

We got to Venice in time to see the sunset, checked into our little hotel right by St. Mark's cathedral, and went out walking to enjoy the atmosphere of the canal city, free of noisy cars. Of course, they have motor boats which spoil the beauty and quiet along the Grand Canal, but they do provide some inexpensive transportation. One just goes along the back "streets" to find the silence. The old-fashioned gondolas can travel in those smaller canals—their only sound being the sound of the oar in the water, and maybe a lovely Italian song being sung by the gondolier.

The second day was lovely and warm. We fed the pigeons and watched the clock in St. Mark's Square strike before we began our adventure. The clock tower was erected in 1496 to1499 from designs by Carducci. It has a dial of blue and gold adorned with the signs of the zodiac. On a platform on the top stand two gigantic bronze figures which strike the hours on the very large bell.

On the island of Murano, we visited a glass factory where we watched men blowing glass into several types of articles, and hand-painting various things like water goblets and dishes. What artists they were! Then to the showroom where a person wished for a few thousand dollars to spend on chandeliers, vases, table ware, lamps, decorative dishes—you name it. Then back to St. Mark's for a quick look inside the cathedral and Doge's Palace. There was a service going on, so we didn't get as close a look at the jeweled golden altar as we'd have liked but saw enough to get a general idea. From the Doge's Palace we walked across the "Bridge of Sighs" down into the dungeons of the prison. The kids decided it wouldn't have been any fun to be a prisoner in those days! We walked up to the Rialto Bridge and crossed it, shopping along the open markets for a picnic lunch we could enjoy later in the car. By gondola we went back to our hotel to get luggage, then to the mainland and our car by a "bus-type" boat. Not enough time there, but then there wasn't enough time <u>anyplace</u>! Gene and I were thankful for the longer visit we had had there in the '50s and wished the children could have also had more time.

The next stop was Florence. Highlights to see there were Michelangelo's statue of *David*, the old Palace Square, Giotto's tower, and the Baptistery with Ghiberti's gilded bronze sculptured doors, which Michelangelo once called "worthy to be the gates of Paradise." People interested in art could spend months in Florence and still never see all the treasures, but we thought we shouldn't try to fill our young ones' heads too full of such things, because it's just too much too fast. That's why we picked only a few highlights in each place.

Rome came next, and we stayed two nights, so we'd have a full day plus a bit of evening on one of them, and a bit of morning on the other. A tour of the Vatican was interesting—especially to see some moon rocks that were a gift from our government; the Sistine Chapel interior; and treasures of old books, paintings, and statuary. One of my favorite works there is the section of the ceiling with a painting called *The Creation of Man*. To me, there's great inspiration and feeling in seeing the forefingers on God's outstretched right hand and on Adam's outstretched left hand just almost touching! And to think what a job that all was for Michelangelo—painting it lying on his back! I think Becky and David were quite awed by the size of the interior of St. Peter's Cathedral, and the fact that Peter's bones are contained under the altar.

One of the most interesting things in Rome was the picnic lunch we took out on the old Appian Way. The sun was warm enough to be without coats, and it was beautifully quiet. The kids had a wonderful time climbing over the remains of old statuary that in some time past was probably decoration for someone's lovely home. We figured we probably sat on a former doorstep to eat our fruit and bread with slices of cheese and Italian sausage. The coliseum was fun, too. And you should have seen the cats! There must have been hundreds of them—all kinds and colors! (David said, "Hey! They still have lions here!")

From Rome we drove down to Gaeta—a little village where one of the 6th Fleet ships has its headquarters—to spend the night with Ginny Maloney. Bill was out on a run with the ship. They are the people who gave us our dog—a Beagle named "Trimmie." They couldn't take her with them when Bill was assigned to this duty station, so she became part of our family with the understanding that when the Maloney's returned to the States, we would give them the pick of a litter of her pups.

Then it was on to Naples for our longest stop. We spent a day on the island of Capri, and another day going to Mt. Vesuvius, Herculaneum, and Pompeii, with an evening out to dinner with friends whom we'd enjoyed visiting in London. A special visit was to the apartment on Parco Lamaro where Gene and I had lived in the '50s. A doctor and his wife live there now. We told them we'd lived there nearly twenty years ago and asked if it would be an imposition if the children could see inside. They were happy to accommodate. They had it jam-packed with furniture and books until one could hardly get around, and the old wash tub in the kitchen had been replaced with an automatic washer! There were also new cabinets and stove. (They really needed a new stove!) It was interesting; and driving up the hill to the house made many years suddenly seem to disappear! Not much change in the houses along the winding street—just taller trees.

Another special stop in Naples was at the little restaurant called the Grottino. It is in an old, old cave that once had a passage from it down the hill to the waterfront. The interior looks like the Blue Grotto. There are real stalactites hanging from the ceiling, and I expect there are some real cobwebs one could see, if their lights were brighter. Gene had been there in December, and the two Russo brothers who are still owners remembered him well. (I remember that one of them is named Pasquale.) When we walked in as a family they just "oo-ed and ah-ed." You've never seen such hand-kissing and bowing and fussing over the children! They wanted to show Becky and David the old guest books we'd signed years before when we used to reserve it for parties. There were even many photos of us and of friends, and we traded stories about all the people whom we'd known then. Becky and David liked them (and their spaghetti, ravioli, and lasagna) so much, we had trouble getting them interested in eating anyplace else! (A new fruit they enjoyed in Italy was

Arancia Rosa, an orange with a slight "blush" on the rind, and an inside as red as a raspberry. Even tasted a little like one.)

From Naples we went to Orvieto—a little medieval hill town between Rome and Florence. Our hotel had been at one time the governor's mansion— and what a place! There were marble staircases, painted ceilings, a big marble bathtub, and numerous other items of luxury. The city, built on the very top of the hill, had been one of the strongholds in its heyday because it was so well guarded from enemies, and could withstand long periods of siege. One reason was that a fantastic well had been dug, deep down through the rock to an unending supply of water. The way down was wide enough to build steps that spiraled down one side and up the other, and donkeys could be used to haul the water up to the surface. Gene was very impressed with the engineering of it.

Pisa was our next stop, and of course the attraction there was the Leaning Tower beside the cathedral. It was started in the year 1174 to be the bell tower for the church and was finished about 1300. It was intended to be built straight up, and to be much higher; but while the work was going on, the ground to the south began to yield, so the building was stopped for about a century. It has been reinforced now with concrete, and from the top one can see the whole town, and as far as the mountains and the sea. The bell tower contains seven ancient bells. From the top, Galileo experimented with the law of gravity.

In Genoa we had reservations on the ferry to travel overnight to Barcelona, Spain. By traveling this way overnight, we'd save about a day of time, plus some tiresome road hours. We had a cabin for sleeping, and many luxuries of a liner, including decks where the children could play and get some exercise. We drove the car onto the ship at 11:30 a.m. and will unload in Barcelona about 10:00 a.m. tomorrow; but before we boarded, we went to see the house where Columbus supposedly lived. We feel like we are "living" history!

After landing in Barcelona we drove around to see some of the city but didn't have time enough to do it justice. When Gene and I visited there before, we really liked the food—especially a rice dish called "paella" that was made with various kinds of meats. We thought the seafood variety was our favorite, so for lunch we gave Becky and David an opportunity to enjoy some, too.

The coast of Spain was very colorful, and the weather was just like spring. We decided we'd just <u>have</u> to go back again someday, because we didn't have time to linger for very long when we stopped. One hotel where we stayed south of Valencia was right on the ocean with acres of golf courses and woods—beautiful! We had picnic lunches on the beach and gave the children time to play for awhile every day that we drove along the coast. We saw Gibraltar from the back side as we drove west and arrived at Wendy's house in Cadiz early in the afternoon on Thursday.

Mike and Wendy Parnell (my brother Ross' daughter and son-in-law) have a lovely, new apartment, and are enjoying the experience of living in Spain very much, although they are anxious to get back to show baby Michael Tracy off to the rest of the family. He's a doll—seems <u>very</u> bright, and they are such good parents. Mike, in the Navy, arranged with the captain of his ship to give us a tour. She's a nuclear submarine tender, and Mike specializes in repairing communications equipment. The "Francis Scott Key"—a nuclear submarine—was tied up alongside, so Mike's captain arranged with her captain for us to tour there, as well. Both ships were very impressive and had more space than I'd imagined. We spent most of Friday with the Parnell's, turned in the car at Seville that night, and took a sleeper on the train to Madrid—arriving about 8:00 a.m. A cab took us out to the air base where we had a leisurely wait, with time to shop a little and relax before our flight left at 2:30 p.m. Saturday for our return trip to the States.

We flew <u>with</u> the sun, so after ten hours in the air, we arrived in Charleston, South Carolina at 6:30 p.m. We had slept a little on the plane, so felt able to "drive on a little further" that evening in another rented car. Gene called Don and Sylvia Diamond in Wilmington, North Carolina, made arrangements to spend the night with them (what was left of it!), and we arrived there a little after ll:00 p.m. They've been good friends for some time—lots of bridge games together, frequent parties, and with their three boys, enjoyed family picnics and outings. It was good to see them—though, again, the time was too short. We visited until they and we nearly fell asleep, and then had a leisurely breakfast Sunday morning before departing.

By mid-afternoon we were back at home again in Springfield, on Calamo Street, to a wonderful neighborhood welcome, including dinner next door with Ed and Bonnie Hardin, and their children, Karen and Wes. Becky and David are very happy to be home again, sleeping in their own rooms, and playing with their friends! They apparently didn't suffer scholastically by missing a whole quarter of school—and their experiences added a whole new dimension to future classes in geography and history. For me, it all now seems like a wonderful dream, but a certain amount of reality soon began with getting back to life in our house that was rented to an Army couple while we were away.

Valuables that we had locked up in a spare room had to be moved back to their places, some damages needed repair, and considerable cleaning had to be done. But hey! The rent they paid made the payments on the mortgage, and I'd do it all over again tomorrow!

Other assignments while still stationed at Headquarters were: Plans Officer, Eastern Regional Team; G-3 Division, Assistant Head of Training and Education Branch A03; Head of Training and Education Branch AO3; and finally, to Head of Inspection Team "B," Inspection Division, MCC 010, from which he retired June 30, 1973. Work on the inspection team required him to be away from home several times during the last year and half of his time at Headquarters. The team traveled to all places in the world where Marines were stationed in order to inspect their working conditions. Travel was provided by a Marine Corps plane that was designated for their use.

In about a week we were able to get unpacked, to begin getting acquainted with the neighborhood, and to discovering opportunities for exploring. We were happy to find it a very friendly neighborhood that included several children near the ages of our kids. Next door on our left lived the Hardin family: Ed, Bonnie, and children Karen and Wesley. Ed worked at the Department of Education in Washington and used one of the then "new" computers that took up considerable space. He was a jovial person and liked to visit with Gene with all kinds of discussions and jokes. He called himself a "Dove," and called Gene a "Hawk." Their house was small but had a large "living" deck with an above-ground swimming pool. Bonnie was from West Virginia, had a lovely southern accent, and was a happy stay-at-home mom. Our kids liked playing together, but if Becky and David were invited to swim in the pool with Karen and Wesley, there was a rule that parents would be nearby. So Bonnie and I spent many hours sipping orange-flavored iced tea on their spacious deck while we talked about everything from cookies to "you-name-it." We four grownups played countless games of bridge, while we snacked and visited, and we still keep in touch.

Next door on the other side was the Ahmed family—Valerie was the American mother, and the father—whose name escapes me—was of some middle-eastern nationality. Jamal was a son about Becky's age, and there was a daughter a few years older.

The family across the street had a diabetic daughter named Jackie who was Becky's age, and in the same Girl Scout troop. I was quite impressed with her. She was very outgoing and had learned to live actively with the diabetes—she responsibly chose her food, and expertly gave herself the needed insulin shots. Jackie's grandmother, named Mrs. Stocks, lived with them. She was a kind, gracious, and fairly active person; and became a frequent, favorite sitter for our children.

We always took advantage of learning about the history, activities, and cultural opportunities in every place we called "home," and this place was one that was really rich! Gene and I had done a lot of exploring when we had lived in that part of Virginia early in Gene's Marine Corps career, but now, with a couple of curious kids, we could do a lot of it all over again, from a different perspective—helping them to enjoy it while we appreciated it all the second time around!

"MY" MARINE CORPS COMMUNITY
(What I would tell a new Marine Corps wife)

I think a woman who marries a Marine realizes that her life as a wife and homemaker will more than likely be considerably different in many ways from civilian life. Even though Gene and I often lived among civilian neighbors, we were sometimes considered "different"; and we found that we needed to be the ones to "reach out" first, in order to get acquainted and assure them that we were "just people"! A book called *The Marine Corps Wife*, published in 1955 by authors who were themselves Marine wives—Sally Jerome and Nancy Brinton Shea—was a very helpful reference for me. There have been many changes in "protocol" and procedures since then—all you have to do is let "Google" show you lists of books and videos that are now available. I wish I could have had access to many of those before I began my "learning from experience"! I'm sure you would find much of the information there to be very worthwhile! You can consider this description of my experience to be just that—what it was like for me—some of which is more than likely applicable to military life now; but I'm sure there are many differences.

As you know, the history and traditions of the Marine Corps itself is very important and precious to every Marine. Learning all you can about that will not only make your life easier and much more interesting, your husband will admire and appreciate your interest in his career and the loyalty that he feels to it. At times, you might even feel that he's "married" to the Marine Corps, as well as to you! You might also sometimes have the feeling that you're an actress, "getting into character," but while some things are different, most will be not unlike making a home and living among civilians.

Living quarters and frequent moves might be one of your most notable differences. It will help if you can be adaptable and be satisfied with living "in the moment." We usually had two or three years at each duty station, but sometimes less; and for one assignment, we were in the same place for four years. Sometimes we had to rent a temporary house or apartment while we were looking for a more suitable one or waiting for quarters on the base. And—I soon learned that more than likely, in any rental apartment, I'd need to "deep-clean" the kitchen stove! Some were unbelievably "grimy"!

A move will be easier if you just know that there will be one—and when. The Marine Corps provided packers for household belongings and paid for the moves that were made as a result of change of station orders. They would also unpack things at the other end, but I chose to do a lot of that myself, in my own time—things like dishes, books, knick-knacks, and clothes. Because the household effects might need to go into temporary storage while we looked for a house, we were able to have a separate small shipment of articles needed for immediate use. Things like a few towels, dishes, pots and pans, a broom, a mop, a steam iron, and such. Of course, all of husband's clothes were moved in a special shipment. We found it wise to invest in furniture that was versatile and took advantage of thrift shops and second-hand stores. My sewing machine was put to good use making simple window curtains from inexpensive fabrics, or for a cover to disguise a packing crate that would be used as a table.

One adjustment, early on, was to husband's overnight and weekend "duty," which seemed to happen most often to the most "junior" officers! As civilians, he and I had never been apart overnight. Our toothbrushes shared the same holder; and in the bed, there were always warm feet that were willing to warm my cold ones! The first time Gene had an order to "stand" overnight duty, he of course, packed up his toilet kit to take with him; and I vividly remember the sort of sad "shock" that I felt to see my toothbrush all alone in its holder—and his toiletries missing from the bathroom! But perhaps that could be considered to be a "drill" for future separations that the military community calls "deployment."

Deployment leads me to advice about maintaining the "business" of homemaking. A deployment might be for a few weeks, or months, or even a year. So a wife needs to be able to "hold the fort" for a while. We had a portable fire-proof strong box for important papers—birth certificates, marriage license, auto titles, wills, and other important legal things. A wife should have a Power of Attorney, know how to manage the bank account, and—if possible—to be able to use a few tools! Husband will probably receive information from his office that might be helpful to you while he's gone. One <u>huge</u> difference for you will be communication with each other when he is deployed. You have the advantage of various types of immediate electronic exchange of information—even to <u>seeing</u> each other by Skype. Each of us wrote a letter to the other almost every day, but it could be several days for them to be delivered. I regularly sent photos—especially after we had children, and he had a few opportunities to send some to me. A few times he was able to make a phone call through radio connection—very happy experiences!

I appreciated Marine Corps Wives' organizations. Socializing was easy—visiting over coffee or tea, luncheons, cocktail parties, dinners, picnic gatherings, and whatever; but being involved with other wives was especially important during deployments, because we provided support for each other. Gene and I found that playing bridge was one of our better ways of getting acquainted in a new place, and of giving our minds some exercise as well. Of course, taking advantage of recreational activities such as bowling, swimming, dancing, and various sports added friendships and fun, no matter if the people were civilians or military.

When we reached a new duty station we made it a point to "be tourists" right away, as we had time. I had never been out of Missouri until after I was married, so <u>every</u> place was exciting and interesting to me! It was amazing how much history I learned, and we were eventually good guides for taking visiting family and friends on sight-seeing trips around our area. When we traveled across country on leave, or to new duty stations, we drove different routes each time to enjoy new places along the way. It was especially interesting to live in the Washington, D.C. area—my husband was stationed at Quantico (home of Marine Corps Schools) several times in different kinds of duty, and also at Marine Corps Headquarters, which is at the south edge of Washington. Quantico is only thirty some miles south of D.C., and there are many good places to live in the suburbs. A really spectacular experience for us one of the times we lived there was seeing, and walking among, the cherry blossoms! And there seem to be "endless" museums, and hundreds of historical places to visit!

Some people think military life might be difficult for children. For some, it might be, but for our two, it seemed good. We were without children for ten years, so our financial base had somewhat improved, and we, ourselves were adjusted to being "gypsies." We had noticed that some peoples' children seemed to be quite "regimented," but we looked for ways to make life for our kids more "normal." We thought it important for them to learn general good manners, but they also needed to be aware of military respect and customs that might not be "normal" for civilians. We didn't want them to be "rank conscious" to the extent that an officer's child should deserve any privileges or feel superior to children of enlisted personnel. We taught them to recognize rank insignia, but that rank was for dads, not for kids. They benefited greatly from living in different places, and from the travel involved between homes. They learned how to make new friends, and a lot of geography and history. Both daughter Becky and son David have great memories of their years of being what is known in the Corps as "Marine Corps Brats."

I hope you'll find being a Marine Corps wife as rewarding as I did! For me, it was an adventure of a lifetime, and I'll always feel that the slogan "Once a Marine, always a Marine" might apply to the spouse as well as to the Marine!

Just be sure you have a good, large-size ironing board and a steam iron! You'll be pressing uniforms often—maybe sometimes even daily! And remember that the Marine Corps motto is "Semper Fi"!

WHAT I WOULD TELL ANYONE ABOUT MILITARY SERVICE – STERLING WYATT

I have an idea that growing up during a time of war might have a strong influence upon a person's opinion about war. My father had not been in military service, but he believed that a man owed his country some time, if he were physically able, in case war was declared. When World War II was declared, he was too old for military service, but was thankful to be able to work in some way to be helpful to the "war effort." So he did carpentry work at Fort Leonard Wood, a new Army base that was near our home in Missouri. I had recently finished business college, and was also employed there in the Post Exchange office. It was a good feeling for us to be doing work to "help in the war effort"! And, of course, there were many ways that almost anyone could "serve" in some way because the War lasted for so many years.

That experience might have influenced my feeling about "duty to country," so I feel proud of my opportunity to be a Marine Corps wife, and to have brothers and brothers-in-law who served. Brothers, Ross and Sterling, were in the Army at different times; sister Barbara's husband was in the Navy; and sister Joy's husband was a Dentist in the Army.

Barbara's grandson, Sterling William Wyatt—son of Randy and Sherry— chose to enlist in the Army, and all of our family grieved very deeply when he lost his life on July 11, 2012, in Kandahar Province Afghanistan when his vehicle was attacked with an enemy IED. He had been promoted to Specialist, and was awarded the Combat Infantry Badge, Medal of Valor, the Bronze Star, the National Defense Service Medal, Afghanistan Campaign Medal with campaign star, Global War on Terrorism Service Medal, Army Service Ribbon, Overseas Ribbon, NATO Medal, and Certificate of Achievement. "I salute all of you who served!"

Sterling Wyatt & his father Randy, 2002

LOVE IS ALL THAT MATTERS

Chapter 5: 1973 to Present

GENE'S BRONZED BOOTS

These are the boots my husband, Colonel Gene Bench, wore in Vietnam from July 1966, to July 1967—when he commanded the USMC Second Battalion, Fourth Marines. During that time he was awarded the Silver Star, two Bronze Stars, Legion of Merit, and Purple Heart. By then, the boots needed to be replaced for official wear, so they became favorites for yard work and fishing.

When he decided upon June 30, 1973, for retiring from the Marine Corps, I decided to have them bronzed for a surprise retirement gift—not easy, I discovered! No shoe-bronzing people had ever <u>heard</u> of such a thing! But I finally found someone in New York who was willing to experiment.

Of course, he missed them one day while they were away for processing and asked me if I happened to know where his boots might be. I said, "Well, I've noticed that sometimes you put things on top of the car when you're loading up after fishing—is it possible you might have accidentally driven away with them there and lost them?" He "allowed as how" that might be possible—and no more was said about the boots.

The surprise came when they showed up as the table centerpiece for one of his retirement dinners! Tall, slim glasses of water inserted inside of them held branches of honeysuckle, trailing around them—representing tangles of wild honeysuckle vines they had waded through when on his feet through many years. Beside them was a letter to him "from them"—now kept inside of one of them. They became unique "conversation pieces," of course—as well as gentle reminders of that special year of life together! The letter said:

"Dear Colonel Bench, For many years we have been two of your closest companions. No matter what time of day or night you've needed us, we have been right with you—doing whatever the activity at hand. Sometimes the experiences were fun things; sometimes difficult ones; often dirty things—whatever the occasion, we were happy to help.

Now that you're retiring from the Marine Corps, which we've enjoyed with you, we'd like to be retired, too. Others will take our place in your new life, and we hope that they will serve you as well and as loyally as we have.

We, however, will continue to serve you in our retirement by reminding you of some places we've been together; of some sea-stories you may or may not choose to tell of our experiences together. The stories will be your choice—we'll keep quiet!

"May the part of your life ahead of you be the best part yet!"

MOON RAINBOW

I wonder how often a person gets to see a Moon Rainbow? In my eight decades of life, I've been privileged to see just one—and it will be a special memory for as long as I live!

Gene retired from the Marine Corps June 30, 1973, so early in July, after the moving truck left, carrying all our possessions, we headed from 7308 Calamo Street in Springfield, Virginia—which had been "home" for four years—to 910 Overlook Drive in Corvallis, Oregon. It would be an almost coast-to-coast trip across country with stops along the way to visit family and a few old friends. Our green 1969 Pontiac sedan's trunk was packed full. A friend would put our Beagle on a plane later, so we would be in Corvallis when she arrived. (I have trouble being with a dog in a small space, so either Trimmie or I had to travel by plane. I was voted to travel in the car, because I would be more useful than Trimmie when someone wanted drinks poured or snacks passed around!) David was just turning ten years old, and Becky was almost fourteen (but "going on 21"). They and I had "carry-on bags" by our feet: "goodies," and things to do along the way. On the back seat, between the kids was a hamster cage, almost as tall as the back of the seat, which housed Tarkio—a three-month-old squirrel that had been rescued as a tiny baby. (The cage actually worked well as a device to keep Becky and David from having quite as many disagreements about who was taking up more than their share of the seat!)

I well remember pulling out of the Calamo Street driveway that last time! David was saying, "Let's go, Dad!" Becky was crying buckets of tears because she was so sad to be leaving her friends there—maybe forever! And I was sad because Becky was sad—so I cried, too!

On other vacation trips we had done some sightseeing in the more southern parts of the country—always allowing time for visiting family in Indiana, Missouri, and Kansas. This time we planned to go through New England, into some of Canada, view Niagara Falls, stop in Indiana, and see Lincoln country in Illinois on the way to our next family stop in Missouri with grandparents and a cluster of aunts, uncles, and cousins. Gene and I had seen some of these places before, but we now wanted to show them to Becky and David. We always thought that we learned more about geography and history by traveling than by reading books, and maybe some of these experiences would help history "come alive" to them.

We wanted to visit Bob and Cidney Brown in Montana on the way to spend time with Gene's family around Tacoma, Washington. The Browns had been neighbors when we had lived in Virginia a few years before. Gene and Bob had worked together, and we often played bridge with them. After Bob retired from the Marine Corps they moved to their home state, and Bob soon became Mayor of Missoula for a few years.

The road between Missouri and Missoula had many interesting places for us to explore, and Interstate 90 seemed to be a good main route for the western adventures. There were some high spots in South Dakota, despite the miles and miles of flat farm land, and very small towns in which were very large grain elevators. In Mitchell there was an elaborate "Corn Palace" that took up almost a whole block. Its outside walls were completely covered with grains of corn and other grains of various colors—dark and light and in-between—arranged in designs of stripes, diamonds, and swirls around the turrets and domes on top in shapes similar to some of Russia's domes. (I'm just now wondering about the origin of dome design in South Dakota! I believe there were many immigrants from northern Europe who settled the upper Midwest—perhaps there was a colony of descendants of Russian immigrants around Mitchell.)

Another stop <u>had</u> to be at Wall's Drug Store in the little town of Wall. I think it was then called the world's largest drug store—the kind that stocked almost anything anyone would ever need. (Sam Walton's Wal-Mart stores hadn't yet become famous.)

We drove through some of the Badlands National Park on a scenic loop highway for close-up views of the grotesque shapes of the peaks, left as a result of erosion that had cut through layers of colorful deposits. The kids enjoyed seeing fossils of various kinds that were displayed at some of our stops.

The main attraction in the Black Hills area was Mt. Rushmore, but we also went to see the beginning of the Crazy Horse monument—a Native American

Chief on his horse—being sculpted from a mountain not far from Mt. Rushmore. We spent a fair amount of time at the Mt. Rushmore memorial grounds and museum—examining with binoculars the sixty-foot high heads of the four presidents, carved from the mountain's granite face by Gutzon Borglum and his son Lincoln. The original idea is credited to Jonah Leroy "Doane" Robinson, who was superintendent of the South Dakota State Historical Society for many years. It was conceived as a "shrine of democracy," with the presidents representing <u>founding</u> by George Washington, <u>expansion</u> by Thomas Jefferson, <u>preservation</u> by Theodore Roosevelt, and <u>unification</u> by Abraham Lincoln. (About a year later we discovered how much it impressed Becky. In an essay she wrote at school describing what she would like to be when she grew up, she illustrated it with a picture of Mt. Rushmore—with a picture of herself mounted alongside the lineup of presidents! When I saw <u>that</u>, I was impressed with <u>her</u>!)

But I started out to describe my Moon Rainbow! By the time we left Mt. Rushmore it was late in the day and we had several miles of mountain driving on the way to our motel. Darkness fell, and we had some intermittent rain. Becky and David fell asleep, but Gene and I were enjoying the cloud formations around us—some very dark and ominous, sometimes a "pile" of white ones; lots of gray ones. Suddenly, some eerie colors seemed to be gathering in the sky in the distance in front of us, and we wondered if it might be some kind of storm approaching. Then the colors lined up into an arc—very <u>grayed</u> colors, but there were red, orange, yellow, green, blue, and violet! Off to the side, some dark clouds had some white ones mixed with them. I turned around and looked behind us—and, guess what! There was a bright, round moon shining from between the clouds! We decided that those unusual night-time colors <u>had</u> to be a rainbow, made from the sun's light being reflected from the moon! We awakened the kids to see it. I wanted to take a picture, but there wouldn't have been enough light for a photograph, and besides, I didn't want to take my eyes off it long enough to look for the camera!

For years I thought I should try to reproduce the scene with something like pastel pencils—but my final decision about that was that it would be impossible to do, and in the "trying to do," I might lose the picture I have in my mind. I wonder if I'll ever be lucky enough to see another Moon Rainbow! I hope you, too, might sometime be blessed with one!

"I REMEMBER READING ABOUT ..."

I would like for my grandchildren and great-grandchildren to know my feelings about the importance of books and reading in my life. I believe that every person one meets becomes, in some way, a part of one's self. And, I think that books have the same effect—considering that the books describe people; their experiences, their joys, their culture, their problems, and how they handle them. As I look back upon the many interests books have kindled for me, and the extent to which my "world" has been expanded by reading, I hope you let books become "best friends," and part of <u>your</u> lives, as well. I'm very thankful for parents, teachers, and others who had a part in encouraging me to read!

Mom and Dad read Bible stories and fairy tales to me from the beginning of my life. When at about age three I began wanting to learn how to "do it myself," they bought a set of several simply written books for children and helped me with the words. The only title I remember of those books was *Dick Whittington and His Cat*. When I was four, Mom added a sister for Ross and me to our family, and since they had given me a name from each of my grandmothers—Ila and May, from Dad's mother Ila Etna, and Mom's mother Oda May—they were planning for the new baby to have the other two: Oda Etna. The book I was reading at the time was about a delightful little girl named Barbara, so I said, "I wish we could name our new baby Barbara! It's such a pretty name!" And they said, "Okay! We'll call her Barbara Oda Etna!" That really made me happy, and Barbara has thanked me many times for that request!

In those days there was no kindergarten in our one-room school. At age six, we began school in first grade. The first-grade reading books included the *See Dick! See Dick Run!* and *See Jane, See Jane Run!* stories, and in math we were beginning with counting and simple addition. Since all grades were taught in that same room, my teacher let me begin "reciting" with the second-grade kids. And before the year was over, I was with the third grade. (It was so interesting for me to listen to the older kids when they were "reciting," I had trouble sometimes concentrating on my next assignments at my desk!)

Our small school had a limited library, in comparison to modern schools, but I managed to always have a library book on hand to read in spare moments. Mom had to make a rule that my chores and my school homework had to be done before I could read for pleasure. Therefore, I volunteered for jobs in which I could read at the same time—like turning the crank on the butter churn or babysitting with the younger children (four of them eventually). Some of the books I remember reading in grade school were Alcott's *Little Men* and *Little Women, Anne of Green Gables, A Girl of the Limberlost,* and *The Legend of Sleepy Hollow.* I liked the feelings that came from sort of pretending I was with them in their adventures. The fact that they could overcome difficulties and problems gave me confidence that I, too, could expect success myself. Laura Ingalls Wilder's books in *The Little House on the Prairie* series seemed to be about country people just like us—a way of life easy for me to understand

One good thing about high school was the well-stocked library! As I began to "notice boys," I enjoyed stories of romance. Grace Livingston Hill was a favorite author for that. I don't remember many of the titles, but one of them was called *Happiness Hill.* I think it is the one that involved a young career woman who met, dated, and became engaged to a wonderful young man. In their learning about each other, they naturally talked about their families, their likes and dislikes, and their dreams for the future; and their "dates" often consisted of just spending time together—walking, exploring the area, and enjoying the out-of-doors. On one such outing, while driving in the country, they came upon the beginning of a new house being built on a hill with a lovely view. Just for fun, they walked through the framework of it, imagining who the owners might be, and how they thought it might look when finished—even about changes they might make. The man suggested that, just for fun, they leave a note for the builders. The "house" became one of their favorite places to go driving. Each time they went back, they noticed that their suggestions had been followed; and each time they left another note, eventually suggesting colors and landscaping designs. Soon after their wedding, he took her to see the "the house," and said something to the effect of, "Welcome home!" before carrying her across the threshold. I thought his gift of a home she had playfully helped to design, was one of the most romantic things I could imagine!

I soon became interested in stories of life in other countries, as school presented studies in history, geography, and classical literature. Pearl Buck's *The Good Earth,* which described life in China, as she knew it from living there with missionary parents, revealed an unimaginable culture to me! Other books and pictures of art, architecture, and life in exotic places like Persia, India, Japan, South Sea Islands, Africa, and the Holy Land "stirred my soul," and gave me a longing to experience those places myself—and I could <u>go</u> there in my imagination! Jan Struthers's *Mrs. Miniver* gave me a look at World War II England; with Alexander McCall Smith, I enjoyed life in Botswana and *The*

#1Ladies Detective Agency series; Oregon's Jean Auel made the time of the Neanderthals come to life with *Clan of the Cave Bear* and *The Mammoth Hunters*. (When we lived for a while in London, I was privileged to meet Antonia Fraser, and hear about the research she did for her delightful book, *Mary, Queen of Scots*.) My daughter, Becky, recently introduced me to *The Red Tent*, by Anita Diamant, which describes the culture, traditions, and womanhood of the Bible in the time of Jacob. It's an intimate description of trials and relationships of what women's lives might have resembled during biblical times, filling in gaps left by the biblical text.

Race relations and cultural differences in our own country became interesting to me quite early, with one of our family "read aloud" books being Harriet Beecher Stowe's *Uncle Tom's Cabin*. We children had <u>heard</u> of slaves but knew nothing of their lives. Needless to say, the book was quite shocking for us, because we were taught that all people were "God's Children." No matter the color of skin, all blood was <u>red</u>, and that made us equal! An old book called *Shepherd of the Hills*, by Harold Bell Wright is a touching story of life in "my" Missouri Ozarks, that I enjoyed reading when I was a teenager. I, of course, identified with one of the residents, being surprised to learn about city life from the stranger who came there to live for a while. Other good stories of racial differences I liked were *To Kill a Mockingbird*, by Harper Lee, and *Gone With the Wind*, by Margaret Mitchell.

Part of the joy of *Gone with the Wind* was probably the time and "setting" of the reading. I had just graduated from high school and had become sixteen the summer that Dad had a defense job near St. Louis. He found an old, dilapidated house in the country nearby where we could live a very simple life for the summer. We moved only very essential furniture—beds, a table and chairs, bicycles, some books and games, lots of scraps for quilt making, a few dishes and utensils, and very little else. The boys had acres of space to explore, but Mom and we three sisters used hours and hours of our time with thimbles and needles, while we girls began learning to piece quilts. But the best part of it all was that, while our needles were sewing, we three and Mom took turns reading to each other from *Gone With the Wind*—the newest edition, printed after the movie was made, so it had many color pictures of various scenes from the movie! It was PURE JOY!

Jan Karon's stories about life in a small town called Mitford, set, I think, in North Carolina, was great fun for me because one of the central characters is Father Tim, bachelor Rector of the Episcopal Church, with a congregation very similar to most of the small churches in my life. People and their relationships are so vividly described, one feels like one of them

Lately, Oregon's Jane Kirkpatrick has provided many hours of pleasure for me with her descriptive historical novels about the settlement of Oregon, Washington, and California. At the beginning of each book she lists the names and relationships of the characters—many of them being the actual, historical people. I've learned a lot of history while imagining the hardships those brave pioneers endured. Oregonians seem to be "different"—courageous, creative, I-can-do-it-myself kinds of people; like maybe "bravery" is a genetic thing.

A great, detailed description of her own life, as well as personalities and happenings in the Washington political arena, is Katharine Graham's autobiography that she calls *Personal History*. Her wealthy father, Eugene Meyer, bought the *Washington Post* in 1933, after having been appointed Governor of the Federal Reserve Board by President Hoover. Katherine worked for some time for *The Post*, and upon her father's death, became, herself, the owner, guiding the newspaper through the critical times of the Pentagon Papers and Watergate, as well as the changes brought about by the young "Women's Movement." She was surely a timely, strong leader in those complicated times—able to stand up to political powers, including a president. An inspiration to any young woman!

Gene, also a voracious reader, devoured adventure, philosophy, history, biography, mysteries, international subjects, <u>anything</u> by John Grisham, psychology—you name it! He gathered a complete collection of Louis L'Amour's stories—some of which I've also enjoyed. I especially like the ones that follow the adventures of the Sackett family as they settled and sort of "tamed" the West. Those well researched stories cover experiences of many different people in the 1600s, the Civil War, into the 1800s.

Our children picked up a lot of our love of books, and we made good use of the many delightful stories and art work of Dr. Seuss! It would be impossible to count the times those books have been opened—even now by our grandsons! Thank you, Dr. Seuss! We've learned a lot about life from you, while we laughed at your clever words and drawings!

I <u>have</u> to tell you that one of my favorite songs is one that was sung by Jimmy Durante—*I'll <u>Never</u> Forget The Day I Read a Book!*

And, wonder of wonders—would you believe I'm even trying to learn to <u>write</u> one?

WHAT WOULD MR. SHAKESPEARE SAY?

I have to admit I'm a procrastinator—and a pack rat—somewhat thrifty, quite curious, appreciative of life in general, and <u>crazy</u> about reading. "Stuff" accumulates in our house because Gene was a pack rat too, and anyway, why would we want to throw something away that we might need sometime? Even after a book has been read, it has value just sitting there on the shelf as a reminder of its contents—it might be useful some day for a reference, or fun to read again sometime. I suppose procrastination leads me to "wait 'til tomorrow" to deal with the "stuff;" and, in some ways, I'm much like my Dad about reading. Mom used to get impatient with his early-morning fire-building in the wood-burning kitchen stove where she'd need to cook breakfast, and in the living room heating stove where we'd do some of our dressing on cold mornings. We saved old newspapers and magazines for fire-starters, and invariably, just before he crumpled it for kindling, he'd notice something interesting that he'd missed reading—delaying the fire-building job.

Today, when I <u>could</u> have been filing papers or sorting through some of my many stacks, the procrastinator in me happened to notice a little book called *Word Power* on a bedroom bookshelf. It's a collection of *Reader's Digest* "Word Power" features that Gene and I always shared as soon as a new *Digest* arrived; and those pages are interspersed with short little essays by various authors—some famous—concerning writing and language. Very interesting. Do you think I put that book back on the shelf and went on to the many stacks that are badly in need of sorting? You should know I didn't!

One of the essays called "Thank you, William Shakespeare!" by a man named Guy Wright, caught my eye. The first sentence reads, "I doubt that there's anyone reading this who goes through a normal day's conversation without quoting Shakespeare." I thought how simple it would be to copy those two pages to share with you, but on the copyright page (the book was printed in 1980), it reads: "This book may not be reproduced in whole, <u>or in part</u>, by mimeograph or any other means, without permission." So, being a law-abiding citizen, I couldn't copy it, and I didn't want to bother with getting permission, so I decided to make up a story of my own to describe it for you.

You will notice that I've written some of the phrases in *italics*. Those phrases, according to Guy Wright, are quotes from William Shakespeare, said to maybe be <u>the greatest</u> cliché inventor of all time.

I'll call the story *LIFE'S UNCERTAIN VOYAGE*, (and you'll also notice, I've plagiarized a good opening sentence):

"It was a dark and stormy night. My name is Dick, and I seem to be having some problems at home. My father is a *man of few words*, but *in my mind's eye* I get the feeling that he'd like to tell me, '*You're eating me out of house and home!*' It was *cold comfort* that he himself was somewhat of a *rotten apple*, but *holding my tongue*, I packed up, *bag and baggage*, and in *one fell swoop*, I was out the door and on my own.

Thinking that *what's done is done*, I realized that I was *poor but honest*. Maybe these were my *salad days*, and I might as well tell myself that *the world is my oyster* as I discover what's out there, even though it is from *grim necessity* that I find myself in this predicament.

As luck would have it, I met a beautiful young girl named Jane, who had a little dog named Spot. People say that *love is blind*, but in my *heart of hearts*, I liked her; and I thought to myself, '*She bears a charmed life.*' Getting along with girls was sort of *Greek to me*, and when I noticed she was interested in a *popinjay* she called Jack, I could tell that something *smelled to heaven!* The way those two acted just was *not in my book!*

Jack was quite a trifling young man—a sort of wolf in sheep's clothing, so I decided to bide my time, knowing that *truth will come to light*. He wasn't *showing his heels*, and he seemed to have *no stomach for a fight*, but I got the feeling that it was *the beginning of the end* of my relationship with Jane.

The unkindest cut of all was when they began *suiting the actions to the words* and told me they had decided to take Spot and go to Reno to seek their fortune.

It may be *neither here nor there*, but I *haven't slept a wink* since they left. I definitely have *seen better days*, and I'm ready to say, '*The long and the short of it is* that it's a *mad world!*' THE END"

So, how often do <u>you</u> quote Mr. Shakespeare? Actually, one of my favorite quotes of his is: *"All the world's a stage, and all the men and women merely players."*

Definitions:

Popinjay- A gay, trifling young man; a talkative, vain person. (From an old dictionary, written before "gay" might also mean homosexual.)

Showing his heels- cowardly.

LOVE IS ALL THAT MATTERS

JAPAN AND HONG KONG — MARCH 1977

By now Gene had been retired from the Marine Corps for almost four years, and we hadn't yet done any major traveling. Becky was a senior in high school and would be off to college—maybe away from home—and we might not have too many more opportunities to travel as a family. We had been to Europe; now might be a good time to experience some of the Orient, and the children agreed. We were eligible to fly space available, with only a very small charge, on military flights, but it would possibly require a few days' waiting period, depending upon flight schedules and what space would be available. It seemed like a worthwhile "gamble," especially since Gene's parents lived but a short distance from McChord Airbase in Washington—one of the likely places for departure to Japan or Hong Kong. We would allow ourselves three weeks, one of which would be the week of Spring Break in order to lessen the time Becky and David would miss school.

On Saturday, March 5th, we checked in at McChord and signed up for the next flight to Japan which would be Tuesday, the 8th, so we had some time to visit with the Bench family. For some reason I had had negative "vibes" about the trip from the beginning of our planning, and it hadn't helped those feelings when three days before departure date, a boy at school let his skate-board get away from him, it hit David and made him fall, breaking his arm. Gene took David to the doctor—a very painful experience for David—plus the fact that he was afraid this accident would cause us to have to cancel the trip he was so excited about! Then, the day we left Corvallis, Gene had a sore throat and couldn't talk much above a whisper for three days. On Monday morning, the 7th, I awakened with pain in my left arch. By mid-morning, I couldn't walk on it. I soaked it for an hour in hot water, which didn't help any, and tried to decide what to do. To start out on a two-week-plus trip with a crippled foot (David already having a luggage-carrying arm out of commission) seemed pretty stupid. I had never had that kind of pain before that I could remember, I hadn't turned my ankle—hadn't done anything but sit around visiting. Gene took me to Madigan Army Hospital (near McChord) and checked me into the Emergency Room where I got into a wheel chair for visits to X-ray, medical doctor, and then to the podiatry department. X-rays showed no unusual bone problem, so the best diagnosis the doctors could come up with was some kind of tendinitis. I was afraid they would tell me to stay off of it, so I told them before they even checked it that we were to leave Tuesday for the Orient, and they <u>had</u> to fix me so I could walk. The podiatrist prescribed a support (which a technician made while I waited) to put into my shoe to put pressure in front of my heel, which helped a little, but even with that, I couldn't do any better than "hobble"—and that, in pain. He told me there was one of the best podiatrists he knew of at the Army base in Japan where our niece Debbie and husband Lonnie lived, so he suggested I let him check it when we got to Japan.

Tuesday, by noon, we'd found out we couldn't get on the military plane! They were carrying cargo that didn't permit passenger space. Gene's throat was improving, my foot was still painful, and the next probable military space available would be Saturday, which would be the whole week spent waiting to get started. We had a conference, called a travel agency, found we could get reservations for Wednesday, the 9th, and decided to buy tickets to fly from Sea-Tac. I awakened sometime during the night Tuesday, and my foot felt hot at the place that had the pain. Wednesday morning, when I wiggled it, it didn't hurt. When I stood on it, it only hurt a <u>little</u> bit. With my shoe and support on, it hurt still less! I had done a lot of hard praying—could it be a <u>miracle?</u> Now came prayers of thanks!

I often wrote lengthy, descriptive letters to my mom and dad, many of which they saved and later returned to me, so I think excerpts from some of those letters would be appropriate to describe some of this "adventure."

March 9-10 (Over the Pacific—I think it's Thursday here). Wish you were with us! We left Seattle-Tacoma Airport at 1:55 Wednesday afternoon, the 9th, in rain mixed with snow. In a very few minutes we were above the clouds in the sunshine, looking through holes in them to see the coastline, mountains, rivers, etc. We followed the coastline north west for quite a while and flew over Adak Island in the Aleutian chain. We cross the date line, so we'll arrive in Tokyo about 5:30 p.m. on Thursday, being in the air non-stop for about ten and a half hours. We're not quite "keeping up with" the sun, but we're near enough behind him, we'll get to see him set about the time we land. (We'll get the extra day back on the return trip—and by then, we'll probably <u>need it!</u>)

It would have been nice to have been able to get a free ride, but the kids and I are getting a nice new experience this way—our first trip on a 747 plane. Boy! Is it ever a <u>big bird!</u> It looks like an awful waste of fuel, though, because there isn't even one-fourth of a load. About one-half hour after we were up we were served drinks and peanuts; then in another one-and-a-half hours came a dinner—choice of chicken or salmon with shrimp cocktail, salad, vegetables in sauce and rice, roll and butter, apple cake, fortune cookie, and "coffee, tea, or milk." When that was cleared away they showed a Telly Savalas movie for which one had to rent headphones if one wanted to hear what was going on. (Becky, David and Gene did *that while I caught up on my reading. The earphones can also be used to plug into a variety of types of music—classical, semi-classical, western, rock, Japanese, and comedy. After the movie David and Becky really enjoyed the comedy channel!)*

There are empty seats all around us, so we are welcome to sit wherever we like—lie down in some of the long ones (armrests fold up) or change about. Gene and I have been playing some gin-rummy, and there has been some napping and reading. Becky has her loom with her and has done some weaving. Right now, she and David are "visiting" happily in the two seats in front of me and Gene is studying some of his Life Underwriter lessons behind me. We've had fresh apples and more Cokes since dinner and are supposed to have a light lunch before we land. I haven't changed my watch yet, and it says almost 10:30—which is bedtime according to the time we got up this morning. We'll probably be a sleepy gang until we get adjusted to the time change. I guess I should feel sleepy, but it's hard to do when the sun is still so bright.

Well, it's soon going to be time to gather up our goodies and get ready to deplane in the "Land of the Rising Sun." My tummy is so full, I'm going to have to stretch awhile. I interrupted my letter long enough to eat another lunch—orange juice, potato salad, roll and butter, cold slices of roast beef, turkey and Swiss cheese, and a glass of milk. It's a good thing this isn't a longer flight—I'd be too fat for my clothes pretty soon! We wrote for reservations at the American Military Hotel but didn't have a chance to get confirmation before leaving home—so we hope they'll have space. It's called The Sanno. I'll add a P.S. after we land.

Saturday a.m. We had a happy landing (Thursday evening). Yesterday we were all like "zombies" because of adjusting to such quick time change and lack of sleep during the flight, so we walked around through some of the nearby little streets and had lunch at a Japanese restaurant—tempura, sashimi (raw fish), and various interesting vegetables and soups. (One of the things David remembers about most of the restaurants was their window displays of some of the items on their menus: colorful, realistic-looking servings made of plastic.) *We also did some phoning and planning. Debbie, Lonnie, and Carmen are picking us up today for a visit with them. Tomorrow we'll explore the Ginza area, which compares to New York's Broadway; go to Kamakura, south of Tokyo on Monday; Tuesday, take an all-day tour of Tokyo, and catch a 7:00 p.m. plane to Hong Kong. We'll be at the Singapore Hotel there for a couple or so days, then back to Japan to Kyoto for more sightseeing and trying for a space available flight home.*

Thursday, March 17—Hong Kong. Too bad about St. Pat's Day today—we all seemed to have "coordinated blue" wardrobes with us and had nothing green to wear—except for David—he has green sport shoes! We at least <u>thought</u> about the occasion; and we <u>did</u> have cabbage for dinner, even though it was Chinese fried cabbage, and with it was Peking Duck, shrimp fried rice, and fried bamboo. The duck is a sort of barbecue style—brought to the table whole, then sliced so that each piece has some of the crisp skin with it. With *chopsticks you put one of the accompanying paper-thin rice pancakes on your plate, dip some leek into a tasty sauce made from beans, sugar, vinegar, and mustard, and put that on the middle of the pancake—then dip a couple of slices of duck in the sauce, put them on the leeks, wrap the pancake around it and eat it with your fingers. Yummy!* (David remembers that a curious thing about that restaurant was its name—The American Restaurant! We liked it so much we ate there several times.)

We had a good time with Debbie, Lonnie, and Carmen in Tokyo. They came to our hotel and took us to their place in their friend's car (larger than theirs, still small Datsun size!). They took us to dinner with them at their NCO Club where we had "Mongolian Grill." We were given a bowl about the size of the blue bowl of a 4-piece mixing bowl set (the smallest one)—maybe a little shorter and a bit more flared. This was at the beginning of a buffet line that had a wide variety of foods: shredded cabbage, Chinese cabbage, thinly sliced carrots, pepper strips. Onion slices, green onions, bean sprouts, thinly sliced beef, pork, and turkey. For marinade sauce there were sesame oil, shrimp oil, garlic vinegar, onion vinegar, soy sauce, hot pepper vinegar, and ginger sauce. The idea seemed to be to pack as much food as possible into your bowl with meat stacked on tip, pour your sauce over it (a mixture of whatever you put together) and send it to the kitchen to be cooked. When it came back, your choice of plain or fried rice was served in another bowl, and you just dug into it with your chopsticks. Really good—depending upon your selection of sauce ingredients. We stayed overnight there on the base at the visiting officers' quarters which was near the McCulley's quarters, had David's arm X-rayed as per his doctor's instructions, and back to Tokyo by train.

Went to Kamakura one day, hoping to see Mt. Fuji, but it was cloudy. Still had fun, though. Saw a lot of interesting things in Tokyo, then came here Tuesday night.

The only trouble with this place is there isn't enough time to see and do all we want to do. Today we went shopping in an old-style market on the other side of Hong Kong Island, did some sunbathing at Repulse Bay Beach (one of the elite beaches), went to Tiger Balm gardens, then to dinner near our hotel—you guessed it—The American Restaurant again. We go so hard all day, we're all ready to rest as soon as we get back to our rooms. Tomorrow we're taking a tour to the New Territories, up to the Red China border, then back to shop in Kowloon.

Saturday we expect to have lunch with a friend of Emma Hollinger's who is a missionary here—teaches in a girls' school on one of the islands near Hong Kong. We're doing that partly for Emma, but we're sure she will also have a wealth of information for us about what it's like to live in Hong Kong.

We've met several interesting people—our tour guide in Tokyo gave us the name and address of his uncle who has recently opened a Japanese restaurant in Kansas City. On the city bus today we chatted with an American lady whose husband is a teacher in the American School here—he's from Kansas City, too. She was from Iowa and Nebraska. Small world, isn't it? Major Martin and his wife Carole have been very hospitable here—he's attached to the Embassy—Executive Officer for the Marine Guard. He got our hotel reservation and invited us to their house last evening. They're full of ideas about places to go and things to do.

We expect to go back to Japan Saturday or Sunday. The time is going so fast—it seems we hardly got started before we have to go home! We thank God daily for our health and energy—especially for my foot that is still holding up!

March 24—Iwakuni Air Base in southern Japan. At this point it's still not possible to say our adventures are over, because we're still not home, and the way things happen to us, any day can be an adventure. Right now we're sitting in the office of Capt. Foster at the Marine air base in Iwakuni Air Base. (Capt. Foster was with Gene on an Inspector General trip in 1972.) We came down here Tuesday the 22nd, after missing a space available (hereinafter called S-A) flight from Yokota (where Debbie and Lonnie live) because there seems to be more S-A out of here. Even that was an interesting experience—riding the "Bullet Train" most of the way, finding the proper tracks, etc. The plane which we hope to get on this afternoon stops in Yakota, then Anchorage, Alaska, and on to Norton Air Base (near Los Angeles) in California. If we get on here, the only people who can "bump" us are active duty people on emergency leave, and people here seem to think we have a good chance of making it all the way.

I should have made some notes about what I've written before, so I don't bore you with repetition, but I don't think I told you about our visit in Hong Kong with Gladys Ward— the missionary friend of Emma's. She was born in 1901 in Canton, China, to missionary parents (also friends of Emma's—in fact Emma contributed lots of financial support to them). She is spry as a chicken, full of smiles and humor, and living in Hong Kong because she likes working with the people there. She teaches classes on various books of the Bible at a seminary and does volunteer work with young people. Her only pay is her Social Security retirement. She lives and works on an island in the Hong Kong harbor, but travels frequently to Hong Kong and the New Territories and Kowloon. She had to go to a funeral in Hong Kong Saturday afternoon, then to a meeting that evening at 7:00, so we had lunch and dinner with her. For lunch she took us to a large downtown dining room where there were hundreds of Chinese people having lunch. Waitresses walked among the tables with trays of various dishes from which you selected what you'd like. It was helpful to see it before ordering— things we might not have been able to figure out from a menu, anyway. Many of the dishes were prepared in little woven baskets and steamed. We insisted that she be our guest for dinner, but she should select the place. This one was a beautiful carpeted dining room with classy decorations and lovely service. Gladys did the ordering after asking about things we'd like—she speaks Chinese as well as she does English, I suppose.

Saturday, March 26 Corvallis. Here I am back under my regular hair dryer where I often at least begin my letters to you. After a week-and-a-half of all kinds of abuse, I'm sure my hair *appreciates it! The only time I had a chance to get it washed while on the trip was in Hong Kong—about half way through the three weeks. That was an interesting experience in a small "neighborhood" type beauty shop which must have been using pretty old equipment. I'd guess the new tourist hotel shops would be more modernized (or "westernized"). I sat in a high, straight wooden chair—with a foot rest stool in front—while the shampoo boy used shampoo and a bottle of water to suds my hair in front of the mirror. He massaged and scrubbed for five minutes or so, then took me upstairs to the wash basin for rinsing and another shampoo application in a chair that laid me back with my head over the basin. The hot water heater was directly overhead—a coil system of water pipe heated with bottle gas flame so that the water was heated as it ran through the pipes. (Americans could sure save a lot of energy by using that kind of water heating system rather than keeping a big tank of it hot all the time! We had that kind when we lived in Woodbridge, Virginia, and it was great.) From there to another chair for curlers to be applied, then to the dryer, and back to a chair for combing. They didn't use a wave set on it, so it was softer than usual, but the stylist who did the setting and combing did a good job on making it look nice. The only problem was that the air in Hong Kong was so humid and warm, my hair was soon fuzzy and wind-blown. Most of the ladies who were getting their hair done there were having it blown dry— a little bit of curl being put into the ends by rolling it over a round brush as they dried it. That's great for people who have a lot of hair, or hair with a lot of "body," but if I tried a style like that I think I would look like I had no hair at all.* (David remembers that in Hong Kong, when I gave him a daily shampoo, the water in the basin looked almost black it was so dirty.)

David was sure excited to get back home. He enjoyed traveling, but I guess the best part of it for him is telling his friends about his adventures. His arm didn't bother him except for the discomfort of carrying around the extra weight and being able to use only one hand. (He was quite embarrassed once when a waitress insisted upon cutting his meat for him!) The X-ray in Yokota showed that it was mending normally. It's time now for it to be put into a shorter cast for the rest of the time—another three weeks, I think.

To tell you about Becky will include "the saga of THE CHAIR." She took a couple of hundred dollars of her own money with her for shopping, and she sure got her money's worth, although sometimes it seemed time-consuming. She loves baskets, so she got a "boodle" of various sizes and kinds of those, including a chest with pretty brass corners and hasp. It's about the size of a foot-locker, large enough to hold 33-1/3" records standing upright. By *taking the lid off and putting it into a separate package, we were able to mail all those bulky things. The surprise came when she decided to bring back a rocking chair! (Bentwood bamboo with cane seat and back). She didn't even ask me about it, and Gene let her buy it on condition she could get it into a bus to get it back to the hotel, which she did by paying for two extra seats' fare. We were lucky enough to get on a minibus from the hotel to the airport (taxis are mostly about the size of a Toyota or Datsun), and the plane took it as baggage. That was from Hong Kong to Tokyo. We must have been an interesting looking bunch, arriving in Tokyo with all our bags plus THE CHAIR! Since it was our second time arriving there, we already knew the best way to get to our hotel—a bus which stopped three blocks from the hotel, and we walked the rest of the way. Next bus would be going in about an hour. Just as we were gathering our gear together for the wait for the bus, three nice looking young men came up and said, "Do you need some assistance?" We explained that we were just waiting for the bus, which would leave in about an hour. They said they had come to meet someone who didn't show up, and had to go back into town anyway, so they would be glad to drop us at our hotel! (Their transportation was a van!) We decided that was Miracle #2 on our adventure! They were a little surprised that we trusted them—and we admit we were somewhat cautious. On the ride to town they explained their business—a new duty-free store which had opened only three weeks before. They insisted that they take us sightseeing the next day and take us to see their store. We thought that to be only fair after the favor they'd done us, but we waited until the next day to tell them that what we <u>really</u> needed most was a ride to Yakota to try to get S-A on the plane. We agreed to promote their business among our friends, which seemed to be all the pay they wanted. At their store we did find the best buy so far on a telephoto lens, so we got one of those, a new tri-pod, and some film (further discounted!) So, I guess we did a good job of "scratching each others' backs"!*

When we weren't able to get on the plane leaving Yakota, we decided to ship excess luggage and the chair before leaving on the train to Iwakuni. But the chair was too large for mailing and too costly to ship. We called Debbie for help. She will keep it until they find some crew-member who might bring it, or they might ship it with their furniture when they come back to the States. What would we have done without her?

We really enjoyed the two short visits with the McCulleys. Carmen is only about eight years old, and a real little doll. I often noticed her studying my face, and once she said, "You seem like Grandma Barbara, but you're <u>not</u> Grandma Barbara!" They all seemed to be enjoying living in Japan. We were glad they were able to read the road signs along the freeway and do the driving! I think I told you earlier about enjoying the "Mongolian Barbecue" with them at their NCO club. I should tell you about another one we had in Tokyo at the Chinzan-so—high on a hill overlooking a lovely garden. A very "spiffy" place. In the middle of each table was a grill where a waitress (or whatever she would be called—sort of combination of cook and waitress) cooked and served as each thing was done, dipping each *into a delicious thin sauce. The various things that were served were: chicken, lotus root, potato, mushrooms, carrots, steak, pork, corn-on-the-cob (about two-inch chunks), green pepper, onion, and rice. (Rice served in a small bowl—not cooked on the grill.) Beverage was tea, dessert was fresh orange. (This was the place David was embarrassed when the waitress cut his meat for him.) We all became quite adept with chopsticks—never used a fork except for breakfast in the hotel where they served rather western style food.*

Well, back to transportation. We did get on the expected plane (a "Flying Tiger" DC-8—considerably smaller than the 747 on the way over, but very comfortable, and delicious food. We left Iwakuni at 3:00 p.m. Thursday the 24th; arrived at Yakota at 4:00; departed at 5:00 p.m.; arrived in Anchorage at about 5:00 a.m. Thursday, the 24th. While they refueled the plane, we watched the sun rise over snow covered hills (temperature 10 degrees) and enjoyed examining a taxidermist's standing specimen of a very large grizzly bear in the airport waiting lounge. About 6:00 a.m. we headed for California and arrived at Norton Air Base a little after 1:00 p.m. David thought it was pretty neat to land two hours before we had taken off from Japan!

Monday evening, March 27. A rented car got us home late Friday evening. We had got our sleeping time turned topsy-turvy, so had to take turns driving and napping, even though we stopped at a motel for Thursday night.

We've spent the weekend sleeping, doing laundry, and putting away. Things were in good order at home—our "house sitters" had kept things running normally—and today Gene and the kids got back to their business and school. It will take still a few more days to get totally back to the time change, but it was all worth it. It's truly a privilege to be able to see how some of the rest of the world lives—if nothing else, one can appreciate home all the more! Each culture has some "assets" and some "liabilities," I suppose. It would be much easier, and would probably cost less, to book a trip such as that with a tour group. They would take care of all the luggage handling, tipping, tours, reservations, interpreters—even most of the food—but we figure the experience the kids received by doing things by ourselves was worth more than could be measured by money. There still wasn't enough time to do and see all we'd like to have experienced, but that's always the case, right?!

I can't really put a period at the end of the story about this adventure yet, because we're minus a car. We'll soon be making another short trip to visit Mom and Dad Bench in Washington to bring back the one we left there at the beginning of the trip. Sayonara!

P.S. So … what happened to THE CHAIR? It came back to the States with Debbie and Lonnie's household effects when Lonnie was transferred to an air base in Florida, and they shipped it to us in Oregon. It is still in use in

Becky's home in Seattle, and has rocked her three children, two grandsons, and a granddaughter!

MAKING APPLE CIDER

Why in the world would I be making apple cider? To answer that I'll back up to see if I can get a "running start" at finding a reason.

My dad, Sterling Kelley, was a journal keeper for most of his adult life and was very interested in genealogy. By the time he retired from his cabinet-maker work with the University of Missouri Maintenance Department in 1974, he had decided to write his autobiography as a gift to his descendants. He had used much of his life working to make a living, and now he had whole days of precious time to use in some really special way. We children had always enjoyed hearing him tell us stories of his many experiences, and one of my brothers (also named Sterling) often said, "Dad, you should write a book!" So he did—teaching himself "touch typing" in order to make the manuscript easier to edit.

When it came time to put it all together he asked me if I would do the final typing and help with details like cover design, arranging the pictures, etc. I had discovered that a friend of ours, who was a writer, used the Maverick Publishing Company in Bend, Oregon to do most of her printing; so after a phone conversation with their manager, Gene and I drove to Bend to have a conference and to receive their instructions for preparation of this publishing project. Dad wanted it to have a hard cover—and to be a real "book" book! He also had a beautiful color photograph of him and Mom together, sitting on their front porch, wearing the colonial costumes Mom had made for them to celebrate the Bicentennial activities in 1976. He thought it would be nice if that photo could be used in some way.

Our next-door neighbor, Alice Hall, and I were what you might call "bosom buddies," sharing all kinds of ideas, discussing all kinds of projects— usually over cups of tea—so naturally, Dad's book became one of our topics. She is an artist, and she had many helpful suggestions. She even agreed— knowing it would need a lot of time—to design and prepare for printing, a dust cover using the Bicentennial photo for the front, and a picture of Dad with his "leaf whistle" for the back. With that much help, Dad and I decided we'd begin!

By now, you're asking yourself, "What has all this to do with making apple cider!" Just hold that thought for a while longer.

Dad and I spent a couple of years of him sending copy to me. I typed it and sent it back to him for approval, making many phone calls, etc. By the end of summer in 1980, it seemed that we were ready to finalize the project. So on November 4th, Mom and Dad came on the bus for a visit in Corvallis, at the end of which Gene and I would take them to Bend, along with the prepared manuscript. On November 12th we would meet with the printer, and "seal the deal." From there, Mom and Dad would take the bus back home to Columbia, Missouri.

In the meantime, one of the attractions of interest in Corvallis while they were here was a "Whistlers'" concert, hosted by Mitch Hider who was a master whistler. For a couple of hours several people whistled tunes from old-time songs, country music, and even classical tunes. Mitch thought Dad had a unique "instrument" that produced a sound that could be called whistling, so Dad was invited to be one of the performers. He had learned as a youngster how to press the folded edge of a hickory leaf close across his lower lip and make a sound by blowing across it—because it has actually become a sort of reed. With his tongue and breath, he formed the tune. (A few years earlier he had recorded some hickory-leaf music with some other folk-musicians for the Smithsonian Institute.)

Well, we're almost to the cider!

Dad, of course, never wanted to miss a new experience, so Gene invited him to spend a day with him on the road to the west of Corvallis, making calls on some of his insurance customers—great scenery, interesting people, and good "togetherness." One of the customers had some apple trees producing more apples than his family could use, so Gene and Dad brought home a bunch of apples—I think maybe two or three bushels! They were no doubt thinking, "apple pie, apple sauce, apple cake," etc. Well, when neighbor Alice saw those apples, they reminded her of the antique cider mill in her garage that she had rescued when her folks closed their winery some years ago on a farm back east. It just seemed natural that on that sunny November day we should experience making cider in her driveway, with that old cider mill!

While Alice prepared the mill, we scurried about collecting empty glass jars and jugs—easy to find at our house because we never threw anything away, thinking we "might need it sometime." Some lawn chairs made places for apple washers and cutters to sit while others took turns turning the wheel that activated the "presser," which began filling the holder of the apple pieces, removing the pulp, pouring up the juice, and swatting yellow jackets (bees!). It would have been an occasion, for someone who had the time, to do a study on the subject of how far away a yellow jacket can smell apple juice! We <u>know</u> that if they smell it, they will come—especially if it's late in summer—and judging by the numbers of them, some must have traveled from quite a distance! Luckily, no one was stung but they did get our attention! Even though the sun was shining, it was quite COLD work for bare hands on cold apples! And, in spite of the chill and the bees, we all had great fun with stimulating conversation about "olden days," Alice and the Kelleys' getting better acquainted, all of us exchanging stories about where we'd lived and things we'd done, etc. etc.!

In a phone conversation yesterday with Alice (who now lives in Portland) I mentioned that I hadn't yet had an inspiration for this week's story for writing class. She said, "Write about making cider with your folks." My reply, "Great idea!" So now you know "why in the world I was making apple cider," as well as "why in the world I am <u>writing</u> about it!"

"THERE'S A FIRE UP HERE!"
May 31, 1994

<u>8:00 a.m. (or so)</u> – A technician came to install the security system we'd recently ordered. We live in the country, and were quite often traveling, and this particular system would sense smoke in the house and automatically call the fire department if a fire should start while we were away. It would also call the police in case of a break-in and had a one-button call for an ambulance in case of emergency.

<u>9:30 a.m.</u> – I received a phone call from a friend named Sylvia. She and her husband Don were Marine Corps friends for many years and were now retired and living in their very large 5th-wheel camper while traveling all over the country—usually wintering someplace in Arizona. This day they were leaving their campsite at Travis Air Force Base in California, heading north, expecting to arrive in Newport, Oregon, about mid-day on June 6, and would be coming to visit us.

<u>10:30 a.m.</u> – Gene was working at something in the garage, I was doing laundry, occasionally watching the technician and visiting a bit. He was a very nice young man who seemed to enjoy his work and seemed very competent about it—drilling various sizes of holes for wires and sensors he'd be installing. I had joked with him at one point about it. I said, "What would happen if you accidentally drilled into a live wire inside a wall?" He said, "No problem. It

would maybe give me a small shock through the drill at the moment it would trip a breaker at the fuse box." And we laughed about it.

He went out to his truck for tools and smelled something burning as he came back through the garage. Gene and I confirmed the smell and checked outside in case neighbors were burning trash, but the odor was only in the garage. The young man climbed into the attic through a large-sized access from the garage, and seeing flames in several places, shouted, "There's a fire up here!" He took a fire extinguisher back up with him, and I ran for the phone— it was dead! Close neighbors were all gone to work. Gene dropped the garden hose he was pulling into the garage to take up into the attic when he remembered the recently acquired cell phone in the car in the shed across the parking area, where he ran to call 9-1-1. By then the smoke was too dense and dangerous to use the garden hose, and too much fire for the small extinguisher.

Time now for emergency procedures: Gene got a wrench and turned off the gas at the meter outside the house, then moved the other car, a VW, out of the garage at the house. I grabbed my purse, threw into it my 47-year-old Bulova watch that happened to be on the dresser top as I went by, picked up a recently received check and folder pertaining to a business deal from Gene's desk, and put the safe-box key in my purse. The workman gathered up his tools and materials and moved his truck to a safe place. By then we were hearing the fire truck sirens on their way.

What a l-o-n-g fifteen minutes it was until the first engine arrived! I had often wondered what I would try to save if our house ever caught fire. Now my mind was racing a-mile-a-minute! Family pictures! Dad's painting! Mom's and Dad's autobiography books! My "marked-up" Bible! I remembered reading an Ann Landers letter about someone who had lost an appointment calendar and an address file in a fire, which had caused a lot of confusion and loss of communication with many friends. My mind processed the thoughts that important documents and papers were already locked in the fire-proof safe; some other valuables were in the heavy, fire-resistant safe. I didn't dare risk my own safety to go deep into the house again for the Bible, books, and pictures; but I did grab the calendar from the kitchen, a jacket from the utility closet, and a quart jar of water, because by then my mouth felt like it was full of cotton from the tension and stress of the moment. Several times I heard myself saying out loud, "Lord! Help! Please help us!"

No flames were visible as yet, so we kept hoping that the smoke that kept pouring from the attic ventilation openings under the eaves, and at several places across the roof, was coming from a "slow burn."

A fire captain in a pick-up truck was the first to arrive, checking out possible entrances for the engines to come close to the house. People who have "little places in the woods" don't always consider such safety features in locating their "hide-away" driveways, etc. Fortunately, we had an easily accessed place, so the first pumper came into the driveway and parked about halfway between the house and the shed. Four other engines—two from Adair Village and two from Corvallis—and an ambulance—lined up on Overlook Drive and down the road alongside the field, so we felt that all that <u>could</u> be done would now be possible. (The extra pumpers were necessary because our well wouldn't support the supply of water and pressure needed.)

Three firemen at a time, using respiratory equipment, took turns in the attic, while a seeming "army" of people—men <u>and</u> women, invaded the main floor. When we next saw the interior, furniture in each room had been moved to the middle of the room, pictures and "things" had been removed from the walls, lamps and our many "knick-knacks" had been safely placed under tables and near supportive furniture. Even the plants were protected! Clothes on their hangers from our bedroom were out of the closet and on the bed, and over everything in each room was a heavy, waterproof tarp to protect from water that might be expected to come through the ceilings.

All we could do was pray and watch the procedure that seemed wonderfully coordinated as communication passed from one place to another via several radio phones. Soon the Fire Captain told Gene he needed to cut holes in the roof because the heat was too intense for the men in the attic and suggested a place on the front side of the house where we were standing and watching. Gene asked if the back side would be as well, and said we had a contract with a carpenter to install two roof windows in another two weeks— that he was thinking of the one that would be over the back bathroom. The Captain said, "Where? And what size?" The place and size Gene indicated worked perfectly for the firemen!

In a couple of hours, though it seemed an eternity, the fire was contained in the attic; holes were cut in the ceiling in a couple of places which drained some water to controlled locations, so that damage was mostly from smoke and some water.

Our insurance agent came while the firemen were still working, and the inspector was looking for the cause. They found that a very large electric wire behind the wall of the hall closet had been severed! In the instant before the circuit breaker was activated, several wires over the living room ceiling became overheated and ignited the old insulation that had become flammable with age. I felt so sorry for that young security system technician!

A month of restoration work followed, while we comfortably lived with some friends—very thankful for the expert work of the Fire Department, insurance company, and for the hospitality of friends! Yes, Don and Syl came for a visit as planned. They parked their camper in a neighbor's driveway, providing a great place for us to visit and play some bridge during their three days in Corvallis! And, yes, the security system installation was completed during the period of restoration—by a different workman.

SUMMERLANE — LOT #6
Camp Sherman, Oregon

In 1996, we received an inquiry about the possibility of selling the farm that we had owned since 1964 on the Alsea River. For thirty-two years it had been one of the joys of our lives, providing a beautiful place for trout and steelhead fishing, picnicking, picking blackberries, raising some beef cows, and a home for son David to experience some much-desired independence when he was sixteen. As much as we loved the serenity of spending time there, it was beginning to need care that wasn't very convenient for us, so we agreed to sell it. But before we did that, we needed to find another property to include with the sale—a land-trade for tax purposes. The areas around Sisters and Bend were becoming popular for retirement and vacation homes, so we spent some time looking, and imagining, among the many high-and-dry hills, what might be attractive for building—for us, or for investment.

Then, by chance, we learned of the opening of a new, small development called 'Summerlane" in the middle of the very small town of Camp Sherman, west of Sisters, near Black Butte. Camp Sherman was founded in the latter part of the nineteenth century, by vacationers from Sherman County, through which the Deschutes and John Day Rivers flow into the Columbia. That county was named for William Tecumseh Sherman, a Union General under General Ulysses S. Grant in the Civil War, who later conducted Indian wars in the West. (His *Memoirs* is considered one of the best first-hand accounts of the Civil War.) In just one visit to Camp Sherman, it's easy to believe how it became populated by vacationers! The Metolius River originates just a short distance upstream, flowing clear and cold <u>out of the ground</u>, providing a home for "feisty" rainbow trout. Tall ponderosa pine trees, green meadows, and views of the unique cone of Black Butte, the snow-capped Mt. Jefferson and Three Sisters mountains, give the place a really special natural beauty!

For several years a stretch of the Metolius River in that area had been a favorite fishing place for Gene and David. Becky's family liked skiing and hiking in the mountains, so it might be a place we could build a vacation home for our own family to enjoy gathering. There would be activities and landscapes for <u>all</u> of us to enjoy! The population had grown to over 3,000 that included many new, beautiful homes in the surrounding countryside. In the center of town are Black Butte Elementary School, a quaint general store, a post office, a volunteer fire department, several small motels, and a fairly new resort that includes the Kokanee Café restaurant and shingled cabins of natural wood color with green roofs. The entrance to Summerlane is off the main road into town. The school property joins it on the west, and the resort is built in the space to the east, down to the bank of the river. There is an active Camp Sherman Community Association that was organized in 1948, with a hall that was built by volunteer members and later expanded to include outdoor picnic tables. It is used for barbecues—of bear, venison, and trout—community potlucks, dances, quilt shows, family reunions, weddings and receptions, 4th of July pancake breakfasts, Saturday night bingo, auctions, rummage sales, and such. We decided it was the kind of place we might find useful! So, on May 21, 1996, after several meetings with our realtor, many phone calls and faxed messages, we met with our farm buyers in Salem to complete the signing of all the documents necessary to buy, sell, and trade the properties that were involved.

The development called Summerlane consisted of nine building lots and three "common" areas, arranged around an oval drive. Deep wells provided water and a large pond. It was a landscape feature, and also served as a source of water for fire emergency. We chose Lot #6 which had a riparian area along a small creek at the back of the lot; and from our back yard and windows, we would have a great view of Black Butte. For a few months the sunny, grassy lot just sat there while we were busy with "life as usual." Then I began to get some "creative" house-planning feelings. So … what kind of house should we build? We had never "built" a house before, beyond choosing some alterations to an "unbuilt" tract house that would be ours. It should be large enough to accommodate all of our family together sometimes; it should be accessible for our use as we aged—maybe needing wheel chairs. And, it needed to be comfortable in any season. There were a few restrictions to consider, such as placement on the lot; height (ours would be limited to one-and-a-half-story so as to not block neighbors' views); a detached garage, and some sort of shrubbery.

We chose Paul Miller for the architect after seeing some of his work at the homes of friends. We liked his vision for taking advantage of views, and for making efficient use of space. He lived in Sisters, so it was convenient for him to visit the site, and to be familiar with the local builders and building codes. With an advertising photo of a bungalow with a porch and dormer windows, we were able to give Paul a general idea of the type of building we would like—except we wouldn't have an attached garage—just a sheltered entrance access between the garage and the house. We definitely wanted a porch, and Paul designed a ramp access to it, as well as the two steps up from ground level.

I'm not able to remember the exact floor plan, but I can describe some of the features. Entering from the front door, to the left was the master bedroom and bath. A central stairway separated that area from the great-room (living and dining space) on the right. The kitchen had a bar extension into the great-room that made a small "nook" from which double sliding doors led to a deck on the rear of the house. It would have electric heat, supplemented with a pellet wood stove in the great-room. (Remembering the heating stoves in our childhood, we wanted one with a flat top that could also provide some space for a teakettle or a soup pot!)

Upstairs were two bedrooms, separated by a full bathroom located on the front side of the house, and a "sitting space" of that same width on the back side, with a glass door to open onto a narrow little balcony. So, from the roof, there would be three dormer windows on the front side, and, I think, one wider one on the back. The one-car garage would have a work bench and storage across the back, and a storage space for sacks of wood pellets along the inside wall nearest the house. The exterior would be stained natural wood color with dark green trim.

We drove to Sisters three times to meet with Paul and were ready to begin building by mid-summer. However, on July 2, 1997, Gene had to have back surgery for spinal stenosis. He wouldn't be able to ride the long distance to Camp Sherman for several weeks, and we wouldn't want to have building beginning for which we couldn't be present a great deal of the time, so we asked Paul to put the project on hold. By the time Gene recovered from the surgery, we had done more thinking about the project, and to the question we were asking ourselves: "Why do you need another house, when you sometimes have a problem maintaining the one you have?" The answer came up, "We don't!" We, and our children, probably wouldn't be able to use it often, and renting it to vacationing people would create a whole new, difficult problem. So, again, the sunny little spot with the Black Butte view was sitting, while other houses sprouted up around it.

In the meantime, Gene's life ended on June 22, 2001, and by late 2004, I began making arrangements to sell the lot, with the idea that I would thus be able to gift the children with some of their possible inheritance which they could use in their own home-building experiences. Ron Roberts and Marti Rawlins, brokers with Re/Max, worked diligently to find buyers who seemed to be very pleased. So, after more phone calls, and more fax messages, that sale was consummated on February 11, 2005, without my personal meeting with the buyers. I have since discovered that they live about two miles from me and have built a home in Summerlane that seems to be similar to our plan—even the same color of stained natural wood with green trim! The new owner was also in the Marine Corps, in Vietnam the year after Gene was there! We still haven't met, but feel like good friends after a long, exciting conversation on the phone—and I have an invitation to visit them at Summerlane when they will be there for a couple of weeks' vacation in September!

FIFTIETH COLLEGE CLASS REUNION
University of Missouri, Columbia, Missouri

How long is fifty years? For some people, it's more than a lifetime. For a few, it's only about half. For most of us, it for sure looks longer when one is looking ahead than when one is looking back!

Gene and I just recently experienced our fiftieth college class reunion at Columbia, Missouri's University of Missouri, which made the last fifty years seem very short, in spite of the many experiences that have filled our lives since that graduation day! After calling some of our best friends from those days and discovering that they were not planning to attend, we wondered if we would find anyone there that we'd know! However, some members of my family live there, so all would not be lost in case the class reunion "fizzled," and besides, we like getting acquainted with new people. So with those thoughts in mind we sent our reservations, looking forward to a good time.

293

My brother Ross Kelley, who lives near Kansas City, met us at the airport on Thursday evening. He and wife Chadna entertained us with dinner at one of our favorite barbecue places—kind of a "traditional" part of their hospitality. (Ross is <u>crazy</u> about barbeque, and often when we travel with them, the evening question, instead of being "What do we want for dinner?" will be "Where will we go for barbeque!") We always have a wonderful time together.

Family in Columbia are sister Barbara and husband Bill Wyatt; their son Randy and wife Sherry, sons Sterling and Chandler; brother Sterling Kelley, wife Jeannette, their daughter Diane, husband Mike McMillen, and their two-year-old son Kelley; Sterling's other daughter Luanne and husband Chris Prestigiacomo, their four-year-old daughter Christiana, and three-year-old son James Michael. A birthday celebration for Bill and one for James Michael provided two family gatherings—one on Friday evening and one on Saturday evening.

We stayed with Sterling and Jeannette, who live on the west side of a small private lake in the country, in a home of their design, built with lumber cut from oak trees grown on their farm. The sights and sounds at that place always conjure up wonderful memories from childhood: cardinals, red-wing blackbirds, mockingbirds, fireflies, frogs, turtle doves, owls, whippoorwills, woodland trails, wild geese and ducks; sometimes a typical Midwestern summer storm complete with <u>great</u> thunder and lightning! This visit, we also watched a pair of foxes playing among the trees across the lake before they loped off through the woods. We wondered if they had come from across the little valley to the east where a neighbor keeps many kinds of exotic (and some not-so-exotic) creatures—a donkey, a llama, guinea fowl, dogs, and an assortment of chickens, some of which would have made quite a nice breakfast for him. (I was reminded of the childhood song about the fox who went out on a chilly night, "He prayed for the moon to give him light; for he'd many a mile to go that night before he reached the town-o, the town-o, the town-o; he'd many a mile to go that night before he reached the town-o!" After some of his exciting adventures and his trip back to his den-home, the song ends with, "And the little ones chewed on the bones-o!")

The reunion activities began with a reception Sunday evening at the Holiday Inn for an opportunity to visit in a casual atmosphere with classmates, or in our case, mostly with new friends. We did find two people, Jean Brand and Bob Brown, with whom we'd socialized in Washington, D.C. when we lived in that vicinity several years ago and then continued a friendship—

knowing they had been students at Missouri University. We hadn't known them when we were all students and didn't know that we had graduated the same year.

At breakfast the next morning Bette Quigley Heck found me and introduced herself. I hadn't realized she was there, because she was in the participant's list under her married name which I had never learned. Her roommate was also there, and the three of us found the many memories of college days, as well as the catching up on our lives after college, to be very exciting. Locating classmates was made easier by having tables designated by "schools." Bette and I were in Home Economics and were both members of the Home Ec honorary society, Phi Upsilon Omicron. Other schools or colleges were Agriculture, Arts and Science, Business, Education, Engineering, Journalism, and Nursing. What was called Home Economics when I was a student is now called HES—Human Environmental Sciences!

After breakfast it was time for "school and college on-site visits" when we went in groups to one of the buildings that had been central in our major studies to hear about current curriculum offerings and to observe many remodeled physical facilities. Bette and I went to Gwynn Hall on the "white" campus which now has an extension called Stanley Hall. How small it looked! How narrow the halls seemed that once led to so many classrooms! Dean Bea Smith, a lovely, vivacious lady who just exudes enthusiasm for her work and life in general, introduced several of the faculty members there who briefly described some of their projects. I decided I would like to see the clothing construction lab. I, a perfectionist person, learned garment construction first from a perfectionist high school teacher, then continued with a perfectionist college professor, Miss Helen Beresford. In those classes we carefully altered paper patterns, cut and stitched clothing for ourselves in order to not only enjoy our own creations, but also to learn how to teach high school students the techniques of sewing well-made garments and other items for homemaking. In this present lab we heard about students learning to design and make patterns by computer, and the new focus which is on commercial garment-making. I noticed the name and address of the Columbia Sportswear of Portland, Oregon, in one of their thick directories of companies for which graduates work.

Gene graduated with a degree in counseling, so he went to see the new College of Education facilities. He discovered faculty members describing the beginning of their educational psychology program, one of the first four such programs to receive accreditation by the American Psychological Association in the early 1950's. Gene had been one of the first students in the program and was awarded a graduate fellowship to work under the leadership of the program's founder, Dr. Paul Polmantier! (He said he corrected the pronunciation of some of the names of early leaders!) Their counseling psychology program remains among one of the top five programs in the nation.

Our final activity was called the Gold Medal Luncheon on Tuesday. After several interesting speakers (Deans and important University officials who all looked much too young to have so many distinguished credentials), we each used a microphone to give name, address, degree and any other remarks, then were awarded the gold medallion suspended on a ribbon of the school colors (black and gold), placed around our necks.

One interesting person we met was Mrs. Arbuckle. Her husband was one of the professors in the dairy department where the making of ice cream has been researched from who-knows-when. For years it has been a source of special ice cream for students and any townspeople who look for a special treat. The Arbuckle family provided a grant to the department to assure the continued production of these wonderful delicacies—now carrying the brand name of "Arbuckle." Mrs. "A" is eighty-five years old, lives near Chesapeake Bay, but owns a farm with some eighty cows near Columbia. Says she never misses an alumni reunion. A very lovely "lady"!

The campus was, of course, very different in many ways: trees are bigger, some older buildings are gone, many new ones filling in almost all of the spaces between what seemed fifty years ago to be a quite nicely planned campus. One thing that has been maintained is the color of buildings. New buildings added to the west area called "Red Campus" are made of red brick; new ones in the east area called "White Campus" are of limestone like the original ones, or of concrete that <u>looks</u> white.

One of the streets near Jesse Hall, the Administration Building, used to be lined with small restaurants, deli-type stores, "watering holes," and such. All of that has now been replaced by a huge building called Reynolds Alumni Center (where most of our meetings and hospitality room were located) with a multi-level parking garage next door. One of Missouri's distinguished alumni is Mort Walker, artist of the comic strip "Beetle Bailey." In the space where a popular hang-out called "The Shack" once stood is now a bronze statue of Beetle Bailey, seated at a bronze table under a spreading maple tree.

The limestone Memorial tower which was the original west entrance to the White Campus now has large wings added to its north and south, housing student center, dining rooms, and other student services, and is called the Memorial Union. The library has been enlarged; and near a place where Gene and I used to sit on the lawn to visit between classes, my family planted a flowering crab tree in 1984 to honor the 60th wedding anniversary of my parents, Sterling and Bertha Kelley.

The football stadium has been greatly enlarged and named for Don Faurot who was coach of a winning team of "Tigers" fifty years ago. One of his team members, Bus Entsminger, was a member of this class of '49 and attended the reunion.

So many years! So many memories! It was in my second year there that I met the man of my dreams. We were married on August 1, 1948, before the start of our senior year; so on graduation day in June of 1949, when we marched into the auditorium in cap and gown, in alphabetical order by schools, we were able to hold hands! His degree was called Bachelor of Science in Education with a major in Math; mine was Bachelor of Science in Education with a major in Home Economics. But <u>my</u> most important title was MRS., received August 1, 1948, when I became "Mrs. Gene Bench"!

L to R: Lloyd Hance, Raymond Law, Bernice Phillips Lubeck, Lester Best, Juanita Goodman Simpson, Blanche Crum Wolfe, Vivian Patterson Bender, Ila Kelley Bench, Winston Alexander, Velma Wilson Williams, Sue Hancock Alexander, Berneice Prewett Brackett

LOVE IS ALL THAT MATTERS

THE BIG "C"
(The writing of this story began on January 11, 2001)

I've often wondered how I would react if a doctor told me that I—or someone in my family—had cancer. Now, I know. I would calmly sit, with my son beside me, almost knee-to-knee with the surgeon returning from the operating room while he described his work and showed us again the "pictures" he'd showed me before he began the procedure to remove what seemed to be a stone from Gene's left kidney. The thing that <u>looked</u> like a kidney stone was actually a blood clot that was blocking the urethra, and the little "camera" that was used inside the passageway showed mass that he needed to examine further, because he suspected that it could be cancer. So, the one-day trip to the Good Samaritan short stay operating room turned into Gene being admitted for further examination, including CAT scan and MRI.

That was October 11 and 12, 2000. With the results of those tests, Dr. Aaberg told us at the hospital the next morning that he recognized the kidney problem as a cancer that had gone beyond the kidney itself, showing up in lymph nodes, on the aorta, and in the fatty tissues that cradle the kidney. There was no panic, no tears, no fainting, no going-to-pieces, as I'd imagined might happen to me, or to Gene. At that moment, the dreaded "Big C" that we'd experienced with numerous friends—many who have survived, and many who haven't—became our "Family Enemy #1," and it was time to declare our war!

But back a month to September, which was a month for us to spend with extended families, and for Gene to go with friend Fritz Bartsch for the five-day antelope hunt in Wyoming that over several years had become an important activity for them.

Labor Day weekend, we went to be with the Bench family at Ocean Shores, Washington—at the same motel, in the same units (with kitchens) where the family has gathered every year for thirty-some years. Children have grown up, married, and now bring their <u>own</u> children, ranging in age from newborn to teenagers and college students. Each year before going home, reservations are made for the following year.

Next, in mid-September, was a trip to Muncie, Indiana, for my Kelley family annual reunion—this year hosted by sister Joy and husband Mark Combs. It was an especially reflective time together because Mark was rapidly becoming the victim of Alzheimer's, as well as Parkinson's disease. Joy was determined to care for him at home as long as possible, so for three days, we just relaxed—thankful to be together, we ate, reminisced, ate, read to each other, and ate. One day was spent thirty-some miles away in Indianapolis with the Combs children: lunch at architect Buddy's newly built home, joined there by Sarah's family; then a barbecue dinner at Marilyn's new home. There were babies we hadn't seen at both places—eleven-month-old Katherine for Buddy; but it was Marilyn's first one—four-month old Andrew.

When we got home, there were only three days left before Gene and Fritz were to leave for Wyoming. Gene was experiencing some blood in his urine, but didn't think too much about it, because it had happened off and on for the last several months—maybe more than a year—but being a "coumadin person," a couple of different doctors who had examined some previous episodes and found no apparent problems, just assumed the blood thinner Coumadin might be causing some ruptured capillaries to bleed. But this time, starting on a trip, and also feeling some pain "in there somewhere," he decided to ask his urologist to at least <u>look</u> at a urine specimen. The doctor was busy in surgery, and Gene's time before departure was short, so the doctor's assistant made a microscopic examination of it and, finding no indication of an infection, told Gene that whatever it was, must be on the way to getting better, so said, "Have a nice trip," and made an appointment to see the doctor upon return.

Well, the hunt wasn't without problems. They caught up with that unseasonably heavy snow storm just after getting to the western border of Wyoming. The road was closed for a while and traffic east was at a standstill. Fortunately, they were near a motel where they stopped for two or three hours, ate some lunch, and put their ever-handy cribbage board to use. Their favorite ranch for hunting—near Medicine Bow, and where they had permission to hunt—was snowed in, and hunting would probably not be possible, so they drove on to another ranch farther to the southeast, and were able to get permission to hunt there, where there was less snow. They bagged one antelope. The next day they went back to Medicine Bow, found the snow melted a lot, but the ground was too slippery to get to their favorite area. Gene was still having considerable pain all this time, so they decided to head home, arriving on the 27th. On the 29th, urologist Dr. Aaberg became suspicious of kidney stones, ordered an X-ray, and made arrangements to do the procedure to remove what appeared to be a stone, and to install some stents to drain the enlarged left kidney on October 11.

Preparation for that began at the short stay clinic about mid-morning, and I stayed with Gene most of the time while he waited. Two friends from church, Lorraine Garrison and Faye McGrath, came to be there to wait with me during the surgery which was scheduled for noon. But by then, surgery was being delayed because of operating room availability, so I assured the friends I'd be okay and didn't want them to give up their time, not knowing how long it would be. (I was very pleased, however, when son David came later to wait with me!) Just before time for Gene to go in, Dr. Aaberg came to show me the X-rays and to describe the procedure to me: the little camera and all of his "tools" would go up the urethra to break up the stone and remove it in small pieces to save the pain of "passing" it, and then to install the stents which would be removed the same way in about a week. I felt relieved to know that finally, a diagnosis had been made, and it would soon be corrected. Then, I heard myself saying, without any previous thought about it, "While you're in there with the camera's eyes to see the area, would you please look for possible cancer?" The doctor looked surprised; but said, yes, he would look, but he was 95% sure the obstruction was a stone, maybe there would be a 4% chance it would be a blood clot, and only 1% chance it could be a cancer. He and the anesthesiologist took Gene to the operating room, and I took my book (and my prayers) to the waiting room.

When the doctor came to me with his report after the surgery, he had a strange look on his face, sat down beside me, and said, "I don't know what to say ... something seems weird about this. Why did you ask me to look for cancer?" I said, "I don't know—the words just came out of my mouth. I hadn't even <u>thought</u> about the possibility before." Then he told me Gene was recovering well from the procedure, but he wanted him to stay overnight in the hospital for more tests. He showed me the pictures the camera had recorded that showed a mass that he thought was more than likely a cancer, though the camera couldn't get close enough for thorough analysis. We'd know more after the next day's tests. And those were the tests that showed the cancerous kidney, lymph nodes, aorta, and fatty tissue around the kidney.

During the next week, on October 16th and the 19th, we had consultations with oncologist, Dr. Howard Fellowes, and with Gene's primary physician, Dr. Clifford Hall. Surgery for removal of the kidney was scheduled for October 24.

Naturally, we were anxious to find out what we could expect, and what would be our best "plan of attack." Dr. Fellowes was new to the Corvallis Clinic staff, and had been chosen as Gene's oncologist—partly, we suspected, because all the others already had as many cancer patients as they could comfortably manage. In consulting with Dr. Hall (who was also a good friend and our next-door neighbor), we asked for his opinion of Dr. Fellows. His reply: excellent résumé with private practice in oncology after training in that field at the National Cancer Institute in Bethesda, Maryland; and he said the Clinic would not have employed him if their oncologist staff didn't have faith in his ability.

The surgery, performed by Dr. Aaberg on October 24th, resulted in the removal of the left kidney, and all possible cancer-affected tissues surrounding it, the lymph nodes, and the aorta. The MRI had also revealed a spot on the liver and a possible small lung lesion. By the pathology report, the name given the "enemy" was <u>Transitional Cell Carcinoma</u>. It also mentioned that there was "some hemorrhage" at the base of the kidney—would that be a possible explanation for the bloody urine? Gene's sister Fern, who had retired from fifty years of nursing, came to be with us for a few days, including the day of the surgery; as did Becky's family, David, and Michelle. After four days in the hospital, Gene came home on the 28th. Relatives went home, and neighbors Grant and Helen Pease brought dinner to us the next evening.

Needless to say, I was having some feelings of inadequacies. The position of Primary Caregiver seemed quite ominous! What if I forgot to give a medication at the proper time? There were often some kinds of conditions that needed to be observed and reported. Bowel movements were to be analyzed and medicated. Pain medication was to be regulated. His heart had had an atrial fibrillation condition for several years. One medication for that was Coumadin which required regular testing and monitoring. We'd need to get a "handicapped" sign for the car to help with parking needs. Maybe we should look for a second opinion of the recommended treatment??

I decided that, in addition to the notes I took during doctors' visits, I should keep a chart of medications, dosages, and the time each one was given. It would also include reports of any side effects, the time and date of such things as bowel movements, nausea, elevated temperature, and sleep. Appointments were noted on the calendar; and prayers were frequent! Medications were modified from time to time, but our bathroom counter usually looked like a small pharmacy! Digoxin and Coumadin for heart; some others for pain; several different choices for bowels; Flomax for bladder; Dexamethasone before chemotherapy; Promethazine as needed for nausea after chemo; Temazepam or Tylenol P.M. for sleep; plus vitamins and supplements he had been taking for general health for some time: Stress Tabs, Selenium, and Vitamins E and C. Some doses were for morning, some for evening, and some "as needed." I'm sure I couldn't have managed all that without "my detailed chart"!

His lounge chair in the living room was a favorite place for him to spend time during the day—near to the TV, a phone, some of the household activity, and his chair-side table full of items for working crossword puzzles, books to read, phone lists, etc.; but the chair was too low for comfort now. A good friend wisely devised a platform that raised it enough for him to easily sit and rise from it. My chair and table were within our arm-reach—and relaxing together there were always special times for us!

In talking with doctors, who seemed interested in a possible cause of the cancer, the first question was, not surprisingly, about smoking. He had never smoked cigarettes, had smoked a few occasional cigars (without inhaling), but that didn't seem to be a concern. They soon all agreed that the most likely cause would have been the considerably heavy exposure to Agent Orange that he received when he was in Vietnam for a year in 1966 and 1967. That would be reason to apply to the VA for service-connected disability, allowing him to receive extra untaxed pay; and at the end of his life, for me to receive an untaxed monthly allowance as his dependent. For this application he had to have a thorough examination by VA doctors, plus letters from physicians in Corvallis, along with medical and pathology reports. David drove us to Portland for that appointment on November 9. We expected results from that to take some time. Government procedures move slowly. However, Gene had a phone call from someone with whom he had interviewed, who said that his papers would be "hand-carried"—separate from the usual ones! Three days before his death, there was another phone call to tell him that the papers had been signed—and they wanted him to know it as soon as possible! He, of course, was very pleased and relieved! Several days later, confirmation came in the mail.

The first chemotherapy was scheduled for November 29th, allowing for further healing of the surgery, and giving time for a family gathering of a few days at Thanksgiving. Drugs that would be used were Taxol, Gemcitabine, and Cisplatin. All three would be given the first week, in a three-hour infusion. Two of them would be given the second week, and the third week, he would rest. As soon as our son David learned the specific name for the cancer, he searched the internet for information about it, including beneficial drugs for chemotherapy treatment. That finding agreed with our doctor's prescription, so we felt confident about the chemo.

LOVE IS ALL THAT MATTERS

We found the "Chemo Room" at the Corvallis Clinic to be a very light, cheery room. It was further softened with several potted plants, and a colorful patchwork quilt that was hanging over a folding screen. Of special interest was a large aquarium containing several kinds of tropical fish which we learned was maintained by Dr. Neville, one of the oncologists. Each patient was made comfortable in a La-Z-Boy-type lounge chair, with a cozy blanket and pillows (as desired), while the cancer-fighting medicines slowly dripped into the bloodstream. Patients were free to bring personal radios or CD players with headphones, and the nurses had a supply of frozen fruit juice bars that the patients could request. Once when Gene was there over lunch time, I brought in a sandwich for him. While he rested there, I could do some errands.

The nurses were all exceptionally cheerful, positive, and attentive. One of them was herself a cancer survivor! At the beginning of Gene's treatment, she was wearing a pretty turban. Later, when she removed it, her head was covered with beautiful, new, soft, baby-fine hair that we watched grow from a length of about one-half inch.

The first treatment went well. There was some nausea, but the medication worked wonders to control it, and he enjoyed visiting with niece Katherine and her husband Don Race who came two days later on Friday for an over-night visit. In the afternoon Gene decided he'd like to walk, with his cane and Don, to the mailbox for some exercise and fresh air; but on the way back, excruciating pain developed in his left leg, and Don had to assist him back to the house and into his chair. Katherine and Don had to leave about 10:00 a.m. on Saturday, but Gene's leg was still painful, so I called Dr. Fellowes who asked me to bring him to the Emergency Room about three o'clock that afternoon. By then Gene was unable to walk well enough for me to help him get into the car, so I called for an ambulance to transport him. I emphasized that it was not an emergency that would warrant their use of a siren, but in a few minutes, here they came with their siren screaming, accompanied by a fire truck! The paramedics, of course, had to do their preliminary examination for reporting "vital signs," so there were, (I think) three of them coming in with their black bags and a stretcher. I followed in my car and met them at the E.R. entrance. After the doctor's examination he was admitted to the hospital again, where a bone scan revealed the presence of cancer in a pelvic bone. There was a large tumor in the right pelvic bone; several small scattered ones, and a small fracture in the left pelvic bone. Dr. Erkkila and Dr. Frey both examined and consulted about it. The second chemo was cancelled, and after eight days in the hospital, preparations were made for radiation treatments of the affected bone. (I had to explain to curious neighbors about the siren!)

Gene came home from the hospital on December 11th, and his sister, Fern, came for a few days. Dr. Erkkila examined the bones and determined it was safe to walk with help. The hospital Home Care department arranged for an aide to give him a bath three times a week; also for a physical therapist to come to our house to evaluate his ambulatory needs, and to show him how to exercise. Part of the exercising was to lift legs while sitting and do "heel pumps." In bed, he was to do "heel slides." Every hour, he was to move around, and walk fifty or so feet. For arm muscles, and some leg exercises he used a wide rubber band called "Theraband." The therapist also ordered a walker and a wheel chair. A lady named Jackie came regularly to bathe him— a very jovial person with a strong back and arms—and used a lot of humor in their bath-time conversations.

Radiation treatments began on December 13th—every week-day for five weeks. A lead protective covering was made for his body, with a small opening where there would be exposure to the rays. Every day I applied aloe vera lotion to the skin that had been exposed and burned. For these treatments we went to the Samaritan Regional Cancer Center located next to the Good Samaritan Hospital. Gene's doctors there were Michael Huntington and Bruce Frey, both of whom seemed very compassionate and skillful. The building has an easy entrance, and cheerful waiting rooms. One of them has ceiling-to-floor windows with a view of a beautiful garden—landscaped with many varieties of shrubs and flowers, among rocks, a small waterfall, and a rippling stream. There is a sound system by which the sound of the trickling water comes through speakers to the inside, making the scene pleasant for ears as well as eyes! Also, in each waiting room is a table with a jigsaw puzzle on it, and some chairs for anyone wanting to look for a few matching pieces. Each day the puzzle was more nearly finished—and eventually replaced with another. Once Gene went to the treatment room, he would be out and ready to go home in just fifteen or so minutes. We were very impressed with the value of those puzzles—not only for waiting patients, but for their caregivers as well, to spend a little time with their minds very peacefully occupied and free from worry that might have so often seemed to totally occupy them. During the time of radiation treatments, a dietician gave me some directions for food intake that included soft diet until one to two weeks after completion of radiation.

On Sunday, December 17th, Becky brought our grandsons (Thomas, age 2½ years, and Evan, six months) from Seattle to spend a week with us. Their presence was very "good medicine" for Gene, and joyful help for me! He liked for the boys to sit on his lap, or to bring toys to play near his chair. He has always called Becky his "Princess," so having her with us was a special treat. Conversations and reminiscing with her was very good for keeping Gene's mind occupied.

One day soon after she came, she took the boys down into the field near the house while we were gone for Gene's daily treatment. Several seedling fir trees had grown there during the last few years, and we harvested one of them each year for our Christmas tree. With Thomas following along, she carried a hand saw in one hand, and Evan in a backpack, until they found the tree they wanted to cut. Off came Evan in the backpack to sit nearby on the ground while she cut the tree, then onto her back again while they dragged the tree to the house. When I came home, we set the tree in a bucket with some water, and the next day she and Thomas brought it inside and decorated it for us. What fun they had! Becky told Thomas some stories about ornaments that she remembered from her childhood.

Brian came on the train from Seattle on Thursday; and Saturday, the 23rd we celebrated our family Christmas a couple of days early, so that the Butlers could be in their own home on Christmas Day.

The final radiation treatment was January 18th, so on Monday the 22nd, we were back to Dr. Fellowes' to prepare for continuing with chemo. A CT scan had to precede that, to see what changes there might have been during the radiation. This time, the chemo medications were Taxol for three hours, and Carboplatin for one hour, added to the continuing Gemcitabine. After a couple of weeks, Procrit was prescribed to stimulate red blood cells and improve "quality of life." Continuing through all of these treatments, of course, were periodic blood sampling for Coumadin protime.

At the beginning of the "bridge-playing season" in the fall we had signed on to be members of a tournament-type schedule called a "Marathon" group. Throughout the season, which ended late in May, couples arranged convenient times to play with each other once each month. At each meeting we followed the rules of playing twenty hands, changing positions at the table after each rubber, but keeping the same partners. We decided we could keep playing when Gene felt up to it, if our opponents could come to our house. His rolling desk chair was used for him to be comfortably seated, and the other couple moved their positions when necessary. We finished (and won second place) by playing the eight games during January, February, and March. Gene's men's bridge foursome also came frequently to play at our home rather than at the Country Club, which was their usual meeting place. We really appreciated the time all of those people gave us, as well as frequent visits from many other friends.

One day in March three of his Masonic brothers visited and brought a small plaque, commemorating his fifty years of Masonic membership.

In February we began thinking more seriously about getting a second opinion. Internet searches verified that he was getting the medications most recommended, but we didn't want to "leave any stone unturned." The Fred Hutchinson Cancer hospital in Seattle was recommended, and we were able to get an appointment there the morning of April 16th—the day after Easter. Becky's family had planned to come to Corvallis for Easter with us, but we're a flexible family, and they became the Easter hosts. Their home has too many steps for Gene to climb to the entrance, so they made a reservation for us to stay at a motel near the hospital. I spent several days collecting X-ray films and copies of medical history from here, which the doctor there wanted to review along with his own physical examinations; so with all of those records, and Easter toys for the boys in hand, David and Michelle drove us to Seattle on Saturday. Just before noon Sunday, the Butler family arrived at our motel toting chests containing hot and cold items for a great Easter lunch time feast of baked ham, home-made rolls, sweet potatoes, salad, broccoli casserole, cake, and sparkling apple cider! The boys brought their Easter baskets of candy treats to share with us, and we had a great party!

Becky came back the next morning to be with us at the hospital—which took until into the afternoon. The advice from Dr. Peter Nelson, after also conferring with another oncologist there, was that the treatment in Corvallis was as good as any that Gene would receive elsewhere. He agreed that the chemo combination was the one recommended for this particular cancer—a very difficult one to treat—and not often cured.

Gene insisted that I take time away from caregiving for some of my own on-going activities, so during times when he could manage for himself at home I bowled on Monday afternoons. Once a week I went to the hairdresser and did shopping for groceries and other various things while I was in town. I kept my cell phone on while I was out, in case he had an emergency, and used it to call him before I started home to ask about anything he might need. He loved

Arby's roast beef-dip sandwiches, so I almost always brought home a couple of those that we could enjoy together for a late-afternoon snack.

Every year since 1989, we had gone to the reunion of the Marines in the battalion he commanded in Vietnam during the last half of 1966 and the first half of 1967—2ndBn 4th Marine Regiment that was fondly called "The Magnificent Bastards." (During the time he was with them, it was called "Bench's Bastards.") The 2001 reunion was to be in Quantico, Virginia, June 21st to 24th, so we made the necessary early reservations to go—with the hope that Gene would be able to manage the trip—even if we needed to use a wheel chair. My Kelley family had planned a large gathering for the preceding weekend—and we made reservations for that, as well—thinking we'd go from there to be with the Marines in Virginia. Gene was even scheduled to speak to a group of young Marine students in Quantico.

Soon after his diagnosis in October, he did let the Reunion committee chairman know about his illness, and it wasn't long until he began to receive phone calls and letters from men who had served with him, not only in Vietnam, but also ones from many years ago! Most of them had gone into civilian careers after their Marine Corps service, had families, and had become teachers, policemen, journalists, engineers, and salesmen, just to name a few. From all of them he heard words of appreciation for the time they had spent together as Marines. Some had been junior officers—many had been sergeants, corporals, and privates. Several of them told him that they attributed their success in their civilian careers to leadership principles they learned from him. One of his junior officers—Walt Boomer, a company commander in Vietnam—had become a general, had commanded all the Marines in the short war in Kuwait, had been Assistant Commandant of the Marine Corps, and by now was CEO of the Rogers Corporation. Similar letters and calls came from extended family members—tributes that meant so very much to him and made him feel that "life was good"!

Early in April one of his lower front teeth became loose, so we went to his dentist, Dr. Cam Little who was also a good friend, to have it removed. I was surprised when he asked Dr. Little how easy it would be to make a replacement for it. Cam described how he thought he could attach one to a small dental plate that could fit into his mouth behind the lower teeth—and he did! A few weeks later Gene told me that it might have been silly to spend money on that little tooth that he wouldn't be using much longer. My reply was, "I think it's one of the best investments we ever made!" I saw it as an indication that his life-long positive attitude about life was still "alive and well"!

Another indication of that desire to make the most of his life was spending two half-days (April 9th and 10th) with the two of us renewing our Senior Driving Certification by taking the AARP 55-Alive driving course for the third or fourth time! (One of the advantages of that certification is a small reduction in the premium of our auto insurance, but it's also a very worthwhile way to emphasize the possibility of a senior person's loss of driving skills.)

On April 13th, we invited our very good friends, Fritz and Winnie Bartsch, along with David and Michelle, to come for celebrating his seventy-sixth birthday.

By the end of April, CT scans showed no shrinkage of the tumors, and now there were spots on his lungs and liver. He talked to me and the children about how we would feel if he decided to stop taking the chemotherapy. He was willing to deal with the sickness caused by the side-effects as long as it might kill the cancer, but it evidently wasn't helping. We told him that we would accept whatever he decided to do, so after conferring with Dr. Fellowes, they decided to discontinue the chemo. Without its side effects, he was quite weak; but without the nausea, he felt better, and wanted to make the most of his remaining time—so May became a very busy month!

For several years Gene and Fritz had gone in the Bartsch "Mini-Winnie" camper to Agnes on the Rogue River the first week in May, to fish for spring salmon with a guide who also became a friend. Without being tied to chemo appointments, they saw no reason Gene couldn't go again this year, if he could travel lying down on the couch at the rear of the motor home. Fishing would be done from the boat that he could get into, with the help of the guide and Fritz. They even put a small portable "potty" in the boat for him! Of course, it wasn't an "easy," adventure, but it was a really appreciated experience for Gene!

We tried to make "life" as normal as possible—our bridge games continued; Becky's family came for another three-day visit; and we went to our neighbor's home one evening for a neighborhood gathering, with desserts. There were frequent phone calls, visitors, TV, etc.

For several years, most people in the Bench family had used the weekend of Memorial Day for a mini-vacation at Fern's home on Mason Lake in Washington. This one became really special when they learned that Gene would feel up to being there for a couple of days! David and Michelle drove us there in our car, with their kayaks tied to the top, and a special foam cushion for Gene's comfort in the front seat. Rooms for the four of us at the Shelton

Inn Motel in the nearby town of Shelton gave us comfortable sleeping arrangements, and most others of the family lived within easy driving distance. Gene's nephew Larry brought his boat, and the weekend progressed in perfect sunny weather, with the usual fun of swimming, water skiing, and fishing from the dock for the young people; everyone visiting with Gene who occupied a comfortable chair, sometimes outside and sometimes inside. Pot-luck food, along with grilled hamburgers and hot dogs, kept everyone well fed. It meant a lot to Gene to be with all of his family, except for one niece in Ohio who was unable to come.

The next weekend, May 31st to June 3rd, was the spring clean-up time, which the families of the Silvies Club called their "work party"—and Gene and I had been a part of that group for many years. Several men who liked to hunt had many years ago bought a ranch near the little town of Silvies in eastern Oregon and built a lodge to use during hunting seasons or for family vacations. A neighbor rancher had grazing privileges in exchange for occasional checking up on the property. Fritz again proposed using his motor home to take Gene for a couple of days with those friends. I decided that this trip should be just for him, so I stayed at home. That outing was another special time for him.

On June 6th, his weakening body and blood tests led oncologist Dr. Neville to recommend that we call Hospice to help with his care. That meant that we'd need to cancel the plans we'd made to go to Missouri and Virginia for those reunions. Jackie, the Hospice administrator, came on June 8th, to determine what our needs would be, and we were surprised to discover the many services that were available from them! One really important blessing was that his nurse would be a veteran Navy Corpsman named Doug, who had served with the Marines in Vietnam during the same time that Gene was there! They hadn't been in the same battalion, but it was great to hear them enjoying comparing their experiences—laughing often and understanding the work the two of them had done during those difficult times!

It was a great relief for our family to have the help of those Hospice "angels"! They cheerfully ministered to all of us, as well as to Gene. For instance—they carried with them a massage chair; and when they came to give Gene a massage, they asked me to sit to receive a back massage myself! One day one of the Hospice volunteers came with a video camera and asked if Gene would like to record some of his memories. He seemed to enjoy that. They had many helpful suggestions for making my work easier, and advice for what developments we could expect.

At about five o'clock on the 13th, a hospital bed from Lincare was delivered. Gene wanted to be situated in the living room where he could enjoy daily "goings-on," and we liked it too. We placed the bed alongside the front of the couch, facing the entrance, with the picture window to his left within his view—it was actually in place of "his chair." The man who delivered the bed had purposely scheduled it as his last delivery of the day, because he wanted to have time to visit with Gene. He also was a Vietnam veteran—a sergeant— and comparing stories was very interesting for both of them. He was really likeable, and often during their visit he remarked, "I can't believe I am talking like this with a 'Colonel'!" At one point he broke into tears, and some hugs followed. (It so happened that he came back again on his way home from work on the 21st, asking if he could "see the Colonel" one last time.)

Neighbors and friends from church brought meals and desserts for us and the many family members who were frequently with us. David and Michelle lived only a couple of miles away; and Gene's sister, Fern, came to stay with us. Becky and Brian, with sons Thomas and baby Evan, cut short their visit with Brian's family on the east coast. It was a great comfort for both Gene and me to be surrounded with our family and friends!

On June 21st, (my birthday) the Hospice people came soon after breakfast, to bathe and dress Gene for the day. He was quite tired, but was also alert, and looking forward to spending rare family time with all of us. About mid-morning we had some special visitors from our church: four high-school boys—who had become close friends with Gene, along with Pastor Marc, his wife, and daughter. The boys' mission was to sing for Gene, as part of their visit. They beautifully and lustily sang, harmonizing "a cappella", a few songs from the church hymnal. Then they surprised us with a martial rendition of *The Marine Corps Hymn!* They said they had looked it up on the internet that morning to learn both the words and the tune! Marines usually just automatically stand up when they hear that music—but since Gene wasn't able to stand just now, I stood up <u>for</u> him! What a thrill it was for all of us! But they had one more surprise: they sang *Happy Birthday!* To me and to Marc! (Marc and I had determined a number of years ago that we shared the birthday date.) Around 4:30 in the afternoon Gene made a point of visiting quite privately with each family member, which turned out to be his farewell thoughts with each of them; and the friendly evening continued, with supper and birthday cake dessert for everyone. What a busy, very memorable day with everyone enjoying Gene's usual jokes that kept spicing up the conversations! By bedtime he was quite tired but seemed to be very happy and relaxed.

I chose to sit by his side holding his hand for an hour or so before I went to bed on the couch that was alongside his bed. His breathing had been quite "noisy" for the last couple of days, but it was peaceful—steady and rhythmic. By midnight, I was realizing that I should probably get some rest myself, because tomorrow would be a very busy day. I must have fallen into a very restful sleep for the next few hours! About 6:30 a.m. I awoke with a "start"! The room was perfectly quiet—Gene was no longer breathing! I felt his body—already cool! I awakened Fern who was sleeping in a nearby bedroom, and with her nursing-experienced touch, she estimated that his life had ended around 6:00 a.m., June 22nd, 2001. I like to imagine that when he received his final orders from the Supreme Commander of us all, it read, "Well done, My faithful servant. I am ordering your spirit to proceed to My Presence on Saturday morning, June 22, 2001, via the 2/4 reunion at Quantico, Virginia. Your 'Magnificent Bastards' will be having their Memorial Service at that time, and they will feel your spirit there with them."

(I later learned from one of the 2/4 members that in fact, at about the hour of Gene's death—three hours later in their time zone they were having their memorial meeting—Gene's memory was being recognized. That thought really "touches my heart"!)

And, what a very special LIFE it had been—for that very special MAN!

A BIT ABOUT COLONEL ARNOLD EUGENE BENCH, USMC

He was "a Marine's Marine," dedicated, compassionate, loyal, and courageous, with great respect and admiration for Marine Corps comrades, both superiors and subordinates. Several of them have told him that principles of leadership they learned from him shaped their own careers—some military, and some civilian. Arnold Eugene Bench (better known, except officially, as Gene) was born in Fordland, Missouri, April 13, 1925, to James and Zula Bench, the youngest of four children. His father was a disabled WWI veteran, and the family became very close as they worked together to survive the depression years. Even as poor as they were, (in Gene's words) "The children were imbued with a fierce sense of patriotism, a catalog of principles and ethics which defy challenge, and a deep respect for our Creator. There was always loyalty to the flag, national holidays, and anything patriotic."

His parents usually tried to keep access to a cow—whether milking a neighbor's or owning one—shared some pork with neighbors and depended a lot upon chickens for food. They sometimes picked cotton in summer; and one winter their main income was from selling walnut kernels they hand-picked from the nuts they gathered from wild black walnut trees that grew in the area. In one of his stories, this is the way Gene described the operation: "Dad devised a clever shucking device to get the outer shells removed from the walnuts. From a car tire, he built a seasoned oak trough that had about 1/2-inch clearance from a car tire, with a flared flume to its front. Then he jacked up a rear wheel of the car off the ground, carefully placing the chute under the tire, with the rear of the car about ten feet from the solid side of the chicken house. With jacked up wheel rotating, walnuts were poured into the front of the chute and the hulls were deftly separated from the shells by the spinning tire, shucking them and throwing them against the chicken house. The shucked walnuts, being heavier than the hulls, piled up against the chicken house, and the hulls fell short. Then the walnuts were spread to dry. A careful balance was sought between keeping enough moisture in the walnut meats to maintain weight, and yet be suitable for picking out. A compression-type nutcracker from Sears Roebuck, which looked very much like a small hydraulic jack, was fastened to a sturdy bench, where Dad cracked washtub after washtub full of walnuts."

Gene's flair for drama was discovered at about age three. In his words: "Dad taught me a little ditty, and at the next community meeting of some sort, I was stood upon a table at the front of the room, and I let forth with, 'When I'm a little man, I'll do the best I can; when I get a little bigger, I'll cut a bigger figger.'" (His life proved those words to be true!) Committing to memory was easy and fun for him. Throughout school years he performed in drama groups, and after they moved back to Ava, he also performed at money-raising socials sponsored by the Ava Lions Club.

If you've ever wondered what happened to the little finger that was missing from his left hand, this is his description: "It was at the Adams farm that Dad added a new cow to our herd. She was bought in Ava, and it fell to my lot to lead her to her new home. The first mile of the trip home was on a paved highway, and although she was gentle, she had become quite agitated by trucks and other traffic. About a mile from town we turned off the paved road, and she decided to run! She ran for about three- or four-hundred yards and turned into a lane. I saw this as an opportunity to get control again and tried to snub her lead rope around a tree. I wound up in a pile at the foot of the tree with a broken arm, a left little finger missing, and the imprint of the tree from my left cheek to my left knee. I gathered up my broken arm in my right hand and walked to the door of the house in whose yard we had crashed. I knocked on the door with my right elbow, and an older couple came to the door. They were both so taken aback that I had to instruct them in how they could help me. The man was able to regain his composure and stopped a boy younger than I who was walking along the road. The boy was asked to go back to the paved highway and request the neighbor there to drive me to the doctor. Someone was sent to notify my folks, and they arrived while I was with the doctor. I was given ether for an anesthetic and the doctor proceeded with repairs. I wore a cast on my arm for a month and went on with my life."

When World War II started, the family lived in the town of Ava. After his two sisters (Lavada and Fern) and his brother (Elby) graduated from high school, they all became "connected with uniforms." Lavada worked in California with the Ferry Command; Fern became a nurse; and Elby joined the Coast Guard. Gene said, "The fourteen months from the start of the war until I entered the Marine Corps were some of the most frustrating ones of my life. I eagerly wanted to 'fix' this Japanese 'thing,' and my nation looked at me as a school kid!" He stayed in school until mid-year and was one credit short of graduation. He appealed to the principal who waived the credit, and with his dad's permission, he joined the Marine Corps in February 1943, at age seventeen.

Boot camp was at San Diego, California. In his words, "From the outset, I was 'chomping at the bit' to get into the war." Through testing procedures he was assigned to a technical school in Grove City, Pennsylvania, and for the next sixteen months attended other technical schools in Corpus Christi, Texas, and in New Bern, North Carolina. He finished the schooling with the rank of Staff Sergeant, and within two months, was awarded another stripe.

Gene's words: "I finally was able to get into the war as an Aviation Radar Chief in a composite air group of F6F night fighters, TBM (torpedo bomber), and Corsair fighters on an aircraft carrier—USS Block Island. A part of the group was formed at Cherry Point, North Carolina, trained at El Centro, California, and Barber's Point, Hawaii, enroute to the carrier which proceeded to the Pacific war zone.

"The planes from the ship were used in close air support for the assaulting troops when there was a landing. As soon as an airstrip was captured or built, the air group, or at least part of it, moved ashore and finished the campaign, operating on land. Our first campaign was in the Philippines, and then we participated in various other landings, including the invasion of Okinawa. I always made it a point to get ashore as soon as I could or take the second sortie of the day by relieving the tail-gunner in a TBM.

"Two days before the war ended our ship was assigned the mission of picking up over 700 prisoners of war being held in Taipei, Formosa (now Taiwan). To accomplish this, a group of us went ashore on the east side of the island, commandeered a train, and crossed the island to Taipei where the Japanese obsequiously turned over the prisoners. Although average-sized men, none of them weighed as much as 100 pounds. We took the prisoners back to the ship where they were very carefully fed five small, carefully selected, meals a day… we proceeded to Manila, and turned them over to a hospital group.

"We again sailed north, awaiting the orders to invade Japan. Then, fortuitously, the dropping of the second atomic bomb convinced a fanatic enemy to end the war."

After discharge at the end of the war, Gene returned to Missouri and enrolled in the Engineering School at the University of Missouri, Columbia, in the summer of 1946. The campus had used temporary buildings to expand classroom and living facilities to accommodate the returning veterans going to school with the benefits of the GI Bill, and Gene found himself living in a wooden frame building in an area that was referred to as "Pneumonia Gulch." There were four men to a unit, and one of his four was named Joe Belshe. Joe was dating Barbara Kelley, one of his high school friends, who Gene met at a basketball game. Gene took a liking to her and asked, "Are there any more at home like you?" It so happened that Barbara was my younger sister, and we lived in the same house on campus. A double date was arranged, and Gene's world—and mine—was at that moment forever changed! After three months we knew we would be married—it was just a matter of when. The wedding date was August 1, 1948, so we finished our final year of college as Mr. and Mrs. Gene stayed at the University for a Master's degree in Guidance and Counseling while I taught high school Home Economics in the nearby town of New Franklin.

In the fall of 1950, Gene began a career in education—setting up a Guidance and Counseling program plus teaching Math—at the high school in Esther, Missouri (a small town southwest of St. Louis). He had maintained membership in the Marine Corps Reserve, so with the Korean War in progress, he was recalled to active duty two months after the beginning of school, with orders to report to the 8th Marines, 2d MAR DIV, Camp Lejeune, North Carolina, where his assignment was First Sergeant. After about a month there, he received a commission, which required attendance at Basic School in Quantico, Virginia; and probably because of his background in education, he was retained there as an instructor for nine more months.

To be back in "The Corps" felt like "home" to Gene, and for the next twenty-two years he enjoyed serving as an infantry officer in various positions around the world including: Guard Officer in Naples, Italy; Staff Officer, 3rd Marines, 3rd Division at Camp Fuji, Japan; Officer Selection Officer, Minneapolis, Minn.; Student, Marine Corps Intermediate School; Operations Officer, 2dBn/2dMar ("Second to None") at Guantanamo Bay during the Cuban crisis; Marine Officer Instructor at Oregon State University from 1963 to 1966; Commanding Officer of 2nd Battalion, 4th Marines in Vietnam from 1966 to 1967; Head of the Briefing Branch at CINCPAC in Hawaii; student at the National War College, Washington, D.C. (where he earned another Master's Degree in International Affairs); Staff duty at Marine Corps Headquarters; Temporary Senior Officer of a detachment in London, England; and finally, a member of the Inspector General Team which traveled out of Washington, D.C.

Along the way he was awarded twenty-one medals, including the Silver Star, Legion of Merit, Bronze Star with gold star and combat "V," the Vietnam Cross of Gallantry, and the Purple Heart.

After Gene retired in 1973, from thirty years of military service, we moved to Corvallis, Oregon. By now we thought our two children, Becky, age fourteen, and David, age ten, would benefit by some stability—especially for their high school years. Some Marine students here at OSU have asked me, what effect their dad's military career had upon our children. From what we have observed, it seemed to be enriching for them to live in different places, learning how to make new friends, adjusting to local customs, and they always seemed to enjoy it. During the considerable traveling we did during leave times, we made a point of observing historical and geographical interests, adding to the benefits of being "gypsies." One day soon after David began school here (in the fifth grade), I was amused when he remarked to me, "Mom, did you know that many of my friends at school have never been out of <u>Oregon</u>?" I had to explain that people have to live where their parents find work. We were able to travel because our dad's work happened to be in a lot of different places.

The year that Gene was in Vietnam was probably more psychologically difficult for them than we realized at the time. Becky was seven; David was three. I didn't allow them to watch news on TV, because there was always more violence than I wanted them to see. (Friends told me that they saw Gene in one of the newscasts.) However, I did keep the radio on a fair amount, and there were often daily reports of the number of Americans killed that day. One day, I realized that even at age three, David was understanding the reporting when he said, "My Daddy is in Vietnam. Is he going to get killed?" After an instant of quick thinking, I said, "Well, Vietnam is quite a large country, and we'll hope he won't be where people are getting killed." After David was grown up, we discovered that he hadn't felt comfortable, as a child and teenager, talking to Gene about Vietnam—fearing the memories might be difficult for Gene; but when there was an opportunity to go with a tour group to the area where Gene was with 2/4 in Vietnam, they went on the trip together. It was a very rewarding and bonding experience for both of them. After that, they were able to freely discuss Gene's original experiences there.

In retirement Gene continued to be active, especially with his favorite hobbies of fishing (salmon, steelhead, trout, bass, clams, crabs, mussels, "crawdads," and such); and hunting (deer, elk, bear, and ducks). He worked as an agent with Farm Bureau Insurance (now Country Companies) for fifteen years and was an area chairman with ESGR (Employer Support of the Guard and Reserve) for several years. Organization interests included the Izaak Walton League (conservation), Silvies Club (hunting group), Marys River Masonic Lodge 221, Retired Officers Club of Corvallis, Boy Scouts, Calvin Presbyterian Church, bridge clubs, bowling, and "puttering" with the computer or around our place.

Being a Marine wife was very enjoyable for me. I loved traveling and living in all of the twenty-some houses we made into "homes" from the time when we were students and educators to this home in Oregon. In each place there were interesting challenges, always love, and a variety of cultures— Naples, London, Hawaii, Minnesota, Virginia, North Carolina, Oregon, and Missouri—more than once in several of the states. In each place, we spent time with sightseeing adventures and local activities, even to picking up some southern accent in the South!

From our home in Naples we toured much of southern Europe; from London, the British Isles and more of Europe. Living in London, we had the added fun of having the children along, when they were old enough (ages seven and eleven) to benefit from experiences there. Also, in London, one of Gene's duties as senior Marine in the area, was to host the Marine Corps Birthday celebration. We made it a very special formal dinner occasion at the Grosvenors House Hotel, with several ranking invited guests—members of the staff from the other services, and from the Embassy office—and, of course, all of the Marines. The guests of honor were Sir Peter Hellings, Commandant of the Royal Marines, and his wife. The consequence of that was equally exciting—being luncheon guests in the Hellings' home with several Royal Marine officers and their wives!

Duty in Hawaii was especially rewarding after the year in Vietnam. We lived in Navy base housing at McGrew Point, in view of the Arizona Memorial; and most of Gene's work was Head of the Briefing Branch of Headquarters, Pacific Command. That meant that early every morning he reported to a "star-studded" audience the previous day's activities and operations of the military units in the Pacific area—including, of course, Vietnam. He was always especially interested in the work of Battalion 2/4, and I remember that he was very sad when he reported the battle at Dai Do. The two years there seemed like a wonderful, long "vacation" when we had time to enjoy the beaches, and to have R & R a couple of times on the Big Island at a resort near the Kilauea volcano.

Being in Cuba during the "Missile Crisis" was quite a challenging assignment for Gene. The battalion had just finished training exercises in Vieques, and was loaded up to return to Camp Lejeune, when they were ordered to proceed to Guantanamo Bay without delay. The troops, of course were "primed for action," so as Operations Officer, Gene and his staff had to use a lot of imagination to invent activities to keep them occupied while waiting to see if they would be needed. The Cubans on the other side of the fence sometimes taunted, which didn't help the situation. To distract them, the Marines did such things as change the numbers on vehicles frequently to make it appear that the vehicles they were using were more numerous; set up a dummy device to look like an electronic receiver of some sort, to which a person periodically walked, as if "checking" it, wrote on a pad, and walked away; they even conducted a mustache-growing contest; and many other things I don't remember.

I could "write a book" about our fifty-three years together! (Who knows, maybe I will!) Life with Gene Bench was an Adventure with a capital "A"! I was a rather conservative, naïve "dreamer," curious about far-away places and the people who lived there. Gene made it possible for some of the "gypsy" in me to be satisfied! I think Gene felt that his work in Vietnam was his most challenging professional adventure. I've heard him say that he "left a large

317

chunk of his soul" with the many dedicated Marines with whom he served—some who even gave their lives to their service. He talked a lot about his "Magnificent Bastards" during his final illness. But we would both agree that our greatest and most rewarding adventure was becoming parents to Becky and David—learning and growing with them and their mates, Brian and Michelle. Then, experiencing the joy of being grandparents to Leah, Thomas, and Evan—and great-grandparents to Maureece, Chelsea, and Chance! All of this isn't to say there haven't been some "down" times—especially separations when Gene had unaccompanied duty, but we discovered that with every problem came some blessings and learning experiences.

Even with the diagnosis of cancer, we didn't panic—it was just another assignment—another battle to try to win. The words "in sickness and in health" became not merely words in marriage vows, but truths that go to the very heart of sharing one's life with another person. They emphasize the truth of *"Love is patient and kind—love bears all things, hopes all things, endures all things. Love never ends." (1 Corinthians 13.)* And after all, <u>love is all that matters</u>! We received an awesome outpouring of love from family and friends, far and near. There were many letters and calls from Marines who had served with Gene in years past. Those helped him more than medicine!

NINE-ELEVEN, TWO THOUSAND ONE

9-11-2001

Few people alive on September 11, 2001, will forget the shock that met their eyes and ears on that beautiful, sunny morning as televisions and radios were turned on across the country! A plane had slammed into one of the World Trade Center twin towers in New York City, leaving the top of it smashed and broken in a mass of leaping flames and billowing smoke! Then, in front of our very eyes, another plane bored almost all the way through the second tower, also exploding into debris and a flaming inferno! Next to be hit was the south side of the Pentagon, and soon a fourth plane crashed in Pennsylvania, believed to have been brought down prematurely because some passengers recognized the hijackers on it and attacked them. What was going on!

When I think about the shocking enormity of that situation, and the extent of the pain and suffering of the thousands of people directly affected by that unbelievably evil attack, I'm almost ashamed to even think about the very small inconvenience it brought to me—visiting family in the Midwest, away from my Pacific Northwest home. But it <u>was</u> a rather significant experience for me that was a new one, and definitely "out of my comfort zone"!

I had left home on August 30, to spend some time in Muncie, Indiana, with my sister Joy and her husband, Mark, who had been ill and house-bound for over a year. The last time I had seen them was a year ago in September, when Joy had hosted our annual Kelley Kids' reunion. Also, Gene had passed away in June, and perhaps some time away from home would help with my grieving process, making this seem like an opportunity for a long-needed visit. Mark's condition had worsened, causing him to sleep most of the time, so Joy and I made use of those periods during the day for "girl talk." I think Mark benefitted as well by having another person in the house to share conversation at meal times. He had lost some ability to speak, but the light in his eyes confirmed his understanding and his great sense of humor!

Joy's children and grandchildren came to visit one of the days to celebrate three of the Combs family's September birthdays—a great treat for me to "catch up" with all of their doings, and to see how the babies had grown into toddlers!

Another idea that came up was to make part of my time there into this years' Kelley Kid reunion. Ross wasn't well enough to travel, so he and wife Chadna wouldn't be there, but the other two couples in Missouri could do it. Barbara and Bill Wyatt rode with Sterling and Jeanette in the Kelley's car for the one-day drive and gave us our 2001 reunion time together! They were even able to give me a ride back to Columbia, for a short visit with their families— to see Diane's new house, celebrate Sterling's and Diane's birthdays, and play with their grandchildren!

On Monday, September 10th, Sterling drove me to Overland Park, Kansas (a suburb of Kansas City) to spend the rest of my time with Ross and Chadna before my scheduled flight back home on Wednesday, September 12th. It was "barbeque time" there! Ross had recently had a couple of strokes and wasn't able to join the rest of us in Indiana, but his appetite for barbeque hadn't been lessened! Neither had his joy of remembering childhood and growing-up escapades, so we looked forward to the next day together, Tuesday, the 11th.

Soon after we were up and preparing breakfast, a neighbor called Ross and excitedly said, "Turn on your TV!" It was unbelievable news! Pictures of the exploding planes at the twin towers! A good part of that day was spent keeping up with developments! Soon we heard the announcement that all planes in the country were grounded, and all flights cancelled—at least until noon on Thursday. I immediately called Delta, and was able to have my reservation rescheduled, provided the conditions became possible. The new time would be 4:15 p.m. on Thursday the 13th from Kansas City, to connect with one of two possible flights from Salt Lake City, to Portland, Oregon. (I also checked the bus schedule—just in case. The buses were swamped, of course, requiring a two-hour's check-in to be reasonably assured of a seat—no reservations; and that trip would take two days.) I preferred taking the chance by air.

I, of course, called my children right away—David at work in Albany, and Becky in Seattle. David said, "Mom! Don't you get on any airplane! Crawl home if you have to—and keep your head down!" I assured them I'd keep them informed, if I could, and I'd be careful!

The news on the local TV showed that planes would be allowed to fly from Kansas City by noon on Thursday, so Ross and Chadna drove me to the airport a couple of hours early, just in case check-in might take more time than usual. Sure enough, the line was long, and security was very tight, so anything carried on the plane was carefully inspected. I'd removed manicure scissors, tweezers, and anything sharp to my checked bag when I packed that morning; but in searching my carry-on bag and my purse, they discovered the safety pin with which I'd secured the checked-bag-key to the lining of my purse where it would be easily reached for use as soon as I got home. Another fairly large safety pin was on my key ring—useful for pinning the keys to some part of my clothing if, for any reason I didn't want to carry a bag, or risk losing them from a pocket. I have never thought of a safety pin as a dangerous weapon, but those inspectors did, so they took them. Actually, they did have a good sense of humor—trying to keep people from being worried, I suppose—so we joked a lot about some of the items in my two bags. For instance, there was a short, compact umbrella. After all, I was headed to Oregon, and I had to have an umbrella handy! (I was surprised that they wouldn't consider it to be useful as a weapon to hit someone in the head! But maybe that wouldn't be "lethal"!)

Before I left the Kelley's house I'd made a peanut-butter sandwich, cut and cored an apple into finger-food pieces, and added a banana to my emergency food supply of a couple of granola bars and the small bag of chocolate-covered peanut clusters that was contributed by Joy in Indiana. I suggested to the inspectors that they treat the sandwich and fruit gently, because that was to be my dinner to supplement the pack of peanuts that would be served with beverage on the plane; and might even possibly be my breakfast!

Ross and Chadna went back home, instructing me to call so they could come back to get me, if for any reason the plane were late, or didn't come at all! Then came the announcements: there would be a delay of maybe two hours. About 7:00 p.m., more news that we'd have to wait for the plane that was expected to leave Atlanta soon! I went to find out about rescheduling for the next day; there was nothing available before Sunday—so I settled in to wait for as long as I'd need to, after calling Kelleys to tell them my plan. I asked them to call my kids and assure them that I'd be okay, and not to worry, because I might not have an opportunity to call until I was back in Oregon. The lady keeping the news-and-snack shop announced to people waiting nearby that she was ready to close, if anyone wanted anything. I picked up another bottle of water and some Ritz-Bits. At the rate I was waiting—I might even need another book to read!

The plane finally came, and we left at 10:00 p.m., and arrived in Salt Lake City at midnight—too late for a connecting flight to Portland. By then, as bad as the national emergency was, I'd decided it wouldn't be of any help to anyone, especially me, if I dwelled on the situation to the point of being worried or depressed. So I made up my mind to be as positive as possible, and to take advantage of the new experiences that seemed to be coming my way. Why should I use the voucher that was being given out by the airline to spend the rest of the night in a hotel? It was already midnight, and I'd have to be back at the airport to get in line at 5:00 a.m. for a ticket on the 8:40 a.m. plane to Portland. Why should I use that small bit of time riding in a shuttle to who-knows-where, undressing for bed, not being able to sleep anyway, then dressing and riding the shuttle again? Besides, I'd never spent all night in an airport terminal before. Life there might be interesting! To be sure, there was life! Cleaning people seemed to "come out of the woodwork" with all kinds of noisy machines—picking up trash, dusting, vacuuming, polishing floors.

A plane landed about 2:00 a.m. with people streaming by in a hurry to get to wherever they were going. Five very nice young men about college age sat in the row of seats across from my "stake-out"; they had a lot of fun playing cards, stretching out on the floor, curling up in seats, going to a wider space to play Hacky-Sac. One of them went out for pizza for their group and had some left, which they passed around to others who were waiting; an Asian girl and a young man sitting nearby visited and played a card-puzzle game; a man and woman came to the area with a cart piled high with a large ice chest, several duffel-type bags, and two gun cases. They had been moose hunting in Canada. A lady sitting a couple of seats away from me seemed to want to just try to rest.

She had on high-topped hiking shoes, khaki pants, and bags that looked "out-doorsy." Some teenage girls made use of time curled up in seats, lying on the floor working word puzzles, eating chips, and "primping." I heard people talking about others who had rented cars to drive on to their destinations rather than fly; some had <u>bought</u> cars, finding none to rent! In the whole country, thousands of people had been stranded <u>in</u> <u>airports</u> for two days ever since planes were grounded on the 11th! <u>I</u> had been able to wait in comfort in my brother's home!

I took a jacket out of my carry-on bag to roll up for a sort of pillow, used the bag for a foot-rest, and felt like I "caught a few winks" as the night wore on. I had eaten half of the sandwich and apple for "dinner" during the waiting time in Kansas City, so about 4:00 a.m. I decided to eat the rest of the sandwich and the banana for an early breakfast before I brushed my teeth and freshened up for the day. People were already lining up, even though the ticket counter wouldn't open until 5:00. I couldn't see why I should use energy standing in line before it even started to move, but soon realized that by 5:00, it would be lengthening fast, so I added myself to it. I thought it was amazing that a surprising number of people were doing a good job of making the best of their many travel difficulties these last couple of days! Two and a half hours later, I had my ticket, found a snack bar near my departure gate, and sat down with some bacon-and-eggs and a biscuit for a "nearly real" breakfast.

Soon I was on the plane! How good it felt to be on the "last leg"—with Portland to be the next stop! It was even on time! Later, I realized that I had actually slept a fair amount on the plane! In another half hour after landing, I was on Anthony's shuttle bus to Corvallis—the only passenger—and I slept again, even as noisy and bumpy as it was!

Thankful to finally be back at home, I had many calls to make to concerned family members. When I called my brother in Kansas City, as I'd promised, to let him stop worrying about my safety, my message started out with, "What an interesting trip! And, I even slept with five <u>very</u> nice young men last night in Salt Lake City!"

Well … so much for my own personal experiences. They seem so insignificant in comparison to the whole picture of that horrible happening! A world-changing event that's unimaginable in scope! But, how is it possible for me to fit "Love is All That Matters" into a terrible demonstration of hate that caused so much suffering! Maybe it has to be reduced to a personal level, realizing that evil has always existed—probably always will—and that only

God's love is able to conquer it. In my opinion, we can help that kind of love to be made manifest in everyday living through our own feelings, relationships, and dealings with our own everyday responsibilities. It would involve respect for others, self esteem, good will, sharing, optimism, and hope. The description of love in the Bible's 13th chapter of I Corinthians is far better than mine! I'm really thankful for parents whose guidance for their family included "love," and that they "walked their talk" in their own actions and behavior!

COLUMBIA RIVER CRUISE—October 20, 2001

Dear Kelley Kids,

I'm going to be bold enough to assume you would all like to hear (read) about my trip last week—cruising up the Columbia River, on the Snake River into Hell's Canyon, back to the Columbia and down to Astoria; then returning to Portland. All the time I was wishing that all of you could have been sharing the experience—it was the kind of thing that would have made a great family reunion!

Early in July—in fact, while Barb and Bill were here—Fritz and Winnie Bartsch asked me to also go, but even though Gene and I have enjoyed traveling on several cruises and tours with them, I felt like I couldn't plan that far ahead so soon after Gene's death—not knowing what and how much time would be needed to take care of family business. As it turned out, the trip was already booked, so I could go on the waiting list, giving me time to think about it for awhile before "putting my money on the line." Fern came to mind as a possibility to share a cabin with me, and the trip began to feel more like a real possibility when I found that she was available, and enthusiastic. In a few weeks, possibility <u>became</u> reality when we were notified of cancellations that moved us up to become passengers.

As you know, weather here in early October can be anything imaginable, which made wardrobe planning a bit of a challenge. It helped that the designated "dress code" was "casual," and we'd have the ship as a "home-away-from-home," so I needed very little more stuff than my summer trip to be with you. And the weather turned out to actually be very good—rain only one of the days during the times we were ashore.

Cruise West, booked through AAA, furnished the transportation on their "Spirit of 98." She was built with all the modern amenities but designed to emulate an early 20th century coastal steamer with carved wooden cabinetry and a Grand Salon complete with a player piano. The dining room, galley, and several cabins were on the first deck; the large lounge (Grand Salon), more cabins, and the bow viewing area on the second; still more cabins (including ours) and the promenade deck on the third; sun deck and Bridge on the fourth. Total passengers, 90. Healthy gourmet meals were beautifully served by various members of the crew, who also doubled as room stewards. There were 26 friendly young people running the ship, including the officers, deck staff, chefs, and two naturalist guides. (One guide wasn't young.)

The senior naturalist was Russell Sadler, partially retired from being a journalist for thirty-five years. I think his column was syndicated, so you maybe have read some of his writing. He's quite a historian—very knowledgeable about the Northwest's development, geology, environment, wildlife, etc. This cruise was emphasizing the "Corps of Discovery" exploration group that was led by Lewis and Clark in 1803—1806, so a lot of Russell's narration contained information about them, including what the area was like when they were here. Every evening after dinner he gave us some background descriptions—often with slides or videos—of what we could expect to see on the next day's excursions. (When I heard his cell phone ring, playing a phrase of Beethoven's *Ode to Joy*, I said to myself, "A-ha! He not only has information—he has SOUL!")

One morning after we docked at Clarkston, Washington, in the heart of Nez Perce country, we enjoyed a presentation by Phil George, a Nez Perce poet and writer, who dramatically shared his peoples' culture. Dressed in full Chief regalia, his movements and descriptions were pure artistry! I felt as if I were in another world in another time! I didn't think to ask him if a video had ever been made of his program; if it hasn't, it <u>should</u> be.

But I'm getting ahead of myself. As we checked in at Portland's Sheraton 4-Point Hotel on Tuesday the 9th, crew members moved luggage we'd tagged with name and cabin number to our cabins, then personally escorted us there as we were again checked in at the gangway at 4:30 p.m. Soon after, a life-jacket safety demonstration (and practice) in the lounge prepared us for a shipwreck emergency. That was followed by the Captain's welcome aboard, the introduction of the crew members, and some announcements about where and when to expect dinner.

We began on the lower stretch of the Willamette River, and soon were headed on down to meet the Columbia. What a lovely beginning, with Russell pointing out some of Portland's places of interest against the rosy sunset sky! All along the way, as we passed historical or scenic points, or maybe sighted some kind of wildlife, his voice came over all the ship's speakers with interesting information for us.

By morning we were in the heart of the beautiful Columbia Gorge. You've driven on the highway (I-84) that follows it a good part of the way, but as you can imagine, it was a real treat to view it from the water! The first of eight locks lifted us up sixty feet early that morning at the Bonneville Dam, and our first stop was for a tour of the powerhouse and the fish ladder. The events of September 11 prevented visiting any more than the museum and seeing the tops of some turbines through a window, but exhibits were quite descriptive, and we did get to see some fish. We noticed that one rather large fish was just lying on the bottom of the passageway and not moving around very much. The park ranger who was our guide (Gene would probably call her a "rangerette"), said it was a sturgeon that had discovered that food often accumulated along there. A sturgeon evidently isn't "programmed" to travel upstream like the salmon that hurry as fast as they can to their spawning place without taking time to eat along the way. Power from the Bonneville is a very important commodity in this area, but Native Americans along the Columbia who have depended upon salmon for food for so many years were grieved to have water from the dam cover the famous Celilo Falls which was one of their best fishing spots. From there the bus took us a short distance for a closeup look at Multnomah Falls. Lots of rain. "Soaked rats" got back on the bus which right away had steamed-up windows. Soon the bus horn began to sound, and the driver was unable to get it turned off! Sometimes if he held it a certain way (Fern and I were sitting on the front seat and had a good view of the whole show), it would stop for a bit. Russell was up there beside him, but no help other than moral support. They finally figured it must have a short because of the rain and decided just to go the short distance to the ship with it blaring! Strange reactions from people we passed! When we stopped at the dock the driver did something to disconnect it. Said he could just use the air horn if he needed one.

Later that day we went through locks at The Dalles dam and the John Day dam and hung up our rain coats to dry. It was the only day all week that we had any significant rain. Other dams and locks along the way were McNary, Ice Harbor, Lower Monumental, Little Goose, and Lower Granite. Altogether we ascended over 700 feet above sea level.

On Thursday morning we were beginning passage up the Snake River through Palouse Indian country—a region of rich grasslands. The Snake originates high in the mountains of Yellowstone National Park and winds its way over 1,000 miles to its confluence with the Columbia. We were told that the high banks of the river appear much as they did when Lewis and Clark saw them in October of 1805. We saw sagebrush and yellow blossoms of balsamroot; also, cormorants, ducks, geese, ospreys, red-tailed hawks, and great blue herons. That evening we docked at Clarkston, Washington. (The town just across the river is Lewiston, Idaho. Not much imagination needed to figure out the origin of their names!)

Friday was spent on a jet boat excursion farther up the Snake and into Hells Canyon. A magnificent journey between steep walls of rock (Idaho on one side, Oregon on the other), seeing dramatic geology, wildlife, and evidence left by prehistoric and historic peoples; through white-water rapids, and quiet stretches of beautiful blue-green water. Our only stop was for lunch at Kirby Creek Lodge. We learned that it is the home of the Luther family, owners of our three jet boats that were piloted by Dad and two sons; the buffet lunch was prepared and served by Mom. Grandma lived in a small house next door, and a sign on her door read, "Grandma's house—children spoiled while you wait"! On the way back downstream—much faster than going up—we saw a family of seven big horn sheep: a huge grandfather ram, a couple of young rams, and four females. Our pilot stopped the boat and turned slowly around a couple of times so everyone could see and take pictures.

By Saturday we were at Walla Walla, Washington, home of sweet Walla Walla onions and many other agricultural products. A large museum there houses collections of early farm and household items, as well as replicas of pioneer homes, school, and places of business. Our lunch was a generous, as well as delicious, buffet served in an elegant dining room in the restored Whitman Hotel. Also nearby was the site of the Whitman Mission—one of the earliest settlements in the Northwest. Many pictures and paintings showed how it looked, but all that was left were foundations and a cemetery. A band of Indians killed all of the people out of anger after many of their people died from smallpox which they thought must have come from the Whitman's. There was also a stretch of alleged "original" wagon tracks with a covered wagon reproduction sitting alone in the middle of a field.

On Sunday we explored around The Dalles. I think its name is French for "The Narrows." Unusual rock formations caused the river to be more narrow there and to form some treacherous rapids, now covered by water from the dam. Nearby is the Maryhill Museum of Art, originally built to be a palatial home on a 6000-acre ranch owned by Pacific Northwest entrepreneur, Sam

Hill. He named the home for his daughter Mary who died before the house was finished, so he never lived there. Artist friends of his (one of whom was Queen Marie of Romania) developed it into the art museum. His replica of England's Stonehenge nearby is a World War I memorial. Next stop was at the Columbia Gorge Discovery Center that was another opportunity to "experience" life in the pioneer west.

We were to meet the ship downriver at Hood River, but a strong wind was blowing which would have made docking there unsafe. So by cell phone communication with the Captain, Russell discovered we'd need to go to the next stop after that which gave us some extra time to "play". He chose to take us to the top of a large, round-topped outcropping of rock, very high up, called Rowena Peak for a breath-taking view of the valley. The roadway was the original old Highway 30—narrow, with many horseshoe shaped curves climbing up the hill, so it was a breath-taking ride even before we reached the top!

That night while we slept, we traveled on down to Astoria, by-passing Portland on the way. I don't need to describe the sights there—you saw those, and more, when you were in Oregon for our family reunion a few years ago. I chose not to go on the walking tour Monday morning, which would have been around the area I explored with you from the Clementine Bed & Breakfast; but Fern, Fritz, and I did walk to the Maritime Museum which was next to the dock where our "Spirit of 98" was tied up. In the afternoon the buses were loaded up for the trip's final stops—first at Fort Clatsop (the replica of the camp the Lewis and Clark party built for a place to spend the winter of 1805-1806). After that, it was south along the coast to Cannon Beach for the benefit of passengers from Illinois, California, Indiana, New Mexico, Arizona, Ohio, Louisiana, Minnesota, Maryland, Pennsylvania, Mississippi, Utah, Texas, Georgia, New York, Florida, and Ontario, Canada to see the Pacific Ocean and to sample the many nice shops.

Back at the ship that evening we were wined and dined at "The Captain's Dinner"—no big formal affair as it would have been on an ocean liner, but wonderful because of the relaxed atmosphere, and the friendliness that had developed during the week of living and exploring together. Then came bag-packing, to have luggage ready to put outside our cabin before we went to breakfast Tuesday morning.

It was interesting to watch the unloading at dockside in Portland. Crew members had gathered all the luggage to the deck by the gangway—red tags for those going directly to the airport, green for those going to the hotel (where our cars were parked), and some other colors for railroad and taxi people. Each bag was handed down a line of crew members to a truck that would move them a short distance to where we would indicate our own bags by <u>touching</u> them before crew members then loaded them and us on our designated buses to go where we needed to go. We left the ship at 9:00 a.m. and were in our cars and headed home by 9:30! Such efficiency! After we left, the crew members would ready the ship for the next trip to begin at 4:30 that afternoon! If you had been there, it would have been perfect! Even so, it was still a really enjoyable week—and I get to "re-live" it by telling you a very little bit about it!

Be good to yourselves—I'm sending lots of hugs! OOO   Love, Ila

QUILTS AND PILLOWS

Quilts have been part of my life for as long as I can remember. In fact, a little pale blue sateen one that my mother made wrapped me and covered me even <u>before</u> I can remember. As I grew up there were one or more quilts on every bed in the house, one or two that could be used for "pallets" on the floor or for picnics, and some extras in case we had overnight company or extra cold weather.

When Mom grew up in the early 1900's, it was customary for a girl to make some quilts for her "hope chest," and a quilt was often a wedding gift from a girl's parents or grandparents. A quilt could be thin and light-weight, or as thick and heavy as seemed to be needed for warmth. <u>Really</u> warm ones were made from patches of wool—more often than not, of pieces cut from worn or old wool clothing. One of the advantages of making quilts was to use small bits of cloth left over from sewing clothes for the family, so that nothing was wasted. And as long as you were fitting various colors and shapes of cloth together, you might as well make it enjoyable by creating various designs!

Putting the top together is called "piecing." Traditional quilters do that by hand—usually in sections called "blocks," although sometimes all kinds of sizes and shapes of the cloth would be patched together making no special design. This was a good way to put together wool pieces that would be heavier than the usual cloth. By keeping scraps, thread, scissors, and needles together in a little basket or bag, the project could be picked up and taken along to work on while one was "resting," or visiting with a neighbor. Finishing the edge is called "binding," and stitching to hold the three layers of it together is called "quilting." (The three layers are top, lining, and batting sandwiched between.

The batting can be a layer of specially layered cotton, or maybe an old blanket. Nowadays, a layer of polyester that comes in various thicknesses is preferred.) The width of the area being quilted is called a "reach." That means you have quilted for a distance as far as you can comfortably reach.

The quilting is easier if the lining, batting, and top are stacked together, then attached to a quilting frame to stretch it and keep it taut. In order to make it manageable, two boards of the frame are long and two are short. As the quilting progresses, the "reach" that is finished is rolled under, over one of the long frames, and an equal amount of unfinished quilt is unrolled from the back side. The short frames form the ends of the work area.

Some frames sit on legs of some kind—some of which look like small "sawhorses"—but Mom quilted in our small living room that didn't have room for the legs or storage space for the project when work wasn't in progress. Dad's invention for support was suspension. Small ropes connected the four corners of the frames to four large metal "eyes" screwed into the ceiling. (It made a great place for small children to play under while Mom quilted!) When she finished for the day, she wound the ropes around the corners of the frames until it was high enough for grown-ups to walk under.

In another story, I've told about the first quilt I pieced—during a relaxing summer in a temporary home. We three girls and Mom took turns reading aloud *Gone with the Wind* while all but the reader pieced quilts. My design was called "Nine-Patch" and my two sisters each made a "Four-Patch." Late in the 1980's I decided I'd like to make another quilt and quilt it with my mother. It took several months to do the piecing—which I wanted to be done the "old" way by hand—and it was a quilt for a queen-size bed—but by spring of 1988, it was ready.

In April, Gene and I drove to Missouri to help celebrate Mom's ninetieth birthday, prepared to stay for a month for Mom and me to quilt while Dad and Gene did "their things." After two days of stitching we realized we could not get it done in a

Barbara, Mom (90 years old), Joy, Ila

month—partly because a beginning quilter can't work many hours at it in a day because one hand has to be available on the under side to "turn the needle" so it goes up to be ready to begin the next stitch on top.

Therefore, my fingers and thumb on my left hand were like hamburger from needle pricks. But once the quilt is stretched, it shouldn't be taken out of the frames unfinished. We figured we could meet our deadline of one month if we quilted around the border, once around each block, and followed the curve of the design diagonally across each block. It was being held together firmly enough that once I was back at home, I could use my large round lap frame to finish. (The design is called "Grandmother's Fan" and it still isn't finished, but I hope it eventually will be!)

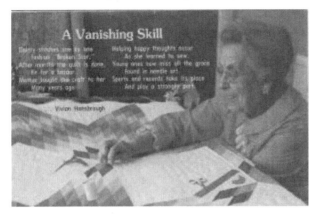

Vivian Hansbrough wrote an article about my mom Bertha Kelley for a magazine and included this picture. She also wrote the poem. Mom was in her late '80s at the time.

There is a wonderful play called *The Quilters* which uses quilts to tell a story of the westward movement in covered wagons. It's well worth seeing in order to understand the role that quilting played in relationships and socializing for pioneer women, and to feel some of the hardships that they endured.

"Picture pillows" had begun to interest me even before I had the big "quilt attack." We Kelley children decided that we'd each "make" something as gifts for Mom and Dad's sixtieth wedding anniversary—and small pillows for their couch or chairs or bed would be good—could be creative and symbolic of something in our relationship with them. I had some quite vivid memories of some of my childhood antics that I could use for my design that would show occasions important to my learning experience. One of those was not getting out of the strawberry patch after I had been told to go. My exuberant four-year-old feet were evidently doing considerable damage to the berries. A small switch applied to my bare legs soon encouraged me to do what I was told! Another unpleasant occasion that was part of my training was when I was maybe about five. Mom usually milked the cow, but for some reason Dad was doing it this time—and the cow was in Grandpa Kelley's pasture a little distance from, but still in sight of the house. I liked to tag along with Dad, and he seemed to like it too, so off we went—he with his milking stool and bucket, and I with my little yellow kitten. Dad warned me that I should keep the cat some distance from the cow, because the cow wouldn't be comfortable with it near. I happily said, "Yes, Daddy," and I suppose I maybe tried too hard, and squeezed the cat too much. For whatever reason, the cat escaped—and in all that open space where she <u>could</u> have run, she chose to run <u>under</u> the cow! Suddenly Dad was on the ground, his glasses bent out of shape, milk was spilled all over, and I was crying because my cat was soaked with milk! I didn't get spanked for that disobedience, but I sure felt sorry for all the trouble Dad and the cat suffered. I think he decided I had learned my lesson without the spanking.

Well, the pillow I created from those experiences includes a little girl with brown-satin hair and a red checked gingham dress (even lace-trimmed panties), very large strawberries, a tan corduroy cow in a flower-strewn pasture behind a fence, a yellow cat, and a large butterfly heading off into a blue sky. The front surface is lightly padded, so that when the pieces were stitched down,

it has a quilted look. The pieces of cloth came from my own considerable stash of left-over-from-sewing scraps, and the motto embroidered on a patch of green grass in the lower foreground is: *"Train up a child in the way he should go...."* (*Proverbs 22:6*.) I didn't have to write the whole Bible verse—we all knew it already!

WHAT DO WE REALLY _SEE_?

It's so easy to take for granted the magical workings of the human body when it is healthy, and all its parts are performing their various specialized duties! Take the eye, for example. Whoever gives a second thought to seeing all the things around us? If the things are far away, the eyes and brain automatically make some adjustments to bring those things into focus. Other automatic adjustments are made to distinguish the many colors that surround us. Poets and philosophers and writers of romantic novels speak of the eyes in ways to make their descriptions and expressions colorful and meaningful. In the Bible there are many passages of scripture that use the eye or eyes to illustrate various principles. Both Matthew and Luke record one of the quotations of Jesus: _"Your eye is the lamp of your body; when your eye is sound, your whole body is full of light."_ The Apostle Paul used sight to illustrate the human inability to fully understand God's purposes when he wrote, _"Now we see through a glass darkly, but then face to face."(1 Corinthians 13:12)_

I recently had a very small sample of "seeing through a glass darkly" when I had a cataract removed from my left eye. A cataract grows so slowly, one doesn't realize how much vision is lost because of it. I knew I didn't feel comfortable driving at night—especially in rain—but otherwise, I only noticed that my distant focus seemed to need adjustment. My doctor said he couldn't correct it because of the cataracts, which we knew had been growing for several years. But the good news was that he said they had developed to a stage that removal would be possible.

Dr. Darrell Gensler in Albany was recommended for further examination and the surgery. I began asking friends about their cataract experiences—especially ones who had been treated by Dr. Gensler. I heard nothing but praise—and simplicity of the procedure, as well as the pleasant surprise I'd find with my vision once it was done. It sounded like they were describing a miracle! I thought I was seeing quite well ... could it possibly be so much improved?

My first consultation with Dr. Gensler was on July 24th. The cataract condition was confirmed but was not urgent. The doctor and one of the nurses described in some detail the condition of my eyes and what would be done for the correction—removing the lens with the cataract and implanting a new lens. I had some trips planned in August and September, so he suggested that I call when I was back into normal routine, and we could make appointments for proceeding. We selected November 7th for the first one; Nov 21st for the second. (The second date was later changed to the 18th because of some needed change for Dr. Gensler.)

The next step was an office visit on October 24th, which included more detailed descriptions of the procedure, a prescription for antibiotic drops for use after surgery, and measurements of my eyes for the new lenses. Meredith, the nurse who was giving me this instruction, showed me a very much enlarged diagram of an eye, and indicated to me where the small incision would be made at the top edge of the iris. This looked to be about 1/4th of an inch in length, which would be the opening through which a tiny vacuum would remove the old lens, after it was broken up with a laser, and through which the new lens would be inserted. Meredith showed me an actual new lens implant which looked to be close to 1/4th of an inch in diameter. It had two curved, hair-sized wire-looking attachments that would hold the implant in place. She said the doctor would be viewing his work area through a microscope–like device that would enlarge my eye to almost the size of a dinner plate!

I was to be at the clinic by 10:00 a.m. on November 7th, wearing comfortable clothing with short sleeves to allow access to my arms for hooking up monitoring devices. I could drive myself there, but someone else had to drive me home. David works about a block from the clinic, and I expected to be finished by noon, so he would walk over and drive me home in my car. At the clinic I was escorted to the surgical wing's waiting room where two men and two women were already waiting. I soon learned that the men were waiting for their wives who were going through the surgical "processing." The two women were friends—one was to have surgery—the other one was the driver. Soon another man came out of the viewing room, all smiles, and pleased with what he had seen of his wife's surgery—said it was a phenomenal procedure. Soon one of the waiting men was called who had requested viewing his wife's experience. The waiting woman was called next, and soon after, it was my turn in the preparation room.

There were four "La-Z-Boy-type" lounge chairs with people in various stages of preparation and recovery. A sanitary cap was put on me to cover my hair; I was covered with a blanket and made comfortable. One nurse inserted an IV port into a vein in the back of my left hand while another one put some drops in my eye to begin dilation. Still another one was asking questions, giving instructions, and describing all that was being done to me. More drops. More waiting. A shot in the IV port began my relaxing. More drops. Three devices connected me to a monitor: a clamp on my left forefinger registered the blood oxygen level; one on my right hand counted heart-beat; a band on my right upper arm inflated periodically to measure blood pressure. More drops began anesthetizing the eye. More waiting. Preparation lasted about an hour. In the meantime, two ladies, about twenty minutes apart, came from surgery to the recovery chair.

In due time my blanket and I were taken into the operating room where I was hooked up to monitoring devices again, given a local anesthetic shot, which deadened the left eye and some of the area around it, and both eyes were "draped." The cover over the left eye must have had some kind of sealer around it. At one point it felt like a bit of fluid was running across the bridge of my nose. I was told it was just a bit of saline water. The eye receiving the surgery was being kept open, making normal blinking impossible; consequently, it wasn't being naturally bathed with needed "tears," so saline water was applied as needed. I was happy to hear the doctor say, "Ila, your surgery is going well. Everything is just as we expected it to be." Then after a couple of minutes he said, "You are now going to hear a buzzing sound that will be the vacuum removing the old lens." In my relaxed state, I guess I felt a little irresponsible, and replied, "Is it a Hoover?" He said, "There is some similarity." In a few more minutes, I heard, "Well, Ila, you're all done. Remove the patch in four hours and put one of the antibiotic drops in your eye every two hours until bedtime." Surgery had taken about fifteen minutes.

Back in the prep room to the recovery chair, my cap and the IV port were removed, and I had a choice of some cool drinks to be sure I wouldn't be sick at my stomach. By then David had arrived, and I appreciated having his arm to lean on to walk to the door where he had the car waiting. With one eye covered, I realized my depth perception was changed, and I thought about my dad who lost one eye due to glaucoma when he was about fifty years old. He never seemed to have much of a problem with depth perception, but his brain probably had worked out an adjustment with his one sighted eye to correct that need.

At home, David made a lunch of soup and toast for me, got me settled with pillows on the couch, and went back to work after I assured him I would be okay, and checked to ask if a neighbor would be available if I had any need. I turned on some pleasant music, slept some, and just relaxed.

David came back about four o'clock to witness the patch removal, but he took my picture first so Thomas and Evan could see what their "Pirate" grandma looked like. My brother Ross called about that time, so while I removed the patch, David was giving Ross a blow-by-blow description of that procedure. I was glad David was there to supervise my "drop" application so I could be sure it was going <u>in</u> my eye. Sure enough, just like I'd been told, there was some double-vision. I had a Kleenex in my hand to wipe away any excess and happened to look down at it. I saw <u>two</u> Kleenexes! One was a pale tan, about the color of a paper bag, but a lot lighter. The other one was snow white! I closed one eye and saw <u>one</u> tan Kleenex. I closed the other eye and saw <u>one</u> white Kleenex. Interesting! When Michelle came from work, she brought a very welcome Chinese food dinner for the three of us. They stayed to visit for awhile and went home only after I assured them I would be able to take care of myself.

Seeing the "tan" Kleenex set me to thinking. What about other colors? I did the "close-one-eye test to some things around the room. The lamp shades that had seemed to be a warm, ivory color were now white! The walls I'd seen as a warm off-white, now appear to be light greenish off-white. My sister-in-law had told me the first thing she wanted to do after she lost her cataracts was to call the carpet cleaners. I looked at <u>my</u> carpet. Yes, the spots I already knew were there now looked darker, but I saw something else—the carpet had been a warm-toned neutral gray. It's now a lighter, bluish gray! Maybe I'll need a <u>new</u> carpet! Yes! It was true what they said about being surprised to see the brightness of colors—and a good time of year to experience it—surrounded by golden big leaf maples, a red-orange sugar maple, a purple-red sweet gum, and a couple of flaming red vine maples! When I came back from the mailbox today I looked out the utility room door window and I couldn't believe my eyes! The sun had come out after a shower and was shining through the millions of droplets of water still clinging to the leaves and tree limbs. A thin vapor was rising from the field beyond as a background for the sparkling droplets, some of which reflected colors from the bright, colorful leaves! I suddenly felt like Cinderella! Or was this maybe a side door to Heaven! It was so beautiful I got a big lump in my throat and felt like crying. A photograph wouldn't do it justice, so I just said, "<u>Thank you, Lord</u>! Help me keep this beautiful sight in my memory forever!" I can hardly wait to see clearly with <u>both</u> eyes—probably with 20/20 vision! What a miracle!

So what do I see in the mirror? All summer I was thinking I was getting quite a nice tan—even got some new "browner toned" cheek color to go with the tan. Now, I see quite a white face, and <u>twice</u> as many wrinkles! Stay tuned—maybe my next surgery will be a <u>face-lift</u>!

SOME MEMORIES—SOME REGRETS

While looking through a long-neglected drawer of miscellaneous "stuff," I discovered a beautiful little blank book, covered with brown-printed velveteen. I'm sure it was very thoughtfully chosen as a gift for me. In it was a folded copy of what was supposed to be its first entry. It said:

"What a lovely little book this is! It was a gift from Becky and Leah on my 55th birthday—June 21, 1980, so it seems appropriate that it begin with a description of the very nice party my family provided. I must be one of the world's most fortunate people to have such a wonderful family!

"Gene said he had to go to town that morning to do some errands, so when he came back, we (Gene, Mom Bench, and I) enjoyed playing a few games of Aggravation. Around 1:00 p.m., I said, 'Well, I better go fix some lunch,' and started toward the kitchen. About that time the back door opened, and David called, 'Anybody home?' Then came Becky and Leah. They brought in a Chinese-food feast—Chicken Chow Mien, Shrimp Fried Rice, Egg Rolls, Beef in Oyster Sauce, and Sweet-Sour Pork. After thoroughly stuffing ourselves with those goodies, Becky and David mixed up some home-made ice cream (with fresh strawberries), then brought in a lovely cream-cheese-iced cake topped with yellow candles, while everyone sang 'Happy Birthday.' Each serving of cake and ice cream was further 'topped off' with more fresh, sugared strawberries that Becky and Leah had picked the day before.

"While Becky and David were freezing the ice cream, 2-year-old Leah and I played in the yard—taking some pictures, watching ants, catching bugs, and appreciating flowers—then took a walk to Hall's house across the road. Leah called my attention to several things along the way—a bird, trees, grass, a stick, rocks—then in Hall's yard she found many interesting things: soccer ball, basketball, beach ball, two baseballs, a toy truck, two toy cars and a large tricycle, all of which she wanted to 'test.' After testing each one she said 'back,' and put it back to go on to another thing. After a short visit with Alice Hall, we started back home. Leah paused in the driveway, turned and waved and said 'Bye-bye, balls! Bye-bye boys'!

"I especially enjoyed and appreciated the attention and love received from Becky and David, because I know they are busy people. Their time is a valuable gift; and it was extra special having Mom Bench with us, sharing her sunny smile and loving greetings.

"Fifty-five must be one of the best years of one's life. Experience has helped one to begin to sort out what things are worthwhile. A grandchild is adding a delightful new dimension by refreshing our memories of the thrills found in sharing the growth and discoveries of children—the wonderful miracle of creation and the development of their unique personalities. One's children are demonstrating that they are independent and capable of handling their responsibilities. It's a time for looking back upon past accomplishments with a feeling of satisfaction of having done the things that seemed best to do at the time—like many wonderful adventures in various parts of the world with a loving, exciting husband, and delightful children; many wonderful friends; and parents who provided a Christian home atmosphere and loving devotion. It's also a time for taking a fresh look at the future and making plans to use the time to its greatest advantage for doing my part to make the world a better place because I was part of it. I want to deepen my faith in God and, with His help to become more sensitive to the needs of others; to be a better wife; to share in community responsibilities; to offer encouragement and comfort to those less fortunate than I. God has richly blessed me, and I want to 'pass it on'!"

Having found this little book—unused for these last twenty-seven years—makes me feel a little sad that I let my time become so filled with such "busy-ness," I neglected to record at least <u>some</u> of the many family "happenings"! There have been exciting things, and some sad things, all of them things that developed the loving family relationships that we've treasured through the years. There were high school and college graduations; the beginnings of careers; marriages, divorces, and then more marriages; births of two grandsons and a great-grandson. We've experienced travels together, illnesses, and death. Many addresses changed while children found other places to call "home."

On August 24th of the year the book was new, Becky became twenty-one, and on September 29th, Leah became two. Mom Bench's life ended on August 27, 1984; and Gene's on June 22, 2001. Now, it's 2007. Becky is the wife of adventurous Brian, grandmother of Leah's eight-year-old son Maureece, as well as the mother of Thomas and Evan, ages nine, and seven. (Leah later had a son, named Chance; and a daughter, Chelsea). David is happily married to his soul-mate, Michelle—an angel without wings. This is my year to become eighty-two.

I think my apology to the little book will be: "I'm sorry I haven't filled <u>your</u> beautiful pages with some of my thoughts and information about our family as the years unfolded. However, in the meantime, I <u>did</u> begin writing memories upon <u>other</u> pages—many of which are, and will continue to be—words that could have first been given to you! I'm still being thankful for every new day, and for the love that inspired the gift of you to me—and who knows—maybe I'll find some very special 'private' things to say to you, in my own handwriting!"

SNOW AND ICE – 2003-2004

I can remember frequently telling people not acquainted with Oregon weather that the mild winters and temperate summers make the Willamette Valley a really delightful place to live. I described summer as "maybe a few weeks in August," having temperatures up into the 90°s. Weather in winter as mostly rainy—not often below freezing—with an occasional snow that might stay on the ground for a couple of days. The last week of December and the first week of January <u>this</u> year gave winter a little different pattern—quite a "wallop," actually.

Snow began falling lightly in the evening, Sunday, December 28th, with a forecast of several inches on the valley floor—much more at higher elevations. About four a.m. I was awakened by beeping and a flashing light from the security system pad on my bedroom wall. The night-lights and clock were dark, so I knew the power was off. I got out of bed and looked outside—four or five inches of very heavy, wet snow everywhere—on fir branches, bird bath, even on the bare maple branches. The beeping and flashing soon stopped, so I snuggled back into bed. Before long I heard loud cracking sounds of tree branches breaking, followed by large and small thuds as they hit the ground—some very near my bedroom; and, I have to admit, it was quite "scary." Further sleep was impossible.

When the power is off, I'm not only in the dark—I have no water and no heat. The well has an electric pump, and the gas furnace runs at the command of the electric thermostat. The "every-day" portable phones are silent—needing power for their electronic "innards" to work. Fortunately, I have two old-fashioned rotary phones—one downstairs and one upstairs—and a cell phone. An important use for one of them is to call Pacific Power & Light to report the power outage. By the time daylight came, I figured it was time to get out of bed, locate some warm clothes, and eat a cold breakfast. I put on a t-shirt under a sweatshirt and covered that with a cozy scarf and a fleece jacket. Next were blue jeans, fur-lined snow boots, and a hat. The house is very well insulated, so it held the heat in the sixties almost all day. Breakfast was juice and cold cereal with banana. In order to keep from opening the fridge more often than absolutely necessary, I moved several things that I expected to use for the next several hours into the garage, which was at least as cold as the refrigerator interior. Another preparation for coping was getting out stowed jugs of water to use in the kitchen and bathroom.

From my windows I could see numerous downed limbs of all sizes in the back yard, so I went outside to inspect further—wondering if any were on the roof or dangerously near it. On the north side of the garage a small tree had broken off, strewing its top and some large limbs down towards the building. The end of one large limb was leaning against the eave but hadn't done any damage.

A snow plow came down the hill and went back up during the day, and I learned later that the reason it went back up the hill was that some large trees had fallen across Hood View Drive—our outlet to Peavy Road and Highway 99W. Three large fir trees had fallen across Mountain View Drive on the west, making it difficult for emergency vehicles like power trucks and snow removal equipment to operate.

What can one "do" on such a day? Kids were happily out sledding and making "snow people," but I thought too much of my old bones and joints to risk a disabling fall outside. No television, no computer for writing letters or stories, and hands too cold for writing with a pen. That left considerable phoning to do, near and far, plus reading. Hard to concentrate on reading— frequently looking out to see what was going on—especially to discover if a power truck might be the vehicle I could hear.

My son David had become interested in astronomy, studying the sky at various times during clear nights to see some special things there—for instance the close proximity of the crescent moon and Venus, just after dark on Christmas evening; Mars being closer to Earth than it has been for a very long time, etc. The sky cleared beautifully Monday evening, so I spent some time getting directions by phone from him for locating Saturn and Jupiter. Without power to light up my photo-cell yard lamp and motion lights, it was possible to see stars better than usual—many of them were even visible from my windows.

Also, on Monday evening, Donna Morse—a neighbor who lived at the west end of Overlook Drive (my road)—called to invite me to spend the night with them. They still had power, plus a wood stove in the living room that was very cozy. Snow had been plowed from the road, and made driving possible, but still tricky; so I walked up to my mailbox with my little over-night bag and flashlight to meet them there. I really appreciated their hospitality and getting better acquainted with their family: husband Terry, teenage daughter Lettie, and younger daughter Lyndie. Power was back on in my area around 1:00 o'clock that night, so I found a nice warm house when they brought me home the next morning on their way to feed a vacationing neighbor's dog.

Rain began melting the snow, but freezing rain soon came into the forecast, arriving Monday, January 5. Before long it became evident that trees were going to be loaded down again—this time with ice. Bowling that day was cancelled, all schools in the area closed—even OSU for two days—and some offices. I thought maybe the snow had taken off all the limbs that would likely cause another power outage, but I made some extra preparations just in case: filled the bathtub with water to use for "flushing," boiled three eggs to use for "cold protein," and took some cooked meat, strawberries and blueberries out of the freezer. I had been able to get to town Friday for a shampoo and restocking my milk, fresh fruit, and bread supply.

Power went out this time on Tuesday about 5:30 p.m., just after I heated soup in the microwave and toasted some bread for my supper. Power was out over a large area in Corvallis, too, so ours wasn't expected to be back on until sometime Wednesday. This time I added some thermal underwear that had belonged to Gene to my attire. <u>Much</u> better! It even was good to wear as pajamas! A t-shirt pulled over the top of my head made a cozy "night cap." (I learned in Girl Scouts that keeping one's head warm helps to warm one's whole body.) On Wednesday evening, Dave and Susi Swanson—my next neighbors to the south—grilled some delicious fresh elk tenderloin, cooked some rice, and heated water on their grill—and shared that with me for dinner. Dave brought it to me nestled among towels in a basket, with the hot water in a thermos, because they didn't want me to risk falling by walking down the road to their house! This time the power was restored to our neighborhood about 9:30 p.m. on Wednesday.

I learned some new things with this storm: how to re-set the electric garage door opener after it has been switched to manual by pulling the red cord; my downstairs is warmer than upstairs when it's below freezing outside; how to replace the batteries in the thermostat that controls the furnace; and how to open the security system control box to unplug the battery if the warning beeping and flashing lights can't be turned off at the pad. Through it all, I was thankful that sometime ago I had bought a battery powered camp lantern which provided quite good, and safe, light. When I went to the mailbox for mail and papers, I walked around the driveway where there was less of a slope than through the backyard path which has a few steps at the beginning of it. My boots, with a good bottom tread, made walking in the snow quite easy, but when it became encrusted with ice, it took some extra effort. I used Gene's cane, which I soon learned didn't work on ice, so as I walked, I jammed the cane down through the crust and dug my heel into the snow with each step. For going back down the hill, I could step safely if I turned my forward foot outward about forty-five degrees and put it down sidewise.

Once (or maybe twice or three times) while I was experiencing the hardship of being cold, I thought about the luxury I enjoyed as a child in a house without electricity or running water. For warmth and cooking, we made a nice fire in the stoves—one in the living room for heat and teakettle or soup pot, and one in the kitchen that had an oven. A grate in the ceiling over the living room stove allowed some heat to go to the upstairs bedrooms. For delicious cool water, we merely turned the crank on the pump in the kitchen. If we wanted a bath, water was heated on the stove and transferred to a round laundry tub on the kitchen floor! It's so easy to take our electric power for granted—when it's <u>ON</u>!

I also realized feelings of fear—hearing the loud snapping of tree limbs breaking—knowing some could be causing damage to power lines or to homes—as a neighbor near me experienced when an oak tree fell on the roof over their kitchen.

I've heard it said that if a month "comes in like a lamb, it will go out like a lion." I don't remember what early December weather was like this year, but I do know it went out like a very vicious lion! Can we hope that January will go out like a lamb?

HOW DID I GET TO BE <u>EIGHTY</u> YEARS OLD!
(My message to family and friends at the birthday luncheon
Hosted by my children and their spouses:
Becky and Brian Butler—David and Michelle Bench)

My heart is filled to overflowing with love and gratitude for family and friends who are honoring my life; and I'm thankful for the good health, peace, and care I've received daily from God throughout my years!

Eighty years ago, on June 21st, 1925, I became the first of five children born to Sterling and Bertha Kelley. I'm so very thankful for that! No family has ever experienced more love! It didn't seem to matter that we didn't have much money—in our community near the small central Missouri town of Dixon, other people didn't have much either.

For a few years I've been writing stories about some of my experiences, to give the younger generations of my family an idea of what my early years were like. They'll have a hard time imagining what my world was like with no computers, TV, or space ships. The closest thing to a Star Wars movie was comic books featuring the adventures of Buck Rogers! (Come to think about it, maybe there isn't <u>that</u> much difference between the two!) Few of our neighbors had cars—and those were usually Model "T" or Model "A" Fords. When I was two years old, the world cheered Charles Lindberg's transatlantic flight in the small propeller plane he named *The Spirit of St. Louis*.

At our home we had no electricity, no indoor plumbing, and no phone. By the time I was a teenager we did have a radio, which was powered by a large battery, charged with a windmill. On laundry day, the washing was done by rubbing clothes and linens up and down on a washboard that was set into a round, zinc washtub of warm water. Soap (home-made lye soap or a large bar of P&G) was first rubbed on to loosen the dirt. That soapy water was squeezed out of each piece by rolling it between rollers on a hand-powered wringer into a tub of clean water for rinsing; rolled through the wringer one more time, and then hung with clothes pins on a line to dry in the wind and sun. We took a bath every Saturday night, whether we needed it or not, using those same wash tubs.

Grade school, Sunday school, church, and community gatherings all happened in the same one-room building, one-and-a-half miles from our house. Our legs were usually our mode of travel. There was only one teacher who taught thirty-some youngsters in all eight grades. Most years there were three people in my class—Richard Vaughn, Helen Vaughn (who were cousins), and I. With the teacher's direction, we students sometimes put on plays and "programs," in which all of us had a part; and we even had art and music appreciation classes, in addition to the "three R's." Every Friday afternoon was devoted to math, spelling, and geography games we called "matches." (Some people call them "bees.")

I rode a school bus to high school in Dixon, where my class of thirty-five students graduated in 1941. Then came business college, work as a secretary at Fort Leonard Wood during some of the World War II years, and University of Missouri in Columbia with a B.S. degree in Home Ec Education. But my favorite "degree" was an "MRS," when I became the wife of Gene Bench—the beginning of a wonderful adventure that included what, for me, has been my most worthwhile accomplishment: being mother to Becky and David! They, in turn, have given me Brian, Michelle, Leah, Thomas, Evan, Maureece, Chance, and Chelsea!

My "motto," which I feel I've received from my Dad's spirit, is: "Love Is All That Matters." Friends and family are important to me because I feel that my relationships with all of them have influenced "who" I am. I believe that life is meant to be lived with a positive attitude, and that Evil can be overcome with Good. I believe that Lady Experience is a great teacher, and I keep learning new things every day! Early on, I learned from her that touching a hot stove wasn't a good thing to do. Just a few days ago, I learned that I should not try to pull a weed that's growing down-hill from me! (That moment of carelessness resulted in a headlong—face-down fall—down a small bank, causing a couple of hairline neck bone fractures, sprained wrist and neck, and other discomforts.) From her I've also learned to be flexible—frequently finding it necessary to "make lemonade" out of an unexpected "lemon." I've learned that very often what seems like a "coincidence" isn't a coincidence at all—it's just part of a plan that hasn't yet been revealed. (Actually, I may need some help, however, to find any good coming from a tumble down a bank! That weed sure doesn't seem to have been worth it! I don't think it even got pulled!)

I've never paid much attention to age—except that eighty used to sound very "old." I've often wondered what that much age would feel like, and so far, it's great! My body may be aging, but my spirit feels young! When I count my "wealth" in friends and family—I'm probably the world's richest lady! I'm unbelievably thankful for each one, and for the love we share! And remember, "Love is all that really matters!"

What a truly lovely eightieth birthday celebration my family prepared for me in June! I think they would have liked for it to be a total surprise, but they decided they needed my help to agree upon a date (to be sure I'd even be available), and to get a list of names and addresses of some special friends— even if the friends might not be able to attend a party in Corvallis. Then, by phone and e-mail, they did all the planning, dividing between their two families "jobs" for everyone. My sister Joy in Indiana helped with the original mailing of "the letters advertising my age." Her list included Kelley family members.

The best I could tell, after it all came together, Becky was responsible for making and sending invitations; then for receiving RSVP's, cards and letters, and assembling them very artistically into a scrap book. For invitations to local church friends, she asked their secretary to print an inclusive one in their newsletter and in the regular bulletin used the Sunday before the party. David did many hours of local "leg-work"—arranging for location, food, and decorations.

My two sisters—Barbara in Missouri and Joy in Indiana—came and planned together for their trip to include arrival and departure on the same plane—connecting in Phoenix for destination in Portland. From there they traveled on a shuttle bus to Corvallis, where I picked them up on Thursday. Unfortunately, their obligations at home didn't permit a very long visit, so on Monday, they reversed the transportation for their return. It was _very_ special for them to be able to be here, even for those few short days! Both of them have lost their husbands, too: Joy's Mark in May of 2002, Barbara's Bill in November of 2004. Brother Sterling's wife, Jeannette, was too ill with ALS for them to be able to come; and deceased brother Ross' widow, Chadna, had previously planned to be on the East Coast with a daughter, also celebrating a birthday that week.

Friday evening and Saturday morning had many hands and legs and heads—David, Michelle, Becky, and my two sisters—all working joyfully together at the Calvin Church fellowship hall. The church just recently completed a remodel that includes extending that area—using moveable walls for dividing it into smaller areas—keeping a lovely fireplace in one end and making one part of the new extension wall open onto a patio area. New white-topped round tables and white folding chairs provides comfortable seating; a sound system is available for amplifying speakers or music; and a piano is there—all resting on new, colorful carpet that is coordinated with the window treatments and scenic mural over the fireplace. Rest rooms were also remodeled and enlarged, so it makes a great place for receptions, church dinners, and such kinds of gatherings.

"Bouquets" of colorful balloons welcomed guests from the parking lot; then inside there were many <u>more</u> balloons, some large flower arrangements, and bud-vase flowers on every white-cloth-covered table. (Many butterflies, too—but not live!) On an oblong table against one wall was a display of family photos showing various eras of my life. The beverage table made coffee, tea, water, and punch available. The buffet table was laden with cold cuts and cheeses, breads, and spreads for sandwiches; also potato salad, mixed fresh fruit and veggie trays, pasta salad, and jello salad. When it was time for dessert, an announcement was made that when I was a child, my Grandpa Kelley, who lived near us and had a peach tree that had ripe fruit in June, always on my birthday brought me a peach for every year of my age. He also brought along enough for Mom to make a large peach cobbler—and then he stayed for dinner! Dessert this day was <u>not</u> birthday cake—it was Peach Cobbler! David had explained to the baker how Mom made it—like a two-crusted peach pie in a large, oblong pan!

Jobs for Becky's husband Brian on Friday evening and Saturday were to provide care and entertainment for their young sons (Thomas, age 7, and Evan, age 5), and to take pictures. Shelby, daughter of Becky's high school friend, Melody, was one of the serving helpers.

Others who came from out of town were Gene's sister Fern, and some of her family from Washington; two couples from Portland; and a couple from California. We calculated that around eighty people celebrated with us on Saturday. It was truly rewarding to me for my family to meet so many of my friends, and for the friends to meet my family. I'm <u>very</u> proud of them and like to "show them off"!

Becky was a speaker for the family's younger generation; my sisters and a few others shared their memories of some of our experiences—even some funny family sort-of-secret stories; and grandson Evan used his first experience with a microphone to say a very loud "Happy Birthday, Grandma"!

MY ZOO

If you come to my house to visit my zoo, you won't find rows of cages with descriptions of the animals. It isn't even like one of those animal preserves where you drive through and find the animals in their natural habitat. The reason is that the animals themselves choose when and where they will make their appearance.

When we moved to Corvallis the second time, after Gene's retirement from the Marine Corps in 1973, we bought a couple of lots on Overlook Drive—one of them with trees and a house; the adjoining one, a field with tall grass. The former owners were bird-lovers, and Garland Nursery had landscaped the area around the house with mostly evergreen types of shrubbery, many of which produced colorful berries for birds' winter dining— also some rhododendron (rhodies), a camellia, some heather, and low-growing juniper that made a ground cover for the long terrace that separated the lawn from the field to the south. A holly tree was beside the driveway a short distance from the house. We also liked birds and kept the bird book handy for identifying them—fourteen-year-old Becky and ten-year-old David joined in the bird-watching. Gene built a birdhouse with twelve nesting compartments and mounted it on a high pole at the edge of the terrace. We discovered that swallows began coming each spring to some of the "apartments" facing the field, and a wren occupied one that faced the house. There was always a lot of activity, and bird songs!

David liked roaming through the tall grass (taller than he in mid-summer) and the woods, noticing animal trails and tracks, even some places where deer had made temporary beds for their afternoon naps. Now and then we saw cotton-tail rabbits, and many gray squirrels. Gene had told the children about his childhood on a farm in Missouri, and about trapping animals for food, and for sale of the skins to provide some pocket-money for himself. That gave David an idea about a way he could get to see some rabbits up close. Gene showed him how to make and set a trap, with the understanding that the animal would have to be released. He soon discovered the trap actually worked—first catch was an opossum, which we, of course called "possum." Gene helped to get it into the dog-carrier for viewing—warning David to keep his fingers clear. It happened to be a mother possum with babies—very tiny ones—some clinging to her fur, and some resting in her pouch. Pretty exciting stuff for a boy interested in animals! A few rabbits were caught when they went for the apple cores he put in the back of his traps, before trapping lost its appeal. He decided to plant a clump of a few little fir trees in the middle of the field "to make some bushes where rabbits could hide." (One tree survived and is now a stately specimen, forty-some years old!) In recent years the rabbits also choose to live in the juniper on the terrace. Every spring one or two young ones hop gingerly onto the lawn early in the morning and late in the evening to nibble grass! That makes for some interesting watching!

We'd had small vegetable gardens in other places where we'd lived, so we were all excited about planting a sizeable one here. The kids had their special areas, and we soon had peas, corn, beans, carrots, lettuce, spinach, beets, tomatoes, peppers—some sweet and some hot—growing nicely. Marigolds are supposed to be a bug repellent, so we made sure some of those also were growing here and there between the rows of vegetables.

But we hadn't yet learned about the habits of deer! They first nibbled at the lettuce; then they added young bean leaves to their salad. I thought, "Well, at least they won't eat the hot peppers! Even the leaves of those plants are quite spicy!" But you guessed it—deer evidently have gourmet tastes—a salad needs a little spicy touch to make it interesting!

We decided we didn't want to be serious enough about gardening to go to the trouble and expense of building a fence that would have to be about eight feet high to keep the marauders out, so after two years, we gave up. The deer are still here, however, and they're very entertaining to our two grandsons. Recently when Thomas and Evan were here, a doe with two playful fawns put on a good show for them. And one morning when I looked out my kitchen window there was a doe lapping up seed that had fallen from the bird feeders; but the exciting thing about that was that her fawn was with her, and nursing! Sometimes as many as five of them—two or three generations—stroll through, going on to visit neighbors' gardens and orchards, and eating various leaves and blossoms along the way. Thankfully, they don't seem to like rhodies, azaleas, daffodils, and some herbs.

Raccoons have frequently visited at night. Their movement sometimes turns on the motion lights, not only announcing their presence, but also providing light for seeing them! I've needed to water shrubs often this summer, and sometimes I've left a hose lying out on the lawn to save the trouble of rolling and unrolling it to use the next day. Once I noticed that the hose was moved from where I left it. The next day, it was pulled all the way off the reel, and the reel was turned over. This time the end was into the juniper over the edge of the terrace. I decided to call the Chintimini animal rescue people to see if they might have some ideas about the hose relocation. Their guess was that a raccoon was trying to get the little bit of water that remained in the hose after it was turned off. The man with whom I talked said that raccoons are very smart animals, and with this summer's dry weather, they don't have many sources of water. I'm just glad they haven't yet learned how to turn on the faucet! I now roll the hose onto the reel and tuck the end into the roll, because they had bitten a hole in the end of the hose trying to get the water out. I decided to make it easier for them: I put out a pan of water for them!

You'd think that inside the house, I'd be safe from animals. I thought so too, until my housecleaner found a small snake resting along the top of a basement window drapery this spring when she began to vacuum there. As soon as the snake was disturbed, it crawled into a hole at the top of the window facing. At least it was no longer loose in the house! With a ladder I looked to see what kind of hole was there. It wasn't visible from the floor. There was a crack where for several inches the window facing wasn't tight against the wall. It is now sealed with a lot of putty!

We've noticed through the years that occasionally a bird—usually a robin—will "fight" with its reflection in a window, or the outside mirror on a car parked outside. This spring one chose my bedroom window for its game. The main thing I didn't like about that was that it was up at the break of dawn— long before I wanted to awaken! It reminded me of Edgar Allen Poe's poem *The Raven* . . . "as of someone gently rapping—rapping at my chamber door." This bird, a young robin, didn't talk to me, so it didn't inspire poetry. I just had to pull the covers up over my ears so I couldn't hear it and try to catch a few more winks.

Another robin built a nest in the honeysuckle vine by the front door. That, we liked! It was fun to hear them "talk" and to watch the baby robins grow. But then another surprise—a second family was there soon after the first one fledged!

The most disturbing visitor I've had appeared in my bedroom one night while I was reading after I'd gone to bed. A small dark thing with wings darted around, about a foot below the ceiling, several times and then left. Needless to say, I was quite startled, but soon realized that it must be a bat. I got out of bed and tried to follow it, thinking I'd open a door and let it go out. I found it in the guest bedroom, clinging to the ceiling. That was good—I'd close the door and deal with it tomorrow. I went back to bed—read some more to settle my nerves—and in a few minutes it was back! I checked the guest bedroom door that had a one-half inch or so crack at the bottom, so it wouldn't drag on the carpet. That bat had managed to squeeze <u>under</u> the door! <u>This</u> time, when the thing left my room, I decided to block the crack under <u>my</u> door and let it have the rest of the house! The next morning, I found it in the kitchen, in a high bowl-shaped light fixture that was deep and slippery enough it couldn't get out. This time David came to the rescue after work, but in the meantime, it had died. For the next few days, when he called to visit and "check" on me, his opening sentence was: "Do you have any bats in your belfry today?" We wondered how it had found a way into the house! Had it come down the chimney and out through the fireplace? A neighbor checked the chimney top and said the screen covering it was still intact, so I may never know how it entered. One pest control person thinks it slipped through the door to the garage sometime when I was going or coming.

One day this week I came home from town about mid-afternoon and went out of the garage in sight of the front lawn to see if either of the two bird feeders needed to be refilled. I stopped suddenly when I saw a fox, the size of a large cat, at the edge of the juniper shrubbery. It started to go away, then turned back to look at me. We stood for maybe two or three minutes, watching each other—I, not moving a muscle, and not looking directly into its eyes. (I've been told than an animal feels threatened if its eyes meet the eyes of its observer.) Soon it turned away and went into the dense juniper, near the place where the baby rabbits come and go. My first thought was that the fox would soon be dining upon some tender rabbit meat. Two days later one of the rabbits had again ventured to the lawn, and I felt happy to see that it was still surviving. I later discovered that a whole fox family had taken up residence in the blackberry thicket behind the shed!

Another day recently I went to my patio door on the way to the mailbox. There, not more than eight or so feet from the door, stood a large doe with a very young fawn in front of her. I stepped back, hoping I could get the camera and take a picture, but they left right away, into the woodsy area of the fenced-in back yard. Several minutes later I again started to the mailbox, noticed that the gate beside the garage was open, and walked over and closed it. On the way up the path I noticed "Mama" deer outside the fence, anxiously watching "Bambi" trying to push through the wire to escape. (It was too young to jump the three feet or so to go over it.) I walked on to the gate near the mailbox and left it opened wide, hoping the baby would find its way out when I went back to the house. But it turned and followed the fence back. Soon "Mama" leaped over, and the two bounded in front of me, running along the other side of the yard until they found the open gate and went on their way. I wonder "who" will visit next? David now calls my place a "safari"!

FOSSILS, FRIENDSHIP, AND FUN
May 31, 2007

Would you believe, that in all of my eighty-plus years of life, I'd never experienced fossil-hunting until this week! Some people in the group probably viewed me as a "fossil" myself! They were the nine children who ranged in age from four years to about eleven or twelve. Others were three teen-age boys—one of whom was a visiting Chinese student—two were brothers of younger children; two ladies were maybe sixty-something—one a teacher from the children's school, the other, her sister who just liked fossil hunting—and eight were parents of the children. The leaders were my geologist son-in-law, Brian Butler, and my daughter, Becky.

By now you're wondering how this group came to be together for this activity—right? At a school fund-raiser, Becky and Brian offered the trip as an item in the silent auction. They made a clever display, calling it "Fossils, Friendship, and Fun," with photos, fossil samples, and information showing the educational value, and what could be expected. The family whose bid bought the trip then invited some others to share it with them.

Just "getting there" was a great experience for me—going from Seattle, north to Bellingham, then east into the foothills west of Mt. Baker. In the back seat, my grandsons, Thomas and Evan, were listening to Lemony Snicket book-reading as we drove. The Skagit River valley was beautiful with springtime growth of vegetable and floral crops in the fertile fields of soil left behind long ago from a major glacier. Brian's geological mind seems to always be analyzing the terrain and formations that have resulted from the travails of Mother Earth as she has changed during eons of upheavals; of extremes of heat and cold; of floods and droughts; of evolution of plant and animal life. A few miles south of Bellingham he pointed out three deep valleys that were cut into the high hills off to the east. He said that is a "fault" that is called the Devil's Mountain Fault.

At around 10:00 a.m., the group of five other cars met us at a small IGA store on Highway 542 (the Mt. Baker Highway) at the eastern edge of Bellingham. Becky had made a sketch map with directions for each driver to follow, but every time we turned onto another road, Thomas and Evan had the duty of counting the cars behind us, to be sure all were still following. Highway 542 took us northeast, across the Nooksack River, then followed it for a few miles as the altitude increased. The next turn was to the right on "Mosquito Lake Road." (When we stopped at our destination, we knew the origin of its name! The mosquitoes weren't all at the lake—they were along the road, too— BIG ones!) The next little road was named "Trickle Creek Road," and sure enough, when we reached the fossil digging place, there was a little creek, trickling along by the side of the road.

The old logging road was narrow but had occasional places to park on the side. There was quite a steep hillside rising on the left where we stopped. It had been cleared, of probably fir trees, some time ago; and scattered over it were many enormous glacial boulders. Some had stumps beside them, showing that trees had put down roots around them, and now had moss and even some small plants growing on them. There were many kinds of vegetation on the hill and alongside the road: several kinds of ferns, grasses, and clovers; salmonberries, blackberries, dandelions, horse-tail, small pink flowers, thimbleberry, plus wild plum and willow trees. It was cool, and cloudy, but no wind—very good weather for a few hours among the fossils!

We all gathered around Brian to hear his description of the kinds of fossils we might find in the digging places that were out-croppings along the hill nearby—just a long step across the little creek. He said we'd find fossils of plants that had been living there in the Eocene era, forty-three million years ago! For each person, he had brought a scientific heavy mesh collection sack, that had a drawstring top and a tag for name and specimen identification and tools. Each person also received a pair of protective safety goggles. As he demonstrated each tool, he described how to use it, and the safety precautions for each one. He asked the children for their ideas about how to keep from injuring themselves or another person who might be nearby. Some of the hammers were heavy, but there were several lighter special ones with a pounding peen on one side, and on the other side, a chisel-shaped peen about five or six inches long—pointed enough to be a good digger. There were also some various sizes of chisels, and one long pry-bar. It was important to wear the goggles always while digging or chipping, and to carry the hammers down at one's side—never across the shoulder. The children were to feel free to ask an adult for assistance, and to ask the leader for answers to their questions. If a car should come into view, anyone seeing it should yell "CAR!" because we were sometimes using the side of the road as a place to examine chunks of rocks for the fossil specimens.

There were several places where others had dug into the hillside, following the striations of the soil. The soil was mostly dark gray, and the fossils were embedded in darker gray layers of what seemed like stone. Pounding gently along one of the lines in a hardened chunk caused it to split, to reveal the fossilized leaf or stems. Some looked like heavy grasses or reeds; some were leaves similar to elm. Some real "prizes" were palm leaves—as much as a foot across. And there beside us was the little creek, handy for washing away dust or soil, constantly bringing clean water!

We began digging about 10:30 a.m., so by 12:30, it was time for the tailgate-picnic lunch the hosts spread for us—various kinds of sandwiches (lots of peanut-butter-jellies and peanut-butter-honeys), chips, pickles, fruit and melon bites, tomato slices, crisp lettuce leaves, varieties of cookies, and drinks.

The enthusiasm of everyone there was a real delight! The kids turned into serious "geology scientists"—really working on the digging, very carefully chipping (some needing parental help), and discovering their treasures with a mixture of excitement and almost reverent awe!

Becky and Brian had prepared for each child a packet of five or six pages of simple fossil history, along with several games and puzzles using geological terms, which they could take with them for enjoying during their drive home.

Yes! It was an experience of "Fossils, Friendship, and Fun"! I'm ready to go again!

MADRONES AND ME

I'm sure everyone has had to do many things they didn't really want to do—things that brought varying degrees of sadness, but nevertheless, things that needed to be done. Maybe it was disciplining a child, or moving from a place you liked to live, or even cutting off really long hair you'd enjoyed for a long time. My most recent one of those things was on September 21, 2007. Well, I didn't actually do it myself—I just "arranged" for it to be done, but that didn't make it any less sad.

As long as I can remember, I've had a "thing" about trees. It probably began from enjoying playing in the cool shade of tall, spreading maples and oaks on hot summer days when I was a child. My dad admired trees and their wood, with which he built lovely furniture and sturdy houses. From him I had my first lessons in identifying various leaves and shapes of trees—in appreciating the different grains and colors of their wood and judging their age by counting the number of rings on the stump after one was cut. On my first trip to the Pacific Northwest when Gene and I were married in 1948, I was fascinated to be among tall evergreens, and to hear the unusual whispering sounds of the wind blowing through their branches. I first saw madrone trees with beautiful large, evergreen, leathery, dark green leaves, and reddish-brown trunks and limbs. The bark is smooth, peeling in thin sheets from older trees. Then—when we bought the house on Overlook Drive, I was so pleased that there were several madrone trees among the Douglas firs on our property! Three of them were growing near the north side of the driveway, and I admired them often, coming and going.

But, after thirty-five years, things changed. They were growing under tall firs, so it was their nature to seek the sun by growing toward the driveway. The tallest one, near the garage, began leaning over the roof, dropping leaves into the gutters. The other two were comfortably growing behind a lilac bush and a forsythia plant, both of which are at least thirty-five years old, and beside a redbud from Missouri that Gene transplanted in 1988. As the trees searched for the sun, they just grew into mingling with the bushes, and on out over the approach to the garage, in the way of a car that might need to park there.

For several years, Rich Holmes, of Holmes Tree Preservation Company has done tree work for us—taking out dead limbs in danger of falling, and trimming where needed; so he became my advisor in the things I had to consider: the loss of the beauty of those big green leaves, their colorful bark, their white blossoms in the spring, and their orange-red berries in the fall; reduction of some of the privacy between the neighbor's house and the road; and whether or not they're needed as a wind break to protect other trees. But I also had to consider the dead leaves that fall into the gutters and make a crunchy mess in front of the garage—the whole year round; being in the way of people needing to use the parking space; and smothering the lilac and forsythia! Rich said they weren't needed as a wind break, but he understood my need to think about it for awhile until I was sure I should do it.

He came on Friday, September 21st, with two of his young helpers and necessary equipment which included a large, enclosed dump truck which towed a heavy-duty chipper. Rich marked the trees and gave the men instructions to cut pieces of a certain diameter (and larger) into stove-wood lengths and stack them. One of the men donned harness for carrying his chain saw and various ropes and straps up into the tree to use for controlling branches, and to anchor himself into safe positions. His spiked boots made climbing look easy, and soon it was obvious that he was a Master Woodsman. (I couldn't help envisioning a young boy's joy—climbing a challenging tree!) On the way to the top, he cut off lower limbs, which had to be dropped straight down to avoid damage to the shrubs underneath. Sometimes that entailed holding onto the limb and swinging it a bit, one way or another.

Meanwhile, the man on the ground stood by to pull on ropes as needed, and to pull the leafy branches out into the driveway, in line for pushing into the noisy chipper. Before they began cutting, I had let them know about my love for those trees—and they said they shared my feelings. My artistic new sister-in-law Susan, who visited in August with brother Sterling, was very much impressed with all our trees, but especially with the madrones, which she had never seen before. I thought it might be fun to save a few small twigs, some pieces of rolled bark, and even some leafy ends of branches to box up and send to her. Soon the man on the ground was helping me select and was saving some good specimens from going into the chipper. One piece that he retrieved was the shape of a Y. He said it would make a good "bean-shooter"! (I felt good about seeing in him the "heart" of a boy!)

Limb by limb, and piece by piece, the trees came down—being dropped safely beside the big shrubs. (Only one small branch of the lilac was broken, and it will never be missed.) All the branches and leaves had been chipped and blown into the truck. As we all three stood among the chunks of trunks that were remaining beside their stumps, I said, "I kind of feel like we're at a funeral." And they quietly agreed. The one who had helped me collect specimens dropped down to the largest stump to count the rings. The wood is so dense, the rings weren't easy to distinguish, but he said that to the best of his ability, he counted between forty and fifty! The top of the stump measures twenty-seven inches across; and the tree was probably about fifty feet tall. I hoped they didn't "hear" the lump in my throat, and I managed to keep my eyes dry, while we visited a bit. I thanked them for their expert work, for understanding my sentimentality, and gave them each a can of cold drink to enjoy as they drove away. (I couldn't help thinking to myself that the main difference between boys and men is the size of their toys!)

When I stood back and looked at the new space, after their machinery was gone, I decided it was good! Too bad it hadn't been done years ago! But guess what? There's a small "grove" of four madrones I see when I look out my bedroom window—far enough away from the house to just be beautiful, without being a problem!

A SPECIAL SEASHELL

On February 14th, 2008, I walked for the second time in the De Soto National Memorial Park on a peninsula at the mouth of the Manatee River in Bradenton, Florida. I was in Florida to visit my long-time good friends, Mai and Arvi Treude, who retired to a lovely home in Bradenton, after living for many years in Minnesota—where we first met.

Mai's neuropathy slows her walking, but it doesn't affect her sincere enthusiasm for enjoying Nature, the seashore, and other activity—and I was happy *to be just strolling, making it possible to examine the native plants like sea grape bushes, mangrove thickets, palms. live-oaks, pines, and beautiful cinnamon-bark gumbo limbo trees! We stopped a few times to sit for a while on a convenient park bench to chat, to watch the birds and lizards, and to soak up some delightfully warm sunshine.*

When I come to this park I can't help being reminded of the man for whom it was named—Hernando De Soto, and his nine ships loaded with six hundred-some men, horses, and live food-animals that landed there over four hundred years ago. It's hard for me to imagine what their lives must have been like—in ships so very small in comparison to ocean vessels that we know! Powered by wind pushing into the ships' sails; the tons of food they would need to carry (without refrigeration); the days and weeks (and more weeks) of seeing nothing but water; using positions of sun and stars for determining their directions, etc, etc, etc! The Florida shore must have been a really welcome sight! But what then*? Strange land, strange food, strange people with strange language! (I've read that some of their pigs that they were carrying for food escaped into Florida woods, and developed into the razorback pigs that are found in the southeastern U.S.)*

As Mai and I walked along one of the sandy riverside trails, I spied a large, apparently very old, piece of the interior of a whelk shell—a little over seven inches long, and a bit more than three inches across at its larger end. It was lying off to the side of the trail, among some grass and weeds; and as soon as I saw it, it seemed to "speak my name," and even "stir my soul"! Being no longer "young in years" myself, we seemed to have a sort of "relationship." I wondered what secrets and information that shell could reveal, if it could speak! I would ask it where it was born, where it had lived, about the other creatures that have obviously shared its existence, and about its need for food and shelter.

According to the Encyclopedia Britannica, whelks begin life deep in the waters of the Gulf of Mexico—but, here is this shell on the shore of the Manatee River, in the northeastern area of the Gulf. How did it come to be here? Did it travel here while it was living? Or did it ride the deep waters of the tides that after maybe many years, deposited it upon that shore?

Judging from its size, I would imagine that the end of its life came in rather old age, and that it rested for some time in water where other sea creatures found shelter and safety on the surfaces of its interior gentle spirals, where its own body used to travel, as if it were on a spiral staircase. At the opening, I see the shell remains of several other creatures—barnacles, and some other shells that look like tiny clams, or scallops, or maybe oysters. Did those creatures live in harmony with each other? Or did they find occupancy at different times? Like the living whelk, they, too, needed to find safety, and food, and shelter.

"Thank you, my whelk-shell friend, for being there upon that beach where I was so happily walking with my very dear friend! I'm taking you home with me to remind me of <u>my own</u> connection to all life!

"I, too, was born into a life that would have needs so similar to yours. Some of my food was available near my home, but effort was required to make much of it useful to me. I could find many other delicious foods by moving about and traveling to other areas.

"When I needed to travel to new places to live, I had to find other safe shelters; and it was to my advantage to live as peacefully as possible with the other creatures who shared my local area, my work, and my interests. Very joyful sharing happened when I was with my birth family, but Nature wanted me to experience deeper sharing that came with finding a mate and guiding the growth of my own children. That required moving to many different areas and living in peaceful community with other creatures: some were my own "kind," many of whom were good friends, but there were some others who didn't share all of my views, or interests, or needs. At times there were animals—some that provided food, some that were family pets, and many <u>wild</u> birds and animals that 'visited' and entertained me and my family with their beauty, their grace, and their songs.

"Like you, my whelk-shell friend, I've now experienced quite a number of years of life, in many different places. I won't be leaving behind a shell, as you have done, but I will hope that I might have provided some 'shelter' for some others in the form of 'food-for-thought' about the process of living—especially of finding ways of living joyfully and peacefully with other creatures upon our lovely planet that needs the attention of all of us, in order to preserve the beauty and life-giving resources that have been so generously provided by its Creator!"

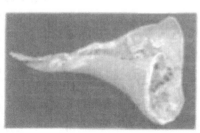
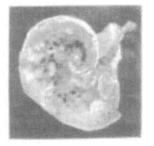

TWO "SLICES" OF LIFE
(One Weekend in Seattle)

I spent the last weekend of March 2008 in Seattle—visiting daughter Becky, Brian, nine-year-old Thomas, and seven-year-old Evan. On two of those days I participated in two very different "slices" of life, poles apart, if judged on an economic scale: a private elementary school, and a "tent camp" of homeless people.

Friday was Grandparents' Day at Meridian School where Thomas is in fourth grade, and Evan is in first. I suppose the students from any private school come from reasonably affluent homes, but among the people I met, I detected no "snobbery," that sometimes exists in such groups. The enrollment of 186 students are in grades Kindergarten through fifth, with specialized departments of music, physical education, Spanish coaching, library, art, and computer lab. African culture was the theme of this winter's global education, which was used in various ways in all the grades—art, music, and social studies.

We grandparents (and "grand-friends") began our visit with coffee and breakfast snacks at a gathering in the gym. I noticed various kinds of P.E. equipment in the room—including a large number of different sizes of unicycles. The Head of School, Mr. Waldman, described the progress of the school's remodeling, the school's mission, and some of the programs and opportunities. We were entertained by music which featured various sizes and tones of marimbas and recorders, with tunes in African traditions; then fifth graders, carrying over-head signs, led us to our grandchildren's rooms.

My first room visit was with Evan. The class sang a lively song for us— first in English, then in an African language. Sitting with our students at their own tables, they were instructed to ask their grandparents about what first grade was like for them. I told Evan about my experience in a one-room country school, with one teacher for all eight grades. It was such a "foreign" idea for him, that his teacher asked me to help with his explanation. The kids were quite surprised, and some asked me more about it later. The amazing thing about that group was our visit to the computer lab to see a video they had made for us, showing some of the skills they were learning, then hearing the teacher describe the types of work they do. I felt like I should be a student in that class, too!

With Thomas, in the fourth grade, the assignment was writing poetry— Haiku style. It was fun for us to "collaborate," and especially rewarding for me to hear his thoughts and ideas! That class had planned to entertain us with launching some rockets they had made, but at launch-time the weather didn't cooperate. Instead, our students took us on personal tours of the library and some other areas of activities. I'm very happy for the special opportunities those children have for education in small classrooms, with teachers who seem dedicated to quality instruction that will give them a well-rounded view of life in a growing global "community."

And then, came Sunday! When I experienced—up close and personal—a "slice of life" very foreign to me! My Seattle family attends Our Redeemer's Lutheran Church, which is located in their neighborhood. Seattle has a "tent city" program to provide shelter for people who make an effort to survive but are unable to afford housing. There are many of these supervised groups, one of which is temporarily located in a section of this church's parking lot. Police help with the camp's security, and they have strict rules of behavior, such as not allowing use of drugs or alcohol. The camp is self-contained, using port-a-potties and wash basins, and taking showers in designated public places other than the plumbing facilities of the church. There are two large dormitory type tents—one for women and one for men—a large community tent furnished with microwaves and coffee pots, and individual tents for couples. No resident children. Some of the people work—others have meager incomes from various sources.

My family's connection: Becky (known in Seattle as Rebecca), is on the church staff in a part-time position of "communication." She prepares the weekly worship service bulletin and the monthly newsletter on her home computer, receiving input from the church office by e-mail and phone, then transferring the completed documents to the office for printing and further preparation. She also volunteers as chairperson of the Social Justice committee—in that way, connected to the Tent City.

It so happened that on the Sunday I was there, the church was serving dinner to the folks of Tent City—about 140 of them, plus several church members volunteering to be table hosts to the visitors. Three women and two men volunteered to help with the food preparation, and several others came to help with the clean-up, but Becky was left to do the planning, shopping, and supervision. She was a little nervous about the project—having never before been in charge of serving food to that number of people, but in her previous employment with Microsoft she had managed office production, so she just used similar techniques to plan and manage this affair. The menu consisted of a hearty casserole of chicken, rice, broccoli, chopped onions, and cheese; mixed green salad, rolls, butter, fresh strawberries, tangerines, cookies, cheese cake, carrot cake, milk, and coffee. I volunteered some help in the kitchen, as well as in assisting with welcoming and visiting; and was proudly amazed with the way everything smoothly "came together"! With their dad's assistance, Thomas and Evan helped by refilling water and milk glasses at the tables, and visiting with some of the guests while eating with them. Becky said she wanted them to experience being with, and helping, less fortunate people.

My own mind was doing all kinds of gymnastics as I compared Friday's experiences with children of comfortable economic means with these ones for whom I could say, "There, but for the grace of God, go I!" I was impressed with the positive attitudes of many of the ones I greeted as they came through the door—men with beards and long hair, everyone dressed in layers of clothing—high-topped shoes, down coats, scarves, warm knit caps, etc. All of them seemed very appreciative of the hospitality and delicious food that was provided for them. They know they are welcome to worship there—and some do. Some take advantage of other social groups that meet at the church, such as AA. I felt so very thankful for my many blessings—for my loving family, and for the countless opportunities it is my privilege to experience!

SIXTIETH WEDDING ANNIVERSARY

of

Gene and Ila Bench

August 1, 2008

Ordinarily, a sixtieth wedding anniversary would be an occasion for great celebration! But what happens when the date arrives, and one of the happy couple is missing? Gene and I had fifty-three adventure-filled years together; and although his life on earth ended seven years, one month, and nine days ago, the date of our marriage is important to me—important enough that it should be commemorated in some way! But how? Wedding anniversaries aren't usually recognized with parties or gatherings of people when one member of the couple is deceased, so there were no plans for any way of celebrating this one. It was just another day—a Friday—and I had an appointment with the chiropractor who was treating me for a low-back ailment. But that didn't keep me from remembering!

Memories began, of course, with the day that was, until then, the happiest, most exciting one of my life—August 1, 1948—our wedding day! For weeks Mom and I had been making the many preparations—sending invitations, cleaning the house, and sewing yards and yards of beautiful fabrics into clothes for my honeymoon, my wedding dress, and the dresses for the three attendants and little cousin who would be the flower-girl. Gene and I were both in summer school at the University of Missouri, but I my "heart" wasn't in my classes! I don't even remember what they were!

I've written another story that describes the day in detail. Truly, it was very happy, though very warm and very busy. Relatives were there from miles around, and my best friend Mary Lou Myer was in charge of the reception which was planned to be at my parents' home. One thing that I remember about it now is that when my sisters planned their weddings, they didn't choose our parents' home for the reception! The church parlor was much more convenient and spacious!

As often happens with my memories, my imagination "took over" at various times of the day! How might we have celebrated our sixty years IF Gene were living and in good health? I couldn't help thinking about what a short time it seemed between his seemingly good health and death! In the summer of 2000, we went to my siblings' reunion in Indiana, and to the annual reunion of the battalion he commanded in Vietnam. In early

August he was salmon fishing at the mouth of the Columbia River with his friend Fritz Bartsch, his sister Fern, and David and Michelle. In September, he and Fritz went antelope hunting in Wyoming. In October, a painful kidney problem was diagnosed as cancer! Winter was spent with surgery, chemo, and radiation. Life ended June 22nd, 2001.

But, back to the IF! I think we would have liked to celebrate by gathering together our two families—and perhaps a few of our many friends, now scattered across the country. If not that many people, at least our immediate family: Becky and Brian; David and Michelle; grandchildren Leah, Thomas, and Evan; and great-grandson Maureece. We would have enjoyed a picnic in a park—maybe at Alsea Falls; maybe a day or two at the ocean. Or perhaps a trip together to Disneyland. We would have even been happy to just all be together at home, playing games, or looking at old photos, and talking about some of the good times we'd had and places we'd lived—North Carolina, Minnesota, Italy, Missouri, Hawaii, London, Virginia, and twice in beautiful Corvallis, Oregon.

Imagining "what might have been" was good, but it wasn't enough. I needed a "souvenir"—something special for myself that I could see and "live with" as a celebration and reminder of that special day. I thought about giving myself a lovely orchid—white with a purple "throat" if possible—like the one I carried on top of Chadna's white Bible at our wedding (the same Bible she carried when she married my brother Ross). But even though beautiful and nostalgic, that would be quite temporary. I've been considering finding a plant for an every-day decoration on the dining table—maybe a small Bonsai tree. So, on the way home from the visit with the doctor, I stopped at Garland's Nursery to see what might be available. Most of their Bonsais were too large or needed environment different from my dining table. But there was one miniature anthurium with perfect heart-shaped leaves and three small, dark coral-colored blossoms that caught my eye. It  was planted "Bonsai fashion" in a shiny black pottery bowl, growing on a dark red porous rock that was absorbing water from the bowl. How unusual and artistic! And appropriate, because it would symbolize our home for two years in Hawaii. (Gene called anthurium blossoms "naughty-boy flowers"!)

It now sits on a tapa cloth mat that I'd brought from Hawaii thirty-nine years ago, reminding me many times a day how very thankful I am for the exciting, adventurous years with my "Knight in Shining Armor" to whom I said, "I do," sixty years ago!

APPRECIATION OF EDUCATION

One way of finding a comparison of some present methods of teaching with the ones that were used when we senior citizens were children, is visiting a few classrooms. I had that opportunity one day last week in Seattle on Grandparents' Day with my grandson Thomas. He began Middle School sixth grade this year in a private school called University Prep. Grades taught there are from sixth through twelfth, with grades nine, ten, eleven, and twelve being called Upper School.

Grandparents (and Grandfriends) gathered in the gym where we were served a delicious buffet lunch—on tables covered with white cloths—and were entertained with music by the U Prep Jazz Band. After lunch, Thomas came to escort me to his sixth and seventh period classes—Geography and Theater. (Theater is this quarter's part of Fine Arts class. In each of the next three quarters, the classes in that period will be Music, Dance, and Art. His other full-time classes are English, Science, Math, PE, and Language—his is Japanese.) After attending the two classes, three of the school's administrators came to meet with us for a period of questions and answers. I liked what I heard about the high standards of the school, and their positive philosophy about education.

I must say, I was impressed! Geography class came first. The teacher there was Mr. Cullen, who introduced himself as the teacher who had been there the longest (thirty-some years, I think). One could tell that he really enjoyed his work. He was courteous, explained things clearly, and maintained attention of the children by seeming to expect their good behavior. He gave them an assignment, to write for the next ten minutes a short paragraph about the thing they found most interesting of this first quarter's learning, while he gave a short explanation to the rest of us about the course content, and his method of teaching.

He began by saying he viewed Geography as much more than what we grandparents might have studied as students—about countries, states, mountains, rivers, memorizing capitals of states and countries, etc. When the children gave their opinions, in turn after raising a hand for permission to speak, some of those methods were revealed.

On the first day of class in September, he had asked each student to draw a map showing the route from home to school, and to describe some things they noticed along the way. Then on the second day, they did the same thing— after having consciously observed the trip to school with a purpose. (This seemed to have been important to the students—several told about that as an important thing they learned, and that they now find themselves noticing more things around them.) This purpose was to give them a "sense of place." "Sense of place" was also achieved by exploring the school grounds—formerly a farm whose owner's name I don't remember, but it began with a "P." One of its former gardens, used for growing vegetables for needy people, became known as "The P-Patch." (Because of that, there are many such gardens now grown in Seattle, and named "P-Patch.") Mr. Cullen says he begins the course by teaching things about the Earth from "the inside, out." If one studies a mountain, for instance, one might like to know how that piece of earth became a mountain—plate tectonics, volcanoes, earthquakes, and such.

Some other things that especially interested the children were learning about earth movements, such as the parting of Africa and South America, and continental "drift." Children had also been impressed with learning about David Attenborough's descriptions of glacial erratic rocks that had been carried by glacial ice to places far away from their origins. (He said one such rock is located nearby in Seattle—respectfully preserved by developers at the time homes were built in that area. That was an important item described by some of the children.) They liked learning that Hawaii (and other islands) are just the tops of volcanoes that have risen in the oceans, and about the discoveries of fossils showing different forms of life in other periods of history.

For seventh period, Thomas took me to his Theater class, located in a very comfortable, small auditorium with descending rows of seats and a sizeable stage with burgundy curtains. Instructor there was Ms. Wyatt. They had spent the quarter learning to write plays. A group of four students worked together planning the plot, the movements of the characters, and verbal expressions. To begin, each one wrote a short description of an episode in the life of some family member or themselves. (We were warned that some of us might happen to recognize some experience of our own!) To develop the writing of the play, the group imagined ways of connecting the information and actions of those four episodes. To demonstrate the result of the work to us, a group was seated on stools on the stage in front of the curtains, each with a copy of the finished script, instructed to read each character's part with appropriate vocal expression and simple movements while seated. It was really amazing to realize how something like that was possible—with people some of us think of as "inexperienced children"! Sure enough, I did recognize the episode Thomas had chosen! He had read about it in my dad's book in which Dad told about one year in his own life when he and his dad traveled in Texas with a minstrel show. Dad, about twelve years old, worked at things like giving shoe shines, and going through the crowds selling peanuts and popcorn. One of the show-people even taught him to "play bones"—holding two beef-rib bones between fingers, shaking them to click together like castanets. Grandpa's work was helping with setting up and taking down the equipment the show company carried with them. I don't remember the other three stories that had to be somehow connected with that one to put the play together—but it worked!

I couldn't help wishing that more public schools could have some of the advantages I saw in University Prep—especially smaller classes. Some things that I observed were good manners, passing through hallways between classes, as well as in the classrooms; respectful behavior between teachers and students; and educational challenges, eagerly met by students seemingly very interested in the subject. I learned some things myself—even in that short time! The best part, of course, was being with Thomas—especially seeing his pleasure in being my guide!

BASEBALL

When I was growing up in the country near Dixon, Missouri, baseball—as we now know it—wasn't a part of my life. I think there were some guys in the community who might have played something similar; but people were poor, they worked hard for a living, and didn't have much time or energy for playing—unless they got together now and then on some Sunday afternoons. Kids at school played something similar to baseball, but there weren't enough people to make teams or to play in all the positions of an official baseball game. There would be a pitcher, a catcher, and one or two "fielders." Any others who wanted to play were batters. The ball was a sponge-rubber one, about the size of a baseball; and the bat was a flat board about three or four inches wide, with one end carved out narrow enough for small hands to hold. The procedure for play was called "work-up." I don't remember all the "rules," but to get a runner "out," he (or she) had to be touched by the ball—hit by throwing it, or by being near him. There must have also been a limit to the number of strokes while batting that would result in an "out." An "out" person traded places with a fielder or the pitcher or catcher, who then went to the end of the batting line, thus giving all players a turn batting and fielding. It was much too active for my participation, so I used my play-time doing jump-rope, or some other thing like Jacks or Tag!

In high school some of the boys played baseball in the spring and fall, and some of the girls played softball as part of the physical education program. The school basketball team sometimes competed with other high school teams in the county, and it's possible the baseball team did too, and I just don't remember. I was grown up before I knew about cities' professional baseball teams—and the first, and most important one, was the St. Louis Cardinals. Through the years I have gradually become somewhat interested in some of those games by hearing male friends and family members talk about which teams were winning—especially at the season of the World Series; but I much prefer to watch student games. My interest rose considerably these past two years, when the Oregon State Beavers became the college World Series champions! I suppose part of my bias began to develop as professional sports grew into "big business," rather than seeming to be played purely for the entertainment of home-town people. When I do watch a pro game on TV, or read about the scores in the news, it's mostly because I want to feel I'm sharing interests with friends or family—especially grandchildren! The games I <u>really</u> like to watch are the ones my grandsons play!

Recently, on Saturday, April 10th, I experienced a quite outstanding game that I will long remember! It was a college student game played by the Oregon State Beavers and the UCLA Bruins at the Goss stadium here in Corvallis—the second of a three-game PAC 10 series. Becky, Brian, Thomas, age 11, and Evan, age 9 came to spend part of their Spring Break with me, and invited me to go with them to the baseball game that started at 2:00 p.m. They had been able to get tickets for high open-stadium seats that were overlooking third base, and I was warned to be vigilant about possible foul balls that could fly into the area where we were sitting. To be on the safe side, Thomas and Evan sat next to me, between me and home plate, and wore their own mitts so they could "protect Grandma" should a foul ball come our way! We had stopped at the souvenir shop on the way to our seats for the boys to buy Beaver baseball caps, and we carried a couple of small blankets—for sitting upon or for warmth, as needed.

The weather was perfect for baseball—sunny with a few scattered clouds, after several days of showers, which in itself was a "spirit-lifter." To add to the excitement, there were maybe thousands of wild geese frequently flying over the stadium in various sizes of "V" formations, either on their way to northern nesting grounds, or moving to some other grass field for fresh food. The first point in the game was scored by UCLA in the top of the fifth inning, and the next point went to OSU in the bottom of the ninth! In almost every inning there were bases with one, two, or three runners poised and ready to move on each time the inning's third "out" was called, and the teams had to change positions. You can imagine the excitement and the "stress" that gradually was building as each inning ended, and then the hope for more scores to be made as each new inning began! All the way to the ninth inning—when OSU finally tied the score, which remained tied to the end, and overtime began!

By then, clouds had begun to move in, and jackets that had been removed in the warming sun began to be replaced. Becky, concerned that I might be getting tired, asked if I would like to leave. I said, "Of course not! Who can leave when we can win the game with just one more run!" So snacks were replenished, and we settled in for more baseball, even though it began looking more and more as if we might also get wet! The tenth inning ended! The eleventh inning ended, with the score still tied! The twelfth inning was played—score still one to one! By then it was 6:30, and Becky, feeling that the boys would need to eat soon—and that I might get too tired—said she thought we should leave. I had intended to cook dinner at home after the game, but now that it was so late, it was agreed that we should go to King Tin for Chinese food instead.

As we drove across town, we listened to the game on the car radio—still no score—and felt some sprinkles of rain as we walked from the car to the restaurant. While we were waiting for our food to be served, the conversation was, of course, about the game. Evan, who has a wonderful imagination, got a "dreamy" expression on his face, and said, "Wouldn't it be cool if, while we are eating, they would keep playing, and when we get back to the car they would still be playing, and we could go back to the game—because we have these stamps on our hands to get into the game again!" Everyone laughed. "Big joke, Evan!"

Then followed the fried rice, the Lemon Chicken, the Beef with Broccoli, and the Fortune Cookies. On the way out, we discovered that while we were inside, a shower had come. In the car, the radio was still describing the game! It was the sixteenth inning, and two runs had given the Bruins a 3-1 victory! It had been a six-hour, twenty-three-minute battle, the longest—by time and by innings—game in the eleven-year history of the Goss Stadium, which opened in March 1999! It was quite a treat for me to have been part of that record-breaking game, of course; but what made it really special was sharing it with my two very enthusiastic grandsons who, themselves are seriously devoted to learning to play the game! And who else ever gets an opportunity to sit by two young, very happy baseball players who are wearing their own baseball mitts in order to lovingly protect their Grandma from being hit by a fast-flying foul ball! Life couldn't be expected to get any better than that!

SOME OF THE ROLES I PLAY

1. Daughter:

I was the first of five children and, as happens with many first children, I had a lot of attention. Dad liked to have me "help" him with projects, and I was often underfoot with Mom, too. I'm thankful for their patience—with my "help" I'm sure I caused their work to take extra time, but I learned a lot! I never doubted that I was totally loved. They read to me, I was included in family prayer time, and taught to sing. Coming home from school was a wonderful time of day when Mom listened to our "outpourings" over a snack—every-other-day the snack was hot, freshly baked bread spread with thick cream or fresh butter and sprinkled with sugar. I think I wasn't much of a "problem child," because I always felt a desire for parental approval, and my parents always showed interest and enthusiasm for my activities, my marriage, and my family. From them I learned to love, how to keep feeling young while aging, and that relationships are more important than material possessions!

2. Sister:

Being the first of five siblings, I became a "little mother" which was appreciated by my two sisters and sometimes by my two brothers, but I've recently learned that my brother next younger than I was quite jealous of what seemed to him to be favoritism shown to me (he thought) because I made better grades than he. (I did make better grades, but I studied more, too!) I sometimes (lovingly) resented my younger brother, the family "baby" because I had to babysit so often when I wanted to do something else. My sisters have in later years told me they especially respected and depended upon me because I was out there learning about life in an unknown "world" and then teaching them about it. When we were children we sang together, and each played a stringed instrument, calling ourselves "The Kelley Quintet." Dad was our coach and manager. Audiences for our gospel style of music were mostly church congregations and Ozark country gatherings called "singings." (Pronounced "singin's".) That younger brother was a little "showman," which helped with our enthusiasm! We really enjoyed the applause and attention, which gave us considerable confidence in ourselves; and I believe that the "teamwork" of singing together gave us a permanent close relationship. Even after all of us married, we have tried to manage to spend some time together—all together—at least once a year (military service interfered during some years.)

3. Student:

Being a student began with being in the first grade at Santee country grade school when I was six years old. I already had learned to read and do some simple math, and I have been eager to learn new things for the rest of my life! It was fun to listen to the older students "reciting" their own lessons in that one-room school! High school was at Dixon, Missouri, followed with a scholarship to Draughon's Business College. Later college was at University of Missouri, in Columbia. I have always wanted to "keep up with the world," and that's becoming more and more difficult with technology so rapidly changing so many ways of living! The mental gymnastics and physical exercise involved with learning new things are more likely to keep minds alert, especially as we age. I'm grateful for the opportunities in Corvallis to find educational assistance and stimulation in every imaginable area of interest.

4. Wife:

This, I feel has been my primary role since marriage on August 1, 1948. During that time, I've been a student-wife, a teacher-wife, a military wife, a salesman-wife, and a retiree-wife. Each phase has had some unique needs to fill: making time for school and homework while still in college; socializing with other teachers (usually on Friday evenings, careful to maintain a teacher's "reputation"—for instance, no visible use of alcohol, etc.); willingness to "wait"—maintaining our home myself when husband's military orders required it; entertaining and being entertained at many official levels; and always keeping FLEXIBILITY. Meeting all of these needs provided personal growth, travel to new places, and sometimes has made me wonder whatever happened to a shy little Ozark country girl who once occupied my body! Sadly, my loving husband's battle with cancer ended our exciting life together on June 22, 2001.

5. Friend:

Friends are wonderful! And I've enjoyed many. I find that a friend helps me "be myself." Sharing problems, achievements, good news, recreation, etc, has a way of putting things into perspective. I still correspond at least once a year (and visit when possible) with a grade-school friend, a high school friend, three from college, one from a place of employment, and many from the Marine Corps years. Local friends are from church, bridge players, bowling, and neighborhood.

6. Secretary:

My first "career ambition" (while still in high school) was to eventually manage a business of some sort; and my young mind thought that it would be well to begin as a secretary and learn the business "from the ground up"! A Draughon's Business College scholarship prepared me very well for that, and my first employment was in the Personnel Office of the Fort Leonard Wood Exchange—a very demanding business, because it was the beginning of World War II. But I soon realized I wanted more challenge; something like teaching Home Economics, even though it would require more college education. That was possible at the University of Missouri; and working part time as a secretary to one of the professors was a source of income to pay for the university expenses! Later secretarial positions were with INA Insurance Company in Minneapolis, Minnesota; in Civil Service for a Law Specialist at Marine Corps Schools in Quantico, Virginia; and at the First Baptist Church in Columbia, Missouri.

7. Teacher:

Even though I had given four college years to learning to be a teacher, it happened that only one year was available for me to play that role—my first year after graduation from the University of Missouri. It was a very rewarding experience to work with high school girls at three different levels of learning the work of "Homemaking"! In my opinion, the "profession" of making an environment for growing a family is one of the most important occupations available—even though it gets so little attention! Just think about all the areas of life that are involved: psychology, child care, health, food, interior decoration, relationships, entertaining, science, etc, etc, etc! My one year of teaching experience was at New Franklin, Missouri; during the time that husband Gene finished his Master's Degree at the University of Missouri. Having been in the Marine Corps during the war, he was still in the Reserve, and was recalled to active duty during the Korean War after his graduation. That ended my teaching career, because I couldn't conscientiously accept a year-long teaching position when he could be ordered to be transferred at any time.

8. Mother:

This is a role that I've considered to probably be my most important and most responsible. Our two children were adopted, so a lot of thought and planning preceded their addition to our family. Daughter Rebecca (Becky) was first, at age five weeks; then David at age seven months when Becky was four years old. Children gave me a new awareness of everything around me—even of myself! For instance, watching a baby yawn or stretch caused me to "notice" my own yawning and stretching. Seeing them experience and discover new things was like returning to the excitement of childhood myself and reminded me of all that I'd been taking for granted. There were also some worrisome times—in occasional illnesses; and then a new kind of worry during their teen years—them testing their independence—I, trying to keep them from making mistakes! They've grown into responsible, caring people with good moral values and work ethic; and I am very pleased to be their "Mom"! Becky has three children, and three grandchildren; and I wonder where the years have gone! Motherhood for me has been like riding a roller-coaster—often scary, but joyful and very rewarding!

9. Grandmother—Great-grandmother:

I haven't had an opportunity to "play" this role the way I'd always hoped, because of living various distances apart, but we've been happy with time together when it has been possible—beginning with new-born time! Each child has seemed like a gift "fresh from Heaven"! What true joy it was to hold those special little people when they must have been wondering, "Where am I? What happened?" Life so fresh and new seemed to be miraculous! Becky's children are my only grandchildren: Leah, Thomas, and Evan. Born September 29, 1978, Leah's first few years in Corvallis, and some of her time in Portland, provided opportunities for her to spend time with us—some over-nights, weekends, or one-day visits. Leah's father is Brad Wilber. In Seattle, a few years after Becky's second marriage with Brian Butler, Thomas and Evan were born: Thomas on July 19, 1998; Evan on June 7, 2000. We felt truly rewarded when any of them visited—thankful for our "country space" with a sizeable yard and field where the kids liked to use their imaginations when they "explored," finding special rocks, worms, bugs, tall grass, and occasional deer, rabbits, and raccoons. Leah liked going to the Alsea River to catch crawdads with Grandpa Gene; and to reading bedtime stories with me when she often spent nights with us. Sadly, Gene's health began failing several years later, by the time Thomas and Evan were old enough to go "exploring" with him, but they liked doing other things together. (I'm writing this in August, 2016—and I'm happy to announce that Thomas is a student Occidental College in Los Angeles!)

I first became a "great-grandmother" when Maureece was born to Leah on April 8, 1999. (He goes to college at St. Martin's University in Lacey, Washington.) His brother, Chance, was born on May 13, 2012; and sister, Chelsea, on December 28, 2014! (Please notice that after three wonderful grand- and great-grand sons, we now have a great-granddaughter!) I like to watch all the children play together—really enjoying each other! The three older boys are only a year apart, and after Chance and Chelsea were born, the older ones became personal "baby-caregivers"—lugging the little ones along and keeping them entertained!

10. Neighbor:

Living with my parents was excellent training for this role! As a child I observed neighborhood relationship—working together, borrowing everything from a cup of flour or an egg to a team of horses or a car, taking food and otherwise helping sick ones, trading child-care, passing along children's out-grown clothes, sharing harvested food, socializing, etc, etc, etc. My childhood home was in a low-income rural area where most people made a living by maintaining a small farm and doing what would be considered menial labor. Later my neighborhoods have been on military bases, in small towns, suburbs of cities, and in a couple of foreign cities. I very much enjoy being a neighbor and sharing the lives of so many interesting people!

11. Deacon:

In our church the deacons are elected members who serve personal needs of certain members of the congregation. Each deacon is assigned to a "parish" that includes ten to fifteen families within a neighborhood. I kept in touch with "my families," sending birthday cards, providing food and other help in times of illness, comforting when bereaved, sharing spiritual experiences, gathering the whole group for occasional socializing, etc. During several years I served three different four-year terms, finding spiritual growth myself, and appreciating the opportunity to be helpful in times of need.

12. Tourist:

From the time I was a child and read about far-away places I've wanted to see-for-myself—to "feel" the flavor of different cultures, to see varied scenery and natural phenomena, to stand in the midst of ruins and imagine the life that was there so many centuries ago! Living in a number of different areas during the Marine Corps years made local travel possible and interesting; and after retirement there was time (and money) for things like cruises, and longer trips. Elderhostels were wonderful ways to have travel and learning experiences all in one package, but time ran out too soon for us to try doing any of them for ourselves.

13. Mother-in-Law:

This is a very rewarding role, and really EASY! It gave me great joy when Becky's and David's marriages added their charming, gifted soul-mates to our family! It's like I have another "son" and another "daughter" to love and enjoy! Nothing is better than to know that one's children have the experience of devoted companions with whom to share their lives!

14. Caregiver:

Giving care to a seriously ill loved one is a skill one hopes will never be needed; but if—or when—it is, there is probably nothing more rewarding or fulfilling! I think Gene and I considered it to be teamwork; and that both of us needed to make a few "adjustments" in the roles we had assumed during our long relationship. For instance, through the years, when we were both riding in the same car, he was the driver. And many other roles had to be reversed—but it was by mutual agreement. When he became ill with cancer, I definitely wanted to preserve his dignity of being "his own man"; and of being "head of the family"—yet, I felt a new kind of quite heavy responsibility myself, because

I had to be the "medication dispenser," a role which I took very seriously! There could be NO mistakes! I used a new spiral notebook to make charts for the many things that needed to be done at certain times; for notes involving treatments, and every other bit of information related to his care and communications with his medical team. At first he felt apologetic, but I assured him that "we were in this fight together," and that I had no feeling at all that I was "imposed upon"! We already had regular housecleaning and gardening help, so I was able to give as much time as I needed to care-giving work. Gene insisted that I continue with my own activities when it was possible—bowling, writing class, and occasional bridge—in fact, Gene's friends often came to our house for their scheduled (and sometimes unscheduled)—bridge games and visits. Soon routines developed; family, friends, and neighbors occasionally visited—sometimes bringing food items to enjoy. There were countless trips to doctors and treatments—for X-rays and chemo. We were thankful that we lived fairly near the Corvallis Clinic and hospital! We were also very thankful that both of us felt God's care and guidance always with us! Thankful, too, that much of the care could be done in our own home; and that I was able to do so much of the "leg-work"! I felt that in a very, very small way, I was being permitted to share a tiny bit of his horrible ordeal! It all gave meaning to, and appreciation for, the marriage vow: "In sickness and in health"!

THE GIFT OF HEARING
(As I Hear It)

Oh! How I appreciate the Creator's wisdom for the gift of the five "senses" we've been given—which we often take for granted, and probably most often use for our physical safety or for our emotional enjoyment! It also seems that if one of the senses becomes impaired, others are heightened to the point of delivering the necessary messages to the brain.

I like to think about some of the sounds that are sharp in my memory, no doubt shaping my appreciation of nature, and giving me an understanding of how to cope with problems—even to learning how to "get along with people."

One of the earliest of important sounds was hearing my mother's voice. How pleasant it was to hear her singing lullabies that made me feel safe and loved! And I liked it when she would say, "Ila, can you help me with this little job?" (It might have been something as simple as bringing a wash cloth when she was changing a baby's diaper and found an unexpected surprise!) By putting her ear to a child's chest, she could hear if she needed to medicate (maybe with a Vicks rub and a hot cloth) for a cold. She often sang while she worked—an indication that she was feeling well and was happy with her family. But as I grew into a "creative" child, I came to recognize a sound of voice that did not "bode well"! That was when I heard her say <u>both</u> of my names in a stern, emphatic voice, "Ila <u>May</u>!" That meant, "Change your behavior, NOW!"

Growing up in the middle of Missouri, I suppose our house was underneath one of the main routes of east-west air traffic. Often when doing chores or playing outside, I'd hear the low droning of a plane flying over. It looked so high and mysterious (although without being "pressurized," it couldn't have been <u>very</u> high)! I always stopped whatever I was doing, shade my eyes with my hand, and stand watching it up there in the sky. I could see the small windows along the side and wonder if the people up there could see me, down here! I always waved, just in case, and longed for the time when I could maybe be one of those lucky passengers!

We lived about two miles from the small town of Dixon, which was an important stop for most of the trains on the Frisco railroad. Depending upon the weather—especially on a foggy day, we could hear their steam whistles. Again, the "gypsy" in me found that a very satisfying, adventurous sound. Once when we lived temporarily in a basement apartment near Dad's work away from home, the house was only a couple of blocks from a railroad that was slightly raised as it went through that part of town. Often there was a "fast train" that rumbled through in the middle of the night. We children, I about six and brother Ross about four years old, sometimes climbed up on the couch where we could see out the high basement window to watch and hear it rushing by—the sound gradually dying away as it swiftly passed by. That was a real novelty for country kids! Another sound of a train in a more recent experience was with a neighbor child named Peter (now a school superintendent in Spokane, Washington). When he was pre-school age, he began to notice that when he heard the whistle of the mid-day train that runs within hearing distance of our homes, it was time for lunch! Still more recently, since I have been traveling by train to Seattle, what an exciting joy it is to hear the whistle of that Amtrak engine as it approaches the stop at the Albany station! My "heart" tells me that in another six hours, I'll be enjoying the very active life of my two young grandsons!

I learned very early in my life to enjoy the sounds of Nature—birds, animals, wind, trickling water in a creek, crickets chirping and frogs singing in the evening. I welcome the early-morning and late-evening songs of robins in the spring and summer; and the enthusiastic song of a wren claiming its territory all day, is music to my ears! (I think I liked it even better before I learned about the "claiming territory" thing—I imagined the song was for the enjoyment of the "wife" who was sitting on the nearby nest!) When I go to visit family in Missouri in summer, I am again reminded of how much I liked hearing the whippoorwills. I have recently learned that at my brother's home, they sing for about a half-hour, beginning about 9:00 p.m. In recent years, I'm often hearing a community of owls hooting at night. I can tell that some are in trees very near my house—others answer from varying distances. Some crows also seem to be nesting nearby. They become very vocal when their young ones begin to leave their nests!

Many kinds of music affect my moods and arouse memories of people and places in my life. Some old hymns remind me of people who were dear friends in my childhood. In our small church, the congregation often was invited to request some favorite song. I can see those people in my "mind's eye," and remember their influence on me in my life. One of those old songs is called *Precious Memories*. Here are some of the words: "Precious memories, un-seen angels, sent from somewhere to my soul; How they linger, ever near me, and the sacred past unfold. Precious father, loving mother, fly across the lonely years, and old home scenes of my childhood, in fond memory appear. Precious memories, how they linger, how they ever flood my soul. In the stillness of the midnight, precious, sacred scenes unfold!"

I even like hearing "squeaky" doors! The sound of that squeak tells me something different is happening! When my children were small, I kept the cookies in one of the high kitchen cabinets—giving me some control over children's sugar intake. If I heard that door squeaking, I knew the cookie supply needed some attention!

If I hear someone say they'll "keep their ears to the ground," I see an image of a pioneer man, or a Native American in the old days, actually putting an ear on the ground. They could thereby calculate the distance between them and whatever was making the sound.

I've been writing about some pleasant sounds—but I'm also thankful for others that can warn of dangers: storms with thunder and lightning; sirens sounding warnings; barking dogs; screams from people needing help; and you can think of many others!

But, some or my most treasured sounds were hearing a door open, and one of my children saying, "Mom! I'm home!" and my husband's words in the evening, "How was your day?"! Very precious sounds to hear—very precious memories!

I might not actually "put my ear to the ground," but I'll keep <u>listening</u>!

THE POWER JUST WENT OFF!

It's a Wednesday morning, about 9:15. Twenty-five minutes ago I heard a "bang" a short distance away; at the same time the radio suddenly became silent and the refrigerator motor stopped running. The only sound I hear now is the battery-driven kitchen clock above the window over the sink as it continues to report the time, second-by-second, with its tick-tock. (That small sound is really noticeable when there is no other sound competing with it!) I had just finished my breakfast of juice and French toast and swallowed my last sip of coffee while I read a magazine article about language expressions and how they've changed during my lifetime.

But then it was time to go into the "power-out-mode." Thankfully, I have two old-fashioned dial phones—one upstairs and one downstairs—that plug into the wall and work without extra electricity. I first called a neighbor to establish whether the problem is in the area, or just in my house, though with the sound of the "bang," I was quite sure the outage would be all over our area. Next, it was time to report to the power company. As I expected, I was put on hold for about a minute while other people were probably doing the same thing. It was good that I had finished my warm, substantial breakfast; but I hadn't yet brushed teeth and bathed, so those things went into the emergency mode—using some of the many jugs of stored water. (Under these circumstances, the bath had to be done with a basin and a cloth!)

Here in the country, the power occasionally goes off at varying times of the day for varying lengths of time, depending upon the cause. In winter, a heavy snow or ice storm might break lines that knock out power for miles around—for several hours, or maybe days. Or, if a local transformer "shorts out," a smaller area will be affected. There is one of those transformers on a pole at the corner of our property, so this outage is probably local and will be short. I hope so, because without power the water doesn't get pumped from the well, the electric kitchen stove and microwave don't work, the garage door has to be manually lifted and closed, and the furnace doesn't run because it's controlled by an electric thermostat. I have ironing I'd planned to do, but it can wait. It seems like a good time to take up my pen and describe the situation!

(In the "olden days" when I was a child, when we wanted to iron, we just set the "iron" irons on top of the wood stove and picked each one up with a special handle when the one we were using cooled off too much to smooth the cloth we were ironing.)

Having grown up without the conveniences of electric power or indoor plumbing, I don't feel as helpless as some who haven't even experienced the few inconveniences they might find on a camping trip. I know that one can live without a daily shower, or without running water to wash off a toothbrush. Dishes can be washed by hand with cold water. Water or food can be heated in a fireplace—if one is fortunate enough to have one. A neighbor of mine cooks on their portable gas camp stove. Gas grills are great, too. To be prepared for any kind of emergency, I use the pantry to rotate things like dry milk, cereal, bottled juice, and canned foods that can be eaten cold.

We keep several jugs of water stored around the house—in empty spaces in the freezer, in bathrooms, and in the downstairs storage room. If there's a wind storm or a snow storm that might result in power outage, I fill bathtubs with water to be handy to use for toilet flushing. (And, of course, a toilet doesn't <u>have</u> to be flushed after every use. Once when we lived in a town that experienced a summertime water shortage, people were urged to cut down water usage—even-numbered houses could water lawns on even-numbered days; odd numbered houses, on odd-numbered days; home car-washing was not permitted; and a popular slogan was, "If it's yellow, let it mellow—if it's brown, flush it down!")

For light, I have several flashlights and a battery-powered lantern with small fluorescent-like bulbs. I'm afraid to carry candles from room to room, in case I should fall and cause a fire, but they're nice on the table or in the bathroom. If the power is off at bedtime, and I can't turn my electric blanket on, I sleep in my long underwear under extra blankets with a cap on my head. (A lot of heat escapes from a body from an uncovered head, you know!) Fortunately, the longest outage we've ever experienced was for four days, so we didn't lose food that was stored in the freezer. Gene was living then, and we used a camp stove in the garage for heating water and cooking. A couple of years ago there were snow and ice storms a week apart that affected a large area for a few days. In my neighborhood we were out of power for about twenty-four hours during the first week, and another twenty-four the second week.

It's fairly warm today—fifty degrees this morning, which will probably reach the high sixties—and the house had warmed to seventy degrees before the power went off, so the temperature is comfortable without extra clothing. In winter, when the power is off, I put on long underwear, wool pants, sweater, fleece jacket, a cap, fur-lined boots, and wear gloves—unless bare fingers are needed.

While I've been writing, the refrigerator started running again, so now it's time to reset some clocks and get out the ironing board. It wasn't all that bad to have a short time of silence—I could better hear the bird sounds where they gather in the front yard around the feeders, the bird bath, and some nesting boxes. Chickadees are chirping, and a wren is making sure the other birds know that part of the area belongs to him and his wife!

FOUR REUNIONS IN THREE MONTHS!
(June, July, August 2015)

I <u>love</u> reunions, and these four groups are really special to me:

The "Kelley Kids" (my sisters Barbara and Joy; brother Sterling and his wife Susan; and sister-in-law Chadna—who was not able to attend this year);

The "Ross Reunion" (descendants of Joe and Oda May Ross, parents of twelve children—one of which was our mother Bertha);

My children—David and wife Michelle; Becky, husband Brian, sons Thomas and Evan and her grandson Maureece. (Becky's daughter Leah with partner Dan, their son Chance, and baby daughter Chelsea will come in August.)

The "Bench Bunch"—family of my husband Gene.

In the early 'nineties, we Kelley kids agreed to take turns hosting (at that time) our five couples, realizing that without Mom and Dad to give us a central location, we might neglect getting together. We definitely agreed upon the importance of "keeping up" with each other! Those reunions have all been very rewarding—three or four days

Joy, Barbara, Ila, Ross & Sterling with Dad & Mom, 1989 at Sterling's home

together in various parts of the country, where local sightseeing was part of our fun—and the five couples of us could fit into two cars to explore together. Loss of a brother and the spouses of the others gradually reduced our number.

This year it was Barbara's "turn" to host us in Columbia, and it was possible for the date of it to include my ninetieth birthday which was on June 21st.

One of the activities Barbara chose for that weekend was a trip to Doolittle, Missouri, to attend the annual reunion of the Ross family. That group has always been important to our Kelley family because it meant so much to our mother Bertha, and our dad Sterling. When we children were growing up, our family and many of those Ross relatives were frequent weekend visitors. What fun it was to have a couple of days now and then to play with so many different cousins through so many years!

The first Ross reunion was organized in 1974, by Paul Hunter and his sister Gloria Camenisch (children of Edna Ross Hunter). It was attended by over a hundred, at the Mountain Grove (Missouri) Church of God campground and lasted a week! Many of the later meetings were at the Flat (Missouri) campground; the time together was reduced to three days, and the date was established to be every Fourth of July weekend. In those days my dad, Sterling became one of the leaders. He put a lot of energy into planning activities—especially games and things of interest to the children. He also brought a large U.S. flag that he reverently raised to the top of the flagpole every morning and took down every evening. There was a large dining hall there, with a wonderful kitchen stocked with pans and dishes; and people took turns helping with meals—in the kitchen and dining hall. In the afternoon an important activity was gathering in the "tabernacle" (open seating area with a stage) to listen to music by several different family members. The Enloe cousins were really good with fiddles and guitars. On a Sunday morning, Cousin Paul Hunter presided in the chapel for us to sing hymns and hear his sermon. (One year, I remember overhearing Aunt Sue say to one of the other aunties that she would like to go hear Paul preach, but she was wearing a pants outfit, and it seemed sinful for a woman not to wear a dress to church!) In recent years, locations have been in various places in that general area, but families have remained faithful, even though attendance has been greatly reduced.

For us Kelley kids, the Ross reunion visit this year seemed to be important; but for some reason, we weren't feeling as much enthusiasm as we had felt about some of the former reunions—most of which we hadn't attended anyway. Would our cousins seem like strangers? Would we even know most of them! But, at least we would be traveling together in the same car, so we could do a lot of valuable "visiting" with each other on the way there and back home.

The trip was from Columbia, to Doolittle, a few miles south of the Ross homestead near Devils Elbow; however, much of the terrain was memorable—very similar to what we had seen when we went to visit Grandma and Grandpa Ross! In those days, some of our trips were made in a wagon, pulled by a couple of horses (or sometimes mules) that were driven by our Grandpa Kelley. In the floor of the wagon bed were some thick, homemade quilts, folded for us kids to sit on or lie down on. Mom and Grandpa sat on the wagon seat, with Grandpa holding the reins and guiding the horses. Within easy reach, were delicious snacks of sandwiches, apples, cookies, and lemonade; and we had unusual scenery—green, forested hills—as far as our eyes could see! I think the trip was probably no more than twenty-five miles, but to us in the wagon, it seemed to be a long, very exciting journey! Just looking across the miles of high hills in the distance was as exciting to us as seeing the Rocky Mountains might have been to Lewis and Clark! Some trips were made in Dad's '29 Oldsmobile, but even those had their own excitement: driving along a narrow road around the side of a high hill that looked like a "mountain" to kids! It felt so scary to look down the hill from the road to a wide, rushing creek! And then to walk up another steep hill after we parked the car by the side of the barn! Memories of those exciting, long-ago trips were discussed again, as we traveled today in a comfortable SUV on a paved highway! It was like we were kids again—even remembering and talking about the great distances we were still able to see!

Well! As soon as we walked through the door of the gathering place in Doolittle, we were greeted by "remembered" cousins! Children of Aunt Sib, of Aunt Nellie, of Uncle Percy, of Aunt Edna, of Uncle Dutch! And some of their children! Memories of "olden days" began to surface! It was as if we were becoming children again, as we remembered so many good times together in our various homes—and especially in the home and on the farm of Grandma and Grandpa Ross at Devil's Elbow! Over a generous, delicious pot-luck lunch the memories continued to pour forth—absent members were talked about and remembered; every person there had great stories about their own families, their careers, and interests!

One cousin of special interest to me was Glenda Ross (a daughter of Uncle "Pert" and Aunt Lola). When she and her sister Jeannie (Imogene) were children, both of them were stricken with polio, which was shocking to all of the Ross family! Those girls were both great inspirations to me, and all of the Ross family, as they grew up. In spite of their need to use crutches, they went to college and became teachers! I remember that they taught at Fort Leonard Wood during some of the years of their careers; and I'm sure that the children who were in their classes must have also been inspired! Jeannie is no longer living, but Glenda lives with her brother, Loren, in the home where they grew up!

Everyone at the reunion was "special"! There's something about the appreciation of family ties that gives a person a feeling of belonging, of connection, of worth! In those few hours of remembering long-ago years, we became kids again—with our brains feeling young again—re-living our youth! By the time the five of us left to return home, our enthusiasm was back! We were rejuvenated—and thankful to be part of that very large Ross family! (Even more "memories" surfaced along the road home to Columbia— requiring a stop at Central Dairy in Jefferson City for ice cream cones, because that was a "Kelley Family Tradition!")

On Sunday, my ninetieth birthday, the Wyatt family—Randy, Sherry, Chandler, and Barbara—had planned several things for us: church at First Baptist; dinner at the Wyatt home; and a focus upon my birthday. In fact, the Wyatt home was actually a gathering place for family members for four or more days of the whole weekend! Several of us slept there—others "came and went"! "Sleeper guests" were Barb's daughter Debbie from Hawaii, son Frank from Vermont, our sister Joy with daughter Sarah from Indiana, and I from Oregon.

But before I tell about Sunday, I want to tell about Friday night! Debbie wanted to make a casserole, to be popped into the oven for breakfast on Saturday morning; so the kitchen and the open area around it became the gathering place for Randy, Debbie, Sarah, and Frank. (It was bedtime for Joy, Barbara, and me—and Sherry had to go to her work at the hospital.) I'm sure that their evening in the kitchen was special time-well-spent for cousins who don't have many opportunities to be together! Before I went to sleep, I often heard a lot of laughing as they worked together on mixing the casserole and talking of who-knows-what! I knew they must be enjoying exchanging stories of experiences and ideas—and getting to know each other better! (No doubt, memories were being made for them to enjoy when they, too, will be wondering "where have the years gone!")

At dinner time, and for the rest of the day on Sunday, others came: Sterling and Susan, Luanne, Diane, Mike, and Kelley. One birthday gift to me was really unique and seemed to be fun for everyone! A large box—an eighteen- or twenty-inch cube, very beautifully wrapped and tied with ribbon—was set in front of me at the table. When I finally got it opened, I discovered layers and layers of different colors of tissue paper. Between each layer I found nine $1.00 bills—each bill crimped in the middle to give it a three-dimension look, like maybe a bird or a butterfly in flight. I dramatically removed each layer and piled the bills upon each other as I removed them. There were <u>nine</u> layers! A total of $90.00! In the bottom of the box I found a small, wrapped box containing a roll of ten more $1.00 bills, with this note: "Here's another ten to get you to 100 years!" What a <u>party</u>! What a <u>family</u>! Those are precious dollars—and I'll find a special use for them that might help to make life more meaningful for someone else! Another precious gift from my sisters was a moonstone pendant—especially meaningful because all of us are what you might call "moon-crazy"! When we look at the moon—especially a full moon—we sense our relationship, knowing that the other sisters (maybe even other members of the family)—are looking at it too!

Sterling and Susan invited Joy, Sarah, and me to spend the next day at their home in the country—to see their flowers and visit with some others of their family and friends. We especially welcomed being able to become acquainted with Luanne's friend, Michael, and to hear about some of his experiences and adventures in several other countries. But time together never seems long enough—our busy lives call us back to every-day-responsibilities, and we feel very thankful for even the few days that we are able to be together—and to wonder where the years have gone!

The <u>third</u> reunion was with my own children: David and wife Michelle; Becky and husband Brian; their sons Thomas and Evan; and one grandson Maureece; —on the Fourth of July weekend. Becky and David rented a lovely, comfortable house on the coast at Seaside, Oregon, for four days! The wall of living-room windows overlooked a large cove, with easy access to its long, wide beach located just across the lightly traveled road. Sunsets were glorious; and the view of the waves as the tide moved in and out was spectacular!

Michelle reading to Thomas

There were hours of walking, wading, sun-bathing, and building sand-castles—according to the desires of each! (After I'd enjoyed some walking along the edge of the water, most of my contribution to the activity on the beach consisted of "overseeing" from a comfortable chair and feeling like the "most fortunate person in the world"!) Sometimes some of the family chose to take short hikes into the shopping area; and on Saturday evening, July 4th, Seaside's famous fireworks show was beautifully visible from the comfort of our living room window! Also, from our window, throughout that day, we had watched hundreds of people carrying umbrellas, chairs, food coolers, blankets, etc. onto the beach below, where they "set up" their own fireworks-watching stations—then lighted up the beach that evening with cozy camp-fires and lanterns.

On Friday evening, I was banned from the well-equipped kitchen, while others prepared meals and snacks that included another ninetieth birthday celebration for me. A "HAPPY BIRTHDAY" banner with rainbow colors of streamers decorated the dining room! After our delicious "Becky's Lasagna" dinner, and there was peach pie which Becky had made earlier in the day! (The peach pie was to honor the peach cobbler my Mom often made from fresh peaches Grandpa Kelley almost always brought to our house for my birthday when I was a kid. He gave me one peach for each year of my age and gave Mom a bagful of them to use for making a peach cobbler! Of course, he then usually enjoyed staying for dinner, and we kids enjoyed playing Chinese-checkers with him!)

The decorations were left in place to enjoy the next day, which was David's birthday! Dinner on Saturday was a bountiful barbeque prepared by David and Michelle, using the electric grill on our back deck—juicy steak, chicken, and "brats"—with all the "trimmings." The yummy dessert was David's favorite cake—German chocolate! Next were the fireworks. The Fourth-of-July fireworks at Seaside are said to be some of the best on the coast. We would endorse that—very colorful, unusual varieties of high-in-the-sky explosions, far-reaching "umbrella" shapes, for quite a long time—and probably really loud sounds, although we at our windows were some distance away.

(One thing we will all remember, about that weekend was a curious item that was part of the decorative furnishings of the house—a funny, life-sized male mannequin, appropriately dressed as a golfer! We all wondered why it was standing in the corner of the dining area—surely, such an unusual thing must be important! I have since wondered if the owner of the house might be one of the golfers who play on the well-used golf course that our rear deck overlooked??)

Who's to say at what age "old age" begins? I used to think that ninety was old—and maybe it is. Maybe I don't know what "old" is supposed to feel like. I know I don't feel "young." Maybe ninety is just a number to count years of life—and age is more like a physical condition. Whatever it is, I'm truly thankful for having been given these many happy, healthy years of experiencing a very special life—and I'm truly thankful for my loving family with whom it is being shared! They live all the way across the country—from Vermont, New York, South Carolina and Florida; to Indiana, Missouri, Kansas, Oklahoma, and Colorado; to Oregon, Washington, and Hawaii! They certainly made my ninetieth birthday special for me!

And now, I must tell you about Reunion Number Four! These people are the dear family I joined on August 1, 1948, when I married Gene Bench! I call them the "Bench Bunch" because they're descended from James and Zula Bench. They've gathered in late August (the weekend before Labor Day) at Ocean Shores in Washington, for more years than I can remember—and for many years before that, at the beautiful Mason Lake home of Gene's sister, Fern Evans for Memorial Days and Labor Days. Actually, I think they don't need a holiday for a gathering—they just like to get together!

For instance: a clam-digging season (often during an extra-low tide) frequently found most of them together at the ocean—arriving just before the tide began receding—or maybe camping overnight! Clams come to the surface to feed; and at low-tide, they can be found closer to the edge of the water. The digging tool was a "clam gun" which might be a special long, slim, shovel-like implement to quickly stick straight down into the sand by the side of a "dimple" in the sand, which indicated a clam was under it; then digging until the clam was visible. (Digging had to be "quick" because the clam was busy digging deeper!) Or the "gun" might be an aluminum pipe, closed at one end with a handle attached. Dad Bench, Bob Beagley, Harry Evans, and some other "old timers" always used the "shovel." Gene was really proud of the "tube" diggers he had made, and some of us younger people preferred those. The tube was held vertically, with the open end placed on the surface of the sand, centered over the "dimple." A small hole near the handle on top was then covered with a thumb—causing vacuum inside the tube, which one pushed down into the sand. When it was then quickly pulled up, the tube of sand had a nice long razor clam hidden in it!

In 1983, we were especially surprised, and excited, on our Memorial Day weekend clam-dig. Several people—Fern, Harry, Helen, Katherine, and "Corky" Evans; Lavada, Bob, Jeannie, Bobby, and Nancy Beagley; Larry, and Sue Beagley and their children; Gene, I, and our granddaughter Leah were there—feeling very happy to have Mom Bench with us! She was not physically able to actively dig; but she wanted to be part of our group—and dressed for the occasion with red rubber boots, carried a bucket and a shovel, and sat in a portable chair near the "action"—cheering us on! Our big surprise came the next day. On the front page of the May 30, 1983, *Seattle Times* was a feature article about clam-digger "Grandma Bench,"—and a color photo of her, sitting on the beach in her red boots, holding her clam shovel!

Well, I "got a little carried away" with describing some typical Bench family fun! This year's reunion didn't include clam digging, but it did include a potluck family-prepared sea-food dinner! (Are you surprised to know that clams were served?)

The third weekend this August, we were again at the Sands Motel in Ocean Shores, Washington; housed in our usual, mostly adjoining units, along one end of the building, alongside the swimming pool. I was the only one of my generation attending—Gene's sister Fern was not able to travel. She was very much missed, of course, as were deceased members—especially Larry Beagley, whose very active life ended so recently on November 23, 2014. He, and his wife Sue, have for many years been our "leaders" for the annual Ocean Shores gatherings; and most of their family came this year. We honored deceased ones with Don Race reminding us of our family's unusual allegiance.

Four generations of the Bench-Beagley-Evans family were represented—the youngest one being my own cute great-granddaughter, Chelsea! Chelsea is eight months old, and it was my first time to be with her. It was a real joy to play with her, especially to be able to watch her learn to crawl! Another "new generation" baby was Kennedy—daughter of Brandon and Miranda Beagley—six or so months older than Chelsea. They, and Chelsea's three-year-old brother Chance, got a lot of attention from grown-up cousin Alecia, as did all the other children of various ages. (All the while, I was remembering when Alecia—and even her mother, Katherine—were the "babies-at-the beach"!) I've always been impressed with the attention the older children give to the young ones!

As always, the children and their young parents kept busy with sand castles that become more and more elaborate every year, as the kids grow older and more "inventive"! After the tide took the castles away, there were games and "rides" in the little town for more adventures, and some had friendly dogs to walk. Dinnertime found each family bringing pots and casseroles and platters of tasty things to share—Saturday evening being devoted to this year's theme— Greek food and dress!

Having now enjoyed ninety years of life, I think I'm learning some things about memory. One thing is that you either have some, or you don't. Another thing is that if you want to find more, try going to a "reunion"—a class reunion, family reunion, workplace reunion, or any other group of people that come to mind. There will be people with whom we shared some really important experiences that we might have never before felt were important! For instance, cousins being children together are <u>more</u> than just kids having fun for a few hours. Even though we don't realize it at the time, it is experience that is helping to shape our lives. At a reunion, we make important connections; we help children develop feelings of "belonging;" and they learn family history; we relax and have fun together; youth is recalled; we're refreshed! Be sure to let me know about our next "reunion"! I'll try to be there, and I hope I'll see YOU, too!

PLANNING AHEAD
End-of-Life

Does it ever seem to you that all through life we quite often find it necessary to "Plan Ahead"? As school children we must study for tomorrow's lessons; we sometimes gather for fire drills—to know how to exit and protect ourselves in case of fire; we rehearse for plays and performances of various kinds; plan the menus for parties; save for purchases; plan our wedding; equip a nursery to be ready for a new baby; plan wonderful vacations; and plan for retirement. Planning ahead makes so many things easier—so, why shouldn't we <u>plan</u> for our end of life! There may never be a need to escape a fire—but we <u>know</u> the end of life is a certainty! A plan might make it all easier; and as for most planning, a few lists are helpful.

My first list consists of answering some questions:

<u>First</u>: What do I want to accomplish in my remaining lifetime?

I feel that I have lived a full life—enjoyed a remarkable family, done some traveling, walked on every continent except Australia and Antarctica, lived in some interesting places, learned a few things, and gathered many great friends—but I do have a few things yet to do!

I want to do something with the Life Stories that I have written—and that will involve editing, recopying, assembling into some "order," and printing.

I want to finish a quilt that I have been working on for longer than I ever intended.

I want to leave a minimum of "after-life" details and work for my children to do.

I want to spend quality time with family: children, grandchildren, and siblings.

I want to spend quality time with friends—local ones, and ones who live elsewhere.

I want to do all I can to maintain a healthy body, a peaceful soul, and an alert mind.

Second: What needs to be done in order for those things to happen?

I need to consider where I want to live:

I have moved to an assisted-living community in Corvallis—but might need even more assistance as I continue to age.

Continue living in Corvallis—near friends, with son an hour away, and daughter in Seattle.

Move to assisted-living near daughter in Seattle. (Advantages—near grandchildren, making it easier to spend more time with them; being near daughter if I needed help for my care—easier from her than from my son.)

If I leave Corvallis, there will be finding another doctor (one who takes Medicare patients); possibly making arrangements for a local bank, and no doubt many other things that haven't yet come to mind.

My house has been sold. In any case, I need to further "down-size." There are keep-sakes for my children; and need for disposal of much other "stuff." Into my assisted-living place, I have moved a small number of things necessary for life here.

Third: Arrange a conference with my attorney to make sure of ongoing financial security; an up-to-date will on file; a Power of Attorney on file for use of a family member, in case of my unexpected inability to contract business; a Living Will on file for care if I were unconscious.

Once the place for living, the down-sizing and/or moving done, and the legal and financial details are in order, the rest of my "wants" can be accomplished, no matter where I live—the "Life Story" work; finishing the quilt; spending time with family and friends, and maintenance of body, soul, and mind! The trick there will be making the best use of time— fighting that devious old devil called "procrastination," and remembering a few uplifting thoughts, such as:

*Life is not about how you survive the storm, but how you dance in the rain!

*Everything can change in the blink of an eye. But don't worry, God won't give you more than you can handle.

*Whatever doesn't kill you, really does make you stronger.

*When it comes to going after what you love in life, don't take no for an answer.

*Time heals almost everything. Give time <u>time</u>!

*Don't take yourself too seriously. No one else does!

*People may forget what you said, or what you did; but they will never forget how you made them feel!

*Remember: LIFE IS SHORT—EAT DESSERT FIRST!

MOVING INTO "ASSISTED LIVING"
Timberhill Place—Corvallis, Oregon

It would take a while to enumerate the times I've moved from one home to another: a few times with my Kelley family as a child; to Mrs. Dunn's boarding house for college; from parental home to creating a new home with my marriage to Gene Bench; to temporary Marine Corps quarters; to so-called "permanent" quarters, and officers' quarters with each of many Marine Corps change-of-duty locations during Gene's years of active duty as a Marine; and finally, to a home in the country near Corvallis, Oregon, when Gene retired. For me, moving was always an exciting experience. Of course, it meant a LOT of extra energy, but I truly enjoyed "turning the house into a home" with our own choices of furniture and "stuff"! We met new neighbors—playmates for Becky and David, and friends for all four of us. There were really valuable experiences at each new place—exploring things of historical and entertaining interest; sometimes adjusting to a different climate; maybe finding a new life-style in a foreign country; and once, even learning a new language!

We had lived on Arthur Circle in Corvallis for three years, from 1963 to 1966, when Gene was the Marine Officer Instructor at OSU—and we loved it! The people; the climate; the recreation; the being near Gene's family! So it was a kind of "homecoming" feeling to be returning to Corvallis and moving into our "forever home" at 910 NW Overlook Drive, on August 1, 1973, which was the 25th anniversary of our wedding! What would it be like to live in one place—year after year, after year! And, it soon felt very comforting to finally be able to "stay put"! Now, we could do landscaping that would be permanent—plant trees we could watch mature to produce colorful leaves, or delicious fruit; change the colors of the house and walls if we liked; invest in recreation vehicles and build new storage for them; and have more space for children and (later) grandchildren to play! It was easy to become very thankful for, and excited about, the view of far-away mountains; the five acres of field and nearby forest, with several kinds of birds, deer, opossums, raccoons, and even a family of gray foxes! There were four bedrooms, three bathrooms, large living room, dining room, large kitchen-dining area, utility room, and lots of storage space—soon filled with our family's collections of "treasures"! The largest house we'd ever had! There were great neighbors! Good schools! Fun friends! Rivers and lakes for fishing! More activities than we had time for! Life was GOOD!

But what needs to happen after thirty-nine years of wonderful, active living? Gene had had a second career as an insurance agent; children had grown up, married, and had children of their own; I had been active in community and church work. We had discussed the various kinds of senior care that might be available, if and when the time came that we might need more help— thinking that we would really like to stay in the home we loved and receive care from visiting aides. But we hadn't made an allowance for the shock of hearing the doctor's diagnosis of Gene's CANCER in October of 2000! Radiation and chemo treatments for six months didn't help enough, and in a few more weeks the cancer took his life—early on June 22nd, 2001.

For the first time in my life I was "on my own"! It was challenging! Much of living was continuing "as usual"—but different because I had to have help with maintaining the house and managing finances—and it was lonely! I could get advice from our children and professional people concerning business; but there was no one "in the house" with whom to discuss problems, or news, or finances, or weather; no one with whom to travel, or to eat dinner! Or to play backgammon! I was very thankful for helpful neighbors and friends—but I didn't want to become dependent upon their generosity, and I certainly didn't want to be a responsibility for my children. I interviewed representatives of a couple of Home Health Care groups, discovering that the cost would include an added travel expense, but it would make it possible for me to continue living in my home. Wearing a "life-alert" button was one way of staying somewhat independent. I had the assurance of receiving emergency help, should it be needed; and I did use it once for an ambulance to go to the emergency room.

I knew the children were concerned, but they never pressured me. Perhaps I should at least do some more exploring; so I began assessing the local care facilities, even to putting my name on the waiting list at my favorite one, Timberhill Place, and assuring my children that I would let them know "when I was ready." (Or, would I ever be ready?) Leaving that special home wouldn't be easy! So much of "ME" was there—the deer, the birds, the open space and stars and sky, the owls that "conversed" at bedtime in the neighbors' trees, the guest-rooms for visiting family, the neighbor-friends, the memories of growing children! Especially the many memories! Even the big-leaf maple tree with the unusual "burl"—outside the kitchen sliding door! And the tall Doug fir that had grown from a tiny seedling that David had planted in the middle of the field when he was ten, "so the rabbits would have a place to hide!" My LIFE was there! And "time marched on."

On March 20, 2012, I got some help with the big decision! I awoke to find everything covered in deep snow! Trees and shrubs were bending; birds were crowding the feeders; and I could hear limbs snapping from some tall oak trees—the snow was evidently very wet and heavy. While I was sitting at the kitchen table eating breakfast, I heard a loud crashing sound up near the road and mailbox. I looked out the glass sliding doors and saw that the very large, old oak tree near the road had broken down the middle, with one half of its trunk and large limbs lying across my driveway! WOW! I wondered what else might soon crash—the whole north side of the property was covered with tall trees! As I was sitting back down in my chair, I seemed to clearly hear a voice say, "Ila, it's TIME!" It was like I suddenly almost felt like a different person— able to realize that living there was going to become more and more difficult with responsibility I didn't need! But I did need to do something about getting that downed "half-a-tree" out of the way! A call to Rich Holmes fixed that problem. He was a neighbor, and a tree specialist who just two days ago had marked several dead limbs that his men would soon remove from other trees. In a short time, while on his way to this day's work, he came with his saw, and cut the part of the tree that was blocking the driveway into moveable pieces. (Thanks, Rich!)

So, okay! I will plan to move! What comes next? When? Where? No need to hurry. Certainly, no use to make very many plans until I knew where I would be able to have a roof over my head! The Timberhill Place apartment had become available three months ago in December, but I felt I couldn't possibly get ready to move then, in the middle of winter; so I had passed it up and remained on the waiting list, giving them freedom to rent it to someone else. One important thing to do was to talk the whole moving idea over with Becky and David. My response from each of them: "What a relief! I've worried for ten years about you living alone away out there!" My next call was to Timberhill Place. The special upstairs two-bedroom apartment that I liked, but had turned down three months ago, probably wouldn't be available, but I might get an idea about when I might expect another vacancy. Still, no hurry.

Well! What a surprise when I did call! "MY" apartment was still vacant! During those last three months it had been entirely renovated—there were freshly painted walls; all new carpet in living room and the two bedrooms; new vinyl floors in the two bathrooms and the kitchen area! It was ready for occupancy! It is in the southeast corner of the upstairs east wing! One block from my bank; three blocks from my church; one block from good shopping areas; assigned parking space for my car; all surrounded by trees and tended gardens and lawns! Called "Assisted Living," it contains sixty apartments (mostly studio and one-bedroom sizes), two dining rooms, a kitchen, an activities room (called the "Friendship Room"), a beauty/barber shop, and offices for the very capable, friendly staff of caregivers and others who keep us aging residents comfortable and safe.

Wow! Decision time! Gene would say, "It's time to bite-the-bullet"! But first, a prayer for continued guidance. (I was beginning to feel that the guidance had already begun!) At my appointment with Debbie, Timberhill's Marketing Director on March 27th, I reserved that upstairs apartment that I liked, giving myself about a month for arranging some of the many things necessary for moving and for selling my house. That beloved home that had been "actively" lived in for thirty-nine years—by two "old pack-rats" and two young ones! Very little had been thrown away through the years—because "we might need it sometime"! Some things even belonged to the children—left over after they moved to their own homes! ALL of Gene's uniforms and military souvenirs were there; many kinds and sizes of luggage; and tools for doing any kind of work you can imagine. Out at the edge of the woods was a tall, three-vehicle shed that still housed a drift boat, two work benches, a lawn mower, more tools, a "Gene-made" fish-cleaning sink, a lifting device that was useful for loading (and unloading) a camper on and off its truck, etc., etc. A formidable collection of many quite valuable things, and some that most people would probably classify as "junk!"

I talked to a couple of men from our church about the contents of the garage and shed—suggesting that if they would like to schedule a "garage" sale, I would donate all the proceeds from it to the church. They said that they would think about it.

After a day or two, one of the men told me that he had gone to a quite interesting estate sale that weekend, and that he had asked for their phone number in case I would be interested in contacting them for help or advice. If they did the sale, it would include the garage and shed contents, as well as the furnishings from the house; and they would do all the work involved with displaying, selling, and cleaning up afterward. When I contacted them, I was told I should leave everything in place—in drawers, hanging in closets, and the pictures in their places on the walls. The people at Timberhill advised me to first move into the apartment—sleep and eat there and go out to the house to do whatever work I needed to do there each day. Then allow my children to take out everything that they would like to keep for themselves. All the rest would be for sale.

Suddenly those three apartment rooms looked awfully small! I was so happy when two long-time friends, Alice and Guy (both architects), told me they were going to "make planning measurements" and they wouldn't take "no" for an answer! They drew a floor plan and cut cardboard pieces of furniture to scale. That made an interesting "puzzle" for us to work with while we sipped cups of tea! Finally, every piece of the puzzle had a place—often with maybe no more than an inch of space to spare! On May 1, 2012, my friendly mover named Chris worked all day packing up the items I'd selected for the apartment. The next day was for last minute packing and moving. I needed to be at the house to supervise the mover, so my dear friend Kim helped by being at the apartment to direct the movers as they brought in items they unloaded from the truck. By looking at the plan Alice and Guy had drawn, she was able to say for each piece of furniture, "That goes right here!" And when it was all in place, there was no space to spare! A couple of the movers put the parts of my bed together, and that night I slept for the first time in my "new home"!

The telephone company transferred my old number right away to the phone at the apartment and gave me a temporary number to use at the house, for as long as I owned it. The picnic table and benches that stayed in the yard became very useful for times when I went back to do whatever work I needed to do. Several times I went back into the house while I waited for the watering to finish—and usually found a few things to retrieve! I kept a couple of shopping bags in the car for such occasions, and when I went home to the apartment I figured I probably looked like a "bag lady"! (As long as the house was on the market, I went out to keep the lawn watered, and my gardener came regularly to mow the grass until the house was sold.)

Gene and I had sold five other homes during the years of Marine Corps moving, so I knew there were a number of manual, legal, and business "chores" involved in selling a house; but he was the one who had taken care of the business connected with of all those other sales. All I had ever done was to sign my name on whatever line where they told me to sign! Now, I was the one who had the "leg work" to do! And that included phone calls, appointments, choosing a real estate sales person, conferences, inspections, appraisals, repairs, house and yard cleanup, estate sale preparation, etc., etc. On May 18th, I signed a contract with Ann Fahy of RE/MAX Realtors to find a buyer and sell the house. In the meantime, "life" kept going on as if nothing else was happening! I really appreciated a thoughtful card from my dear friend Mai with whom I had worked and spent happy times since the 1950's—letting me know her thoughts were with me, which was great for "keeping my spirits up"!

Two days after moving, I had the pleasure of presenting a scholarship and a leadership award, in honor of Gene's memory, to two NROTC students at the OSU awards program (the leadership award went to a young woman for the first time!). The next day David and Michelle took me shopping for a new "flat-screen" TV and a computer desk, helped with setting up some electronic devices, and hung one of my large paintings. (Michelle said she had heard that getting some pictures on the wall right away helped one to "feel at home" in a new place!). A week later they took me to dinner to celebrate Mother's Day, and again helped with my "settling-in"). The next week, my friend Gay asked if she could come and help with hanging pictures—I had learned that there were no restrictions on how many nails could be driven into the walls, so my apartment soon looked a little like a museum! Gene's medals and photos; other photos—children, grandchildren, great-grandchildren, Kelley family, Bench family, diplomas, more paintings, and souvenirs. Also in May, there was an appointment for an eye examination, resulting in new glasses. On Memorial Day weekend I took the train to Olympia, Washington, to attend the annual gathering of the Bench family at the home of nephew Larry and his wife Sue.

The estate sale happened on the first three days of June—stressful days for me, even though I was not allowed to be there. With the house now stripped of all contents, my regular housecleaning team gave it their final treatment. They were exceptional experts, and we had become quite good friends, so it was a kind of "bitter-sweet" day for them, and me.

July began with the Butler family coming for a visit that included celebrating David's birthday on the 4th of July. The rest of the month was busy with appointments with my doctor and dentist; some bridge games with friends, several evening trips to "the house" to water shrubbery and fruit trees; unpacking boxes at the apartment; and being surprised how much time would be spent at Timberhill Place just eating meals! Each meal needing the better part of an hour, by the time salads were served, orders were taken, and the food was served! After all, I felt that I should take some time to begin getting acquainted with residents at Timberhill and try to "be a good neighbor"! From time to time the realtor let me know that quite a number of people were looking at my house, and at one time a quite low offer was made; but it was still early, and we decided to wait for a better one.

During the second week in August, my kids and I received invitations from the Wyatt cousins in Columbia, Missouri, to attend a memorial service for their son, Sterling, who was killed in Afghanistan in July. (Sterling was my sister Barbara's eldest grandson.) There had been an earlier memorial and burial in Columbia, but this service was to be at Fort Lewis, from which Sterling's unit had departed when they were ordered to go to Afghanistan; and the Army was flying his family to Fort Lewis to attend it. I went with my Becky's family, Brian, and teen-age sons, Thomas and Evan. It was a really rewarding experience for all of us—an opportunity to meet two of Sterling's friends who had been with him and were severely injured in the explosion of the IED that killed Sterling. During a family dinner after the service we were able to have time for a relaxing visit. My grandsons were especially impressed with the military formalities of the memorial, and with chatting with Sterling's teen-age brother Chandler and a very friendly Sergeant who was the driver for the family while they were at Fort Lewis.

Later in August we had an offer from a family who seemed to be very interested in the house. The offer was a little low, but I had accidentally had a chance to meet them and visit a bit. (They seemed to be very nice people.) They lived in Washington and were staying in a motel while they were house-hunting. Two school-age sons were with them, and two older daughters were still in Washington. However, there was a bit of a problem—it wouldn't be possible to close a sale that would give them possession until sometime in October, but they were hoping to be able to get the boys enrolled in school early in September. They wondered if it would be possible for them to live in the house, and pay rent for a month, while waiting for the paper work to be done for the sale. My real estate agent privately, strongly, advised me against it—said she had seen some serious problems that resulted in the sale "falling through." But my daughter and I talked it over and decided we would be willing to take a chance. We didn't like the thought of those children being without a "home" during their first month of adjusting to a new school; so an agreement to buy was signed, and they moved in.

I rested for a few days in Missouri with my Kelley family; and spent time the week before Labor Day in Seattle and Ocean Shores, Washington, enjoying the annual reunion of the Bench family. The Flemings family moved into my house the first of September; and the sale of the house at 910 NW Overlook Drive was closed on October 12, 2012! I've heard that "all's well that ends well," but I do believe that moving from that house was the most stressful period of my LIFE! I am so very thankful to my Higher Power for keeping me "sane" and healthy that summer—for helping me write this story (even with a "lump in my throat")—and for the years of happiness our family enjoyed with the birds, deer, and squirrels at 910 NW Overlook Drive!

Now, six-plus years have passed. Trees are taller! The red-maple that we planted in the front yard is an especially beautiful sight with its yellow-orange-red leaves in autumn! The people who bought the house have been happy to live there—and have become well-liked in the neighborhood. They invited me once to see the remodeling they have done! (I had the feeling that they might be sort of hoping for my approval!) Actually, some of it was similar to what I might have done myself! It is certainly better now for accommodating their family that is larger than ours. And we are good friends! (Another neighbor has told me that it has become known as "Ila's house"!)

I've even given up driving and sold my beloved car—a gray 1995 Subaru station wagon! That was a different kind of "stress"—for awhile, there was a feeling like someone had died! But Gene would say, "This, too, shall pass;" and I know it's true! Timberhill Place is a really comfortable, delightful home!

Chapter 6: Holidays

SOME NEW YEAR EVES AND DAYS

New Year's Day was a very important day when I was growing up because it was so important to Dad. He was a thoroughly optimistic person, and he put enthusiasm into almost every moment of his life. I'm sure he thought that his enthusiasm would "rub off" on the whole family—and a lot of it did—but as I age, I understand and appreciate his philosophy more and more. He taped little "positive thoughts" around the edge of the bathroom mirror until there wasn't much space left to see one's face! One of those which he also often quoted to us was, "*Act* enthusiastic, and you will *Be* enthusiastic!" Key words that were on the bathroom mirror were, "*Act—Be*"! So it was no surprise to hear his words of advice often on New Year's Day—"Be kind on New Year's, and you'll be kind all year"; "Be cheerful on New Year's, and you'll be cheerful all year"; "Make your room tidy on New Year's and you'll tidy it all year"; "Read something worthwhile on New Year's, and you'll read good things all year"; "Do a good turn"; "Pray"; "Eat healthful food"; "Spend some time outside in the fresh air"; "Get some exercise"; "Think about it being a new year! No one has ever seen it before—and wonderful new things will be invented; many things will be done for the first time"!

With thoughts and conversations like that drifting around all day, you can imagine some of our activities, as well as some "constraints." It certainly wouldn't have been appropriate to pick a little fight with a brother or sister! A lot of house-cleaning got done, wood got carried in for burning in the heating stove and the cook stove, snow got shoveled (there usually was some), and Fox and Geese was a favorite game for exercise in the snow. For a few hours of the day a pot of black-eyed peas with some chunks of ham cooked on the living room heating stove, or on the back of the kitchen stove.

In the south, it was considered a sure provision for good luck all year to eat black-eyed peas on New Year's Day. Who is to say all those things aren't true? I still find myself following the "rules"—even to cooking black-eyed peas and adding cornbread to the dinner menu! Sometimes our kids, or some friends, are with us for the "feast." If we're invited to eat with someone else, they'll usually let us bring some peas to fill a place in their menu—for instance a cup of pea soup as an appetizer before dinner!

I'm sure most other cultures have their own good-luck traditions. One that Gene and I experienced when we lived in Naples, Italy during the 50's was more a New Year's Eve happening than a New Year's Day one. Our Italian friends had told us a bit about what to expect and recommended that we participate to whatever extent we might choose.

The military community maintained an Officers' Club, which happened to be located on top of one of the higher hills on a plaza called The Vomero. We lived a short distance down the hill, on Parco Lamaro—one of the streets leading into Vomero, so it seemed reasonable to begin the evening up there with a nice view of much of the city below. It was, of course, a very dressy formal occasion—dinner, dancing, champagne, entertainers, and a good time with American friends. At midnight we put on coats and went outside where the fireworks looked and sounded like war! All over the city, in almost every piazza (an open, park-like space) there were fireworks bursting in air, making great reddish and orange glows as the smoke rose and reflected the colors! This went on for probably thirty minutes or so. Then, when we finally got into our car to drive down the hill to our house, we appreciated the warning from our friends to watch out for broken glass. One of the Italian traditions was to throw their empty wine bottles out the window at midnight—to symbolize giving up the old year with mistakes or whatever and welcome the new year with new hope. In most of the city people lived in quite high apartment buildings—seven, twelve, stories or more—that rose with maybe no more than a sidewalk between the building and the street. When those bottles went out the windows, a goodly number of them landed, and, of course, crashed, on the street below!

In Hawaii, 1967 and '68, we lived in Navy quarters near Pearl Harbor, down the hill from the town of Aiea. One of the New Year's Eve traditions there was also a display of fireworks. The idea, a Chinese one, I think, was to encircle one's house with firecrackers which, when ignited at midnight, made a path of explosions all the way around the house—which would frighten away the evil spirits. These weren't the kind of firecrackers we are allowed to use now in Oregon or in most of the states—these were the old-fashioned real firecrackers the Chinese people have been famous for making. The Navy regulations wouldn't have allowed them in our neighborhood, but we were near enough to Aiea, that we experienced a great view—with sound effects—from outdoors in our yard! Again, it looked and sounded like a raging battle—the whole hill looking like it was going up in smoke! Becky, age eight, and David, age four, were ecstatic! Gene and I were awed!

My mother and dad came to visit us in December of 1968, and stayed a few weeks, also experiencing the Hawaiian Christmas-New Year season. If Gene and I were <u>awed</u>, I could describe them as <u>super-awed</u> by seeing the bright, smoking lights and hearing the explosions! They had never seen fireworks like that before!

When Gene retired in 1973, and we made our "permanent home" in the country near Corvallis, we began a "tradition" of ending each year with a bridge party. By inviting ten of our friends who were crazy about playing bridge, we could have three "tables" of people, all enjoying a favorite game while visiting and "sipping," and snacking upon delicious "goodies" that each couple brought. We kept the TV on so that those who wished could have a peek at New Year goings-on in some other part of the world as the evening progressed. A few minutes before midnight we took a break from cards to watch the Times Square gathering on TV. Gene and I filled crystal wine glasses with sparkling cider for all of us to "toast" the New Year, and each other, while the "ball" dropped at Times Square! But that wasn't the end of the evening. Gene announced that we shouldn't tempt Fate when it came to "luck." So to make sure we played bridge all the next year, we should play some bridge to begin the year! So right then—the first thing we did on New Year's Day, was to sit down and play one "round" of bridge before departing for the night!

Becky, and my grandsons Thomas and Evan, came to spend the last weekend of 2007 with me. Thomas was nine and Evan was seven years old, and they seemed sad that they had never had the experience of "seeing a New Year in." They easily persuaded their mom to allow them to stay up until midnight! That made the occasion special for me, too! We all went to town to shop for some sparkling cider, some various kinds of noise-makers, and some "party" treats; then, after dinner and the dishes were done, we settled in the living room with some games to play, and the TV turned to a channel with a program showing New Year celebrations that were going on in some other parts of the world as midnight arrived there. At midnight for us, the TV channel showed the New Year "ball" descending at Times Square in New York City! What excitement! What noise! The boys wanted to go outside and make some "celebration" noise, too! We didn't have any fireworks to explode, but we found some pans we could bang together, and drum-types of things to beat upon to make quite a lot of noise out in our big, open yard under the stars!

And now we've experienced the beginning of a new Millennium! The "hype" about the Y2K "bug" that some people thought might cause problems in these new times when so much of our world is being controlled by computers, proved there was nothing to fear about the arrival of the year 2000! I wonder if we might be neglecting to appreciate the marvels of these times! I've always enjoyed thinking about our "place" in history—with help from things like *Time* magazine's choice of "The Man (or Woman) of the Year," The "Happening of the Century," or "The Person of the Century"—and there can now be opinions about "The Man (or Woman) of the Millennium!"

By now, you might be thinking that I believe it's important to "actively" celebrate a new year. I hope that you think that I <u>believe</u> a new year <u>is</u> important enough to celebrate! A celebration can be noisy, shared, formal, public, festive, ceremonial, solemn, or private—so long as it's recognized as important to one's life. So, what happens when I'm alone on New Year's Eve or New Year's Day? I still "celebrate"! I might choose to read a special something; have a dessert treat; talk on the phone to friends or family members—almost always spending some time watching TV shows of celebrations in other places, or a concert. My thoughts center upon being thankful for the many blessings, family, and friends that I have enjoyed! And, of course, those thoughts contain a sincere prayer for guidance in the New Year—for myself, my family, and for the world we live in!

NEW YEAR'S DAY–2006

Once upon a time there was a little old lady who lived in the country a few miles outside of a pleasant, small city, that was a lot like a large small town. The people there were friendly, and so many different activities were available, that they could choose many exciting and interesting things to do. The little old lady had lived there for many years with her actively retired husband while their two children were getting through school; so even after she became a widow, and the children were out on their own, she was still quite busy, healthy, and happy—because she knew from experience that "what a person gets out of life depends pretty much what one puts into it."

During her childhood the little old lady lived in a family that gave considerable enthusiasm to life—celebrating birthdays and most holidays in special ways. For instance, a new year was important for "getting a new lease on life"—maybe even planning ways that life in this new year could be even better than in the one just past. But on one New Year's Day, she had an unpleasant dose of humility.

LOVE IS ALL THAT MATTERS

It was a Sunday, and she had been to her church at Calvin Presbyterian on Dixon Street. The music was uplifting; the sermon on something about "acting like a Christian" was inspiring; a few minutes of fellowship after the worship service was refreshing, and she happily started home, looking forward to writing some letters after a quick lunch. In her little Subaru station wagon, she made her way over to Highland Drive—her usual route out of town to her home. Heading north, in front of Linus Pauling Middle School, she soon came to a stop at Circle Boulevard where the traffic light was red. She had seldom seen so little traffic in that area, and while she waited for the light to turn green, she thought to herself that a lot of people must be sleeping in after New Year's Eve celebrations. There was one car beside her waiting to turn left, and another one crossed on Circle from east to west before the light turned.

In the next block, she saw no cars or people, but had to stop for a traffic light again before crossing Walnut Boulevard. Soon after she crossed Walnut, continuing north up a small hill, she saw flashing blue lights in her rear-view mirror. She said to herself, "I must pull to the curb and stop to give that police car room to pass, because it must be in quite a hurry to get somewhere!" But it didn't pass—it stopped right behind her!

A nice, quite young-looking woman officer came and stood beside her— a little behind the left door—as the little old woman wondered why she was being stopped. The pretty, young officer authoritatively said, "Do you know how fast you were driving back there?" The little old lady replied, "I know I was driving very slowly past the school, and I didn't <u>feel</u> like I was speeding any other place." The officer then asked, "Do you know the speed limit along there?" "I know," said the little old lady, "that it is 25 mph south of Circle and 20 by the school, and that it is 35 a little north of where we are parked." She then heard from the young officer that the speed limit in the block just covered is 25, and the little gray Subaru was clocked going 47! The little old lady was so surprised, all she could think of to say was something like, "I'm really shocked, because it didn't <u>seem</u> that fast!"

The officer asked to see the little old lady's driver's license and registration, which she readily produced, thinking that she would be receiving a warning— and maybe a lecture. But the young officer took the credentials back to her car and returned with a citation! Attention was called to the recorded location and speed, plus the date and time to appear at the Municipal traffic court on January 25, at 8:30 a.m. The little old lady noticed that written in the "Base Fine" box on the ticket was $237.00.

By now you might have guessed that the "little old lady" was ME—and the date of the "crime" was this last New Year's Day. After talking to a clerk at the court, I found that I could appear in court on an earlier date, and that a letter to the judge describing the incident in my words might be helpful. So I chose to appear on Thursday, the 12th at 3:00 p.m. which would be a more convenient hour for me—maybe a less crowded docket—and just get it all over with. In the letter I emphasized that I couldn't believe that if I had been going 47 miles per hour, it couldn't have been for more that just a moment, because I had gone from being at a standstill at Circle, then would have been slowing down for the red light I saw at Walnut. I also said I would greatly appreciate the prevention of the citation being recorded by my insurance company or by the DMV, if at all possible.

The judge had a bad cold and began the proceedings by apologizing and saying we would get to business as rapidly as possible. I was wishing someone else would go first, because I didn't know "how to act," but I had checked in several minutes before court time just to be efficient, and soon learned that the docket must have been arranged by order of checking in. Yes, my name was the first one called. It was quite humbling—and, being first, I felt like a "lamb being led to the slaughter"! There were a few questions that I don't even remember; the judge read my letter, and said, Mrs. Bench, I think you must be a very good driver, but I can't ignore the citation. I will reduce your fine to the minimum of $178.00. Be sure to wash your hands after handling these papers that I'm handling and take this to the desk at the entrance to make your payment."

I've heard that a criminal often returns to the scene of the crime, so the next time I drove north on Highland between Circle and Walnut, I watched my speedometer as I progressed, and I truly believe the officer was parked on Sequoia, doing the "clocking." I remember thinking at the time I was cited that the police might be still expecting to stop someone who had partied late and might still be a DUI.

I believe in "positive thinking," so I can consider this incident to be a blessing in disguise. I know that I often "push" the speed limit—maybe so much that I need to work on re-learning the "feel" of various speeds. I'm telling the story of the experience in the hope that it might influence someone who reads it to consider driving habits. I know that I'm not the only person breaking speed limits!

MEMORIAL DAY—2004

Memorial Day has had a significant place in my life for as long as I can remember. As children, we were taught that it was a special day for remembering and paying respect to family members and friends who had passed on, as well as for honoring veterans who had fought in wars to preserve freedom for us—many of whom "paid the supreme sacrifice" with their lives.

In our mid-Missouri community, it was called "Decoration Day." It was customary to load up with as many flowers as we could find in our yard (along with a bunch of tall tin cans for holding water) and make a trip to one or two cemeteries where family members were buried. Mom's people were mostly in the cemetery at Hooker Church at Devils Elbow; Dad's people were mainly at Fairview Church near Dixon. For several days before, Mom kept a sharp eye on her peonies—hoping they would be bloomed in time—or that they wouldn't bloom too early! Each family also packed a generous picnic lunch. After graves had been "decorated," long tables (usually church pews, placed with the seat parts facing) were set up on the lawn for the "basket dinner." What a feast! And all of it looking so delicious, it was hard to choose what to eat! Fried chicken was very popular (especially good, because most people used lard for frying in those days); many potato salads, made with mashed potatoes, rounded over and covered with slices of boiled egg; there were slices of home-smoked and baked ham; chicken and dumplings; chicken pie; maybe even some fried squirrel or rabbit; green beans cooked with ham or fat meat until they were dark brownish green; cole slaw; maybe some early radishes. At the other end of the table were desserts: every imaginable kind of pie—apple, cherry, blackberry, banana cream, chocolate cream, lemon meringue; many cakes— chocolate, banana, spice, coconut covered, etc., etc. Children ate and then played; grownups ate and then talked—doing a lot of remembering and telling (or re-telling) stories of past good times (and bad) with family members now resting out there in the cemetery.

This Memorial Day I happened to be house-bound with an aggravated case of bronchitis, which kept me from being with the Bench family for an annual gathering at Fern's place at Mason Lake in Washington—so the TV was my companion. Watching the many Memorial Day-related programs for the three-day celebration gave me a chance to probably think more deeply about the meaning and value of this annual time that is set aside for remembering and honoring those who worked, and even died, to preserve freedom. It was also

403

a date to salute men and women of today's armed forces, now at war against terrorism, defending our homeland, and still dying.

CNN televised live the dedication of the World War II Memorial on the Mall in Washington, D.C. on Saturday. What a grand monument it is—and it's dedicated to all who served during WWII: 16 million military people, more than 400,000 who died, and the millions who supported the war effort from home. It is hoped the Memorial will inspire future generations, deepening their appreciation of what the WWII generation accomplished in securing freedom and democracy.

Designed by Friedrich St. Florian, it is constructed with marble, plus bronze artwork to symbolize the work and dedication of all Americans in unbelievable unified efforts, not only to preserve our own freedoms, but to liberate millions of others suffering under dictatorships. Two huge marble arches, opposite each other across the reflecting pool and fountains, represent the Atlantic and the Pacific areas of conflict. Each state and territory is represented by a marble pedestal hung with a double bronze wreath—one of oak leaves to represent the contributions of industry; one of wheat representing the contributions of agriculture. Twisted bronze ropes connect the upright pedestals, denoting the unity of all the states.

The Master of Ceremonies, and one of the speakers, was retired General P.X. Kelley, a former Marine Corps Commandant, who for a few years has been Chairman of the Memorial Commission. (In the summer of 1966, Gene received command of the 2nd Battalion, 4th Marines from him in Vietnam, so I've had the pleasure of knowing him for the past fifteen years when we've attended annual 2/4 reunions.) Bob Dole was a Commission Chairman before General Kelley and was another speaker—relating some of his personal experiences as a WWII veteran. Tom Hanks, after starring in the movie *Saving Private Ryan*, became dedicated to the idea of the memorial and contributed greatly in many ways to the project. He had stirring words to say about the war effort, and about the great work of reconstruction at the end of it. It was the largest war of all time, and in many ways, defined the character of our nation. Many aged veterans and their families were present, some were interviewed, and all were honored.

On Sunday evening the annual Memorial Day concert was televised by PBS, live from the west lawn of the U.S. Capitol. This was its fifteenth year on the air, and it offered a special segment on the 60th anniversary of the D-Day landing on Normandy beaches on June 6, 1944. Tribute was paid to troops serving now in Afghanistan and Iraq—with special focus on wounded service members, and stories of children who have lost parents to war. The host for this program was Ossie Davis, actor and WWII veteran. Some guests were the U.S. Joint Chiefs of Staff; actor Charles Durning, a U.S. Army veteran of Normandy; and actor Joe Mantegna. Music was provided by the National Symphony Orchestra, directed by Erich Kunzel. Some principal singers were Brian Stokes-Mitchell and Marin Mazey of Broadway musicals, who sang many WWII era songs, sometimes asking the audience to join in. Violinist Joshua Bell made several romantic war-time songs come to beautiful life; and country music star Brad Paisley, playing his guitar, sang two of his touching compositions that gave tribute to wives and families: *When You Say Nothing At All*, and *I Live For Little Moments*. At the end of the concert, combined choruses and soloists with the orchestra sang, *Let There Be Peace on Earth, And Let It Begin with Me.*

The next hour on PBS showed a video of the history of the construction of the Memorial—eleven years in the making. There was an interesting interview with a WWII vet who was one of the construction workers. At the beginning of the project there was a lot of criticism of its location between the Washington and Lincoln Memorials—worry that it would obstruct the grand view of that space with the reflecting pool. The designer then suggested lowering the "floor" of it to six feet below the street level, maintaining the almost unobstructed view of the Mall. Washington D.C. will host a summer-long salute to those who served during WWII that will include more than a hundred WWII-theme exhibitions, performances, and walking tours in the D.C. area. Hotel packages will be offered, and a parade salute to America's Greatest Generation will be offered on July 4.

As uncomfortable and weak as I felt with that "Bronchitis Bug," it almost seemed that it might have been a "coincidence that really wasn't a coincidence." Staying at home with it gave me an opportunity to experience some touching thoughts, reviving memories of those war days that made them more meaningful now than when I was part of the whole thing as a late teenager. Who knows where these present military actions will eventually lead? It's good to remember the unity and strength of Americans in the past, and to hope that it might some day be possible for all people of the world to live in peace!

THANKSGIVING DAYS—2003 and SOME OTHER YEARS

Thanksgiving Day this year (2003) with my children and two grandsons was a very special time. With Becky's family living in Seattle, Thomas in his first year of school, and everyone busy with work and various activities, we sometimes find two or three months had gone by without being together. Thomas and Evan always look forward to seeing Uncle David and Aunt Michelle, because they know they're going to have some quality "play time"! In the past, their play has been mostly active—outside, running, chasing, hiding, batting or throwing balls, etc. Weather this year, and the boys' increasing maturity, made indoor games more pleasant, with building blocks, a Bingo-like game using picture cards, and even some chess added to the "inside" action.

Dinner was a whole-family activity, which was great for me (still recovering from Shingles on my face). Some food was traditional, some was new. Traditional turkey, dressing, and gravy; Becky's cranberry-orange sauce; David and Michelle's usual pumpkin and apple pies; sparkling apple cider served in the Waterford wine glasses; Brussels sprouts—made with a <u>new</u> recipe, combining them with baby carrots and pearl onions. New additions were David's fruit salad with honey-lime dressing, and mashed potatoes instead of sweet potatoes because the little ones like them better. The kitchen and dining rooms were like bee hives with people moving among each other doing table setting, cooking and cleaning up, visiting, and managing to stay out of each others' way. I mostly got to play with Thomas and Evan!

The day got me to thinking about other Thanksgiving days. For some reason, my memories about celebrations as a child, when we lived in the country near Dixon, seem quite "foggy." I even called my sisters and a brother for some reminders from them—but they weren't much help. This makes me think that maybe there wasn't very much "tradition"—especially concerning dinner; but all of us remember Grandpa Kelley and Ross going hunting early in the morning and frequently bringing back some squirrel and/or rabbit for Mom to fry. At school, we studied about the Pilgrims and the first Thanksgiving. That project covered reading, history, and art—drawing pictures, making construction-paper cutouts of Pilgrim families, Indian guests, turkeys, and corn for pinning to the bulletin boards, and sticking to the windows. Sometimes a few children put on a little "play," and often someone read (or memorized) Lydia Child's "Thanksgiving Day" poem that begins,

"Over the river and through the wood." I don't remember ever being at my grandparents' farm at Devils Elbow, Missouri, on Thanksgiving. Part of the reason might have been that it was twenty-five or so miles to their place, the cold weather, and the fact of our frequent lack of transportation.

Mom and Dad moved to Columbia, Missouri, in 1947, when Barbara and I were there in college, and Ross was in the Army. By that time, Thanksgiving dinners for them had been somewhat "modernized": turkey, if several people were there, a roast chicken or a duck if Mom and Dad were alone. And, there were always many kinds of "trimmings"—dressing, gravy, sweet potato casserole topped with baby marshmallows, home-canned pickles, and vegetable relish, green beans, pumpkin pie, mincemeat pie, and more than likely, a blackberry or peach cobbler. Mom's mother and Dad's father lived with them at different times in their later years, so we looked forward to being with all of them when we could—hearing many colorful stories from them about "back when"!

In 1952 and 1953, Gene and I lived in Naples, Italy, in an upstairs apartment with a very modest kitchen. The stove was gas with two burners on top, and an oven not much larger than an average modern microwave oven. It would cook two layers of cake, or one cookie sheet-size pan of something, or a small roast at a time. A Thanksgiving turkey was <u>not</u> one of the <u>Italians'</u> traditions. But, at our American commissary, frozen American turkeys were available—and we wanted to enjoy that special "touch of home" if we could just find a way to cook a bird that large! Gene had made friends of the chefs at some of the local restaurants where he and various friends frequently went for lunch, so he asked one of them for a suggestion—and a pizza oven that would do it was found. Gene wrote down for them the 325-degree temperature, and the time it would need to roast. The pizza chef said, "Oh! No, no, no! No po-si-bi-le!" He then explained that the heat in his oven would be more like 450 degrees, or more; and the turkey would be perfectly cooked in a much shorter time—something like an hour or two, as I remember. We had invited some American friends to come for dinner, which we tried to make as "traditional" as possible, with the foods and preparation equipment that were available to us. The men went to pick up the turkey at the appointed time, and a juicier bird, none of us had ever tasted! It was beautifully browned, with a crisp crust, and had been baked with celery, garlic, and rosemary inside it. What a feast we had! I don't remember all the side dishes, but I doubt there was gravy, and I'm sure there was delicious Italian wine!

I've never since had the courage to try roasting a turkey in such a hot oven! Maybe I just haven't had enough wine!

THANKSGIVING—2005

I'm reading a book in which the author listed, in the front of the book, the names and relationships of the people in the story before beginning with Chapter One, so I'll try that technique with this one:

Rebecca (Becky) Butler—my daughter, whose family lives in Seattle;

Brian Butler—Becky's husband;

Thomas—their seven-year-old son;

Evan—their five-year-old son

David Bench—my son, who lives in Crawfordsville, Oregon (a very small town between Brownsville and Sweet Home;

Michelle Bench—David's wife.

In "the olden days" (when Becky and David were children), we frequently spent Thanksgiving with Gene's parents in Puyallup, Washington. But after they left home, our house became the usual meeting place for the family Thanksgiving gathering. It has seemed an especially good location, since grandchildren (and one great-grandson) joined the family.

This year I had a phone call from Becky early in November saying that Thomas seemed especially interested in his school's celebration of Grandparents' Day and wondered if I would like to come share it with him on Tuesday, the 22nd. Well, of <u>course</u> I would! She said I could go to Seattle on the train and ride back to Corvallis with them, to be at my home for our family Thanksgiving later that week. That meant some extra logistical planning in order to have everything in place at home for serving Thanksgiving dinner on the 24th! The house cleaners were due to be here on Tuesday of that week, so I had to provide them with a house key to use in my absence. David and Michelle traditionally bring fruit salad and a couple of pies, so that helped with the food preparation. The turkey was a major concern. I usually reserved a fresh one from Richey's, which I picked up on Tuesday or Wednesday; but for me to be able to leave on the 6:30 a.m. train on Monday, the bird would need to be in my refrigerator on Sunday—or be picked up before 9:00 p.m. Wednesday evening. Both of those plans seemed risky. What if the power should go off while I was gone, and the bird would get too warm? Or, even more likely, what if traffic delayed us and we'd not get back to Corvallis by 9:00

p.m.? The answer seemed to be a <u>frozen</u> one to be thawing in my fridge. And we'd need a quick supper when we got to Corvallis on Wednesday evening.

Monday morning was one of those quite foggy ones so typical in Oregon, so I allowed myself a little extra time for driving to the Amtrak station in Albany. The old building has recently been restored with some remodeling; and a large, well-lighted, paved parking lot has been added where travelers can leave cars without charge—but they don't open the station doors until 8:00 a.m., so the "waiting room" is outside under a wide eave. Thankfully, it wasn't raining, and conversation with other people who were waiting made it pleasant. We had a scenic ride to Seattle, only a few minutes past the scheduled arrival time. (Passenger trains have to give right-of-way to freight trains on this route, which sometimes requires some short delays on side-tracks.) Becky and an excited Evan were waiting for me.

Tuesday morning, I rode with Becky to drop the boys off at their respective schools—Thomas and me, first. Grandparents were to register in the school auditorium, enjoy some beverages and pastries, and visit together while waiting to be escorted to the children's rooms, or to tour the campus. Thomas was in the second grade at Evergreen School, which serves grades from kindergarten to eighth grade. This was his third "Grandparents' Day." His room was ready for guests at 9:45. Six students were present; six were absent.

Each child introduced his grandparent (or in some cases a "grand-friend") and went to the wall map to mark the location of the grandparent's home. Thomas was chosen as the first volunteer to make his introduction. His teacher, Mrs. Debbie Reddy, gave us a summary of some of the things they are studying, then grandparent and child looked through folders of work, with time to talk about each thing.

After that came two "presentations" by the children. The first one was an in-unison reading of a poem the children had completed, having been given the first four lines. It was titled "Pickles." The kids were almost too "giggly" to read it, so it was great fun. The next presentation was called "Furry Flyers...All About Bats." The different lines were read by various individuals, with all of them joining in for the end. It was obvious that they had had a "learning experience."

Next, was an early lunch of "Stone Soup"—vegetables having been brought by the children. With that, we had rolls, veggies and dip, cranberry muffins, and chocolate turkeys the children had made with cookies, chocolate rounds and chips, with a red-hot candy for the waddle. Butter for our rolls was provided at the child's table from a jar containing butter they had churned themselves the day before, by shaking whipping cream in a baby food jar!

Becky came to pick me up on her way to bring Evan home after his half-day school.

Wednesday was Evan's turn to entertain. His school served a Thanksgiving "feast" for parents and other family members. Thomas was off from his school, so he was also with us. The children had made simple costumes for themselves with a large, decorated paper bag as a jacket. Appropriate hats, along with the jackets, described their characters—Indians or Pilgrims. They had also made place mats of colorful woven construction paper, and small candy cups shaped like Pilgrim hats. Parents and guests lined up in the hall, and when we reached the door, Evan was there to meet us, and to escort us to our table. He had told us the day before that we would sit at "the long" table. He said, "I just can't wait to see what it will be like!" It was long enough for four people on each side—and had built-on benches for seating—high enough for a 5-year-old's feet to touch the floor! Evan introduced each one of us. About me, he said, "This is my Grandma Bench, but you can call her Ila."

Children here entertained us with a little song:
"Hello, Mr. Turkey, how are you? Hello, Mr. Turkey, how are you?
With a gobble, gobble, gobble, and a wobble, wobble, wobble,
Hello, Mr. Turkey, how are you!"

Another presentation, in unison was:
"Mr. Turkey ran away—what shall we eat Thanksgiving Day?"
That was followed with someone saying,
"Pumpkin Pie!"
The next time someone said,
"Brussels Sprouts"
Etc, with various things, until the last one was:
"CANDY!"—shouted in unison!

The "feast" consisted of "Friendship Soup" (contributed and made with children's assistance); corn muffins; Little Sizzlers in blankets; a small stem-shaped cup of apple juice; and pumpkin pie that some of the mothers had contributed.

LOVE IS ALL THAT MATTERS

Our car was packed, and ready to leave for Oregon when lunch was over at noon. We found <u>very</u> heavy traffic, which slowed at times to just creeping for awhile—arriving in Corvallis at 7:30 p.m.—two hours longer than normal driving time—but with the various things they carried with them in the car for entertainment, the boys were very patient.

I was really impressed with the boys' enthusiasm and "public" social graces, and I knew the trip was totally worth while when Thomas said to me while we were in his class-room, "Grandma, this is the <u>first time</u> I've had a grandparent with me for Grandparents' Day!"

CHRISTMAS TREES—THEN AND NOW

This past Christmas season, in 2006, has been for me a time of considering Christmas trees. For the past four years, I haven't had one. One of those years I was invited to Seattle to be with Becky's family and Brian's mother who came from Maryland. The other three years, I suppose a tree just didn't seem important to me. I hung swags of greens and holly outside by the doors, made greens and holly arrangements for tables, and bought some nice poinsettia plants. But this year, I felt that I should get back to having a tree, because a tree really adds so much to the Christmas spirit. Decisions, decisions—should it be a small, fragrant fresh one that I would really <u>like</u>, or should it be a fake one that might be easier to manage? With those thoughts, many memories came to mind of other Christmas trees that had been in my life—some of them quite important.

I don't remember much about the Christmas decorations during my earliest years in the country near Dixon, Missouri. The house was so small, there wouldn't have been very much room for a tree, but I think there might have been small, table-sized ones of fresh cedar from our nearby woods. I do remember some delicate glass ornaments of various shapes. One was a colorful bird with a tail made of a bunch of long, soft, bristle-like stuff, sitting on a metal clip to use to attach it to a branch. Some ornaments were spherical with two sides that looked "pushed in," making shiny, raised designs inside of them. Some others had an elongated lower section that came to a point at the bottom. And I remember that a large red, honey-combed tissue paper bell (that folded flat for storage) was always hung in the middle of the ceiling; and twisted streamers went out from there to each corner of the room.

After we moved from there, and lived in towns, we had trees about six feet tall, and even had strings of electric lights for them—in addition to collected ornaments and the decorations we made ourselves, such as popcorn strings, and chains made of links of colored paper. Some of Mom's quilting cotton was sometimes used underneath—to look like snow. One of my sisters remembers beating Dreft suds into thick foam and putting it on branches to represent snow.

A very special tree was the one Gene and I had on our first Christmas together. We lived on a farm for a short time that fall and winter of 1948, so we cut a small cedar from the woods, and placed it on an end table by the couch. It was no more than about two and a half or three feet tall and was quite "fat" with branches growing close together. We were too poor to buy decorations for it, so we made our own: strings of popcorn and cranberries, and ornaments of colored paper and shiny foil. Central Dairy at that time was using crimped foil covers on their milk bottles. A special color was used for each different product, such as red on whole milk, gold on cream, blue on buttermilk, green on chocolate milk, and silver on skim milk. Mom used a lot of milk of different kinds for the meals she served to some college boys, so she saved the bottle covers for us. They could be cut, shaped, or combined into all kinds of decorative, shiny things to "dress up" our little tree! We even invited my family (eight adults and a small child) to come for Christmas dinner! The people who had lived on the farm before we moved in had a sizeable garden that still had some vegetables we could harvest: there were greens, potatoes, carrots, and cabbages that had the original heads cut out. Each of those cabbage plants continued to grow tiny little heads, about the size of Brussels sprouts, around the center where each leaf grew from the stalk. Very tasty! Gene took his "22" rifle out around the farm and "harvested" some of the hundreds of rabbits for our meat, and Mom brought some pies, so we had an interesting "feast"! Roasted rabbit with dressing is what one might call "gourmet"!

Christmas in Minneapolis in 1959, was special because it was our first one with our first child—Rebecca Anne! She was just four months old but was really attracted to the lights and shiny things on a tree that occupied space on the floor by the living room picture window. We decided we should spend Christmas that year with my Mom and Dad in Missouri. Gene was especially conscious of careful driving with our precious baby in her little portable bed in the back seat. (No seat belts or child restraints in those days.) Suddenly a car in front of us caused him to suddenly slow down, and our car went into a skid, and headed down an embankment. He managed to keep it from overturning, bumping along over rocks and rough ground. It so happened that there was a small bridge across the ditch at the bottom of the bank that the car just happened to be aligned with for crossing into a business parking area, where he was finally able to stop. In the meantime, I was on my knees, hanging over the back of my seat, holding Becky down in her bed! We discovered the car had a dented gas tank and some other damages, but was drivable, so we continued the day-long drive safely—only emotionally "going to pieces" after we arrived at the Kelleys'.

Our first Christmas with David was in Corvallis in 1964. He was born July 4, 1963 but didn't come to live with us until February 1964. Having a little brother made that Christmas special for Becky—and for us!

In 1966, while Gene was in Vietnam, Becky, David, and I lived in Columbia, Missouri on Proctor Drive. We had a tree, but I don't remember anything spectacular or "abnormal" about it. My Dad must have helped me get it into the house and onto its stand. Mom and Dad came to spend Christmas Eve night with us, were great helpers for Santa, and then we all enjoyed Christmas Day "playing" together. David was three, and Becky was seven years old.

In Hawaii we had the same tree for two years in a row—1967 and 1968. The cut trees that were for sale there had come from Oregon or Washington and were already beginning to dry out when they arrived. We decided to get a potted Norfolk Island pine which we could move outside after Christmas, and let it continue to grow in its pot. By the next year it had grown about a foot and was even more beautiful! We didn't want to use lights that would maybe make the boughs unhappy with their heat, but its open branches made a great way to enjoy special ornaments we'd been collecting through the years. Its place of honor was in the corner of the living room where two windows met. It was so warm we often had the windows open, and it seemed quite strange to have the shiny "icicles" blowing off the Christmas tree! My Mom and Dad came for a Christmas and New Year vacation with us in 1968. By that time Gene knew he'd be getting orders in the spring, so it was a good time to put our special tree into the ground. One of Dad's hobbies was planting trees wherever he went, so he and Gene planted this one as his "Hawaiian tree" in our yard which was a large corner lot. It liked its permanent home and grew to be much taller than the house. Friends sent us a photo of it several years later, and Gene visited it again in the early 1990's when he was in Hawaii on business.

Our Christmas in 1970 was in London, where we lived for three months. There we had a tiny tree, about two or three feet tall, which we decorated with home-made things and chocolate ornaments wrapped in colored foil—made for that purpose. Becky and David thought it was quite novel that when we took the tree down, we ate the ornaments! Another story tells about Christmas fun that year, including a surprise of snow on Christmas morning!

We finally "settled down" on Overlook Drive in Corvallis in 1973. Becky was fourteen, David was ten. For the next few years we had fun going for family treks and finding our special U-Cut tree. Some of the farms served hot chocolate and cookies.

We had bought the grassy vacant lot that adjoined us to the southeast, and before long we discovered fir seedlings coming up here and there. When they became Christmas tree size, the field became our tree source. We didn't prune them like the professional tree farmers do—they just grew naturally, making the branches far enough apart to allow ornaments to "swing free." New trees were growing every year, so there were varying sizes, and we still had many left to stay for full growth. In September 2000, Gene became a victim of cancer and had surgery in October. He was battling that with chemo and radiation treatments that kept him house-bound. Becky brought her boys to stay the week before Christmas with us, which was a really special treat! Having them here was Gene's best medicine! Thomas was two, and Evan was just six months.

One day while Gene and I were gone for a radiation treatment, Becky took the boys with her and went down into our field where she cut a Christmas tree from the ones growing there. Evan rode in her backpack while she carried a saw in one hand and held Thomas by his hand with her other one. While she worked with the saw, Evan watched from his parked backpack, and Thomas played nearby. By the time we came home she had dragged it to the garage door, and the next day, she and Thomas decorated it while Gene and I played with Evan and joined in the fun. And so, another special tree lifted our spirits! Brian came on the train, and with David and Michelle, we had our family Christmas a couple of days early so the Butlers could be in their own home on the 25th.

In the fall after Gene's death in 2001, I discovered a small fir tree that had been damaged by loggers who had cut some dead firs behind our shed. It looked to be a perfect size for a Christmas tree, so my yard-man cut it for me and helped put it into the stand. I called it my "Charlie Brown" tree. I "helped" its shape on the lower right-hand side by adding a branch that I stuck into the stand and secured it with some wire!

But what about THIS year? After some shopping around, I decided to buy a small artificial Noble Fir. I <u>had</u> to have one with wide-apart branches so ornaments could hang free! But ... I waited too long to get it. In every place I looked, it had sold out. So, I bought a small Doug fir from the Boy Scout Troop 3 lot. (I discovered that the same size of Noble fir was too heavy for me to lift with both hands, and it <u>had</u> to be light enough for me to handle alone.) After it sat in water for a few days, I decided to bring it in on the Saturday before Christmas. First, I had to saw off some lower branches to give it room to go into the stand. Then, after struggling with it for the best part of an hour, trying to get it straight in the stand—holding the trunk of it with left hand, bending down to turn the screws into place on the stand, my back began giving me some messages that it was getting unhappy. And I didn't even have it into the house yet! I said to myself, "Self, how important is this tree? Is it possible someone else might enjoy it more? You'd even get a bonus of the hours needed for decorating it! If you find a charity that can use it, you'll know it's the right thing to do!"

I first called Love, Inc., a group to whom I've donated things before. Answering machine. I had to talk to a <u>person</u> for this project. Community

Outreach had all they could use, but they knew of a group trying to get a shelter for homeless men ready to open that night where it might be of use. I called that number, and the lady who answered said they would be delighted! I even included with it a box of new LED indoor-outdoor lights, and a bag of holly that was left over from what I'd cut from my trees for my own use—and it was picked up the next day by the Coalition for Sheltering Homeless People! I felt almost "giddy"! A great load had been lifted, and I hoped those people felt as happy as I did! (Next year I'll shop earlier to find my "fake" tree!)

Several years later: I DID shop earlier that next year and found a quite nice-shaped small tree that was "just my size"! Then, in 2012, when I moved to my apartment in an assisted living facility, even that little tree was too large for the space available for it. But I want you to know that I discovered it's very important to my "spirit" to celebrate Christmas with a tree—and I DID find an even smaller one that I've happily enjoyed here! For decorations I use my "old" star (that Gene made long ago); and load the branches with some small angels, and some ornaments my kids made when they were small children. With that, there's no doubt about my "my Christmas Spirit"!

Chapter 7: Other Family

MY PARENTS' "WORKING" HONEYMOON

Bertha Ross and Sterling Ray Kelley were married on June 22, 1924, in Dixon, Missouri, which was near my Dad's home. Mom was born, and lived her life until then, at Devils's Elbow, Missouri, on a homesteaded river-bottom farm; and in that community they met and carried on their courtship. When we children were small, our favorite thing about bedtime was hearing Mom tell us "bedtime stories"—and the ones we almost always asked for were the ones about her meeting Dad, their courtship, and marriage! It must have given us a good feeling to imagine the two of them, being young, and having fun together!

I have often thought about what it must have been like for Mom to become involved with a man like Dad. She has said that her first impression of him was that he was a real "smart aleck"—always teasing and playing tricks on his friends, "taking charge" of conversations, or choosing the songs when they were together at music parties at some neighbor's home. Those parties were called "singin's." She just wasn't interested in those "rowdy" boys who were temporarily in the area, working for farmers. (Dad, and his cousin, Lee Kelley, were working at gathering in the corn for the Hunter family—good friends of the Ross family.) Mom said that one of Dad's tricks the first time they were together was slipping the chair out from under one of the "boys" as he started to sit down, causing him to fall to the floor instead! However, they found themselves together at other parties—where she was the one who played the organ for their singing—so it wasn't like she was going to just tell him to "stay out of her life"!

I suppose I have some idea of her feelings, remembering how I felt when I first met Gene Bench who was to become <u>my</u> husband. Both Mom and I were studious, rather quiet, and not what one would call "adventurous." I had never traveled out of my home state, but Mom had hardly been out of her home county! These new men in our lives were "different"! They had both had many "worldly" escapades: Dad and his father traveled with a circus for a few years when Dad was grade-school age, and later worked in the Kansas wheat harvest—traveling north with the threshing crews as the wheat ripened. Gene had lived in Oklahoma, as well as in southern Missouri, and had been in the Marine Corps for about three years with duty in the South Pacific during World War II. Both Gene and Dad were full of life and eager to live life "to the hilt," which included girls, and living what we might call "on—or near—the edge"!

Dad, no doubt, during conversations when they were getting acquainted, told her about what it was like to live in Corpus Christi, Texas—where it was warm, even in the winter, and you could just pick oranges and lemons right off the trees—about walking on the sandy beach of the Gulf shore, finding pretty shells and watching water birds that people in Missouri had never seen! He liked meeting new people, and found them all interesting in their own special ways; so he must have told her about the circus entertainers, the comedians, and the musicians in the minstrel show that was part of the circus program—especially the lively rhythm man who taught Dad how to "play bones," how to hold them between certain fingers and shake his hands in a certain way to make them click together. And, he no doubt would have told about the excitement of traveling to different towns on the circus train—and about <u>his</u> job of going through the grandstands selling popcorn and peanuts!

For much of her life, one of Mom's choice jobs on the farm was the late afternoon hunt for the cows and bringing them in from woods and meadow pastures for the evening milking. On these excursions, with only her Collie dog as a companion, she must have wondered about the world beyond those lovely hills and valleys—places she would have read about in her school books. So she would have found Dad an exciting person, who brought to her probably monotonous life, some answers and reality to her curiosity.

In the meantime, becoming more interested in Mom, and realizing that some of the entertainment he'd found with many of the other girls he'd met wouldn't be available with her, and discovering that she didn't like his drinking and smoking, Dad toned down his behavior when he was with her; and made friends with the rest of the family, too. Church was important to Mom and all of the Ross family (there were twelve children), so if Dad was to be able to use his one day off to spend with her, he had to go to church with them. As a result of that, he, too, became a Christian; and gave up his alcohol, cigarettes, and "riotous living."

Mom has said she felt sorry for Dad because he had no mother, so she must have been very happy to see the very close relationship that developed between him and her own mom. (His mother and dad separated when he was four, and his "mothering" had come from his Grandmother Kelley.)

I heard the story of Dad's proposal, and Mom's acceptance, so many times as a child, I almost feel as if I were there—maybe from up in the branches of the cherry tree under which they were sitting and visiting in the shade! Dad was making plans to go to Kansas to work in the wheat harvest for the summer, and they were sort of saying their "farewells." Mom sang for him the song, *"Red River Valley,"* which begins with, "From this valley they say you are going; I shall miss your brown eyes and sweet smiles." That must have struck like an arrow right into Dad's heart, as their separation became more of a reality to him. So he said, "Why don't you go with me?" She said, "What could I do if I went?" and he answered, "You could cook!" He kept talking about how nice it would be if they could both go—and I can imagine that Mom was thinking about how much fun it would be to have an adventure like that! But being the demure person she was, she said, "The folks wouldn't want me to go." That makes me think she was deciding that going would be <u>her</u> choice but needed to feel more secure with the family blessing.

That evening Dad walked with Grandpa to the barn at chore time, and along the way, asked if Bertha could go with him to Kansas. Grandpa said, "Well … you'd have to get married first." I can imagine that it was all Dad could do to keep from jumping up and down with joy, as he seriously assured Grandpa that marriage was, of course, in his plan!

They had only one week to prepare—the harvest train would leave from Dixon the next Sunday—but Mom told him she would be ready!

When I think about the months of planning that went into my own wedding, I can imagine that Mom must have been almost frantic—the first problem being what to wear! She didn't have time to sew anything new! She consulted a dear friend, Mrs. Gilkey, for whom she had done a lot of house work, sewing, and quilting. Mrs. Gilkey suggested Mom's nearly-new brown satin dress which she had trimmed with gold and red beads around the neck, on the sleeves, and in panel designs on the skirt. There wouldn't be time for her to change before boarding the train, and the brown color of the dress would be good for traveling. Dad had recently bought a new "Hart-Shafner & Marx" dark gray suit with narrow, black satin bindings on the lapels. I remember both the suit and the dress! They were worn for several years—maybe ten! (My sister Barbara even still has the dress!)

Dad made the arrangements for the wedding in Dixon at his Great-aunt Sarah Mitchell's home; and his Uncle Jim Kelley performed the ceremony. Mom's sister Cora was her Maid of Honor, and sister Nellie made a little basket of red roses for her to carry.

After the ceremony and wedding dinner, Mom began her first train ride! How exciting it must have been—looking out the window as new and strange countryside came into view! The train would have stopped in many of the small towns where she could see people going about their business—horse-drawn wagons and buggies, and more cars than she had ever seen around her home. Soon the landscape would have drastically changed to flat terrain, fewer trees, and miles of golden wheat looking like large waves as the wind blew over it. She would have noticed sunflowers growing along the way, because she dearly loved all kinds of flowers.

Their first stop was in Garfield, Kansas. They began the harvest with Mr. Richards, where Dad had made his first harvest in 1919. Next, they worked for the Charley Aldrich family. There, they had a private room, and Mom worked in the kitchen. The farmers gave their farm hands a generous, hot dinner at noon, so extra kitchen help was needed, too. Mom was paid $2.00 per day, and Dad's pay was $5.00 for a day. When threshing was done there, Dad went to harvest in Dodge City, leaving Mom to work longer at the Aldrich farm.

While in Dodge City, Dad bought a Ford touring car, which was a big help for their transportation. Mom must have had fun trying to learn to drive! The dirt roads weren't very wide, and about the only time she had to practice was after work in the evening. She used to tell us stories about learning all about how to put on the brakes, and give it gas, but there were so many jack-rabbits—and the rabbits looked so funny with their long ears—she would get to watching the rabbits hopping along down the road in front of the car, and would almost follow them when they decided to get off the road! She decided she didn't want to bother with learning to drive, and I think she never even tried again.

After wheat harvest ended, they drove to Manford, Oklahoma, where Mom's Aunt Minnie and Uncle Pony were working. Dad went to work building oil tanks, and Mom again worked in a kitchen. Along the way, they visited some cousins of Dad's in Lyons and Chase, then headed back to Missouri; and arrived in Dixon, close to Grandpa Kelley's birthday, November 26th. They stayed with him while they began clearing trees and sprouts, then building their house on the nearby little 10-acre farm Dad had bought. Friends and relatives pitched in to help, because Mom and Dad wanted to be settled in time for their first baby to be born in June! They even had a couple of months to spare! The baby was me—Ila May! on the first day of summer—June 21, 1925—one day before their first "happy anniversary"!

GRANDMA ROSS

My Mom's mother, Oda May Delancy, was born on November 8, 1868, in Tennessee, to Andrew Jackson DeLancy and Lydia Ann Drolsbaugh. Andrew was a tailor by trade, born in Pennsylvania, January 17, 1846, and was in the Confederate Army. Soon after Grandma's birth they moved from Tennessee to Pea Ridge which was about ten miles east of Devil's Elbow, Missouri. Andrew rented a farm on the Gasconade River which was a few miles from their home, and when Grandma was a teenager, she often went with her dad to the farm and did their cooking while they worked a few days at a time. I don't remember hearing how she met my Grandpa, Joseph E. Ross, but in my mom's stories of her life, she says that the Hooker school house was half way between the DeLancy farm and the Ross farm, so she thought that Hooker was probably where they met. After they were married, on March 16, 1889, they lived on the Ross farm that Grandpa's parents (Daniel and Sarah Callahan Ross) had homesteaded at Devil's Elbow.

According to Mom's story, Devil's Elbow is named after a bend in the Big Piney River that winds through lovely south-Missouri hills. The tall bluffs, blue river, and rich bottom land make "The Elbow" a picture of colors and life. The Piney is fed by many pure springs and runs clear, over gravel shoals. It lies calm, and full of fish in the deep eddies. The farm had fine fields along the river banks and rocky, wooded hills that overlooked that valley. Mom's story says, "When God created the world, he must have been really proud of 'The Elbow'!"

Grandma must have been a really hard worker. About six years after they were married, and the birth of three of their twelve children, Grandpa got something wrong with his eyes, which they called "granulated lids." He became nearly blind, and wasn't able to run the farm, so the neighbors built a smaller log house for the family up on the hill, and they rented out the farm. The blindness lasted for several years and Mom said Grandpa spent many days lying under the bed so the light wouldn't hurt his eyes. In evenings after chores were done, the children did school lessons, and Grandma often read to Grandpa.

She loved to read and was a good scholar. The doctor couldn't find a cure for his eyes, but Grandpa later met an old Indian who told him to bathe his eyes three times a day in warm salt water. He did, and that cured him. For the rest of his life he continued to bathe his eyes daily. I can remember seeing him take his wash pan of salt water outside for eye bathing when he was doing his morning face and hand washing.

It's hard for us with our many homemaking conveniences to imagine the energy Grandma must have had to put into rearing a family of twelve children. I wonder how many pairs of stockings she must have knit—how many BIG meals she cooked—how many dishes she washed—how much butter she churned—how many clothes she laundered—how many clothes she sewed and mended—how many noses she wiped (usually with the skirt of her apron)—how many "owies" she kissed—how many times she swept and mopped floors—how many buckets of water she

Ross Family: Jess, Dutch, Hub, Pete, Tuck, Nellie, Edna, Bert, Bun, Cora, Syb, Sue

carried from the spring—how many geese she plucked to get feathers for pillows and featherbeds—how many bars of soap she made—pretty much all by herself until the children began growing old enough to help with the unending hard work. Mom tells so much in her life-story book about their family life as she was growing up, you can get a good idea from that what kind of lady Grandma was!

In some of my childhood memories of Grandma at their home, I see her preparing the corn for feeding her chickens. She always wore a generous apron with big pockets, which was useful for many things. (Mom's book has a quote about the uses of "Grandma's Apron.")* She sat down in the kitchen with a sack of ears of corn by her side, her lap made a little wider and deeper. She took two ears of corn and used one of them to push the kernels of corn off the cobs and into her apron-covered lap until she had a sufficient amount shelled. Then she lit up her little clay pipe (carried in an apron pocket), gathered up her apron full of corn, and went out to the barnyard where she called, "Here, chick, chick, chick," as she took hand full after hand full of corn and swished it out to spread over the ground. That done, she went into the chicken-house and gathered the eggs—into her apron—to bring into the house. Mom told me that Grandma began smoking to ease the pain of some bad teeth when she was young, but she continued to smoke after she had dentures, seeming to find that time alone outside with her pipe a good time for her own relaxing.

Waking up in the morning, after sleeping upstairs on a fluffy featherbed, was a great experience for me! She always ground coffee from beans, so the fragrance from that pot that was brewing on the back of the wood cook stove was even better than from a Starbucks coffee shop. Mixed in with that, was the smell of home-smoked bacon and ham being fried; and big, buttermilk biscuits just ready to come out of the oven to be spread with fresh butter and homemade jam. There were many people of various ages and sizes to eat at the long table. For seating behind the table there was a bench that would seat maybe ten people—to give you an idea of the table's length. Various kinds of chairs, and stools were moved up to the ends and the other side of it. Sometimes there might be more people than could sit at the table at once, so there would be a "second sitting." Small children could stand up by their mothers.

After Grandpa died, and Grandma moved from the farm, she did a lot of visiting with several of her children, and our home seemed to be one of her favorite places. She finally moved in with Mom and Dad when she became unable to keep up her own place. To Dad, she had always seemed like a "substitute" mother, and he loved her deeply. They had great times discussing things like news, or politics, or books. She always met him at the door when he came home from work and took his lunch bucket to the kitchen for him. One of her greetings that Dad loved was, "There you are, you old Pup!"

To pass her time during the days when both Mom and Dad were at work, she read, pieced quilts, and kept the house totally free of dust. Mom and Dad subscribed to the Reader's Digest Condensed Book Club to help keep reading material for her, and she read the newspapers from cover to cover. She was a joy for all of us—never critical, always interested in our activities, and her wonderful sense of humor kept us happy with jokes and funny stories.

She passed away on November 20, 1955, just a few days after her 87th birthday, never recovering from a broken hip. Thank you, Grandma for giving me such a wonderful mother who learned from you how to work and laugh and manage, and especially to love!

* "*Grandma's Apron*" *(from Mom's book)*

There were a few things that Grandma had that modern ingenuity hasn't as yet replaced. Fast disappearing today is the old-fashioned apron Grandma used to wear. And Grandma's *apron was something she wore <u>every</u> day! It was big and had a hundred different uses. Principal use was to protect the dress underneath, but along with that, it served as a holder for removing hot pans from the oven. It was wonderful for wiping children's noses, drying children's tears, and also was used for cleaning out dirty ears.*

From the chicken coop the apron was used for carrying eggs, fuzzy chicks, and sometimes half-hatched eggs to be finished in the warming oven. When company came, those old aprons were ideal hiding places for shy kids, and when the weather was cold Grandma wrapped it around her arms.

Those big old aprons wiped many a perspiring brow bent over the hot wood stove. Chips and kindling wood were brought into the kitchen in that garment. From the garden it carried all sorts of vegetables. After the peas had been shelled, it carried the hulls out. In the fall, it was used to bring in apples that had fallen from the trees.

When unexpected company drove up the road, it was surprising how much furniture that old apron could dust in a matter of seconds. And when dinner was ready, Grandma walked out on the porch and waved her apron and the men knew it was time to come in from the field. It will be a long time before anyone invents something that will replace that old-time apron that served so many purposes.　　　　　　　　　　　*-Author Unknown*

GRANDMA KELLEY

Charley E. Kelley and Ila Etna Warren, my dad's parents, were married January 9, 1898, in Reynolds County, Missouri. They first lived in Flat River where daughter Tressa Rose was born on November 7, of that year, and a daughter named Golda was born on February 19, 1901, but died that same year on October 16. Then their son Sterling Ray was born on December 14, 1902, and they moved to St. Louis near the end of 1903.

When Dad was about four years old, his parents separated. The way Dad tells that story in his autobiography is that they were living in St. Louis where Grandpa had work in a packing plant and later as a motorman on a streetcar. He says, "On my parents' seventh wedding anniversary, January 9, 1905, Pop took my sister Tressa and me back to Dixon, his old home town. Mother stayed in St. Louis working, I think. My Dad expected her to come to Dixon after he built a house on his father's farm, but she never came back to us."

Grandma did return a few years later, and unbeknownst to any of the family or neighbors, took Aunt Tressa away, and was never heard of again until I was in high school.

Even in her absence I think hearing <u>about</u> her influenced my thinking, and no doubt a lot of that thinking was a result of my Mom's opinion of the whole thing. She, of course, couldn't imagine a mother leaving her two- and six-year-old children, and in her opinion, Grandma was "a poor excuse for a woman," an opinion that wasn't kept as her secret. I was aware as a child that Dad had many questions in his mind about what his mother might be like, and what life would have been like with her, because he wasn't able to remember her at all. Dad was close to his Aunt Zilla, Grandma's sister, who assured him that Grandma was a "good" lady, which didn't satisfy all of his curiosity, but helped his feelings. He must have had deep feelings of loneliness and wrote numerous poems from his imagination of her and of life with her. (Mom felt sorry for him and called his poetry-writing "brooding.")

But soon we were to have some curiosity satisfied. In the fall of 1937, Dad received a letter from his sister Tressa who then lived near their mother in Michigan! Aunt Tressa had had a "tiff" with Grandma and in their disagreement, Tressa used as a weapon the threat of revealing their whereabouts. She wanted to come to visit, if it would be O.K. with Dad and Grandpa Kelley, who lived only a quarter of a mile from us! Of course that was like a miracle to Dad—overjoyed with the prospect of at last meeting his long-lost sister who could possibly make it possible to also meet the mother he so longed to know! <u>My</u> mother wasn't so sure about the whole experience. There was no excitement in it for her. She was reserving her reactions for later when she actually got to know these two mysterious women now coming back into Dad's life.

Aunt Tressa's visit was exciting to us children. She had gifts for all of us, of course, and stories about some of the places they'd lived. She told about leaving Dixon with her mother so long ago; said her mother dressed her up as a boy and disguised herself with heavy makeup and a veiled hat before they went to catch the train out of Dixon. Grandpa had suspected the kidnapping when Aunt Tressa disappeared, so he went to the railroad station to intercept them—that being the only reasonable means of transportation available to a woman and a little girl. Aunt Tressa said she could have easily touched him as he stood there seeing them board the train, but not recognizing them!

Grandma had changed her name to Violet Smith, had married, and had another daughter named Bonnie who also lived in Michigan. Aunt Tressa's name had been changed, too, and she had married a man with the last name of Jamison, but I don't now remember their first names. (She had no children.) Dad didn't mention it in his autobiography, but if anyone in the family has access to any of his old address books, it might have been recorded there. Maybe even in some of his diaries which Joy has now.

I could tell Mom wasn't very happy with the whole visit, but she was a loyal wife, preparing "company" meals, and packing lunches for Dad and Aunt Tressa to take with them when they went out exploring the areas where they had lived and played as children. Looking back, I can probably realize Mom's feeling—Aunt Tressa didn't seem to include Mom as a very important part of Dad's life. She was so wrapped up in childhood memories and in analyzing Dad as a grown-up man, Mom was just sort of left out of her picture. Even Grandpa felt left out because her opinion of him had been colored by her mother's opinions.

When it was time for Aunt Tressa to leave, they decided that Dad would drive her back home to Michigan for him to meet his mother and half-sister. That further developed into him driving Aunt Tressa, Bonnie, and Grandma back to Missouri to visit Grandma's family (the Warrens) in Reynolds County, and to meet Mom and us children.

Their visit with us was quite short, so it took me a long time afterwards to get acquainted with the lady for whom I was named—and I'm not sure I ever did really know her. She was a devout Christian, wrote a lot of poetry, and seemed to be a quiet, very private sort of person. She eventually came back to live in Missouri around her childhood home where Dad (sometimes with Mom) visited her frequently for the remainder of her life. She and Grandpa never met again—by mutual agreement. Grandpa's assessment of the situation, expressed in his slow, country drawl was, "Well...it just seems to me that it's pretty often better to just let sleeping dogs lie."

I'm really sorry for the sadness my Dad suffered for so many years of not knowing his mother—or even knowing of her whereabouts—but I'm very pleased that by finding and knowing her in later years helped him to be happier and more content with memories of his life! Even though there wasn't time for me to really "know" her, I feel thankful to her and to Grandpa Kelley for some "good genes" that even now are part of me and my Kelley family!

GRANDPA KELLEY

My dad's father, Charley Edward Kelley, was pretty much a no-nonsense, no-frills kind of man. He believed in "don't talk if you've nothing to say," and the opinions he expressed had been wisely considered and were briefly stated. His philosophy consisted of "do unto others as you would have them do unto you," and he dearly loved his family, often coming to our house to play board games with us five children, or just to "set a spell."

Grandpa Kelley (far right) with Kelley cousins

His house that I knew was about a quarter of a mile south of ours, although most of his property was just across the road. "The road" was a country dirt road, occasionally maintained by the County—or the WPA—sometimes graveled, but still muddy in places after a lot of rain. His "land" was about five acres, and the little all-season creek that ran across our place crossed the road and continued east though his woods which was also a pasture for his Black Angus milk cow named "Blackie." A barbed wire fence enclosed his property, but we liked to go through the gate near the creek, walk on the path that went alongside the creek for a way, then curved through the woods, up a gently sloped hill to a gate that opened into his orchard. (I can still remember the feel of the cool ground on my bare feet, imagine the fragrance of the soil and forest, and hear the songs of several different kinds of birds.) Many of his orchard trees were peach, some of which ripened early enough for him to give me a birthday gift of a peach for each year of my age, on June 21. He also brought along enough peaches for Mom to make a peach cobbler, and, of course, he stayed for dinner, which we called "supper." (A few days later he would bring most of the rest of his peach crop, which Mom canned, giving half of them to him.) The path through the orchard ran along the fence on the east, soon coming to his yard and house.

One of the attractions in his yard was his croquet court. I don't know the size of it, but according to the Britannica Encyclopedia, an official regulation-size court is 40' by 75', so I expect that was the size of Grandpa's. It looked <u>level</u>, kept that way with an old grader blade which he dragged over it to cut

427

any grass or weeds that had the audacity to grow there. The soil contained enough clay that it was quite hard and packed. A ball didn't need to be hit very hard to send it to the next wicket, or even the length of the court! Grandpa's yard was a favorite place for men from the community to gather on summer Sunday afternoons to visit and play croquet. He was also a very good barber, so some of the men took time out from talking and playing croquet to get a haircut—the charge, a dime. At least three or four dogs usually lived with him—various kinds of hounds that he liked for hunting, and other strays that were looking for food and love which he generously gave.

There were several tall trees in that section of his yard—most of them White Oak, I think. Not far from the croquet court was a large workbench, a pile of mostly metal junk he sometimes bought at a sale, a vice, and a forge for blacksmithing. He frequently put new shoes on neighbors' horses, and my brother Ross thinks he made them himself. I've often watched him working at his forge, pounding shape into whatever it was he was making, then sticking it into water to cool it. I also liked to watch him sharpening saws, which were held in the vice while he pushed his file skillfully across each tooth. Every summer, a one-legged Mocking Bird sat in the tip-top of one of those tall trees—probably had a nest nearby. We knew it had only one leg, because Grandpa had a very strong telescope through which we could watch it!

To enter at the front of his house from the road, there was a "people-sized" gate made of wood near the mailbox, and a path leading straight to the door. A little to the north—straight out from the croquet court—was a wire gate we called a "gap" that opened wide enough for a car to go through. A curved path led from that gate to the door.

I'm having trouble remembering what flowers or shrubs there were— maybe some lilacs and/or snowball bushes. He liked flowers, and he had a small garden where he grew some things, so he might have had some flowers there among his vegetables. He grew one thing that was unusual to us—and delicious—a little orange and yellow striped fruit about the size of a tennis ball that was like a miniature melon and tasted something like a sweet cantaloupe. He called it pomegranate. He mowed his lawn grass with a reel push-mower from Montgomery Ward. To cut the orchard grass, which grew tall, he used a scythe—a reaper with a long, curved handle that had a curved cutting blade. If he wanted to bundle the grass as he cut it, he used a similar reaper with a "cradle" attached. The cradle had long teeth that held a bundle of cut grass together, which could then be picked up and formed into a "shock" which was several bundles, standing together upright. He let the grass dry for awhile, then put it into a haystack from which he fed his cow during the winter. He often helped us, as well as other neighbors, during the hay season.

Now, I'm about to get to the house itself. I always imagined that it was much like many of the houses that were built by the pioneers. Grandpa was content to live simply, and living alone, didn't need much space. None of us in that community had electricity or indoor plumbing, so that part of his life-style didn't seem unusual. He used a kerosene lamp inside the house and carried a kerosene lantern when he needed light outside, or for walking at night. The house was one room, built of hewn logs, chinked and filled between them with mud. There was one window on the south side, and the one door, made of solid wood, was on the west. To enter, one stepped over a threshold about eight inches high onto the packed-dirt floor. The interior walls were just the interior side of the logs.

To the left of the door along the wall were hooks for his coats and hats. There was also a professional barber's chair—black leather seat, back, padded arms, head-rest, and foot-rest. Much of the metal was chrome, in fancy curved shapes. The foot-rest could be folded toward the chair to expose the padded part for resting one's legs or left up to make a step for feet. With a lever, the back would recline. And it swiveled! You can imagine what fun that was for small children—for as long as Grandpa would allow!

On the north wall, behind the barber chair was a big walnut wardrobe for his clothes. Most of the rest of that wall was taken up by his high double bed that had a tall walnut headboard against the east wall. There was a large hanging of some sort on the wall behind the bed. It might have been a tapestry, but I don't remember the design.

An old organ with its "insides" removed made some storage space on the east wall. On it sat an eight-day mantel clock that chimed on the hour and half-hour. He kept pens and pencils, paper and various odds and ends there. In one of the drawers were some pistols. The seat in front of it was a rotating organ stool. Between the organ and the bed stood his guns—a twenty-two rifle, and two muzzle-loaders, one was a rifle, the other a double-barreled shot-gun. A stove occupied space in the middle of the room, a small distance from the east wall—the stove pipe going up through the attic and on through the tin roof. The stove had a flat top that always had a black iron teakettle sitting on it, and he baked biscuits in the oven almost every day. Near the corner was a built-in ladder that went up to an opening in the ceiling that was the access to the attic. Also on that wall was a picture of a boy holding a rifle, a dog sitting by his side, watching some flying ducks. It was a sort of Norman Rockwell style of art that Ross says was put out by the Hercules Powder Company.

Along the south wall were some tables. There was a small one that had a wash basin and soap dish on it, with a mirror hanging over it and a small shelf with toilet articles, razor, etc.—under it, sat a large bucket called a "slop bucket" for waste water. Next, under the window, was a large table for food preparation and eating. The water bucket sat on the left end of it and held a blue-enamel dipper. (He carried his water from a spring that ran into the creek.) There were two or three chairs—I think one was a wooden stool. In the corner, that would be to the right as one came in the door, was a cupboard that supplied storage for dishes, pans, and food supplies. He didn't have screens on his door and window—said that if flies came in, he wanted them to be able to get out.

Grandpa never had a car, and no horses when he lived in this house, so he often walked the two miles to town, riding home with a neighbor if he had many things to carry. Ross sometimes went with him and says that the first place they stopped in town was at Sport Gilbert's general store where Grandpa bought a bag of donuts, which they ate while sitting on a bench outside the store. At the edge of the sidewalk was a hitching rail for horses, as well as parking space for cars. From there they might do some grocery shopping, eventually ending up at the pool hall where Grandpa picked up saws people had left for him to sharpen, or delivered ones that he had already finished, and bought a pint of Hill and Hill whiskey to drink on their walk home.

His income came from odd jobs—handy-man, railroad crews, or road work—and later from what was then called "the old-age pension." His life-style was so simple, he had few needs—denim overalls and chambray shirts were his every-day wear, and one suit with a tie and some dress shirts made up most of his wardrobe. For winter he wore long underwear, had some warm jackets and a rain- coat, one hat for everyday, and one for "Sunday."

I've often wondered what might be his inner feelings. Was he lonely? If so, he didn't complain about it. Did he feel he was "enjoying" life? He never said he wasn't. I don't think he did much reading, but he was proud of my dad's "self-education" and achievements, and he was very interested in our school work—praising us when we brought home good grades. He was friendly to neighbors and helpful to anyone who needed help. By the time I knew him he had already done quite a lot of travelling, working with a circus that traveled through Texas, and several other states; so if he had ever wondered what some of the rest of the world was like, he might have learned enough to satisfy his curiosity. He gave his family a special kind of stability and lots of love—probably the most valuable gifts a man could give. Thanks, Grandpa!

AUNT NELL AND UNCLE SCOTT

During our dating period, Gene spoke often of various family members, but his Aunt Nell and Uncle Scott seemed to be two of his favorites. His dad, James C. Bench, was one of six children, including Will, Mary (who married Henderson Osborn), Ben, Virgil (whose wife was Susie Toppas), and Nell, who married Scott Delman. They grew up in southern Missouri, and most of them continued to live in and around Fordland—twenty or so miles east of Springfield. Virgil and Susie worked in the bank her father owned in Fordland. (Virgil died young from appendicitis, and later Susie became the owner of the bank.) The Delmans lived on an 80-acre farm a few miles west of Fordland.

Both Uncle Scott and Aunt Nell were hard workers. They arose early in the morning; and then in the afternoon, Aunt Nell rested on their screened-porch bed, and read the paper. They had a few dairy cows, and also raised chickens and some pigs. The milk, cream, and eggs provided  part of their income. Cows were milked by hand, requiring attention at six o'clock every morning and at six o'clock every evening—summer and winter, rain or shine. Every morning a large can of milk was taken by wheelbarrow to the end of the driveway and left by the mailbox to be picked up and taken to town.

Their main meal was at noon—farm vegetables, fried chicken or pork chops, and always a large pan of cornbread—enough for supper later, and some for the dog. Cooking was done on a wood stove, with a large box for the wood beside it. When Aunt Nell put something in the oven to bake, she always put a stick of wood in the middle of the kitchen floor to remind her to keep an eye on whatever was cooking. Rural electricity came to their area several years after I first met them, and they felt really fortunate to have many new-fangled conveniences—a radio; power in the shop and barn; lights in the house and yard; a refrigerator, and especially an electric cooking stove! She could now

431

adjust the heat in the oven without regulating the number of sticks of wood she put on the fire! It even had a timer to set for when the baking might be finished! But Aunt Nell had her own way of giving attention to the oven—and why change something that had always worked so well? When the wood-box was moved out, she kept one stick of wood out of it lying by the new electric stove—and when she put something in the oven to bake, that stick of wood went to the middle of the floor as a reminder!

Aunt Nell called her younger brother (Gene's dad) Jip. They had no children of their own, so their nieces and nephews were all special to them. Jip's kids frequently stayed with them part of the summer to help with the farm work and earn a little money. One of the big seasons for work was the strawberry season. They had a large field of the berries, which brought in one of their largest seasonal incomes. It was really a treat to visit them then, as we often did!

Uncle Scott was a thin, wiry man who was really proud of his farm and home. When we visited, he often took us walking along the creek, through the pasture; and showed me the corner of the farm that he had promised to Gene for a place to build a home, when he "settled down," if he chose to live in that part of the country. One place Gene always wanted to go was to the "sink-hole." It was at the edge of one of the fields—several feet across, with some trees and brush growing around it. It was <u>very</u> deep and was somewhat of a mystery as to how it came to be there. Uncle Scott had some stories about it that I don't remember, but one of them was about an even deeper sink-hole on a neighbor's farm, with a lot of water in the bottom of it. It has been said that many years ago someone put a note in a bottle and threw it into the sink-hole; and that it eventually was discovered on a Pacific Ocean beach! Some people might call Uncle Scott "hen-pecked"! Aunt Nell was quite "bossy," and very critical of some of Uncle Scott's ways—in a scolding kind of voice, that seemed to me to "put him down." But he seemed to "let it in one ear and out the other," joking, or smiling, or just not paying attention. However, even with her criticizing and scolding, we knew that they were truly devoted to each other.

When they were married, Uncle Scott drank quite a lot, and Aunt Nell "dipped snuff." They made an agreement that if he would stop drinking, she would give up snuff. He stopped, but before long, she began what she thought was secretly continuing to "dip"! I can't imagine how she could think that he didn't know! Did they never kiss? They slept together—surely she'd realize that a snuff-dipper's breath was revealing! She even threw her empty cans out the truck window someplace along the road to town, so he wouldn't find them in the trash! But Uncle Scott—being the sweet person he was—never admitted that he noticed her habit. Even when they went shopping in Fordland, he always managed to leave her alone with her shopping for awhile to give her an opportunity to "secretly" buy her snuff!

It was always fun to visit there, hear stories of their families, and help with the chores. The house was always clean, the yard neatly kept, and work was seemingly done with dedication and without stress. Sometimes, one of my jobs was to go the cellar to bring in some fruit, vegetables, or a home-canned something. It was located a few feet from the back door, down a couple of steps into a large, cool room that was framed and mounded over with a thick layer of soil that had grass growing over it. There they stored potatoes, apples, carrots, cabbage, cream, butter, and milk (before their electric refrigerator). Shelves held many quarts of canned vegetables, and fruits.

Aunt Nell—who some "city" people might consider somewhat undignified—and she wouldn't have won a beauty contest in her cotton dress from Penney's or Sears, and her flat, comfortable shoes—but she was one of the most unselfish, generous, bighearted persons I have ever known. Yes, she was quite opinionated, but then, aren't we all! She had lived through hard times, with little formal education; but she was wise, and kind. We never knew much about her health, but she was frequently complaining about having "female" trouble which she described as "feeling like her insides were falling out"—but evidently there wasn't pain enough to keep her from hard work. She didn't want to go to the doctor, because "she feared he'd say she had cancer"!

When we were married, they were delighted! From Aunt Nell we received the very practical gift of a covered, three-quart, aluminum sauce pan, with a bowl-shaped insert to make it into a double boiler. It's still one of my most-used pans that I couldn't have lived without. But that gift wasn't good enough for Uncle Scott—he thought we should have some silver spoons! Six of them!

Their neat little farm is now home for a grand-nephew—Sammy Kindall (son of Helen, the daughter of Virgil and Susie) and his sweet wife Debbie. I'm happy that those young people can rear their children in that place that was so loved and holds so many happy memories of the love Aunt Nell and Uncle Scott gave to their extended family!

FAMILY TALENTS AND INTERESTS

I've "heard tell" that sometimes by noticing a child's favorite playthings, or their interests in things they like to do, we might be able to get a clue about their choices of careers or hobbies when they grow up. So, to test the theory, I decided to analyze some of the members of my family—two sisters, two brothers, and myself—now that our ages range from eighty-five to ninety-three years, and we've all seemingly enjoyed "playing the cards Life dealt us"!

Living in the country, with no other children living very nearby, our amusement mostly came from playing with each other—after helping with chores around the house. Mom and Dad sometimes turned those chores into challenging games. There were things like small-coin rewards for digging dandelions out of the lawn, picking bugs off the potato plants, carrying in wood for the stoves, picking huckleberries and wild blackberries, and such. We three girls often sang and harmonized while we washed and dried dishes. The boys built go-carts, "rolling-hoops," and various inventions from things retrieved from the junk pile behind the barn. And there's no way to forget the play-houses under trees in the nearby woods, and mud pies made in discarded lids and small tin cans. (There was a place at the edge of the woods where there was some light-brown colored, very fine-textured soil that we liked to use for the mud-pie "frosting." And a bit of dry dirt in the bottoms of the pans made the pies come out of their pans easily after they dried and hardened.) But we also were often sort of "left to our own devices"—free to choose our own <u>favorite</u> kind of play or activity if we weren't needed to help with chores.

Sterling is the youngest of our group, and he could amuse himself hour after hour with building winding roads and small villages in the open space between the fences that bound the cow pasture and the yard around the house. Part of that space was the dirt driveway, and the chickens, dog, and cats were free to roam there. I suppose it would be called a "barn-yard," because it also contained the combination barn and garage. Sometimes others of us played with him—he had plenty of little cars to share! "Santa Claus" had even brought the boys a dump truck and a steam shovel one year! We "sputtered" the sound of our motors, and "walked" our forefinger and middle finger for our "people" who carried on conversations when they met along a road or in a town.

By the time Sterling approached teen years, we had acquired a piano. Some of us, including Sterling, took lessons from a neighbor, but Sterling never learned to "read" the notes. Our teacher would usually play the homework assignment so we could hear how it should sound, and that was all Sterling needed to be able to play it back to her at the next lesson. When he grew up, he bought a baby grand piano for himself (guitars, too). Playing music that was popular as we grew up—sometimes singing along with it and composing fancy flourishes—became one of his cures for stress. Some stress, and a lot of pleasure, came to him in his career of sales and maintenance of automobiles— five different franchises (Pontiac, Datsun, GM trucks, Mercedes, and motor homes. His hobby became collecting and restoring classic cars.

Younger sister, Joy, likes to travel. Her first trip alone was a surprise visit to the elderly neighbors across the road when she was about four years old. She just disappeared from our house one sunny afternoon; which, of course, was quite a worrisome thing for the rest of the family who began searching and calling her name in the house, in the barn, and even in the woods. After a short time, brother Ross spied her strolling down the neighbor's driveway on her way home. When questioned, she casually explained that she "just went over to Hiles' house to see if they had any new kittens"! Other trips on her own have been to visit Gene and me—including a camping trip with us in Minnesota and spending a summer together when we lived in Naples, Italy. As a child she dearly loved her dolls, and spent hours dressing them and making new clothes for them with scraps from Mom's sewing projects. In college, she chose to major in Textiles and Clothing, earned a Master's degree from Wisconsin University in Madison, and then spent several years as a Textiles and Clothing professor at Ball State College in Muncie, Indiana.

Middle sister, Barbara, was the genius in our "mud-pie bakery"! And she was one of Mom's best helpers in the kitchen, as well. Dietetics was her major in college, and her first career position was Dietitian in the Hallmark Cards cafeteria in Kansas City, Missouri. Wonderful, sometimes quite unusual, edibles appeared regularly on her dining room table! This food-gift of hers appears even in the next generation—her son, Randy, earned a degree in

Restaurant and Hotel Management at the University of Missouri, managed several restaurants, and now sells restaurant equipment in mid-Missouri.

But that wasn't all there was to Barbara's talent. From the time she was a toddler, she has kept the family laughing with her jokes, and her special comedy. In mid-life she became a professional clown—calling herself "Peaches." Her official costume is a gaudy black-and-white, old plaid jacket that once belonged to Dad (or some other man's coat), topping a pair of baggy pants. For hair she chooses between a wig of yellow short, curly hair, or one of red, long and curly. On her feet she wears clunky men's shoes; sometimes she wears a Derby style hat; she colors her face white, paints on large, over-size lips, and  sometimes clips on a round red nose. She's great with entertaining children, and for a few years was a "grandparent-volunteer" at the elementary school in her neighborhood—helping kids who needed a little extra attention with reading or math.

Brother Ross—who created the junk-pile go-carts and wagons—rebuilt an old car into a farming machine when he was a teenager. Dad often worked away from home, and with this motorized "thing," Ross could haul stuff, plow, or rake hay. After returning from a tour of duty in the Army at the end of WWII, he used his GI Bill for a complete course in automobile repair and painting. For several years he ran his own shop (was probably the world's most expert auto painter), and then began a new career as an auto-claims adjuster with State Farm Insurance. He could estimate damages almost to the penny!

So—what about "big sister" Ila? One of our "group" games as kids was "playing school." Being the oldest, and already in school, I was naturally the "teacher." Do you sense the power and control that came from that? And how about the control developed as being a "sitter" for the younger ones when Mom was working in the garden? Yes, I became a teacher—Home Ec— thinking I'd like a career to help underprivileged Native Americans on some reservation to learn things about homemaking. After one year of teaching in a high school near home, I found myself "practicing what I preached" as wife of

436

a career Marine—with no regrets! Still plenty of opportunities for controlling, helping "fix" things for people!

It seems I <u>should</u> have inherited more talent than I did for writing poetry. My dad, who didn't know his mother while he was growing up, loved writing poems—often about missing his Mom. When he did meet her, as an adult, he discovered that she had written poetry throughout her lifetime.

My grandsons are showing talents that are yet to be developed. Judging from the speed with which Thomas built all kinds of things with Lego pieces, he might grow up to be a construction engineer. I predict a career in dancing and acting for Evan. When he hears music, his body starts moving to the rhythm. I hear frequent "concerts" of his piano practicing by telephone. And when he tells me about a play he's been in at school, or a movie he's seen, he doesn't just tell me a brief description—he recites the whole script! (As those two have been growing up, Thomas has developed a talent for pitching baseball; Evan has studied in France and likes team-rowing. I'm still looking forward to the interests of my Great-grandchildren!)

DAVID AND MICHELLE
Crawfordsville, Oregon

Early in the week David called to ask if I had plans for that Saturday—the 13th—and asked if I would like to spend some time with him and Michelle. (He didn't have to tell me that their purpose was to be sure I didn't sit at home being lonely while thinking of Gene because it was his birthday.) I, of course, jumped at any chance to be with those two, anytime; so he instructed me to be ready at 9:00 a.m. when they would pick me up. He said to bring some "off-road" shoes and an umbrella; that we would drive through some little towns east of here, go to see the tulip fields along Peoria Road, and be back to Corvallis in time for a Chinese lunch at King Tin's.

Two of the "little towns" he planned to drive through were Brownsville and Crawfordsville. He and Michelle had recently bought a home in Crawfordsville, and Brownsville is nearby. The area is near some hills where there were once some very active gold mines, and the highway goes on to the east. Crawfordsville is a very small town, and the highway is the main street; but there is another street parallel to it a block to the south, and there are six cross streets. But listen to this: they have a fire station, a post office, a small store, a community church, and an elementary school with two small school buses parked in the parking lot on Saturday. Just before you enter the west edge of town, you cross the Calapooia River at a covered bridge. That bridge is no longer in use by the highway but is part of a river-bank park that has picnic tables—and more than likely some good places to stand while you drop a fishing hook in the river.

The Crawfordsville Bridge

Sometime during the winter, David and Michelle began looking for a home they could buy—preferably in the country. They looked around Corvallis first, but weren't very hopeful of finding anything they wanted to afford because Corvallis has the reputation of being Oregon's most expensive place to live. The Albany area where they work was searched—as far east as Lebanon. Finally, by coincidence (that maybe wasn't a coincidence at all) they noticed an ad in one of those local, low-cost advertising papers: this one-acre place in Crawfordsville was being sold by an elderly woman whose husband had recently passed away, and she was unable to continue living there without help. It's a two-bedroom, plus sunroom, rambler style, about the vintage of my place. It has a large shop with a wood heating stove in it, a sort of "decorative" little tool shed, some chicken coops, a large garden, several shade trees and fruit trees, beautiful lawn with various shrubs—all of it enclosed within a shoulder-high cyclone fence. But before they told me much about it, or made any serious commitment to it, they "felt me out" about them living that far away from me! (30-some miles, I think!) They wanted to be sure I'd be comfortable without them being here in Corvallis. I really admired their concern, so I assured them that I'd be fine—with good neighbors, and other friends, who "watch out" for me. Gene and I really appreciated the freedom my family—and his—gave us to live where we wanted or needed to live; and to rear our family without interference from them. We've always felt that we could never do less for our own children.

After poking around in their very well-maintained house and yard and shop for awhile, we left to see the tulip fields. They had taken me on some "back" roads on the way over—arriving by way of a hill from which there was a great view of the town. We'd also gone through grain-field country and spotted some Bald Eagles waiting for a late breakfast of a rabbit or some field mice. Now, as we left town, driving along the river, we soon came to another park that was a camping park. David pointed out that it was the place his Boy Scout troop camped when they rode their bicycles there from Corvallis when he was maybe eleven or twelve years old. (You may or may not remember the yappy little Fox-Terrier-looking dog David used to have? It was on that trip that he found the dog—a tiny puppy—along the side of the road, put it in his coat pocket, and took it with him to camp! Then brought it home! The scout master wouldn't allow him any food from the troop's dinner for the dog, so David divided his own dinner and breakfast with it. He named her "Peanut" because she was so little.)

West of Brownsville we crossed I-5 to Peoria Road that runs north and south, between 99-E and 99-W. It has always been my favorite route between Corvallis and Eugene—large farms with various styles of homes, most of them surrounded with flowers and nice landscaping. (Some of them were customers of Gene's when he was an insurance agent.) A couple of the farms raise bulbs—several acres of rows and rows of many colors of tulips, daffodils, and other bulbs now in full bloom. It was like looking across a rainbow that was lying on the ground! Naturally, I had my camera handy, and when we were ready to leave, I was instructed to choose a couple of bunches of flowers to bring home with me. My choices were one bunch of large, long-stemmed, "orangey-coral" tulips with pointy petals; the other a bit shorter, with ivory colored double blossoms that were tinged with a rosy-coral color. I mixed

439

them into two beautiful bouquets—one for the kitchen table and one for the living room.

The Chinese lunch, which started with a bowl of warm egg-flower soup and a cup of hot tea, was a perfect ending of a great outing on a chilly, occasional-showers day!

(I haven't told David and Michelle yet that if I get too lonely here without them nearby, I could easily find a place in Crawfordsville to build a house for myself that wouldn't be any more than six blocks away from them! Maybe even less!) And all the time, everywhere we went, we felt Gene's spirit there with us! (Thank you, Gene!)

* * * * * * * * * * * * * * * * *

Crawfordsville was founded on the land of Philemon Vawter Crawford in 1870 by Crawford and Robert Glass. When the post office was established in 1870, it was named for Crawford. He was born in Madison, Indiana, in 1814, and arrived in Oregon via the Oregon Trail in 1851. His son, Jasper V., was the first postmaster. Philemon Crawford had previously helped establish the Boston Flour Mill near Shedd. In 1915 there was a population of 300—two saw mills, a flour mill, a high school, an elementary school, and three churches. In the early 20th century, the population included Sikhs from Pakistan and India who worked for the Calapooya lumber Company. (From *Wikipedia*)

GRANDCHILDREN & GREAT-GRANDCHILDREN

I'm a grandmother—and grandmothers are known to believe their own grandchildren are far superior to anyone else who ever lived. Well, I do, too—but I'm going to be perfectly truthful when I write about mine!

Leah Elizabeth Wilber was born September 29, 1978—our first grandchild! We had thought her mother Becky was the most beautiful baby we had ever seen—but here was her child who was just as beautiful! What a joy it was to hold her and admire those perfect little fingers and toes! And those beautiful blue eyes! We were happy that we lived in the same area and could experience her growing! As she developed into a very active toddler, I found walks with her to be as exciting as they had been with her mother, Becky! There was endless excitement with rocks to throw, anthills to watch as the ants came and went in their searches for food, birds to watch, flowers of various weeds to pick—always, she had a very active curiosity!

Along the way, she and her mom moved to Arizona when Becky wanted to finish college in Tucson, so my time with Leah became really limited. We were always happy when she was able to visit with us from time to time.

Another move for Leah and Becky was to the Seattle area—Graduate school for Becky at the University of Washington, and marriage to Brian Butler in 1989. As part of that lovely island wedding, Leah was a really beautiful ten-year-old "flower-girl," wearing a blue, silky dress that I made for her!

My grandsons are Thomas Eugene and Evan Nelson Butler, with whom I spent a few days in autumn 2003. Thomas was born July 19, 1998; Evan on June 7, 2000. You can imagine how much fun they are now at ages five and three!

Thomas has been a very active person almost from birth—very curious and observant. I call him a study in perpetual motion. When it comes to toys, he seems to prefer things that need to be put together, or ones that "do" something like movements or sounds. From the time he was very young he liked the "Thomas, the Tank Engine" videos, and the "Veggie Tales" series. Some of his first words were "big boulder" (said with enthusiasm and excitement)! It was his description of a scene in the tank engine video when a huge rock rolled off a cliff, down onto the railroad, and then rolled along chasing the Thomas engine and his train down a long grade. He always anticipated that scene, with loudly saying, "Big boulder, Big boulder!" just before it showed up on the screen. Luckily, the Thomas railroad was made into hands-on toys, just the right size for small hands, and in pieces that could be added as his imagination and coordination developed. It was a much-loved toy, later enjoyed by younger brother, too!

This year, at age five, he likes robots, Lego toys, Rescue Rangers, Hot Wheels, and Pirates. He has several Star Wars types of vehicles and people that he has put together—with his mother's help—from Lego kits. She has patiently helped him learn to follow the step-by-step instructions, to identify the many different shapes of the pieces, and to visualize how they attach to each other; so he's learning "space relations" without realizing it—as well as great eye-finger-muscle coordination! He brought the most recent unfinished one when they visited me this last weekend, so I had a chance to be his "helper" part of the time. There were over one thousand pieces in the kit! I mostly just

441

watched, or helped look for certain pieces that he showed me on the directions—which he called "inshtrukshuns." He often spotted the pieces before I did, and deftly popped them into place.

When I was in Seattle in August, he was taking swimming lessons—continuing from the previous summer. This time he was learning crawl strokes, swimming on his back, and diving. Again, I could recognize his good muscle coordination. On the way home from swimming we made a ritual stop at McDonalds for a Happy Meal—two Happy Meals, because brother Evan got one as well—chicken nuggets, French fries, and a milk shake. The most important part of the order, of course, was to see which toy came with it! Both boys have collections of Happy Meal pirates, cars, and such!

Kindergarten started for Thomas in September at Evergreen School in Seattle, which is for students from preschool to eighth grade. If he continues to like school as much as he has enjoyed these first few weeks, he'll do very well!

Evan, at age three, is a joyful little fellow—full of life, with a definite mind of his own; and he loves to talk—about everything! He seems to have finally learned that he shouldn't make a game of wrecking things that Thomas has built, but he likes to build up towers of blocks himself, then have the fun—and freedom—of knocking them all down! Dinosaurs have been favorite toys of his for a long time; and now he's sharing Thomas' interest in pirates and ships. At the ocean or aquarium, his favorite things are starfish and octopuses. He has a small play house that opens out to give access to the various rooms. One day I watched him for probably twenty minutes or more, squatting on the floor, moving the miniature people of the family around, "talking" for them while they cooked, ate, drove a car, or played. If he's playing with several cars—he likes "little" ones—he sometimes "parks" them in a row and uses only one at a time.

He looks forward to preschool where one of the activities provided is listening to music and adding rhythmic dancing and movements. Consequently, any time he hears music, his whole body goes into motion! I like to enjoy books with him. If it's one he's heard a few times before, he knows all the words, but we have to stop to identify all the pictures before turning a page. He especially likes butterflies—and sees a lot of them around my house, because I like them, too! And, he likes rainbows. One day I was wearing my white nylon windbreaker that has bright-colored stripes sewed around the upper body and sleeves—colors are yellow, orange, red, green, and blue (in descending order). Evan's mom called his attention to it: "Look, Evan, Grandma's jacket has a rainbow on it!" Evan's reply was, "There's no <u>purple</u>!"

Things that are out of place attract his attention—he closes open doors, puts the arm cover on the couch if it has slipped off, and such. One day when we were at the pool while Thomas had a swimming lesson, I noticed that Evan busily picked up a large leaf that had blown from a nearby tree and took it to put into a nearby trash container.

Riding with their family to the coast, and sharing their apartment for the annual Bench family gathering was a real treat. Their new Toyota van is equipped with a video screen for the rear passengers to enjoy—and it is great for making a long trip seem pleasantly shorter. It was my privilege to share it! On short jaunts, radio music entertains the passengers. One favorite song is a cute rhythmic thing called, "Tickle, tickle, wump, wump." A repeated line in another one is "Down in Louisiana, in them old cotton fields back home." And, would you believe, "Oh, beautiful for spacious skies—for amber waves of grain!" When Evan asks for it, he says, "Play 'Brotherhood'!" The annual three days at Ocean Shores was a great time for the boys to be with cousins of all ages—grown-ups, teenagers, and several kids their own age.

Being a Grandma is very rewarding—and, yes, one's own grandchildren <u>are</u> special! I <u>know</u> it when Thomas wants to show me how deep he can dive! And when Evan says, "Me-Me," and I know he's calling ME! (2019 "update"—Thomas is now in college, and is an expert baseball pitcher. Evan spent his high school junior year studying in France, will graduate high school this year, and is in the process of selecting a college! Rowing is his choice sport. My two grandsons are suddenly young "men"!)

Evan, Thomas, Becky & Brian in France 2018

But children have a way of growing up and moving away into lives of their own, and so we weren't surprised to hear from Leah about our first "great-grandchild"! Maureece! He is now an industrious college student, and an outstanding basketball player! (Another young "man"!) His very enthusiastic brother, Chance, is in first grade; and his feisty, really cute sister Chelsea, is age four!

Chelsea, age 3

Chance, age 6

Leah, Maureece, Chance & Chelsea 2018

Maureece, 2018 High School
Graduation

ANTELOPE HUNTING IN WYOMING

September 25th, for the past twenty-some years, has reminded me of antelope in Wyoming because, for at least that many years, that has been the opening day of the season for hunting them. Today, in 2004, is no different. It's a memorable date for me because, in most of those years, Gene was one of the hunters.

A few years after we moved back to Corvallis in 1973, an Izaak Walton friend of Gene's, named Frank Parks, stirred Gene's interest in the adventure of antelope hunting. A brother of Frank's son-in-law, Bill Willoughby, lived in Lander, Wyoming, and had hosted Frank a few times for some fishing and antelope hunting, so in 1982, Frank made arrangements for Gene to go along. Frank had "fallen in love" with trout fishing in the Popo Agie (pronounced Po-**pa**-jee) River near Lander, so he naturally wanted to introduce Gene to it. I think <u>that</u> part of the trip was almost as important to Frank as the antelope. Gene later said that it <u>was</u> a truly beautiful, pristine river—well worth the time and the experience. And, of course, Gene found the antelope hunting to be especially enjoyable and challenging. I think that one of the things he liked most about hunting was learning the habits of the animals, appreciating their physical beauty, and being challenged by the various ways they were able to outsmart a hunter! (For one thing, an antelope is <u>very</u> "fleet of foot," and if the animal is running, one has to aim some distance <u>ahead</u> of it to bring it down!) He liked the experience so much, he persuaded my brother Ross, who lived in Kansas, to meet him there a couple of years later after Frank's health caused him to have to give up going on those trips. Ross and Gene changed their hunting location to the Medicine Bow-Rock River area, obtained permission to hunt on some nearby ranches, and camped in a trailer-camper. For the following few years, Gene's friend Bob Carey went with him from Corvallis; and in Medicine Bow, met Ross and his "party" which by then included his son, two sons-in-law, and a grandson.

In 1987, Ross and Gene decided it would be fun if just the two of them and their wives, Chadna and I, extended the hunt into a few days' vacation. We did our "camping" in double motel rooms in Rock River—a <u>very</u> small town ten or twelve miles north of Interstate 80. We ate our meals in a cozy little café across the street, except for some picnic lunches we made ourselves.

"Sightseeing" was the goal for the four days we were there before the 25th, and we found a surprising number of sights to see and things to do. Ten miles or so south of Rock River, and a little bit north of the Interstate, we explored some of the original tracks of the "Overland Trail," now partially grown over in brush and woods. A sign hanging on the fence that was across the trail near the parking lot said that in some difficult places, the earlier wagons were hoisted up to get over such terrain as cliffs. The trail began in Atchison, Kansas, went through Laramie, and connected with the Oregon Trail at Fort Bridger, Wyoming. Stage coaches ultimately traveled it in the late 1800's. A meadow extended beyond the parking lot in one direction, and while we were exploring in that area, a pheasant walked across in front of us.

Of course, viewing antelope was a very important activity. We spent <u>hours</u> just driving around the countryside in Gene's 4-wheel-drive SUV, spotting herds of them, sometimes in valleys, sometimes on the rolling, sagebrush-covered hills. <u>What beautiful sights!</u> Usually the animals were too far away to photograph very well (partly because they blended so well into the landscape), but one day when Chadna and I were out along a road near Rock River, we saw a buck inside a pasture very near the road. He seemed as interested in us as we were in him, so while he was just satisfying his own curiosity, I snapped a picture that I later had enlarged and framed for Gene. On one of the ranches, there was a field of tall windmills, built to generate electricity. Ross and Gene really enjoyed showing Chadna and me some of the ranches where they had hunted in the past, and where they expected to hunt this year. They had made a point in past years of getting acquainted with the ranch owners, and Gene frequently took a box of Northwest apples or a bag of Walla-Walla onions as a gift to the family.

One experiment the guys conducted that has provided hilarious enjoyment every time the memory has been brought up between us, was an attempt to attract antelope to come to them. Gene said he had heard that antelope are very curious animals, and they will investigate something unusual and unfamiliar in their vicinity—something like maybe a white flag. Gene had a very long extension fishing rod with him, to which they tied a white rag that was in the car for cleaning purposes. They soon spotted some antelope on a hillside; then drove around the hill, so they were out of sight of the animals, to begin their advance up to where they could lift their "flag." The thinking was that the antelope would be surprised, and curious, to see the flag waving in the breeze, while the two of them were still out of sight. This, of course, meant going on hands and knees part of the time—eventually lying on their stomachs. Then they took turns lifting their heads to observe the behavior of the animals. For Chadna and me, something about watching those two grown men—presumably fairly intelligent ones—creeping and crawling up that hill, just really "tickled our funny bones"! By the way, the antelope just looked at the waving white flag for a couple of minutes and went back to their grazing! The experience was worth the while, if for no other reason than to give us a great memory!

A few miles east of Rock River was a lake called Wheatland Reservoir. Part of one day was spent there with a picnic lunch and fishing. I was <u>very</u> surprised at the size of trout we were catching—<u>much</u> larger than the Rainbow we usually caught in Oregon. I think they were called "Lake Trout." Chadna won the prize for the biggest one, between 18 inches and two feet long! We released most of the ones we caught, but we took Chadna's fish back to the motel and cooked it in an electric skillet she had brought with them. With some applesauce and bread to go with it, we had a real feast!

Another adventure was shooting prairie dogs with pistols. Ranchers hated them because their animals sometimes got broken legs from stepping in their holes. It was "sport" for Ross and Gene. Chadna and I thought the little "dogs" were too cute to destroy!

Medicine Bow, the next town west of Rock River, was a good "tourist stop". The Virginian Hotel there is preserved as an historical building. Not only was it an important place for travelers on the Union Pacific Railroad, but it was also the site for the filming of the TV series "The Virginian," which was based on the book of the same name by Owen Wister. James Drury played the part of the character called "The Virginian," Doug McClure played the part of Trampus. The story featured the West of the 1890's. In 1929 a movie called "The Virginian" starred Gary Cooper, and in 1946, a new one was made starring Joel McCrea. A motel next door to the hotel is called "The Trampus." It is where our family hunters have always stayed for the several years they have met there.

Early in the morning of the 25th, Gene and Ross went off to do their hunting. They were later getting back than we had expected, but we found out the reason when they finally returned. When they tried to start the car to come back, it had a vapor-lock, and wouldn't start. Repeated efforts with the car's starter soon ran the battery down. Ross started walking, hoping to be able to wave down some motorist. Meanwhile, Gene began getting chilly, but was unable to close the electrically powered window lifts. After some time, Ross connected with a passing rancher in a truck who was able to go to the car and get it started with jumper cables. Once back with their "harvest," they dressed the animals behind the motel at scaffolding provided by the motel for that purpose. From there they went to a cold storage place, either in Medicine Bow or in the neighboring town of Hanna (again, my memory fails), where the meat was cut, packaged for freezing, and kept cold for us to pick up on our way home the next day.

Gene's last antelope hunt was with Fritz Bartsch in 2000—with heavy snow on the ground in Wyoming. In addition, Gene was experiencing considerable pain from what was thought to be an infection. Soon after, it was diagnosed as cancer. Ross also had had to give up hunting about that time, but one of his sons-in-law, Brice Shriver from Pennsylvania, will be there today with his sons Bryan and Brandon to continue the family Wyoming antelope tradition! Good luck, guys! My heart is there with you!

P.S. (Later) In looking at the map of that part of Wyoming, some distance southwest of Medicine Bow and near the southern border, there is the small town of Dixon. Near there is Battle Lake. On its shores, in 1878, as a member of the Henry Draper Eclipse Expedition, Thomas A. Edison, aided by the frayed ends of his bamboo fishing rod, conceived the idea of a non-conducting enduring carbon filament resulting in the later perfection of his incandescent electric lamp.

A FAMILY JOURNEY

I am reminded of this journey because it all happened during this time of the year in 1991. Early in the spring, probably early March, Gene and I had planned a trip to Missouri to attend one of his high school class reunions at Ava, Missouri. We would fly to Kansas City on Delta Airlines, rent a car, spend a night with my brother Ross and his wife Chadna in Overland Park, Kansas, then go on to Columbia to be with Mom Kelley and the families of brother Sterling and sister Barbara for a few days. The Ava reunion would be on Mother's Day weekend, so we would be celebrating with my mom a few days early. (I was even having a lot of thoughts about Mom, especially about her hands that had done so many wonderful things. I was trying to put some of them into a poem, but nothing was working, so I gave up, having learned that if I were supposed to write a poem, it would "come.") On the way to Ava, we planned to see Gene's cousins Helen and Dale Kindall in Fordland, Missouri, and spend a night with them. Helen had been a favorite playmate and friend of the children in Gene's family, and we always had a good time reminiscing with them and maybe meeting some of their several children and grandchildren who lived nearby.

But in mid-April, our journey had to take some different directions when we heard by phone that my Mom was in the hospital with a kidney problem. I hadn't been able to share final moments with Dad, who lived only two days following a heart attack from which, at first, it seemed he would recover; so when I heard about Mom, I decided I wanted to BE there—no matter WHAT! We decided I would go the next day, and Gene would go as originally planned.

Other than being very arthritic and becoming progressively feeble, her health had been unusually good for her age. She occasionally lost her balance, and had fallen a couple of times, which her doctor thought might possibly have been caused by some "TIA's" which we in the family called "mini-strokes." After those experiences she agreed to wear a "Life Line" device with which she could summon help in case of some emergency. Barbara and Sterling who lived in Columbia took her shopping, to church, and helped in various ways. We all had been encouraging her to move to a retirement facility, even taking her, by appointment, to visit and have lunch at a nice one where several of her friends already lived, but she was adamant—insisting that she <u>didn't want to leave her home</u>! She said she would get someone to stay with her if she got to where she shouldn't be alone. One time several months before, when we were visiting, we asked her permission to inquire about home help. A very friendly lady from an organization called Kelley Services came to describe their program, which seemed to us a possible alternative, but evidently it didn't suit Mom. Behind our backs she called her 80-some year-old widowed sister (Aunt Inez, better known as Aunt Bun) who lived alone in Dixon. Aunt Bun, who had stayed with other family members to help them as needed through the years, agreed to come to stay with her "for awhile" which by now had been close to eight months. That had made TWO people for Barbara and Sterling to assist! But the two of them seemed to be happy—visiting with each other, watching T.V., reading, quilting, doing light gardening, and whatever two little old lady sisters could find to do to pass their time.

Lately Mom seemed to be losing her stamina along with her appetite, and for over a week just didn't feel well. One night, on her way back to bed, after going to the bathroom adjoining her room, she fell and wasn't able to get up. Instead of using the Life-Line device, Aunt Bun called Sterling to come help her get back into bed, but Sterling decided to call an ambulance to take her to the hospital. A blood analysis revealed an infection, requiring an intravenous antibiotic to which it soon became obvious she was allergic. Now to add to her discomfort, her whole body was covered with a very itchy rash!

I arrived the next day, by way of Kansas City, where Ross and Chadna picked me up and took me to Columbia. Then sister Joy came from Indiana prepared to stay a few days, and Aunt Bun decided she should go check on her own home, as long as we could take care of Mom.

With all of her children around her, Mom seemed somewhat content to wait for the doctors to help her recover, until after a few days her kidneys stopped functioning. A nephrologist was called in to assist her own doctor, and his advice was to try dialysis. He said that sometimes that would cause the kidneys to return to normal function. It was a frightening experience for Mom, but she agreed to do it, if it seemed the best thing to do. The results of that first procedure were really amazing! She felt good and her mind seemed to be refreshed and wonderfully clear! We all had such fun with her, listening to her talk with us about good "old times" and memories of many experiences of her life!

During these days of spending time with her, we realized we were also spending very high-quality time with each other, creating bonds that we hadn't even felt as children. We took turns being with her, giving her time for resting, and we continued with work and caring for families who lived there. Joy and I stayed at Mom's house, did some cleaning and gardening, and kept fresh flowers from her garden in her room. One night when it was my turn to sit with her from midnight to 7:00 a.m., I placed my chair where I had some light from the bathroom with the door opened just a bit—enough light to see to read. Soon words about her hands began to tumble around in my mind, and I started writing. By the time Sterling arrived for his "shift" at 7:00, my poem was done, and needed only a minimum of correcting. I would have it ready for Mother's Day after all!

After three dialysis treatments the doctor decided the only way she could continue to live would be to continue the dialysis on a regular basis. He called all of us children into a conference about it, explaining that he suspected that she wouldn't want to do it, and IF she didn't, he wanted to prepare us for thinking about what to expect as her life came to an end. We had a feeling that she was suffering through the frightening treatments because she felt that we thought it the best thing for her to do, but in reality, we knew in our hearts that it was probably time for God to take her home. The doctor arranged for himself and all of us together to talk with her about her wishes. Her answer was that she had had a wonderful life with her loving family, and that she was happy to now look forward to going on, to finally be with Dad and her Lord.

She was moved from the hospital to a lovely skilled-care facility, to a room that had an empty bed and space for our family gatherings. We took turns being with her around-the-clock, and with each other for the remainder of her life. She thanked all the doctors and nurses for the care they had given her—

said she was soon going to be in Heaven, and she hoped she would someday see them there, too! The doctor had estimated it would probably be about ten days, but she had a strong heart that kept going for fourteen and was conscious until the last few hours of it.

Gene's journey also took a different turn. He went to Ava as planned, met his sister there, and visited with the cousins as planned. Then he came to Columbia to be with the Kelley family to stay until I was ready to return home, all the while every few days calling back to Corvallis to cancel some appointment.

Several "treasures" were discovered on this journey. For one thing, we learned that many things we consider important in our every-day living are not important at all, and life can go on perfectly well without us, if need be. Another treasure was discovering deeper bonds with family as we shared these life-and-death moments with Mom. We made a decision then to keep those bonds alive by taking turns hosting a family gathering of siblings and spouses for three or four days at least once a year. Family ties mean a lot to all of us, and we seem to grow even closer as we ourselves age—and find our families extending to two more new generations!

Chapter 8: Other People

DIXON NEIGHBORS

When my Mom and Dad built their first home on a little ten-acre farm, two miles north of Dixon, Missouri, the Lynch family already lived on another small farm just across the winding country road. Dad's father, Charley Kelley, lived about a quarter of a mile to the south, and Dad's uncle Jim Kelley lived about a half-mile north, with Aunt Ada and their family of seven children: Hosea, Lee, Josie, Oral, Opal, Pearl, and Dallas.

Not long after I was born in June of 1925, the Lynch family moved away, and our new neighbors across the road were Earl and Mary Hile. This story will be especially about them. To my parents, they were "Dad" Hile and Mrs. Hile. They wanted us children to call them "Granddad and Grandma." They came to our community from Trenton, Missouri—a small town to the north, where Mr. Hile had spent many years working for the railroad. I don't know which one, but I seem to remember them talking about the Rock Island. He had retired with a pension, which made them seem to us like quite wealthy people. They had a comfortable monthly income—many people in those parts often didn't even have a job. Both of them were white-haired, so seemed very old to us children—but they were active and lived probably another twenty years or more. I think they were a lot of help to my young parents who were busy clearing their land, building a house and outbuildings, planting their garden, and doing all the work of beginning farming. My dad had to work away from home sometimes in order for us to have an income.

Hiles' place was already an established farm, having a very nice bungalow style house with a fenced-in lawn; and a large barn with room for their team of horses, a cow, equipment, and hay loft. There was a special chicken house equipped with nesting boxes, water and food space inside the house away from marauding wild animals, and plenty of "roosting" space; and there was an outhouse that we children thought was "the lap of luxury"! The "seats" were not just shaped sawed-out holes—they were "store-bought," "donut-like" hole-covers with lids. But the most interesting thing was a roll of regular bathroom "tissue"! (Our outhouse was supplied with last season's Sears Roebuck catalog!)

I don't know the farm's acreage, but it must have been more than ours. They had a large field for growing hay, a couple of pasture areas, some woods, and a sizeable gardening space they called the "truck patch." They also had a Model "T" Ford touring car—used every Saturday for shopping in town two miles away, and for going to the Baptist Church in town every Sunday morning. They always offered my Mom a ride on Saturday for shopping; and most of the time, when she went, one of us children was privileged to go along. More than once Granddad Hile used his car to go get the doctor to come to our house when a child was sick, or when Mom was giving birth to a baby.

Granddad Hile used his team of horses for many farming jobs— plowing, disking and harrowing to prepare soil for planting; pulling a mower for cutting hay; pulling a wagon for hauling hay to the barn or for hauling feed from town. He even sometimes did some plowing for us when we didn't have our team of mules.

Behind the chicken house was a sizeable orchard and grape vineyard. There were apples, peaches, pears, plums, and raspberries that I remember. Grandma did a lot of canning and making jam and jelly. In the yard around the house—fenced to keep the chickens out—was lush green grass, several kinds of roses, peonies, pansies, dahlias, asters, zinnias, petunias, and beautiful sweet peas. I remember that there were many different colors of sweet peas, and that they were some of my favorite flowers. They were usually blooming in June, so she often gave me a bouquet of sweet peas for my birthday. (My sister Joy sometimes gives me sweet peas for my birthday, just for memory's sake!)

Going to their house was a special treat for us children. They had a playful little white and tan mongrel dog, and several cats and kittens of various colors. In their living room and bedrooms were wool Oriental carpets, lamps with pretty shades, and a pull-down lamp with a dome-shaped shade over the middle of their round dining table. (Lamps all burned kerosene—electricity hadn't yet come that far out of town.) They always gave us the colored comic section from their Sunday paper—which was delivered with the Monday paper on Monday. They even had a battery-operated radio and invited us sometimes to listen to *Fibber McGee and Molly* or *Amos 'n Andy,* or to play dominoes with them.

Almost everyone had some pigs they could feed inexpensively from food scraps, garden weeds, and dishwater (which was called "slop")—then they were fed extra grain for fattening before butchering in the fall. Hiles not only grew pigs for meat, but also used their annual calf for veal when it was old enough to butcher. Pork could be smoked or salted for preserving, but without refrigeration or freezers, beef meat was more difficult. It had to be canned in a pressure-cooker. But they did it. We always enjoyed the gift of a few fresh cuts of meat at butchering time. I especially liked the stew Mom made from back-bone!

Eggs were a quite regular product from the Hile's farm. They sold them by the crate to the market in town, and to us for about a dime a dozen—but their "dozen" was usually a count of thirteen eggs. Milk was another thing that we sometimes shared. Cows have to be "turned dry" for a while before a calf is born, so when our cow was dry, we'd get milk from the Hiles. When their cow was dry, our cow also had enough milk for them. (I never noticed if the cows were ever dry at the same time!) Our mail boxes sat side by side on a support on our side of the road at the end of both driveways, so if we expected to be away for a few days, Hiles held our mail for us. If they were gone, we did the same for them.

We sometimes helped Grandma Hile with her spring housecleaning. Those wool rugs were regularly cleaned with a push-type carpet sweeper with a rotating brush inside that picked up some dirt, but much dust just went deeper inside. So they had to be carried outside once a year for deep cleaning, and it was quite heavy work. They were hung across a clothesline, and then beaten with a broom or a special rug beater, something like a tennis racquet, to get the dust out. As I remember, their rugs were rolled up and stored through the summer, then put back on the floor for warmth in the winter.

Granddad and Grandma Hile were just wonderfully friendly, helpful neighbors! She was kind of quiet and "proper," never "talked down" to us children, and seemed to like to entertain us. Granddad was more boisterous, had a great sense of humor with lots of jokes, and used <u>generous</u> profanity that we didn't hear in our family—things like "God damn" and "hell." And he almost always had a large "saxophone shaped" pipe in his mouth. Mom and Dad explained to us that using those profane words was just Granddad's way of talking, so we mustn't be critical of it to <u>him</u>, but that <u>we</u> should never talk like that! He loved to tease my younger brother Sterling, whom we called

"Junior" then. Granddad's pet name for him was "Squarehead." When our family was quarantined with scarlet fever, Grandma Hile often left a pot of stew or a pie or a cake at our door.

A wonderful memory of mine is looking out the front door window towards their house the first thing on a winter morning. The sky was often pink in advance of the sunrise, and a column of smoke was either slowly rising, and curling from their chimney, or falling quickly towards the ground. Mom said that if the smoke was going up tall and slim, we would have a nice day. If it fell to the ground, weather would probably be bad. Whatever the smoke was doing, it was a very comforting feeling to know the <u>Hiles</u> were there!

We moved away from that community in the fall of 1944 and didn't have frequent contact with the Hiles after that. Another very good younger neighbor who lived a mile or so away had by that time become a friend of Hiles, sharing farming interests, and giving them some assistance as they aged. Her name was Adele Buss. I am unable to recall (if I ever knew) any details about the life of the Hiles in those later years. I seem to remember that at the end of his life, Granddad was living in a retirement home near Rolla, Missouri, that people called the Baptist Old Peoples' Home. Mrs. Buss had moved to another farm near St. James, Missouri, by then, and perhaps she had something to do with his residence there. I do remember that she visited him there. I'm quite sure that Grandma died before he did—possibly while they still lived on the farm.

Many years later I went with my parents to see the changes that had been made to the little farm where we had lived. The Hiles' house and outbuildings were still much as I remembered them to be and was now occupied by a person we'd known from her birth as Cora Dale Rollins! She wasn't at home that day, so we didn't get to visit with her. I remember thinking that some of the goodness and solid values that we think of as "American Life" lies in the stability of country and small-town neighborhoods, where everyone knows everyone, and eventually become connected through work, friendship, and even marriage!

LOVE IS ALL THAT MATTERS

ADELE BUSS
A Very Special Friend

Into our Santee community, in the late thirties, came a new neighbor who seemed to be totally "out-of-place." Her nearest neighbors didn't know how to go about getting acquainted. They thought her to be "uppity-uppity" and "high-toned"—and to us country folks, she <u>was</u> "different"! "Wonderfully different"!

Her name was Adele Buss—tall and slim with short stylishly bobbed, sandy-colored hair—bubbly personality, and eager to learn how to manage the small farm she and her husband Henry had recently bought. They came from St. Louis, where Henry had for years been a school custodian, and Adele was an executive secretary in a high-level office of a large business. (This, in an era when many were without work—and not many women were employed outside their homes.) Her work was so stressful, she was headed for a nervous breakdown, so changing to a quiet, country lifestyle was recommended as a way for her to use some of her unending energy. Since neither of them knew anything at all about farming, it was decided that Henry should keep his job in St. Louis until a farm could be established; and she hoped that she might find some children to whom she could give piano lessons. She had a married daughter named Betty, who lived in St. Louis, was a professional organist, and taught piano lessons.

Adele was a perfectionist; so naturally, if she was going to learn a new job, she wanted to learn how to do it <u>right</u>. That meant gathering printed bulletins of all kinds from the County Extension Office, reading other farm papers, and hiring helpers from whom she could learn what she needed to know.

I don't remember how she and my folks met, but very soon they became really good friends, and she appreciated advice from them. Mom knew a lot about gardening, canning, and almost everything else about living on a small farm—and Dad soon recognized that she was an educated person with much more enthusiasm for life than most of our country neighbors. She was "cultured," and she had "class"! She and our family soon became very close.

Before long, it was arranged that during the summer between my sophomore and junior years in high school, I would live with her Monday through Friday to help with her many chores—cleaning and dishwashing inside; feeding chickens, and some other animals, pulling weeds, planting, and harvesting outside. I knew how to milk a cow, so I shared that twice-a-day job, as well. In return for my work, I was paid a small amount of money each week, but most of my pay was a daily piano lesson, with some time allowed for practice. When school started in the fall, I continued piano lessons once a week—and was offered the same job the following summer, too! My two sisters and one of my brothers also took lessons for a few years—for which she received pay from Mom and Dad.

What kind of conversation goes on between employer and employee working side-by-side almost all day every day, beginning no later than 6:00 a.m.? For us, it was more like she did the talking, and I did the listening, as she drew out some of my opinions and ambitions and described things about "The World" that I could only imagine! She was a devoted Christian of a Protestant faith but told me that she had joined the Catholic Church in order to encourage Henry to attend services. Of course, it was in her nature to study the Catholic religion, as well, and to pass on to me many of their beliefs. What a wealth of experience and knowledge flowed down those rows and rows of garden plants while we pulled those pesky weeds! Her sense of humor was always on the surface, peppering all her conversation with positive viewpoints and plenty of funny stories! I remember that one of those silly funny little sayings was: "Airplanes should always have their underneath sides spread with butter, in case they should fall. We all know that if you happen to drop a piece of buttered bread, it always falls butter-side-down!"

Her house was furnished with valuable, quality things totally foreign to my country lifestyle—richly polished table tops; beautiful hand-made linens; sterling silver, fine crystal, and hand-painted china—the likes of which I had never seen! In her closet were lovely furs and silks and delicate, high heeled shoes. "But," I thought to myself, "those designs were in style ten years ago! Why does she still wear them?" (Little did I know that one day I'd be wearing some of my own clothes for twenty years!)

Occasionally, some of her city friends came to visit for a day—or maybe over-night. Those occasions called for all-out hospitality! The best vegetables from the garden; special home-grown meat; home-baked bread and dessert; all served using her best linen and china! Mrs. Buss had, herself, worked in her early years as a maid for wealthy people where she wore special uniforms—including a frilly apron when serving food to people seated around the table. (Guess who learned to properly set a table and to formally serve food to her guests! She even had a frilly apron for me to wear!)

A few years later, they moved to a larger farm near St. James, Missouri. Henry left his job in St. Louis, and they enjoyed farming until Henry's death. Adele continued to live there, for a few years—had a stroke while in her kitchen and was moved to a private nursing home where she lived a few more years as an invalid—still smiling, joking, and passing along her positive thinking!

By now, you won't be surprised to hear me say that I consider Mrs. Buss to be one of the most important people in my life! From her I learned about "The World"! About famous authors; about composers and appreciation for good music; about a positive philosophy of life and faith in God that I'd already begun learning from my parents. I could not have had a better mentor, and I'll be eternally grateful for her influence and her friendship!

TO MY FRIEND AND SUPER-TEACHER—MISS WILDA FLINT

What a super role-model you were to a shy little country girl at Dixon High School—a freshman in 1937! I had come to high school from the Santee one-room grade school where I had been advanced from 1st Grade to 4th Grade in two years. So I was a couple of years younger than my classmates, but I <u>felt</u> very mature and serious. I soon realized that you, Miss Flint, were not only a very good teacher, but you seemed to be the kind of person <u>I</u> would like to be. In a word, you had "class"!

I <u>so</u> admired your poise, and your self-confidence. Your eyes twinkled when you smiled—and you were almost always smiling. Although you were very friendly and relaxed with students, you maintained wonderful respect, and made us each one feel special. You encouraged conversations and never "talked down" when we expressed our own opinions or interpretations of whatever was the subject at hand.

To look at you, one would think you had just stepped out of a fashion magazine—not <u>high</u> fashion—just clothes that were beautifully appropriate: simple, colorful, comfortable things like pleated skirts, sweaters, suits, and often loafers that looked freshly shined. Your grooming was all a part of your persona: simply styled hair, just-right makeup, polished nails, and, of course, silk stockings with perfectly straight seams.

As a freshman, my required subjects didn't include any with you, so I was a sophomore by the time I began to benefit from being in your classroom— second-year English and World History that year, followed later by third-year

English, American History, and English IV. Your English classes weren't just boring grammar and sentence diagramming; they were loaded with great literature. You often read to us—poetry, stories, or portions of Shakespeare's plays. You could make those readings really "come alive." By the time you finished Edgar Allen Poe's poem, *The Raven*, one almost expected a sleek black bird to appear at the door saying, "Nevermore"! When you read from *Snowbound*, I felt like reaching for my sweater. I had a hard time at first making sense of Shakespeare, but during your reading of parts of *As You Like It*, I could envision the scene that described, "All the world's a stage—and all the men and women merely players; and one man in his time plays many parts…"

History, in your class, wasn't merely a list of important happenings and their dates to memorize—it was about <u>real people</u> with motives and problems and solutions. Sometimes their opinions differed so much, there were wars. We learned about adventures of all kinds, about discoveries of new places and new cultures, and about inventions of things to make life more comfortable. You certainly could make life more <u>understandable</u>! And you seemed to <u>enjoy</u> it!

How thankful I am to have been privileged to be one of your students! Your enthusiasm and positive attitude seemed contagious; and it's <u>mind-boggling</u> now to think about how many <u>hundreds</u> of people have benefited from your influence!

Thank you, Miss Flint—you were a "Super-teacher" and a very "Classy Lady"! I'm a better person because of you, and if my family could all be here, they would agree with my words!

Respectfully, Ila Kelley Bench, daughter of Sterling and Bertha Kelley; sister of Ross Kelley, Barbara Wyatt, Joy Combs, and Sterling W. Kelley

LOVE IS ALL THAT MATTERS

TWO BEST FRIENDS

"Well, Hello! Who are you two—
Looking so happy and confident!"
"Why <u>shouldn't</u> we look happy and confident?
We're best friends—and "Indispensable Secretaries"!
Ila May Kelley, and Martha Nell Malone.
We're both helping the Army
To win World War Number Two.
Martha Nell helps the Post Commander
Of Kentucky's Camp Campbell Base;
Ila's boss hires the personnel
For Fort Leonard Wood's Post Exchange.
"Martha's home was in Cadiz, Kentucky;
Ila's was Dixon, Missouri—
But we met at Draughon's Business College
In Paducah, Kentucky; to learn
The skills we would need—
Steno pads and sharp pencils in hand.
How many hours did we listen
To dictation we wrote in shorthand?
The faster the reading, the faster we wrote—
Until the top speed we could write was
One hundred twenty words in one minute!
We soon became masters
Of file cabinets, typewriters, and phones.
Our aim was the same—
An office to tame!
"We were "sisterly" friends,
And this photo will prove
We even had similar "tastes"—
Both suits were beige tweed;
And our business type shoes
Were leather of stylish brown.
"In sixty-four years, we're still "sisterly friends,"

LOVE IS ALL THAT MATTERS

Connected by visits, by letters, and phone.
Life is good—and so thankful are we
For the special joys that we've known!"

Ila Kelley Bench
February 13, 2009

EMMA VIOLA HOLLINGER

It must have been the Voice of God which led me to the very special friendship with a retired Evangelical minister named Emma Viola Hollinger!

Sometime in 1974, a friend in our church women's group, who was a volunteer helper at the Corvallis Care Center, told me about a ninety-three-year old resident there, who had written one book a few years ago, and had more material that she hoped to publish. However, poor health and failing eyesight was making it impossible for her to pursue her plan. Even though I'd had no experience with writing or publishing, I felt curiously compelled to offer my assistance—to at least meet the lady to find out what she needed, and what she expected of a helper. My friend, Nancy, went with me on my first visit to introduce me to the Care Center people, who would in turn, introduce me to Emma.

Then came the shock of my life! Emma, extremely frail and withdrawn, occupied a very small space in her hospital-type bed—curled up in a fetal position—with almost inaudible responses to the nurse's questions! She was almost deaf, as well as blind. There was practically no response as the nurse introduced me and told Emma that I had come to get acquainted, and to write letters for her to her family. She was too sleepy for visiting that day, so I left after a few minutes, <u>thankful</u> to get out into the fresh air! There was an odor inside the building—a mixture of disinfectant with all the other odors there that were being disinfected—that completely took away any appetite I might have had for lunch and made me wonder how long it would take to adjust to the atmosphere there! Only a few more visits convinced me that Emma "was worth it"!

Midmorning visits on Tuesdays seemed a good time for both of us—after her bath, and during her "sitting-in-her-chair" time. The chair was a large, soft "nest" for her, among some fluffy pillows. She had two books in her room— a large-print Bible near her bed, and a padded, leather-bound book titled, *The*

Poetical Works of Henry Wadsworth Longfellow. (There's a handwritten date of Dec. 25, 1903, in the front of the book, published by Hurst and Company of New York, but no copyright date.) My early visits were short, always with reading a few passages of scripture—sometimes my choice, but usually hers—and some kind of small-talk like the weather, or local news that day. I liked to ask her about her many very interesting memories. She told me she was born December 21, 1881, in Iowa, to Benjamin and Julia Paige; was orphaned at the age of five, and was reared by an aunt in Garwin, Iowa. She taught in Iowa schools for a few years, later graduated from the Moody Bible Institute in Chicago, and was ordained to preach in the United Brethren Church of Christ. Her dream was to be a foreign missionary, but she was unable to pass the rigid physical requirements of her denomination; but she developed friendships with a number of missionaries. Some of them still wrote letters to her.

For a while she was a church pastor, then began working as an evangelist; and in 1934, at age fifty-three, she married the Rev. Dallas C. Hollinger who had a daughter named Virginia who never married. Emma and Dallas worked together as pastors and evangelists in Ohio and retired in 1945. Emma then opened a private Bible school in her home until failing health no longer permitted her to continue with that ministry. Her husband worked with Boy Scouts, and she often traveled with him to their camps. She told me that one of her poems, "Listening to the Voice of God," came as an inspiration on one of those trips in the mountains of Idaho.

After her husband passed away, and her arthritis was worsening, she came to the west coast and lived for some years. I can't recall the name of the place she discovered along the northern Oregon coast where there were warm springs and mineral-rich mud that helped to relieve her arthritis pain; and I have forgotten what brought her to Corvallis to live. But I seem to remember reading an article about her that was written at the time her first book was published in 1970. I think she was then living in a place we would now call "assisted living." The book was written and published while she was living there during her eighties.

Shortly after meeting her I discovered that a member of her local church, the Evangelical Church, was her guardian; that another member did her laundry, and some others visited her occasionally. Her only relatives were the step-daughter in Florida, and three nieces—all "senior citizens" themselves—who lived in Nebraska, Wyoming, and Arizona. It took a number of visits for her to feel comfortable with dictating letters for me to send to these family members, but after receiving some answers back from them, she seemed to have more enthusiasm and more awareness. She even began to realize that if I were there, it must be Tuesday! Sometimes in good weather, an aide would put her in a wheelchair so I could take her outside!

Reading to her was an interesting procedure! One needed to almost <u>shout</u> in order for her to hear (she had no hearing aid), so I moved my chair alongside hers, my face near her left "good ear," and held the book back behind her head. As time went on, she became more accustomed to my voice, and we could carry on conversation "away from the ear," but still up close. She soon asked me to expand the reading to include poetry. That's when she directed me to her book of Longfellow poems, whereupon I discovered she had memorized many of them—including *Psalm of Life* and *Thanatopsis*! She also asked me to "check her memory" on some scriptures. She had memorized whole chapters of the Bible! And with a bit of prompting from me, she rapidly recovered an amazing lot of it! What a change from the time I first met her! It was very rewarding to have her anticipate my visits, and to see some sparkle coming back into her once empty-looking eyes, and a smile on her "skin-and-bones" face! Sometimes we even sang some of the old songs we both remembered!

We talked often about her writing—she asked me to get some of the things from the high shelf in her closet to read to her again. There were several "ream-size" boxes full of double-spaced sermons, a box of poems, and the obituary she had written for herself. (Also, hanging farthest back in the closet, in a plastic zippered bag, was a dark green, silky dress with a satin collar that she said was the dress she had saved for her burial. When she said she was "ready to meet her Maker," she really meant it! Not only spiritually, but even to the final earthly requirements for her body!)

There were pages and pages of poems revealing her deep devotion to her Lord, philosophy of life, every-day living, appreciation of nature, etc. She thought it would be nice to have some of them printed into "a little book—not too costly—that people could use for gifts and as a devotional aid." I chose several of them to send to three different publishers—one was to the people who had published her first book—but after each one came a letter saying they couldn't use them. Then, one day, in a little magazine called "Sunshine," I read an ad for a small book of poetry that seemed similar to Emma's collection. I ordered a copy and told about Emma and how I was looking for a publisher— thinking <u>his</u> publisher might be interested. The letter I received with the book was written by the author's wife, who said they had simply taken his manuscript to a printer, and then managed the sale of the book themselves. They had already sold more than six hundred copies in less than a year! I decided that if they could do it, I could do it! Maybe I'd even start with a thousand copies!

After many estimates and much research as to how to organize an attractive, inexpensive little book (which led to a very interesting friendship with Corvallis historian, Ken Munford, who then worked in the OSU Printing Office), I found that CH2M-Hill was the best printer for the money. A good square-dancing friend of ours was in charge of printing there and gave me instructions about how to prepare camera-ready copy for their press. (We could save about fifty dollars if I did this part of the work.) I discovered a typist whose grandmother had once been a roommate of Emma's. She was very excited about the project and had some better fonts than I had on my typewriter. My daughter Becky, who was a high school junior, was able to squeeze some time from school work to do a few simple drawings, and to take a photo of Emma (which she developed as a photography class project) for the book.

The next thing was to find money to pay the printer. Since it seemed like a sort of "love" project, I wondered if the people of her church might like to be included as helpers—and they did! Emma asked me to select a title and some of my favorites, to which she added some of hers, and we came up with twenty-nine poems that represented a variety of themes! She suggested that after we repaid the printing cost, all of the income from sales should go to the Mission Fund of her church. The church was doing some remodeling at that time, which was to include a library, and Emma was really thrilled (as was I) when they decided to name the new library for her! (There was over $500.00 available for her to contribute to the church Missions!) Emma and I agreed that it was the Lord who made all this possible! Perhaps you have heard the expression: "God works in mysterious ways, His wonders to perform!"

On August 1, 1976, Becky and I were invited to attend Emma's church, to share during the service our relationship with Emma, including the introduction of her latest book, *Listening to the Voice of God;* and to remain afterwards for the congregation to examine the books, to buy some, or to arrange for us to send copies to friends. Emma wasn't up to attending, but she was a very happy lady and gave me names of several people to whom she wanted me to send gift books.

I visited one of her nieces in Nebraska once when we made a cross-country trip and corresponded with the other nieces and the step-daughter, inviting them to be my guests to visit Emma, but none of them felt physically able to come.

What a joy it was for our family to know Emma! Gene and the children visited occasionally, and the children made Christmas cookies and decorated little Christmas trees for her. In August of 1978, she suffered a massive stroke from which she never regained awareness of her surroundings. I, and several from her church, took turns sitting with her, reading and talking some—in case she was more aware than she was able to communicate. After about a week— on August 29, 1978, at age ninety-seven, the Lord called her "home," where she had prayed for so long to go. I felt a great relief that she was no longer trapped inside her disabled body—her spirit now free to enjoy the love of her God she had shared with so many people for so many years! And I was thankful that I had been privileged to help her continue her influence through a little book of poems, even when she was almost blind, nearly deaf, and unable to care for herself. I'm especially thankful that in the words of her poems and in hearing stories of her life I found many hidden "blessings in disguise" and found myself "listening to the Voice of God" in new and different ways!

FRITZ AND WINNIE BARTSCH

Fritz and Winnie Bartsch became two of our very good friends soon after we came to live in Corvallis, in 1973. I think Gene met Fritz as a member of the Izaak Walton League—a wildlife/conservation group. Both of them enjoyed fishing and hunting, so in a short time they were spending a lot of time together in fields and streams. Both Fritz and wife Winnie loved playing bridge and traveling, giving all four of us common interests and very close friendships.

Fritz grew up in Wisconsin, where he learned to enjoy nature and the out-of-doors. He helped his dad in his sheet metal business—giving his very sharp mind freedom to become inventive and creative. A PhD, after WWII, qualified him for high level scientific work with the EPA, specializing in water problems.

Winnie was loads of fun in a down-to-earth sort of way. She loved to cook exotic meals and was a dedicated member of the Corvallis Garden Club. Both she and Fritz were wildflower enthusiasts; and wherever they lived, they spent many hours hiking to photograph them. They even had several varieties growing in their yard. Oklahoma was Winnie's childhood home, and during WWII, she was a secretary. From her mother she inherited macular degeneration, which gave her a deep appreciation for sight—as hers slowly deteriorated. But she never let that loss slow her down very much. She "read" books on tape; her clock "spoke" the time on the hour and the half-hour. To play bridge, she used large-print cards and a special very bright lamp that Fritz invented for her use.

A "Mini-Winnie" Winnebago motor home gave them wonderful vacations together—which they liked because they could take their beloved cats, which had come to them as strays. It became their home-away-from-home for hunting trips with long-time friends. Winnie didn't hunt, but she liked camping in the woods, and helped with meals.

Our travels with the two of them were mostly by Holland America—two cruises in the Caribbean to various islands that included Colombia, the Panama Canal, and Costa Rica; one was along the inside passage from Vancouver, Canada to Juneau; and two tours of Alaska that included travel by plane, bus, and train; exploring gold mining country in western Canada, boating down the Yukon River, visiting Fairbanks, Anchorage, and Denali Park, including views of Mt. McKinley. I remember that on one cruise we were waiting in a gathering area with many other passengers for our turn to debark. Being "bridge-nuts," one of our guys pulled a deck of cards out of his carry-on bag, and some kind of horizontal space was created with other bags where we began playing bridge—attracting a few onlookers, of course, but we had fun! Other frequent activities together included bowling in a senior league, crabbing, and digging clams on several different beaches in Washington State—sometimes being joined by some of Gene's family.

Fritz and Gene spent a lot of time with each other fishing and hunting—in rivers, lakes, and the ocean for trout, bass, perch, steelhead, sturgeon, salmon, and anything else that "took their bait"! For hunting, it was to eastern Oregon for deer and elk; to Wyoming for antelope; and to a "blind" for ducks that Fritz had built many years ago on an arm of the Willamette River. With Fritz's ingenuity, you could imagine that it was the "ultimate" in convenience and comfort! A small stove inside provided warmth and a flat top for a coffee pot or a pan of soup! (Or for heating wax with which to remove feathers from ducks.) Stove wood was within easy sheltered reach of the door. A small table, placed near the camouflaged window overlooking the river, served many purposes, including a surface for playing cribbage while they waited for ducks to come into range. And, back at home, what a treat it was to dine upon wild duck roasted with orange sauce, using Winnie's recipe!

On May 31st, 1994, during installation of an alarm system in our house, we were surprised by an attic fire, evidently from old insulation that was ignited by an electrical spark. Gene was preparing to leave soon to play bridge with a foursome that included Fritz, but with the fire emergency, he called Fritz to cancel—and, of course told him the reason. The Fire Department had arrived and were busy with their work, but we were quite surprised that within fifteen or twenty minutes of the call to Fritz (driving time), both Winnie and Fritz were also there to offer assistance, which included insisting that we move into their home to stay while ours was again made liveable! That turned out to be a month! Just one of the many examples of their friendly helpfulness!

The final Wyoming antelope hunt for Fritz and Gene was in September 2000. Soon thereafter, Gene was diagnosed with cancer, which he fought with chemo and radiation until the following May, when he decided to give up the chemo that was really debilitating. But still, he and Fritz had a couple of outings in the Mini-Winnie. It had a couch in the back where Gene could lie down most of the time and make travel possible. They went to the Rogue River to fish for salmon when the fish started upstream to spawn in May. Then early in June, they went to their hunting lodge in eastern Oregon where the members of the Silvies Club gathered for a weekend of opening the lodge for summer use—mending fences, cutting dead trees and bringing them in for fireplace wood, cleaning the spring that supplied water, and general cleaning. Of course Gene wasn't able to do any of the work, but just being with those good friends for the weekend, was better than medicine for him!

While Gene was still living, Fritz began making arrangements for a wrought-iron railing to be made for the steps by our back door—to make going in and out easier and safer for Gene. However, the craftsman didn't get it finished until about a week after Gene's death. Fritz and Winnie both came one afternoon to install it, and it so happened that my sister Barbara and husband Bill Wyatt were here from Missouri for a visit with me. It was a lovely, sunny July afternoon that is still as vivid in my memory as if it were yesterday! The plan was for Fritz and Bill to work on the railing while we all gathered at the picnic table nearby to enjoy some cold drinks with conversation mixed in. Fritz brought with him a very heavy drill with which to drill into the concrete steps, for inserting the bolts that would hold the railing in place. Just holding that drill level for a few minutes was very tiring, so when one hole was drilled, Fritz would say, "Well, let's rest awhile." Then in a few minutes, they drilled another hole, followed by another rest. They needed holes for five bolts. When it was finally installed, we all rejoiced! It was so beautiful—and it looked as if it should have always been there! Perfectly designed, and so very useful! The most special thing about it was the love that Fritz put into the project for the benefit of his friends! It will always be a fond memory for me!

A few weeks after Gene's death, Fritz and Winnie invited me to join them on a riverboat cruise up the Columbia River and into the Snake River. Gene's sister Fern, also a friend of Fritz and Winnie, shared a cabin with me. It was a very enjoyable cruise—limited to ninety-some passengers, with a naturalist on board who called attention to visible wildlife and told great stories of the travels of Lewis and Clark when they had traveled these same rivers with the Corps of Discovery.

With age came physical problems. Winnie had a successful knee replacement, and with housekeeping and gardening help, they were able to stay in their lovely, spacious home. Several weeks later, when Fritz was in the hospital recovering from a hip replacement, their son and daughter-in-law from Portland were in Corvallis for a weekend visit. On Sunday morning, they and Winnie were preparing to go visit Fritz. While Winnie was in her bedroom, the children heard a "thud," and discovered Winnie on the floor. Soon she was taken by ambulance to the emergency room where doctors were not able to save her life. I can only imagine the shock and grief Fritz felt when he was told of her death!

After Fritz recovered from his surgery and the period of therapy, he became a resident at Stoneybrook Assisted Living, by then needing dialysis for failing kidneys. Being a very outgoing person, he was soon surrounded by old and new friends, enjoying many of the activities provided there. But after several weeks, a stroke further disabled him, and he was moved to an assisted living place near his children in Portland. His busy, productive, adventurous life ended peacefully on February 1st, 2009, at age 95.

Life with Fritz and Winnie gave me and my family an abundance of memories to treasure! There were so many very good times with those two people who lived enthusiastically and joyfully to make the most of every minute of life! (Winnie was born October 19, 1915; Fritz, on November 30, 1913.)

PHOTOGRAPH
of
TWO WORLD WAR II MARINES
Colonel (Ret) Arnold ("Gene") Bench and Cpl (Ret) Charles (Chuck) W. Lindberg

What do I notice about this picture? For <u>me</u>, the first thing is the familiar smile and laughing eyes of my husband, Gene—handsome even without the top of his head! The second thing is the happy face of a new friend, Chuck Lindberg—a former Marine I first met only the day before. The next thing is their two hands in the center of the photo—I notice that each hand has part of a finger missing: the left little finger on Gene's hand, the left forefinger on Chuck's. But the <u>real</u> story here is the black-and-white photograph that Gene is holding.

Meeting Mr. Lindberg was one of the thrills of my lifetime! He had served in the 3rd platoon of "E" company, 28th Reg in WWII, and was one of the six Marines present at the <u>first</u> flag-raising atop Mt. Surabachi on Iwo Jima on February 23, 1945! Notice that I said the <u>first</u>. The famous photo that we all know about that occasion was taken four hours later by AP photographer Joe Rosenthal, when the original flag was being replaced by a larger one. The photo Gene is holding is an autographed copy of the original one in which Lindberg participated. He is standing behind the Marine holding the rifle, and himself had the duty of carrying a flame-thrower, as part of a forty-man patrol, led by 1st Lt. George Schrier, that had been ordered to climb the mountain.

Just before the patrol began its climb, Colonel Chandler Johnson called Lt. Schrier aside, gave him an object taken from his map case, and said, "If you get to the top, put it up." The object was an American flag from the USS Missoula—a relatively small one. A Marine staff sergeant named Louis Lowery, a photographer for *Leatherneck Magazine*, asked permission to come along and record the ascent. One person in the group was Corpsman John Bradley, carrying his medical supplies, and wondering how many of the group would return alive. The group naturally attracted the attention of the Marines on the beaches below—and even men aboard the offshore ships trained binoculars to follow the thin line's winding trek, and many expected it to be a slaughter.

The patrol reached the rim of the crater about 10:00 a.m., from which they could see the devastation and rubble left from the American bombing. The Japanese had constructed a catch-system for rainwater on the crater's surface, and fragments of pipe lay scattered about. One of the men found a fragment of usable length for a flag pole and lugged it to their spot—noticing that there was a bullet hole in the pipe through which the rope could be threaded. The rope was from Doc Bradley's kit—rope he carried for using with stretchers.

Lt. Schrier, Platoon Sgt Thomas, Sgt Hansen, and Cpl Lindberg converged on the pole. They shook the folded flag out and tied it in place. Louis Lowery documented the proceedings with a steady succession of camera shots. He moved in close, suggested poses, and cajoled the boys into self-conscious grins with his patter. Louis Charlo joined the four. At 10:20 a.m. they thrust the pole upright in the gusty wind, the first foreign flag ever to fly over Japanese soil. Lowery, wanting added drama for his shot, motioned to Jim Michaels, who crouched dramatically in the foreground with his carbine.

When that small swatch of color fluttered, an amazing cacophony arose from the island below and from the ships offshore—whistles, cheers, and ships' whistles! Chuck Lindberg remembered it as a big wave of noise washing over them. He said it gave him a happy chill, the likes of which he'd never experienced before or since!

Japanese soldiers then began coming out of nearby caves and the men of the patrol became involved in a fierce firefight, with no American casualties. Lindberg and some comrades spent time using flamethrowers and demolition charges to secure the mountain.

From below, the Secretary of the Navy, James Forrestal, decided he wanted to go ashore, and he wanted the Suribachi flag as a souvenir. But Colonel Johnson disagreed. He felt that the flag belonged to the battalion. He decided to secure it as soon and possible, and sent his assistant for operations, Lt. Ted Tuttle, to the beach to find a replacement flag— saying, "And make it a bigger one."

Meantime, the AP photographer, Joe Rosenthal, was having a bad day. Nothing seemed to go right for him. He slipped on a wet ladder and fell into the ocean between the command ship and a landing craft. When he was fished out, he unzipped his camera from its waterproof bag and clicked some shots of Forrestal, then heard the news that a patrol was climbing Suribachi. With a magazine correspondent named Bill Hipple, he headed toward the mountain until they reached the command post of the 28th Regiment. Being too late for the flagraising, Rosenthal said he'd still like to go up, and talked two other armed photographers to go with him.

When Lt. Tuttle returned, he was carrying an American flag he'd obtained from LST-799 on the beach. As it happened, this flag—a good deal bigger than the one now planted on the mountain—had been found in a salvage yard at Pearl Harbor, rescued from a sinking ship on December 7th, 1941. Col Johnson handed the flag to his runner, nineteen-year-old Rene Gagnon, to put inside his field pack, with orders to take it to Lt. Schrier on top of the mountain, and to "tell Lt. Schrier to put this flag up, and I want him to save the small flag for me."

When Rosenthal reached the top, he found two Marines dragging a length of drainage pipe that weighed more than a hundred pounds. The replacement flag was attached to that pole, so that it could be raised simultaneously with the lowering of the first one. Three photographers, including Rosenthal, milled about taking pictures of the operation. No one else on the summit paid much attention to what was going on. One photographer filmed it as a movie. The four squad-members circled closer to the pole, and another one moved up—wearing his Indian-style blanket stuffed through his military belt on his rump. Doc Bradley was walking past with a load of bandages in his arms and was asked to come and help. Rosenthal spotted the movement, grabbed his camera, and clicked off a frame at the instant the flagpole rose upward in a quick arc. The banner, released from their grip, fluttered out in the strong wind! The six people in that photo were Ira Hayes, Franklin Sousley, John Bradley, Harlon Block, Mike Strank, and Rene Gagnon.

Joe Rosenthal was unsure about his photo. He hadn't even had a chance to glimpse the image in his viewfinder. The six continued to struggle with the heavy pole in the whipping wind. Some looked for rocks to add support. Doc offered ropes he'd brought along to tie casualties to stretchers, and they secured the pole. No one paid attention. It was just a replacement flag! It flew for three weeks, eventually chewed up by the strong winds. The important flag—

the first one raised that day—was brought down the mountain and presented to Colonel Johnson, who stored it in the battalion safe.

I have another "connection" to this important historical happening. When I was reading *Flags of Our Fathers*, written by Doc Bradley's son James, I thought to myself that Gagnon is such an unusual name, I should call one of my sister's family members named Chris Gagnon. Sure enough, Rene Gagnon who was part of the second flag-raising, was a second cousin to Chris' father! Chris is the husband of my sister Barbara's granddaughter Carmen!

Charles Lindberg was awarded the Silver Star for bravery, and after World War II, returned home to Grand Forks, N.D., moved to Richfield, Minnesota in 1951, and became an electrician. In 1954, he was invited to Washington D.C. for the dedication of the Marine Memorial. It carries the names of the second group of flag-raisers, but not the first. His death came on June 24, 2007, at age eighty-six. He had spent decades explaining that it was his patrol, not the one captured in the famous photograph by Joe Rosenthal, that raised the <u>first</u> flag over the island.

(I used information from *The Flags of Our Fathers*, by James Bradley, to refresh my memory of the visit with Lindbergh.)

LOVE IS ALL THAT MATTERS

MAI & ARVI TREUDE
FLORIDA—2005

What a treat it was to have ten sunny, summery, February days with my long-time friends! I met Mai and Arvi Treude in 1957 when we lived in Minneapolis; in fact, Mai and I worked in the same office at Insurance of North America for over a year before I became a mother to Becky. The Treudes had come from Estonia as teenagers with their families, by way of being refugees in Germany, to escape the occupation of Estonia by Russia at the time of World War II. We soon became close friends and have maintained that relationship ever since—they visiting us and we visiting them—enjoying outdoor activities like picnics, fishing, crabbing, walking; theatre, comparing reading adventures, and discussing our various experiences and travels. When it came time for them to retire, they moved to Florida, bought a home in Bradenton, which is near Sarasota, and near Anna Maria Key, in sight of Palma Sola Bay. Soon they were offering their warm hospitality to friends from the North and to extended family members still living in Estonia. Just being in their lovely home, tastefully decorated in serene, harmonious colors with collections of art and items from their travels, was a vacation in itself!

This was my second visit with them in Florida and having done a great deal of sightseeing a few years ago while Gene was living, it was especially rewarding this time to just be together doing "everyday" activities, visiting with Arvi's 97-year-old mother Alma, and meeting several Estonian friends who have moved to that area.

"Getting there" on Monday, February 14th, was pleasant and uneventful all the way across the country, until I got to Atlanta where I had to change planes to go on to Sarasota. It was beginning to be foggy when the plane landed at 8:15 p.m., but I soon learned that my connection would be late, or maybe wouldn't arrive at all, because of the fog. The originally scheduled arrival time in Sarasota was near midnight, for which I felt apologetic because it seemed so late, but now it would be ridiculous! How thankful I am for cell phones! With the connection so uncertain, we decided they should just go to bed, and I would call when I got to Sarasota, whatever time it might be. It happened that I finally arrived at 2:00 a.m. Poor Arvi was awakened and picked me up in due time in their sleek, silver Jaguar!

Needless to say, there were no early risers on Tuesday! Late breakfast included fresh-squeezed juice that came from oranges from a friend's yard! Mai likes a daily "adventure," so we spent time that day driving around for me to see various kinds of homes—from small bungalows to gated condominiums, to large "estates" with three- or four-car garages, and screen-enclosed patios with swimming pools. Landscaping everywhere was colorful with blossoming trees; fruit-laden orange, grapefruit and lemon trees; Norfolk Island pines; palms of many sizes and kinds; hibiscus; azaleas; impatiens, poinsettia, and things I don't remember. Mai and Arvi specialize in growing various kinds of orchids— some now in full bloom. One purple Cattleya had five large, fragrant blossoms. (And, it's February!)

Our first stop was at a one-acre farm for fresh-picked strawberries. Many of the surrounding larger farms have recently been sold for housing developments. (New housing developments seem to be everywhere!)

Nearby De Soto National Memorial Park, on a peninsula at the mouth of the Manatee River, was our main destination. At the entrance were hut-like rush shelters—replicas of those that De Soto's entourage (and local Native Americans) lived in when De Soto landed there in 1539 to explore the area for gold, and to establish colonies for Spain. A short movie described their adventure and showed their long, difficult journeys into what are now South Carolina, North Carolina, Alabama, Georgia, Tennessee, Arkansas, and Texas. They traveled back again to the Mississippi River, and down to New Orleans, and sailed along the Gulf coast to a colony on the eastern coast of Mexico. De Soto died of a fever after three years, and was buried in the Mississippi River, having traveled about 4,000 miles on native trails, meeting and battling hostile Indians, leaving behind disease and acts of inhumanity in his overzealous pursuit of riches. Half of the soldiers were lost to sickness and battles and continued on for another year after De Soto's death. No gold was found, and no colonies were established. The only "Indians" Mai and I encountered were life-sized, painted flat replicas in surprising places along the nature walk around the park. Those would especially interest children who were frequent park visitors. The path wound through mangrove thickets, sea grape bushes, palms, live-oak trees, and pines; then along the white sand river beach. Occasional benches along the way provided places to rest and enjoy the sights. We spent several minutes viewing the river, the city of Bradenton in the distance, sailboats and motor boats, pelicans diving for—and catching—fish, and small lizards (maybe Geckos) darting over the rocks in the sun. Geckos were numerous everywhere—occasionally even in the house, which interested Keesu, the cat! An unusual tree there in the park was called Gumbo Limbo with wide-spreading branches and bare, cinnamon colored, smooth bark.

Mai has neuropathy, which is affecting her feet, and she likes to walk for exercise, even though it's sometimes slow. I <u>need</u> to walk more for exercise myself. But <u>think</u> about it—<u>shopping</u> is walking, too! And we both like to shop 'til we drop, whether we buy anything or not. What fun it was, nosing around a very large Sarasota mall—in Sak's and Chico's for clothes, shoes and jewelry; in specialty shops of unique housewares, art, and crafts; and in shops along the beaches catering especially to tourists. At one pricey jewelry store I found a very beautiful, uniquely styled gold pendant made of the Black Hills colors of gold. It was concentric circles, alternating the three colors, about two inches in diameter, thin and flexible—on a yellow gold chain. I just <u>had</u> to investigate it—even possibly <u>invest</u> in it? $1,750.00! Some of the jewelry was on special for 50% discount, but this piece wasn't—not until March 1st. The saleswoman eagerly offered to hold it for me and ship it to me later—including, of course, the 7% sales tax. I told her I'd <u>think</u> about it! No, it didn't come home to my jewelry box, but I did find some things to add variety to my Clothes Tree-and-Sears wardrobe.

Our Saturday special activity was a luncheon and fashion show at the elegant El Quistador Country Club, overlooking (I <u>think</u>) Palma Sola Bay. It was a benefit for the Bradenton Art Center. Before we sat down at our table we surveyed the view from the second-story dining room windows. Pink Flamingos frolicked in and out of the trees along the beach in the distance, beyond the grounds landscaped with grass, trees, shrubs, and large decorative pools. Lunch was delicious quiche, Caesar salad, chunks of fruits, scones, and "sinful" layered raspberry cake. A number of artists had tables loaded with various unique hand-made things such as jewelry, handbags, paintings, and scarves. I discovered that I was sitting next to June Morse who had a display of hand-painted silk scarves of various shapes and beautiful colors. I had been warned to take with me a cozy sweater of Mai's, but it was almost 80 degrees outside, and I couldn't imagine I wouldn't be comfortable in my short-sleeved dress. It turned out to be really uncomfortably <u>cold</u>, so I decided that one of those large silk squares—the one with white magnolia blossoms painted on a purplish-rose background—draped around my shoulders, would feel <u>just right</u>! (June later told me that the blossoms of the magnolia tree in her yard inspired the design.) The fashions were well displayed by various Art Club members; colorful, original designs—even reasonable prices—that would be a lot of fun to wear if one lived in the "Florida Culture"!

A couple of dinners out were delightful: one was near "home" at a small white-table-cloth place with Greek and Italian specialties; but the really special one was at a place called the Sand Bar on an Anna Maria Island beach. A small group played music while we enjoyed seafood followed by Key Lime pie, and watched the sun sinking over the water into a flaming sunset.

On Sunday, I read in the paper about an annual tradition that commemorates the return trip of cattlemen who used to drive their cattle across the state to markets to sell in Tampa. It's called The Cracker Trail Ride, 120 miles, lasting a week. There are about 100 horses and "Cracker" members, as well as some non-riders. The youngest children ride on mules or in family wagons. Experienced teen-age riders handle their own horses. They arise about 6:30 a.m. and ride out about 8:00 o'clock each morning. A caterer follows with trailers and a smoker. The nights' activities can include story telling, music, or whatever "strikes their fancy." As they ride through communities, they draw a lot of attention, which inspires them to do entertaining riding to show off for the bystanders.

Perhaps some of my most thrilling experiences happened every morning—hearing bird songs, especially those of mocking birds and cardinals, through the open windows! Being a "midwestern girl," I really miss those songsters, and the bright color of the cardinals. It seemed that the songs were longer and more prevalent at the start of my second week there, as if the birds realized that it was now spring and time to sing! Doves' calls in the distance were common, as were eastern bluejays and crows, but maybe the very best scenes were of occasional yellow butterflies, and a pair of doves sipping water from the sculpted white birdbath just outside the window that was one of my frequent spots to read.

LOVE IS ALL THAT MATTERS

Florida isn't a place I'd choose to live year-round, but I really like being there with my special friends in the winter! Thanks, again, Mai and Arvi!

Chapter 9: Miscellaneous

DID I REALLY DO <u>THAT</u>?!

I feel very humble and thankful for the active, eventful life God has given me to enjoy for ninety-plus years! He placed me in a caring family, surrounded me with inspiring people, provided a lifetime of rewarding experiences, gave me a loving husband, and brought me two wonderful children! I've never been one to "blow my own horn," so this seems a bit unnatural; but I realize that some of the things that He has helped me accomplish, should maybe be said. They are part of "who I am"!

*My first award was birth (June 21, 1925) to the position of first sibling in the Sterling and Bertha Kelley family. In this position I had undivided parental attention—but later, many family responsibilities as well, when joined by two brothers and two sisters.

*Age three: Began singing in public—at church: "Will the Angels Let Me Play?"

*Started to school in 2nd grade; and began second year in 4th grade.

*8th Grade graduation—Attended special awards meeting with County Superintendent and teachers in County Seat of Vienna, Mo.—was one of highest ranking for grades in Maries County. While there, Dad took me to the office of a friend of his who was a well-known attorney. He praised my accomplishment and ambition and gave me a pencil with a special replaceable eraser—I'd never seen that type before.

*In high school, selected for a part in a school play—a child who wore a pinafore with ruffles and a big bow in back. (My "credentials": the smallest and youngest student in school.)

*Played violin and cello in school orchestra and sang in school Glee Club. (Sometimes went to competitions with other schools.)

*Valedictorian of the class of 1941—Two boys and I had grades so close together the winners' grade totals were figured to four decimal places. I was given a full scholarship to my choice of college. I chose Draughon's Business College in Springfield, Missouri.

*First employment was Secretary to the Post Exchange Personnel Manager at Fort Leonard Wood, Missouri.

*College at University of Missouri, Columbia: Selected by Phi Upsilon Omicron (Home Ec Honorary) for scholarship and citizenship award as a sophomore. (Received a prize of an electric alarm clock in a walnut case.)

*Worked part time as secretary to Dr. Bertha Bisbey, Professor of Dietetics to earn college expenses. Typed theses for her graduate students which had to be four copies with no errors and no apparent erasures.

*Elected to Phi Upsilon Omicron (Home Economics Honorary) in Junior year.

*Elected to Mortar Board (Womens' Scholastic Honor Society) in Senior year.

*Honored for high grades and participation in honor societies at Honors Convocation at graduation.

*Vocational Home Economics teacher at New Franklin High School (1950)

*Marine Corps wife—Hostess for husband's social needs; gave support to families of officers who worked for him, especially when the men were deployed away from base; corresponded with wives of officers in his Battalion during the year he was in Vietnam.

*One social occasion was hosting a USMC birthday banquet in London where the Commandant of the Royal Marines and his wife were honored guests.

*Another: Invited to tea at U.S. Ambassador's home in London with military wives. Honored guest Antonia Frazer, author of *Mary, Queen of Scots*, spoke about writing that book and one about other English notables.

*Secretary to Law Specialist (Navy Cdr.) at Quantico, Virginia (1951)

*Secretary to Supervisor of Civil Service office (Mr. Shuttler) at Quantico, Virginia (1953)

*Secretary to Manager of Safety Dept., INA Insurance Co, Minneapolis, Minnesota (1957-1958)

*Mother—Adopted two children: Rebecca Anne (Becky) in Minnesota in 1959; David Eugene in Oregon in 1963.

*Grandmother—Leah Elizabeth Wilber, 1978; Thomas Eugene Butler, 1998; Evan Nelson Butler, 2000.

*Great-grandmother—Maureece Shavalya Wilber, 1999; Chance Armel Francois, 2012; Chelsea Violet-A'ree Francois, 2015.

*Visited a retired minister (Emma Hollinger) in a nursing home for several years. Designed and arranged to have a book of her poems published and marketed. She donated the income from those books to her church—Evangelical in Corvallis.

*Served on board of Elders at Calvin Presbyterian Church for six years.

*Served on board of Deacons at Calvin for eight years.

WHERE CAN A TRAIN TAKE YOU?

I'm writing this on March 7, 2002, and just yesterday returned home from spending a few days with the Butler family in Seattle. Most of my six days there were sunny—unexpected in Seattle at this time of year, so we made the most of our time to be outdoors. They live only a short distance from a wide, sandy beach-park along the eastern shore of Puget Sound, so that was a destination for most of a whole morning. It's a place where almost-four-year-old Thomas and almost-two-year-old Evan like to use some of their non-stop energy: swinging on different designs of swings; digging and running in the sand; discovering unusual rocks and shells; feeding ducks in a little lake made by a small creek; flying a yellow and red airplane shaped kite, watching sailboats and steam ships passing by on the water; and counting cars on an occasional train rushing by on the land-side of the beach. Part of their usual beach ritual is to finish with a stop at the little shore-side fish'n chips place near the parking area. A lunch of batter-dipped fish, French fries, coleslaw, and drinks was topped off with soft ice-cream swirled into small cones.

Other days I joined into play-dates with Kid-friends and Mommy-friends, shopping and nearby playground exercising. And, of course a few cartoons, puzzles, books, and games. I welcome every opportunity to enjoy time with all of them, but especially Thomas and Evan who are growing so fast and seem so eager for new experiences!

A train from Albany seems to be my safest and most comfortable way to travel to Seattle now—and I like seeing some "sights" that show views of towns and countryside not seen from the freeway.

Quite frequently, I find that one experience leads me to be reminded of some similar one from "away-back-when." Riding home yesterday reminded me of an unusual train trip along the East coast a number of years ago. I think it must have been shortly after school was out in June of 1972. We lived in Springfield, Virginia; Becky was about thirteen, and David about nine years old. Disney World in Orlando was becoming a popular place to visit by then, although far from its present development; and a special train made travel there more interesting for us, because if we were going to be in that part of Florida, we'd like to enjoy more of the state, beyond the areas reachable by the train. So we made a reservation for an unusual train ride.

We drove to Lorton, a small town a few miles from our home, late in the afternoon, arriving there around 6:00 p.m.—in time to watch our car, along with many others, being loaded aboard the train! We were to sit in a coach-type car in seats that adjusted to a very comfortable angle for sleeping and were given pillows and blankets. But first, before the train was ready to depart, we were invited to the dining car to be elegantly served a delicious dinner on white-cloth-covered tables. One car on the train was set up to provide entertainment for children—movies, pop-corn, etc. A lounge car was available for adult movies, drinks and socializing. Come morning, we had breakfast in the dining room, and were each given a box-lunch just before arrival in Orlando about noon. We were surprised to see how rapidly and efficiently the cars were unloaded, so we were soon on our way to other adventures.

Disneyworld, of course, was our first one. After being at Disneyland in California about three years before, we had an idea of what to expect, and knew some tricks for making the most of our time—trying to avoid long periods of standing in lines. We had allowed time for two days there, but we were so "efficient," we discovered we'd seen all we wanted to see after one day.

The Everglades was one of our important stops, and was very impressive to David, who was especially interested in the alligators and crocodiles! A boat-ride took us through the marshes for close-up viewing of the water animals and many kinds of tropical plants—many of them with blossoms.

Driving through orange groves was new and different, and a trip along some of the Keys gave Becky and David a chance to play in the sand. (Key lime pie was good, too!)

Becky was happy when we stopped for a couple of nights at Homestead Air Base. Being in the Marine Corps, Gene was entitled, with his family, to stay in quarters in the Officers' Guest House if space was available (and it was), so we had very comfortable rooms for a fraction of the cost of a motel. Meals were served in the nearby Club, and Becky was very happy to see the swimming pool. She, being "13-going-on-20," was also happy to find a late-teen-age bikini-clad girl to share her interest in sun-bathing. It didn't take as much southern Florida sun—and a lot more sun-screen—to get a sun tan than it did in northern Virginia!

On the way back north, St. Augustine was a stop for a short tour of the "old town" and a bit of history—the oldest city in the U.S., and originally a Spanish colony.

A tour of Cape Canaveral was exciting for all of us, even though we had to use our imaginations as to what it might be like to see a rocket or a space ship launched!

My niece, Wendy Parnell, whom we'd visited in Cadiz, Spain a couple of years before when her husband Mike was stationed there in the Navy, now lived in Charleston—another Navy assignment for him. Wendy enjoyed giving us a short tour of Charleston, and all of us—except maybe David—enjoyed their "bed and breakfast" hospitality. David's problem was their dog—a full-grown Great Dane "puppy" who liked to play. All was well for awhile, until the dog pushed David down and stepped one of his huge feet into David's face. That even frightened me and ended the fun with the dog for David! He was thankful to get back home to play with his Beagle.

It's interesting how a commonplace ride on the Amtrak yesterday afternoon reminded me of that overnight ride so long ago on the "piggy-back" train to Orlando—the beginning of a great vacation with our growing children who seem to have grown up too fast!

MY NOSE KNOWS

I wonder how many of us think very often about the value and the blessing of our five senses! No doubt their presence in our bodies is for the purpose of survival—to warn us of impending danger, to make it possible to see, to hear, to smell, to taste, and to feel what we need to know for safe living. Most of the time those things are doing their work in our behalf even if we don't consciously "call" them into action. The smell of smoke alerts us of nearby fire; the sight of flames shows us where it is! Judgment is necessary to know what action we take. If a bite of bread tastes moldy, we don't swallow it, or eat the rest of that piece of bread. Hearing a siren warns of a speeding vehicle, and we make sure we're out of the way. We can certainly be thankful for those life-saving warnings! But if you stop to think about it, used in those ways, those senses create an emotion of a certain amount of fear or caution.

But what of the pleasures that come from those five senses! We can add gratitude for happiness as well as thankfulness for safety by taking some time to consciously notice and enjoy the many feelings aroused by one or more of those five senses. I'll give you examples of a few of my favorites, and you'll probably be reminded of a <u>multitude</u> of your own! I expect the <u>emotion</u> or experience that accompanies the "sense" is the reason for the pleasure!

For me, the fragrance of bacon and coffee cooking stirs many childhood memories—an especially fond one is of waking up in Grandma and Grandpa Ross' house. Other long-ago memories are of smelling freshly cut grass and hay. (I was often the one behind the hand-pushed lawn mower or helping with getting the hay to the barn.) I remember the smell of Tabu lipstick—the light-pink color of "natural" was the first one I was allowed to use. And there's a vivid memory of Arrid underarm deodorant fragrance. I felt so "grown-up" when I first used that! Several years later, I learned that my Avon bath oil fragrance traveled half way around the world! When Gene was in Vietnam for a year, I frequently took my bath and relaxed in pajamas after putting the kids to bed—then there was time to write my daily letter to Gene. He soon let me know that he especially looked forward to my letters because "my fragrance came with them"! Flowers that are special for me are honeysuckle—its fragrance wafting through my childhood home's bedroom window; daphne—because it blooms so early in the spring; Christmas greenery; and some kinds of roses. Baby powder gives me very precious memories of my children. I remember the kind of comforting smell of the cow when it was my turn to do the milking; and I love the smell of the earth after a rain when the ground has been dry for a long time. (Not long ago a friend told me that she remembered really liking the smell of <u>concrete</u> after a summer rain! I realized at least <u>one</u> difference between a country girl and a city girl!) Mom was smart to time her bread-baking so that we'd come home from school to that wonderful aroma! (And then enjoy a slice of it covered with home-made butter and jelly—especially if lucky to get a "heel"!)

By now you get my idea about positive uses of sensory perception, so I'll simply name some others:

"Sight"

-Moonrise—especially over a lake in October.

-Sunrise—every one of them different!

-Sunset—one of my favorites, standing with Dad one June evening on the Connemara coast of Ireland, looking at my watch to see that the time was 10:30 p.m.!

-A toddler trying to learn to walk.

-Soaring hawks.

-A bald eagle perched on a dead "snag."

-A clear, mountain stream—(is that a "sight" or a "sound"?)

-A rainbow—a really special sight for me because it's not only beautiful, but spiritual. Biblically, it was a message from God, and it speaks to me of faith, hope, and love!

"Taste"

-Chocolates in Perugia, Italy—with my sister Joy

-Chocolate covered peanuts—with <u>anyone</u>, or with <u>no one</u>!

-Cracker-Jacks—a treat from Mom coming home from grocery shopping – even a prize inside!

-Potato soup and dumplings for dinner—cooked in a black, iron pot on the wood stove.

-Peach cobbler—almost always one on Mom's kitchen counter!

-"Snow-cream" as soon as the snow stopped falling

-Succulent, fresh lobster or crab—on a Maine coast, or self-caught Oregon Dungeness

"Sound"

-A cardinal's song—I really miss that while living in Oregon!

-A robin's song on a long, summer evening—often in Oregon!

-A whippoorwill singing—in Missouri, almost always about 9:00 p.m.

-Owl hoots late at night

-A high-flying plane—in Missouri when I was a kid. Who are the people on it? Where are they going? Can they see <u>me</u> down here waving at them? Will I ever be riding on a plane? (I don't wave at the people any more, but I <u>do</u> think about the people and where they might be going!)

-Applause—when my siblings and I sang together as children!

-A laughing baby!

-Gene's laughter!

-"Ila May!"—When Mom or Dad said it, it meant some kind of trouble for you-know-who!

"Feel"

-Fur—my new mink stole one Christmas

-A baby's skin, and its hand in mine

-Warm sun on a cold day

-Mud between my toes

-Dixon Drug Store—in summer – small, glass top tables and wrought iron chairs with round seats, in the back of the store where it was sort of dark and cool! Of course, with a dish or a cone of ice cream!

-Gene's stolen kiss on the back of my neck!

-Warmth of a campfire—that covers exciting sight, crackling sound, warm feeling, smoky smell, and even taste, if you put hot-dogs and marshmallows with it!

Well, a positive attitude is supposed to help keep us from stress; and appreciation of the "little" things deepens our joy! May you frequently find abundant joy in many bright spots that you happen to come upon unexpectedly!

SOME GARDENS

Gardens have been part of my life for as long as I can remember. Mom used to tell us bedtime stories from her life experiences, and one that somehow really interested me was the one about choosing a spot to build their first house and planning the use of their ten acres two miles north of Dixon, Missouri. It was a right-triangle shape, having sloping hills on the north and south, with a fairly wide flat "creek valley" in between. Oak woods bordered all of the west side, and the road defined the east side that was the triangle's hypotenuse. It was February 1925, and she and Dad had just returned from living in Kansas and Oklahoma for the first eight months of their marriage. (Their honeymoon was spending the summer following the Kansas wheat harvest as it moved north. After that was finished, they went to Oklahoma where Dad worked in the oil fields with some of Mom's uncles and cousins.) They were expecting their first child in June and were eager to get the house built to get their own roof over their heads!

There was some snow on the ground, and as they walked around to explore the site, they noticed a small area on the south slope where the snow was melted off. Mom stepped up on a big rock that was there and said, "Right here is where the house should be!" From there they had a view of all the property, and it would be a cozy place for catching the winter sun. Dad agreed.

That northernmost angle was chosen for the garden, lawn, and house; then came the barn and "cow lot." This garden was for some perennial things like rhubarb, asparagus, raspberries, and strawberries; then in the spring they planted potatoes, peas, carrots, beans, okra, cabbage, lettuce, radishes, onions, tomatoes, and things that could grow without a lot of space per plant. In part of the "bottom" field, which was actually better soil, they planted things like squash, pumpkins, melons, cucumbers, sweet potatoes, and corn. A couple of climbing beans were planted by each corn stalk to be helpers for each other—the beans put nitrogen into the soil for the corn; the corn provided the "pole" for the bean vines to climb.

One of my earliest garden memories is of the strawberry patch when I was about three or four years old. Mom and Dad were working there, either picking berries or weeding; I don't remember which, because that wasn't important to me at the time. I had been playing on the lawn nearby, but decided I'd like to be more sociable, so I found my way through various plants and rows to where they were working. Dad showed me how the plants grew with little runners going out all around and said I shouldn't step on them. In fact, he told me I should go back to the yard to play! But the birds were singing, and there were butterflies to watch and try to catch, so I didn't do what I was told to do as soon as I was expected to do it. I had even forgotten to watch where I stepped, so I soon felt some persuasive "swats" to remind me. Needless to say, I learned two lessons right there: to listen to parental instruction and do as I was told, and to watch where I stepped in a garden!

As I grew older, there were plenty of opportunities to watch where I stepped! All five of us children were expected to help in various ways with planting, tending, and harvesting. One source of money was picking bugs off the potato plants and worms off the cabbages. The potato bugs were especially prolific—they were soft, reddish colored, about ¼" long and almost as wide. (Real fat ones might have been a little bigger.) I think they were probably the larvae of the Colorado Potato Beetle. Each child carried a tin can with a little kerosene in the bottom of it, held it under a branch and flicked the bugs into it with a small stick. We kept thousands of those little pests from growing up, and were paid, I think, a nickel for each can full.

Setting out tomato and cabbage plants Mom had started from seed early in the spring was a "child-labor" assembly line affair. Mom dug the holes; one of the younger kids put a plant into it; an older one with more experience held it upright, pulled soil around it and firmed it in place; the next one came along with a bucket of water and put about a cupful on each plant to "water it in;" the fourth one followed, covering the watered spot with dry soil.

At harvest time we learned to appreciate the work of growing so many good things to eat. It was fun to climb up into the cherry trees that grew in the yard to help Mom (and the birds) pick the juicy, red jewels that Mom turned into delicious pies. Some of us had fun ripping open the fresh pea pods to enjoy the awesome order of peas attached so neatly in a row—then having some for dinner in a delicate white sauce with just a touch of pepper. (Opening a pea pod and appreciating the beauty of the neat row of peas was a great experience for a child, but as an adult, I preferred the newer variety called Sugar Peas with edible pods. They saved a lot of the work of shelling, plus making use of those delicious pods ourselves rather than giving them to the pigs!) Corn was more of a challenge, to rip off the tough husk and pick away all the silk. The "pay-off" came when we cleaned up the debris and could save the tender inside husks for making dresses on clothes-pin dolls. Now and then, alongside a full ear, we'd find a small, undeveloped ear that was a "ready made" doll with a silky fringe at the bottom of her dress!

After we were married, Gene and I didn't often have the space or the time for a garden. As children, the garden had provided a large percentage of our food—eaten fresh during summer, then canned or stored in the cellar—enough to last all winter. As adults, living in towns, it seemed better to work for money to buy food someone else worked to grow. Our limited gardening then became growing a few flowers or herbs or small amounts of things like peas, green beans, lettuce, radishes, and tomatoes just for summer enjoyment. One such garden was in Minnesota. It is lake country, and we liked to fish for the bass and pike, so Gene frequently "planted" some fish remains alongside the plants. Plants really liked that! Here, in the country near Corvallis, Oregon, we joke that the little bit of gardening we do is for the deer. Some of the things we'd like best to grow—like petunias—are favorites of the deer, too. They drink from the bird bath, sleep under the big fir tree in the field, rest on the front lawn, and just generally make themselves "at home." Gene says he has to chase them out of the driveway to get his car out of the garage when he goes deer hunting! So …we learn to live with them. After all, they were here first!

Mom and Dad didn't move very often, but wherever they lived, there was a garden. Their last one, in Columbia, Missouri, for the last forty some years of their lives was extra small by their standards, but by making less space between rows, snuggling things together, letting cucumbers climb on the fence, etc, they grew surprisingly many things—and weren't satisfied. So when Dad retired, they rented a vacant lot a couple of blocks away to get the space they wanted for vegetables and flowers for cutting—much of which they shared with friends and the Food Bank. Then, the yard around the house became their floral showpiece. The summer of their 50ᵗʰ wedding anniversary they planted a raised garden, shaped like two overlapping wedding rings. That one was planted with many kinds of just white, yellow, and gold colored flowers.

Gardening, for my parents, for my sister Joy, and for most gardeners, seems to be a combination of physical therapy and the enrichment of one's spirit. The soil and water and air of the good Earth are the life support for all of us, and she deserves our respect and appreciation. A fancy little sign among the flowers in my parents' garden read, "A kiss of the sun for pardon, the song of a bird for mirth. One is nearer God's heart in a garden than anyplace else on Earth." I truly believe that! I'm sure that growing up with gardening parents in the Depression era gave me a great subconscious knowledge of the miracle of plant life that carried over into a greater appreciation for all life (except for those pesky potato bugs)!

(You might like to think about comparing gardening to the nurturing and rearing of children??)

FROM OREGON TO VIRGINIA—2003

I'm writing this for two reasons: first, of course, is to remember the rewarding visit with my very dear friend, Carla Spicer—but another value is that it was the first time in my life that I had made a long trip to an unfamiliar location, without assistance at the end of it, such as being met by a friend or family member with the transportation to take me to my final destination! I was quite surprised to have that feel so "scary"! Planning it was interesting, but it was really challenging!

Another story will tell about living in Naples, Italy, in the early 1950's when Gene was an officer in a Marine Corps detachment that was assigned to guard some of the international offices that had moved to Naples from London. The Commanding Officer of the guard detachment was Capt. Raymond Spicer, whose young wife, Carla, was a lovely Italian lady from Genoa, and we rapidly became very good friends. Even being Italian herself, she seemed a bit lonely in Naples because the culture, food, and language dialect were quite different from those of her life along the Italian Riviera— sort of "lower class." I, of course, felt like a total stranger—this being my first experience of even being in a foreign country, much less living there, needing to learn my way around, and how to shop for daily needs. I was very thankful for Carla's help in learning the language and ways of "fitting in."

After two-and-a-half years together there, our husbands' assignments never again coincided, but we called ourselves "sisters" and maintained our friendship through phone calls, correspondence, and several short visits.

During this last summer, the thought occurred to me that I would like to visit her in Virginia. Her husband had died of a heart attack about seventeen years ago, and she maintained their home at Triangle (near Quantico), which included <u>learning</u> to drive. Sons Michael and Raymond were on their own by then: Michael had graduated from Harvard Business School, married, and was working; Raymond graduated from the Naval Academy and was now in the Navy. Occasional visits to Italy through the years kept her in touch with her family there.

For a few weeks, I had called her several times and found no one at home, I tried writing a letter. Still no answer. After several days I received a call from Michael who had happened to be at her house and checked the answering machine. From him I learned that she had had a stroke, was in a hospital, and was getting dialysis three times a week! Not long after that, her sons arranged for her to be in Greenspring Village, an assisted living facility in Springfield—a few miles north of her home, and in the town where our family had lived for four years before moving to Corvallis.

The thought about visiting her was still in my mind, but from phone conversations with her, she sounded very unhappy, and once said, "I would like to see you, but I wouldn't want you to see me like this!" So I contented myself with phone visits, seeming to be still getting "internal messages" that said, "Visit Carla." I did have a Frequent Flyer certificate that needed to be used before February, so my air fare would even already be paid.

I called Marge Jones, another friend who still lived in Springfield, and asked about the location of Carla's new home, nearby motels, etc. Marge would have given me a place to stay, and transportation, but she was soon leaving to spend extended time in Arizona. I then called the Greenspring Village and discovered that they had some guest rooms for visitors—one could be available on November 4, 5, and 6. Next, a call to Delta for a reservation. Answer was "yes"! This almost seemed like a "sign" for proceeding! In the meantime, Carla's son, Raymond, had been selected for Admiral—and transferred to Washington, D.C. I asked him for his opinion about the trip. He said Carla might feel "guilty" if she thought that I would go "all that way just to see her." So I told him I could tell her I had other friends in the area I'd like to visit, too, in which case he thought seeing me would be very good for her.

Now, it was "nail-down" time—early in October. I chose to leave on Tuesday the 4th of November, and return on Saturday, the 8th. That would give me one extra day if I should be able to see some other friends. From a few more calls I learned that a good shuttle service, the Super Shuttle would be convenient transportation from Reagan Airport, would cost only sixteen dollars, and would deliver me to the main entrance to Greenspring Village. (The shuttle had an interesting phone number: 1-800-BLUEVAN—and the vans are actually blue!)

About three days before I left, a small cluster of blisters appeared on the right side of my upper lip, and I had some occasional shooting pains around my right ear; but I couldn't let a little fever blister stop me, and if my ear was still bothering me when I got home, I'd see a doctor. After all, I'd only be gone for five days.

My plane left Portland at 7:00 a.m., which meant I'd have to catch Anthony's 3:00 a.m. shuttle from the Ramada Motel in Corvallis. I set my alarm for 2:00 a.m.—time to eat something before leaving home—and the pain in my ear felt better. There was some spare time at the airport after checking in, and I had a new book with me to begin reading: (*The Secret Life of Bees*, by Sue Monk Kidd). On the plane a small breakfast of cereal, yogurt, a banana, and a granola bar was served, but I was too sleepy to read much along the way. I changed planes in Cincinnati, arrived at the Reagan airport in D.C., and was ready for a shuttle by 4:30 p.m.

I was happy to find the weather warm and sunny for my first look at that city since 1973. There were awesome changes—an elevated Metro train, many more multi-lane freeways, and bumper-to-bumper evening traffic moving at a snail's pace. Thankfully, the shuttle could use express lanes and move faster. I tried to call Carla from the airport, but she wasn't in her room. Another call to her nurse's station assured me she'd get my message of my whereabouts.

I found Greenspring Village to be truly a "village," located not far from where we'd lived in Springfield, in an area that we'd seen as woods. I wondered if I'd ever be able to find my way between Grove Terrace and Carla's area! When I arrived at my room after checking in, I found a lovely, large arrangement of flowers that Carla had ordered for me! One of the residents took me to the Renaissance Gardens area where Carla lives. We had a joyful greeting, a light supper, introductions to some of her friends and aides, and a lot of catch-up talking until bedtime—and agreed to meet in her dining room for breakfast at 8:00 a.m.

What a surprise met my eyes when I awakened and looked in the mirror! The right side of my face was covered with many red blotches and some blisters of various sizes! My first thought was that it could be an allergic reaction—maybe from the shrimp that had been in last evening's meal—but I'd never before been allergic to shell fish! At that point there was nothing to do but to "grin and bear it" for the time being.

After breakfast we found a cozy little sitting room where we could visit and look at some pictures I'd brought with me. When Carla had to go for dialysis after lunch, I decided I should look for some medical advice about my face. Greenspring had a medical staff, but it was only for residents. However, one of the pharmacists said my rash looked to her very much like Shingles and said I should see a doctor. She told me about a nearby clinic with an emergency room, and it was easy to call a cab to take me there. (The triage nurse who checked me in liked my address—she was from Portland, Oregon, married to an Air Force man who had graduated from OSU!) Their Dr. McGuire's diagnosis was Shingles, with an explanation of its origin as chickenpox—the virus remaining in the body and hiding at the roots of nerves until something like stress aroused it to action. His prescription was an anti-viral medication to take five times a day for a week. He also said that I should see an eye specialist soon, and that I would only be contagious to someone who hadn't had chickenpox or hadn't had a chickenpox vaccination. He thought I probably needn't worry about the people at Greenspring as long as I didn't touch them.

It so happened that Becky's family had planned to be visiting Brian's mother in Towson, Maryland, near Baltimore while I was in Virginia, and wanted to pick me up Friday to spend that afternoon and night with them. I decided I couldn't expose my grandsons who were ages five and three, but a call to Becky assured me they had had vaccinations. Another call to my doctor's nurse here in Corvallis got an appointment for me with a Corvallis Clinic ophthalmologist when I got home. His prescription was one drop of an antiviral liquid every two hours, nine times a day. I also was told that the blister cluster on my lip was the first Shingles eruption, and that the ear pain was an early symptom.

Thursday was a good day with Carla, even though my appearance was so grotesque. That evening a friendly volunteer with a guitar gathered a few residents in a sitting room for some socializing. She led some "camp-type" group songs, and then introduced a game that reminded me of some of my writing class exercises. The idea of the game was to develop a story. A person

494

drew one of the slips of paper she held that had one word on it. The person drawing it added to the story using that word in some way. To begin, someone had to suggest a name for the main character in the story, and "Red Riding Hood" was suggested. It was amazing and funny to hear about all the things that happened to her—getting lost, being found, her conversations with several animals in the woods, etc.!

Becky came to pick me up on Friday and stayed for a short visit with Carla herself. Carla hadn't seen her since she was a small girl. Butlers took me to visit a nearby old home—The Hathman House—now owned by the National Park Service, and one of the oldest homes in the country. The estate had been famous for its iron works. That evening, a really tasty dinner was prepared by Margaret (Brian's mother) and Brian—Crab Imperial, young asparagus, fresh green salad, rolls, and chocolate cake! Thomas and Evan frequently seemed to be studying my face which must have looked awfully strange to them. Becky simplified my appearance to them by describing the splotches as "owies"! I was able to change my departure location from Washington's Reagan airport to Baltimore, and still get back to Portland about the same time as originally scheduled. Margaret very helpfully called her shuttle driver to pick me up for the ride to the airport to begin the flight back home.

Except for the Shingles outbreak, it was a very rewarding trip—and, as I often find, a valuable learning experience! When doing something for the first time, it helps to make a plan, and gather as much information as possible to have an idea of what to expect; and to not be afraid to ask questions! From the Shingles, I learned I need to reduce stress when possible. Maybe stress comes from just the way I take some things more seriously than I should—or maybe I try to make things "too perfect." I also made two decisions: unless it's a matter of life or death concerning me or someone in my family, I will (1) never live in a large city; and (2) never live in a large nursing home. But wait! Some advice to me that Gene stressed until the end of his life was, "Never say 'never'!" and, "Stay flexible"! So maybe I should re-word those two decisions: "I hope I will never need to live in a large city"; and "I hope I will never need to live in a large nursing home"! But just those few hours with my dear friend Carla, made that "adventure" with its surprises and some inconveniences totally worth all my effort!

BUGS

Some bugs just "bug" me! I know that the human mind probably cannot comprehend the number of various insects that inhabit Earth, and I know that life as we know it couldn't possibly exist without them—so I have tremendous respect for <u>almost</u> all of them. Mosquitoes are a nuisance, but they at least provide food for swallows I like to watch darting over my field in the spring. Spider webs are sometimes kind of unsightly indoors, so I don't <u>encourage</u> spiders to take up residence in my house; but still, I frequently find some of their "maternity wards." Outside is different. Spiders trap all kinds of bugs that do various kinds of damage, so that's good. And, what a joy it is to look or walk outside on a frosty morning and find a lacy, delicate-looking web— intricately designed, securely attached in several places for stability, just waiting for "the catch of the day"! I'm also a good friend to a praying mantis, a ladybug, or even snakes and bats—when they're outside!

Box elder bugs are a different story. A few years after we moved into our house on Overlook Drive, we noticed that in the spring and fall there were large congregations of them around for a few weeks. They especially seemed to enjoy the warmth of the south and west sides of the house. That meant having them ready to come inside at the doors we most often used and finding residue where they had been sitting. We learned from pest control people that box elders do no structural damage, so they aren't dangerous like termites or carpenter ants; and that living at the edge of woods, it would be almost impossible to be totally free of them. Someone suggested that sometimes spraying them with soapy water helped to discourage them, but it didn't seem to deter these. We decided to adjust to living with them—even as ugly and messy as they are. Evidently, they have chosen our house as their "heaven on earth," because it seemed to have facilities to their liking for their hibernation and breeding.

So, several years passed, but during October 2003, they have been especially numerous. On a Saturday about two weeks ago—a day that was unseasonably warm after a few cool days—the south and west sides of the house were just <u>black</u> with them. They must have been enjoying a really special festival of some kind—they were lined up along the boards, even piled upon each other in clumps in some places, and flying hither thither and yon, visiting with all of their friends! When I opened the back door, some of them dropped inside, and some of them flew onto my clothes and into my hair when I went out. I soon found myself using an unhandy door to get to wherever I needed to be outside and began to feel like a prisoner in my own house!

I said to myself, "Enough is <u>enough</u>! I called pest control and got some estimates and evaluations of their products. I wanted to be sure their method would be environmentally safe. Evidently, most birds don't use those bugs for food, so there wouldn't be danger of "treated" dead bugs killing birds. One company sent a person to make an estimate after seeing the situation and making accurate measurements. He was also quite a salesman. He thought the really best solution would be for me to sign up for monthly service which would also take care of bugs other than the box elders—but that wasn't what <u>I</u> thought I needed. I have no cockroaches, I live well with spiders, and the box elders are only a problem during one month in the spring and one month in the fall. I agreed to a one-time treatment which would include a follow-up one in two weeks. The entire outside of the house and the inside of the garage would be sprayed—some of the small areas with a hand-pumped sprayer, most of it with a power sprayer that would get some of the solution into crevices. The bugs only had to touch the solution for it to be effective. Even the residue that lingered on the surface of the house would have some effect. (I have to confess that I suppose I actually signed a paper to authorize the use of a "Weapon of Mass Destruction"!)

The result was truly a "mass destruction"! Even though that spray-day was cooler, and there were only about a fourth as many of the critters out as had been out on the warm Saturday before, it was amazing to see the numbers now piled along the concrete walk and driveway by the house! And the next morning, all those who came out to warm themselves in the sun, soon fell down on top of the ones already there! I wanted to get them out of my sight, but some were still "wiggling," and I didn't want to use a blower to move them onto the grass, in case they might recover to harass me again. So I swept them onto a dust pan and put them into plastic bags I could tightly close. I didn't bother to clean up the ones that fell onto soil around most of the house, but I thought it might be interesting to see what these captured ones would weigh— it was almost two pounds!

The mass destruction was administered eight days ago—and I'm still seeing dead bugs and sweeping them up. I don't even want to <u>think</u> about what a terrorist could do to Nature (including the human race), with a device as simple as a power spray! But it's sure a relief to be rid of at least <u>some</u> of those <u>BUGS</u>!

LOVE IS ALL THAT MATTERS

THE MUSIC IN OUR LIVES
(Kaleidoscopic—Often Changing)

Music is defined as a rhythmic sequence of pleasing sounds. That can even include the song of a bird, or the babbling of a brook. Some early mathematicians supposed there might be ethereal musical sounds produced by the movements of the heavenly bodies. They called this "The Music of the Spheres." Pythagoras discovered that vibrating strings produce harmonious tones when the ratios of the length of the strings are whole numbers, and that those ratios could be extended to other instruments. I think they opened doors to unlimited imaginations of beauty and inspiration!

The rhythm of music has been used for centuries. Some of the ways have been on early ships and boats that required oars to be used for power. The larger the boat or ship, the more oars. Two people in a canoe can easily strike a rhythm with their paddles for smooth movement, but the many oarsmen on a ship needed a leader to provide a rhythmic sound for them to all be able to pull their oars at the same time. Martial music has been associated with military activities for maybe centuries, as well. In early wars, rhythm provided by drums—or the use of certain tunes—gave soldiers directions for action: charging, retreating, etc. Other musical tunes gave directions for things like time to eat, time to go to bed, time to get up, an important officer is near, etc. The practice of precision marching, to the rhythm of music and drums, helps with the training necessary for unity of activity for soldiers—even unity of thinking. A child's first response to music is probably the rhythm of it—and its use is helpful in developing coordination. How about, *Here We Go 'Round the Mulberry Bush*, or *Pop! Goes the Weasel?*

I experienced the use of music for developing rhythm in learning touch typing—typing without looking at the keys. The Dixon high school teacher, Mr. Bell, wrote on the black board the letters to be typed for each exercise—for instance: JHJ-space, JHJ-space; FGF-space, FGF-space. Then he started music on his portable record player. On the wall over the blackboard was a large diagram of a keyboard which we were to use to find the proper keys from the "home" position of fingers on our typewriter keyboard. Fingers of the left hand were to be on A,S,D, and F (little finger on A). The fingers of the right hand, starting with the forefinger, were on J,K,L, and ;. These simple exercises continued until we'd used all the fingers to find all the keys adjacent to them— always beginning with fingers in "home position." (The modern keyboard has added many letters and symbols, of course, for using computer operation.) Mr. Bell played several different tunes—always marches—but the two I remember most clearly are: *The Stars and Stripes Forever*, and *The Wedding March* from the opera *Aida*. Creative kids often put words to *Stars and Stripes*" like: "Be kind to our web-footed friends, for a duck may be somebody's mother; Be kind to our friends in the swamp, where it's always cold and damp." Even after we became familiar with the keyboard and had advanced to typing from printed copy, he still played music to help us maintain rhythm—which would ultimately help in increasing speed. To pass the course, we had to type sixty words per minute, if I remember correctly. Sometimes when I'm typing, one of those tunes will still creep into my head!

Watching the movie *Fantasia* is a real kaleidoscope of "visual sound"! I really enjoy the artistry of the projected moving shapes and colors, and I appreciate the imagination of the composers—using their art to guide and stimulate my own thoughts as I connect the movement and color with the beautiful musical harmonies!

I'm happy when I see children's cartoons that are made with classical music in the background. In these times of "new music"—hip-hop, heavy metal, and such—I think it's good for young brains to get subconscious imprints of music that has inspired people for so many years. One of my favorite "educational" musical pieces is *Peter and the Wolf* with the story being told to background music by Prokofiev.* What a "fun" way to learn to identify the sounds of various instruments, and to "feel" the emotions conjured up by those sounds!

In a similar way (without so much description of instruments) the musical sound tracks of movies express moods and emotions of the stories being acted out. Think about *Star Trek, Oklahoma!, Sound of Music, Wagons West, Bridge Over the River Kwai, Lawrence of Arabia, Frankenstein, Fiddler on the Roof*—and various operas!

Singing hymns not only establishes certain desired moods in a church service—like praise or contemplation—but it also is a method of uniting group thoughts, preparing the minds of the congregation for receiving the message of the scriptures and the sermon.

I am often reminded of the close relationship of members of my family. I feel sure that the music we experienced as we were growing up was instrumental (excuse the "pun") in forming lasting bonds! As babies, Mom often held us close and sang to us in her rocking chair while she fed us from her breast and rocked us to sleep. Joy, Barbara, and I liked to "harmonize" while we washed and dried dishes. (The dishwashing job probably took a little longer, but we sure had fun!) Our whole family enjoyed singing together, with Dad playing a guitar. Sometimes we sang hymns; sometimes comical songs and folk songs. We really liked hearing Dad sing a song he wrote about the wreck of the "Sheffield"—the car he and other workers rode on when they did work on the railroad. He could make us laugh when he sang *Cotton-Eye Joe* and *My Name is Ticklish Rueben*! The chorus of that song was a bunch of laughing "ha, ha, ha's" which Dad made into a couple of lines of "tune." By that time we all were laughing! I've been thinking lately that we children probably experienced a special "bonding" when we sang together for a few years— harmonizing, and each one playing an instrument. Even though we don't often sing together now, we sure are good friends!

I can't imagine a life without music, because it is so useful and enjoyable in so many ways! But there's one kind that I heard <u>about</u> when I was a teenager that I never actually <u>heard</u>! It must have been whatever it was that Mom meant when she said, "Be home by eleven o'clock, or you'll 'have to face the music'!" I wonder what the <u>tune</u> to that music would have been?

*Russian composer Sergei Prokofiev (1891-1953), composed *Peter and the Wolf* in 1936.

TRIGGERS FOR MEMORY

I often think about the magic of memory, and what a great gift it is. Without memory, I suppose even survival might not be possible, because we learn early in our lives which experiences give us pleasure, and which ones give us pain. If we are lucky, we'll remember which ones to avoid, if at all possible. Of course, as I age, I'm realizing that many memories of childhood are still vivid to me; but I'm embarrassed when I can't remember the name that goes with a familiar face I meet when I'm grocery shopping!

For the most part, I've been blessed with happy, pleasant memories—and for that, I'm ever so thankful. I really feel compassion for people whose memories are of abusive experiences so extreme they still feel mental and emotional pain, perhaps even physical pain. And how does a memory come into our minds? I feel like there might be "triggers."

What "triggers" <u>my</u> memories? Things I see, things I smell, things I hear, things I taste, things I feel, things I do, things I read about. My house looks like a museum, so I have no trouble finding memory triggers when I'm there—a pleasant memory is connected with just about everything I see! Here are a few of them:

Approaching the garage doors at my home I think of my Dad when I see the old <u>Navy ship's bell</u> he gave Gene as a retirement gift.

I think of my mother and my family when I see the <u>quilts</u> on all of my beds. They have Mom's tiny stitches in the quilted designs; and the many colorful pieces came from scraps left from sewing some of the clothes she made for us as we grew up.

I think of granddaughter Leah when I <u>grind coffee beans</u>. Once when she was visiting—maybe five or six years old—I used my fore finger to wipe the last bits of the grounds out of the coffee grinder. She was watching, and said, "Grandma, we use a little brush to get those out!" I said, "Why didn't <u>I</u> think of that!"

Another reminder of Leah comes with <u>doing laundry</u>. When she was three or four, she liked to "help" me put things into the dryer. As I shook out each item, she identified its owner.

Sometimes when doing my laundry, I'm reminded of childhood laundry day when Mom rubbed home-made soap on each piece, and then pushed it up and down on a washboard. After rinsing, things were hung to dry on a wire line, with clothes pins holding each piece in place.

<u>Peeling a banana</u> brings Peter Hall to mind. He became an award-winning principal and superintendent of schools; but I first knew him as a neighbor in diapers—and then I enjoyed watching him grow up. As a child, he hated the banana "strings," and had to have every one of them removed.

My old <u>Betty Crocker Cookie Cookbook</u> gets many people remembered. It has grease spots, dough stains, notes for adjusting recipes, and most of the pages are loose. I've used it almost every Christmas since the 1950's to make four or five different kinds of cookies to share with neighbors. So, not only do I remember my many neighbors, I think of children—neighbors' children, my own children and grandchildren, and even Gene who helped with decorating them!

Almost every time I <u>travel across country</u>, by plane, or by car, I think about the pioneer wagon trains. Would I have been brave enough to have been in one of them, had I been living then?

My <u>large, steamer trunk</u>, now holds treasures like baby shoes and first toys, children's clothes, my own baby quilt, special formal dresses that I designed and made, and some square dance "originals." It reminds me of its original purpose—for shipping clothes and personal items to Italy when Gene had an assignment there in 1952.

We had bought a piano when we lived in Italy, and I took lessons there. I no longer have that piano—it was a gift to Becky for her 21st birthday—but I still have the <u>bench</u> that went with it. I helped Dad make it to match the piano's lovely curved legs and deep, reddish-brown color. The wood for it came from a walnut tree that had grown on my mother's family farm. My special job was to do the sanding. Dad was a perfectionist, and I learned how smooth, "smooth" can be—much smoother than I ever expected! He taught me <u>so</u> much about so many things!

I have several <u>Hoya plants</u> that my mother called "Christ's Tears" because from each of the small, velvety, pink flowers that grow in a round bunch, there drips a tiny drop of sticky fluid. I still have the one which was a gift from Mom when she and Dad came for their first visit with our daughter Becky when she was a tiny baby. Mom had started it with a cutting from her own quite old plant. I call it my "Becky Plant" because they are the same age.

I even get memory triggers from smelling <u>Jergen's</u> original-scent hand lotion—Jergen's was the first lotion I ever used. And <u>Tangee</u> lipstick still has the fragrance and "taste" I remember from my first lip color!

Almost all decorative items around my house have stories: Some examples: the now <u>bronzed boots</u> that Gene wore in Vietnam.

The <u>African painting</u> he brought back when he was a student on a trip that was sponsored by the National War College.

We discovered the <u>Neapolitan street scene painting</u> when we lived on Parco Lamaro in Naples, Italy.

The large painting of a <u>Red flowered cactus plant</u> attracted our attention at a sidewalk art sale in London.

An antique blue-green <u>cloisonné vase</u> from an early-morning Saturday sale in London.

Two antique <u>railroad lanterns</u>, also from the Saturday sale in London.

A hammered <u>brass pot</u> we found in a quaint shop in Venice, Italy.

A bronze statuette called <u>Dancing Faun</u>—a replica from Pompeii.

A small marble statue of Michelangelo's *David*—from Florence, Italy.

A Teak wood carving of a <u>laughing Buddha</u> Gene brought from Japan—gives me a happy feeling when I look at it!

Two pairs of large, <u>porcelain elephants</u> that Gene brought from Vietnam.

On a wall in the kitchen-dining area are a couple of treasured works of my children's high school art: a <u>batik wall hanging</u> that Becky made—dark green background with lighter yellow-green plants, curved as if moving under water, around a yellow and white fat tropical fish (similar to "Nemo"). David's project is a <u>decoupage picture of a leopard</u> in a background of a sunny field with dark green trees, done on a piece of wood.

Two <u>linoleum block-print</u> pictures that were made by neighbor-friend Alice.

A <u>desert scene pen and ink-water color print</u> from Becky when she lived in Tucson, Arizona.

A Frances Hook charcoal drawing of <u>Jesus, the Carpenter</u>—a beloved gift from Gene.

A truly treasured "memory" item that I see every day is the folded and framed <u>United States flag</u> that was presented to me by a Marine Corps officer at Gene's memorial service. I like to think of it, not as a symbol of his death, but as a symbol of his love for our country, and the dedicated life he lived—as a Marine for thirty years, with combat in World War II and Vietnam—as the father of two wonderful children, and as an interested citizen in everyday community life in the many locations where he lived! He loved and respected nature, and lived "large," with an incredibly positive attitude! One of his mottos was, "There are no problems—only interesting situations"! The greatest of my memories is my fifty-three years of life with him! It was "Adventure" with a Capital "A"!

Of course, the book from which you are reading this story is filled with a great many of my memories—most of which are happy ones. Naturally, there have been many memories that are less than happy, but nonetheless rewarding for the value of the experiences that went with them.

WAGONS IN MY LIFE

The idea for this story came to me in 2004, on my way home from the Portland airport in the shuttle bus after a trip to Columbia, Missouri. I want to be sure that I am in <u>no</u> way critical of the shuttle service, because it's a real life-saver for me when I take a plane trip, which is at least two, and sometimes four or more times a year. It's just that the shuttle is a great place for "thinking"! I'm not comfortable reading while traveling in an automobile—too much side-to-side movement, I suppose; so all there is to do on that two-hour shuttle trip is to observe the scenery as we rush by, and to <u>think</u>! I feel quite a great need to be with my Kelley family more often that I did when we were all younger, with longer life expectancies; and sometimes I like to visit far-away friends I haven't seen for a long time. On this particular trip the bus was one of their smaller ones—and no doubt one of the older ones—a little noisy, and a little "bumpy"! That's what reminded me of my childhood, and of the many times I rode in wagons in those long-ago days—those wagons were noisy and bumpy, too!

This ride was not without a lot of <u>thinking</u> and <u>remembering</u>. Have you ever wondered how fortunate many cities are to have quite wide streets between their rows of brick buildings that were built a century or more ago—before there were automobiles that would need room for two, three, or four lanes of space that came to be known as streets? A look at some photos of Main Streets in frontier towns will show why they had to be wide, even then. You will notice horse-drawn wagons and buggies, some traveling, and some stopped along the street—their "power systems" tied to hitching posts in front of the buildings which were merchandise stores, taverns, hotels, barber shops, furniture stores, feed stores, garden stores, harness shops, blacksmiths, restaurants, and such. The street space then needed to be wide enough for a horse-drawn wagon to turn around, and wide enough for a wagon to be parked with the horses still hitched to it.

My mom and dad had a Model "T" Ford early in their marriage when they lived in Kansas and followed the wheat harvesting as it moved north. Now, back in Missouri when they began building and settling on their small farm, they sold the car to buy needs for the farming they would do—lumber for the house, horses, a wagon, farm implements like plows, a cow, some pigs, and some chickens. So when we traveled to town or to church, or to visit family and friends, it was by wagon. If a family could afford <u>two</u> wagons, one of them might be a buggy—lighter and more comfortable for riding—probably with a top over it for shade, or shelter from rain. We only had the "work" wagon that was needed for hauling heavy things connected with farming. One year they had two or three acres of tomatoes planted, and during the summer, as the tomatoes ripened, Dad frequently took a wagon load of them to the cannery in town and brought home bags of grain for the hogs and food for the cow.

Sometimes—usually on Saturday, we <u>all</u> rode to town in the wagon. What a bumpy ride it was on that rocky, dirt road—but what fun! My "mind's nose" can even now imagine the odors—fragrance of some hay in the wagon bed to make it a softer place for kids to sit, and the "animal" smell of the horses that were right in front of the wagon. (Actually, they were mules—a brown one called "Jack," and a mottled white and gray mare named "Beck." Kids, naturally, thought it quite amusing when the animals had to relieve themselves while they just continued walking along, pulling the wagon!) If hay had been cut and was ready to haul from the field to the barn, a hay-frame was attached to the wagon to widen the base for the load, since hay was light weight enough to be stacked for a high load.

The wagon was also used for our ride to church. For quite a number of years some of us children were too small to comfortably walk the one and one-half miles. Of course, when we started to school at age six, we were considered "big enough to walk."

Some people made a more comfortable wagon by attaching it to the frame of a stripped-down automobile. Therefore, the "wagon" had springs and rubber tires—and as you rode along, maybe with the horses trotting, you felt like you were just gliding or floating! What a luxury! Those vehicles were called "Hoover wagons." Herbert Hoover was president at that time, and many people were out of work. That era was called "hard-times." There was a story that people were too poor to pay for gas for a car, so they built a wagon out of it!

One very nice occasional wagon trip was visiting Mom's parents and family about twenty-five miles away on the Big Piney River. That was an almost all-day journey that included scenery of rivers and bluffs, of farms and woods. The road we traveled crossed a bridge over the Gasconade Rive that was peaceful, flowing, blue-green colored water. Along the way, we munched on a picnic lunch and snacks, and some of us children maybe took a nap in the wagon bed on the hay that was covered with some old quilts. Sometimes Grandpa Kelley went with us to drive the wagon if Dad was busy working. Grandpa really liked gingersnap cookies, so when he was with us, Mom included a bunch of those cookies in the lunch basket! I didn't care for them— too "spicy-hot" on my tongue!

Sometimes when I seem to have too many things that I need to do, in the time available to do them, I think about those days when life seemed to move more slowly, and without so much noise. People seemed to have time to sit and "visit" while children created games to play—and the men folk gathered someplace outdoors and talked "man-talk." Right now, I have to stop writing and get going to town in my car—writing class starts in fifteen minutes, and this story will be ready for me to read!

WHAT'S WITH WATER!

There's something about water that holds a universal interest and fascination for almost everyone—young and old! Do sights like lakes and rivers, hard rain storms, or gentle showers—or Niagara Falls—come to mind? How about oceans? The fact that it's necessary for supporting life is no doubt responsible for a large part of our interest. On the other side of its fascination is its capability of destruction when it gets into places where it shouldn't be—in amounts that can't be handled! You might be reminded of devastating floods and typhoons. Some of that thinking might concern scientific aspects. I want to think now about the enjoyment of it!

A small creek ran across our little ten-acre farm near Dixon, Missouri. Its beginning was from springs and drainage located in several acres of oak woods that bordered the west side of our property. A small trickle of it even ran during most of the summers and supported a small pond (which we called a slough—pronounced "slew") to the side of it about the middle of what was called "The Bottom." (The Bottom was a field in the middle of the property from which small hills sloped to the north and to the south.) The creek ran along the south side of the field where the hill to the south began. Rocks in that area were mostly flint, but now and then we found some limestone pieces, soft enough to write or draw pictures on something like a concrete porch! (For some reason, Mom usually thought it would be well if we washed those off when the art session was finished!) Occasional summer rains turned the creek into what seemed to us children like an exciting, roaring river! The water was quite muddy at first, and not much fun to play in—except to make boats and watch them float rapidly down—sometimes bumping into land on one side or the other, or into branches or large rocks along the way. At the east side of the field, the creek—also sometimes called "the branch"—crossed the dirt road that ran by our house. No bridge was necessary there because that part of the road was stabilized with rocks and gravel, and the land was level enough that the creek had some space to spread out.

The most fun there was just wading when the water was clear, looking for "pretty" rocks along the way, and noticing the tiny little waterfalls that caused it to "sing" with wonderful trickles! But it wasn't enough to just wade, and look, and listen. We often built some dams or re-routed its small channel. Just before it crossed the road, it deposited sand and silt when the water was high; and when the water was low, that sandy place was the next best thing to being on a beach beside an ocean, because we could build castles with the wet sand and mud. In the slough we found more adventures—catching tadpoles and saving them for awhile in jars of water. As summer progressed, we noticed the changes in their bodies as they grew legs and became frogs!

In due time I grew up, lived in towns, and became busy with many things; but I still enjoyed just "looking" into the water of rivers and lakes and oceans wherever we lived or traveled. Then, when Gene and I were married, water came into my life again—"BIG TIME"! He also had grown up by a creek and near rivers where he and his older brother often spent hours fishing, swimming, and loving the water! And he still loved it!

You can only imagine what a treat it was for us to live in Minneapolis, Minnesota, for three years—from 1957 to 1960! Our home was in the middle of the state called "The Land of Ten Thousand Lakes"! We felt like we had "died and gone to heaven"! Gene's assignment there consisted of visiting colleges in a five-state area, giving students information about the military program that would earn a commission in the Marine Corps upon their graduation. He spent a considerable amount of time out-of-town during the school year, but in summer, I frequently prepared a picnic supper to take with us to a nearby lake as soon as he came home from work in the office. There, in a small motor boat, we fished for bass among reeds near the banks, listened to frogs, watched and listened to the loons, and dined on sandwiches until glorious sunsets—happier than if we were guests of the Queen of England! (And the mosquito repellent Gene carried in his fishing tackle box made the evening possible! Minnesota mosquitoes are giant ones!)

My brother Ross and his wife Chadna, who lived near Kansas City, were good fishing friends. They came to Minnesota to "open the trout season" with us one year. We rented a cabin on one of the larger northern lakes for that adventure. (Nothing better than a dinner of freshly caught rainbow trout, sautéed in a bit of butter, and served with some apple sauce on the side!) They've also fished for salmon with us in Oregon; and we joined them one winter for two weeks of bass fishing and sightseeing in Florida. Our motel cabins were located on Lake Okeechobee—a large, smooth lake a little west of West Palm Beach, and east of Fort Myers.

It was our first trip to Florida, so when we rested from fishing there were many other things to enjoy! All around us were tropical varieties of beautiful flowers, and along many roads were the (unusual to us) citrus groves—oranges, grapefruit, lemons, etc. The Everglades and jungles were new kinds of sights—and driving for several miles along the highway that connects the islands of the Florida Keys was especially scenic! It is said to be one of the longest overwater roads in the world. We spent a lot of time in Fort Myers, finding some history of the neighboring vacation homes that belonged to Thomas Edison and Henry Ford. They must have been great friends—both of them having unusually creative minds that gave the world so many new inventions! The local museum was a good place to learn about them—their many mutual friends, and to see samples of some of their creations, from light bulbs to automobiles!

Sometimes while I waited for fish to be interested in the delicious bait I was dangling in the water for them, I'd find a few creative, poetic thoughts about fishing coming to my mind. Maybe I'll share some of them on some following pages. It was easy to "get hooked" on fishing when I was with special people who also liked it! There was time to feel refreshed, "in the lap of Mother Nature," and to enjoy some beautiful water—in rivers, lakes, and oceans!

Early in 1952, Gene received an assignment to Naples, Italy—and I was really happy that I could go, too! Soon we had "water, water, everywhere"—traveling there on a military ship—leaving from New York! There was Atlantic Ocean water for several days, then we entered the Mediterranean Sea! We had never seen water that was that blue! Unbelievably blue! From our apartment windows, high on a hill in Naples, we continued to be able to see it—every day for two and a half years! When we traveled in Europe we enjoyed seeing some famous rivers—Danube, Rhine, Po, Tiber, Thames, Shannon, Arno, Avon, Seine, Marne, to name a few; and Switzerland's Geneva Lake and Lake Lucerne were delightful. On one of our trips to Switzerland we took a chair lift to a beautiful high lake (whose name I don't remember at the moment), spent much of a day in a small boat just exploring and fishing. I wanted to "get some sun on my shoulders" for my summer tan—and kind of lost track of the time of exposure! Luckily, I had a silk dress with me that would touch my fiery shoulders VERY lightly. I had to wear something to dinner in the dining room—and even that very soft touch was painful! (That was in the days before "sun-screen.") I really enjoyed those few hours floating around on that beautiful blue-green lake, though! Water is truly "WONDERFUL"!

HOUSE PLANTS

I suppose I was born into a world of house plants—I know I have lived with them ever since! One of the earliest ones that I remember was a thriving Angel Wing begonia that was probably about four feet tall, and still growing. My mom had a very "green" thumb, and that Angel Wing was her pride and joy! As the sizes of our homes increased, so did her indoor "garden." By the time I was in college Dad had built an extension on the back of the Hickory Street house in Columbia, Missouri, that included a dining room large enough for a bank of various plants in front of the wide picture window, with a view of more flowers in the back yard. Some of the tall plants sat on the floor in the dining room, some were on stands and tables, and some hung from hooks in the ceiling: There was a very large, very old Boston Fern; some philodendrons; sansevieria that she called "Mother-in-Law's Tongue," pots of various colors of coleus; Christmas cactus; a purple-leafed Wandering Jew (Zebrina); geraniums; a Crown of Thorns (euphorbia); a gardenia, and a covered terrarium—maybe other things that I don't remember! In the kitchen window grew a collection of six or more African violets of several shapes and colors. When she and Dad visited us in Hawaii, at Christmas time1968, our five-year-old David gave her a gift of some Bird of Paradise seeds. They are native to Hawaii, and several were growing in our back yard. Before long she had a very large potted one growing, with beautiful blue and orange "bird" blossoms! In winter, it lived in the dining room "garden alcove"—in summer, it was moved to the partially shaded car port. I think that from the love it received, it must have truly <u>thought</u> it was in Paradise!

While we still lived in Dixon—and I was in high school—our friend, Adele Buss, gave Mom a cutting from her hoya (wax plant) that she called "Christ's Tears." It's highly fragrant, and its velvety, pink blossoms grow in a cluster with a small drop of sticky liquid in the center of each small flower. When we brought our baby Becky home, Mom and Dad drove from Columbia, Missouri, to Minneapolis in Minnesota to see her the very next day! Mom brought with them a small hoya plant she had started from a cutting from her own treasured hoya. That special vine still grows in my living room window, after over fifty years of being moved around the country! Hawaii didn't allow foreign plants to be brought in, so Mom kept our hoya for us for the two years we lived there. I call it my "Becky Plant." I gave a start from it to Becky when her daughter, Leah, was born; and now her hoya is over thirty years old.

Dad was a plant lover, too, so he never objected to helping Mom with moving large plants or helping with re-potting. Her "green thumb" meant that she wanted her plants to "be all that they could be"! When she watered them, it was done carefully and lovingly. If one of them looked like it was "unhappy" for some reason, she'd actually <u>talk</u> to it—maybe say something like, "What's the matter with you? Would you like to move to someplace else?" Or, to another one, "You sure are looking good today!" as she carefully turned it to get light on its other side.

A house never seemed like a home to me without a few plants growing in it, so we always had various varieties. I've heard Gene joke that he felt like he should sleep with a machete within reach in case he had to cut his way out! Because we had to move every two or so years, I wasn't able to get <u>too</u> sentimentally attached to very many of them during our Marine Corps years. But as soon as we moved into a new place, it wasn't long before things were growing. Plant-moving hadn't yet started when we lived in Naples, but even though we lived on the fifth floor, I talked our landlord into installing some window-boxes for geraniums. Several years later in London, we hadn't lived in our little apartment very long before Becky and David said, "Mom, we need some flowers in here!" So ... they went shopping with me, and we began keeping flowers in there!

Philodendron was good for trailing over the top of a window, or for hanging near one. English ivy was another easy vine. I liked palm plants for giving variety of texture and shape; and a hanging spider plant (chlorophytum) was fun with all the baby plants growing at the ends of its branches. I also had African violets that I displayed on a special plant stand at varying heights. Peperomia, with its darker color made a good accent, and Crown of Thorns (Euphorbia) reminded me of Christ. It has small red flowers that are said to symbolize the blood that came from wearing the crown made of sharp thorns. A sweet potato immersed in a pot of water will sprout and grow into an interesting vine—easily disposable at moving time. At one time Becky and David had fun growing avocado trees from seeds. If they were allowed to grow without pruning, they became quite tall. If one were pruned back early in its growth, it grew branches. Prayer plant (maranta) was another "fun plant. Not only is it a beautiful, dark blue-green color with some reddish veins in the leaves, it folds it's leaves up as if in prayer in the evening.

In Hawaii, there was not much space in the house for plants, but many flowering things grew in the yard—plumeria (white and pink), hibiscus, banana trees, and Bird of Paradise. Philodendron vines covered the utility fence. I sometimes cut pieces of philodendron branches and kept them in a pot of water indoors. One day I discovered that mosquitoes were breeding in one of the pots—water hadn't often been changed—just "added to!" I was stunned! Of course, once I thought about it, I realized what a perfect set-up it was for a "mosquito city"! There were at least two generations of them—in all stages of development! How interesting! I decided to wait until the kids came home from school so we could enjoy a "science lab" together before I "sent the skeeter-babies to skeeter-heaven"!

When we moved to Corvallis in 1973, we had more space, as well as stability, for some larger plants! A rubber plant made a good filler for a corner in the living room. We grew a large dish of various cacti from starts brought from Tucson when we went to be with Becky at her graduation from the University of Arizona. A lovely, large peace lily (spathiphyllum) grew from a small potted one that David brought from the garage sale of a gold-mining friend of his when David was in high school. Two Christmas cactus plants were from one that Gene's mother gave us when she and Dad moved to a retirement home. Becky gave me a small pot of String of Pearls for my birthday in about 1975. Another special Christmas cactus was grown from a small branch of a very old one in the library at Dixon, California. It was a gift to David when he and Gene visited friends there in about 1980, while on a trip to explore "Big Foot" country in California. A fig tree (ficus) was from neighbors who couldn't take it with them when they moved away.

I'm sure that one of the important things about the value of house plants in my life is that I so appreciated Gene's willingness to allow room in the car at moving time for me to keep those plants that I especially prized! We usually looked like Gypsies as we drove across country, stopping for family visits along the way—unloading and reloading, and watering plants at every stop! So, you can see that many memories are living ones—living in the form of green leaves and vines, especially with an understanding, appreciative husband!

FAMILY PETS

I, myself, have never been your average lover of pets, but I've always felt a respect for animals—and as I've learned more about the intelligence and capabilities of many different ones that are used for therapy, or ones that perform special tasks, I realize their importance and value. When I was a child, living in the country during Depression years, our animals seemed to be there for a source of food—milk, eggs, and meat. A team of mules, Jack and Beck, helped with crops and transportation. In the barn, there was no need for rodent extermination—cats took care of the mice! There always seemed to be kittens to play with (and give away), and it was interesting to discover the many various colors of cats! (I thought the calicos were prettiest!) One problem with barn cats was that sometimes stray tom cats raided the barn and killed baby kittens. But even our working animals became good friends, were named, and given special attention! Someplace I learned about Bantam chickens—I thought they were really pretty, and were also curious, because they were so small—so Dad bought a pair to add to our collection of bigger chickens. They were called "Ila's Banties." The rooster became quite "feisty" and liked to hop up on little brother Sterling's back when he was bent over playing with his cars. That eventually became a problem, so I lost my rooster—to a pot of dumplings for dinner.

We always had a cow for the purpose of producing milk to drink, cream to sell, and calves to sell for income. Dolly and Babe were two memorable ones. Babe was Dolly's daughter—old enough to take over production when Dolly's age became a disadvantage. Their breed was a mixture of Jersey and Guernsey—the best for giving milk with rich cream. For producing calves to sell for meat, the cows were bred to Herefords—a good breed to sell for the best meat. Dolly and Babe were gentle, with big, beautiful brown eyes—and easy to manage when moving them between pastures and barn. I was even an occasional "milk-maid"! I realize that a cow isn't really what most people would call a "pet," but she can be a "friend"!

For Grandpa Kelley, who lived alone about a quarter of a mile away, dogs were his "family"! He wasn't able to turn away a stray dog, so at his place there were always four of five, and sometimes more of them! He did quite a lot of hunting for rabbits and squirrels for his own food, and dogs were helpful for that. They all had names—Spot, Coondog, Black Dog, and Rover, to name a few—and were of various known and unknown breed mixtures, basically hounds of one kind or another.

Dad frequently worked away from home, and once when he came home for a weekend, he brought a beautiful brown-and-white cocker spaniel—an adult dog given to him by a friend who was looking for a good home for her. Her name was Brownie, and she very soon became loved and happy in our family. My brother Ross spent a lot of time with her, taking her with him when he hunted rabbits in the woods or worked around the farm. Before long we discovered that she hadn't been spayed—when she gave us a litter of puppies of unknown parentage! That was a great experience for us children, and we were allowed to keep one puppy that we named Patches. When our family moved to Columbia, it didn't seem fair to take a freedom-loving country dog to live in a city, so Patches joined Grandpa's family of dogs for many more happy years.

Joy claimed a white cat—a gift to her from our piano teacher, Mrs. Buss. The kitten had been left in Mrs. Buss' mailbox, and she already had all the cats she wanted for herself.

Another time, Dad brought home an adult dark, smoke-colored Persian cat named Janie. What a beautiful thing she was, with her blue eyes and long, fluffy hair! She had been a "house cat," but with us, she was also allowed to go outdoors. She didn't seem to mind the extra time it took for grooming her—removing burrs and stickers she picked up from her hunting and foraging around the farm.

Mom liked having caged canaries—yellow ones—and through the years had several pairs of them. About the time Lindbergh made his famous ocean flight, Mom had a new bird she named Lindy. He was handsome, and soon became a favorite, often filling the house with his beautiful songs—sometimes even before the morning alarm clock! He and his mate once produced a nest full of babies. Mom helped by installing a cup of some kind in the cage and providing a variety of materials for them to build the nest to their own specifications! She kept birds again in her later years—this time a pair of parakeets that she called "lovebirds."

After we moved from the farm—and Mom had more leisure time, a bigger house, and running water—we had a small aquarium with tropical fish of several varieties: a snail and a bottom-feeder for cleaning the sides and gravel in the bottom of the bowl, some angel fish, and some guppies. For some reason, Mom's pets seemed to develop "maternal" instincts—the guppies began to produce babies, too! Mom had learned that the newborn babies would be in danger of becoming food for the larger ones, so she crocheted a tiny net to use for transferring certain fish from one aquarium to another.

Brother Sterling had become a teenager by the time we lived in Columbia, and a young beige-colored dog he named Smokey soon became his companion. They spent many hours playing together. Smokey liked to run, and Sterling also trained him to pull. With a rope tied to his collar, Smokey learned to tow Sterling on his bicycle!

When our daughter Becky was small, Gene and I got some goldfish for her to enjoy watching. We thought it well to have <u>some</u> form of life in the house, and fish were less work than some other possibilities. She liked watching them and feeding them, but one day, when she was about six years old, she climbed into Gene's lap and said, "Daddy, could I have a pet?" Gene replied, "Well, Princess, you already have some pretty fish." To which she emphatically answered, "Daddy! You can't hold a fish and play with it!" Her birthday was coming soon, so we decided to celebrate it with giving her a kitten. When Gene went to select one, he decided that maybe two-year-old David should also have one; so he came home with <u>two</u> kittens! Becky chose the dark gray colored one with stripes, and gave her a name she made up herself, "Trendi." David named his multicolored one "Patches." Needless to say, those two kittens were <u>loved</u>! It took considerable attention to help David learn how to play with it! It didn't <u>like</u> to be grabbed up by its middle and carried by an active toddler to wherever he wanted to go to play!

In Hawaii, Becky and David each had a pet guinea pig—one was black and one was an orange color—inherited from neighbors who were moving back to the States. Those cuddly little animals must have had many friends, because in due time, we had to also pass them on to another family when <u>we</u> moved.

When we lived in Springfield, Virginia, a registered beagle named Trim-Tab (Trimmie for short), was given to us by a Marine Corps friend who had orders for duty in Italy for a couple of years. They couldn't take Trimmie with them, so we agreed to breed her and give them the pick of a registered litter when they returned. Later, in Corvallis, Trimmie lived happily in the country with plenty of deer, possums, and coons to get her attention! One day we learned from a neighbor whose house was robbed, that the kids who had broken in said that they had planned to rob our house—because they knew we weren't at home—but because they were afraid of the barking dog, they went next door.

Our only other dog was a terrier-type puppy that son David found by the side of the road on a Boy Scout bicycle hike-campout trip. He had recently chosen a "deodorized" skunk for a pet, but he carried the little puppy home in his back-pack, and begged permission to keep her. The bargain was that he would have to choose between the dog and the skunk, so he advertised the skunk for sale (and sold it) and named the puppy Peanuts. Peanuts grew up to look almost exactly like a small fox—very cute—and liked playing with Trimmie inside the fenced back yard and barked at everything that moved. She later developed cancer and had to be put down.

For a while there were pet mice in our house—one white and one black—living together in a glass aquarium-house. They were an experiment to see what color their offspring would be. We thought there would likely be some white ones, some black, and probably some with both white and black markings. Surprise! I think there might have been one black one, but the others were solid gray—the color of the ones you don't want to find in your house!

Probably one of <u>my</u> favorites of our children's pets was Becky's black, gray, and yellow striped cat that she named Sarang. The name was inspired by a story Becky had recently read about a tiger who was a friend and protector  of a blind boy in India. She was a kitten Becky chose about a year after we moved to Corvallis, and she remained with us after Becky left home. Becky thought (and we agreed) that Sarang would not like leaving this place where she so loved hunting and roaming in the field and woods. Sarang lived to be eighteen years old. She has now been gone for another eighteen years, and I still miss her!

I'm happy for my many memories of all these animals—and for the pleasure they brought to the people who cared for them. When all is said and done, I guess we are just "all God's creatures" together!

A SPECIAL BOOK

A little book that has been on one of my shelves since I was eleven years old is titled *Good Cheer Birthday Book*. It was edited by Edwin Osgood Grover, copyrighted in 1913, reprinted in 1916, and 1931. It's only four by six inches, one-fourth of an inch thick, and is a collection of "upbeat" quotations and poems by some well-known authors. Also, alternate pages provide six dated lines for recording birthdays—from January 1, to December 31. It was a birthday gift from my grandpa Charley E. Kelley, June 21, 1936, when I became eleven years old. The cover has been gone for so long, I don't even remember what it looked like, but when I leaf through it, I discover familiar quotes that I recognize as words that, even at that young age, I considered to be important. And it appears to have been used often!

It's interesting to notice the names I chose for recording birthdates: all of my mother's twelve siblings, her mother and dad, and many cousins are recorded; my dad's mother and dad, his sister, an aunt, an uncle, and some of his cousins; many of my school friends, neighbors, and some other people who were important to me in those days. Most are written in pencil—I suppose because I probably didn't often use a pen. However, some names of people I met during college are written with ink. Dad and Mom each had a fountain pen, but we children just dipped a pen in a bottle of ink, which was very unhandy and messy, so pencils seemed better.

Thinking about those pens reminds me of the "very modern" dark green Shaeffer fountain pen Mom and Dad gave me for a high-school graduation gift. It has a vacuum device for filling—a great improvement over the older ones with a small lever on the side which helped draw ink into the interior rubber bladder. It was a constant companion until ball-point pens were invented! (Actually, I still have it, though it's never used!)

As I have now been leafing through this little book—reading the names of the people whose birthdates are recorded there—a vivid memory of each one comes to my mind! I could write a long story about what each one of them meant to me—and for some of them, stories have already been written!

Neighbors: Earl and Mary Hile, Dixon, Missouri; Mrs. Espey, her sister and brother the Fausbourgs, in St. Joseph Missouri.

High school friends: Lucille Cross, Lena Mae Jones, Bernice Phillips, Marion Veasman, Juanita Goodman.

College friends: Mary Lou Dunagin (Springfield), Mary Bourn, Lois Hansen (my wonderful roommate from Louviers, Colorado), Gerald Hook (roommate's boyfriend), T. D. Hendrix (my boyfriend), Pat Innes, Martha Nell Malone (Paducah, Kentucky).

Fort Leonard Wood: Russell and Margaret Johnson (youth group leaders), Sgt. Harold White (a soldier fifteen years older than I, but I had a crush on him, anyway! He was expert with playing an organ and piano, and helped with our youth group), Capt. Harry Ooms (another youth group helper. He died of a brain tumor while at Fort Wood.), Clarence Jennings (a young carpenter from Oklahoma who came to work at Fort Wood when it was being built and had room and board at our house. We liked each other a lot, but I was only fifteen, and wasn't allowed to go out with him.)

Mr. I. N. Richey (Newton—called "Newt") was a very special person in our community when I was a child. His sons worked with my dad on several projects, so <u>Mr.</u> Richey was a sort of grandfather-type of friend. A very devout Christian, he taught the adult Sunday School class at our little church from the time of my earliest memory—and he dearly loved to sing. I remember that his favorite song, which he often requested, was on page seven of our paper-back song book, but now I don't remember the name of the song! His wrinkled face always had a joyful smile! His birthday was June 26, 1860.

I noticed that my dad evidently thought that the birthdate of the Dionne quintuplets, May 28, 1934, was important enough to record. I think those five little girls, who were born in Canada, were famous because they were the first known quintuplets.

The birth date (that I recorded *in ink*) of a *really* important college friend was April 13th, 1925—Gene Bench! He was special because August 1st, 1948 became our wedding day!

The last birthday that I recorded in the book was *very* special to me then, and still is—Jesus, December 25th!

I'm feeling a bit like a song Jimmy Durante used to sing — "I'll never forget the day I read a book!" I'm realizing how some of the quotes and poems in this little book might have been important in the formation of my philosophy of life. By age twelve I was feeling very grown-up and, I thought, wise! Those quotes and poems with their authors' positive attitudes seemed really important to me. Here are just a few of some quite special ones:

"If I cannot do great things, I can do small things in a great way."—James Freeman Clarke

"If winter comes, can spring be far behind?"—Shelley

"They can, because they believe they can."—Virgil

There were two quotes that reminded me of a book I read in grade school: *Mrs. Wiggs of the Cabbage Patch:*

"I believe in gittin' as much good outen life as you kin—not that I ever set out to look for happiness; seems like folks that does, never finds it. I jus'do the best I kin where the good Lord put me at, an' it looks like I got a happy feelin' in me 'most all the time."— Mrs. Wiggs

"Looks like ever'thing in the world comes right if we jes' wait long enough."— Mrs. Wiggs

Here's one that I penciled in on the back of the fly-leaf:

"Don't put off until tomorrow what you must do today."—Joseph E. Ross (my mother's father)

So, thank you again, Grandpa Kelley, for this little book that seems to have been so important in my life!

TOTAL ECLIPSE
August 21, 2017

If you have known me very long, you have no doubt heard me talk about how thankful I have always been for my parents—Sterling and Bertha Kelley. From the two of them I began learning from my earliest life to love and appreciate the wonders of "Nature": warm sunshine, tiny ants, rippling water, busy birds, cool grass, colorful flowers, the far-away moon, the millions of tiny stars, etc, etc, etc.! So you won't be surprised that they were in my thoughts yesterday as I watched with wonder the often taken-for-granted TOTAL ECLIPSE of the sun! It's undoubtedly one of Nature's most spectacular displays but is often overlooked because it takes so little time to view and is so seldom within our range of sight. I remember that when we were children, an eclipse was an interesting thing to Dad—and he knew the importance of guarding our eyes from the danger of the bright rays of the sun. He fashioned viewing devices for us with pin-holes in cardboard and kept us from "looking" too long at a time. Thank you, Dad! Yesterday I had the convenience of special spectacles—but I still limited the time!

My home now is with sixty-some very interesting people who need various kinds of assistance, but still enjoy mobility and care from a very capable staff. For yesterday's eclipse viewing they provided comfortable seating for all of us in our parking area, along with the special eclipse-viewing spectacles, cinnamon buns, and bottles of water. The sky was blue, the breeze was comfortably cool, and music was playing from the area by the serving table. Caregivers were on hand to give any needed assistance, and we were safely away from the crowds of thousands of people and traffic in our city and throughout the country who were also waiting for viewing this unusual sight.

You more-than-likely live with a "handy-dandy" I-phone or other hand-held device with which you can (and probably already have) located good descriptions and photos of the many happenings that were associated with this unusual eclipse. People now are able to travel long distances and communicate in many ways to experience special activities that I was not able to enjoy as a child. The "totality" area began near Newport on the coast of Oregon and extended all the way across the country to the coast of South Carolina. Thousands of people (even from foreign countries) reserved rooms and camping spaces many months ago all along that space—and my home in Corvallis, Oregon, happened to be sitting right in the middle of it! In this town Oregon State University had some vacant dorm rooms that they made available, as did many citizens, and thousands of people just drove into town from miles around. Many places provided entertainment and food during hours before and after the short time that the center of attraction was the eclipse!

I expect that during a few days earlier many newspapers had publicized the event with descriptive diagrams and photos so that even people who had never seen an eclipse could understand just what was happening and know what to expect. Our paper also had information like photos and articles about the behavior of various animals—for instance the fact that animals would be surprised when darkness began to fall earlier than usual, but they would still begin to prepare in their usual way for night. Birds would stop singing, temperature would begin dropping, etc. I remember my mother telling about an eclipse she saw when she was young and lived on a farm—the chickens began going to roost! In our area we had no animals to observe, but as the moon slowly covered the sun, the temperature became noticeably cooler, and darkness remained for a little less than two minutes, which gave us time to view the moon totally covering the sun, with the bright circle of sunlight surrounding it. (Of course, during that very brief time, we could safely view the sun with our bare eyes. Otherwise, we watched only with the special very dark eclipse glasses!) Darkness had begun gradually—like a normal twilight—until the sky was quite dark, and the area around us was what I might call "light-dark." When I looked up into the sky it was dark enough that I saw a star! (A planet, no doubt.) Soon, the untimely "dawn" began until the surrounding light was back to normal brightness!

I wonder how many people might have had feelings similar to mine? It was almost like I had been in the presence of magic, or "spirit"! Kind of "other-worldly"! It had certainly been an occasion that "brought people together," regardless of nationality, class, or age—standing or sitting shoulder-to-shoulder—watching a magical natural phenomenon that not one of us could produce or duplicate! I wondered what it must have been like for people in ages past to see an eclipse—before scientists had discovered the workings of at least some of the miracles of the universe! I can imagine that it could have been frightening to many! I'm very thankful to our Creator for the development of imaginations and enquiring minds of the many generations of people who have discovered ways to learn at least a "little" bit about the greatness of the Creation that we are privileged to experience and enjoy! I'm also very thankful that I saw that one star that was shining within the area of the sky that was being darkened for a few minutes by the exciting ECLIPSE!

MY FAITH STORY

Having been reared in a Christian home in mid-Missouri, my story is one of *growth* in faith. From my parents I learned about God's love; and from their example, about faith in God, neighborly love, and the power of prayer. I experienced answers to their prayers in such things as the healing of my little brother when he was near death with scarlet fever, and of financial help in the Depression years.

Our church was a non-denominational, community variety which met in the local school house; and attendance was never in question. There was church school every Sunday morning, and sometimes a training-union type Bible study on Sunday evenings. Visiting ministers came to preach—some regularly, and some by invitation. From these basic, Bible-teaching ministers and parents, I was taught that even though I personally believed in God and Jesus, to be assured of eternal life, it was our belief that I must repent of my sins, make a public confession, and be baptized. I felt "called" to take this step during a revival meeting when I was twelve years old. Soon after the series of meetings closed, all the converts from that week met with friends and families for baptism by immersion in a lovely little river near our community. I don't remember all who were baptized that day, but I do remember that my seventy-year-old grandmother Ross was one of them! I had never felt that I was a very "bad" person, but the experience of repentance and baptism was very real and gave me a new enthusiasm to follow Christ. I felt His presence especially through high school when I prayed for help to win a scholarship, because my family was not financially able to pay for me to go to college. Yes—my prayers were answered!

For a few years during World War II, our family lived at Fort Leonard Wood, Missouri. Our church there was also a non-denominational one, and we met many wonderful Christian people from all parts of the country who were stationed there. Through study and fellowship with some of them, my faith was deepened, and I was encouraged to assume some leadership roles with the youth group.

When I was a student at the University of Missouri, I discovered that the First Baptist Church had a very active student program that I liked; and the leader's message was "love with enthusiasm!" I met Gene Bench the next year, and the two of us enjoyed the fellowship of that group. Soon we became members of that church, along with my mother, dad and two sisters; and we were married there on August 1, 1948. The pastor, Rev. Lee C. Sheppard, was a loving person who did a lot to help us develop faith to live abundantly. For the next twenty-five years of moving about, First Baptist was our church "home," to which we returned for the dedication of our children—Rebecca Anne in 1959, and David Eugene in 1964.

Having been reared in community churches, I felt very comfortable worshipping in military chapel congregations during the years of Gene's career with the Marine Corps. I was thankful for my faith during those years, because it turned many experiences which might have been fearful into interesting adventures. Prayer helped me feel a soul-to-soul link with Gene when he had to be away from home—in Japan for more than a year in 1956, during the Cuban crisis in 1961, and in Vietnam for a year in 1966.

Here are some examples: The children didn't watch news reports with me on TV because I didn't want them seeing the close-up pictures of the Vietnam fighting and casualties that were always dramatically shown as part of the news. Even so, they occasionally heard radio news, and there were frequent reports of the number killed that day. After hearing one such report, our three-year-old David's eyes became teary and he said, "My Daddy is in Vietnam! Is he going to get killed?" (I managed to "keep-my-cool" to answer that quite logical question: "Vietnam is a big place, and we just have to hope Daddy was safe!") Needless to say, our prayers always included, "Take care of Daddy today." One day soon after Gene went to Vietnam, while doing dishes at the sink—my mind upon Gene, as it usually was—I sensed a special "presence." I seemed to hear a voice just to the left of the window in front of me saying, "I'll take care of him—you take care of the children." Suddenly it seemed that a heavy load was lifted! I could free my mind of worry and concentrate upon spending really quality time with the children, my family, and friends.

In 1973, Gene retired from the Marine Corps, and we came to Corvallis to live. The years of experience in non-denominational worship groups gave us a feeling that belief in Christ and in neighborly love transcends identification with a religious denomination, so we did some "shopping around" for a church home in Corvallis. Our family decided upon Calvin Presbyterian as our preference, because the people seemed to really enjoy being Christians. They were friendly and loving, and there were many opportunities and areas for study and service.

As I have aged, I've learned even more about letting go, and letting God guide my life. It often seems that "coincidences" later seem to have been part of a "plan." I've admitted weaknesses and found them replaced with His strength. I've trusted Him to solve problems and have been rewarded with patience to wait for His timing. I have many more weaknesses, and I'm sure I'll have many more problems, but I will continue to praise the Lord daily for His love and many blessings; and I will trust that His spirit will help me to continue to grow! I believe that all people are "God's children" regardless of color of skin, of economic fortunes, of physical abilities, or of nationality. I believe that "Peace on Earth" depends upon the ability of all people to practice tolerance and acceptance of our various beliefs—and that it has to "begin with me."

I like to think of this scripture as my motto: *"Trust in the Lord with all your heart and lean not on your own understanding. In all your ways acknowledge Him, and He will direct your paths!" (Proverbs 3:5-6)*

Chapter 10: Family Photos

Top Row: Ila Bench, Barbara Wyatt, Jeanette Kelley, Chadna Kelley, Joy Combs
Bottom Row: Gene Bench, Bill Wyatt, Sterling Kelley, Ross Kelley, Mark Combs
at Joy's home, 2000

Kelley Kids, 2003
Standing: Barbara, Ila, Joy
Seated: Ross, Sterling

Ross & Chadna with a big fish

The Family

Ila Kelley Bench – the Big Sister and author of this book
Ross Kelley – Ila's brother
Barbara Kelley Wyatt – Ila's sister
Joy Kelley Combs – Ila's sister
Sterling Kelley, Jr. – Ila's youngest brother
Bertha Ross – Ila's mother
Sterling Ray Kelley – Ila's father
Charley E. Kelley – Sterling Ray Kelley's father & Ila's paternal grandfather
Ila Etna Warren – Sterling Ray Kelley's mother & Ila's paternal
        grandmother and namesake)
Joseph E. Ross – Ila's maternal grandfather
Oda May (DeLancy) Ross – Ila's maternal grandmother

Arnold Eugene ("Gene") Bench – Ila's husband
James C. Bench – Gene's father
Zula Bench – Gene's mother
Lavada Bench – Gene's sister
Fern Bench Evans – Gene's sister
Elby Bench – Gene's brother

Rebecca ("Becky") Anne Bench Butler – Ila & Gene's daughter
Brian Butler – Becky's husband
Thomas Eugene Butler – Becky & Brian's son & Ila's grandson
Evan Nelson Butler – Becky & Brian's son & Ila's grandson
Leah Wilber – Becky's daughter
Maureece Wilber – Leah's son & Ila's great-grandson
Chance Francois – Leah's son & Ila's great-grandson
Chelsea Francois – Leah's daughter & Ila's great-granddaughter

David Eugene Bench – Ila & Gene's son
Michelle Bench – David's wife

Made in the USA
Lexington, KY
05 November 2019

56599727R00293